Data Communications and Networking Fundamentals Using Novell NetWare

Emilio Ramos
Al Schroeder
Lawrence Simpson

Macmillan Publishing Company
New York

Maxwell Macmillan Canada
Toronto

Maxwell Macmillan International
New York Oxford Singapore Sydney

Editor: Ed Moura

Printed in the Republic of Singapore

Macmillan Publishing Company
866 Third Avenue
New York, NY 10022

Macmillan Publishing Company is part of the Maxwell Communication Group of Companies.

Maxwell Macmillan Canada, Inc.
1200 Eglinton Avenue East
Suite 200
Don Mills, Ontario M3C 3N1

Library of Congress Cataloging in Publication Data

Ramos, Emilio
Data communications and networking fundamentals using Novell NetWare/
Emilio Ramos, Al Schroeder, Lawrence Simpson.
p. cm.
Includes index.
1. Local area networks(Computer networks) 2. Netware(Computer file)
I. Schroeder, Al. II. Simpson, Lawrence. III. Title
004.6'16—dc20 91-43455
CIP
ISBN 0-02-407791-7 (Hardcover Edition)
ISBN 0-02-946389-0 (International Edition)

IE Printing: 1 2 3 4 5 Year: 2 3 4 5

ISBN 0-02-946389-0

Preface

During the past decade, businesses have experienced unprecedented growth in the use of computer workstations by their employees. Although data communications and networking previously had been an integral part of data processing systems, this new growth area has brought these topics to the forefront in both the business and personal-use sectors.

While communications has been taught at the college level for many years, courses in networking only recently have become part of the core curriculum. This change has caused a shift in course structure for computer students. Some colleges have developed a networking course, while others have modified their data communications course to place a greater emphasis on networking. Whatever the approach, colleges and universities are trying to provide a strong introduction to both communications and networking for the computer literate student.

This book was written to serve both needs. The first half of the book serves as an orientation to communications and networking. The second half focuses on the use of networks. It features Novell's NetWare to illustrate local area network applications, and it provides hands-on tutorials for the student to implement NetWare.

Netware was chosen as the software to use because it currently has the largest share of the market. Therefore, it is likely that a student not only would want to study it, but would see it again in business use.

Objectives of This Text

1. To teach the fundamental terminology of communications.
2. To present the components needed to establish communications and the options available in applying each component.
3. To show the uses of both wide area and local area networks.
4. To teach the fundamental terminology relating to networks.
5. To illustrate the components required to configure a local area network and the options available in applying each of them.
6. To present fully the characteristics of NetWare.
7. To show the student how to install and operate NetWare.

Organization of the Text

The book is written in two parts, which provides the flexibility of using either or both of them, depending on the situation. The first half is an introduction to communications and networking. It provides the essential terminology and concepts for an introductory course in communications and networking. The second half of the book provides an introduction to the use of NetWare, including installing, managing, and using the software. This provides the student with a how-to look at applying the knowledge gained in the first half of the book, and it reinforces the concepts and terminology from the first half, particularly with respect to LANs.

The organization of the book assumes a level of computer literacy usually attained in college level Introduction to Computer Science courses or an equivalent continuing education course. This book provides a foundation in the concepts and terminology of communications and networking; it follows that with the study of a specific LAN product and the opportunity for hands-on use of that product. Exercises in the first part of the book focus on grasping communications terminology and studying specific network components. Hands-on tutorials in the second half of the book focus on installing, managing, and operating a specific local area network.

A degree of flexibility is inherent in the book's organization, which allows use of either the first or the second half or both parts, as need warrants. Chapters 1 through 6 and chapter 14 can be used to teach a course in communications and networking through a variety of scenarios. Chapters 7 through 13 can be used to teach an introductory course in Novell NetWare to persons who already have a knowledge of networking concepts. The entire book provides an introduction to both communications and networking, with hands-on use of the most popular LAN product.

Appendices

Appendix A provides a reference to NetWare's commands, rights, and attributes. It can be used as a general reference when studying and using NetWare.

Appendix B explains a few features associated with using NetWare on the Macintosh.

Appendix C contains lists of vendors for a variety of network products. You should review this material for familiarity, and use it as needed to identify vendors in any area of communications and networking.

Supplements

For the instructor there is a comprehensive instructor's guide that includes

1. Suggestions on how to organize the course, depending on the desired emphasis and focus;
2. Answers to all end of chapter questions;
3. Solutions to projects;
4. Transparency masters of the art in the book and the chapter outlines;
5. Hints for the presentation of material in the classroom;
6. Test bank questions for examinations.

Acknowledgements

Our greatest source of support and encouragement has been our families. Without them we could not have written the book.

Rhonda Ramos' encouragement and moral support throughout the writing process were invaluable in making the book a reality. Christopher, a new addition to the family, provided the incentives for and, at the same time, a few obstacles in the way of writing this book.

Rose, Clint, Matt, and Sarah Schroeder gracefully forgave the late nights, the weekend hours, and the home chores left unattended. Rose did double duty at work and at home, and the children accepted many conspicuous absences from baseball, soccer, basketball, and dance events.

The family of Lawrence Simpson provided support and tolerance when necessary. Missed family gatherings and a delayed anniversary present can never be repaid in full. But in such a loving family, these debts are quickly forgiven.

We would like to thank the reviewers of the material, who provided quality feedback during the development process. They include

Scott D. Ahrens, Solano Community College
C.T. Cadenhead, Richland College
Pat Fenton, West Valley College
Seth Hock, Columbus State University
Stephen Jordan, Cooke County College
James Koerlin, Golden Gate University
Richard Meyer, Hartnell College
Brenda D. Scott, Lamar Salter Technical Institute
Ward Testerman, CalPoly Tech

We would also like to thank the Macmillan staff who participated in this project and provided the opportunity to publish this book. Vernon R. Anthony believed in our ability to meet the challenge. Ed Moura, Linda Ludewig, Cindy Peck, Ben Shriver, JoEllen Gohr, Russ Maselli, and others provided much needed support and guidance throughout the development process. Thank you all for your efforts in completing this project.

Emilio Ramos
Al Schroeder
Lawrence Simpson

Table of Contents

1

Introduction to Communication Concepts

Objectives

1. Understand the concept of data communication.
2. Obtain an overview of the history of data communication.
3. Understand the basic requirements of a communication system.
4. Understand the basic concepts of networking.

Key Terms

Computer	Data Communication
E-Mail	EBBS
Home Banking	Host
Interchange Channel	Modem
Network	Public Network
Satellite	Telecommuting
Teleconferencing	Terminal
Transmission Medium	Videotext

Introduction

This chapter provides an overview of data communication from a historical perspective. It also describes the main components of a data communication system. The chapter introduces terminology and concepts required to understand the progress of data communication up to the 1990s. Mastering this chapter will enable the student to have a good understanding of the technological concepts pertaining to the configuration of data communication and networking systems.

The chapter begins with an introduction to the concept of data communication and its importance in the business world. It then provides a brief history of the most important developments that have shaped the data communication industry, followed by the most important functions that a data communication system must provide. Then the major requirements of a data communication system are discussed. Finally, the basic technological concepts of networking and data communication are presented, and examples of different types of systems are explored.

What Data Communication Is

Data communication is the transmission of electronic data over some medium. The medium can be coaxial cable, optical fiber, microwaves, or some other. The systems that enable the transmission of data are often called data communication networks. These networks are an important component of today's information based society, a society dominated by computers and the need to have access to information.

Information is a commodity that can be sold and purchased. It can be generalized that the value of the communication system depends on the knowledge transmitted by the system and the speed of movement of the knowledge. High-speed data communication networks transmit information that brings the sender and the receiver close together. Therefore, a good communication system is a major component of a successful business organization. The ability to provide information in a timely and accurate fashion is the key to survival in the 1990s and the decades ahead. Because of this, data communications is one of the fastest growing segments of the communication market.

Functions of a Data Communication System

The functions of a data communication system in the business environment can be categorized by the features associated with them.

1. **It must provide information to the right people in a timely manner.**

   Having information at the proper place in a timely fashion can mean the difference between making a profit or sustaining a loss. Today's companies have networked data communication systems that can deliver text, voice, and graphical information at speeds that were thought impossible just a few years ago. By integrating communication and computer technology, a letter or report can be delivered anywhere in the world in seconds or minutes. Sometimes the information is delivered instantaneously as it is being produced (e.g., video conferencing).

2. **A data communication system needs to capture business data as it is being produced.**

   Data communication systems are being used more and more as input mechanisms to capture data about the daily business operations of a corporation as the data is being produced. Online computer applications allow a business to enter customer information, produce an invoice to the customer, and provide inventory and shipping information while the customer is performing the transaction. In addition, once the information is entered into the system, it is available to other users instantaneously.

   Many businesses depend for their survival on having data available on a real-time basis. In these systems, data must be available as soon as it is entered into the system. Imagine, for example, an airline reservation system that cannot provide timely notification of flight information to passengers or a bank that cannot post deposits for several days. Transportation, finance, insurance, and other industries require complex, fast, and accurate data communication systems for their business survival. As a result, companies have developed parallel systems and proper backup systems to ensure that their communication networks have a minimal amount of "down time" (time when the network is not functioning).

3. **Data communication systems allow people and businesses in different geographical locations to communicate with one another.**

   Data communication systems allow employees of companies separated by large distances to work as if they were in close proximity. Corporations can communicate with manufacturing operations in a geographical location far away from their administrative headquarters. Inventory, personnel, and other company data can be transmitted from one location to another through high-speed data communication networks. In this manner, the corporation can operate as a single entity. Managers can instantly review inventory levels in the manufacturing location. Engineers can deliver new designs in real-time, and managers can share timely and accurate information in order to make strategic decisions.

Data communication systems combined with computer technology are an integral part of today's companies. These systems can provide data accurately and in timely fashion to any desired location. As a result, a business can become more effective and efficient in the world market than was possible a few years ago.

A Brief History of Data Communications

The first data communication systems were created in 1837 as a result of the invention of the telegraph by Samuel F. B. Morse. Even though the United States government declined to use the telegraph, in 1838 Morse created a private company to exploit his invention. By 1851, over fifty telegraph companies were in operation. Today's Western Union Telegraph was formed in 1856 and became the largest communication company in the United States ten years later.

In 1876, the U.S. patent office issued a patent to Alexander Graham Bell for his invention of the telephone. In 1877 the Bell company was formed, and by 1878 Bell installed the first telephone exchange with an operator.

In 1885, American Telephone and Telegraph Company (AT&T) was formed to build and operate long distance lines in order to interconnect the regional phone companies.

The vacuum tube was invented in 1913, and in 1941 came the integration of computer and communication technology. This was an important step in the evolution of communication systems. The computer enabled the creation and management of faster and more sophisticated systems. With this integration, the usage and development of new systems accelerated, lowering the cost of communication and increasing quality and efficiency.

In 1943, submersible amplifiers and repeaters were developed, facilitating communication across large distances and among international customers. In 1947, the invention of the transistor allowed for the development of smaller and faster computers. Integration of communication systems and computers would not be what it is today without the invention of the transistor and subsequent developments in integrated circuitry. The first satellite was launched in 1957, and this expanded the opportunity for worldwide data communications.

In 1968, an important decision, known as the Carterfone Decision, was made by the Federal Communication Commission (FCC). The FCC decided that a small Dallas based company (Carter Electronics Corporation), could attach its Carterfone product to the public telephone network. The Carterfone allowed the connection of private radio systems to the phone network. When AT&T refused to allow Carter Electronics to attach its product to the phone system, Carter Electronics sued and won. This decision opened the door for the attachment of non-AT&T equipment to the public phone system and spawned a new era in the communication industry. It also broke the monopoly that AT&T and the Bell companies had over the phone system. In 1984, AT&T divested itself from the Bell companies. This allowed many other companies to provide phone services to individuals and companies, ultimately increasing the quality, sophistication, and types of offerings that a communications company could provide. It also helped in reducing the cost of using data communication systems. Table 1-1 shows a summary of the history of data communication.

	Summary of Data Communication History
1837	Invention of the telegraph
1856	Western Union was created
1877	The Bell company was formed
1885	AT&T was created
1913	Invention of the vacuum tube
1941	Integration of computing and communication technology
1947	Invention of the transistor
1957	First satellite was launched
1968	Caterfone decision
1984	Divesture of Bell company

Table 1-1. Summary of history of data communications

Today, the network of available telephone lines, microwave stations, and satellite stations continues to expand. Computer technology continues to become faster and more economical. And data communication has become a worldwide enterprise.

Basic Components of a Data Communication System

Data communication systems can be divided into three major components:

1. The source of communication. This is the originator of the message to be sent.
2. The medium of communication. This is the physical path through which the message has to travel.
3. The receiver (sometimes called the sink or host) of the communication. This is the receiver of the message.

In many situations a computer is both the sender and receiver. The medium can be a leased line from the telephone company (also called a common carrier), a proprietary coaxial line, optical fiber, microwave, satellite, or other facilities. Fig. 1-1 depicts a basic data communication system. This system includes computers or terminals that act as senders, modems, connector cables, telephone switching equipment, interexchange channel facilities, a receiver, and a host computer. The items in Fig. 1-1 will be explained in more detail in further chapters, but a general description follows.

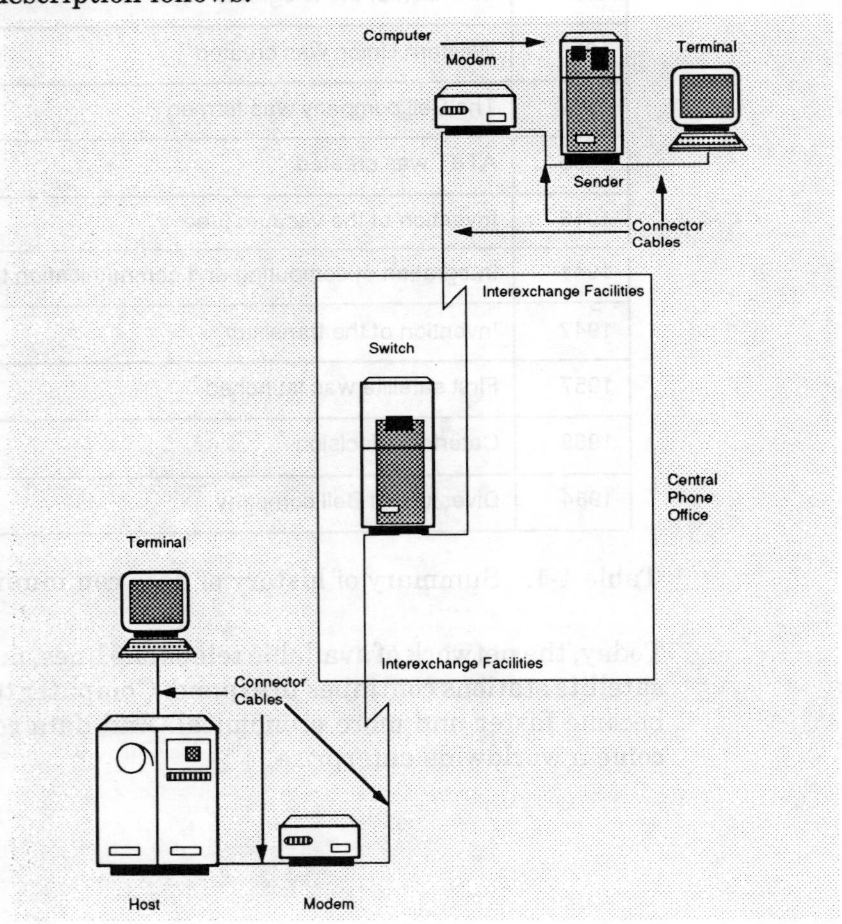

Fig. 1-1. Data communication system

The computer and terminal are used to enter information. This device can be a terminal attached to a minicomputer or mainframe, or a microcomputer with a keyboard and a printer, or it can be a FAX machine, or any other input device.

The connector cables in Fig. 1-1 connect the sender to a modem. The connector cables can be simple copper wire, twisted pair wire, coaxial cable, optical fiber, or other media.

The modem is an electronic device that converts digital signals originating from a computer or FAX machine into analog signals that the telephone equipment can understand. The signals go from the modem to a local telephone switch that connects the home or office to the telephone company central office or some other carrier.

The central office (sometimes called the exchange office) contains switching and control facilities operated by the phone company. All calls and data exchanges have to flow through these facilities unless there is a leased line. If there is a leased line, the phone company wires the line around the switching equipment in order to provide an unbroken path.

The interexchange channels (IXC) are circuit lines that connect one central exchange office with another. These circuit lines can be microwave, satellite, coaxial cable, or other physical media.

Finally, the receiving end has another modem to convert the analog signals from the telephone company back to digital format. These signals are then transferred to a host computer that processes the received message and takes appropriate action.

There are many other components that can be incorporated into the data communication system depicted in Fig. 1-1. Chapters 2 through 6 provide further details of these components, as well as an in-depth discussion of communication networks that incorporate computer technology.

Introduction to Data Communication Networks

A network is a series of points that are connected by some type of communication channel. Each point (sometimes called a node) is typically a computer, although it can consist of switching equipment, printers, FAX machines, or other devices. A data communications network is a collection of data communication circuits managed as a single entity. The collection of data communication networks and the people that enter data, receive the data, and manage and control the networks make up the communication system. Fig. 1-2 shows examples of multiple networks which are part of a data communication system.

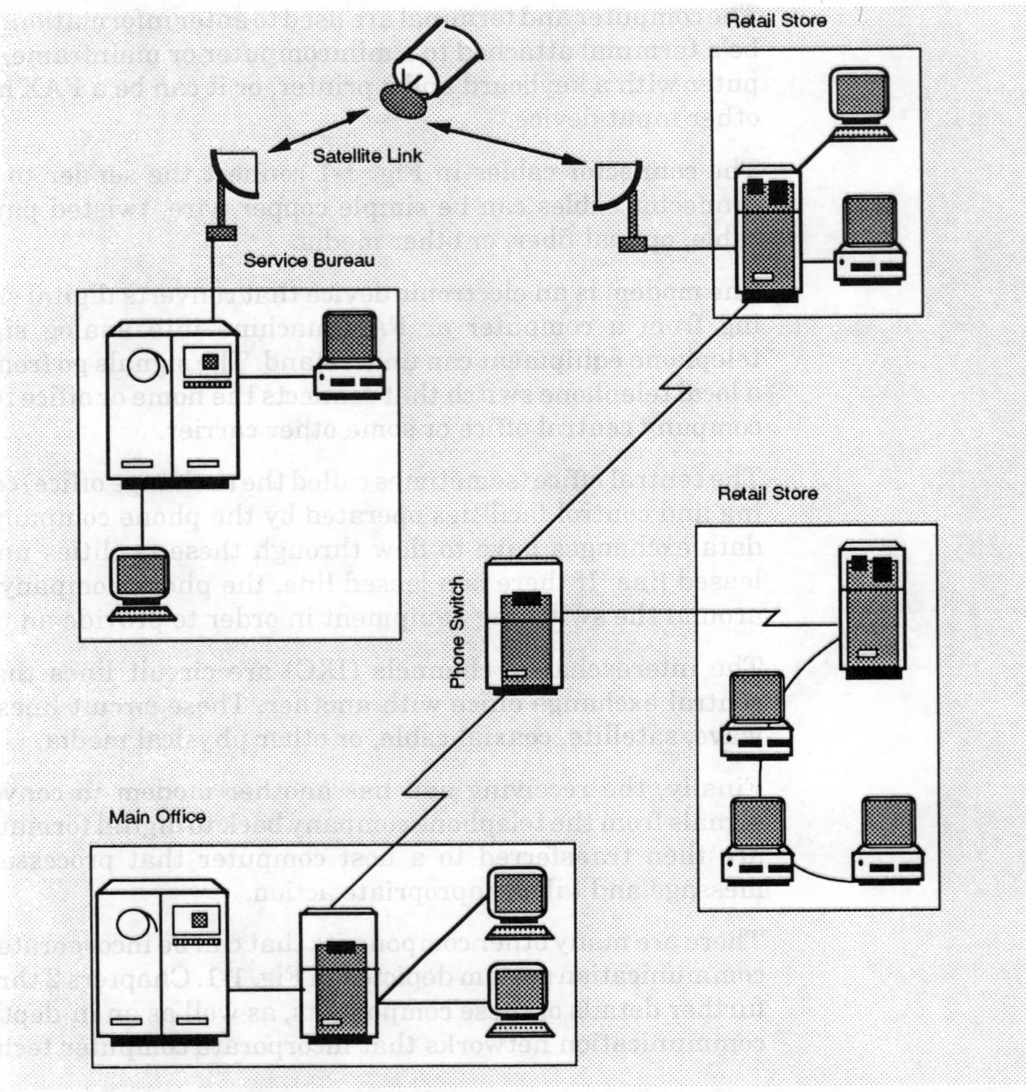

Fig. 1-2. Network system

Requirements of a Data Communication Network

There is a set of major criteria that a successful data communication network must meet. These are performance, consistency, reliability, recovery, and security criteria.

Performance

A data communication network must deliver data in a timely manner. Performance is typically measured by the network response time. Response time is normally considered the elapsed time between the end of an inquiry to the network and the beginning of the response from the network or system. The response time of a communications network must match the expectations of the users. Many factors affect the response time of a network. Some of these factors are the number of users on the system, transmission speeds, type of transmission medium, and the type of hardware and software being employed.

Consistency

Predictability of response time, accuracy of the data transmitted, and mean time between failures (MTBF) are important factors to consider when choosing a network. Inconsistency of response time is annoying to users, and sometimes it is worse than a slow but consistent response time. Accuracy of data is important if the network is to be deemed reliable. If a system loses data, then the users will not have confidence in the information generated by the system.

Reliability

Network failure is any event that prohibits the users from processing transactions. Network failure can include a breakdown in hardware, the data carrying medium, and/or the network controlling software (network operating system). The mean time between failures (MTBF) is a measure of the average time a component is expected to operate between failures.

Recovery

All networks are subject to failure. After a failure, the network must be able to recover to a prescribed level of operation. This prescribed level is a point in the network operation where the amount of lost data is non-existent or a minimum. Recovery procedures and the extent of recovery will depend on the type of hardware and software that control the network.

Security

Network security is another important component in communication networks, especially when computer data is involved. A business's data must be protected from unauthorized access. Therefore, companies are placing more stringent security measures on networks in order to safeguard their data. When a communications network is being designed, security must be carefully considered and incorporated into the final design.

Applications of Communication Networks

During the 1990s, data communication networks will be a faster growing industry than computer processing itself. Even though both industries are now integrated, we are moving from the computer era to the data communication era.

There are many business systems that use data communication networks as the "backbone" for carrying out their daily business activities. Data communication networks can be found in every segment of industry. On-line passenger systems, such as American Airlines' SABRE, have changed the way people travel. In addition, an airline's computer is normally connected via telecommunications to all other airlines. In this manner, reservation agents from United Airlines can make reservations for flights on American Airlines. Car rental companies, such as Avis, and hotel chains, such as Holiday Inn, could not function effectively without their reservation systems. Other types of applications discussed below include videotext, satellite, public networks, teleconferencing, and telecommuting.

Videotext

Videotext is the capability of having a two-way transmission between a television or computer in the home and organizations outside the home. It allows people to take college courses at home, conduct teleconferences from the home, play video games with players in other locations, utilize electronic mail, connect with the bank and grocery stores, do on-line mail shopping, utilize voice store and messaging systems, and carry out many other functions. Fig. 1-3 shows a screen display of a bulletin board that is used for discussing expert advice on computer topics. The conferencing system can be accessed from a home by using a microcomputer and special hardware to call a host computer and use it to "talk" to other people on the system.

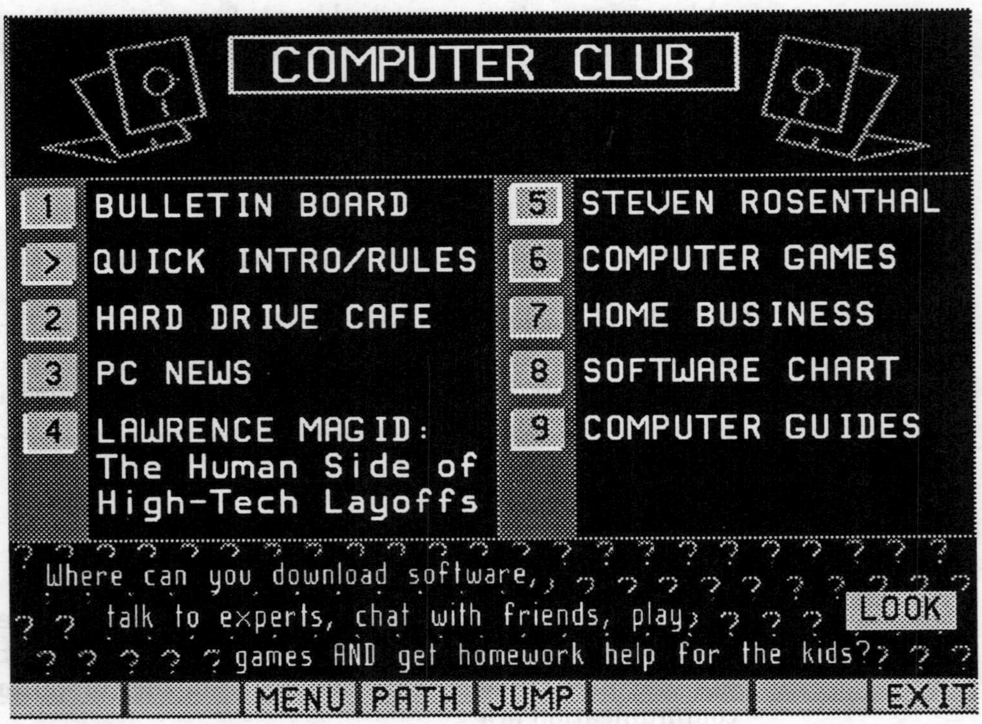

Fig. 1-3. Screen of a bulletin board

Satellite

By using a home satellite TV receiver and transmitter, people will be able to communicate with other people via a satellite disk located on their property. This antenna can receive and transmit voice or data to any other part of the world by relaying it to other satellites orbiting the earth.

Public Networks

Public networks have standard interfaces that allow almost any type of computer or terminal to connect to other computers or terminals. Many companies already have their own private telephone branch exchange (PBX). These systems can connect terminals and computers in the company to other systems anywhere in the world by using satellite, radio, and microwave transmission. In addition, cellular radio loops can be used to replace copper wire as the communication medium for computers.

Teleconferencing

Video teleconferencing allows people located in different geographical regions to "attend" meetings in both voice and picture format. Documents can also be made available to all people attending the teleconference almost instantaneously.

Telecommuting

This application allows employees to perform office work at home. Through the use of a terminal or a personal computer, an employee can be in constant communication with the company and perform his or her work more efficiently and without wasting the time required to travel to and from the office. This allows employees to have greater time flexibility, less stress, optimized scheduling, and many other benefits.

Electronic Mail

Electronic mail (e-mail) provides the ability to transmitt written messages over short or long distances instantaneously through the use of a microcomputer or terminal attached to a communication network. The people communicating through electronic mail do not have to be on-line at the same time. Each can leave messages to the other and retrieve the replies at later times. Fig. 1-4 shows a screen that is typical of many electronic mail systems.

Electronic mail has the capability to forward messages to different locations, send word processed or spreadsheet documents to any user of the network, and transmit the same message to more than one user by using a mail list. A mail list contains the names and electronic mailbox addresses of people that the message must be sent to. The electronic mail system reads the names and addresses from the list and sends the message to all users on the mail list. Electronic mail improves corporate and individual communications significantly. See chapter 15 for additional information on electronic mail.

Home Banking

Computers can handle the traditional methods of making payments through home banking. A user with a terminal or microcomputer can connect to his or her bank's computer network through electronic mail and pay bills electronically, instead of writing paper checks. The user can indicate the amount of a payment and the receiver of the payment electronically, and the bank processes the transfer of funds. Additionally, new home banking systems offer many other services besides personal fund transfers. Some of these services are providing checking account balances, ticket purchasing, and stock information services. Fig. 1-5 shows a screen of a home banking service software program. The banking service display in the figure has services for bill paying, credit card acquisition, money markets, IRAs, loans, mortgages, and others.

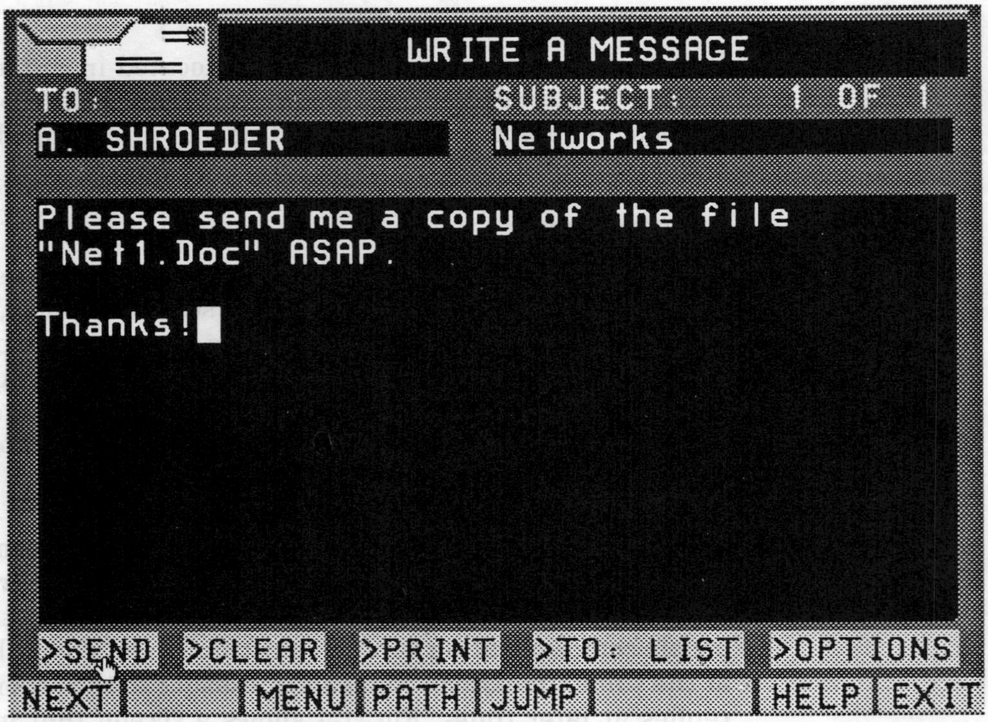

Fig. 1-4. Electronic mail screen

Electronic Fund Transfer

The ability to transfer funds electronically from one financial institution to another has become a necessity in today's banking world. Commercial banks transfer millions of dollars daily through their electronic fund transfer (EFT) system. The large number of transactions that are made every day by banks require the use of computers and communication networks to increase speed and cost efficiency.

Information Utility Services

Information utility services offer general and specialized information that is organized and cross-referenced, much like subjects are in libraries. Items are organized into data bases and contain several categories of services such as access to news, legal libraries, stock prices, electronic mail services, conferencing, and games.

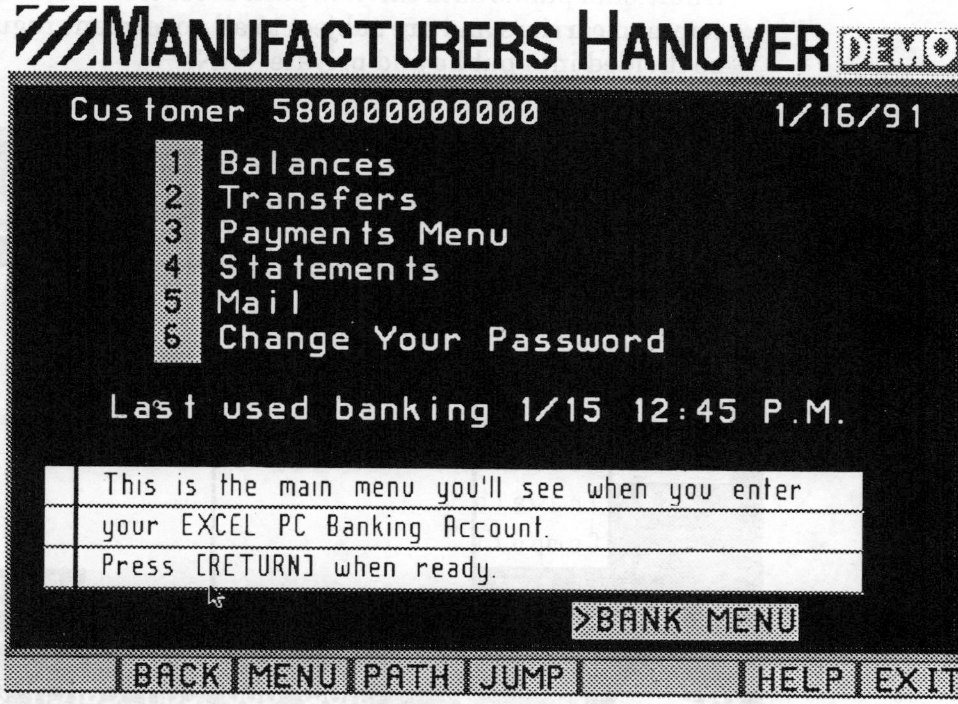

Fig.1-5. Screen of an electronic home banking system

The desired information is located by signing on to the information service and then selecting the topic of interest from a menu. Once the topic is selected, search criteria can be entered and the system will display the information on the screen. This information can then be captured (downloaded) onto the hard disk of the user's microcomputer for further examination. See chapter 15 for more information on this topic.

Electronic Bulletin Boards

The electronic bulletin board system (BBS or EBBS) consists of a computer or microcomputer that is used to store, retrieve, and catalog messages sent in by the general public through their modems. The telephone company provides the link between the person using the BBS and the host computer of the BBS. The primary purpose of BBS is for people to leave notes to others. Also, some BBS are now being used for group conferencing. They offer a variety of messages and services to their users. Some of these services are electronic "chat" with other users, making airline reservations, playing games, and sending and receiving messages. Fig. 1-6 displays some of the services offered by a privately owned information utility service.

Value Added Networks

Value added networks (VANs) are alternative data carriers to the traditional public data carriers such as AT&T. VANs are now considered common carriers and are subject to all goverment regulations. They can be divided into public and private VANs.

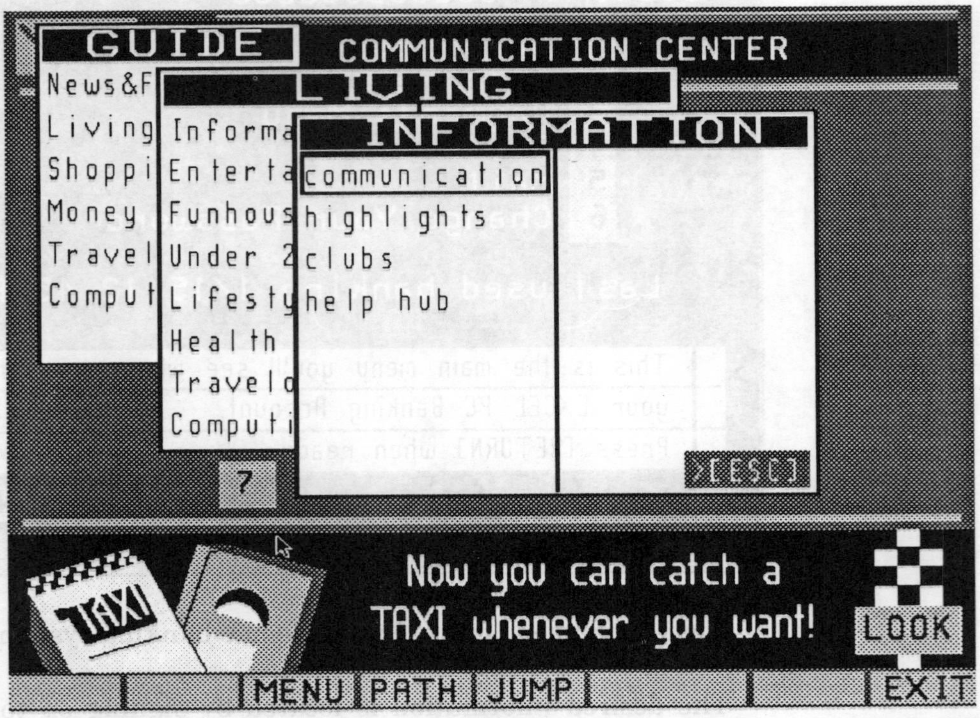

Fig. 1-6. Screen showing some of the offerings of a private information service

Private VANs own and operate their networks and are not accessible to the public. One example of a private carrier is the SABRE system used by travel agents to make reservations and check prices. Public VANs offer a wide variety of communication services to the general public. These services include access to databases and electronic mail routing. An example of a public VAN is Telenet.

Summary

Data communication is the transmission of electronic data over some medium. The systems that enable the transmission of data are often called data communication networks. For a data communication system to be effective, it must provide information to the right people in a timely manner, capture business data as it is being produced, and allow people and businesses in different geographical locations to communicate with one another. The basic components of a data communication system are the source of communication, the medium of communication, and the receiver of the communication. All data communication systems must meet a minimum set of requirements which include performance, consistency, reliability, recovery, and security requirements.

Data communication systems are composed of data communication networks. A network is a series of points that are connected by some type of communication channel. Each point is typically a computer, although it can consist of many other electronic devices. A communication system is a collection of communication networks and the people using and managing the networks. There are many examples of data communication networks. Some of the most popular are airline reservation systems, videotext services, satellite systems, public networks, teleconference systems, and telecommuting systems.

Questions

1. Briefly describe the concept of data communications.
2. Name some of the possible data transmission media.
3. What are the functions of data communication systems?
4. Briefly name the most important historical events that shaped the communication industry up to the 1990s.
5. Describe the basic components of a data communication network.
6. What is a communication network?
7. What is the difference between a communication network and a communication system?
8. What are the major requirements that a data communication network must possess?
9. What is meant by mean time between failures (MTBF)?
10. Discuss three applications of a data communication network.

Projects

Objective

This project will make the student familiar with a currently implemented data communication system. It provides a way to visualize the concepts and hardware discussed in the chapter. In addition, it allows the student to acquire a "feel" of how people use the components of data communication systems and to observe some of the equipment and processes that will be explained in more detail in subsequent chapters.

Project 1. Understanding an Existing Computer Communication System

Visit the data center at your institution and find what types of network and data communication facilities are available for the private use of the institution and which facilities are available for general public access. Try to answer all the questions below by asking data center personnel or by observing the daily operations and hardware present at the center.

a. What types of mainframes or minicomputers (hosts) are available?

b. What types of personal computers are available?

- ❑ Laptops
- ❑ Macintosh Classic/SE
- ❑ Macintosh II family
- ❑ IBM PC/AT
- ❑ IBM PS/2
- ❑ IBM-compatible clone
- ❑ Other

c. Are the hosts networked?

d. Are the personal computers networked?

e. How are the personal computers connected to the host?

f. Is electronic mail available?

g. How is the electronic mail accessed?

h. What data bases are available in the institution library?

i. How often do they experience down time?

j. Find out how the staff conducts business when their computer or terminal is down.

k. How is the data protected from unauthorized access and accidents?

Project 2. Understanding an Elementary Computer Network

Contact your local bank and write a report that describes how the bank personnel perform their daily routines. Use the outline below as a guide for your report.

a. Computer systems in use at headquarters and at the branches:
   - ❑ Mainframes
   - ❑ Minicomputers
   - ❑ Personal computers
   - ❑ Terminals

b. Networks used at each branch and between branch and headquarters:

c. How is electronic fund transfer handled?

d. What types of value added networks and public networks are used to perform e-mail and electronic fund transfer?

e. Are there any facilities available for home banking?

f. What types of disaster recovery plans do they have?

g. How do the managers at different branches communicate with each other?

2

Essentials of Data Communication

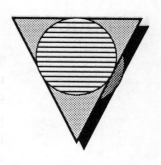

Objectives

1. Understand the different types of transmission modes.
2. Understand the function of modems in a communication environment.
3. Understand the function and composition of the standard RS-232 I/O port.
4. Obtain a general overview of standard digital logic and control codes.
5. Have a general understanding of the different types of terminals.
6. Understand the role of front end processors and their functions in a communication network.
7. Understand the importance of the mainframe or central processing computer in data communications.

Key Terms

Async/Sync Transmission	**Communication Control**
Digital Code	**FAX**
Front End Processor	**Half/Full Duplex**
Light Pen	**Mainframe**
Microcomputer	**Modem**
Mouse	**Parallel Transmission**
RS-232 Port	**Scanner**
Serial Transmission	**Terminal**
Touch Screen	**Voice Entry**

Introduction

This chapter introduces the concepts of protocols and transmission modes. There is also an in-depth discussion of modems and serial communication considerations.

In addition, the chapter presents a discussion of some of the basic hardware required for data communications. This basic hardware includes a host computer, front end processors, terminals, microcomputers, modems, transmission media, and software to control the hardware.

Modes of Transmission

There are different ways in which the transmission of data can be classified. They can be grouped into three major areas:

1. How the data flows among devices.
2. The type of physical connection.
3. The type of timing used for transmitting data.

Data can flow in simplex, half-duplex, or full-duplex mode (see Fig. 2-1). The physical connection can be parallel or serial (see Fig. 2-2). The timing can be synchronous or asynchronous.

Data Flow

In simplex transmission, data flows in only one direction on a data communication line. Examples of this type of communication are commercial television and radio transmission.

In half-duplex mode, transmission is allowed in either direction on a circuit, but in only one direction at a time. This type of transmission is widely used in data processing applications.

Full-duplex mode allows for the transmission of data in both directions simultaneously. Most terminals and microcomputers are configured to work in full-duplex mode. This type of transmission requires more software and hardware control on both ends.

Physical Connection

Input/output ports can transmit data bit by bit or send the entire byte in a single parallel operation employing eight lines, one for each bit. The benefit of parallel transmission is its simplicity. A byte is placed on the output port of a device and a single pulse transfers the data to a receiving device. However, because of the number of wires involved, it is expensive and impractical over long distances.

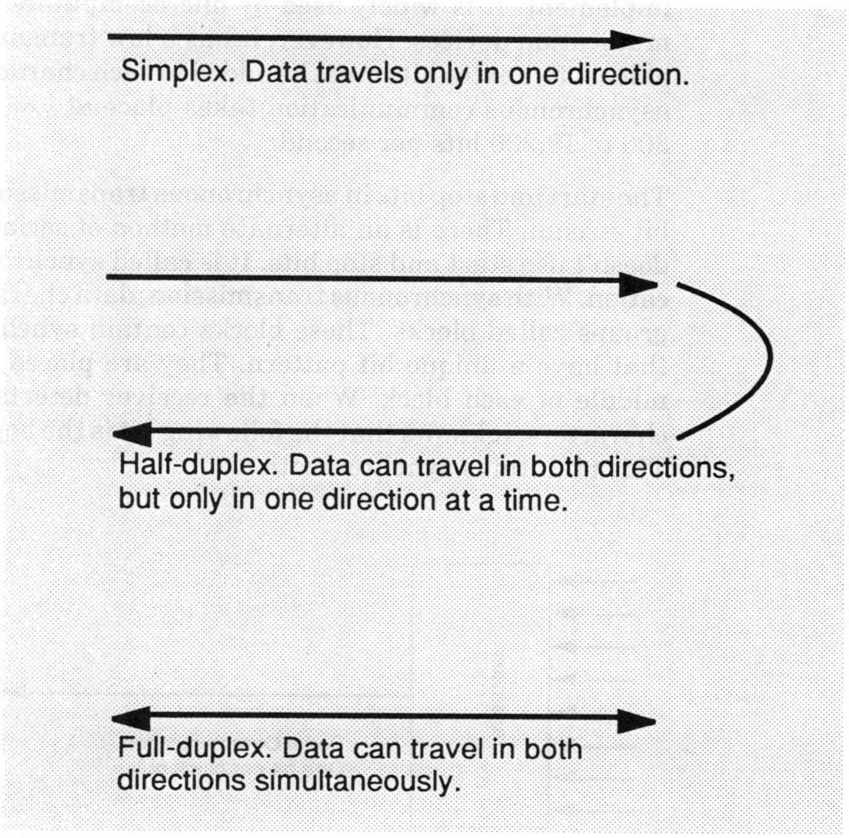

Simplex. Data travels only in one direction.
Half-duplex. Data can travel in both directions, but only in one direction at a time.
Full-duplex. Data can travel in both directions simultaneously.

Fig. 2-1. Data flow modes

In serial transmission the data is sent one bit at a time. It uses a single conductor to provide communication between devices. Standard telephone lines can be used to transmit data serially. Transmitting data in this mode is more complex than parallel transmission, but it is currently the most widely used type of data transmission.

Timing

Asynchronous communications is characterized by the use of a start bit preceding each character transmitted. In addition, there are one or more stop bits which follow each character. In asynchronous transmission, (sometimes called async), data comes in irregular bursts, not in steady streams.

The start and stop bits form what is called a character frame. Every character must be enclosed in a frame. The receiver counts the start bit and the appropriate number of data bits. If it does not sense the end of a frame, then a framing error has occurred and an invalid character was received.

Asynchronous transmission is relatively simple and inexpensive to implement. It is widely used by microcomputers and commercial communication devices. However, it has a low transmission efficiency since at least two extra bits must be added to each character transmitted. Also, asynchronous communication takes place at low speeds, ranging from 300 to 19,200 bits per second.

The start and stop bits in asynchronous transmission add overhead to the bit stream. There is an alternate method of serial communication that doesn't use start and stop bits. It is called synchronous serial communication. With synchronous transmission, data characters are sent in large groups called blocks. These blocks contain synchronization characters that have a unique bit pattern. They are placed at the beginning and middle of each block. When the receiver detects one of these special characters, it knows that the following bit is the beginning of a character. This maintains synchronization.

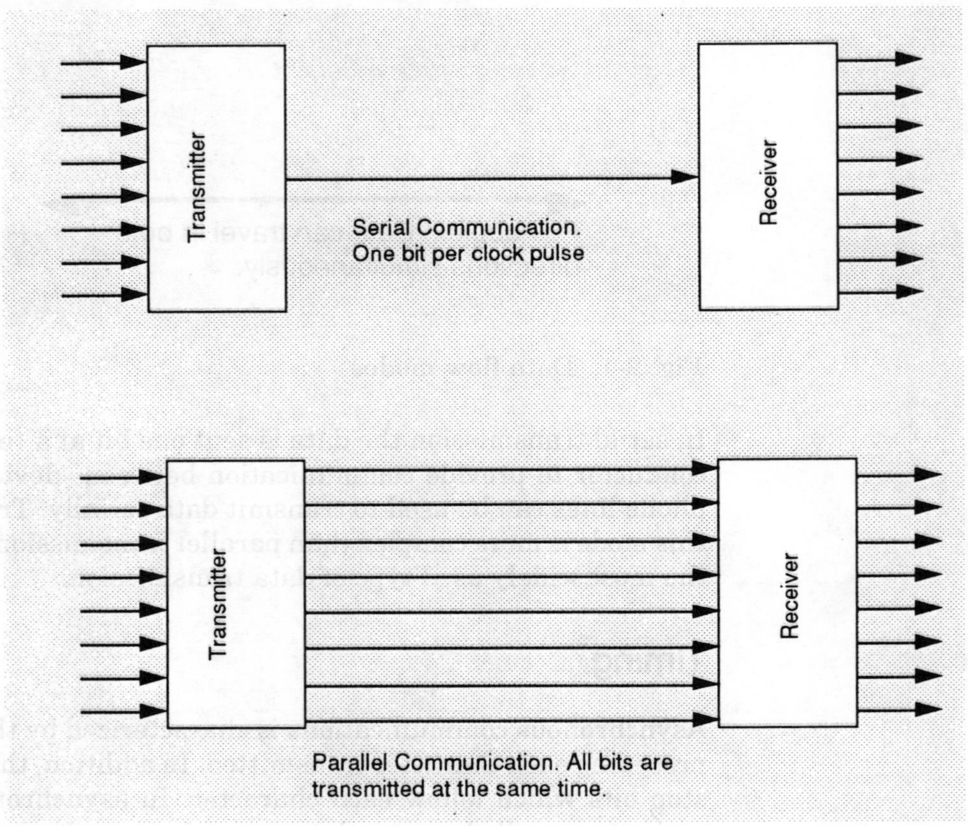

Fig. 2-2. Serial and parallel connections

The synchronization characters range in number from one to four. This type of transmission is more efficient than asynchronous communication. As an example, assume that 10,000 characters are going to be sent serially. If the characters are sent via asynchronous transmission, then 10,000 char x (7 data bits + 2 bits per char) yields 90,000 bits that are sent in asynchronous communications. Using synchronous communication, the calculation (10,000 char + 4 synchronous char) x 7 bits per char yields 70,028 bits that are sent.

In this example, the synchronous transmission has a 22 percent increase in transmission efficiency over asynchronous transmission. The efficiency of synchronous over asynchronous transmission increases as the block of data gets larger. Many terminals use synchronous communication, including the IBM 3270 series.

Modems

Fig. 2-3 depicts the connection of a remote terminal or microcomputer to a host system via standard telephone lines. The terminal and host systems are separated by devices called modems. A modem is an electronic device that converts (modulates) the digital communications between computers into audible tones that can be transmitted over telephone lines. The received data is then converted (demodulated) from the audible tones into digital information. This is the origin of the name modem (MOdulator-DEModulator).

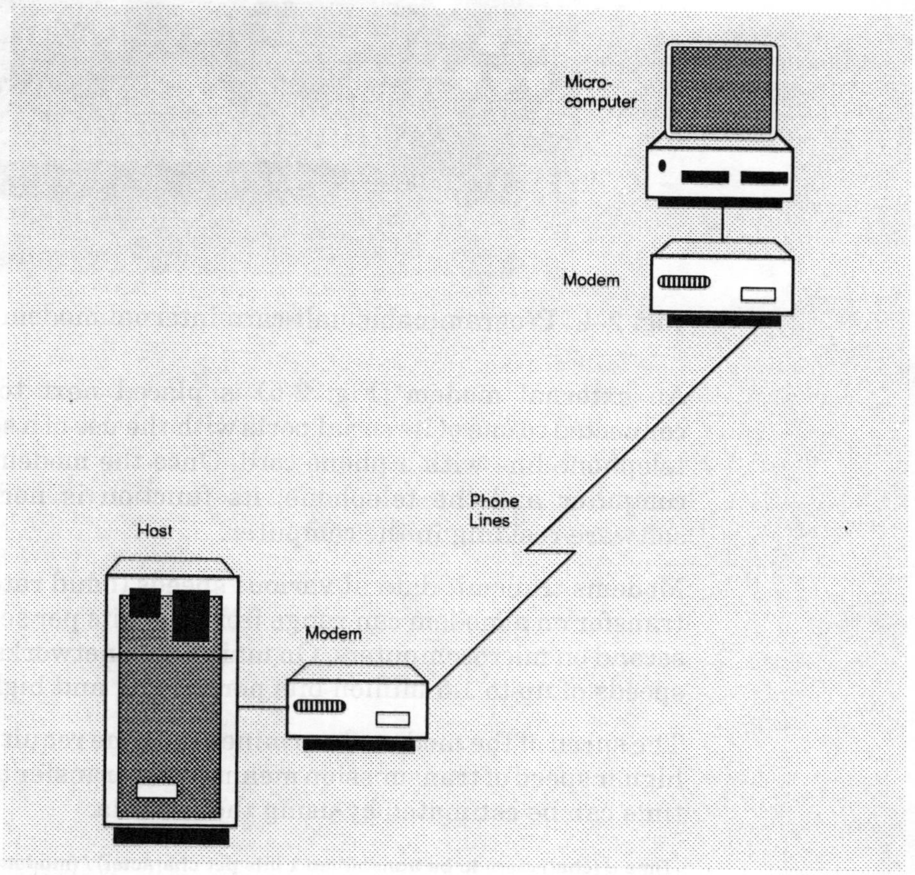

Fig. 2-3. Connection between a remote station and a host system

Most modems can dial phone numbers automatically. Additionally, they can redial busy numbers and automatically set the proper communicating speed.

Modems can be external or internal. An internal modem (Fig. 2-4) is placed inside the computer by using available bus expansion slots. Then it is connected to a phone line with the use of a standard phone cord.

The AT&T programmable half-card modem fits inside a personal computer. The modem can be operated directly from the keyboard. (Courtesy of AT&T).

Fig. 2-4. Programmable half-card internal modem

An external modem (Fig. 2-5) is placed next to the computer and connected to one of its serial ports with the use of a serial cable and to the telephone line with a phone cord. Once the modem is connected to the computer and the telephone, its function is normally controlled by software residing in the computer.

Modems transmit data at various speeds (baud rate). The speed of data transfer on a modem can range from 300 bits per second to 9600 bits per second on microcomputers. On mainframe networks, modems operate at speeds of up to 1.5 million bits per second, and higher.

The speed of the modem determines the time required to transfer files. A higher speed of transmission means lower transfer time. The file transfer time can be estimated by using the formula:

Time = (characters to be transmitted x bits per character) / (modem speed in bits per second)

The AT&T 4024 modem transmits data asynchronously or synchronously at 300, 1,200, or 2,400 bps. Transmissions can be either full-duplex or half-duplex. (Courtesy of AT&T)

Fig. 2-5. External modem

As an example, assume that a 100 page document is to be transmitted. Further assume that each page contains approximately 3300 characters and each character requires seven bits for storage. This means that there will be 2,310,000 bits to be transmitted. The following table displays the approximate amount of time required to transmit the file.

Bits per second	300	1200	4800	9600
Time (seconds)	7700	1930	480	240

These are just approximate times. The actual time required to transfer a file depends on many factors such as noise in the communicating lines, how the data is packed, how many times a character must be retransmitted, and so forth. However, the times shown in the table can be used to obtain an idea of how the transmission time is reduced by increasing the speed of the modem.

Types of Modems

Optical Modem

An optical modem transmits data over optical fiber lines. This type of modem converts electrical signals from a computer into pulses of light to be transmitted over optical fiber lines. It operates using asynchronous or synchronous transmission modes.

Short Haul Modem

This type of modem uses wire pair cable to transmit electrical signals. It is also called a 20-milliamp or line driver circuit. It interfaces an RS-232 port (see the section on RS-232 in this chapter) to standard 20-milliamp loop systems. A short haul modem transmits at speeds of 19,200 bits per second. This type of modem is used to connect computers between different offices in the same building.

Acoustic Modem

This is an older type of modem, also called an acoustic coupler. It interfaces with any handphone set and it is used for dialing up to another computer.

Smart Modem

A smart modem can perform functions by using a command syntax language. The language can be accessed through communication programs and adds functionality to the modem. Among microcomputer users, the Hayes modem has become the standard. This device can automatically answer or dial other modems, switch communication parameters, set the modem's speaker volume, and perform many other functions under software control.

Digital Modem

If, instead of using analog conversion, the communication circuits use digital transmission, then a digital modem is used. This type of modem modifies the digital bits as needed. Its function is to convert digital signals into more precise and accurate signals suitable for transmission.

V.32 Modem

A V.32 modem works at full duplex at 9,600 bits per second over normal telephone lines. It is typically used to back up leased phone lines on networks. That is, if data transmission through a leased line is interrupted, a V.32 and normal phone lines could be used as a temporary replacement for the lease line.

Features of Modems

Speed

Modems are designed to operate at a set speed or a range of speeds. The speed can be set via switches on some modems or fall under program control. Typical speeds for modems under microcomputer control are 300, 1200, 2400, 4800, and 9600 bits per second.

Automatic Dialing/Redialing

Some modems can dial phone numbers under program control. If the modem encounters a busy line, it automatically redials the number until a connection is made.

Automatic Answering

Modems can automatically answer incoming calls and connect the dialing device to a host system.

Self-testing

Most new modems have a self-testing mode. That is, the modem has electronic circuitry and software in ROM that allows the modem to check its electronic components and the connection to other modems, and to report any problems to the user. This includes memory checker, modem-to-modem transmission tests, and other self-tests.

Voice-over-data

Newer modems allow the simultaneous transmission of voice and data. This allows a conversation to take place while data is being transmitted over the same phone line.

Other

Newer modems contain many other features in addition to the ones outlined above. Some of these features are:

Auto-disconnect
Manual connect/disconnect
Speaker
Full- or half-duplex
Reverse channel
Synchronous or asynchronous transmission
Multiport

The RS-232 Port

On most microcomputers that use the ASCII code, the connections between external modems, computers, and other devices conform to what is called the RS-232 standard. The RS-232 is a connector that is found on the back panel of most computers. Fig. 2-6 shows a diagram of a 25-pin RS-232 connector.

The important pins to consider are pin numbers 1, 2, 3, 4, 5, 6, 8, and 20. Following is a description of these connectors with the capitalized abbreviations corresponding to the modem front panel.

Pin 1. Frame ground: FG. It is used to connect the frame of the terminal or modem to earth ground. It protects the device from dangerous voltages. Normally, this pin is left unconnected.

Pin 2. Transmit data: TD. Outgoing data travels from the terminal or computer to the modem via pin 2.

Pin 3. Receive data: RD. Incoming data travels from the modem to the terminal or computer via pin 3.

Pin 4. Request to send: RTS. This is used to indicate to the terminal or computer that the modem has activated its carrier and that data transmission can start.

Pin 5. Clear to send: CTS. This pin is taken to an active level when the terminal or computer is ready to accept data.

Pin 6. Data set ready: DSR. An active DSR indicates to a device that it is connected to an active modem.

Pin 8. Data carrier detect: DCD. This pin is used by the modem to inform the computer or terminal that a remote connection has been made.

Pin 20. Data terminal ready: DTR. An active DTR indicates to the modem that it is connected to an active device.

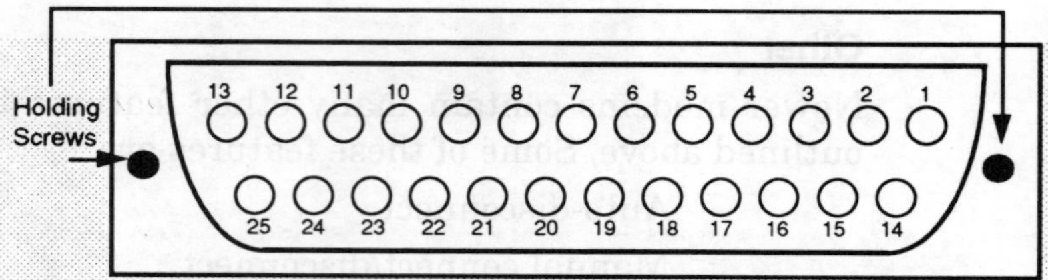

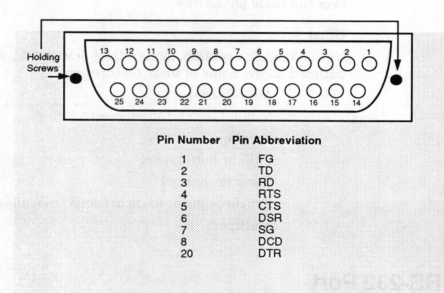

Pin Number	Pin Abbreviation
1	FG
2	TD
3	RD
4	RTS
5	CTS
6	DSR
7	SG
8	DCD
20	DTR

Fig. 2-6. RS-232 connector (25 pins)

Handshaking is the manner in which the communicating computer knows when the other machine is sending or receiving data, or when it is doing some other task that might interfere with the transmission signals. This is also referred to as the communications protocol. Handshaking can be accomplished through the use of software by using control characters (X-On and X-Off). Pins 4, 5, 6, 8, and 20 are used for hardware handshaking. That is, these pins are used to make sure that there is cooperation between the devices exchanging data.

Another type of RS-232 connector is the nine-pin RS-232 connector found on some microcomputers. By using nine pins instead of twenty-five pins, space is saved on the back panels of computers and peripherals. The layout of the pin connections on this type of RS-232 differs from manufacturer to manufacturer. Fig. 2-7 shows the layout of the nine-pin RS-232 connector found on the IBM PC-AT.

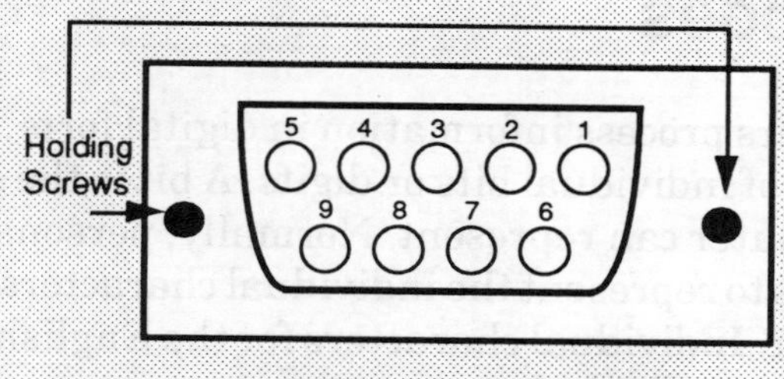

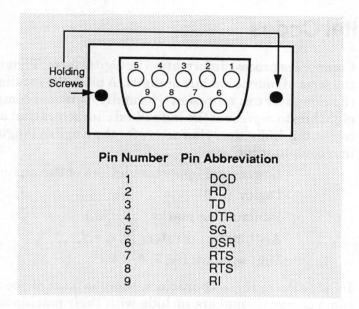

Pin Number	Pin Abbreviation
1	DCD
2	RD
3	TD
4	DTR
5	SG
6	DSR
7	RTS
8	RTS
9	RI

Fig. 2-7. RS-232 connector (9 pins)

The nine-pin connector in Fig. 2-7 has an extra pin (pin 9, RI) beyond the eight defined above. This is the ring indicator. This pin becomes active when the modem has received the ring of an incoming call.

The process of using a modem to connect a microcomputer or terminal to a host system is as follows:

1. When the communicating devices are powered up, the terminal's DTR signal and the modem's DSR signal are activated.
2. When the terminal is ready to send data, it activates its RTS signal.
3. The modem activates the CTS signal of the analog carrier.
4. The user's modem dials the phone of the remote modem and waits for its response.
5. When the user's modem senses communication over the phone line, it activates its DCD signal.
6. A high level DCD signal tells the microcomputer or terminal that it is connected to a remote device and the data exchange can begin.

Standard Digital Codes

Computers process information in digital form. That is, information is in the form of individual bits or digits. A bit is the smallest unit of data that the computer can represent. Normally, personal computers use seven or eight bits to represent the individual characters that are stored inside the computer. Individual characters for the English language that are stored in a computer include:

Lower- and uppercase letters of the alphabet (a...Z)

Digits (0...9)

Punctuation marks (., ?, :, ...)

Arithmetic operators (*, -, +, /, ...)

Unit symbols (%, $, #, ...)

In addition to these characters, there is a set of special characters that some computer makers include with their machines. These are mostly graphical and language specific characters.

For many years, the computer industry has tried to standardize the representation of digital codes. As a result, two major code representations exist in the market today. The most popular and widely recognized is the code system employed by the American Standard Code for Information Interchange (ASCII). The other major code is the Extended Binary Coded Decimal Interchange Code (EBCDIC), which is used by IBM mainframes and compatibles. Most other types of mainframes, minicomputers, and microcomputers employ the ASCII code.

ASCII is a seven-bit code in which 128 characters are represented. EBCDIC uses eight bits to represent each character. Table 2-1 shows the standard ASCII code representation. In addition, there is a set of special characters used by IBM personal computers and compatibles called the Extended ASCII. The characters represented in Extended ASCII vary among computer manufacturers.

In this chapter we will concentrate on explaining the ASCII representation since it is the most popular. The ASCII code in Table 2.1 contains 128 unique items. The table shows 32 control characters and 96 printable characters. Table 2-1 uses the hexadecimal system to represent the ASCII value of each character. To find the ASCII value of a character the process is as follows. Assume that the ASCII value of "A" is required. The column number of "A" is four, therefore four is multiplied by 16 giving 64. The row number of "A" is one, so one is added to the previous result. The total is 65 and that is the ASCII value of the character "A". Notice that the rows jump from 9 to A, B, C, D, E, and F. In this case A represents 10, B is 11, C is 12, D is 13, E is 14, and F is 15. Using the example above it is easily verified that the ASCII value of the character "O" is 79, because 4 x 16 = 64, and 64 + 15 = 79.

	0	1	2	3	4	5	6	7
0	NUL	DLE	SP	0	@	P	`	p
1	SOH	DC1	!	1	A	Q	a	q
2	STX	DC2	"	2	B	R	b	r
3	ETX	DC3	#	3	C	S	c	s
4	EOT	DC4	$	4	D	T	d	t
5	ENQ	NAK	%	5	E	U	e	u
6	ACK	SYN	&	6	F	V	f	v
7	BEL	ETB	'	7	G	W	g	w
8	BS	CAN	(	8	H	X	h	x
9	HT	EM	)	9	I	Y	i	y
A	LF	SUB	*	:	J	Z	j	z
B	VT	ESC	+	;	K	[	k	{
C	FF	FS	´	<	L	\	l	|
D	CR	GS	-	=	M	]	m	}
E	SO	RS	.	>	N	^	n	~
F	SI	US	/	?	O	-	o	DEL

Table 2-1. ASCII codes

The printable characters can be generated by pressing the corresponding key on the keyboard, or by pressing the shift key and the appropriate key. The control characters are generated by pressing a key labeled Control or CTRL on the keyboard and a corresponding key. For the rest of this chapter, the character ^ will be used to denote the CTRL key. Control codes are used for communicating with external devices such as modems, printers, and additional codes.

The control codes can be further subdivided into format effectors, communication controls, information separators, and others as described below.

Format Effectors

The format effectors provide functions analogous to the control keys used in document preparation. Each code name is followed by its hexadecimal representation, then a colon, and finally the key combination that can generate the code. A description of each follows.

BS (backspace) 08H:^H. It moves the cursor on a video display or the print head of a printer back one space.

HT (horizontal tab) 09H:^I. This is the same as the Tab key on a keyboard or typewriter.

LF (line feed) 0AH:^J. It advances the cursor one line on a display or moves the printer down one line.

CR (carriage return) 0DH:^M. It returns the cursor on a display or moves the printer head to the beginning of the line. This code is sometimes combined with the line feed to produce a new line character that is defined as a CR/LF sequence.

FF (form feed) 0CH:^L. It ejects a page on a printer. It also causes the cursor to move one space to the right on a video screen.

VT (vertical tab) 0BH: ^K. It line feeds to the next programmed vertical tab on a printer. It causes the cursor to move up one line on a video screen.

Communication Controls

Another series of control codes is used for communication. These codes are:

SOH. It indicates the start of a header.

STX. It indicates the start of text.

ETX. It indicates the end of text.

EOT. It indicates the end of transmission.

ENQ. It indicates the end of an inquiry.

ACK. It indicates acknowledgement by a device.

NAK. It is negative acknowledgement.

EXT. This is an interrupt.

SYN. It is synchronous idle.

ETB. It indicates the end of a block.

These control codes are used in building data-transfer protocols and during synchronous transmission.

Information Separators

The information-separator codes are:

FS. It is used as a file separator.

GS. It is used as a group separator.

RS. It is used as a record separator.

US. It is used as a unit separator.

Most of the communication control and information separators codes are not relevant to the material presented in the rest of this chapter. However, they are shown here for general information purposes.

Additional Control Codes

The most important additional codes are

NUL (null) OOH: ^@. It is used to pad the start of a transmission of characters.

BEL (bell) 07H:^G. It generates a tone from the speaker on the video monitor or the computer.

DC1, DC2, DC3, and DC4 (device control): ^Q, ^R, ^S, ^T. These codes are used to control video monitors and printers. Of these four, the first (DC1) and the third (DC3), are of special interest. DC1 is generated by ^Q, and it is called X-On, and DC3 is generated by ^S, and it is called X-Off. If a computer sends information to a printer too fast, then the printer's buffer gets full before it can print the characters stored in it. The result is that characters are lost before they can be printed. In this situation, the printer sends a ^S (X-Off) to the computer before the buffer is completely full. This causes the computer to stop sending characters. When there is room in the printer buffer for more characters, a ^Q (X-On) is sent to the computer. This indicates to the machine that it can resume sending characters. This use of X-On and X-Off is called software handshaking.

ESC (escape) 1BH: ^[. Video terminals, computers, and printers interpret the next character after the escape code as a printable character.

DEL (delete) 7FH. It is used to delete characters under the cursor on video displays.

When two computers talk to each other, the information will be exchanged by passing the individual bits that make up the characters. The flow of information is controlled by the use of control codes between communicating devices. The conventions that must be observed in order for electronic devices to communicate with one another are called the protocol.

If the communicating devices are in close proximity, coaxial cable, twisted-pair cable, or optical fiber can be used to connect them. If the computers are far apart from each other, then microwave, satellite, or telephone line connections are used to connect the machines.

The phone company provides one of the most common and inexpensive methods of connecting machines. However, if analog phone lines are used, a modem must be employed.

Terminals and Microcomputers

A terminal is an input and/or output device that can be connected to a host computer. The terminal may depend on the host system for computational power and/or data. Obviously, many devices can meet this definition of a terminal. Among them is the microcomputer. Both the terminal and the computer to which it is connected are known as data terminal equipment (DTE). This type of equipment operates internally in digital format and produces digital output. The modem used to connect the terminal or computer to the communication line is known as data circuit-terminating equipment. Because the definition of data terminal is broad, there are several categories of terminals, each of which is defined in the following section.

Classifications

Microcomputer Workstation

A microcomputer workstation is a general purpose microcomputer or specialized input/output workstation with "smart" circuitry and a central processing unit. Technically, there is a difference between a microcomputer workstation and a microcomputer. The workstation includes the tools necessary for a professional to perform his or her daily work. These tools are specialized software applications such as CAD systems and mathematical modeling systems. In addition, today's workstations have the ability to multitask software programs. This means they can run multiple programs simultaneously and can switch among them as the user needs to. The microcomputer may not have all of these capabilities built in. It may only be used for word processing or database access. Regardless of which system we are discussing, the microcomputer is an integral part of communication networks. It can be used as part of a local area network or as a terminal device connected to a host system. Fig. 2-8 shows a picture of a typical microcomputer system.

Microcomputer workstations are being increasingly used in networks since they can perform many processing functions internally before the data is passed on to a host system. Some of the ways in which they are used are:

1. Data stored in central systems is transmitted (downloaded) to the microcomputer. The data can be processed by the microcomputer using a word processor, database, spreadsheet, or some other software application. After processing, the data is transmitted back to the central system for further processing or storage.

2. Data stored on the microcomputer can be submitted as a batch job to the host system as required.

3. Applications on the microcomputer can be assisted by the processing power of the host system. For example, a scientific data base can reside in part on the microcomputer system, but when large calculations or repetitious calculations are required, the microcomputer can rely on the host system for assistance.
4. Large projects can be divided among several microcomputers. The completed pieces can then be assembled on the host system.
5. Microcomputers can work as terminals to the host computer. In this role they emulate the native terminals of the central system.
6. Microcomputers that are part of a local area network can share storage and printer devices on the network or devices on the central system.

This IBM PS/2 model 70 contains a powerful processor and comes with a minimum of 1 megabyte of memory. (Courtesy of IBM Corporation)

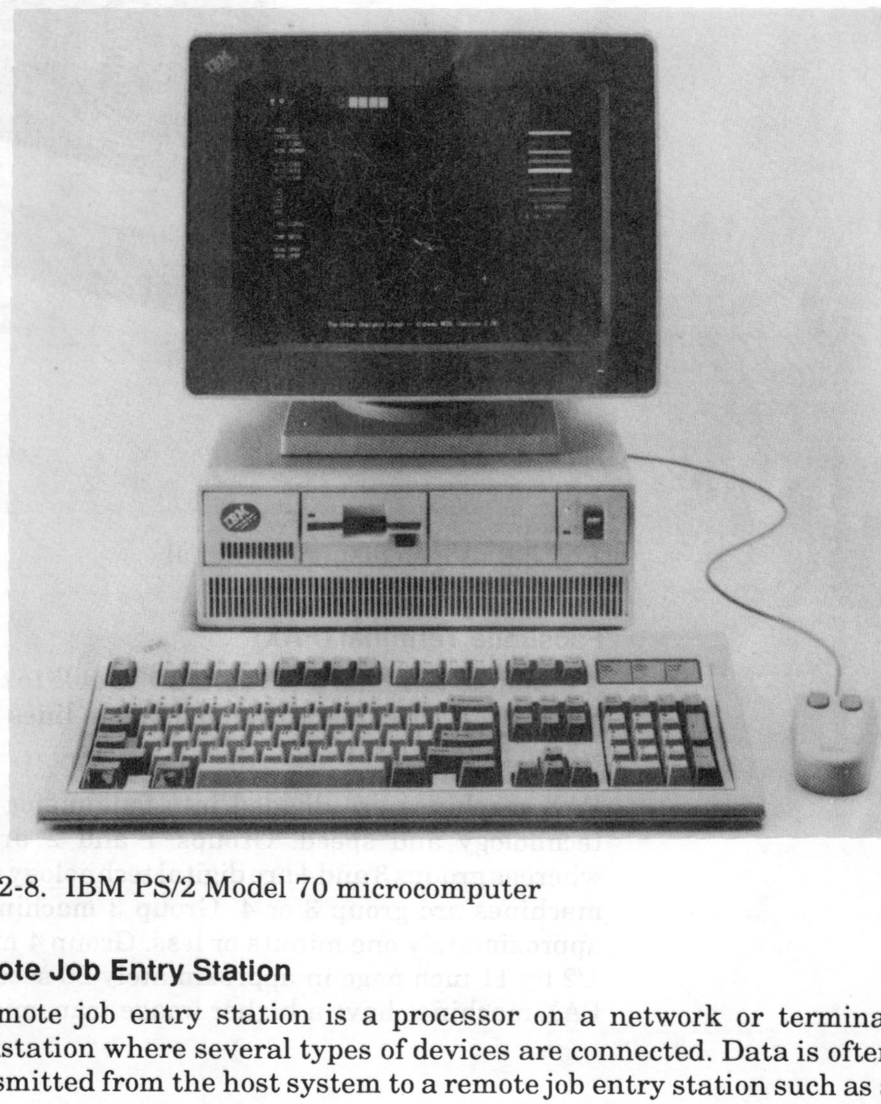

Fig. 2-8. IBM PS/2 Model 70 microcomputer

Remote Job Entry Station

A remote job entry station is a processor on a network or terminal workstation where several types of devices are connected. Data is often transmitted from the host system to a remote job entry station such as a video display terminal (VDT) or printer. Input can also be received by the host in a batch mode from entry stations.

Data Entry Terminal

This is a low cost terminal used in homes or offices. This device can establish an interactive dialog with the host system and obtain data from a business application and at the same time provide data to the application. Fig. 2-9 shows a picture of a data entry terminal. An example of a specialized data entry terminal is the transaction terminal employed by ATM machines in the banking industry for cash dispensing.

The IBM 3192 VDT is a low-cost terminal designed for general use. The 3192 can display eight colors and graphics. (Courtesy of IBM Corporation)

Fig. 2-9. Video display terminal

Facsimile Terminal (FAX)

A facsimile terminal (see Fig. 2-10) is able to transmit an exact picture of a hard copy document over telephone lines and satellite circuits anywhere in the world.

FAX machines are divided into four major groups according to their technology and speed. Groups 1 and 2 are older analog machines, whereas groups 3 and 4 are digital technology machines. Most newer FAX machines are group 3 or 4. Group 3 machines can transmit a page in approximately one minute or less. Group 4 machines can transmit an 8 1/2 by 11 inch page in approximately 20 seconds. Additionally, group 4 FAX machines have a higher image transmission quality. Some newer models of FAX machines use "plain paper" to produce a hard copy of a digital transmission. This type of machine, also known as a laser FAX, can double as a scanner for the computer or as a plain paper copier. Its circuitry is based on laser printer engines, and it can serve as a multipurpose machine on a network.

This FAX35 facsimile machine can transmit a page of data in 15 seconds. It contains a 30-page memory for sequential broadcasting and a 124-station autodialer. (Courtesy of Ricoh Corporation)

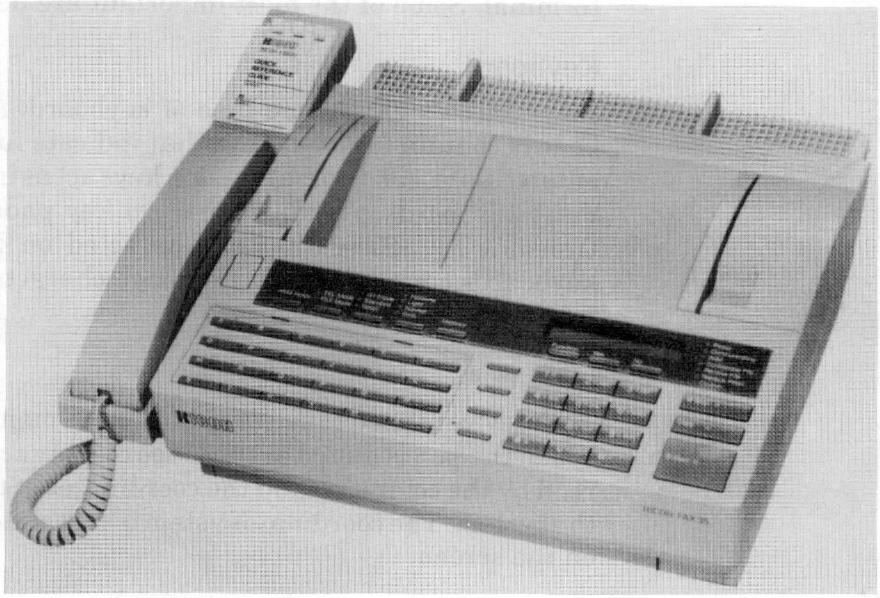

Fig. 2-10. Facsimile terminal

Signals from a digital facsimile device can be read into a computer and stored because they are made up of bits. This has led to the development of FAX boards that can be added to microcomputers. With these boards, any document created on a personal computer can be transmitted to any FAX machine through phone lines. Messages sent by FAX machines can also be received by the FAX boards inside microcomputers and a picture of the document can be stored on a disk or sent to an attached printer.

Dumb/Intelligent Terminals

Dumb terminals are video terminals that do not participate in control or processing tasks. They do not contain storage systems, internal memory, or microprocessor chips. When a character is typed on one of these terminals, it is transmitted immediately to the host system. This forces the host or central system to create buffers for this type of terminal so the message can be assembled before acting on it.

Intelligent terminals are able to participate in the processing of data. These terminals contain internal memory and are capable of being programmed. Many intelligent terminals also contain auxiliary storage units and fast central processing units. Most of today's intelligent terminals are microcomputers and specialized microcomputer workstations.

Attributes of Terminals

Many terminal attributes should be considered when purchasing a terminal. Some of the most important are described below.

Keyboard

All terminals have some type of keyboard. Advanced or extended keyboards contain function keys that indicate functions to be performed on entered data. Also, some function keys act as interrupt keys. Additionally, most keyboards contain numerical key pads and control keys used to transmit sequences that can be acted on by a program. Specialized keyboards contain foreign language characters and job specific characters.

Light Pen

This device is used to select options from menus appearing on the screen. When the pen is aimed at the video display screen, the light image can be read by the computer and the coordinates of the point are determined by the system. The coordinate system is translated into a selection displayed on the screen.

Touch Screen

Such a screen works in a similar manner to the light pen. A portion of the screen is touched with a finger to make the selection.

Mouse, Joy Stick, and Trackball

The mouse allows the user to control the screen cursor by moving the mouse on a table surface. When the screen cursor is on a selection, a mouse button is pressed. The coordinates of the cursor are read by the computer and this location is associated with some software option. The joy stick moves the cursor by moving the stick in a specific direction. A trackball is similar to the mouse except that the cursor is moved by rotating a ball mounted in a fixed holder. The cursor moves in the direction of rotation of the ball.

Voice Entry

Data can be entered into the system by using a microphone. Special voice recognition software is required in the system.

Page Scanner

A page scanner can scan an image and translate it into a digital format. The image can be stored and later processed by the computer.

Front End Processors

Front end processors are often employed at the host end of a communication circuit to perform control and processing functions required for the proper operation of a data communication network. Fig. 2-11 illustrates the location of a front end processor in a communication network. The front end processor provides an interface to the communication circuits. It relieves the host computer of its communication duties, which allows the host to perform the data processing function more effectively.

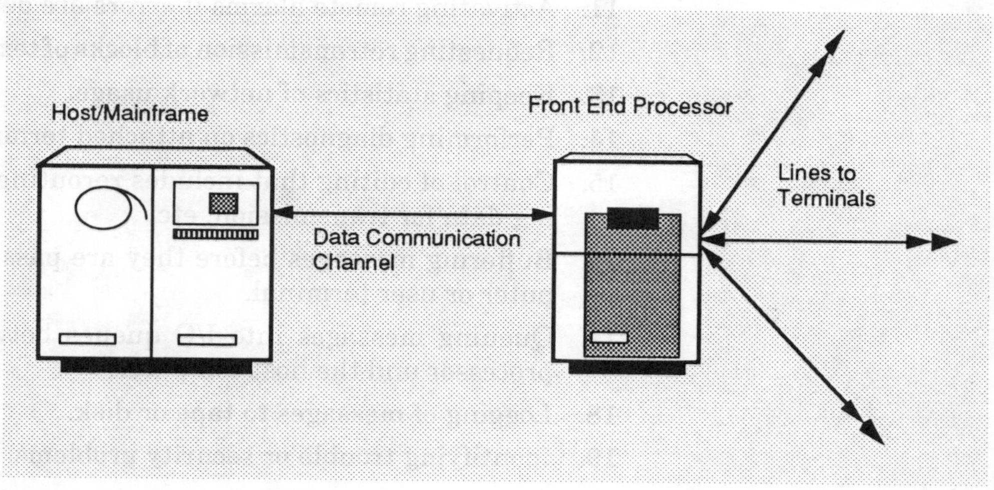

Fig. 2-11. The front end processor in a communication network

The typical duties of the front end processor are message processing and message switching. In message processing, it interprets incoming messages to determine the type of information requested. Then it retrieves the information from an on-line storage unit, and sends it back to the inquiring terminal without involving the host system. In message switching, the front end processor switches incoming messages to other terminals or systems on a network. It can also store messages and forward them at a later time.

Functions of the Front End Processor

The functions of the front end processor includes the following:

1. Circuit polling and addressing terminals. Polling involves asking each terminal if it has a message to send. Addressing involves asking a terminal if it is in condition to receive the message.
2. Answering dial-in calls and automatic dialing of outgoing calls.
3. Code conversion from ASCII to EBCDIC or EBCDIC to ASCII.

4. Circuit switching. This allows an incoming circuit to be switched to another circuit.
5. Accommodating circuit speed differences.
6. Protocol conversion, such as asynchronous to synchronous.
7. Multiplexing (see chapter 3).
8. Assembly of incoming bits into characters.
9. Assembly of characters into blocks of data or complete messages.
10. Message compression for more efficient communications.
11. Activating remote alarms if errors are detected.
12. Requesting retransmission of blocks of text containing errors.
13. Keeping statistics of network usage.
14. Performing diagnostics on attached terminals.
15. Control of editing that includes rerouting messages, modifying data for transmission, etc.
16. Buffering messages before they are passed to the host computer or user terminal.
17. Queuing messages into I/O queues between the front end processor and the host computer.
18. Logging of messages to tape or disk.
19. Identifying trouble or security problems.

There are many vendors of front end processors. Some of the best known models are the IBM 37xx family of communication controllers and the NCR COMTEN 3600 series of front end processors.

Mainframe Computers

Mainframe computers are considered central computer systems that perform data processing functions for a business or industry. In some networks, several mainframe computers can be found sharing the responsibility of processing information as a distributed system. In such systems the hardware, software, processing, and data are normally dispersed over a geographical area. The individual technologies are connected through some type of communication network. As part of this network, mainframe computers can perform networking functions as well as the more traditional processing functions.

A mainframe computer that is built to perform "number crunching" routines may not be suitable to perform communication routines. The type of processing required for communications differs greatly from that required to perform mathematical calculations. For a computer that is built to perform traditional data processing functions, additional or auxiliary hardware is required. The type of auxiliary hardware will depend upon the configuration of the network.

There are three types of configurations, the first of which consists of a computer that is not part of any local or wide area computer network. The circuitry required to handle all communications is built into the machine. Fig. 2-12 shows a typical configuration for this type of centralized system. This configuration uses dedicated hardware to handle the interaction between the host system and the data entry terminals.

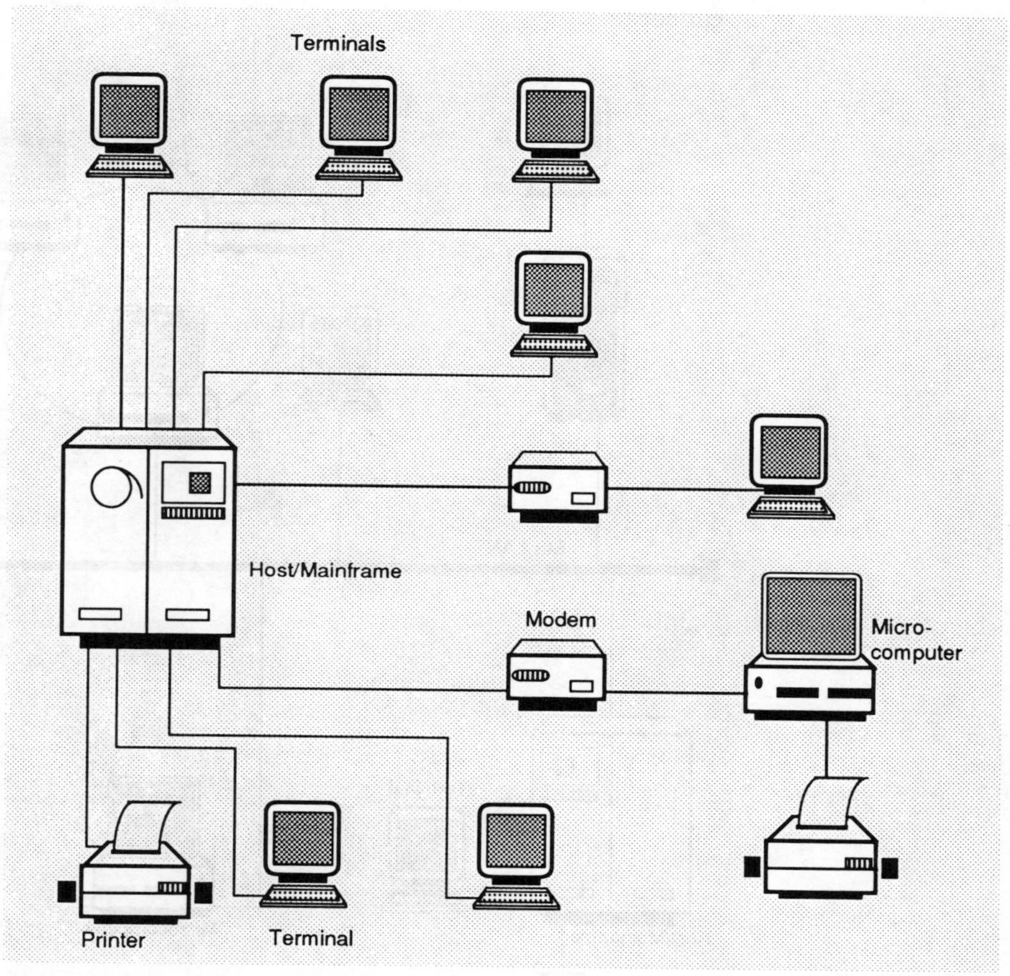

Fig. 2-12. A stand-alone centralized system

The mainframe computer can store users' programs as well as the software to handle communication with the users. The type of configuration shown in Fig. 2-12 can be found in manufacturing environments and in dedicated database systems. Even though we refer to the computer as the mainframe computer, this central system is often a minicomputer system.

The second type of configuration is a network that employs microcomputers, minicomputers, and mainframe computers connected through some type of local area network (LAN). Fig. 2-13 depicts this type of system. The network is usually confined to the business office or business complex where the processing is taking place. Users can communicate to the outside world by sending their message to an outside system through the local telephone exchange or some other medium. The local exchange then routes the message through long distance networks until it reaches the local exchange of the receiving system. Finally, the message is routed to the receiving computer or local network. These systems are important, and there are several chapters in this book that further explore the concepts.

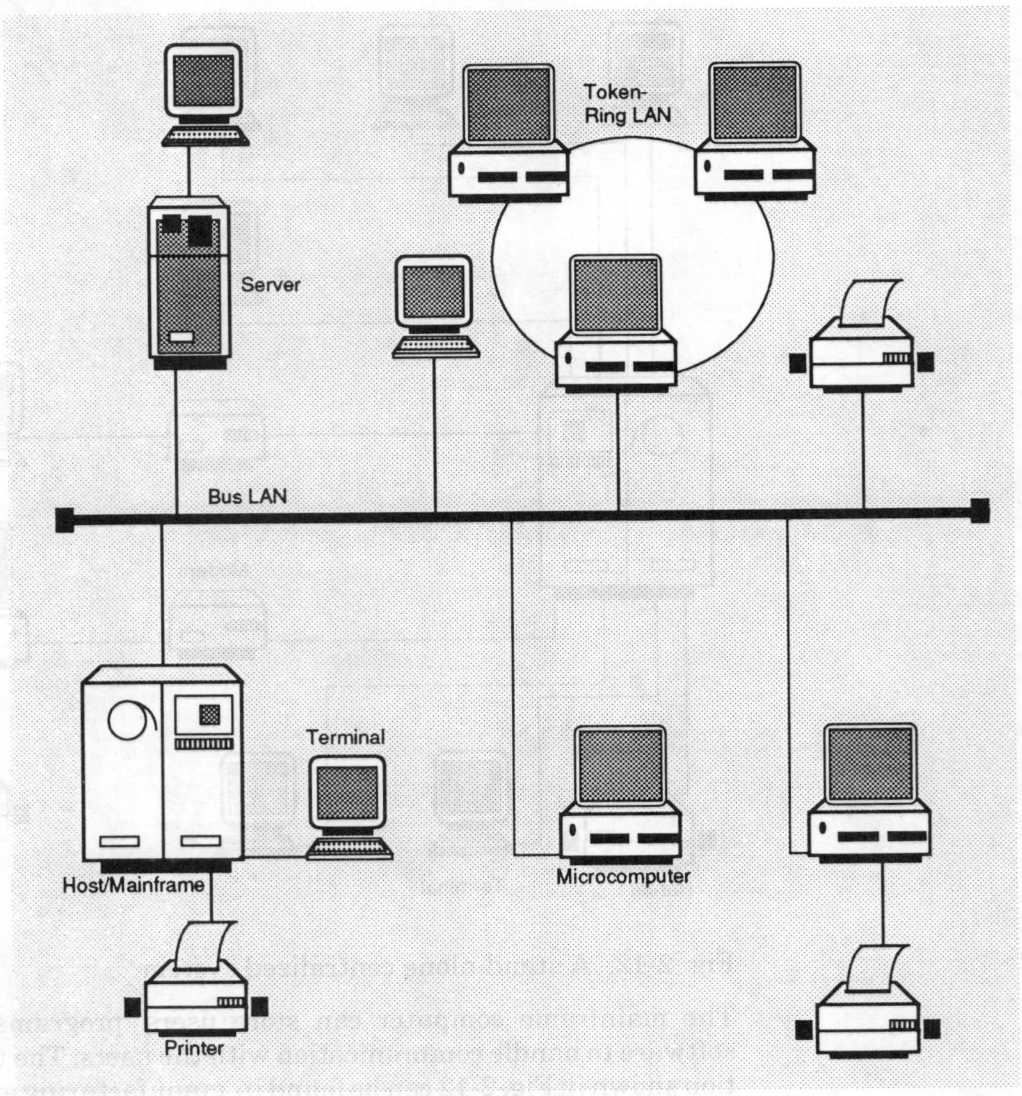

Fig. 2-13. Computer systems connected by a LAN

The final type of configuration is one that employs a large general purpose computer along with a front end processor (FEP). Fig. 2-14 shows a diagram of this configuration. The front end processor is known by names such as line controller, communications controller, or transaction processor. The function of the FEP is to interface the main computer to the network where the users' communication equipment resides. It can be a nonprogrammable device that is built to handle a specific situation. Or the front end processor can be programmable and it can handle some processing functions in addition to input/output activities.

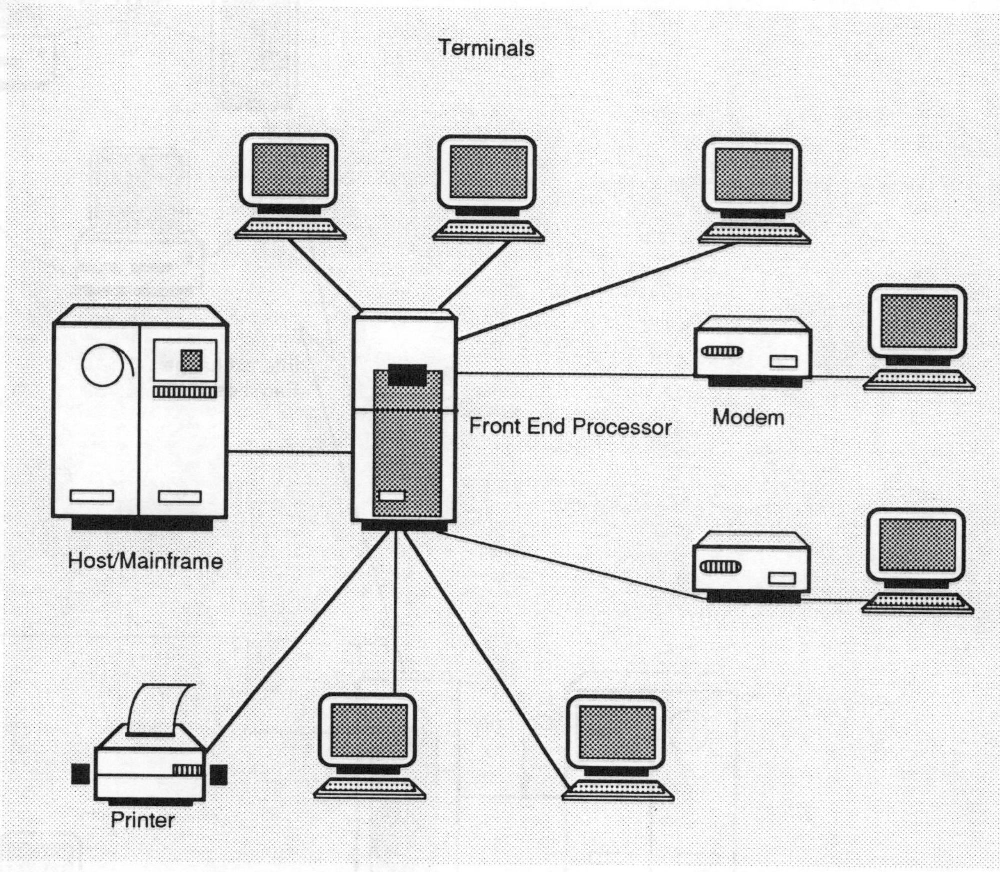

Fig. 2-14. Computer network employing a front end processor

During the past few years, network designers have opted to remove as much processing as possible from the host computer. The idea is to distribute the processing hardware along a network, making the entire system more efficient.

Fig. 2-15 shows an example of this type of network distribution. The front end processor handles the control of all communication functions. The data channel between the front end processor and the host system handles the movement of data into and out of the main processing computer. Remote terminal controllers handle users' terminals. Microcomputers process data locally and later transmit the results to the host system. Telephone exchanges, multiplexers, and other devices are used throughout the network to handle communications efficiently between users and the host computer. Further in this book, chapters on networks and local area networks explain the terminology and concepts in more detail.

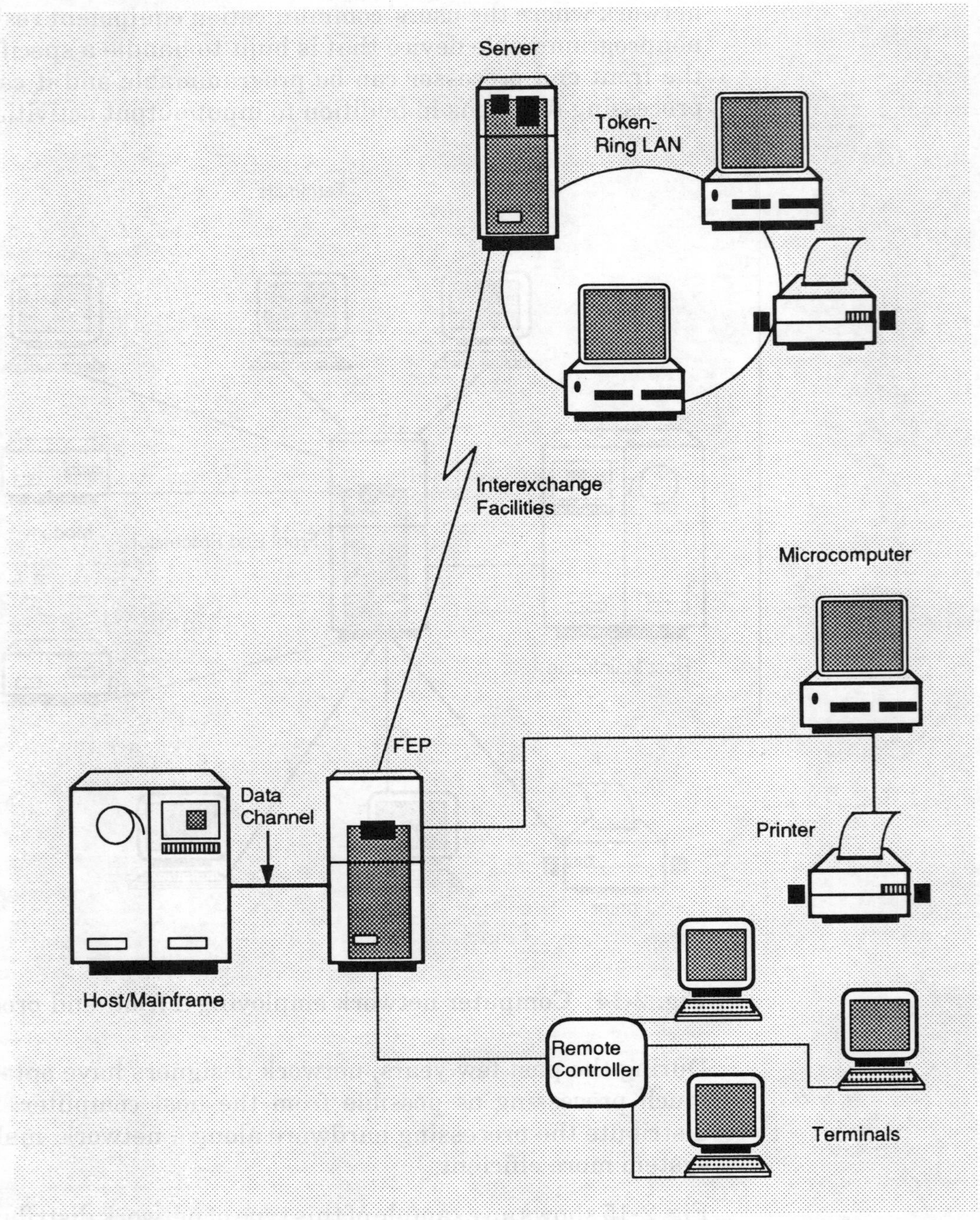

Fig. 2-15. Distributed network system

The trend in computer technology is toward faster, smaller, and distributed network systems. However, the central or host system plays an important part in network strategies. The processing and data throughput power of minicomputers and mainframes is superior to that of microcomputer systems. This makes the mainframe or the minicomputer a key component of a successful network configuration. In addition, many network managers rely on a central or host system for security, backup, and maintenance purposes.

Summary

There are many modes of transmission. The most common types are simplex, half-duplex, full-duplex, synchronous, and asynchronous transmission. Much of the communication performed by microcomputers and terminals is through the standard RS-232 port found on the back panel of most terminals and computers. Terminals can be classified as remote job entry terminals, microcomputer workstations, data entry terminals, facsimile terminals, and dumb/intelligent terminals.

A modem is used to transmit digital data over telephone lines. A modem is a device that allows computers to communicate over analog transmission media. They can be external or internal. Their transmission speed varies from 300 to over a million bits per second.

All information processed by computers and front end processors must be in digital form. The ASCII and EBCDIC formats are the most widely used for representing characters. Many of the control codes of the ASCII format are used for communication control by computers and modems.

Typical electronic devices used in data communication are microcomputers, terminals, front end procesors, and mainframes. The terminals are used strictly to send and receive data to and from a host computer. There are many variations in terminal attributes. These include keyboards, light pens, touch screens, mice, joy sticks, trackballs, voice entry devices, and page scanners.

Front end processors are employed at the host end of a communication circuit to perform different control and processing functions required for the proper operation of a data communications network.

Mainframe computers are considered central computer systems that perform data processing functions for a business or industry. Mainframe computers are used in networks as host systems or as controllers. There are three types of configurations in which a mainframe can be used. The first is a configuration where the mainframe is a stand-alone system. The second configuration employs minicomputers and microcomputers in a local area network. The third configuration includes a front end processor to help with the communication.

Questions

1. Briefly describe the different types of network configurations in which a mainframe can be used.
2. Describe the function of a front end processor.
3. What are the differences between dumb and intelligent terminals?
4. Describe the function of a modem.

5. List and define three different types of modems.
6. What is asynchronous communication?
7. What is synchronous communication?
8. What are the main features that can be found in smart modems?
9. How can microcomputers be used in a network configuration?
10. What are the advantages and disadvantages of serial and parallel communication?
11. Briefly define the main attributes of terminals.
12. List three different types of terminal configurations.
13. What are half- and full-duplex communications?

Project

Objective

This project provides the student with hands-on practice in setting up and using a microcomputer and a modem to access a bulletin board service. The number of a BBS must be provided to the student in order to complete the assignment. To find the number of any BBS in the area, contact a local computer user group. It is important that students understand the uses and benefit of the BBS since they are being used by corporations as services to their employees and as a means to do business.

Connecting to an Electronic Bulletin Board System.

The Communications Process. Computers process information in digital form. That is, information is in the form of individual bits or digits. A bit is the smallest unit of data that the computer can represent. Normally, personal computers use seven or eight bits to represent the individual characters that make up the alphabet and other special characters.

If two computers talk to each other, the information exchanged will be done by passing the individual bits that make up the characters. If the computers are in close proximity, then coaxial cables can be used to connect them.

If the computers are far apart from each other, then telephone lines are typically used to connect the machines. If the phone company is used as the bridge between the computers, then another small problem arises. The signals that travel through the phone lines are audible tones which a computer cannot interpret. Moreover, the phone lines cannot carry digital signals. In order for two computers to communicate over phone lines, a modem must be used.

The hardware and software required to connect your computer to the outside world are as follows:

1. Your personal computer.
2. A modem connected to your computer.
3. A telephone line.
4. A host (receiving) computer with a modem.
5. Communications software (Communications tool in Microsft Works).

The Modem. A modem, as discussed previously, is an electronic device that converts (modulates) the digital communications between computers into audible tones that can be transmitted over telephone lines. The received data is then reconverted (demodulated) from the audible tones into digital information. Most modems for personal computers can dial numbers for you, redial busy numbers, automatically answer calls, and set the proper communication speed.

Modems can be external or internal. An external modem is placed next to the computer and connected to its serial port with the use of a serial cable and to the phone line with a telephone cord. An internal modem is placed inside the computer by using an available expansion slot. Then it is connected to the phone line with the use of a phone cord. Once the modem is connected to the computer and the phone line, its function is controlled by the communications tool in Works. Your modem will come with instructions on how to unpack it and an explanation of the type of port it can connect to. Refer to these instructions to make sure the modem is properly installed.

Software Communications Terminology. By following the general steps outlined below, you will be able to communicate with electronic bulletin boards or services (BBS). Before an actual connection is used, your modem and software need to have the same settings as the receiving or host computer that you are trying to access. These settings are common to all communications setups; they are:

1. Baud rate. This is the rate of transmission of data. One baud equals one binary bit per second. Typical settings are 300, 1200, 2400, 4800, and 9600. As the baud rate increases, the rate of transmission also increases and the shorter the time you have to spend waiting for information to appear on the screen. Some BBS services charge more per hour when you use higher baud rates.
2. Data bits. This is the number of bits that make up a character. Most mini- and mainframe computers use seven bits.
3. Stop bits. This is the number of bits used to indicate the end of a character. In most cases, one stop bit marks the end of the character.

4. Handshake. The term refers to the manner in which the communicating computer knows when the other machine is sending or receiving data, or when it is doing some other task that might interfere with the transmission signals. This is also referred to as the communications protocol. The protocol refers to all the conventions that must be observed in order for the computers to communicate with each other. If two computers communicate over phone lines, then Xon/Xoff is used. If the machines are connected with coaxial cables, then Hardware is used.
5. Parity. This is a method of checking for errors in data communications. If the number of data bits is eight, then parity should be None. Otherwise, you need to refer to the host machine and find out which type of parity it is using, and then set this selection appropriately on your computer.

Setting up the Hardware. External modems have an RS-232 or serial connector that is normally found at the back of the modem. An RS-232 cable will be required to connect this type of modem to the RS-232 or serial port on the back of the PC. You will need to use the appropriate serial cable for your computer. The IBM PC and compatible microcomputers use a cable that has end connectors that are different from the connectors found on Apple computers. Check with your local dealer or your instructor to find the right cable.

1. Connect the modem and the PC using the serial cable as outlined in Fig. 2-16.
2. Connect a telephone cable from a wall outlet to the phone connector normally found at the back of the modem.
3. Turn the modem on. The front lights of the modem labelled MR (modem ready) and either LS (low speed) or HS (high speed) should be on. These lights may vary from modem to modem.

If you have an internal modem,

1. Remove the protective case of the computer and install the modem in one of the empty slots located at the back of the machine.
2. After it is securely placed in the expansion slot, replace the computer cover.
3. Now connect a phone cord to the phone connector port found at the rear of the modem.

The next step is to obtain a bulletin board phone number and then set up the communications software to connect the computer to the BBS.

There are many communication software packages on the computer market. Some of the more common are Crosstalk, ProComm, and Smartcom. There are also public domain and shareware communication programs that perform many of the functions of the more expensive packages. You can contact your local computer dealer or computer magazines for a listing of such programs. Additionally, many integrated programs such as Microsoft Works contain communication software built-in along with other productivity programs. This type of application program can also be used to perform most, if not all, of the communication requirements that you may have.

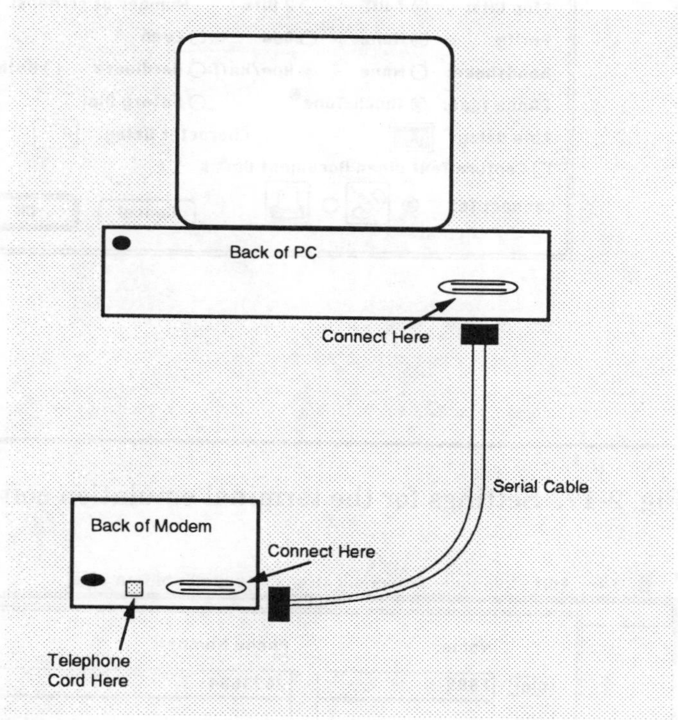

Fig. 2-16. Connection between PC and modem

Regardless of which communication program you have, the application will contain a screen similar to Fig. 2-17. The screen in Fig. 2-17 displays the type of terminal emulation desired, the baud rate or speed of transmission, and the other items discussed previously in this section. Some additional items are the phone type and the handshake. The phone type indicates whether the modem will use touch-tone or a rotary dialing method. The handshake indicates the protocol that will be used. If a modem is used to connect two systems, typically Xon-Xoff is selected. If the two computers are connected directly through a cable, then hardware is selected.

The value of each parameter is found by calling the bulletin board operators or by trial and error. The values shown in Fig. 2-17 will work in most cases. If one of the parameters is initially set incorrectly, the screen will contain "garbage" characters. In this case, change the number of bits, stops bits, and parity until the screen looks right.

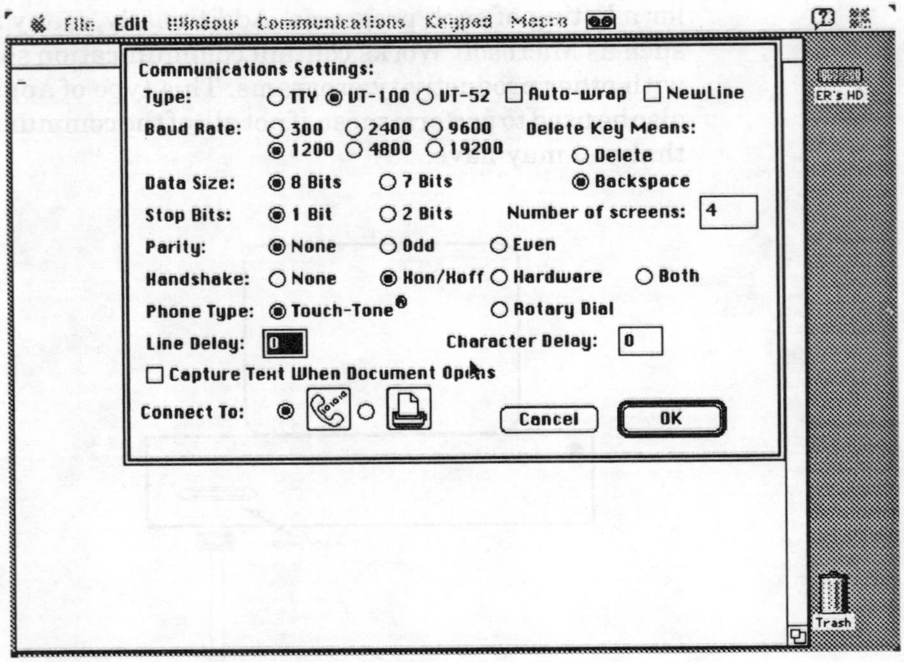

Fig. 2-17. Settings for the terminal emulation software

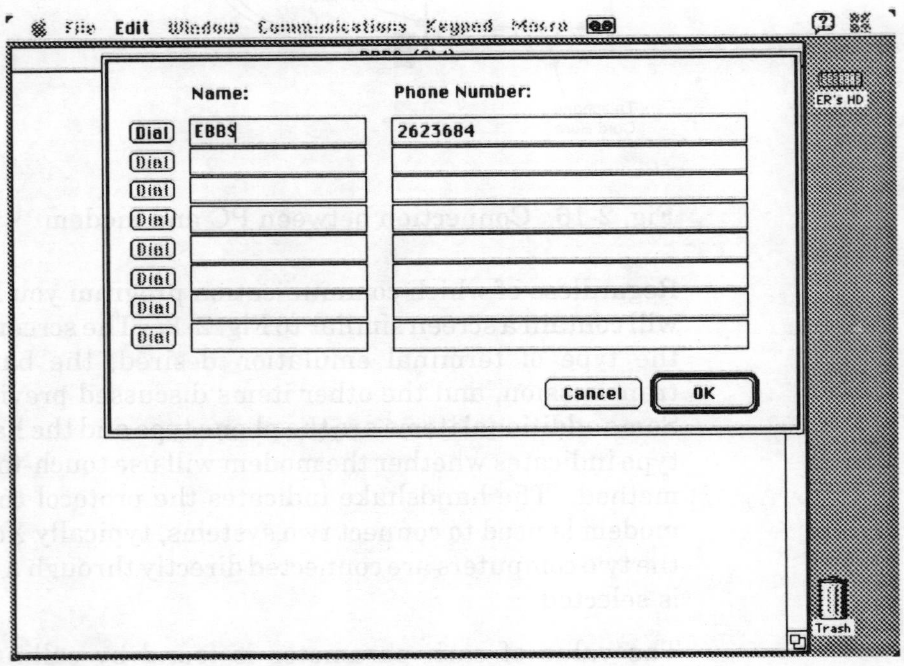

Fig. 2-18. Automatic dialing system provided by communication software

The software that you use will have a provision to type the phone number of the data line for the BBS. You may have a screen similar to Fig. 2-18 or your dial menu may be different. In either case, the function is to type a phone number and indicate to the computer to dial it. Type the phone number for the BBS at this point and instruct the software to dial the number. This last function is usually accomplished by pressing a key combination that indicates to the modem to dial the number automatically.

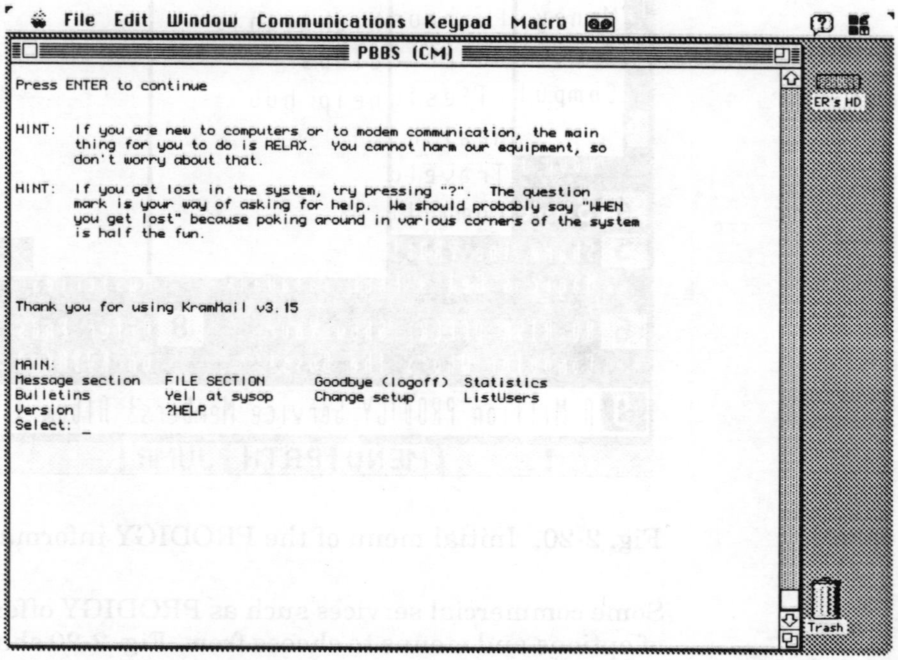

Fig. 2-19. Welcoming (initial) screen from a BBS

After the number is dialed (and assuming a response from the BBS host computer), a screen similar to Fig. 2-19 will appear. The BBS will display a general menu of services that are available to users. The type and amount of service provided depends on the type of BBS. If it is a large commercial BBS system such as DIALOG or PRODIGY, then numerous services are available. If the BBS is set up by an individual or small group of individuals to service a local user group, then the number of services is limited. Normally, these services include electronic mail, conferencing, games, and special interest sections. To use the BBS follow the instructions below.

4. In most instances typing the first letter of a menu item and pressing the [Enter ←] key will activate the desired menu.
5. At this point you can navigate throughout the BBS at your own pace. To perform a desired function, most BBS have on-line instructions that indicate the procedure to follow.
6. When the session is over, select Quit and hang up from the communication software menu.

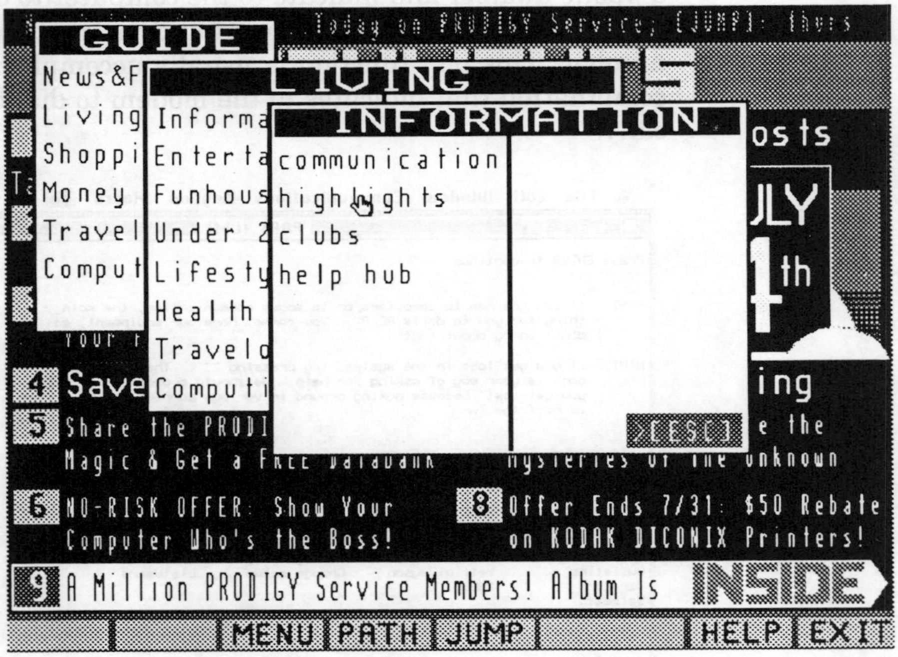

Fig. 2-20. Initial menu of the PRODIGY information service

Some commercial services such as PRODIGY offer many different types of options and menus to choose from. Fig. 2-20 shows the initial menu of PRODIGY and some of its choices and Fig. 2-21 shows some of the many options available.

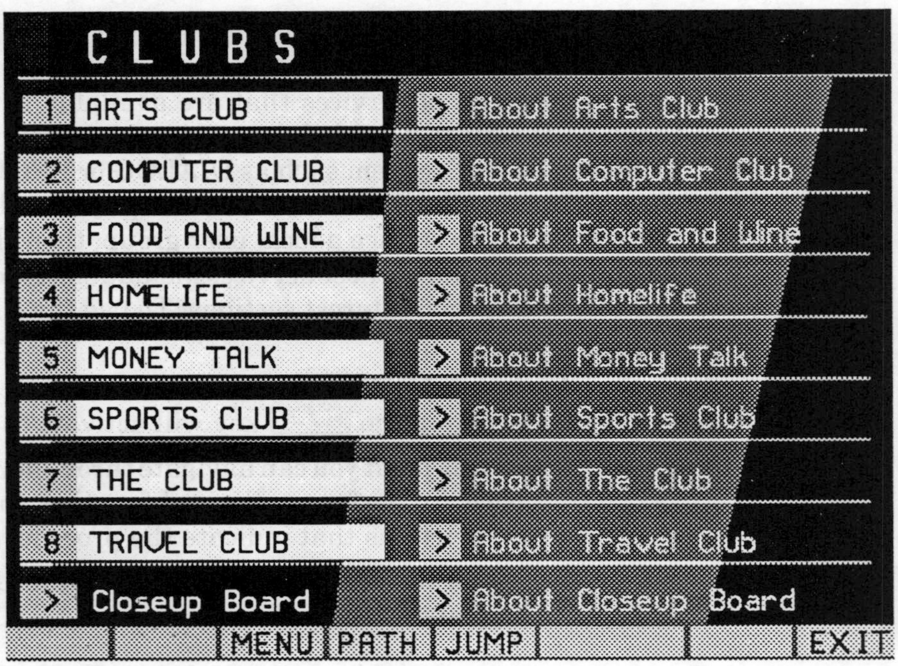

Fig. 2-21. Options available from the PRODIGY information service

On-Line Services and EBBS

The following is a list of some of the most popular commercial information services available.

GEnie	301-340-400	800-638-9636
CompuServe	617-457-8600	800-848-8990
BIX	603-924-9281	800-227-2983
Prodigy	914-993-8848	NA
Delphi	617-491-3393	800-544-4005
America	800-227-6364	NA

3

Advanced Data Communication

Objectives

1. Understand multiplexers and their function.
2. Understand concentrators, protocol converters, PBXs, cluster controllers, and matrix switches.
3. Understand the different line adapters that can be placed on a network.
4. Understand the different types of circuit media available in the market place.
5. Develop criteria for selecting communication media.
6. Have a general knowledge of the concepts related to networking hardware .

Key Terms

Channel Extender
Cluster Controller
Concentrators
Encryption
Line Monitor
Matrix Switch
Multiplexer
PBX
Satellite
Circuit Media
Coaxial Cable
Digital Line Expander
FDM/TDM/STDM
Line Splitter
Microwaves
Optical Fiber
Protocol Converter

Introduction

This chapter introduces concepts that enhance the topics discussed in earlier chapters. The student needs to have a general understanding of the field of data communications before moving into networking and Novell NetWare.

Today's data networks have increased in sophistication and take advantage of equipment that was formerly reserved for voice communication systems only. Multiplexers, protocol converters, PBXs, matrix switches, and concentrators are among these devices. Additionally, the educated network user and manager must understand the different devices that can be used to monitor networks and the transmission media available to them. The chapter concludes with a description of different criteria that need to be considered when planning data communication networks.

Multiplexers

Function

Multiplexing technology allows the transmission of multiple signals over a single medium. Multiplexers (see Fig. 3-1) allow the replacement of multiple low-speed transmission lines with a single high-speed transmission line. The typical configuration includes a multiplexer attached to multiple low-speed lines, a communication line (typically four-wire carrier circuit), and a multiplexer at another site that is also connected to low-speed lines. Fig. 3-2 depicts this configuration. In addition, the figure shows a remote site that is connected to a multiplexer through the use of modems. The remote site contains terminals, microcomputers, modems, and printers attached to a multiplexer. The host site has a multiplexer, FEP, and a host CPU.

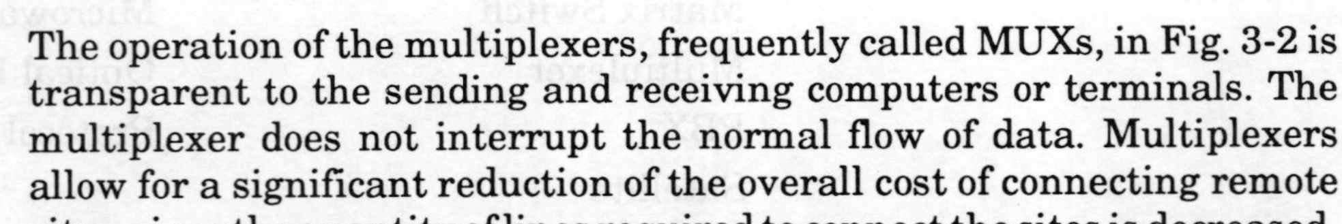

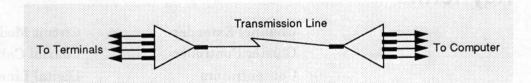

Fig. 3-1. Communication using multiplexers

The operation of the multiplexers, frequently called MUXs, in Fig. 3-2 is transparent to the sending and receiving computers or terminals. The multiplexer does not interrupt the normal flow of data. Multiplexers allow for a significant reduction of the overall cost of connecting remote sites, since the quantity of lines required to connect the sites is decreased.

Multiplexing techniques can be divided into frequency division multiplexing (FDM), time division multiplexing (TDM), and statistical time division multiplexing (STDM).

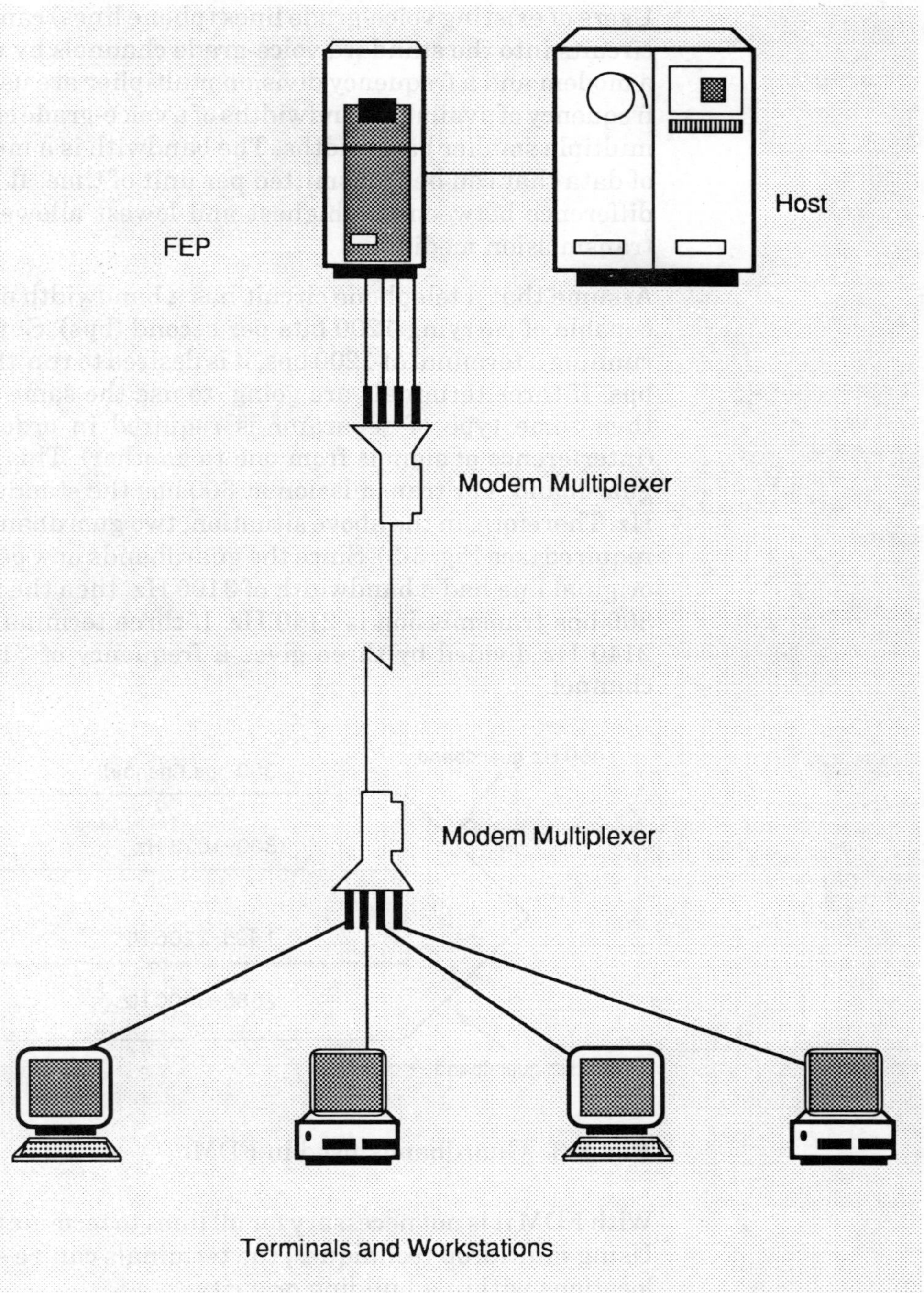

Fig. 3-2. Workstation connectivity using multiplexer

Techniques

Frequency Division Multiplexing (FDM)

Users of existing voice-grade lines (phone lines) can multiplex low-speed circuits into the standard voice-grade channels by using FDM. In FDM, a modem and a frequency division multiplier are used to break down the frequency of available bandwidths of a voice-grade circuit, dividing it into multiple smaller bandwidths. The bandwith is a measure of the amount of data that can be transmitted per unit of time. It is determined by the difference between the highest and lowest allowed frequencies in the transmission medium.

Assume that a telephone circuit has a bandwidth of 3100 Hz, and a line capable of carrying 1200 bits per second (bps). Suppose that instead of running a terminal at 1200 bps, it is desired to run three terminals at 300 bps. If three terminals are going to use the same communication line, then some type of separator is required in order to avoid crosstalk (interference of signals from one to another). This separator is called a guardband. For transmission at 300 bps the standard separation is 480 Hz. Therefore, in the above situation, two guardbands of 480 Hz each are required (see Fig. 3-3). Since the guardbands now occupy 960 Hz, and the original line had a bandwidth of 3100 Hz, then the frequency left for the 300 bps transmission is 2140 Hz. If three terminals are required, then 2140 Hz divided by three gives a frequency of 713 Hz to be used per channel.

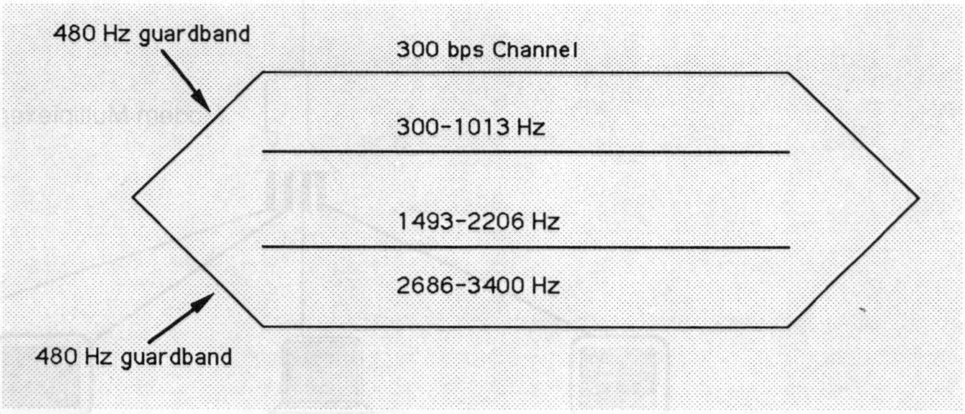

Fig. 3-3. Guardbands used in FDM

With FDM it is not necessary for all lines to terminate at a single location. Using multidrop techniques, the terminals can be stationed in different locations within a building or a city.

Time Division Multiplexing (TDM)

Time division multiplexers are digital devices and therefore select incoming bits digitally and place each bit into a high-speed bit stream in equal time intervals. (See Fig. 3-4.) The sending multiplexer will place a bit or byte from each of the incoming lines into a frame. The frames are placed on high-speed transmission lines, and a receiving multiplexer, knowing where each bit or byte is located, outputs the bits or bytes at appropriate speeds.

Time division multiplexing is more efficient than frequency division multiplexing, but it requires a separate modem. To the sending and receiving stations it always appears as if a single line is connecting them. All lines for time division multiplexers originate in one location and end in one location. TDMs are easier to operate, less complex, and less expensive than FDMs.

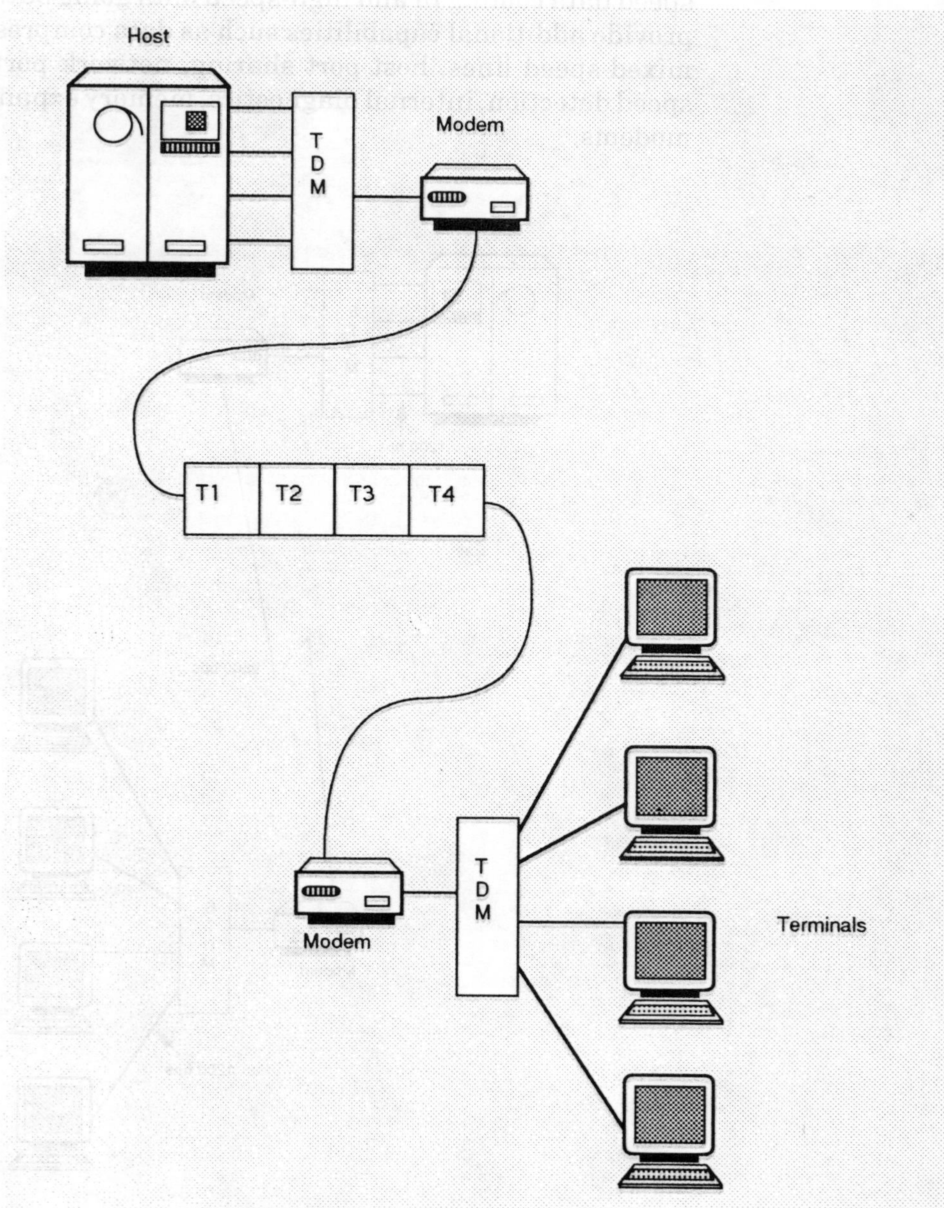

Fig. 3-4. Network using TDMs

Statistical Time Division Multiplexers (STDM)

In any terminal-host configuration the terminals attached to the host CPU are not always transmitting data. The time during which they are idle is called down time. Statistical time division multiplexers are intelligent devices capable of identifying which terminals are idle and which terminals require transmission, and they allocate line time only when it is required. This allows the connection of many more devices to the host than is possible with FDMs or TDMs (see Fig. 3-5).

The STDM consists of a microprocessor based unit that contains all hardware and software required to control both the reception of low-speed data coming in and high-speed data going out. Newer STDM units provide additional capabilities such as data compression, line priorities, mixed-speed lines, host port sharing, network port control, automatic speed detection, internal diagnostics, memory expansion, and integrated modems.

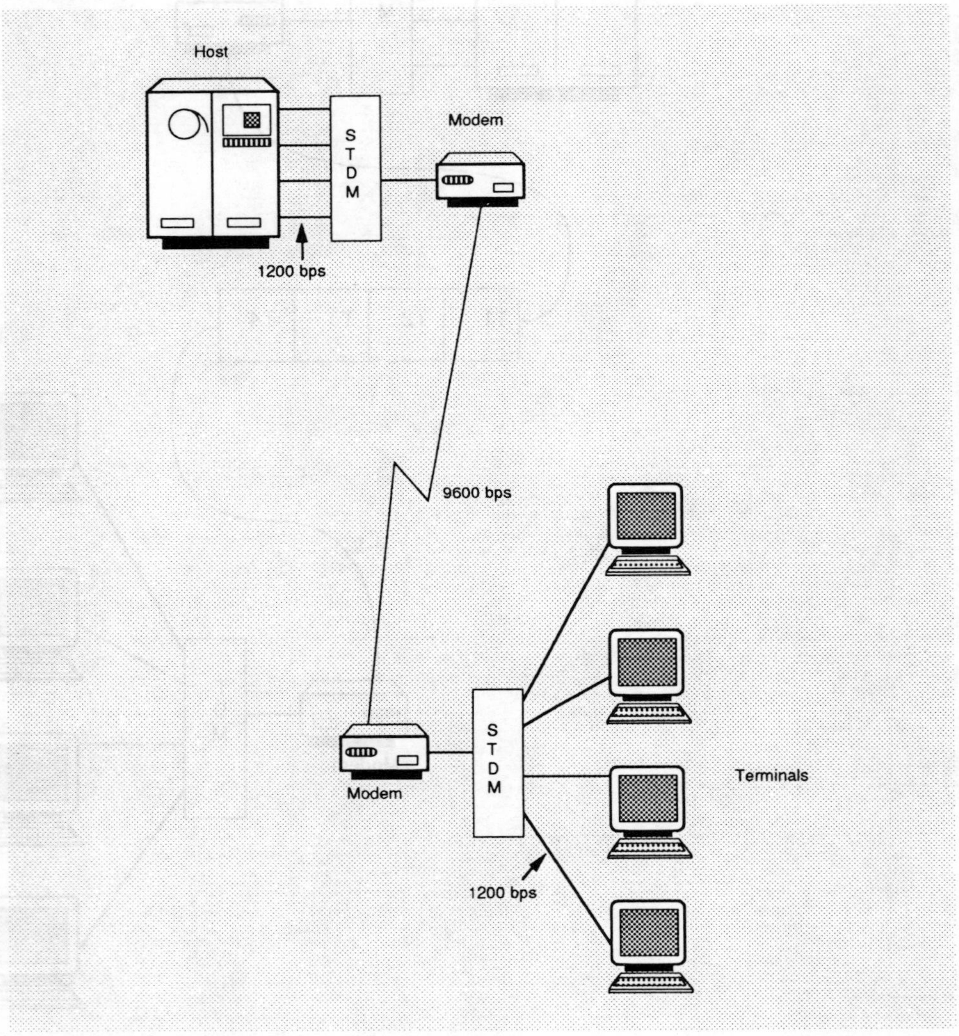

Fig. 3-5. Network using STDMs

The number of devices that can be multiplexed using STDMs depends on the address field used in an STDM frame. If the frame is 4 bits long, then there are 16 terminals (2 to the power of 4) that can be connected. If 5 bits are used then 32 terminals can be connected.

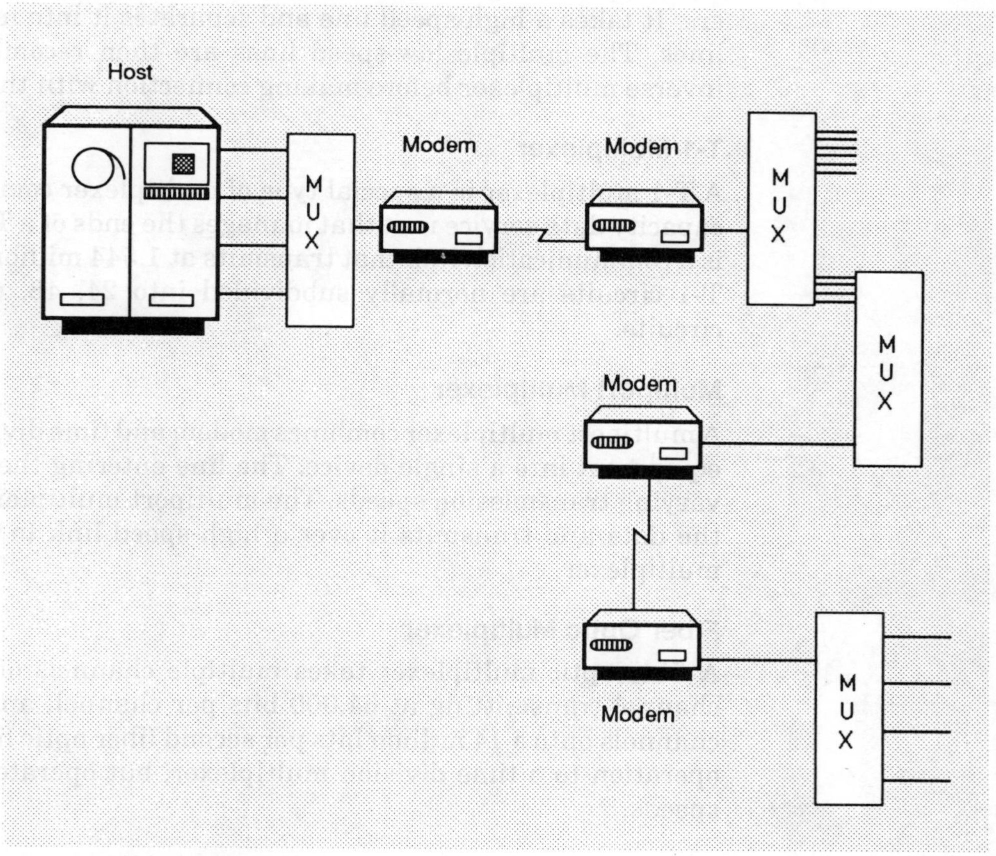

Fig. 3-6. Cascading multiplexers

Configurations

Multiplexers can be used in a variety of configurations and combinations. Cascading is a typical configuration used to extend circuits to remote entry points when there are two or more data entry areas. Fig. 3-6 shows an example of cascading multiplexers. In the figure, data entry terminals in a geographical location are multiplexed, and a single carrier sends the data to a temporary receiving location. The data is then demultiplexed and multiplexed by a third multiplexer before being sent to the final destination. Then a multiplexer receives the data and distributes it among the ports of the host system.

The number of ports that a multiplexer can accommodate varies. Commonly there are 4, 8, 16, 32, 48, or 64 ports. The price of a multiplexer will vary with the number of ports in it.

Types

Inverse Multiplexer

An inverse multiplexer provides a high-speed data path between computers. It takes a high-speed line and separates it into multiple low-speed lines. The multiple low-speed lines are then recombined by another inverse multiplexer before making connection with the other computer.

T-1 Multiplexer

A T-1 multiplexer is a special type of multiplexer combined with a high capacity data service unit that manages the ends of a T-1 link. A T-1 link is a communication link that transmits at 1.544 million bits per seconds. T-1 circuits are normally subdivided into 24, 48, or 96 voice-grade circuits.

Multiport Multiplexer

A multiport multiplexer combines modem and time division multiplexing equipment into a single device. The line entering the modem can be of varying transmission speeds. The multiport multiplexer then combines the data and transmits it over a high-speed link to another receiving multiplexer.

Fiber Optic Multiplexer

A fiber optic multiplexer takes multiple channels of data , with each channel transmitting at 64,000 bits per channel, and multiplexes the channels onto a 14 million bits per second fiber optic line. It is similar in operation to a time division multiplexer, but operates at much higher speeds.

Concentrator

A concentrator is a line sharing device with a primary function that is the same as a multiplexer. It allows multiple devices to share communication circuits. In addition, a concentrator is an intelligent device that sometimes performs data processing functions and has auxiliary storage. Some of the earlier concentrators were statistical multiplexers. That is the reason some vendors call a concentrator a statistical multiplexer or stat mux.

In addition to having a CPU, concentrators are used one at a time, whereas multiplexers are used in pairs. Also, a concentrator may vary the number of incoming and outgoing lines, while a multiplexer must use the same number of lines on both ends.

A typical concentrator configuration is depicted in Fig. 3-7. The example shows multiple terminals using a concentrator to access several host systems. Concentrators perform data compression functions, forward error correction, and network related functions in addition to acting as a line sharing device. They are considered data processing devices, and newer types of concentrators are built around microcomputers and minicomputers.

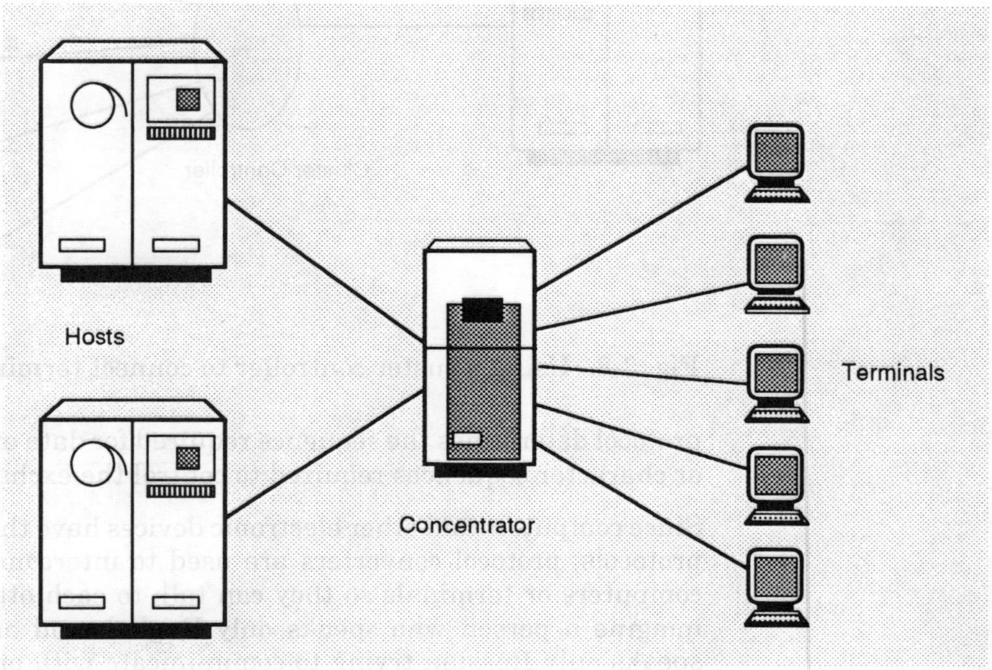

Fig. 3-7. Concentrator used to connect multiple terminals to hosts

Cluster Controller

A cluster controller is designed to support several terminals and the functions required to manage the terminals. Also, it buffers data being transmitted to or from the terminals, performs error detection and correction, and polls terminals (see Fig. 3-8). Polling is a technique by which the controller checks to see which terminals are ready to send data. If a terminal needs to send a packet of data to a host, the cluster controller ensures that the packet gets to its destination.

Protocol Converter

In order for electronic devices to communicate with one another, a set of conventions is required. This set of conventions is called the protocol. A

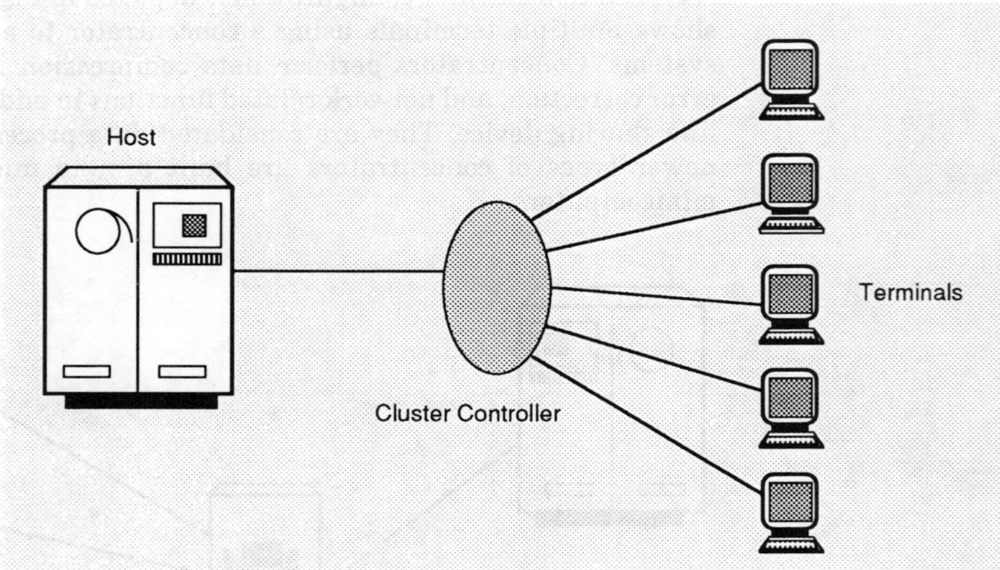

Fig. 3-8. Using a custer controller to connect terminals to a host

protocol determines the sequence required for data exchange and the bit or character sequences required to control the exchange.

Since computers and other electronic devices have their own proprietary protocols, protocol converters are used to interconnect two dissimilar computers or terminals so they can talk to each other. As an analogy, imagine a person who speaks only English and another person who speaks only Russian trying to communicate with one another. For the communication to be effective and efficient, a translator who understands both languages serves as the bridge between both persons. The protocol converter assumes the role of the translator in the electronic data exchange.

Two prevalent protocols are used in the computer environment in theUnited States: ASCII and EBCDIC. The EBCDIC protocol is used by IBM in midrange and mainframe systems. The ASCII protocol is used by virtually every other computer manufacturer. Therefore, to connect an IBM personal computer that uses the ASCII protocol to an IBM mainframe, an ASCII-to-EBCDIC converter is required (see Fig. 3-9).

Protocol converters can be hardware or software designed. A hardware protocol converter is treated as a "black box" on the communication line. It performs its function in a manner that is transparent to the system. For example, third party vendors offer asynchronous to synchronous protocol conversion boxes. This allows an inexpensive async terminal to access an IBM mainframe. There are also add-on circuit boards that fit inside microcomputers that perform communications and protocol conversion at the same time. These boards allow a personal computer to emulate a 3278 terminal and connect to a 3270 controller via a coaxial cable. Some of the cards have the controller built in and can access the mainframe directly.

The other method of protocol conversion is achieved through the use of software. Typically, this software resides in the host system and converts incoming data to the language that the host system can understand. This is an inexpensive manner of achieving protocol conversion. However, it requires attention from the host computer, reducing the amount of time it can apply to other tasks. Whenever possible, hardware protocol converters are used.

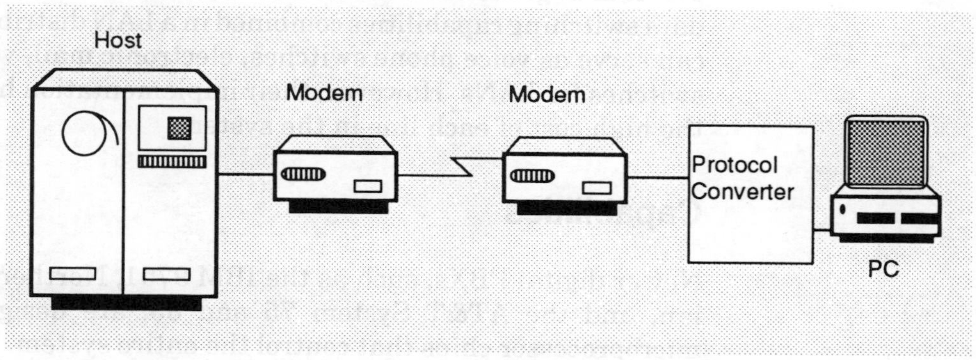

Fig. 3-9. Using a protocol converter to connect a PC to a host using the EBCDIC protocol

Private Branch Exchanges (PBX)

A private branch exchange is an electronic switchboard within an organization. All the telephone lines of the organization are connected to it. Normally, several of the telecommunication circuits of the PBX go from this switchboard to the telephone company's main office. These are called trunk lines when they are devoted to voice transmission. If they are used for data communication, they are known as leased lines, dedicated lines, or private lines.

PBX History

PBX systems have been in offices for a number of years. As organizations developed and grew, PBX equipment was upgraded and enhanced to meet users' demands. The evolution of PBX equipment can be categorized into several generations.

The first generation of PBXs was placed in service prior to the mid-1970s. They carried only voice and were capable of handling only analog signals. Their design was electromechanical, and they used analog circuitry for switching signals.

The second generation of PBXs was designed between the mid-1970s and the mid-1980s. These were also voice-only PBXs, but they digitized voice signals before transferring them through the switch. This PBX equipment could be modified to carry digital data signals as well as voice. However, the transfer rate for data signals was slow.

The third generation of PBXs has been in existence since the early 1980s. They have the capability to move voice and data at relatively high speeds. Incoming analog signals are converted to digital signals, and therefore offer great flexibility and capabilities. Most of today's PBXs are from this generation.

The fourth generation of PBXs is characterized by having all voice and data switching capabilities combined in a LAN distribution system. They can serve as voice phone switches, electronic mail, voice mail, and data switches for LANs. However, their implementation has been slow due to the high cost of each line in the system.

Capabilities

Newer digital PBXs, such as the IBM 9751, Northern Telecom's Meridian, and the AT&T System 75 and 85, are designed around 32-bit microprocessor chips that control the entire system. They contain many features, including the following:

1. They can transmit voice and data simultaneously.
2. They can perform protocol conversion allowing equipment from different vendors to communicate.
3. They can control local area networks from within the switchboard.
4. They have voice and electronic mail.
5. Asynchronous and synchronous transmission can be performed simultaneously.
6. Automatic routing is available, ensuring that calls are routed through the least costly communication system.
7. They can switch digital transmission without the use of modems.
8. They can provide security by requesting and maintaining security access codes.
9. They can connect digital signals to high-speed circuits such as T-1 circuits.
10. They allow computer users to select different host computers or destinations without the need to rearrange cables.
11. They also offer many other features such as call forwarding, call holding, conference calling, and paging.

Besides digital and analog PBX systems, there are other categories into which PBXs can be placed. These are voice only, voice and data, and data only. Even though PBXs offer many advantages for digital data communications, they have limitations in the speed of data transmission. Typically, PBXs work at about 8 to 256 KBPS (kilobits per second). As distance of transmission increases, the rate of transmission decreases.

Matrix Switch

A matrix switch allows terminals and other electronic devices to access multiple available host processors without the need to physically move any communication line. Matrix switches operate in a manner similar to early PBXs.

Matrix switches evenly distribute users over multiple processors. If one processor becomes overloaded, users can be quickly and efficiently moved to another processor. If a line fails, the terminal connected to that line can easily be switched to another available line. Additionally, more terminals can be distributed using matrix switches than using physical wire.

Line Adapter

A line adapter is a device that is placed in the line of data transmission to perform monitoring functions, extend the range of data transmission, perform security functions, or allow the sharing of a data line. Some of the most commonly used types of line adapters are line monitors, port sharing devices, line splitters, digital expanders, and security devices such as encryption systems and call-back units.

Line Monitor

A line monitor is used to diagnose problems on a communication line or link. It attaches to a communication circuit, and a digital format of the data flowing through the circuit is displayed on a screen, printed to paper, or stored on an auxiliary device for further analysis.

There are two categories of line monitors, active and passive. Active line monitors can generate data, are interactive, and can emulate various types of monitors. Passive line monitors gather data and store it for analysis at a later time.

A typical line monitor can work with data speeds of up to 64,000 bits per second, and has video displays, has memory, supports synchronous and asynchronous transmission, has breakout box capabilites, and is capable of being programmed.

Microcomputers can be enhanced to function as line monitors. A PC adapter board, internal RS-232, and software can convert a standard microcomputer into an active and intelligent line monitor and response time analyzer.

Channel Extender

A channel extender links remote stations to host facilities. It connects directly to the host system and operates at high speeds. It functions like a small front-end processor. In addition to connecting remote work stations and computers to a host, it can support auxiliary devices, including printers. Fig. 3-10 shows the placement of a channel extender in a communication circuit.

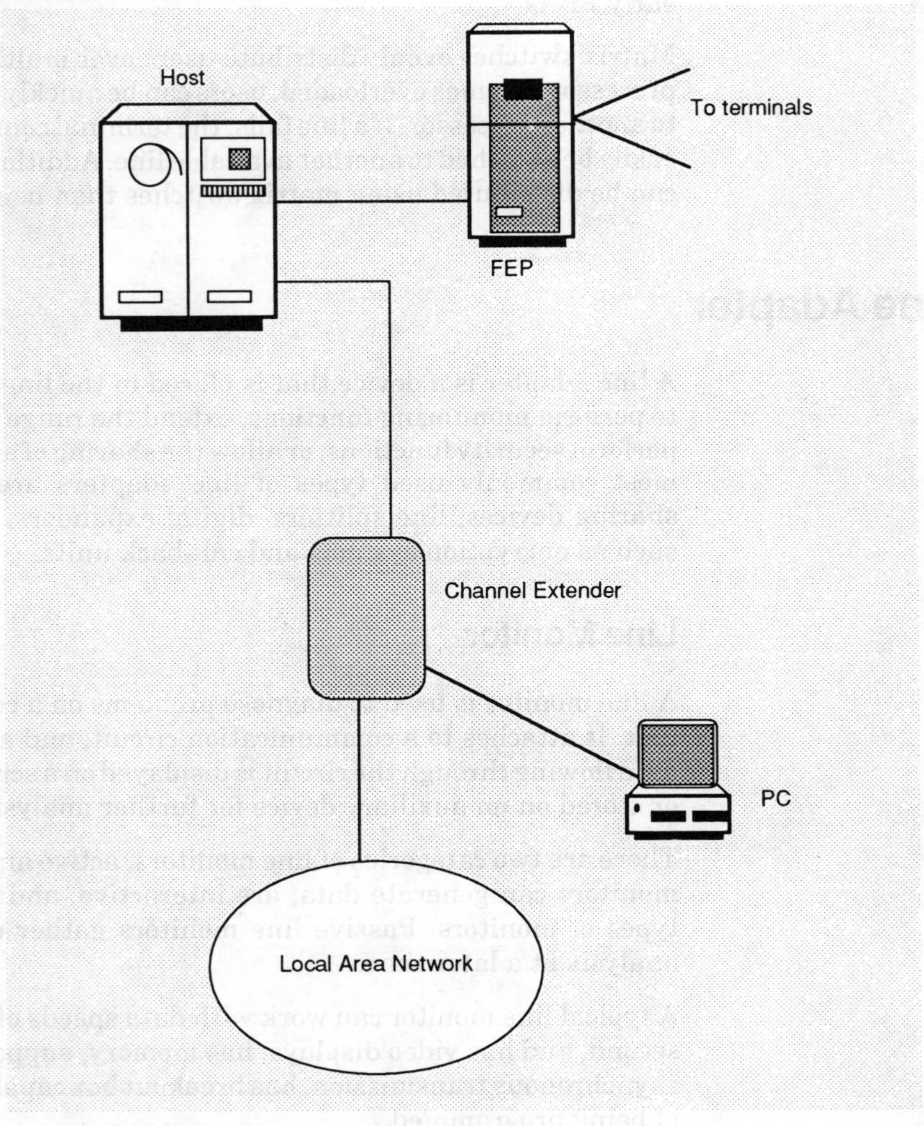

Fig. 3-10. Distributing data processing beyond the typical 400 feet limitation

Channel extenders are slower and less powerful than FEPs. They are a method for improving response time and offloading data communication processes from networks, and provide a less expensive alternative to FEPs. In recent years the software that controls channel extenders has increased in sophistication and power. This allows the new generation of channel extenders to compete directly with communication front end processors.

Fig 3-10 shows how distributed processing can be achieved beyond the typical 400 feet limitation for a mainframe data channel interconnection. The mainframe channel can be extended to another mainframe channel by using a channel extender. This device can also connect microcomputers and terminals at remote locations. Moreover, local area networks can be connected to the mainframe channel through a channel extender.

Port Sharing Device

A port sharing device allows multiple terminals or stations to use a single port on a FEP. It is used when the capacity of a FEP needs to be exceeded. For example, if a front end processor has 32 ports, then 32 incoming lines can be attached. If the number of users increases to 48, and there are no resources for extending the FEP or creating a LAN, then a port sharing device constitutes a temporary fix until a more appropriate solution is designed. Channel extenders can serve as sophisticated port sharing devices.

Line Splitter

A line splitter works in similar fashion to a port sharing device. The difference is in the location of the line splitter. It is typically found at the remote end of a communication line, where the terminal or work station is located. Port sharing devices are normally located at the host end of the communication line.

Line splitters act as switches that allow several terminals to connect to a modem to access the host system. Even though multiple terminals are attached to a line splitter, only one communication line exists. Therefore, only one terminal can be communicating with the host at any one time.

Digital Line Expander

A digital line expander allows users to concentrate a larger number of voice and data channels into the bandwidth of a standard communication channel. If a communication site has only two leased lines between two terminating points, then it can save money by using a line expander to increase the carrying capacity of those lines. One digital line expander can provide up to eight intermixed voice and digital data transmission circuits over a single digital communication circuit.

Security Devices

Securing data transmission lines is an important aspect of data communications today. Several pieces of hardware can assist in protecting data flowing through communication circuits.

Call-Back Unit

A call-back unit is a security device that calls back the user after he or she makes a login attempt. If the phone that the user is on is an authorized number, then the system permits the user to login.

The procedure that this unit goes through to secure lines is as follows:

1. A person attempting to access the system makes a connection from a remote terminal.
2. The person is required to provide an identification number (ID) and a password.
3. The connection is severed after the ID and the password are entered.
4. The ID and password are checked in a table to verify that the user is authorized.
5. If the user is authorized, the dial-back unit calls the user's registered phone number. The phone number is stored inside the host and authorized by the company's security personnel.
6. The user's modem is accessed and the session between the terminal and the host begins.

Dial-back units provide access only to authorized users, inhibiting access by hackers, unless they are using an authorized phone. However, these units have some problems. First, the host system becomes responsible for the cost of the connection. Second, if a person is on a business trip and tries to access the host system with a portable computer, the computer won't be able to make the connection, since the phone number being used is not registered.

Encryption Equipment

Some data communication networks, such as those employed by the government and military, require very secure communication. Encryption equipment is used to scramble the data at the sending location and reconstruct it at the receiving end. Fig. 3-11 depicts this configuration.

Encryption devices expect digital information as input, and produce digital information as output. The U.S. National Bureau of Standards (NBS) has set a standard called the data encryption standard (DES), which uses 64 bits. Eight of the 64 bits are used for error detection, and a 56-bit pattern is used for the encryption key. This provides 2^{56} possible different key combinations.

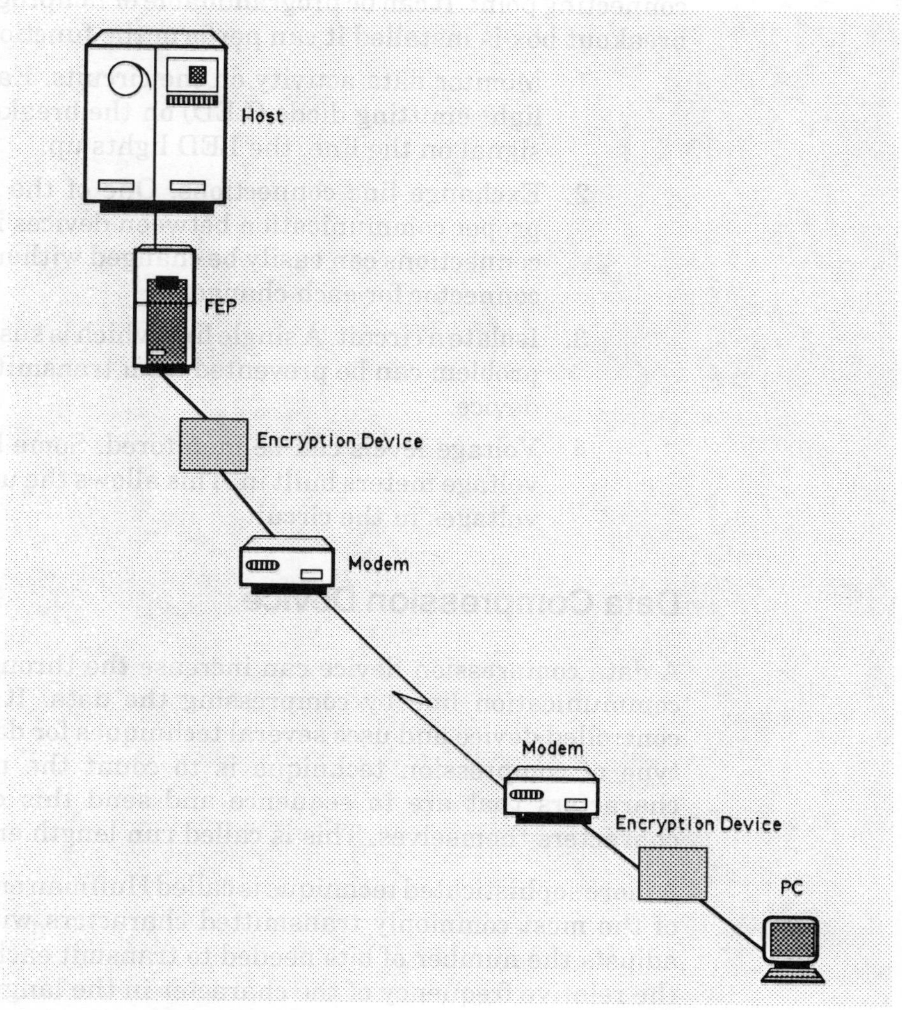

Fig. 3-11. Encryption equipment being used to protect data transmission

Miscellaneous Equipment

There are other hardware devices that help in the installation and maintenance of data lines. Two of the most common are the breakout box and data compression devices.

Breakout Box

A breakout box is a passive device that can be attached to a circuit at any connecting point. It can be programmable or nonprogrammable. Once the breakout box is installed it can perform the functions below:

1. Monitor data activity on the circuits. Each line circuit has a light emitting diode (LED) on the breakout box. If there is a signal on the line, the LED lights up.
2. Exchange line connections. One of the major causes of improper communication between devices is crossed lines. Line connections can easily be changed without the need to build a connector for each change.
3. Isolate a circuit. A single line which is suspected of causing the problem can be prevented from transmitting to the receiving device.
4. Voltage levels can be monitored. Some breakout boxes have voltage meters built in. This allows the user to detect unusual voltages in the circuit

Data Compression Device

A data compression device can increase the throughput of data over a communication line by compressing the data. It is a microprocessor controlled device and uses several techniques for data compression. One type of compression technique is to count the number of repeating characters that are in sequence and send this count instead of the characters themselves. This is called run length encoding.

A more sophisticated technique is called Huffman encoding. It uses tables of the most commonly transmitted characters within a language and adjusts the number of bits needed to transmit each character, based on the relative frequency of the character in the language.

Circuit Media

The primary medium used for communication lines is wire conductors. Wire conductors can be classified into four major groups: open wire, twisted pair cable, coaxial cable, and optical fiber cable. There are also microwave and satellite media.

Open Wire

Open wire lines have been around since the inception of the data communication industry. An open wire line consists of copper wire tied to glass insulators. The insulators are attached to wooden arms mounted on utility poles. While still in common use throughout the world, they are quickly being replaced by twisted pair cables and other transmission media.

Twisted Pair Cables

A twisted pair cable is composed of copper conductors insulated by paper or plastic and twisted into pairs. These pairs are bundled into units and the units are bundled to form the finished cable. Fig. 3-12 shows a terminal connector where twisted pair cables are being used.

A variation of twisted pair is called the shielded twisted pair. Normal twisted cable is placed inside a thin metallic shielding and then enclosed in an outer plastic casing. The shielding provides further isolation of the signal-carrying wires. It is less susceptible to interference signals produced by electrical wires or nearby electronic equipment.

Transmission frequencies can be high for long distances. In this case, electrical interference in the form of crosstalk between adjacent circuits is a problem for twisted pair cables. Coaxial cable solves this problem.

Twisted pair wires are connected together at this punchdown block in the telephone equipment room.

Fig. 3-12. Terminal connector for connecting twisted pair cables

Coaxial Cable

Coaxial cable consists of two conductors. The inner conductor, normally copper or aluminum, is shielded by placing it inside a plastic case or shield. The second conductor is wrapped around the plastic shield of the first conductor. This further shields the inner conductor. Finally, the outer conductor (shield) is covered with plastic or some other protective and insulating cover (see Fig. 3-13).

Coaxial cables are normally grouped into bundles. Each bundle can carry several thousand voice and/or data transmissions simultaneously. This type of cable has little signal loss, signal distortion, or crosstalk. Therefore, it is a better transmission medium than open wire or twisted pair cables.

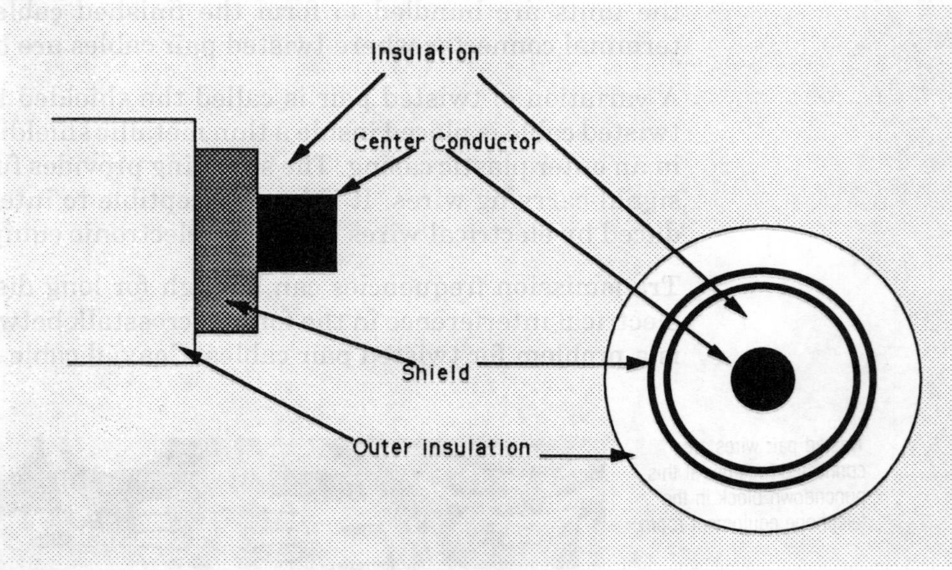

Fig. 3-13. Coaxial cable

Optical Fiber

Optical fiber consists of thin glass fibers that can carry information at frequencies in the visible light spectrum. The data transmission lines made up of optical fibers are joined by connectors that have very little loss of the signal throughout the length of the data line.

At the sending end of a data circuit, data is encoded from electrical signals into light pulses that travel through the lines at high speeds. At the receiving end, the light is converted back into electrical analog or digital signals that are then passed on to the receiving device. The typical optical fiber consists of a very narrow strand of glass called the core. Around the core is a concentric layer of glass called the cladding (see Fig 3-14). After the light is inserted into the core it is reflected by the cladding. The light follows a zig-zag path through the core. The advantage of optical fiber is that it can carry large amounts of information at high speeds in very reduced physical spaces with little loss of signal.

There are three primary types of transmission modes using optical fiber, although many more are being developed. They are single mode, step index, and grade index.

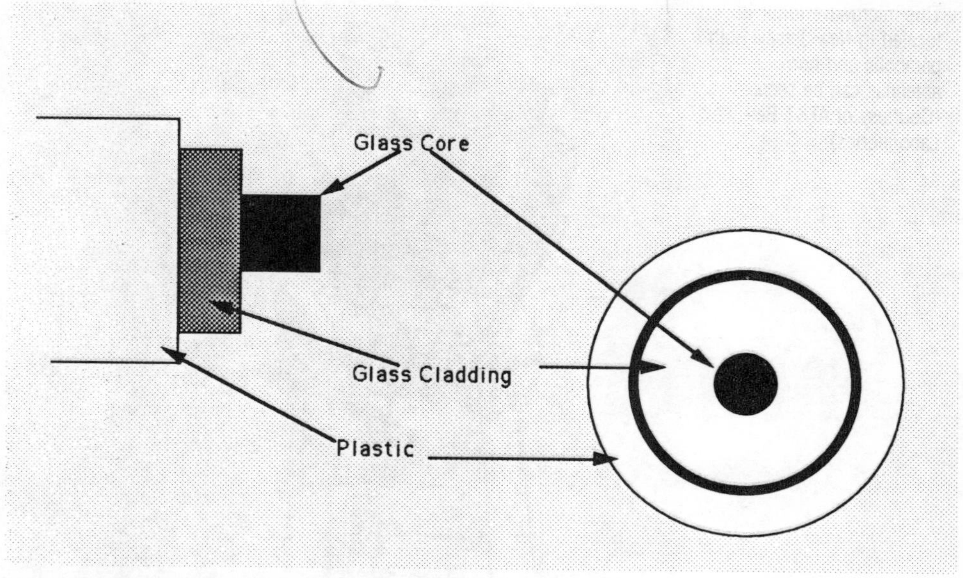

Fig. 3-14. Optical fiber cable

Single mode uses fibers with a core radius of 2.5 to 4 microns. Since the radius of the fiber is so small, light travels through the core with little reflection from the cladding. However, it requires very concentrated light sources to get the signal to travel long distances. This type of mode is typically used for trunk line applications.

Step index fiber consists of a core of fiber surrounded by a cladding with a lower refractive index for the light. The cable has an approximate radius of 30 to 70 microns. The lower refractive index causes the light pulse to bounce downward back toward the core. In this type of transmission, some of the light pulses travel straight down the core while others bounce off the cladding multiple times before reaching their destination. This mode is used for distances of one kilometer or less.

Grade index fiber has a refractive index that changes gradually as the light travels to the outer edge of the fiber. The cable has a radius of 25 to 60 microns. This gradual refractive index bends the light towards the core instead of just reflecting it. This mode is used for long distance communication.

Microwave

Microwave is a high frequency radio signal that is transmitted over a direct line-of-sight path between two points. Since the earth has a curvature, this necessitates that microwave stations be no more than 30 miles apart. Fig. 3-15 shows a picture of a microwave tower and transmission station.

This microwave tower is located in New Jersey. Both parabolic and horn antennas can be seen. (Courtesy of AT&T Bell Laboratories)

Fig. 3-15. Microwave tower and transmission station

There are three main groups of radio systems used for communications lines. They are broadcast, beam, and satellite. Broadcast radio is limited to a unique frequency within the range of the transmitter. Beam radio transmission needs to be repeated if the signal is to travel farther than 30 miles. Normally, radio beam repeaters are found on top of buildings, mountain tops, and radio antennas. Satellite microwave radio is employed to avoid the limitations imposed by the earth's curvature.

Microwave transmission offers speed, cost effectiveness (since there are no cables), and ease of operation. However, it has the potential for interference with other radio waves. Additionally, commercial transmissions can be intercepted by any person with a receiver in the line of transmission. This creates security risks.

Satellite Transmission

Satellite transmission is similar to microwave radio transmission, except that instead of transmitting to an earth-bound receiving station, it will

These satellite dish antennas are about 5 meters in diameter. Other dish antennas are as small as 1 meter. (Courtesy of Contel ASC)

Fig. 3-16. Satellite dish antenna

transmit to a satellite several thousand miles out in space (normally approximately 22,300 miles). Fig. 3-16 shows a picture of a transmitting satellite dish antenna.

The basic components of satellite transmission are an earth station, used for sending and receiving data, and the satellite, sometimes called a transponder. The satellite receives the signals from an earth station (uplink), amplifies the signal, changes the frequency, and retransmits the data to another receiving earth station (downlink). The change in frequency is done so the uplink does not interfere with the downlink.

In satellite transmission, a delay occurs because the signal needs to travel out into space and back to the earth. Typical delay times are 0.5 seconds. There is an additional delay due to the time required for the signal to travel through ground stations.

As stated before, satellites use different frequencies for receiving and transmitting. The frequency ranges are from 4 to 6 gigahertz (GHz), also called the C-band; 12 to 14 GHz, also called the Ku-band; and 20 to 30 GHz. As the value of the frequency decreases, the size of the dish antenna required to receive and transmit the signals needs to increase. The Ku-band is used to transmit television programs between networks and individual television stations. Since signals in the Ku-band have a higher frequency, their wavelength is shortened. This allows receiving and transmitting stations to concentrate the signals and use smaller dish antennas.

Security poses a problem with satellite communications, because it is easy to intercept the transmission as it travels through the air. In some cases, a scrambler is used to distort the signal before it is sent to the satellite, and a descrambler is used in the receiving station to reproduce the original signal.

Circuit Media Selection

Many factors influence the decision of a medium for a communication network. These factors include cost, speed, expandability, security, and distance requirements. Decisions regarding these factors cannot be made independently. However, for pedagogical reasons, each factor will be considered individually.

Cost

The cost of a given communication network will include not only the cost of the medium itself, but also the supporting hardware and software required to manage the network. The cost of further expansion must also be taken into consideration. For example, a business that is established in Dallas, may consider Dallas, Houston, Chicago, and New Orleans as its target cities. To connect its regional offices to its headquarters, this emerging company can use leased lines from a common carrier. However, if it is projected that within five years their contact offices will be in many more cities, then a satellite network will be more cost effective than leased lines.

Speed

The transmission speed of communication networks ranges from a low 300 bits per second to several million bits per second. Some media, such as twisted pair cable, are less expensive than optical fiber. However, optical fiber can transmit at much higher speeds than twisted pair cable. The cost of increased speed must be balanced against the needs of the network and its users.

Two factors dictate the speed of a medium: the response time expected by users and the aggregate data rate. Response time is the time it takes from the moment a terminal sends a request to the time the response from the host gets back to the user. A good response time is two seconds or less. However, longer response times may be tolerated to save on the cost of the medium. Aggregate data rate is the amount of information that can be transmitted per unit of time. A company's users may be satisfied with transmission speeds of 9600 bits per second. But at peak processing times, with large files, the speed requirements may range as high as 19,200 bits per second. The same communication medium may not work for both speeds.

Some transfer rates for common media are:

Private and leased lines	300 to 80,000 bits per second
T1 type media	1.5 to 300 megabits per second
Coaxial cable	1 to over 500 megabits per second
Optical fiber	over 2 gigabits per second
Microwave	up to 50 megabits per second
Satellite	up to 50 megabits per second

Expandability

Eventually, most data communication networks need to be expanded by adding more devices at a location or by adding new locations. Some media offer more cost effective expandability than others. For example, coaxial cable and satellite based networks are easier to expand into new locations. Leased telephone lines make expansion into new areas more difficult and costly.

Future expansions must be considered whenever a data communication network is being designed. For example, a company can install twisted pair cable throughout an entire building. Two or three years after installation it finds that it needs coaxial and optical fiber media. In this case the cost of rewiring the building is larger than it would have been to install it initially. When planning communication networks, both short-range and long-range needs must be considered..

Security

The lack of security in a data communication network will allow hackers or unauthorized persons to have access to vital data. The data could be used to gain an advantage in the market place, or it could be altered or destroyed with catastrophic consequences for a business.

Providing a completely sealed network where unauthorized persons can never access the network is impossible. However, some media, such as optical fiber, are more difficult to penetrate than other media, such as coaxial cable or satellite. The most vulnerable medium to the average hacker is switched lines.

Distance Requirements

The distance between a sender and a receiver can determine the type of medium used for data transmission. In addition, distance affects the number of devices that must be served. For short distances twisted pair, coaxial cable, and optical fiber may be used. For long distances, the average business may have to rely on local carrier lines, microwave, or satellite media.

Environment

The environment in which a medium must exist will eliminate some options from consideration. For example, local building codes may prohibit a company or educational institution from laying cables under streets. In this case, microwave radio transmission may need to be used. Another example is a case where phone lines are sharing conduits with electrical wires. This may cause too much interference with digital data transmission. During the planning stages of a data communication network, the location of the medium and local constraints must be taken into account to avoid costly modifications during installation.

Maintenance

The type of maintenance required for a communication network must also be considered during the planning stage. If a coaxial line is broken or becomes defective, it can be repaired easily by finding the trouble section and replacing it. However, if a satellite malfunctions and needs repair, the time required to place it back into normal operations may be lengthy. This is why many communication companies have multiple media backup networks.

Leased vs Switched Lines

When using telephone lines for the transmission of digital information, the options are to use a leased line or to use a switched line. Both of these must be rented from the phone company. A leased line, also called a dedicated line, is treated specially to carry computer information. The leased line is set up to bypass switching equipment at the phone company and it is dedicated to connect two systems 24 hours per day and seven days per week.

If the line is not leased, then a phone call must be made to the computer that will become the host during the transmission. After the connection is made, digital data is transmitted and routed over any available telephone lines. These types of lines are called switched or dial-up lines because the data transmitted must pass through switching equipment at the phone company so it can be routed to available lines.

If a connection between computers needs to be kept for very long periods of time such as 12 hours per day or more, and needs to be kept during the entire week, then a leased line will be more cost effective than a switched line. However, if the connection between computers is performed during short intervals of time or occasionally, the switched line will be a better alternative.

Summary

Several types of electronic devices are used in the design and installation of communication networks. The most commonly used are multiplexers, concentrators, cluster controllers, PBXs, matrix switches, line adapters, and security devices.

Multiplexing technology allows the transmission of multiple signals over a single medium. Multiplexers allow the replacement of multiple low-speed transmission lines with a single high-speed transmission line. The typical configuration includes a multiplexer attached to multiple low-speed lines, a communication line (typically four-wire carrier circuit), and a multiplexer on another site that is also connected to low-speed lines. There are several techniques by which a multiplexer can be used. Multiplexing techniques can be divided into frequency division multiplexing (FDM), time division multiplexing (TDM), and statistical time division multiplexing (STDM).

A concentrator is a line sharing device whose primary function is the same as that of a multiplexer. It allows multiple devices to share communication circuits. Unlike multiplexers, concentrators are intelligent devices that sometimes perform data processing functions and provide auxiliary storage.

Cluster controllers are designed to support several terminals and the functions required to manage the terminals. Also, they buffer data being transmitted to or from the terminals, perform error detection and correction, and poll terminals.

A private branch exchange is an electronic switchboard which connects to all the telephone lines of the organization.

A matrix switch allows terminals and other electronic devices to access multiple host processors without the need to physically move any communication line.

Line adapters come in different varieties. Some of these are line monitors channel extenders, line splitters, and port sharing devices.

Securing data transmission lines is an important aspect of data communication today. Several pieces of hardware can assist in protecting data flowing through communication circuits. These devices include call back units and encryption equipment.

Other devices used in monitoring and improving line channel performance are the breakout box and data compression device. The breakout box is a passive device that can be attached to a circuit at any connecting point. A data compression device can increase the throughput of data over a communication line by compressing the data.

The primary medium used for communication lines is wire conductors. Wire conductors can be classified into four major groups: open wire, twisted pair cable, coaxial cable, and optical fiber cable. Microwave and satellite are also used for communications. Many factors influence the choice of a medium for a communication network. These factors are cost, speed, expandability, security, and distance requirements.

Questions

1. What is a multiplexer?
2. Describe four different types of multiplexers.
3. How are multiplexers used?
4. What are concentrators?
5. What is the function of a protocol converter?
6. What is the function of a PBX?
7. What is a cluster controller?
8. Describe four different types of line adapters.
9. How does a line monitor work?
10. Why is hardware encryption used?
11. Describe four different types of circuit media technology.
12. Describe the different modes of optical fiber transmission.
13. What criteria should be used when selecting the media needed for a data communication network?
14. What advantage does optical fiber has over coaxial cable?

Projects

Objective

The projects in this chapter are intended to familiarize the student with the basic hardware required to connect computers and printers using standard RS-232 ports. The basic equipment required to perform the projects is outlined in project 1. As an additional challenge, the instructor may provide unknown or lesser known serial printers and instruct the student to design the interface between the printer and a microcomputer.

Project 1. Interface between an External Modem and a Microcomputer

There are two methods of connecting an external modem to your computer. The first method is to purchase a serial cable from a local computer store, and connect the RS-232 or serial connector at the back of the computer with the serial connector at the back of the modem. This is the easier method. The second method is to construct your own serial cable. The tools required to make this cable are as follows:

1. Soldering iron and solder material.
2. Nine-wire (or more) cable.
3. Two serial connectors of the right gender. The gender can be "male" or "female." The male has pins coming out of the connector. In most cases the connector required for the PC will be female and that for the modem will be male. However, the gender of the connectors is not standard among all equipment manufacturers.
4. Wire strippers.
5. Clamps to hold the wires and connectors.
6. Breakout box (optional).

After all the tools and materials are gathered, use the connections outlined in Fig. 3-17 to connect a modem and a terminal.

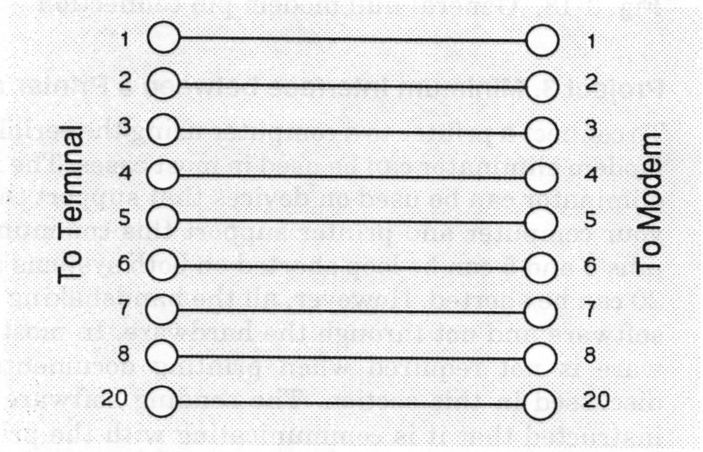

Fig. 3-17. Modem and terminal interface pin connection

Project 2. Serial Interface between Two IBM or IBM-compatible Microcomputers

To connect one computer directly to another without a modem, a modem eliminator or null modem is required. A null modem is a cable that has at a minimum the wires that connect pins 2 and 3 on both computers crossed over. Pin 2 on both computers is responsible for sending data, and pin 3 receives data. As you can imagine, if both of these pins were not crossed, then both the computers could talk but neither would be listening. Make these two connections now.

(Making the connecting cable is only one aspect of connecting two microcomputers. Communication software will be required to perform the communication functions. The project in chapter 4 explores this topic further and provides some hands-on experience. A general null modem can be created by crossing pins 2 and 3, 20 and 6, and connecting 8 to 6 on the RS-232 cable as in Fig. 3-18.)

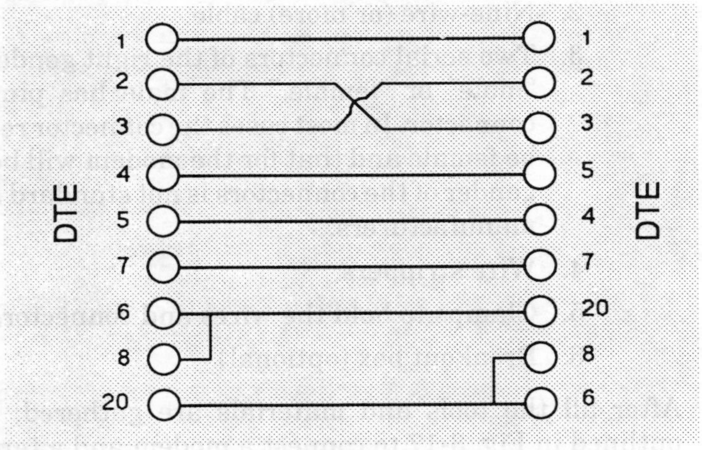

Fig. 3-18. General null modem pin connection

Project 3. Minimum Interface between a Printer and a Microcomputer

To connect a printer to a computer using the serial port, a minimum null modem eliminator can be used in most cases. The minimum null modem eliminator can be used on devices that support the Xon/Xoff protocol. If your computer and printer support this communication protocol, then pins 4 and 5 can be loop shorted on both systems and also pins 6, 8, and 20 can be shorted. However, all the handshaking must be done through software and not through the hardware. In most cases additional software is not required when printing documents using the interface discussed in this section. The sending software program needs to be instructed that it is communicating with the printer serially and that Xon/Xoff should be used in addition to the typical serial parameters (see project in chapter 2).

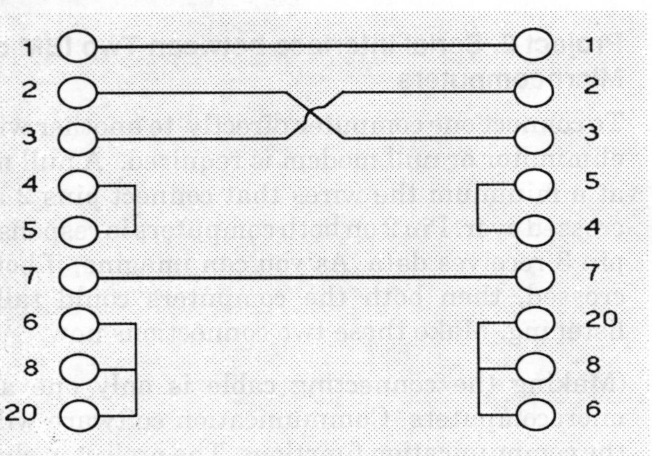

Fig. 3-19. Minimum null modem

To construct the minimum null modem eliminator, follow the configuration in Fig. 3-19.

Project 4. General Interface between a Printer and a Microcomputer

In some situations a minimum null modem eliminator is not sufficient for the printer and the computer to communicate. If the printer seems to "lose" characters or if it prints correctly for a while and then it stops, the configuration in Fig. 3-20 may solve the problem. Some printers require pin 11 (printer ready) to become active by a signal from the union of pins 6 and 8 as in Fig. 3-20.

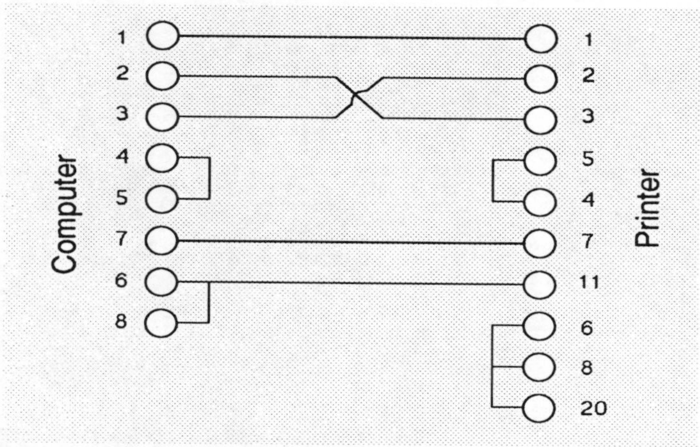

Fig. 3-20. Pin connection for a printer to PC serial interface

4

Network Basics

Objectives

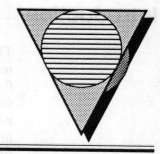

1. **Understand the benefits of networking.**
2. **Understand the difference between local area networks and wide area networks.**
3. **Learn the standards that are used in designing networking technology.**
4. **Know the different types of network topologies.**
5. **Understand the different devices used for interconnecting networks.**
6. **Obtain a general overview of design considerations for hybrid networks**

Key Terms

Bridge
Brouter
Bus Network
Gateway
Local Area Network
Metropolitan Area Network
Network
PDN
Ring Network
Router
Software
Star Network
Wide Area Network

Introduction

This chapter explores the benefits of using networks in the work environment. The terminology acquired in previous chapters becomes the foundation for understanding the importance and functionality of networks. The information system industry is being shaped by the use of networks for interconnecting workstations, peripherals, mainframes, and minicomputers. Students in all areas of business need to understand network connectivity issues and the advantages and disadvantages of different configurations.

This chapter presents the benefits of having a networked environment and the basics of understanding networks. The difference between wide area networks and local area networks is explained, along with the different types of network topologies that are found in the workplace. Finally, the technologies required to connect dissimilar networks are discussed, along with related design concepts.

The student should read the material in this chapter thoroughly before starting the next chapter and before covering the section on Novell's NetWare. Those chapters assume knowledge and understanding of the general networking concepts explored in this chapter.

Benefits of Networking

The microcomputer, with all of its benefits and usefulness, has serious shortcomings. The microcomputer was designed with a single user in mind. It was not designed to share its resources among other computers. If a printout is required, the personal computer must have its own printer. If a file must be stored in a hard disk, the personal computer must have its own hard disk. To a lesser extent, mainframes and minicomputers have the same problems. Even though a mainframe has many terminals that share disk space and printer capabilities, users of other computers within the same corporation may have a need to share resources in an efficient manner.

For example, assume that a corporation has an IBM AS-400 minicomputer, a Digital Equipment Corporation VAX minicomputer, and many personal computers and terminals. On many occasions the data stored in the AS-400 may be required by users of the VAX minicomputer and vice versa. In addition, some data processed in microcomputers and the resulting information must be shared by users of both minicomputer systems. This type of scenario creates many different types of information needs that must be resolved in an efficient and cost effective manner. Users should not be expected to duplicate data entry procedures or to master the use of multiple diverse and difficult-to-use systems.

How does a system manager resolve the information needs of the users? One solution is to provide two terminals for each user, one for the AS-400 and one for the VAX. This solution does not solve the problem of sharing data among the minicomputers. Another is to provide every user a personal computer. Each user can access one minicomputer, download the data to a personal computer using a communications program, modify the data locally, and, using a different emulation-communication program, upload the data to the second minicomputer. This solution may eventually work, but it assumes that every user is proficient with both minicomputer systems and the personal computer. In addition, to perform the entire transaction properly, the user must have a good knowledge of microcomputers and communication software. These assumptions typically cannot be made. Finally, even though a user may accomplish the entire transaction without errors, the method employed is not very efficient.

The isolation described in the example results in duplication of hardware, software, and human resources by the user. If the company has 100 microcomputers and all users need to run a specific package, the company must purchase 100 individual programs if it wishes to remain within the limits of the law. Similarly, each user must be provided with a printer and any other peripherals required to use the software.

Even small companies will find that using computers in an isolated format is inefficient. As an example, imagine a small company that purchases a microcomputer to keep track of inventory. In this scenario, one person keeps the inventory updated, and others occasionally use the microcomputer to check the inventory level and monitor availability of a product. As users find the application useful, the demand to use the inventory database increases. The company also grows and expands its product line, adding more inventory items to the database. As the database is used on a continuous basis and the inventory grows, it becomes increasingly difficult to keep the inventory updated. If more computers are purchased to handle the demand, then the complication emerges of needing several computers, each with a current database.

A computer network can change a group of isolated computers into a coordinated multiuser computer system. A network user can legally share copies of the software with other users if network versions of the software are purchased. Data can be stored in centralized locations or in different locations that are accessible to all users. Printers, scanners, and other peripherals connected to the network are available to all users. If the inventory system described above was placed on a network with several other computers, the system could be kept updated and could be accessed by many users simultaneously.

Hardware Sharing

A network allows users to share different types of hardware devices. The most commonly shared items are hard disks, printers, CD-drives, and communication devices.

Sharing Hard Disks

Today's sophisticated software applications require large amounts of disk space. As companies require more information about their operation, larger disks are required. Although, the price of disk technology has dropped dramatically in recent years, disks with a capacity to store billions of bytes are still relatively expensive. In addition, it is not uncommon for microcomputer users to require hard disk capacities of many megabytes. It would be too expensive to purchase large disk space for all users or all possible situations that may arise within a corporation. In addition, the security and backup of storage devices becomes more difficult to manage when the devices are isolated.

Today's networks are based on the concept of sharing access to storage devices. These disks are typically installed on special devices called file servers, which will be discussed in the next chapter. As outlined above, sharing disk space has several benefits. The most obvious are costs, integrity of the data, and security. Costs are reduced by purchasing hard disks to be shared among all users, instead of purchasing one for each user or location. The safety of the data is improved over having it on isolated disks, since a network administrator can make constant backups of all files on the device. Security of the data is enforced by using the network's built-in security systems. Data on isolated disks is an easy target to anyone who wants to damage it.

Sharing Printers

Printer sharing is common on networks. Printers can be attached to a file server, or connected to the network independently of the file server (see Fig. 4-1). Any user in the network depicted in Fig. 4-1 can use any of the printers in the system. Instead of each user having a low-cost printer attached to a terminal or microcomputer, a few high-speed, high-quality printers can be purchased and connected to the network. Any user that needs a fast printout can send the output to the printer nearest to the station. In addition, other input and output devices can be shared on a network. These include facsimile machines, scanners, and plotters.

Sharing Communication Devices

Personal computer users on a network often need to access remote systems or networks. One possible solution is to provide them with modems and terminal emulation software to access other systems. This is expensive. Users on a network can share modems, gateways, bridges, (these devices are more fully discussed in this chapter) and other network and data communication devices without the need to purchase one for each user (see Fig. 4-2).

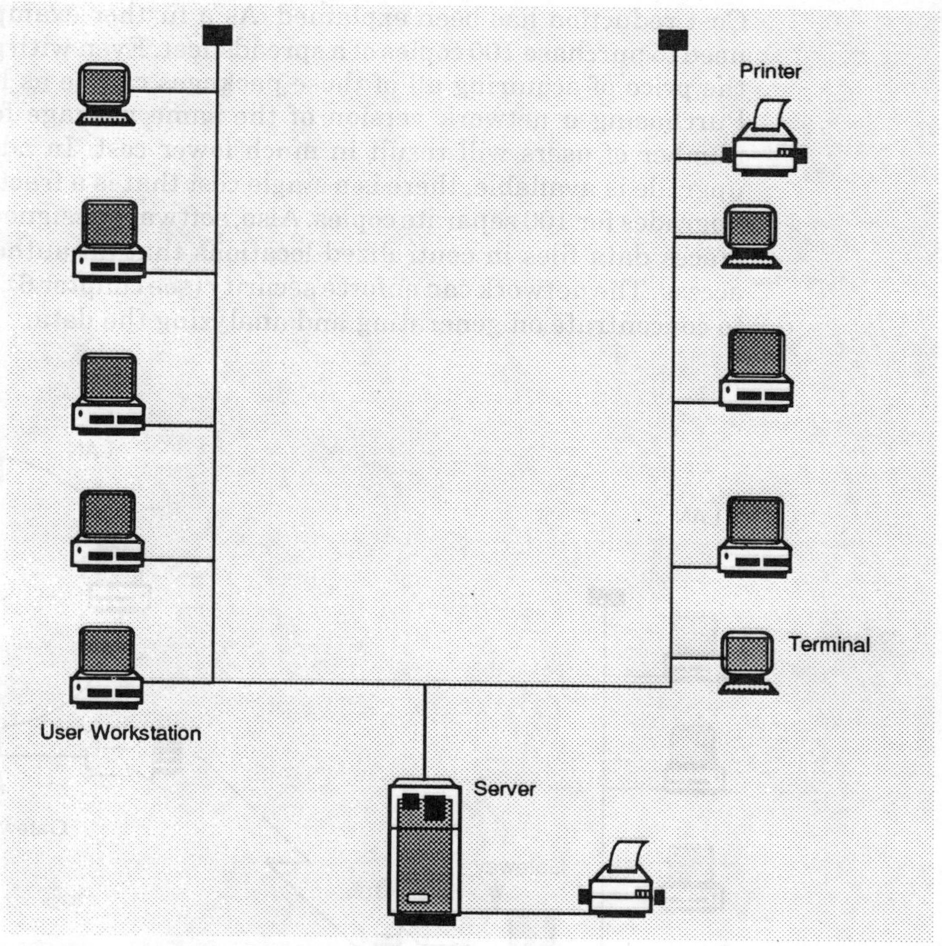

Fig. 4-1. Sharing printers with a network

The benefits of sharing hardware on a network are clear. Costs can be reduced by avoiding duplicate hardware, and at the same time users can have access to a variety of devices. Also, data security and safety are improved by having up-to-date backups and enforcing the security measures that come with each network.

Software Sharing

Instead of purchasing an individual application program for every user in a company, a network version of the program can be obtained. Software designed for networks allows multiple use of the software simultaneously. Users can share the data produced and used by the package. There are many advantages of sharing software. The most important are cost reduction, legality of the product, sharing data, and having current upgrades.

Cost reduction has been explained. As a further example, imagine the need to purchase 100 copies of a spreadsheet. Even with group discounts, the price of acquiring all of those packages can be as high as $50,000. Purchasing a network version of the same package for an unlimited number of users will result in much lower cost. In addition, when an upgrade is available, there is a single cost that is a fraction of the cost of upgrades for 100 separate copies. Also, software designed for networking places data files in centralized locations that all authorized users can access. The network can enforce security (see chapter 6), leaving the user to concentrate on generating and analyzing the data.

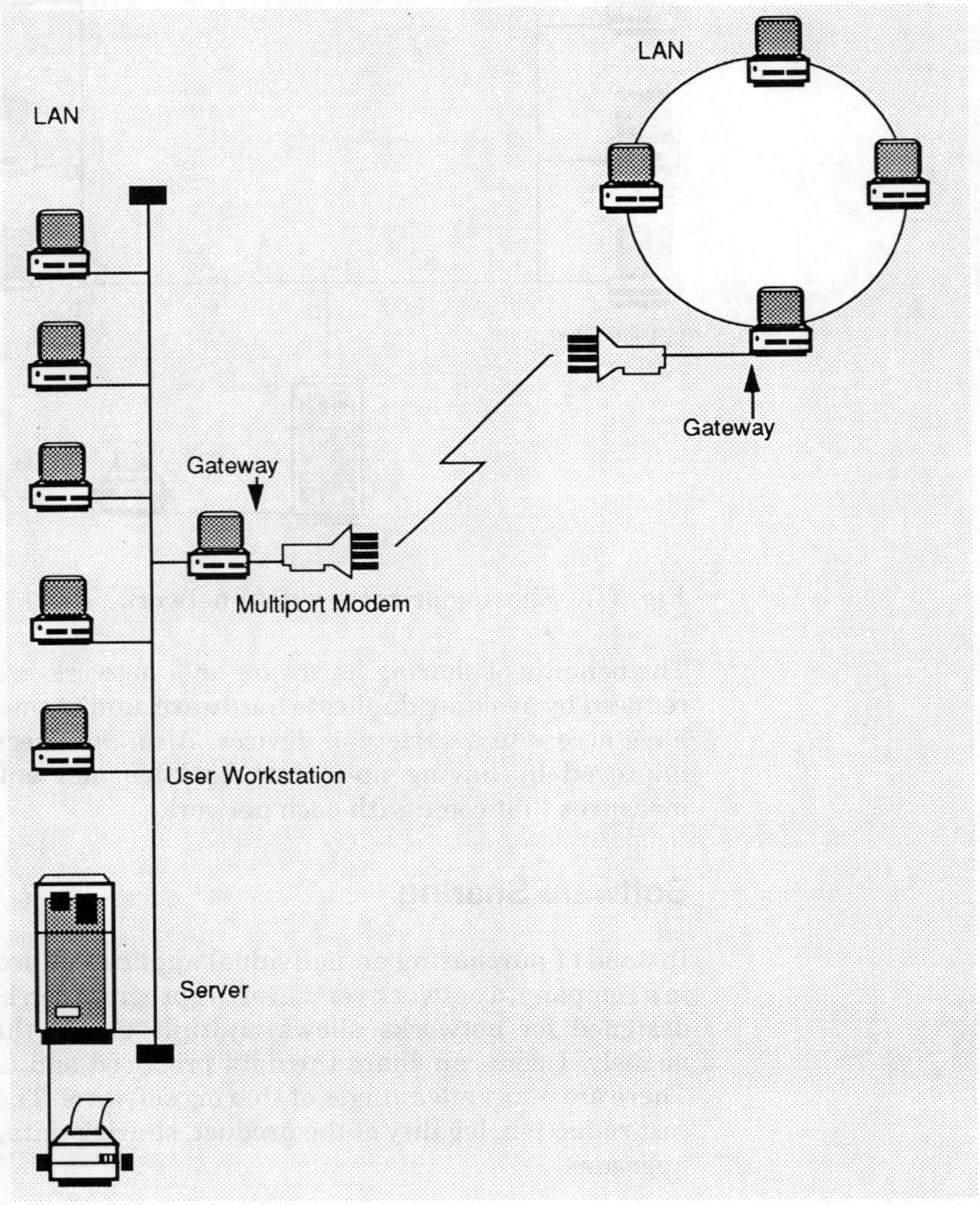

Fig. 4-2. Sharing computing resources with a network

Networking multiple computers also has an added advantage. The productivity of users can be enhanced by taking advantage of groupware. Groupware software includes electronic mail (e-mail), calendar, appointment, word processing, alarm clock, and other time management software. It allows a user to manage his or her time electronically, and communicate this information to other users in the network. It is intended to eliminate much of the inter-office paperwork, making information available to all users faster.

Challenges of Networking

Although the implementation of a network carries many benefits as outlined in the beginning of this chapter, its introduction into the work environment presents new challenges and costs that are sometimes not anticipated. These challenges can all be summarized as the cost of networking.

The cost of networking includes, but it is not limited to, these factors:

1. The cost of acquiring and installing cables and associated equipment for the transmission of data. The purchase of transmitting media is just one aspect of this cost. Specialized personnel may be required to lay the cable. Also, if the distances are large, additional equipment such as line adapters may be required.
2. The cost of purchasing the network operating system, and network versions of individual software packages. Software applications that were running on an individual basis may need to be upgraded in order to obtain network licenses. Additionally, many software programs designed for an individual computer will not execute on a network without modification of the source code.
3. The cost of personnel to manage software installation, expand and reconfigure the network, and provide backup, maintenance of hardware and software, and maintenance of the network/user interface. As users are added to the network, the security and safekeeping of data becomes critical. Personnel will be required to maintain the network on a full time basis and to ensure that proper backups are made in a consistent and timely fashion. The network interface will need modification as types and quantities of users change.
4. The cost of bridges and gateways to other networks, and the software and other equipment required to implement the connection. After the network is implemented, there may be a need to connect it to other communication systems. The cost

and challenge of performing this connection are an additional burden to network managers, and additional personnel and training may be required.

5. The cost of training users of the network and the personnel required to manage the network. This is an ongoing cost due to the turnover of personnel in companies. If the company has a high turnover ratio, then this cost will be large.
6. The cost of maintenance including installation of future software upgrades, correcting incompatibilities between the network operating system and new software upgrades, and correcting hardware problems. As new versions of the network operating system become available, old software programs may not be able to coexist with the new OS. In such cases, new versions of application software must be secured. (Of course, if the number of users is large, then having a network license can provide substantial savings over purchasing many individual copies of the same program.)
7. The cost of hiring a network administrator or specialist to manage the system or to solve problems as they occur. Although many companies use existing personnel to manage new networks, these people will have to give up a minimum of approximately 10 to 20 hours per week to manage and back up the network. Their absence from a task for which they were hired will eventually have to be compensated for by hiring assistants or by increasing the salary of such personnel.
8. The cost of network versions of software. Software designed to work on a network is normally more expensive than individual copies of the application. For a network that contains large numbers of users working with a software application, there are cost savings in purchasing a single network version of the program. But for a network with a small number of users, such cost saving may not be realized.

In small companies the task of implementing and managing the network can be performed by one or two persons. In large companies, there will be a need for several full time employees to perform network management duties; therefore, the above costs will become a sizable portion of the operational budget of the company.

Types of Networks

The geographical area covered by a network determines whether the network is called a wide area network (WAN--see Fig. 4-3), metropolitan area network (MAN), or a local area network (LAN). Wide area networks link systems that are too far apart to be included in a small in-house network. Metropolitan area networks connect across distances greater than a few kilometers but no more than 50 kilometers (approximately 30 miles). Local area networks usually connect users in the same office or building. In some cases, adjacent buildings of a corporation or educational institution are connected with the use of LANs.

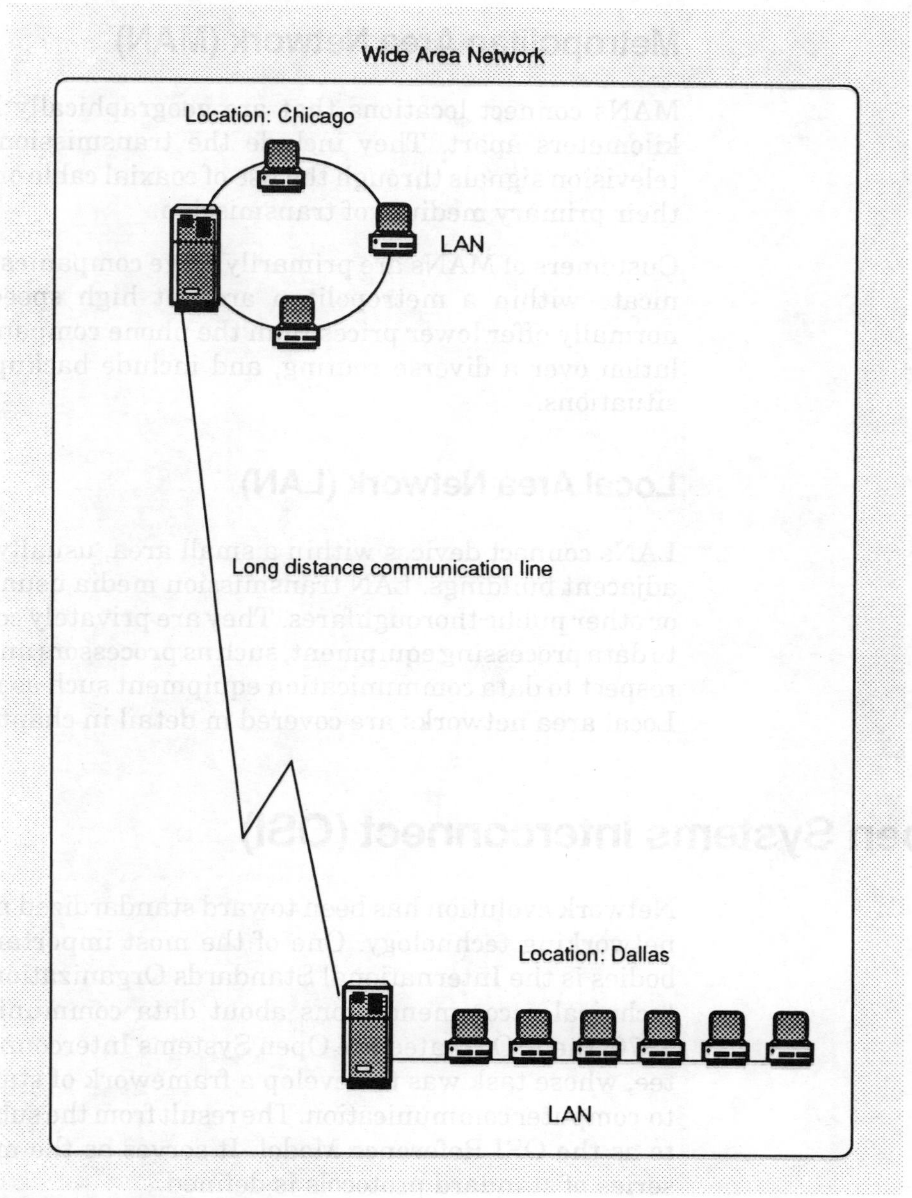

Fig. 4-3. Wide area network

Wide Area Network (WAN)

WANs cross public right-of-ways and typically use common carrier circuits. They use a combination of the hardware discussed in chapters 2 and 3. They use a broad range of communication media for interconnection that includes switched and leased lines, private microwave circuits, optical fiber, coaxial cable, and satellite circuits. Basically, a wide area network is any communication network that permits message, voice, image signals, or computer data to be transmitted over a widely dispersed geographical area.

Metropolitan Area Network (MAN)

MANs connect locations that are geographically located from 5 to 50 kilometers apart. They include the transmission of data, voice, and television signals through the use of coaxial cable or optical fiber cable as their primary medium of transmission.

Customers of MANs are primarily large companies that need to communicate within a metropolitan area at high speeds. MANs providers normally offer lower prices than the phone companies and faster installation over a diverse routing, and include backup lines in emergency situations.

Local Area Network (LAN)

LANs connect devices within a small area, usually within a building or adjacent buildings. LAN transmission media usually do not cross roads or other public thoroughfares. They are privately controlled with respect to data processing equipment, such as processors and terminals, and with respect to data communication equipment such as media and extenders. Local area networks are covered in detail in chapter 5.

Open Systems Interconnect (OSI)

Network evolution has been toward standardized networking and internetworking technology. One of the most important standards-making bodies is the International Standards Organization (ISO), which makes technical recommendations about data communication interfaces. In 1970, the ISO created the Open Systems Interconnect (OSI) subcommittee, whose task was to develop a framework of standards for computer-to-computer communication. The result from the subcommittee is referred to as the OSI Reference Model. It serves as the model around which a series of standard protocols is defined.

The OSI Reference Model is known as a layered protocol, specifying seven layers of interface, wherein each layer has a specific set of functions to perform (see Fig. 4-4). Each layer has a standardized interface to the layers above it and below it, and it communicates directly with the equivalent layer of another device.

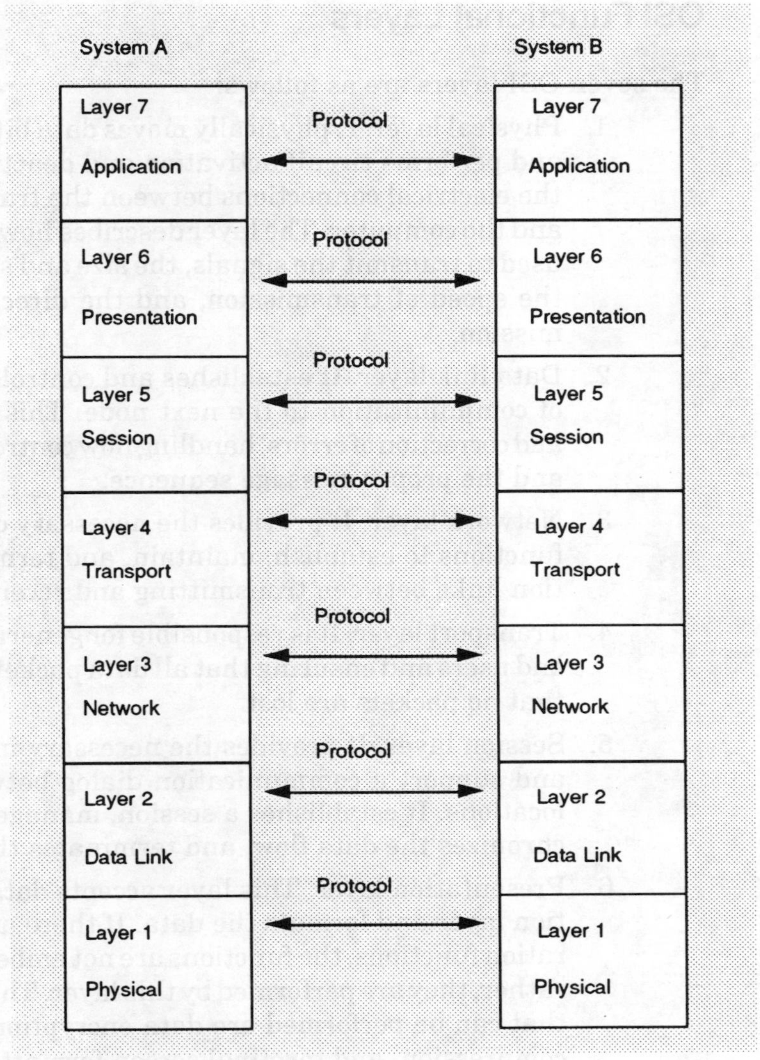

Fig. 4-4. OSI reference model

Having a layered framework, the OSI model offers several benefits:

1. Network hardware and software designers can allocate tasks more effectively among network resources.
2. A network layer can easily be replaced by a layer from another network vendor.
3. Processes from mainframes can be off-loaded into FEPs or other network control devices.
4. Networks can be upgraded easier by replacing individual layers instead of the entire software system.

OSI Functional Layers

The seven OSI layers are as follows:

1. Physical layer. It physically moves data bits between modems and performs circuit activation and deactivation. It specifies the electrical connections between the transmission medium and the computer. The layer describes how many wires will be used to transmit the signals, the size and shape of connectors, the speed of transmission, and the direction of data transmission.
2. Data link layer. It establishes and controls the physical path of communication to the next node. This includes detection and correction of errors, handling flow control between modems, and the proper message sequence.
3. Network layer. It provides the necessary control and routing functions to establish, maintain, and terminate communication links between transmitting and receiving nodes.
4. Transport layer. It is responsible for generating the address of end users and ensuring that all data packets are received, and that no packets are lost.
5. Session layer. It provides the necessary interface to manage and support a communication dialog between two separate locations. It establishes a session, manages the session, synchronizes the data flow, and terminates the session.
6. Presentation layer. This layer accepts data from the application layer and formats the data. If there are any data preparation functions, the functions are not embedded into the data; rather, they are performed by this layer. The types of functions that can be performed are data encryption, code conversion, compression, and terminal screen formatting.
7. Application layer. This layer provides network services such as file transfer, terminal emulation, and logging into a file server. This layer is functionally defined by the user, and it supports the actual end-user application.

Network Topology

The configurations used to describe networks are sometimes called network architecture or network topology. Networks can have many different logical and physical configurations. However, regardless of how they are implemented, networks can be placed into one of the general categories below. The most common network topologies are

1. Ring
2. Bus

3. Star
4. Hybrid

Regardless of the configuration used, all networks are made up of the same four basic components:

1. The user workstation that performs a particular operation.
2. The protocol control that converts the user data into a format that can be transmitted through the network until it reaches the desired location.
3. The interface that is required to generate the electrical signals to be moved on the medium.
4. The physical medium that carries the electrical signals generated by the interface.

Networks can be further categorized into narrowband networks and wideband networks. On narrowband networks only one device on the network can be transmitting at any point. This means that only one user can be communicating through the network at any given time. The typical transmission speed for this type of network is up to a maximum of 10 megabits per second. In wideband networks multiple users can be communicating at the same time. Microcomputer networks such as Novell and IBM's PC LAN are considered narrowband.

Ring Network

The ring architecture is depicted in Fig. 4-5. This configuration is typical of IBM's Token-Ring network. Each device in the network is connected sequentially in a ring configuration that is shown in Fig. 4-5 as the solid line connecting all devices.

In a ring network, each node (receiving/sending station) can be designated the primary station and the others as secondary stations. Also in this type of network, the wire configuration is a series of loop-type connections from a centralized location called a multistation access unit (MAU). This is done so that if a station in the network malfunctions the ring will not be broken. The MAU provides a short circuit to ensure the integrity of the network in case of a malfunction in any location on the ring. In this type of network, data travels around the ring in one direction. The time required for the data to travel around the ring is called the walk time. The message knows the destination because each workstation in the ring network has a unique address.

Reliability is high in ring networks, assuming that the integrity of the ring is not broken. Also, expanding a ring network is easy to achieve by removing one node and replacing it with two new ones. Finally, the cost of the ring network is usually less than that of the star and hybrid networks.

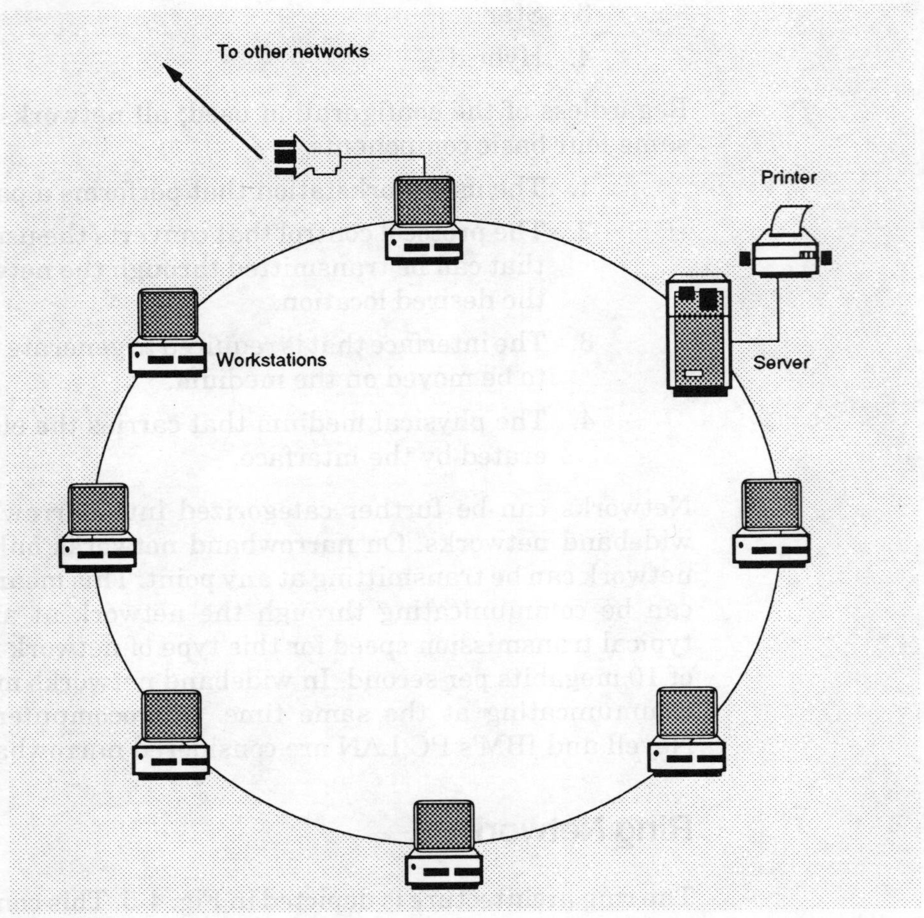

Fig. 4-5. Ring network

Bus Network

A bus topology (also called a tree topology) connects all networked devices to a single cable (called the bus) running the length of the network. Fig. 4-6 depicts this configuration. Cables running between devices directly connect them to the bus. Therefore, data may pass directly from one device to another without the need of a central hub. With some applications, however, the data must first be moved in and out of a central controlling station.

In the typical implementation of the bus configuration, all nodes on the bus have equal control. One end of the bus is the head end. The head end returns the message back into the bus travelling in the opposite direction. Most personal computer networks use the bus topology.

The reliability of bus networks is good unless the bus itself malfunctions. Losing one node does not have an effect on the rest of the network.

Expandability is the strength of the bus topology. A new node can be added by simply connecting it to the bus.

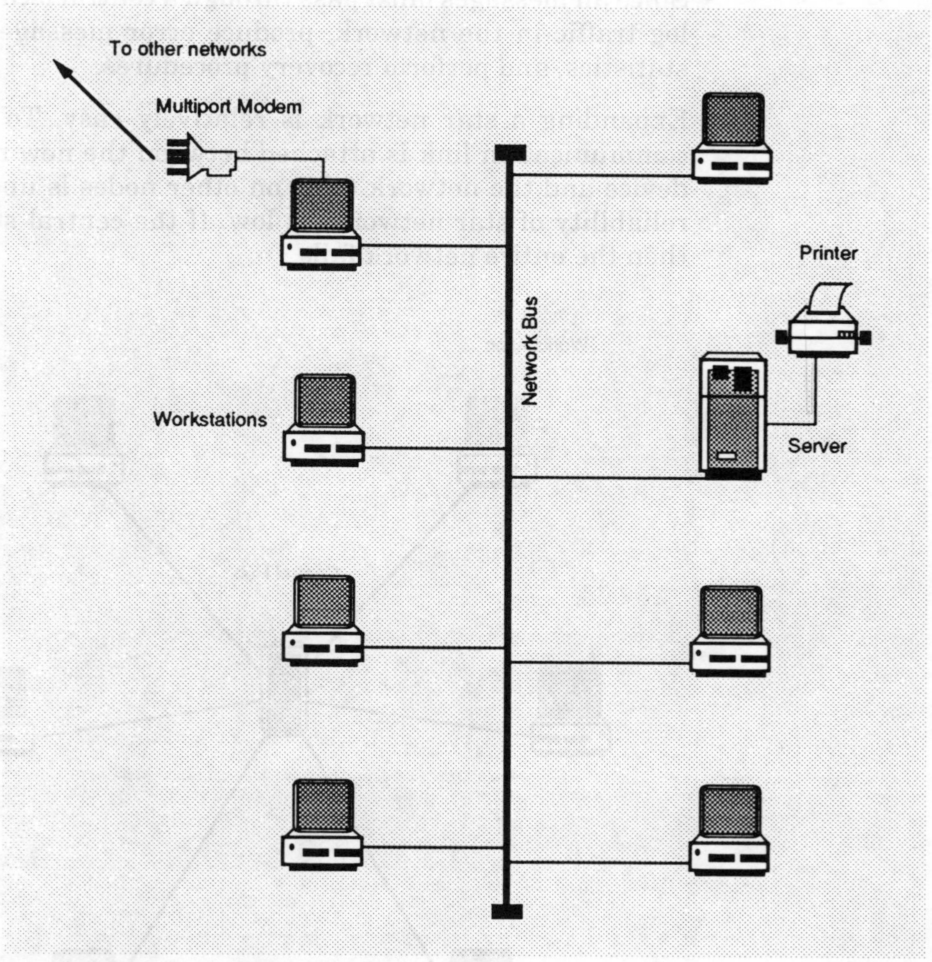

Fig. 4-6. Bus network

Star Network

In a star network (sometimes called a hub topology) all devices on the network are connected to a central device that controls the entire network (see Fig. 4-7). The central location receives messages from a sending node and forwards them to the destination node.

The star topology is a traditional approach to interconnecting devices in which each device is linked by a separate circuit through a central device such as a PBX. In this case the PBX receives a message from a workstation and switches it to a receiving station.

Star networks have several advantages. They provide the shortest path between nodes in the network. Messages travelling on the network must only pass through one hub to reach their destination. Therefore, the time required to get a message from the source to its destination is short. A star network also provides the user with a high degree of network control. Since all messages must pass through a central location, this station can log traffic in the network, produce error messages, tabulate network statistics, and perform recovery procedures.

Expanding a star network is relatively easy. To add a new node, a communication link is attached between the new node and the central device and the network table on other nodes is updated. However, the reliability of star networks is low. If the central station malfunctions, then the entire network fails.

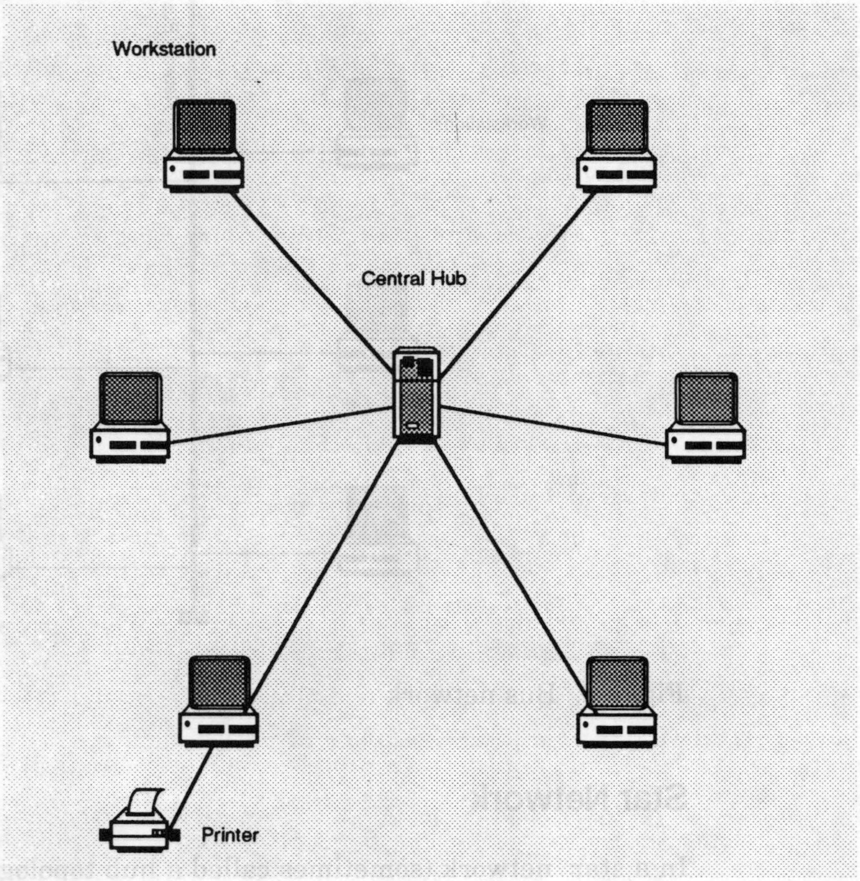

Fig. 4-7. Star network

Hybrid Networks

A network with hybrid topology (Fig. 4-8) contains elements of more than one of the network configurations outlined above. For example, a bus network may have a ring network as one of it links. Another type of hybrid topology is a star network that has a bus network as one of its links where a workstation is normally found.

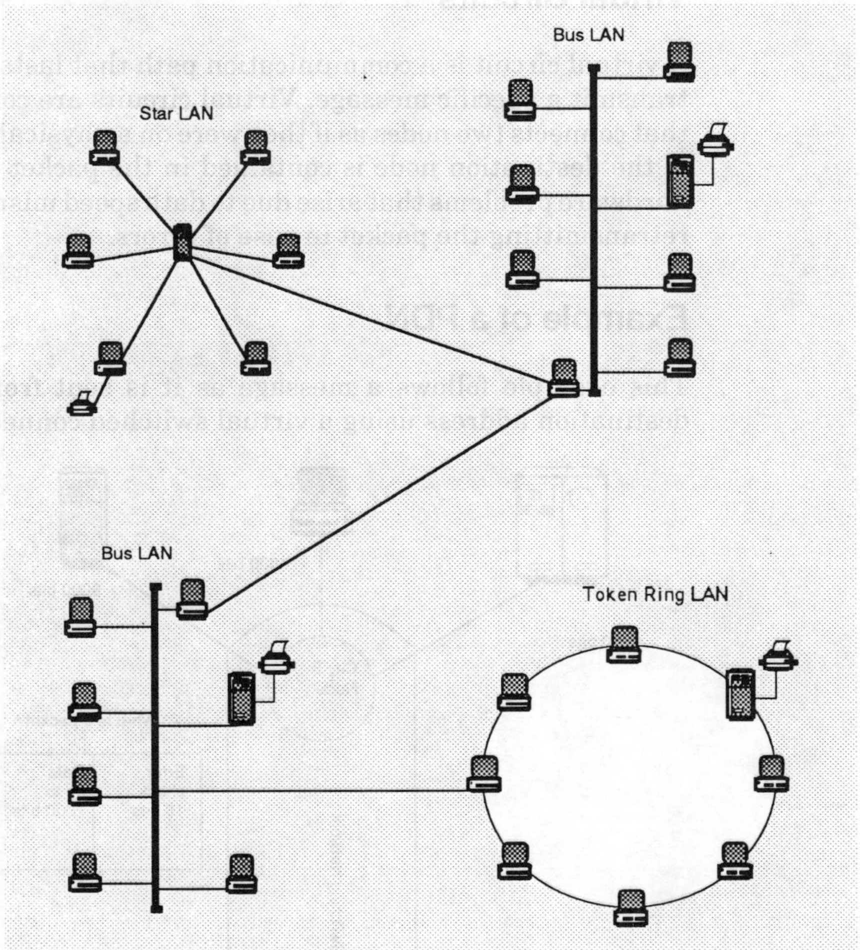

Fig. 4-8. Hybrid network

Packet Data Networks

Packet data networks (PDNs) are based on packet switching technology. Packet switching is a store-and-forward data transmission technique in which messages are split into small segments called packets. Each packet is transmitted through the network independently of other packets, whether or not the other packets are part of the same transaction. The packets belonging to different messages travel through the same communication channel. The communicating terminals or workstations are connected via a virtual circuit.

Virtual Circuits

A virtual circuit is a communication path that lasts only long enough to transmit a specific message. Virtual circuits are controlled by software that connects two nodes as if they were on a physical circuit. The address of the destination node is contained in the packet of data. This avoids hardware problems that arise due to data speed mismatches and helps in retransmitting the packet in case of errors.

Example of a PDN

This example follows a message as it is sent from a terminal to its destination address using a virtual switched connection (see Fig. 4-9).

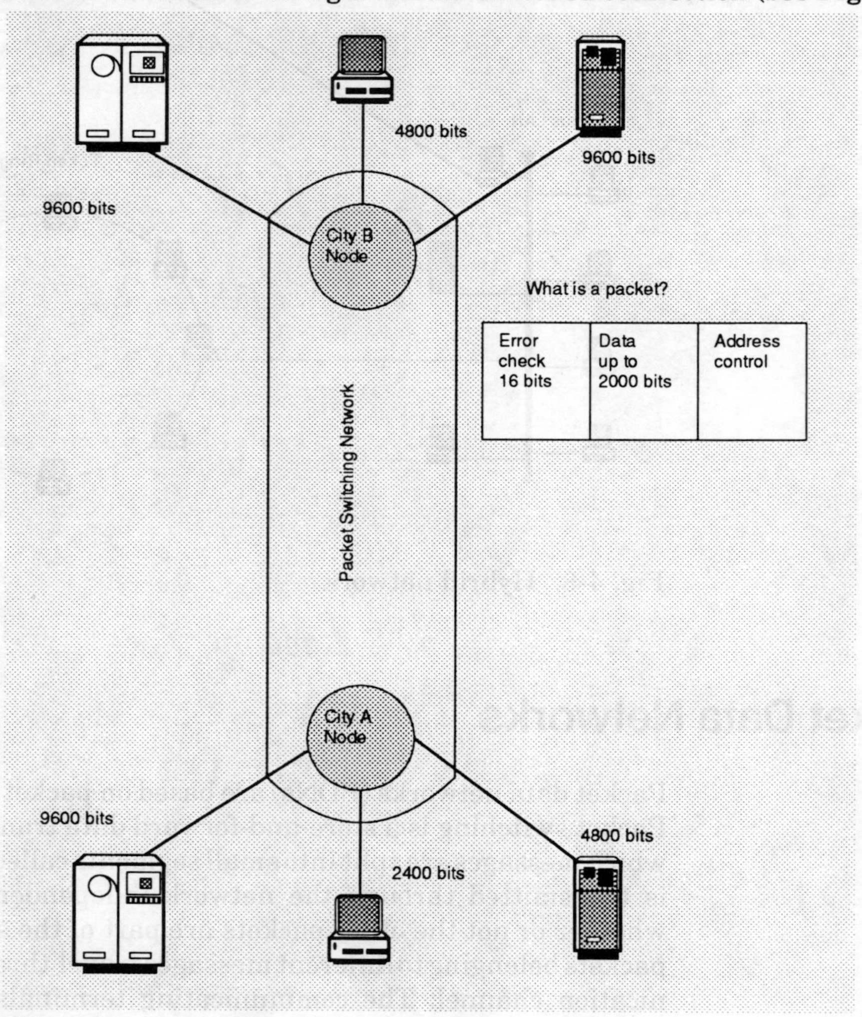

Fig. 4-9. Message path from terminal to destination address

The user connects to a packet switching network. After the login procedure, the address of the receiving node is provided. The PDN then performs a call request packet from the sending node to the receiving node. The call request is delivered to the receiver as an incoming call packet. If the receiver accepts the call, it sends a call accepted packet that the sender node receives as a call connected message. Then the data exchange may begin.

After the data is transmitted, either node can transmit a clear request to the other node. The receiver of the request acknowledges the disconnect with a clear confirmation control packet and the transmission is completed.

During data exchange, the process of splitting messages into individual packets is called packetizing. Packets are assembled and disassembled either at the sender's terminal or the receiver's terminal, or sometimes by a packet assembly/disassembly (PAD) facility. In either case, packetizing is performed almost instantaneously, and data is transmitted in a virtually uninterrupted stream.

By using PDNs, users are only charged for the amount of data transmitted and not for the amount of connection time. Also, PDNs provide access to many different locations without the cost of switched connections. However, since PDNs are usually shared networks, users must compete for circuits. Therefore, it is possible for traffic from other users to block the transmission of a message. Also, if the number of data packets to be transferred is large, then the cost of using a PDN can exceed that of leased lines.

Network Interconnectivity

As networks proliferate in the workplace, homogeneous networks are no longer the rule, but rather the exception. Heterogeneous or hybrid networks have become prominent. They are composed of several network segments that may differ in topology, protocol, or operating system. For example, some networks contain a mixture of personal computers running on a bus network using Novell's NetWare, UNIX workstations using Ethernet on a token ring, and minicomputers running any of the several large-platform protocols.

These systems were originally designed to communicate with devices using the same topology and protocol on a homogeneous networked environment. To network these types of topologies into a single seamless environment is an almost impossible task.

Connecting Hybrid Networks

Before any attempt is made to interconnect a mixture of network configurations, some basic network characteristics need to be understood. The topology is the way a network is configured. Different topologies were outlined previously in this chapter.

Another network characteristic is the protocol. Recall that the protocol is a set of conventions or rules for communication that includes a format for the data being transferred and the procedures for its transfer. When interconnecting networks, the protocol, as well as the topology, must be considered. Two networks that use the same topology but different protocols cannot effectively communicate without help.

Heterogeneous networks can be thought of as building blocks connected by "black boxes." The building blocks are self-contained local area networks with their own workstations, servers , and peripherals. Each consists of a single topology and a single protocol.

To connect two of these boxes, a boundary must be crossed. A connection must be made with both boxes either by a physical cabling scheme or by radio waves. The device that makes the connection, the black box, does not change either interconnecting network. It simply transfers packets of data between the networks. It not only satisfies all the physical requirements of both networks, but also transfers the data safely and securely from one network to the other.

The ability to connect two heterogeneous networks depends on two requirements. First, the topologies must be able to be interconnected. Second, there must be a way to transfer information between dissimilar systems of communication (protocols). This means that at some point a common protocol must be employed. There are several ways to accomplish this. Most use high-level protocols for moving data and employ tools for internetworking such as bridges, routers, brouters, and gateways. Each of these devices has its characteristics and specific applications. The type of device used in connecting dissimilar networks will depend on the amount of transparency desired and the cost that a company is willing to pay for such devices. A rule of thumb is that the more sophistication a device has, the higher the transparency will be to the users and networks and the more expensive the equipment will be.

Bridges

Bridges are normally employed to interconnect similar networks. Both interconnecting networks must have the same protocol. The end result is a single logical network (see Fig. 4-10). A bridge can also be employed to interconnect networks that have different physical media. For example, a bridge may be used between an optical fiber based network and a coaxial cable based network.

Bridges may also be used to interconnect networks that use different low-level communication protocols. Therefore, under the right circumstances, a bridge may be used to connect a token ring network and a star network running different communication protocol software.

Bridges feature high-level protocol transparency. They can move traffic between two networks over a third network that may exist in the middle of the other and that does not understand the data passing through it. To the bridge, the intermediate network exists for the purpose of passing data only.

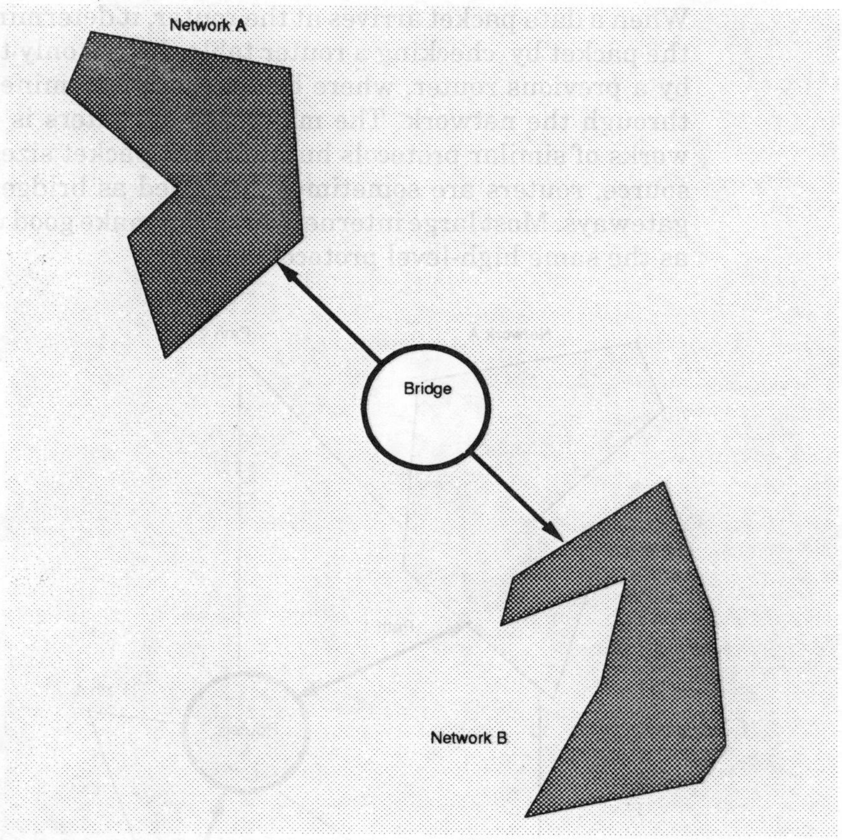

Fig. 4-10. Networks connected by a bridge

Bridges are intelligent devices. They learn the destination address of traffic passing on them and direct it to its destination. They are also employed in partitioning networks. Assume that a network is being slowed down by excessive traffic between two of its parts. The network can be divided into two or more smaller ones, using bridges to connect them. Since bridges must learn addresses, examine data packets, and forward messages, processing is slowed down by these functions.

Routers

Routers don't have the learning abilities of the bridge, but they can determine the most efficient data path between two networks. They operate at the third layer of OSI. (see Fig. 4-11).

Routers ignore the topologies and access levels used by networks. Since they operate at the network layer, they are unconstrained by the communication medium or communication protocols. Bridges know the final destination of data packets; routers know only where the next router is located. They are typically used to connect networks that use the same high-level protocol.

When a data packet arrives at the router, it determines the best route for the packet by checking a router table. It sees only the packets sent to it by a previous router, where bridges must examine all packets passing through the network. The major use of routers is to interconnect networks of similar protocols but different packet sizes. Depending on the source, routers are sometimes described as bridges and sometimes as gateways. Most large internetworks can make good use of routers as long as the same high-level protocol is used.

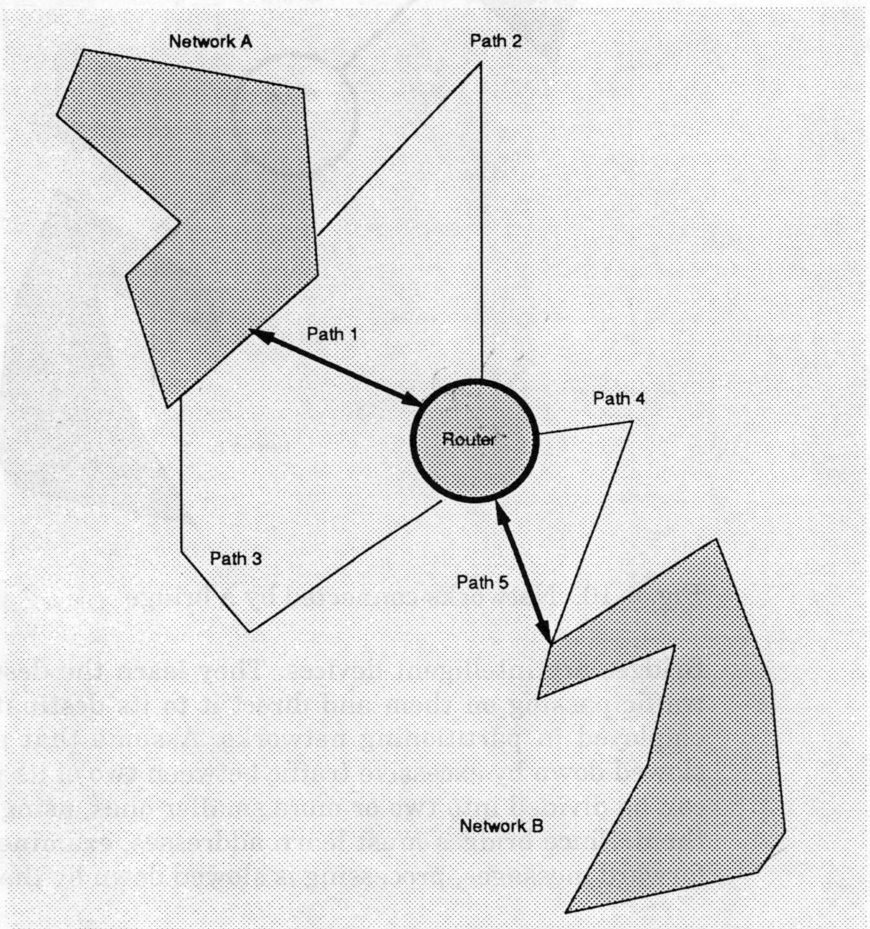

Fig. 4-11. Networks connected by routers

Brouters

Brouters are hybrid devices that incorporate bridge and router technology. Often they are improperly referred to as multiprotocol routers, although, in fact, they provide more sophistication than true multiprotocol routers. They provide the advantages of routers and bridges for complex networks. Brouters make decisions on whether a data packet uses a protocol that is routable. Then they route those that can be routed and bridge the rest.

Gateways

Gateways are devices that provide either six or seven layer support for the OSI protocol structure. They are the most sophisticated method of connecting networks to networks and networks to hosts (see Fig. 4-12). Gateways can interconnect networks of totally different architectures. It is possible to connect a Novell PC based network with an SNA network or Ethernet network using a gateway.

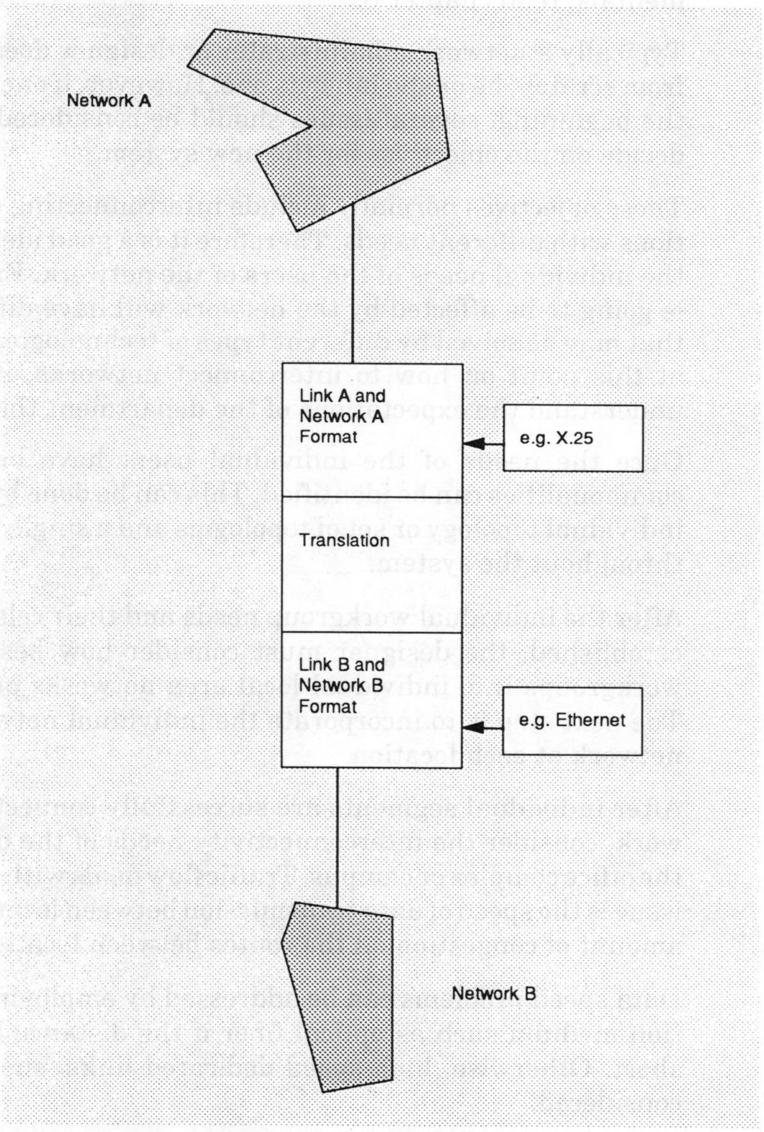

Fig. 4-12. Networks connected by gateways

Gateways do not route data packets within networks. They simply deliver their packets so the network can read them. When a gateway receives a packet from a network, it translates it and routes the packet to a distant-end gateway. Here the packet is retranslated and delivered to the destination network. A gateway is the most sophisticated method for interconnecting wide-area networks.

Planning a Hybrid Network

Even though chapter 6 in this book deals with the different concepts of network design, this section provides a general overview of planning a heterogeneous network. For an in-depth view of network design fundamentals, read chapter 6.

Typically a network administrator or designer does not plan a network from scratch, he or she inherits one. However, if one can be planned from the beginning, several issues should be considered. The first step is to decide on the objectives for the new system.

These objectives normally include interconnecting different work situations with different needs. Therefore it is a good idea to start by defining the individual needs of the users of the network. Each department that is going to be affected by the network will have different requirements that may be solved by different types of technologies. Instead of deciding at this point on how to interconnect networks, it is a better idea to understand the expectations of the department that will use them.

Once the needs of the individual users have been established, the commonalities can be identified. This can be done by considering how an individual topology or set of topologies and a single protocol may be used throughout the system.

After the individual workgroup needs and their related needs have been established, the designer must consider how best to incorporate the workgroups into individual local area networks or network segments. The next step is to incorporate the individual network segments into a network at each location.

After individual segments are successfully connected into a single network, consider the interconnectivity needs of the different buildings in the office complex or campus. Traffic flow deals with two main issues. One issue is the speed of data transmission between locations. The other is the amount of congestion on the routes between locations.

Data speed problems can be addressed by employing a fast communication medium such as optical fiber if the distance between buildings is short. Otherwise, high-speed dedicated links, such as T-1, need to be considered.

Congestion of traffic in the lines becomes a concern when public data communication circuits are used. Alternative methods of traffic routing need to be considered. For example, if the network spans an area from Chicago to Dallas, alternate routes such as through Kansas City or Memphis are possible paths.

Using a technique called the spanning tree algorithm, bridges can be placed between both long haul locations. Under the control of the spanning tree algorithm, the bridges making up the alternative routes between Chicago and Dallas conduct tests to determine the best communication path at any given time. The one with the best path becomes the forwarding bridge, and the others stay in a holding pattern. If the communication link begins to deteriorate, then the other bridge starts forwarding messages and the original bridge stays on hold. This technique can also be used between buildings that are short distances from each other in order to have a consistent throughput efficiency in the communication circuit.

Managing Hybrid Networks

Today's network managers have a large array of sophisticated tools to manage and correct problems in homogeneous and heterogeneous networks. The type of management tools utilized fall into three general levels of sophistication and flexibility of usage.

The first level consists of simple performance monitors. Performance monitors provide information on data throughput, node errors, and other occurrences. A product that falls into this category is Novell's LANtern. LANtern offers a cost effective way of monitoring individual networks or network segments and reporting the existence of problems. This solution is good for small to medium sized networks.

The second level consists of devices or software that perform network analysis. These add meaning to the data generated by the network monitor. An example of a network analyzer is Novell's LAN analyzer. Network analyzers provide a large amount of information about the network operation, but require skillful and knowledgeable network operators to interpret the data. Also, network analyzers are very expensive.

The third level of network management tool is designed for wide area hybrid networks. These tools come in two different types. One is a new array of global network management tools that allow a network administrator to obtain a global and sometimes graphical view of the operations on the entire network. The other type of management tool comes in the form of two emerging standards called The Simple Network Management Protocol (SNMP) and the Common Management Information Protocol (CMIP). Both techniques have the same goal, that is, to move information across a network so the network manager can find problems in the system. They have different designs and reporting options, but they will play an important role in future management of wide area hybrid networks.

Summary

A computer network can change a group of isolated computers into a coordinated multiuser computer system. A network user can legally share copies of the software with other users. Data can be deposited in centralized locations or in different locations that are accessible to all users. Printers, scanners, and other peripherals connected to the network are available to all users. Additionally, a network allows users to share many different types of hardware devices. The most commonly shared devices are hard disks, printers, and communication devices.

Software designed for networks allows multiple users to access programs simultaneously and share the data produced and used by the application. The advantages of software sharing are many. The most important are cost reduction, legality of sharing the product, sharing data, and up-to-date upgrades.

The geographical area covered by the network determines whether the network is called a wide area network (WAN) or a local area network (LAN). Wide area networks link systems that are too far apart to be included in a small in-house network. They can be in the same city or in different countries. Local area networks connect devices within a small local area, usually within a building or adjacent buildings.

Network evolution has been in the direction of standardized networking and internetworking technology. One of the most important standards-making bodies is the International Organization for Standardization (ISO), which makes technical recommendations about data communication interfaces. The OSI Reference Model, created by the ISO, is known as a layered protocol, specifying seven layers of interface, where each layer has a specific set of functions to perform.

The configurations used to describe networks are sometimes called network architecture or network topology. Networks can take on many different logical and physical configurations. However, regardless of how they are implemented, networks can be placed into one of the general categories below. The most common network topologies are ring, bus, star, and hybrid.

One commonly used technique that networks use to transmit data to users' workstations is called packet switching. Packet switching is a store-and-forward data transmission technique in which messages are split into small segments called packets. Each packet is switched and transmitted through the network, independently of other packets belonging to the same transaction or other transactions. The packets belonging to different messages travel through the same communication channel. The communicating terminals or workstations are connected via a virtual circuit.

As networks proliferate in the workplace, homogeneous networks are no longer the rule, but rather the exception. Heterogeneous or hybrid networks are prevalent. They include several network segments that may differ in topology, protocol, or operating system. The ability to connect two heterogeneous networks rests with two requirements. First, the topologies must be capable of being interconnected. Second, there must be a way to transfer information between dissimilar systems of communication (protocols). This means that at some point a common protocol must be employed. There are several ways to accomplish this. Most use high-level protocols for moving data and employ tools for internetworking such as bridges, routers, brouters, and gateways.

Questions

1. Why should individual microcomputers be connected into a network within an organization?
2. What is a local area network?
3. What is a wide area network?
4. What are the most common network topologies?
5. Describe the bus network topology.
6. What is a gateway?
7. What is a bridge?
8. What is a router?
9. What is packetizing?
10. Describe the operation of a PDN.
11. What is a hybrid network?
12. What tools are available to manage a hybrid network?
13. What is a communication protocol?
14. What is the first consideration in designing a hybrid network?
15. What is OSI?
16. What are the different layers of OSI?

Project

Objective

This project will familiarize the student with the software techniques required to transfer files and establish a two-way serial communication between computers using different operating systems but the same communication protocol. It is important that the student understand the individual concepts of basic file transfer and communication between two microcomputers using a direct serial or a modem connection. If two different computers are not available, then the project can easily be modified to accommodate two computers of the same type. In this case the student should be instructed that the process for dissimilar systems is the same and the process of file transfer among different systems will be simulated.

Communication between a Macintosh and a MS-DOS Based PC through the Serial Port

Several methods allow you to connect a Macintosh and a MS-DOS based PC or compatible through the serial port to provide file transfer capabilities. One of these methods is to purchase a commercial product specifically designed for this purpose such as Maclink PC and follow the instructions in the manual to perform file transfers. This package comes with all the cables and software required to perform the connection.

Another method is to use your existing communication software to perform the connection and the transfer. In addition, you will need to make a cable to physically connect the two machines. In this section we will take the second approach (the first methodology is outlined in appendix B under PC to Macintosh data transfer).

The cable can be constructed in two phases. The first step is to purchase a Mac to modem cable from your local computer store. This is done because of the small serial interface on the Macintosh side. The cable costs approximately $5.00, making this a simpler approach than working with the small Mac interface.

The serial cable by itself will not work (see projects in chapter 2). A null modem will be required to complete the circuit. To build a null modem refer to chapter 2 projects. Connect the serial cable and the null modem together and then connect one end of the serial cable to the Mac and the free end of the null modem to the PC (see Fig. 4-13).

Now you are ready to establish the connection using whatever communication software is available. For this example, use the communication tool in Microsoft Works for the Macintosh and Microsoft Works for the MS-DOS based PC. We have chosen Works on the Mac and the MS-DOS based PC due to their popularity and availability. If your system does not have these two software products, use any type of communication software for both systems. The screens will look different depending on your communications software, but the procedures are basically the same.

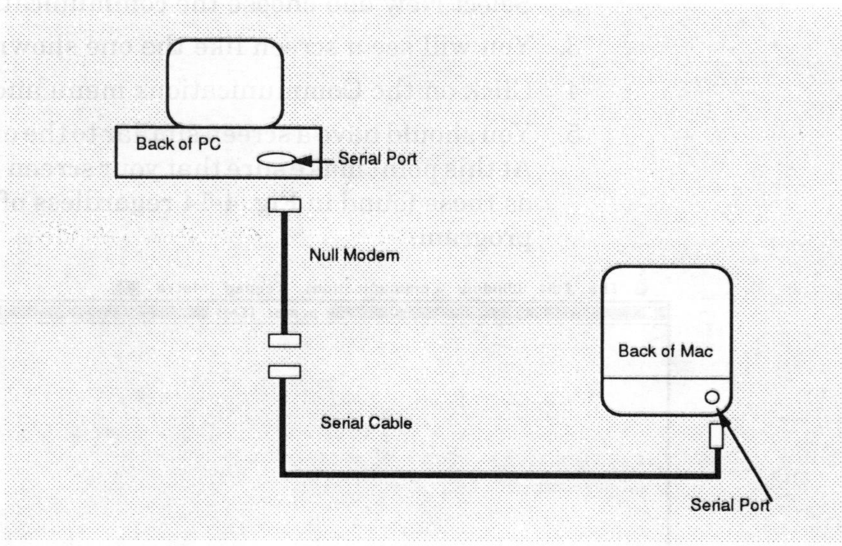

Fig. 4-13. Diagram to connect a Macintosh and an MS-DOS based PC

Before the communications link can be established, both systems must have the same communications settings. Fig. 4-14 shows the communication settings that will be used for this project.

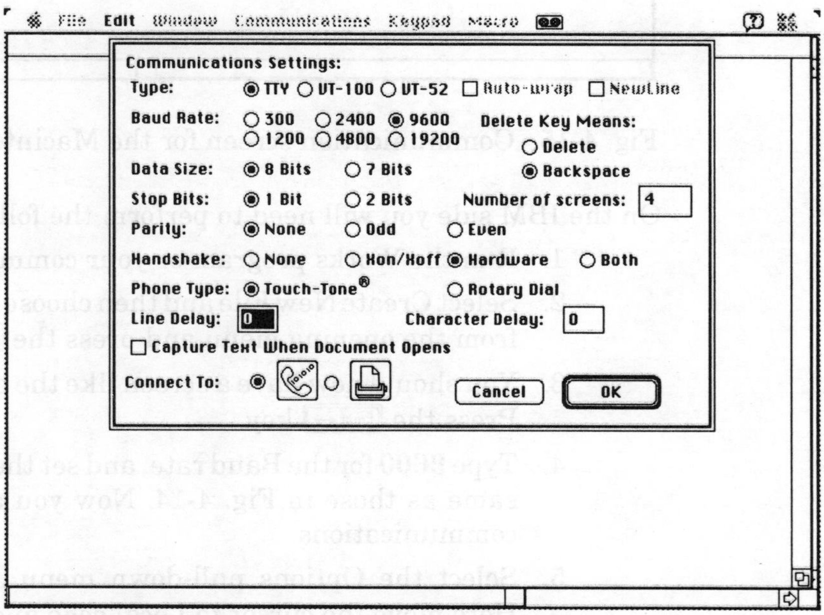

Fig. 4-14. Communication settings for PC and Mac

To set the right parameters on the Macintosh you will need to perform the following general steps:

1. Launch the Microsoft Works program (or your communication software).
2. Select New and choose the communications tool.
3. You will see a screen like the one shown in Fig. 4-15.
4. Click on the Communications menu and select Settings.
5. You should have a screen similar to the one shown in Fig. 4-14. At this point make sure that your screen has the same settings as those found in Fig. 4-14 regardless of your communication program.

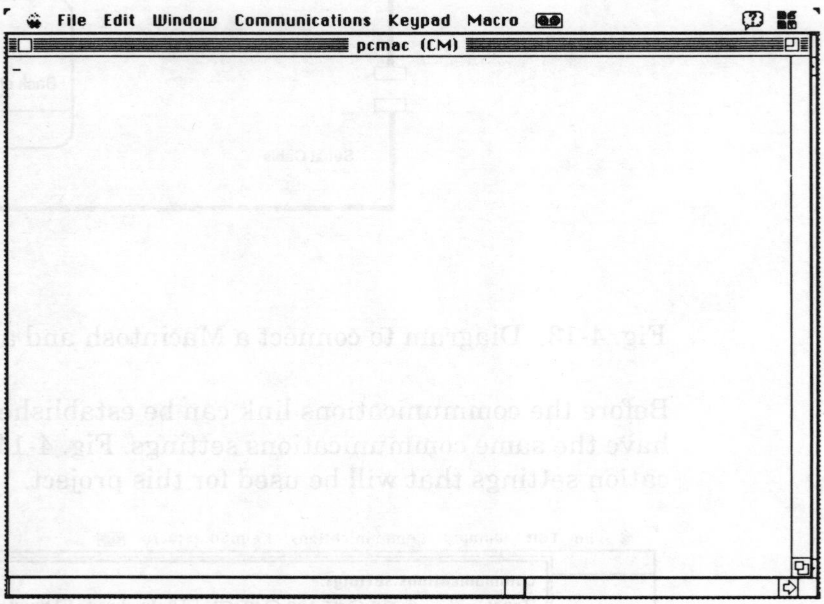

Fig. 4-15. Communication screen for the Macintosh

On the IBM side you will need to perform the following steps:

1. Run the Works program or your communication application.
2. Select Create New File and then choose New Communications from the opening menu and press the [Enter ←] key.
3. You should now have a screen like the one shown in Fig. 4-16. Press the [Enter ←] key.
4. Type **9600** for the Baud rate, and set the other parameters the same as those in Fig. 4-14. Now you are ready to establish communications.
5. Select the Options pull-down menu and choose Terminal. Here move the cursor to Local echo and press the [space] key to place a ⊠ mark.
6. On the IBM PC side select the Connect pull-down menu and choose Connect.

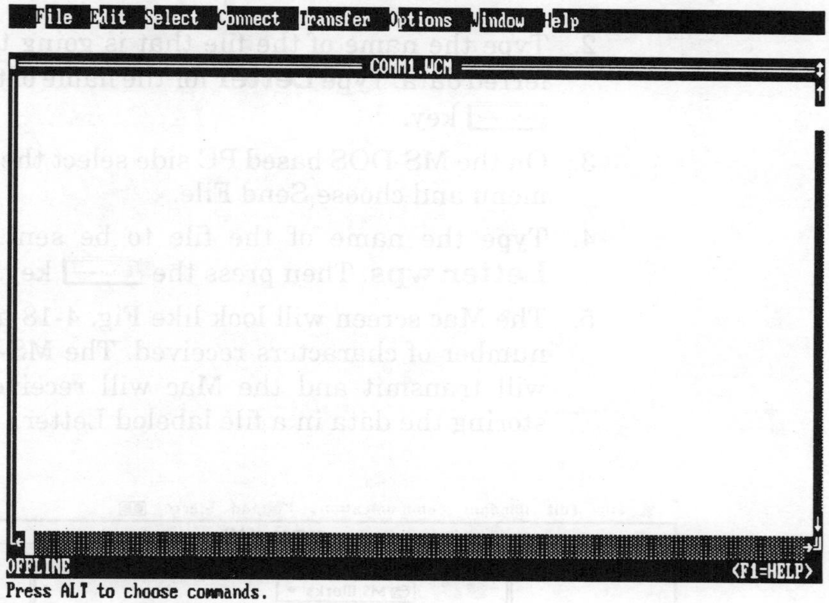

Fig. 4-16. Communication screen for the MS-DOS based PC

7. Type the following on the MS-DOS based PC side: **"Now is the time for all good men to come to the aid of their country."**

You should see the same text you typed on the MS-DOS based PC side displayed on the Macintosh side as you type. This is a successfull connection.

Now we will transfer a file from the PC to the Macintosh. The file to be transferred can be of any type you desire. For this exercise we will transfer the file created by typing the following text using the word processing tool in Works for the PC and then saved as Letter.wps.

"To whom it may concern,

This is a sample data file to test the communication capabilities of the Works program. Files can be transferred with any type of communications program that supports uploading and downloading of text and binary files.

We are copying the same paragraph again below this one.

This is a sample data file to test the communication capabilities of the Works program. Files can be transferred with any type of communications program that supports uploading and downloading of text and binary files."

To transfer this file from the PC to the Mac, follow these instructions:

1. Click on the Communications pull-down menu on the Mac and select Receive File. You should get a screen like Fig. 4-17. Make sure that you select Xmodem.

2. Type the name of the file that is going to receive the transferred data. Type **Letter** for the name of the file and press the [Enter ←] key.
3. On the MS-DOS based PC side select the Transfer pull-down menu and choose Send File.
4. Type the name of the file to be sent. In this case it is **Letter.wps**. Then press the [Enter ←] key.
5. The Mac screen will look like Fig. 4-18 and will indicate the number of characters received. The MS-DOS based PC side will transmit and the Mac will receive the transmission, storing the data in a file labeled Letter.

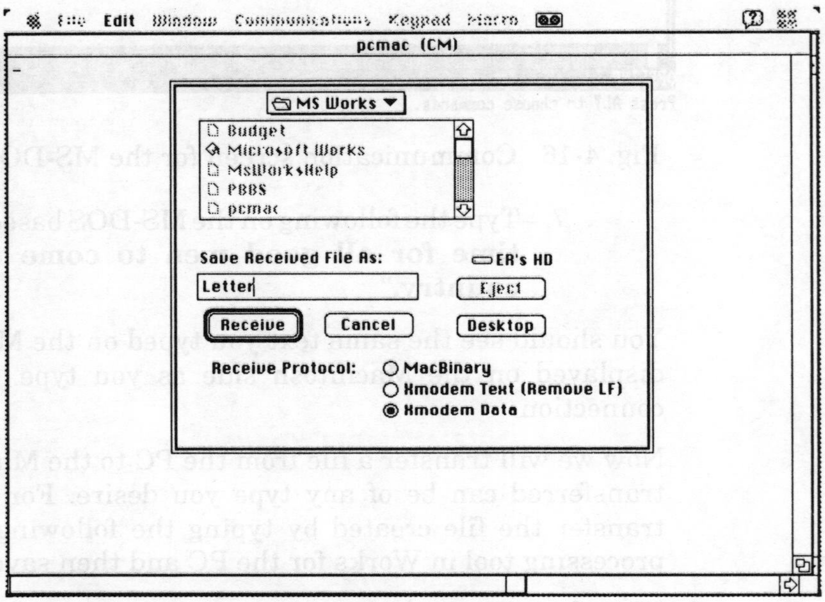

Fig. 4-17. Macintosh dialog box to initiate file transfers

After the transmission is completed, the Mac will sound a short beep to indicate the end of transmission and you will have a file called Letter in the Works folder on the Mac. The same process can be repeated in reverse order to transfer files from the Mac to the PC.

To transfer files using a modem, the process is virtually the same, except that a modem connection must be made. The serial cable developed in chapter 3 can be used to connect the modem to the computers. One of the computers will be the host and its modem will be set to answer mode. This can be done by activating a switch on the modem. The software on the host will be indicated to receive and the sender will transmit using the procedure outlined above. Even though we used a Mac and an MS-DOS based PC in the example above, the same procedure can be used to connect any types of microcomputers.

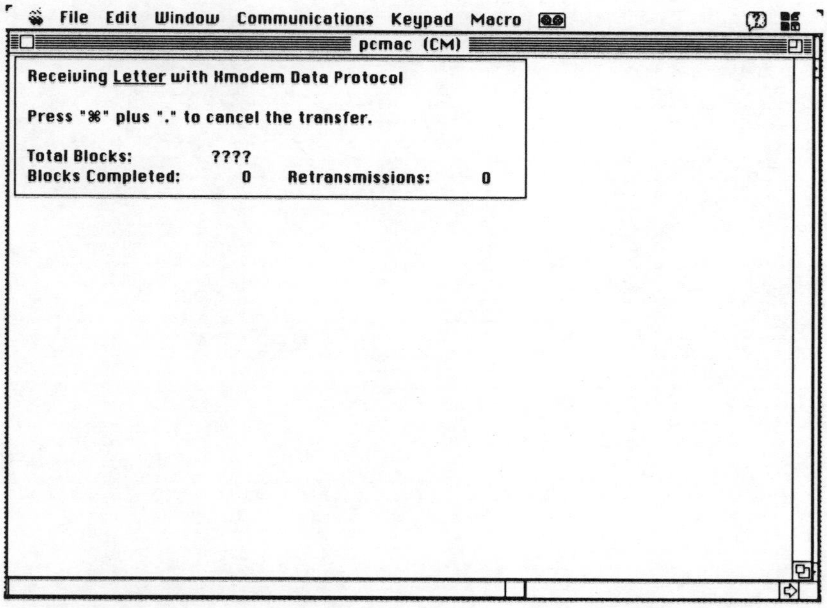

Fig. 4-18. Macintosh dialog indicating file transfer statistics

5

Local Area Networks

Objectives

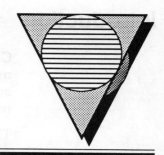

1. Understand the importance of a local area network.
2. Understand the function of a local area network.
3. Obtain a general view of the types of applications running on a local area network.
4. Understand the hardware and software components of a local area network.
5. Understand the different topologies of local area networks.
6. Understand the standards that guide the design of local area networks and their protocols.
7. Have a general understanding of how to install a local area network.
8. Understand the components required to have an efficient local area network.

Key Terms

3COM 3+	AppleTalk
Bus Topology	CAD
CSMA/CD	File Server
Local Area Network	MS LAN Manager
Network Operating System	Novell
Office Automation	Ring Topology
Star Topology	Wide Area Network
Workstation	

Introduction

Chapter 4 introduced general concepts that applied to all types of networks. This chapter describes local area networks in detail. The rapid acceptance of local area networks has made networking a common event in the workplace and especially in education.

The local area network allows individuals to share resources and offset some of the high cost of automating processes. An individual at any computer in a local area network can create a document and send it to another computer in the network for editing or printing purposes. The access provided by local area networks is controlled and to some extent secure.

These concepts, as well as some of the inner workings of the hardware that makes up the local area network, are explored in this chapter. Additionally, the IEEE standards are defined and their impact on network design is explained.

Finally, the chapter provides a general overview of the implementaion of a local area network and a discussion of efficiency considerations for file servers and server software.

LAN Definition

One of the largest growth segments of the communication industry since the early 1980s is local area network (LAN) technology. This growth has resulted in lower prices for the hardware and software required to implement a LAN. The lower prices in hardware have translated into less expensive microcomputers. That is the reason most LAN workstations today are microcomputers. It is not intended to say that all LANs are composed of microcomputers, for many LANs contain a mixture of microcomputers, minicomputers, and mainframes.

Local area networks interconnect devices that are confined to a small geographical area. The actual distance that a LAN spans depends on specific implementations. A LAN covers a clearly defined local area such as an office suite, a building, or a group of buildings. To better understand LANs, it is important to know their uses.

LAN Applications

Most LANs are implemented to transfer data among users in the network or to share resources among users. A LAN implementation can provide high-speed data transfer capability to all users without the need of having a system operator to facilitate the transmission process. Even when connecting a LAN to a wider area network that covers thousands of miles, data transfer between users of the network is time effective and in most cases problem free.

Another reason for implementing a LAN is to share hardware and software resources among users of the network. Even though the price of microcomputers and their peripherals has dropped in recent years, it is still expensive to provide every user with disk space, printers, CD drives, scanners, and plotters. Although the cost of some of these items is relatively inexpensive, it is not cost effective to purchase ten laser printers for ten workers in an office, since the printers will be idle for large periods of times. In this scenario, it is more practical to implement a local area network so all users can share one or two printers (see Fig. 5-1).

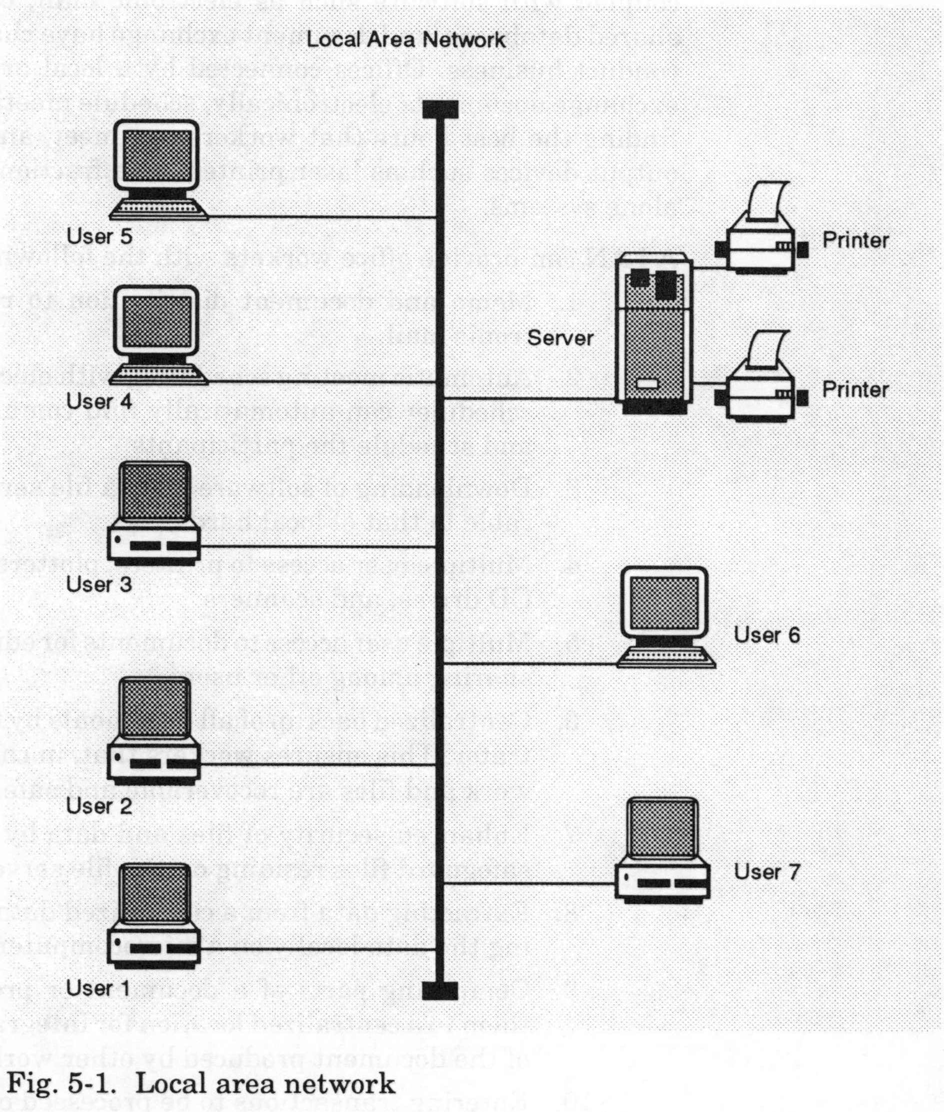

Fig. 5-1. Local area network

LANs also allow users to share software and the data produced by the software. Software for which a site license has been obtained can be placed on a shared hard disk drive. The software can then be downloaded to any workstation that requests it, provided that license agreements are observed. This facilitates backups of network installed software and the installation of software upgrades as they become available.

There are many LAN applications. Some of the more common types of applications are office automation, factory automation, education, computer-aided design, and computer-aided manufacturing.

Office Automation

Microcomputers have provided office workers the ability to automate their processing needs. The local processing power of the microcomputer coupled with software such as electronic mail, calendar automation, shared databases, and document exchange have changed the way offices conduct business. Offices connected by a local area network can now exchange documents electronically, schedule meetings electronically by finding the best hours that workers can meet, and share high-quality output devices such as laser printers at a fraction of the cost of stand-alone systems.

A LAN can provide office workers with the following capabilities:

1. Memo and document distribution to recipients using electronic mail.
2. Automatic meeting scheduling with electronic calendars. The scheduler can automatically find commonly available times and schedule the participants.
3. Downloading of software from a file server at speeds comparable to that of local hard disks.
4. Multiple user access to printers, plotters, facsimile machines, CD drives, and scanners.
5. Multiple user access to documents for editing purposes and for sharing among other users.
6. Centralized backup of all documents by the network administrator. This ensures workers that, in case of a disaster, their work and files are recoverable and safe.
7. Enhanced security of files and data by allowing the LAN to safeguard files residing on the file server.
8. Extracting data from a centralized database and manipulating the data locally on a microcomputer.
9. Composing parts of a document or project and submitting them to a centralized location for integration with other parts of the document produced by other workers on the network.
10. Entering transactions to be processed on other LANs.
11. Sending data from the LAN to other users on a WAN or other LANs.

Education

Educational institutions have found LANs to be an invaluable tool in the education process. Colleges and universities use LANs to provide students access to a centralized server from where they can communicate with faculty or other students through electronic mail, access software required for class assignments, and place assignments on a centralized disk for faculty retrieval and review.

Research faculty and students have access through LANs to the local library and through gateways to electronic libraries throughout the world. In addition, the academic community has access to information located in large geographical areas through wide area networks such as Bitnet.

CAD

Computer-aided design (CAD) software allows users to have a workstation to create drawings, architectural blue prints, and electronic maps without the need of pencil and paper. A LAN used to connect CAD stations allows designers to place notes and instructions to drafters on a centralized server. Each drafter can retrieve the information, ask for further clarification, and complete a portion of the drawing. Then the drawing can be sent to other workers on the LAN for completion and finally sent to a plotter. In most cases, many engineers work on portions of a single project. A LAN enables them to quickly exchange and share information among themselves and to complete the project. CAD systems are used extensively by car manufacturers, aerospace workers, and computer corporations.

CAM

Computer-aided manufacturing (CAM) systems are used to control assembly lines, manufacturing plants, and machinery. A LAN in a computer-aided manufacturing environment allows the automatic control of scheduling, inventory, and ordering systems. Errors that are found by the individual system in the manufacturing process can be transmitted by the LAN to a centralized location for analysis and correction. Instructions can then be transmitted through the LAN to correct the problem and continue the manufacturing process.

LAN Characteristics

Today's local area networks have a number of characteristics that are common among most of the topologies that form their configurations. When a LAN is purchased, the following characteristics should be kept in mind. LANs can provide users with:

1. Flexibility.
2. Speed.
3. Reliability.
4. Hardware and software sharing.
5. Transparent interface.
6. Adaptability.
7. Access to other LANs and WANs.
8. Security.
9. Centralized management.
10. Private ownership of the LAN.

Flexibility

Many different hardware devices can be attached to a local area network. A station on the LAN can be a terminal, a microcomputer, a printer, a facsimile machine, or a minicomputer.

Many types of software applications can also reside on a file server on the LAN. In an automated office, as one user is performing electronic mail, another user can be accessing a database, while another may be manipulating data in a spreadsheet and sending output to a shared laser printer.

LANs can handle applications with different processing and data transfer capabilities. As an example, some users may be transferring text files through the network at the same time other users are transmitting high resolution images from a CAD system. This flexibility is inherent on most types of LANs and is one of the reasons for their success.

Speed

LANs can have high-speed data transfer. This speed is required because of the large number of bytes that must be downloaded when a workstation requests a software application. A good rule of thumb is to have a LAN that downloads files at a speed comparable to the transfer rate from a hard disk to the memory of a microcomputer.

Reliability

A LAN must work continuously and consistently. For a LAN to be considered reliable, all stations must have access to the network according to the privileges established by the network administrator. No station should consume the majority of the processing capacity of the LAN, since that would inhibit access by other users and increase the response time experienced by network users.

Also, LANs should be able to recover from a system failure without losing jobs or files located on the server. If a station malfunctions, the rest of the network should continue operating without problems.

Hardware and Software Sharing

Sometimes there is a specialized device called a server to facilitate sharing. A server is a computer on the LAN that can be accessed by all users of the network. The server contains a resource that it "serves" to the LAN users. The most common type of server is the file server. Using the office automation example, there may be a node located in one of the offices where a file server resides. The file server can contain software applications and data files, and it may have printers, plotters, and other devices attached to it. Other users on the network access the application software and data files stored on the file server. When a user's workstation requests a file, the server "serves" the file to the user's workstation (also called the client).

Other service functions include printers and other output-device services such as plotters. When a document from a user needs to be printed on one of the printers attached to the file server, the document is printed from the user's workstation in much the same manner as if the printer were attached locally. The document reaches the file server and it is transformed into a file that is then "served" to the printer.

Additionally, when software upgrades become available, the upgrades can be placed on the server. When a user requests the software, the user automatically receives the latest release of the product. In this manner, file servers become repositories for software applications. The software residing on the server consists of software products with a site license for a predetermined number of users. For example, a company may decide that of their 200 employees, only 50 will be using a word processor at any given time. Therefore, instead of buying 200 copies of the same program, it can purchase one copy with a site license for 50 simultaneous users. The one copy of the software is placed on the file server, and downloaded to a user workstation whenever it is requested. This avoids the need to pass diskettes or to keep large inventories of application software and hardware.

Transparent Interface

Having a transparent interface implies that network access for users should be no more complicated than accessing the same facilities using a different interface. A user should not be expected to learn a series of complicated commands to print a file. Instead the system should use the same commands or similar commands to the ones that he or she used when the workstation was not attached to the LAN. For example, if an application is invoked from a local hard disk by typing its name and then pressing the ENTER key, then the same procedure should work when requesting the application from a file server.

Adaptability

A well designed LAN has the ability to accommodate a variety of hardware and can be reconfigured easily. If a new device such as a plotter or a facsimile machine needs to be added to the network, it should be done without disruption to the users. Additionally, if a node needs to be removed, added, or moved to another location, the network should allow any of these changes without affecting existing users. A LAN should also be capable of expansion without regard to the number of users. That is, the number of users should not inhibit the need for expanding the services of the LAN.

Access to Other LANs and WANs

In many situations a LAN is just a small component of a much larger network distributed through the corporation facilities. A large corporation may have LANs of different topologies and using different protocols, including packet switching and wide area networks. A LAN should allow user access to the global facilities in the corporation by connecting the local area network to the wide area network facilities using some type of gateway. This connection should also be transparent to the user.

Security

Connectivity and flexibility of a local area network should not be accomplished at the expense of security. If data and user communication is allowed to be accidentally or intentionally disrupted, then the LAN loses its integrity.

The LAN should have provisions for ID and password security mechanisms. File security should be enforced with the use of read, read-write, execute, and delete attributes. Additionally, virus detection mechanisms should be always in place.

Security should also be extended to hardware devices attached to the network. The LAN should be able to restrict access to hardware devices to only those users that have proper authorization.

Centralized Management

Most LAN installations are intended to reduce costs and promote ease of use. A LAN should minimize operator intervention and contain several management tools that provide a synopsis of the operation of the network to the network operator. Additionally, the network operator should be able to perform backups of the entire system from a centralized station.

Private Ownership

The hardware, software, and data carrying medium is normally owned by the corporation or institution that purchased the LAN. This is in contrast to wide area networks in which the hardware is owned by the corporation but the medium belongs to a public carrier. All repairs, maintenance, and new connections are the responsibility of the owner of the LAN.

LAN Components

There are two major items that must be considered when planning or installing a LAN: the network hardware components and the network software. There are three major categories of devices that make up the hardware components of a local area network (see Fig. 5-2). These are the server, the LAN communication system, and the workstations.

Servers

As stated before, servers are computers on the network that are accessible to network users. They contain resources that they "serve" to users that request the services. The most common type of server is a file server. Most LANs have at least one file server, and they often have multiple file servers. The file server contains software applications and data files that are provided to users upon their request. For example if a user needs to use a spreadsheet, a request for a specific spreadsheet package is sent to the file server. The server finds the requested application on its disk and downloads a copy of it to the requesting workstation. As far as the user is concerned, the spreadsheet behaves as if it were stored on a local disk.

The file server is simply a computer with one or more large-capacity hard disk drives. Normally, it is composed of a minicomputer or a fast microcomputer. This is done since many users will be accessing the server at the same time, requiring a high performance machine with fast hard disks.

If a LAN relies on the server for all of its functions, then this type of technique is called a dedicated server approach. Other LANs do not require a distinction between a user workstation and the file server. This type of approach is called a peer-to-peer network. In a peer-to-peer network any microcomputer can function as the file server and user at the same time (sometimes called a nondedicated server).

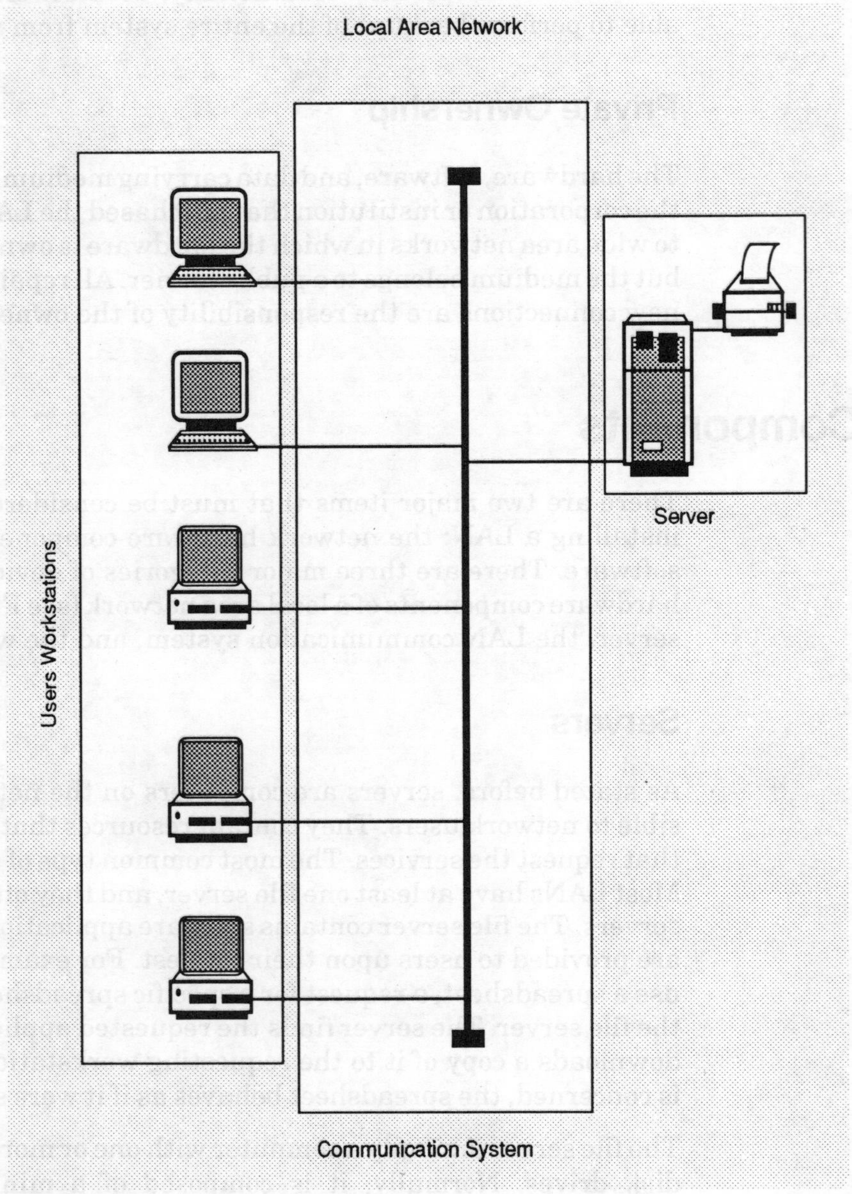

Fig. 5-2. Major components of a local area network

File servers are not the only type of server that can be present on a network. Any computer that has a sharable resource is considered a server. For example, if users of a LAN need to have access to modems, it is possible to have a computer that contains several modems for user access. This is called a modem server. Gateways are also called servers. Also, a network can have compact disk (CD) servers. These consist of an array (2 to 14) of CD drives attached to a microcomputer. Users can then access any of the CD disks in the server from their workstations.

As mentioned above, file servers can be nondedicated or dedicated. If a file server is dedicated, then it can only be used as a file server and not as a workstation. This is typical when a LAN has many users. For small local area networks, a file server may function in a nondedicated fashion as a file server and as a user workstation.

Workstations

The typical LAN workstation is a microcomputer, and, for the remainder of this book it is assumed that file servers and workstations consist of some type of microcomputer. Terminals can also be used to communicate on a LAN, but the cost of a personal computer is usually low enough to be justifiable, since a complete computer with increased capabilities is obtained. Once the microcomputer is connected to a LAN, it is used in similar fashion to a microcomputer in stand-alone mode. The LAN just replaces the locations from where files are retrieved. Some LANs, such as those that use Novell NetWare, can have workstations from different vendors, such as IBM and Apple. Users of NetWare can attach an IBM PC or clone and a Macintosh and use their machines the same way they used them in their stand-alone configuration.

The responsibility of the PC workstation is to execute the application served by the LAN file server. On most LANs the workstation typically does the processing. On distributed LAN networks, the file server and the workstation can share the processing duties. This scenario is typically found on LANs dedicated to database functions only.

After an application is served to the PC workstation, the application begins execution. During the execution of the program, the user may want to store a file or print a file. At this point the user has two options. To save a copy of the file, the user can save it on a hard disk or floppy disk local to the workstation that he or she is using. The other option is to save it on the file server's hard disk. In the latter case, the file could be made available to all other users on the LAN, or kept for private use by using file security attributes. If the user decides to print the file, it can be sent to a printer attached to the server, or printed locally if the workstation has a printer attached to it.

The LAN Communication System

When two or more computers are connected on a network, a special cable and a network interface board or card (NIC) are required in each computer and server. The cable is used to connect the network interface board to the LAN transmission medium. Most microcomputers are not equipped with an interface port that can be connected to a second microcomputer for networking purposes (except the Macintosh computer that has a built-in AppleTalk port). As a result, a network interface card (see Fig. 5-3) or network adapter must be installed in the microcomputer. There are many different types and brands of NICs, but each performs the same function. It transmits data between computers at high speed.

The speed of transmission will depend on the type of medium, the capabilities of the NIC, and the computer that it's attached to. Typical speed ranges for LANs are from 1 to 16 megabits per second and a few are even higher. However, since the workstations in the LAN are connected by a cable, the geographic range the LAN can cover is limited to buildings or campuses where the cable can be laid.

Data is transmitted from a workstation to a file server and vice versa by packetizing it. When a file is requested from the file server, the NIC translates this file into data packets. Normally, the data packets are of fixed size, although they could be different sizes. Most adapters use packets of 500 to 2,000 bytes. The file server's NIC places the data packets on the network bus (cable), where they are transmitted to the workstation NIC. Here the data packets are assembled back into the original data file and given to the workstation.

Each data packet (see Fig. 5-4) contains the address of the workstation on the network that is to receive the data packet. The address of each node in the LAN is provided by the NIC. This address can be set with switches on the NIC when it is installed. Some NICs already have the address set at the factory before they are shipped to a customer.

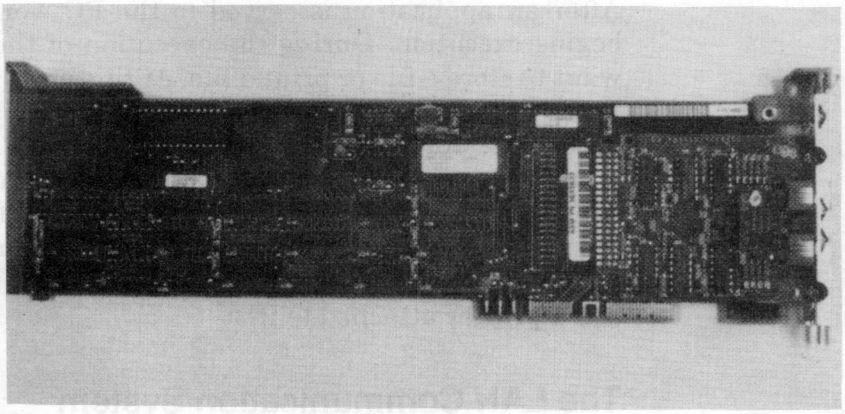

Fig. 5-3. Network interface card (NIC)

The NIC address uses a combination of 8 bits, and therefore can have a value of from 1 to 256. This limits the number of users on the LAN to 256. Large LANs can be created by joining two or more LANs into a single network using one of the network interconnecting devices explained in

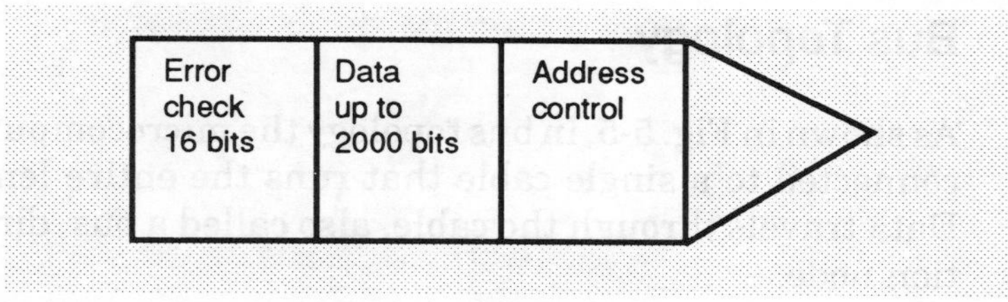

Fig. 5-4. Data packet

chapter 4. Some new network adapters have larger addresses by using more bytes to form the address. However, most LANs use the system outlined above.

LAN Software

The processes that take place on the hardware devices of a LAN must be controlled by software. The software is the network operating system. One of the most widely used network operating systems is NetWare by Novell, Inc.

The network operating system controls the operation of the file server, and it makes the network resources accessible and easy to use. It manages server security and provides the network administrators with the tools to control user access to the network and to manage the file structure of the network disks.

The network operating system controls which files a user can access, as well as how the user accesses these files. For example, a user may have access to a word processor file, but it can only be read and not modified. At the same time, another user may have access to the same file and be able to modify it.

In most cases, the network operating system is an extension of the PC workstation operating system. The same commands used to retrieve, store, and print files on the microcomputer are used to perform these functions on the network. The network operating system also provides extensions to the PC operating system to do some functions more efficiently.

LAN Topology

Network topologies were introduced in chapter 4. Three of these topologies, the bus, ring, and star are used extensively in LAN implementations.

Bus Topology

As shown in Fig. 5-5, in bus topology the microcomputer workstations are connected to a single cable that runs the entire length of the network. Data travels through the cable, also called a bus, directly to the destination node.

The bus topology is the most widely used of all LAN configurations. The reason for its success is the early popularity of protocols such as Ethernet that used this configuration.

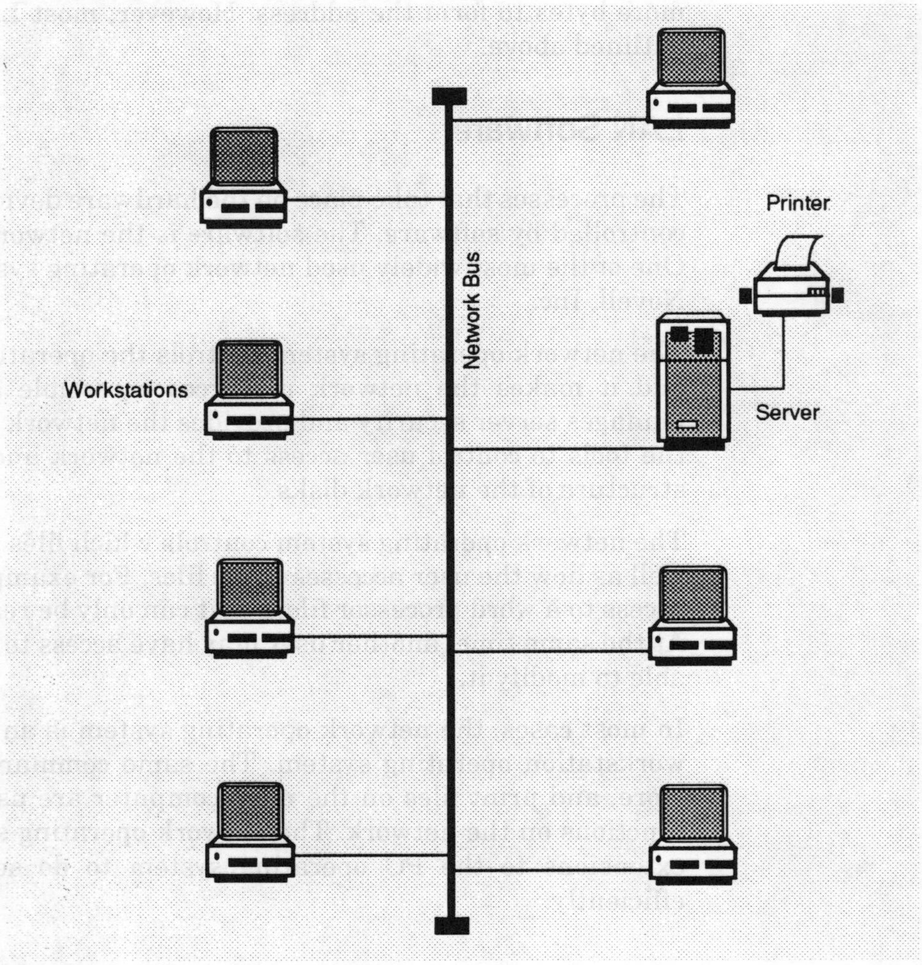

Fig. 5-5. Bus topology

Ring Topology

A ring configuration uses a token passing protocol (see next section). It is the second most popular type of configuration. As shown in Fig. 5-6, the ring topology connects all nodes with one continuous loop. Data travels in only one direction within the ring, making a complete circle through the loop.

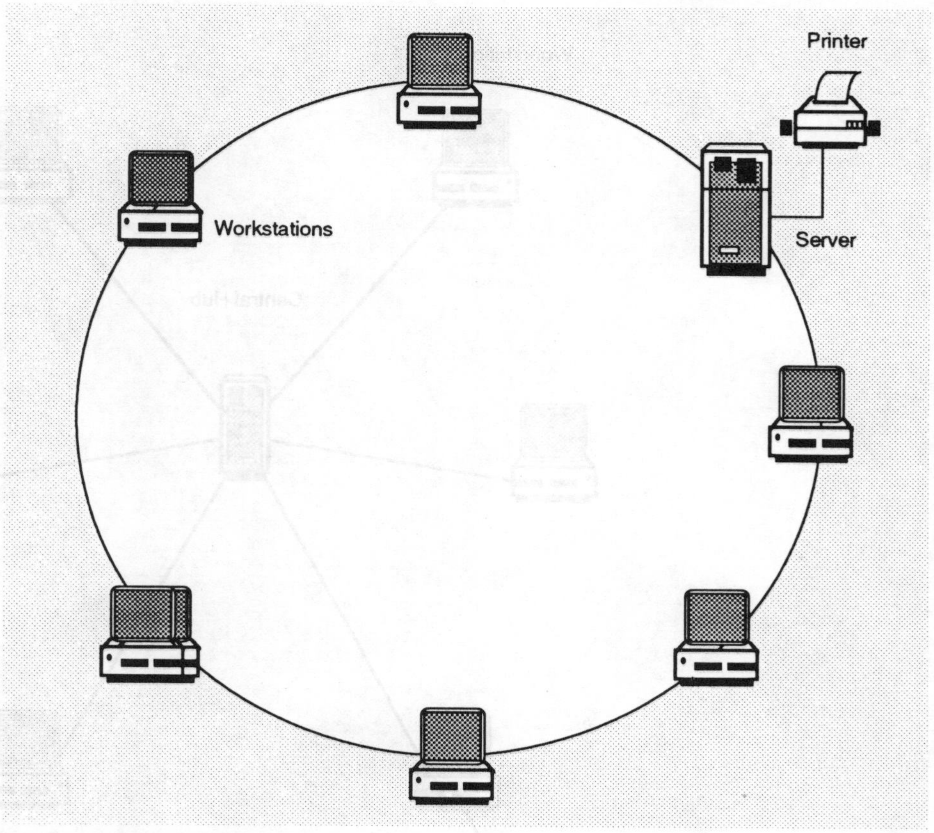

Fig. 5-6. Ring topology

Star Topology

The third major topology is the star (see Fig. 5-7). In a star configuration, each node is connected to a central server. Data flows back and forth between the central server and the nodes in the network.

LAN Protocols

Local area networks have a variety of configurations. Regardless of the LAN configuration, every message transmitted contains a destination address. In addition, each node in the network looks for its address in each message. If the address is present, then the station picks up the message. The hardware that makes up the network must be controlled by a protocol so that all stations on the system can communicate with each other whether they are from the same vendor or not. The protocol consists of the set of rules by which two machines talk to each other. It must be present along with the LAN hardware and the network operating system. Some communication protocols were discussed in previous chapters.

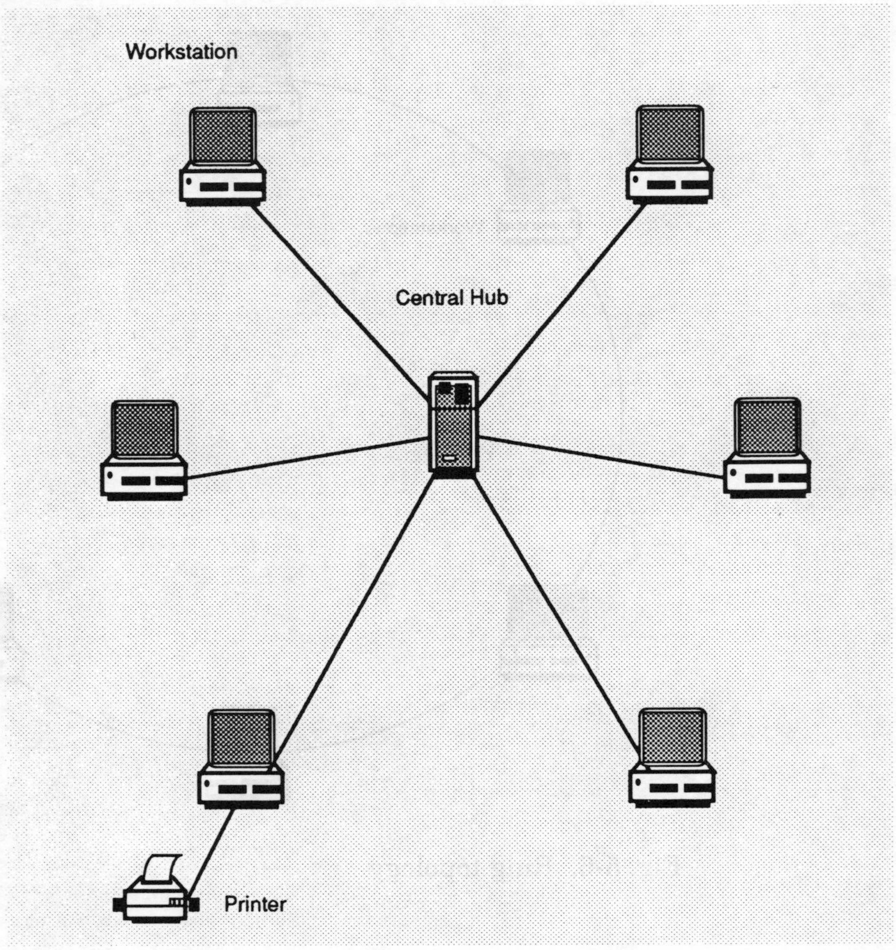

Fig. 5-7. Star topology

Other common protocols used in LANs are the logical link control (LLC) protocol established by the Institute of Electronic Engineers (IEEE) 802 Standards Committee, the carrier sense multiple access/collision detection (CSMA/CD) protocol, and the token passing protocol.

LLC Protocol

The most important aspect of LAN protocols is the logical link control or LLC. This is a data link protocol defined for local area networks that is bit oriented. An LLC's frame, also called a protocol data unit, contains the format shown in Fig. 5-8. The destination address identifies the workstation to which the information field is delivered, and the source address identifies the workstation that sent the message. The control field has commands, responses, and number sequences that control the data link. The information field is composed of any combination of bytes.

CSMA/CD Protocol

As its name indicates, the CSMA/CD protocol uses a technology that allows a node in a LAN to gain control of a communication circuit. It uses frames as its basic data format (see chapter 3). The header cf the frame, also called the preamble, synchronizes the transmitter and receiver. The control field indicates the type of data being transmitted.

Token Passing Protocol

The token protocol is based on a message (token) being placed on the communication circuit of a LAN. Here it circulates until acquired by a station that wishes to send a message. The station changes the token status from "free" to "busy," and attaches the message to the token. The token moves from station to station, with each station examining the address. When the message arrives at the receiving station, the station copies it. The receiving station passes an acknowledgement to the sending station. The sending station accepts the acknowledgement and changes the token status from "busy" to "free." The token then continues looping on the circuit until another station needs to send a message.

Header (size is variable)	Destination Address (8 bits)	Source Address (8 bits)	Control Field (8 or 16 bits)	Data (8 x n bits)	Trailer (size is variable)

Fig. 5-8. LLC frame

LAN Standards

The type of protocol and access method used depends on which LAN standard a specific vendor follows. The standards are set by the Institute of Electrical and Electronic Engineers (IEEE) 802 Standards Committee.

802.1

This is known as the highest-level interface standard. This specification is the least well defined because it involves a lot of interfacing with other networks and it is still under consideration.

802.2: LLC Protocol

It is equivalent to the second layer of the OSI model and was described just previously in this chapter. It provides the point-to-point link control between devices at the protocol level. Many of the applications designed for data on LANs use the 802.2 standard so that they can interface with the other layers of the OSI.

802.3: CSMA/CD Baseband Bus

This is known as the carrier sense multiple access/collision detection (CSMA/CD) baseband bus. It describes the techniques by which any device on a bus can transmit when the medium interface determines that no other device is already transmitting.

This type of LAN uses coaxial cable or twisted pair wire as the transmission medium. At the physical level, this standard also defines the types of connectors and media that can be used.

The 802.3 standard is based on research originally done by the Xerox Corporation. Xerox called this type of local area network Ethernet. It is among the most popular and is widely used.

802.4: Token Passing Bus

This standard describes a method of operation where each device on a bus topology transmits only when it receives a token. The token is passed in a user-predetermined sequence and guarantees network access to all users. Since the bus topology does not provide a natural sequence of stations, each node is assigned a sequence number, and the token is passed from one station to another following the sequence numbers assigned to the stations.

802.5: Token Passing Ring

This is the mechanism utilized on IBM's Token-Ring LAN. It uses a token to pass messages between workstations as outlined previously. Several types of cables can be used for token ring LANs, but twisted pair is the most commonly used.

802.6: MAN

This is the metropolitan area network standard. The specifications were developed to create standards for networks whose stations were more than five kilometers apart. The criteria include standards for transmitting data, voice, and video.

Commercially Available LANs

There are many vendors of local area network hardware and software. Although the vendors are many, a few commercial vendors control a large segment of the LAN market, especially in the personal computer market. Some of the most prominent commercial products available are Novell NetWare, Microsoft LAN Manager, 3COM 3+, IBM LAN Server, AppleTalk, and Banyan VINES.

Novell NetWare

Novell NetWare was originally designed around hardware using a star topology to communicate with a single file server. The file server simply allowed client computers to store and share files. NetWare has become largely hardware independent, allowing many topologies and file servers to be used simultaneously, but communication on the network is still handled almost entirely through a primary file server with all user's workstations, called clients, accessing the server to perform network functions.

Netware's original structure has influenced all of Novell's products to date. Even in new NetWare configurations the file server manages the network. In other words, two client computers may be connected directly to each other by a network cable, but for a file to be transferred from one to the other, that file must be first sent to the file server, then to the target client computer. Of course, the network provides many other functions, but they are generally centered around the idea of a client computer connected to a file server.

By far, the most common client on a Novell network is an IBM PC or PC-compatible computer running DOS. Compatible, in this case, means that other manufacturers have designed computers to work almost exactly like the original IBM product. Even IBM has produced computers with much more power and flexibility, while maintaining this compatibility with the PC. DOS (usually pronounced as a single word) stands for disk operating system. It is the software that handles all of the low-level functions of the computer such as reading and writing to the disk drives, loading and executing application programs, and handling input from the keyboard. When running an application program such as a word processor, DOS allocates memory, reads the program from the disk drive, and then allows the program to begin. The application program can then use the resources of the computer through what are known as DOS function calls. This system allows the application program, and the person who wrote the application program, to be freed from worrying about the messy details of operating all the peripherals attached to the computer. For instance, there are many different types of disk drives and dozens of companies manufacturing them. To the application program, this is irrelevant. It will simply make a DOS function call to read or write data to the disk drive and DOS will handle the input and output to the device.

NetWare runs on a large number of hardware platforms in addition to the IBM PC. These platforms include DEC, VAX, VMS and IBM's VM and VMS, and the Apple Macintosh personal computer. In the case of the Macintosh, NetWare allows Mac applications to reside on an IBM or compatible computer (the server) and uses Macintosh computers on the LAN to run the applications. This allows a single network and server to provide applications that are DOS specific and Macintosh specific. Additionally, NetWare drivers are also available for nearly all network interface cards currently available for PCs. These include ARCnet, Ethernet, Token-Ring, G-Net, and ProNet.

NetWare was designed and optimized as file server and network management software. It uses proprietary directory and file schemas designed for quick access. To users, the network functions of saving and retrieving files appear as DOS structures. NetWare provides services for security, printing, file server access, access to other networks, electronic mail, and communications.

With more than 35 percent of the market, and new partnerships with IBM, Novell is the largest provider of LAN operating systems. Therefore, this book concentrates in its second half on the Novell NetWare operating system.

Microsoft LAN Manager/3COM 3+ Open

3COM's 3+ Open is a network operating system based on OS/2 LAN Manager developed by Microsoft Corporation. Therefore, 3+ Open is related to IBM's OS/2 LAN Server since the LAN Manager is the core of IBM LAN Server.

3COM provides directory services through a Network Control Server (NCS). This is a different approach than the one taken by most other network vendors. While other vendors opt to have a distributed directory service, 3COM uses a centralized system. If the NCS goes down, the entire network is also down.

The workstations can be OS/2 or DOS based. However, to take full advantage of all the network functions, OS/2 should be the operating system on the workstation instead of DOS.

LAN Manager provides services for security and controls access to the network. It also provides services for accessing SNA, X.25, X.29, and other MS-Net networks.

IBM LAN Server

The IBM LAN Server, like 3COM 3+ Open, is based on Microsoft's LAN Manager. Like LAN Manager, LAN Server runs under the OS/2 operating system. It supports OS/2 workstations or DOS workstations. However, DOS workstations cannot take full advantage of all features of the network operating system.

Even though LAN Server is based on LAN Manager, IBM has changed many of the features of LAN Manager, making the product different in how it provides several of the functions of the network.

LAN Server provides services for security through a global Domain Controller. This is a technique that uses one server to provide security for all other servers. This is a departure from LAN Manager, where each server maintains its own security.

The other services provided by LAN Server are similar to those provided by LAN Manager, but many of the commands used by LAN Server are different from its counterpart, making the management of both systems difficult.

Banyan VINES

Banyan Systems developed VINES (VIrtual NEtwork System) in an effort to provide high-quality communications among personal computers and to link their LAN to other LANs, minicomputers, and mainframes. In order for their LAN to work properly, Banyan recognized that they needed a multitasking operating system. Banyan settled on UNIX V as its platform for connectivity strategy.

VINES includes file and print services, a global naming and access system called "StreetTalk," and built-in connectivity services to have:

1. PC dial into the VINES network.
2. SNA access.
3. Asynchronous communication and file transfer.
4. TCP/IP support.
5. X.25 and X.29 support.
6. Token-Ring bridge support.

In addition, VINES provides services for security through VANGuard, as well as NETBIOS emulation, time service, and chat and backup facilities. Also, it includes some optional services such as electronic mail, network management, and communication services.

The core of the VINES system is StreetTalk. This is a directory and naming service that allows access to applications, files, printers, gateways, bridges, users, servers, hardware resources, and communications. StreetTalk is responsible for making the network transparent to the user by integrating all services and users. This allows users to use the network facilities as natural extensions of their own workstations.

Banyan's VINES LAN hardware supports a wide range of third party vendors that includes ARCnet, Ethernet, IBM Token-Ring, Omninet-1B,

Pronet 4, 10, and 80, VISTA LAN-PC, and StarLan network interface cards.

AppleTalk

All Macintosh computers have built-in circuitry for connecting the machine to a LocalTalk network. LocalTalk is one of the network types available in the AppleTalk network system. The AppleTalk system is a way of connecting computers, printers, and other peripheral devices so that users can share information and resources in a transparent manner.

LocalTalk under AppleTalk works by using a file server approach. The server, which can be any of the computers in the network, provides services for printing, file sharing, and some security services.

Since every Macintosh comes with the capability of connecting to LocalTalk, it is relatively simple to use the network and to perform network functions. However, the network has limitations in the type of services that it provides and the speed of data transmission is slow when compared to other networks in the market.

General Installation of a LAN

Installing the LAN Hardware

Assuming that a complete LAN kit is available, the first step is to install the NIC in each microcomputer that is going to be part of the LAN. The NIC is installed in one of the expansion slots inside the machine. If the NIC's address was set at the factory, the NIC can be installed as is. Otherwise, a set of dip switches on the NIC must be set to a combination that has not already been used on the LAN. It is suggested that each NIC on the network follow a sequence. Then if something goes wrong during the operation of the network it will be easier to identify problems.

After the NIC is installed, each microcomputer must be connected to other microcomputers on the LAN. The most common way of doing this is to connect each microcomputer in a daisy chain configuration. The first and the last of the microcomputers are given an ending plug. This indicates to the network that there are no more nodes in the network beyond these points. The cable used to connect the microcomputers can be coaxial or twisted pair cable, depending on the requirements of the LAN and anticipated upgrades.

Protecting the Hardware

Electronic equipment is suceptible to power sags, power surges, and electrical noise. A power surge is a sudden increase in power, which in many cases can destroy the microchips that make up the computer circuitry. A power sag is a loss of electrical power. A power sag can force a computer reset, or a network shutdown. Information stored in RAM prior to a power sag is lost and in some situations, a network can't automatically rebuild itself so it can continue operating. Electronic noise is interference from other types of electrical devices such as air conditioners, transformers, lights, and other electrical equipment.

There are several devices that protect computers against the problems outlined above. These are power surge protectors, power line conditioners (PLCs), and uninterruptible power supplies (UPS). The type of device used depends on the equipment to protect, the importance of the data stored in the equipment, and economics.

Power surge protectors are the least expensive of all protecting devices. They range in price from a few dollars to approximately $150. They protect equipment from short duration electrical surges (called transients) and voltage spikes. Their price depends on the type of materials used to make up the device and how fast these components react to a power surge. The faster the reaction time, the more expensive the item. Whenever possible, the protector with the fastest reaction time should be purchased. Power surge protectors are normally found at the user's workstations.

Power line conditioners (PLC) are more expensive than surge protectors. They protect equipment against electrical noise and interference from other equipment. Most PLCs also protect against surges and sags in electrical power. They tend to filter out electrical noise while maintaining power within acceptable levels for the computer to operate. Many user workstations and servers use PLCs to guard against temporary and very short duration power spikes and sags.

Uninterruptable power supplies allow a system to continue functioning for several minutes even when there is a total loss of power. Normally, the additional running time provided by the UPS is enough to safely shut the system or network down; on many occasions, the time is long enough that power is restored without having to shut the system down. They should be used by all servers to protect users' data and the network from a sudden and unexpected loss of power. Additionally, a UPS protects against power surges and electrical noise.

Installing the LAN Software

To install the LAN software, the network operating system must be installed, a station profile for each microcomputer needs to be created, and a profile for each microcomputer logging onto the LAN also needs to be created. The process required to install the network operating system varies according to the type and size of the LAN.

On networks such as Novell's, the network operating system replaces the workstation native operating system. This involves reformatting the hard disk of the computer that is going to act as the file server. In this case, installing the network operating system consists of following instructions displayed on the screen after placing the network system disk in the drive and turning the computer on. The procedure consists of loading the LAN kit disks in the sequence requested. The entire process is normally self-explanatory after the first instructions are displayed on the screen.

On smaller networks, the network operating system is loaded when the user turns on the microcomputer, or it is done automatically by using a batch file that is executed automatically. The network operating system manuals that come with the LAN kit indicate which files must be placed in batch files and which files must reside on the file server.

The Network Profile

A network profile must be established for each microcomputer on the LAN. The profile indicates the microcomputer's resources that are available for other network users. This profile is set up once when the network is installed, but it can be changed later if necessary.

The profile contains information about user access privileges and password requirements. Additionally, it indicates which devices are printers, which hard disks are shared, and the access mechanisms for these. For example, if a user has a hard disk called C:, and it is not included in the network profile, then this disk is not accessible to other users.

Also, each user has a profile which adds security to the LAN. Each device has a name code and each user has a name code. During normal execution of the network operating system, only users with the correct codes and security access can use specific devices.

Login to the Network

The last step in installing the local area network software is the login process. Assuming that there are no hardware problems, each microcomputer on the LAN has, in its autoexecutable batch file, a copy of the network files required to incorporate the microcomputer into the LAN. When the computer is booted, these files take over the operation of the microcomputer hardware and make a connection through the NIC and the network cable to the file server.

The first network request found by the user is a login ID that is unique to each user and then a password which may or may not be unique to each user. In some set-ups, the password may be requested from each user. If the user profile software on the server acknowledges an authorized user, then the microcomputer becomes active on the network and can perform any functions authorized for the specific machine.

LAN Security

One of the most important functions of LAN software is the security of the network against accidental or unauthorized access. One methodology is to split the file server's hard disk into sections, or volumes. Each volume can be given public, private, or shared status. If a volume is made public, then everyone on the network has access to its contents. Private volumes can be accessed only by single users for read or write functions. Shared volumes allow all users to have read and write access to the contents. Some file servers have more sophisticated security levels. Network operating systems, such as Novell's NetWare, allow not only volume security attributes, but extend the security attributes to individual files on any volume.

Another type of security employed by LANs is volume, file, and record locking. Volume locking is a technique by which a user can lock all other users out of a volume until he or she is through with the volume. Some networks allow locking to be placed at the file level. Others allow locking at the record level. Record locking is preferred under normal circumstances since a user can control one record while other users have access to the rest of the records and the rest of the network files.

Other types of security that LANs can provide are data encryption, password protection to volumes and files, and physical or electronic keys that must be inserted into a network security device to gain access.

Remote LAN Software

Remote software offers microcomputer users the ability to operate programs and access peripherals on a remote system by using a modem. In addition, remote LAN software allows users to have node-to-node communications so users can share networked applications.

This type of software can be used for technical support, group conferencing, and training. Also, network managers can control network functions from locations other than a network station or the file server. Additionally, technicians at remote locations can access a LAN experiencing problems. This is done to conduct diagnostic tests and software repairs.

Legal Issues

Software installed on a LAN needs to meet certain legal criteria. Some network administrators feel that a single legally purchased copy of an application can be placed on a file server and made available to all users. This is illegal. An application software program can only be used on a LAN when a site license exists for the package. Furthermore, the number of users accessing the application program needs to be limited to the number of users stipulated in the licensing agreement. Honesty and integrity are the best paths to follow in this area.

Server Hardware

The primary function of a server is to provide a service to network users. The most important server in a LAN is the file server. The file server has a much higher workload than that of a typical stand-alone microcomputer. The stand-alone PC takes care of the needs of a single user. The file server takes care of the needs of all users on the network. Therefore, careful consideration must be given to the hardware that constitutes the file server.

First, a network designer needs to decide whether a dedicated or non-dedicted file server is going to be used. Since a nondedicated server functions as a file server and as a user workstation, a dedicated server will outperform a nondedicated server. For example assume that a MS-DOS based PC is being considered as the server, and NetWare is the operating system. If the clone is not 100 percent compatible with the IBM PC, interrupts used by NetWare may conflict with the software.

For large networks, the file server should be a dedicated server, and the fastest and most efficient hardware should be considered. Also, to avoid execution problems, a new dedicated server should be compatible with the network software.

Since the file server is just a computer with some added hardware and software, the main components of the server that will affect speed are the central processing unit, RAM caching, the hard disk and controller, hard disk caching, and the random access memory installed on the server.

The Central Processing Unit (CPU)

The central processing unit performs the calculations and logical operations required of all computers. All programs running on a computer system must be executed by the CPU.

In the personal computer market, the CPU classifies the computer. In the IBM market area, the original IBM PC had a CPU that consisted of 16 bits with a bus consisting of 8 bits. This meant that 16 bits were used to perform the calculations, and data moved inside the computer 8 bits at a time. The processor used in the original IBM PC was the Intel 8088. When the IBM AT was introduced, it had a 32-bit CPU with a bus of 16 bits. Today, the fastest IBM microcomputers and compatibles use a CPU and data bus, both of which process 32 bits. The processors of choice are the 80386 and the 80486.

The size of the data bus and the CPU's clock speed govern the speed of a microcomputer. The bus is the pathway that connects the CPU with the network interface card and other peripherals attached to the microcomputer. The size of the bus determines how much data can be transmitted in each cycle of the CPU's clock. A larger bus size can move data faster and provide better performance.

The CPU's clock speed is the other factor that affects performance. The clock speed determines how frequently cycles occur inside the computer and therefore how fast data can be transmitted. The clock speed is measured in cycles-per-second or Hertz (Hz). The original IBM PC had a clock speed of 4.77 MHz. Recently produced microcomputers have clock speeds of 33 MHz and higher.

Whenever installing a new file server, a computer with a faster CPU clock and the largest possible data bus should be utilized. Of course, the computer with the faster CPU and the larger bus is going to be more costly. For small networks, clock speeds of 8 to 20 MHz and a data bus of 16 to 32 bits should be considered. For large networks, clock speeds of 16 MHz or more and a data bus of 32 bits should be considered.

The Hard Disk and Controller

A fast computer with a slow hard disk will deteriorate the performance of a LAN. The hard disk is a mechanical device that contains metal platters where data is stored for later retrieval. The hard disk controller is a circuit board that directs the operation of the hard disk.

As data moves inside the server at speeds of up to 10 million bits per second, data moves to and from the hard disk at speeds of approximately 1/20th of that in the best of situations. This can create a bottleneck that slows the LAN for all of its users. A fast hard disk and controller is essential to the performance of a LAN.

The average time required for the disk to find and read a unit of information is called the access speed. Most drives today have access speeds that range from a low of 15 milliseconds to a high of 80 milliseconds.

Hard disk controllers come in four different categories with varying performance, and they vary in the size of hard disk that can be attached. The categories are these.

1. ST506. Standard on most IBM ATs and compatibles. This drive controller has a transfer rate of approximately 7 megabits per second and supports a maximum of two drives, each with a size up to 150 megabytes.
2. ESDI. Enhanced Small Device Interface. This is standard on most 80386 based computers. The controller has a transfer rate of 10 megabits per second and supports a maximum of four disk drives. Typical drives have 300 megabytes.
3. SCSI. Small Computer System Interface. This controller has data transfers of approximately 10 megabits per second and support up to 32 disk drives. This type of controller supports drives having a capacity of 700 megabytes and more.

4. IDE. Intelligent Drive Electronics. IDE controllers combine features of the other three interfaces and adds additional benefits. They are fast like ESDI drives, intelligent like SCSI drives, and look like standard AT ST506 interfaces to the system. With capacities of up to 300 megabytes and even larger disks in the near future this type of controller is become increasingly popular. However, they suffer from a lack of standardization. However, there are new proposals in the market that attempt to create a better standard for this type of drive.

In addition to considering the speed of the hard disk and the hard disk controller, drives with enough size to support future upgrades and expansion should be considered.

Random Access Memory

Random access memory (RAM) is used by the file server to store information for the CPU. The speed of the RAM installed in the CPU determines how fast data is transferred to the CPU when it makes a request from RAM. If the speed of RAM is too slow for the type of CPU in use, then problems will arise and LAN deterioration will take place. Care should always be taken to match the speed of RAM to the speed of the CPU clock for optimum performance.

Some network operating systems, such as NetWare, use RAM as buffer areas for print jobs and for disk caching. Disk caching is a method by which the computer will hold in memory the most frequently and recently used portion of files, increasing the efficiency of the input/output process.

If a file server has only the minimum amount of RAM to run the network operating system, performance will deteriorate as users are added to the LAN, due to the increased access to the hard disk by the file server. Adding extra memory will dramatically increase the performance of the network by increasing efficiency of the input/output operations.

Server Software

To effectively provide file sharing services, the software that controls the file server must provide security, concurrent access controls, access optimizing, reliability, transparent access to the file server and peripherals attached to the server, and interfaces to other networks.

The file server software should provide user access to those elements necessary to perform job functions, while restricting access to items for which a user does not have access privileges. This means that some users do not know that more files exist. Other users are allowed to read them, and still others are allowed to delete or rewrite them.

Concurrent access controls allow users to access files in a prioritized fashion using volume, file, and record locking. These controls allow a file to be changed before another user reads the information. Otherwise, a user may be reading data that is no longer current.

Access optimization is achieved by having administrative tools in the LAN that allow the fine tuning of the network. This provides users with the best possible response time while safeguarding the contents of users' files. Some of these tools are fault tolerance, file recovery, LAN to mainframe communications, disk caching, and multiple disk channels.

The software in the file server and the server itself need to have a continuous and consistent mode of operation if users are to trust the network. In some situations, multiple servers offer each other backup services and increase the reliability of the LAN.

Transparent access means that using the LAN should be a natural extension of the user knowledge of the individual computer system. LAN users are typically not computer experts. Access to the file server should be no more difficult than accessing a stand-alone computer. This includes accessing peripheral devices such as printers, plotters, and scanners.

Often the LAN needs to interface with other LANs. The server software should have extensions that allow this to take place.

Summary

Local area networks are networks that interconnect devices that are confined to a small geographical area. The actual distance that a LAN spans depends on specific implementations. LANs are implemented in order to transfer data among users in the network or to share resources among users.

A LAN implementation can provide high-speed data transfer capability to all users without a system operator to facilitate the transmission process. Even when connecting a LAN to a wider area network that covers thousands of miles, data transfer between users of the network is time effective and in most cases problem free. The other reason for implementing a LAN is to share hardware and software resources among users of the network.

There are many LAN applications. Some of the more common types of applications are office automation, factory automation, education, computer-aided design, and computer-aided manufacturing.

When a LAN is purchased, the following characteristics should be kept in mind. LANs can provide the user with:

1. Flexibility.
2. Speed.

3. Reliability.
4. Hardware and software sharing.
5. Transparent interface.
6. Adaptability.
7. Access to other LANs and WANs.
8. Security.
9. Centralized management.
10. Private ownership of the LAN.

There are two major items that must be considered when planning or installing a LAN: the network hardware components and the network software. There are three major categories of devices that make up the hardware components of a local area network. These are the server, the LAN communication system, and the workstations.

LAN servers are computers on the network that are accessible to network users. They contain resources that they "serve" to users that request the service. The most common type of server is the file server. Most LANs have at least one file server, and many have multiple file servers. The file server contains software applications and data files that are provided to users upon request.

When two or more computers are connected on a network, a special cable and a network interface board are required in each computer. Connect the server to the cable and then connect the cable to these boards. Most microcomputers are not equipped with an interface port that can be connected to a second microcomputer for networking purposes (except the Macintosh). As a result a network interface board (NIC) or network adapter must be installed in the microcomputer.

The processes that take place in the hardware devices of a LAN must be controlled by software. The software comes in the form of the network operating system. One of the most widely used network operating systems is NetWare, which is provided by Novell, Inc.

The network operating system controls the operation of the file server, and it makes the network resources accessible and easy to use. It manages server security and provides the network administrators with the tools to control user access to the network and file structure.

Network topologies come in many different configurations. The bus, ring, and star topologies are used extensively in LAN implementations.

The LAN protocol is the set of rules by which two machines talk to each other. It must be present in addition to the LAN hardware and the network operating system. Some communication protocols used in LANs are the logical link control (LLC) protocol established by the Institute of Electronic Engineers (IEEE) 802 Standards Committee, the carrier sense multiple access/collision detection (CSMA/CD) protocol, and the token passing protocol. The type of protocol and access methodology used depends on which LAN standard a specific vendor decides to follow.

A file server is a computer with some added hardware and software. The main components of the server that will affect speed are the central processing unit, the hard disk and controller, and the random access memory installed in the server.

To effectively provide file sharing services, the software that controls the file server must provide security, concurrent access controls, access optimizing, reliability, transparent access to the file server and peripherals attached to the server, and interfaces to other networks.

Questions

1. What is a LAN?
2. What types of applications can be found on most LANs?
3. Describe the major characteristics of LANs.
4. What is a file server?
5. What is the function of the network interface card (NIC)?
6. What is the purpose of the network operating system?
7. What are protocols?
8. What is the LAN communication system?
9. Briefly explain two different LAN topologies.
10. What is the 802.2 IEEE standard?
11. What is token passing?
12. Describe three characteristics that affect file server efficiency.
13. Describe four characteristics of server software.
14. Why is it important to have a fast hard disk and controller in a file server?

Project

Objective

This project provides hands-on knowledge of software that allows remote access of a personal computer from another personal computer. This type of software is becoming more common in the workplace as it is employed to provide assistance to users from remote locations or to help users to run programs that reside in computers located at remote sites, and can be used to transfer files between computers that have incompatible disk drives.

Remote Access to a PC

There are situations in the workplace in which for instructional or error-checking needs it would be desirable to control the functions of one personal computer (host) from another personal computer (remote). The remote computer can be located next to the host computer or miles away in a different geographical location.

To perform such operation, the host and remote computers need to run special software that allows the host to become a "slave" or extension of the remote system. There are several commercial programs available to perform such functions. One of these programs is a shareware program called The TANDEM Remote System (TTRS).

The TANDEM Remote System is shareware software. This means that it can be acquired in most cases free of charge from local user groups or dealers that sell public domain software at nominal prices. The software can be tried, and if found usable, it is expected that the user will send a contribution back to the author of the program. In return, the author provides, in most cases, a program documentation and new enhancements to the software.

The main components of TTRS are two programs TANDEM.EXE and TMODEM.EXE. TANDEM.EXE is the host program and TMODEM.EXE is the remote program. The function of the system varies slightly depending on whether the remote and host systems are connected directly with a null modem or through the telephone lines.

Direct Connection. Before the remote computer can access the host system the proper hardware must be connected to both computers using the standard RS-232 port. Follow the steps below to see if you have all the required items.

1. Write down the port number (COM1 or COM2) that you are going to use in the host computer.
2. Write down the port number (COM1 or COM2) that you are going to use in the remote computer.
3. Using a null modem cable (see chapter 3 projects), connect the two computers using serial port 1 (COM1).
4. Boot up both systems.
5. Make two copies of the original software. One copy will be used in the remote system and the other in the host computer.

With the TTRS diskettes in the computers' A drive or installed on their hard disk you will need to launch the TMODEM program in the remote computer and TANDEM in the host computer. The command lines are as follows.

For the remote computer the command line is

d:>TMODEM port, baud-rate, , D

d:> is the drive where the program is located

port is the serial port

baud-rate is the baud rate of the serial port

D indicates that the two computers are connected directly

For the host computer the command line is

d:>TANDEM port, baud-rate, , D

d:> is the drive where the program is located

port is the serial port

baud-rate is the baud rate of the serial port

D indicates that the two computers are connected directly

6. In the host computer type **TANDEM 1, 9600, , D**
7. In the remote computer type **TMODEM 1, 9600, , D**

At this point a password will be required. The passwords available are in a file called PASSWRDS.DAT that is in the original distribution disks.

8. Type any of the original passwords provided on the original disk.

Telephone line access. To access the host computer through the telephone lines a modem must be present at the host site and at the remote computer. You may want to refer to projects in previous chapters that show you how to connect a modem to a microcomputer.

1. Write down the port number (COM1 or COM2) that you are going to use on the host computer.
2. Write down the port number (COM1 or COM2) that you are going to use on the remote computer.
3. Make sure that the host system is attached to a modem set in the "answer" mode, and the modem is connected to a telephone line.
4. Make sure that the remote system is attached to a modem set in the "originate" mode, and that the modem is connected to a telephone line.
5. Boot up both systems.
6. Make two copies of the original software. One copy will be used in the remote system and the other in the host computer.

With the TTRS diskettes in the computers' A drives or installed on their hard disks you will need to launch the TMODEM program in the remote computer and TANDEM in the host computer. The command lines are as follows.

For the remote computer the command line is

d:>TMODEM port, baud-rate

d:> is the drive where the program is located

port is the serial port

baud-rate is the baud rate of the serial port

For the host computer the command line is

d:>TANDEM port, baud-rate

d:> is the drive where the program is located

port is the serial port

baud-rate is the baud rate of the serial port

7. Assuming that the host's modem is connected to COM1 and that your modem can transmit with a speed of 1200 baud, in the host computer type **TANDEM 1, 1200**
8. Assuming that the remote's modem is connected to COM1 and that your modem can transmit with a speed of 1200 baud, in the remote computer type **TMODEM 1, 1200**
9. The remote modem program will ask you to enter the phone number of the host modem. Type the number correctly without spaces or extra characters. If the connection is successful you will see a CONNECT message on the screen.

For Both Cases. At this point a password will be required. The passwords available are in a file called PASSWRDS.DAT that is on the original distribution disks.

10. Type any of the original passwords provided on the original disk.

At this point the two computers should be connected together. Under the TTRS control several commands can be used to control the host system, run programs on the host from the remote computer, and transfer files. These commands are as follows.

CLS. Clears the screen.

DIR. Displays directories of the host computer. It uses the same specifications as the DOS DIR.

DOS. Takes you to the operating system. This allows the remote computer to run programs that reside on the host computer.

BYE. Hangs up the phone and waits for the next call.

SHUTDOWN. Terminates TANDEM on the host computer from a remote location.

CHAT. Provides a clear screen so that the remote computer can communicate with someone at the host computer.

SEND. Transfers files between the host and the remote computers.

To transfer files between the host and the remote, the command line is as follows:

TANDEM:>SEND direction d:FILE.EXT [d:FILE.EXT]

The direction parameter uses the smbol ">" to indicate "to" or the symbol "<" to indicate "from." In addition, the words "HOST" and "REMOTE" are used to establish the direction in which the file is to be transmitted. For example, if a file named "data.dat" resides on the host main directory and it needs to be transferred to the remote computer and placed in a subdirectory named "c:\datafile" the command line is as follows:

11. **TANDEM:>SEND >REMOTE c:\data.dat c:\datafile\data.dat**

This procedure can be used to transfer files between desktop computers and portable computers.

To run a program from the remote computer that resides on the host computer the process is as follows:

12. Type **DOS** and press the Enter← key.

You will be taken to DOS and any DOS commands you type will affect the host system but will be displayed on the remote computer.

13. Type the name of the program that you wish to run and press the Enter← key.
14. When you are ready to return to the TANDEM environment, exit the program, type **EXIT**, and press the Enter← key.

The TANDEM Remote System is useful in many situations in the work environment. It can be used to run demonstrations on two computers simultaneously, to run programs that reside at the office from home, and to provide assistance to users at remote locations.

6

Network Design Fundamentals

Objectives

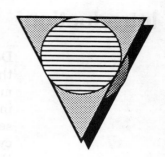

1. Be familiar with the life cycle of network design and implementation.
3. Understand the importance of response time, network modeling, message analysis, and geographic location in network design.
4. Know the different types of security threats to a data communication network.
5. Know some standard controls for unauthorized access to a network by users and by computer viruses.
6. Understand the basic principles for developing a disaster recovery plan.
7. Understand the basic principles for developing a network management plan.

Key Terms

Computer Virus	Disaster Plan
Encryption	Feasibility Study
Life Cycle	Network Management
Network Modeling	Network Security
Password/ID	Response Time

Introduction

Designing or upgrading a network is a complex and time consuming task that must follow standard system analysis methods. The typical planning methodology includes the following of the system life cycle and its inherent phases. Although the phases are not always followed in the sequence provided, it is important that network designers follow the life cycle process if the end result is to be successful. This chapter describes the different life cycle phases of system analysis and correlates them to network design and planning. Also, some specialized topics of network design such as response time and network modeling are explored.

The introduction of computer processing, centralized storage, and communication networks has increased the need for securing data stored in these systems. This emphasis manifests itself in the increase of available techniques and methods for detecting and deterring intrusions into the network by unauthorized users. Several types of network security enforcement techniques are explained. Additionally, a discussion of viruses is presented.

An additional measure of network security is the implementation of a network disaster recovery plan. The plan must be implemented within the framework of the system analysis approach. Several ideas on how to design a recovery plan are presented in the chapter.

The Life Cycle of a Network

The life cycle of a network is an important planning consideration because of inevitable technological changes that will have to be dealt with. Each network is a representation of the technology at the time of its design and implementation. Eventually, the network will become obsolete. New technologies and services will emerge, making it cost effective to replace outdated equipment and software with newer, more powerful, and less expensive technology.

During its life cycle, a network passes through the phases outlined in Fig. 6-1:

1. The feasibility study involves the subphases of problem definition and investigation. The problem definition attempts to find the problems that exist in the organization that caused management to initiate the study. The investigation subphase involves gathering input data to develop a precise definition of the present data communication conditions and to uncover problems.

2. The analysis phase uses the data gathered in step 1 to identify the requirements that the network must meet in order to have a successful implementation.

3. During the design phase, components of the network are defined.
4. The implementation phase consists of the installation of the hardware and software that make up the network system. Also, during this phase all documentation and training materials are developed.
5. During the maintenance and the upgrade phase the network is kept operational and fine-tuned by network operations personnel. Additionally, updates of software and hardware are performed to keep the network operating efficiently and effectively.

The life cycle concept can be applied to network design as a whole or in part. As a network moves through these phases, the planner becomes more constrained in the alternatives available for increasing data capacity, in the applications available, and in dealing with operational problems that may arise. These restrictions are the result of increased costs and difficulty in changing the operational procedures of the network. In addition, although the phases of the life cycle are presented here as a series of steps, the designer may have to go back through one or more phases of the design process. This feedback mechanism is important in order to incorporate concepts or ideas that may surface during the design and installation of the network.

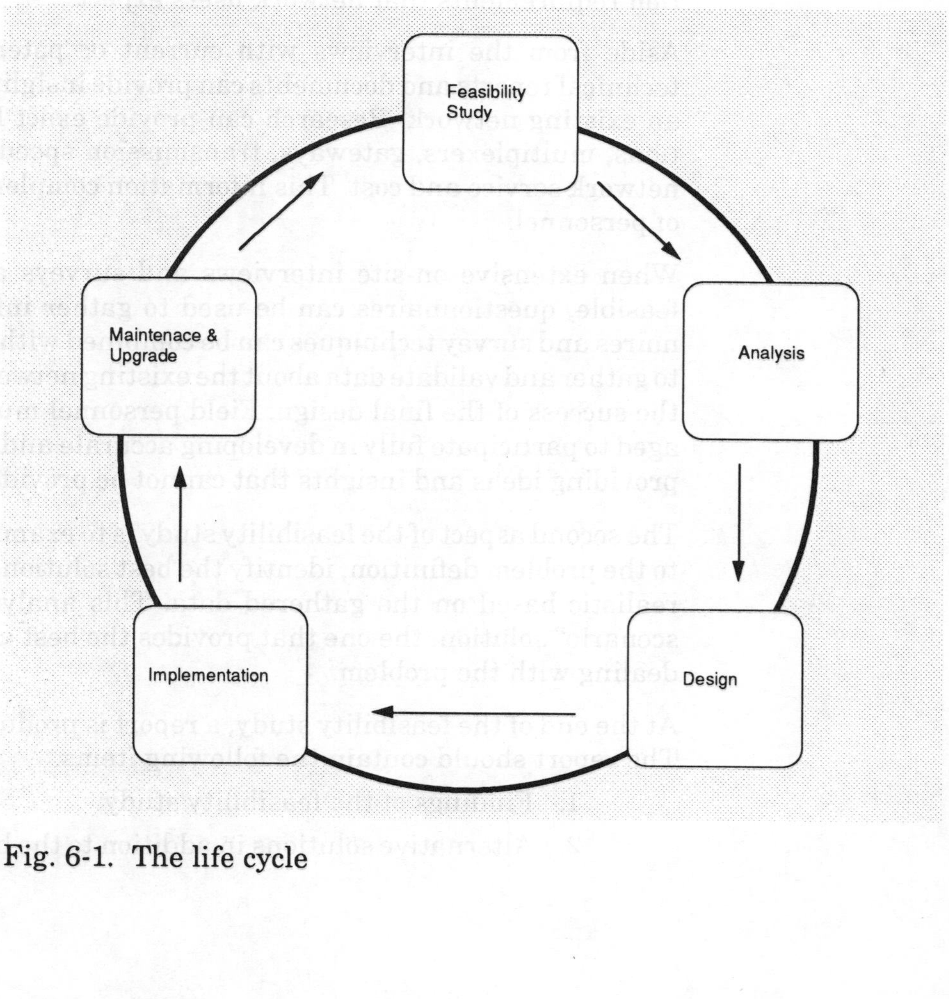

Fig. 6-1. The life cycle

The Feasibility Study

The feasibility study is performed in order to define the existing problem clearly and to determine whether a network is operationally feasible for the type of organization that it plans to serve. This is not the place to determine the type of network that may be implemented. Rather, the designer needs to fully understand the problem or problems that are perceived by management who initiated the request for the study.

Problem definition is the first step in the feasibility study. It is important to distinguish between problems and solutions. If a solution is made part of the problem definition, analysis of alternative solutions becomes handicapped. The problems need to be analyzed to determine whether and how they may point to the formulation of a new network or the upgrade of an existing network. The investigation of the current system takes place by gathering input data from the personnel involved in the use of the network and from the personal observations of the designer.

Interviews with users help to develop a precise definition of current data processing needs and to identify current problems. This process emphasizes only the information that is relevant to the network planning and design process. The data gathering process concentrates on terminal or workstation location, the current type of communication facilities and host computer systems, and the future data processing and communication requirements that network users expect.

Aside from the interviews with current or potential network users, technical reports and documents can provide insight into the operation of an existing network. Research can provide exact locations of workstations, multiplexers, gateways, transmission speeds, codes and current network service and cost. This information complements the interviews of personnel.

When extensive on-site interviews and surveys are not economically feasible, questionnaires can be used to gather information. Questionnaires and survey techniques can be combined with follow-up interviews to gather and validate data about the existing network. This helps ensure the success of the final design. Field personnel must always be encouraged to participate fully in developing accurate and complete data and in providing ideas and insights that cannot be provided in questionnaires.

The second aspect of the feasibility study is to examine possible solutions to the problem definition, identify the best solution, and determine if it's realistic based on the gathered data. This analysis provides a "best-scenario" solution, the one that provides the best all-around method for dealing with the problem.

At the end of the feasibility study, a report is produced for management. The report should contain the following items.

1. Findings of the feasibility study.
2. Alternative solutions in addition to the best possible solution.

3. Reasons for continuing to the next phase of the process.
4. If a realistic solution was not found, recommendations for another study and the methodology to follow in order to arrive at a feasible solution.

Analysis

This phase encompasses the analysis of all data gathered during the investigative stage of the feasibility phase. The end result is a set of requirements for the final product. These requirements are approved by management and implemented by the designer or designers of the network.

The formulated requirements must relate computer applications and information systems to the needs for terminals, workstations, communication hardware and software, common-carrier services, data input/output locations, data generation, and how the data will be processed and used. As a result, the formulated requirements identify the work activities that will be automated and networked. They relate the activities to the information input/output, the medium of transmission, where and how the data resides, and the geographic location where the information must be generated and processed.

Since data communication networks serve many types of applications, the volume of information for all applications must be combined to determine the final network design. Analyzing the raw data acquired in the investigation section of the feasibility study helps identify the total data volume that must be moved by the network.

The final product of this phase is another document, sometimes called a functional specification report, that specifies the functions that must be performed by the network after it is implemented. The report can include the following sections.

1. Network identification and description.
2. Benefits of proposed network.
3. Current status of the organization and existing networks.
4. Network operational description.
5. Data security requirements.
6. Applications available for this network.
7. Response time.
8. Anticipated reliability.
9. Data communications load that the network will support.
10. Geographic distribution of nodes.
11. Documentation.
12. Training.

13. Network expected life.
14. Reference materials used in preparing the report.

Many other requirements can be incorporated into the report. The number and complexity of the requirements will vary according to the type and size of network being recommended.

Design

The design phase of the life cycle is one of the longest phases. The outcome of this step depends on the expectations of management. At a minimum it will include a set of internal and external specifications. The internal specifications are the "blue-prints" of how the network operates, including modules used for building the network. The external specifications are the interfaces that the user will see when using the network. Both of these specifications may include data flow diagrams, logic diagrams, product models, prototypes, and results from network modeling.

At this point, designers should have a detailed description of all network requirements. These requirements should now be prioritized by dividing them into mandatory requirements, desirable requirements, and wish list requirements.

The mandatory requirements are those that must be present if the network is to be operational and effective. The desirable requirements are items that can improve the effectiveness of the network and the work of the users, but can be deferred until later if other priorities warrant. The wish list requirements are those provided by workers who feel that such items could help them increase their individual productivity. However, the small increase in productivity might be gained at a large cost, and the moneys could be expended in other areas.

The design phase will also indicate how the individual network components will be procured and the procedures for installation and testing of the network. The final document produced during this phase will become the "blue-print" for the remaining phases of the life cycle.

Response Time

One of the most important requirements in network design is response time. Response time is the time that expires between sending an inquiry from a workstation or terminal and receiving the response back at the workstation. The total response time of a network is comprised of delay times that occur at the workstation end when transmitting a message, the time required for the message to get to a host, the host processing time, the transmission back from the host to the workstation, and finally the time required for the workstation to display the information to the user. Usually, a shorter response time requirement will dictate a larger cost of the system. A typical cost versus response time curve is found in Fig. 6-2. The graph shows that the cost of a network is exponentially proportional to the average response time required.

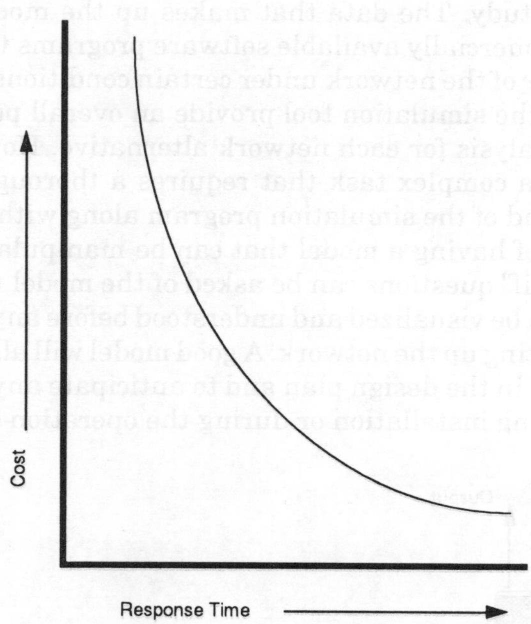

Fig. 6-2. Cost vs response time graph

To find the response time for a network that has yet to be implemented, the designers should look at statistics from other operating networks with similar work loads, a comparable number of users, and similar applications being run. Although the scenario may be difficult to find, comparing similar networks will provide statistics with approximate average response times and some indications as to where pitfalls are for the network being designed. In situations where a similar network is not available, predicting techniques must be used. These techniques are based on network modeling and simulation methods.

Simulation is a technique for modeling the behavior of the network. The response time is viewed as an average of the time elapsed for certain discrete events. (Fig. 6-3 depicts some of the causes for increasing response times.) Simulation programs are written to emulate a series of real life events, and the elapsed time for each event is added up to provide a measure of the response time and behavior of the network.

Network Modeling

One of the major uses of the data gathering process is in developing a network topology. The load (the number of messages that need to be transmitted) and site data are used as input for network modeling programs. Network modeling programs are application software that model a network, using mathematical models.

The network design alternatives are mathematically modeled for performance and then for cost, using public network tariffs and the geographically distributed peak loads found during the investigation step of the feasibility study. The data that makes up the model can be placed in several commercially available software programs to better understand the behavior of the network under certain conditions. The model created along with the simulation tool provide an overall performance capacity and cost analysis for each network alternative. However, simulating a network is a complex task that requires a thorough understanding of networks and of the simulation program along with its limitations. The advantage of having a model that can be manipulated electronically is that "What if" questions can be asked of the model and the effect of any changes can be visualized and understood before any money and effort is spent in setting up the network. A good model will allow designers to find weaknesses in the design plan and to anticipate any problems that may appear during installation or during the operation of the network.

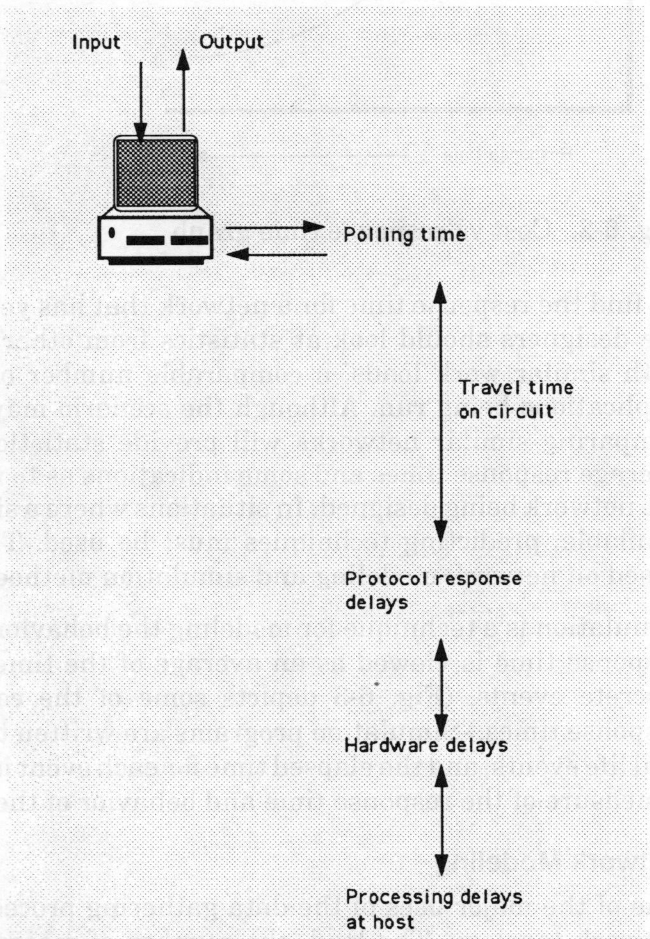

Fig. 6-3. Reasons for increasing response time

The output from the model is the basis for recommendations of a particular network design to be implemented. All aspects of the network should be included in these recommendations. Some of these factors are least-cost alterative, short response time, technical feasibility, maintainability, and reliability.

Once the overall network topology has been determined, it is manually fine-tuned to achieve the levels of operational performance required. The modeled network may place hardware in locations where it is not cost effective due to the time and cost of maintaining such equipment. In this case it would be better to incur the additional cost and place the items in a location where they are more accessible for maintenance purposes.

Network modeling tools are limited in their capabilities to analyze all the different data communication requirements. They normally model one aspect of the system, such as the speed link between workstations and servers. To model the other aspects of the network, subsequent iterations of the model are performed. The results of each analysis are combined to produce a final network configuration.

Geographic Scope

A geographic map of the scope of the network should be prepared at this point. The geographic scope of the network can be local, city-wide, national, or international. Normally, a map showing the location of individual nodes is prepared. The individual items that connect each node, such as gateways and concentrators, do not have to be indicated on the map (see Fig. 6-4).

The next map to be prepared indicates the location of nodes within the boundaries of the country. It needs to show the different states or provinces that will be interconnected and a line must show each connection from state to state.

The third type of map that may be required shows the location of the individual cities that are part of the network. The map should contain lines that connect each city in the network in the same logical fashion that the actual communication lines are distributed.

The last map shows the local facilities and the terminal or workstation location. It can be as wide as the boundaries of a city or as specific as the individual buildings and offices that are part of the network. Individual network connectivity items such as concentrators and multiplexers are not required to be displayed on the map. It is possible that, at this stage, the location of these items is not yet determined.

Message Analysis

Message analysis involves identifying the message type that will be transmitted or received at each terminal or workstation. The message attributes are also identified, including the number of bytes for each message. Message length and message volume identification are critical to determine the volume of messages that will be transmitted through the network.

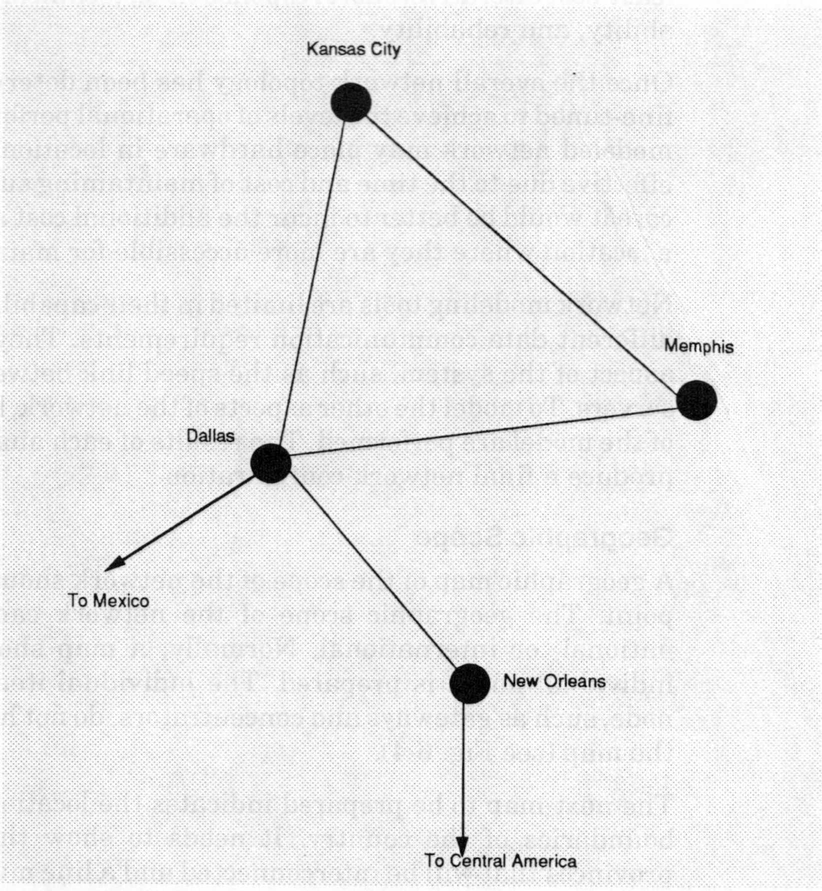

Fig. 6-4. Geographic scope of the network

The daily traffic volume is sometimes segmented into hourly traffic to provide the designers with the peak traffic hours. This information is used to identify problems with data traffic during peak hours.

It is important to note that most networks are designed based on average traffic volumes instead of traffic volume during peak hours. For most organizations it is not cost effective to purchase a network based solely on volume during peak hours.

Software/Hardware Considerations

The type of software purchased for the network will determine the operation of the network. It will specify whether the network will perform async or synchronous communications, full-duplex or half-duplex communications, and the speed of transmissions. Additionally, the software will determine the types of networks that can be accessed by the network being designed.

The network designer should select a protocol that is compatible with the OSI seven-layer model and one that can grow as the network grows within the organization. The protocol is a crucial element of the overall design, since the server architecture must interface with it. If the protocol follows accepted standards, the addition or replacement of multiple platform servers can be accomplished.

The pieces of hardware that are part of a network are:

1. Terminals.
2. Microcomputers and network interface cards.
3. File servers.
4. Terminal controllers.
5. Multiplexers.
6. Concentrators.
7. Line sharing devices.
8. Protocol converters.
9. Hardware encrypting devices.
10. Switches.
11. PBX switchboards.
12. Communication circuits.
13. FEPs.
14. Port sharing devices.
15. Host computers.
16. Channel extenders.
17. Testing equipment.
18. Surge protectors, power conditioners, and uninterruptible power supplies.

Each of the listed devices has a unique graphical representation that varies slightly according to the designer (see Fig. 6-5). The designer should prepare a graphical representation of the network hardware using the symbols outlined in Fig. 6-5 or similar ones.

The final hardware configuration needs to take into account the software protocol and network operating system that are going to be implemented in the network. The results should be the least-cost alternative that meets all the organization's requirements.

Before ordering any hardware, the designers should decide how to handle diagnostics, troubleshooting, and network repair. Most new network hardware has built-in diagnostics and testing capabilities.

Finally, selecting hardware and software involves selecting more than just a system. It involves selecting a vendor. The vendor's ability to maintain, upgrade, and expand the network components will determine the overall success of the network.

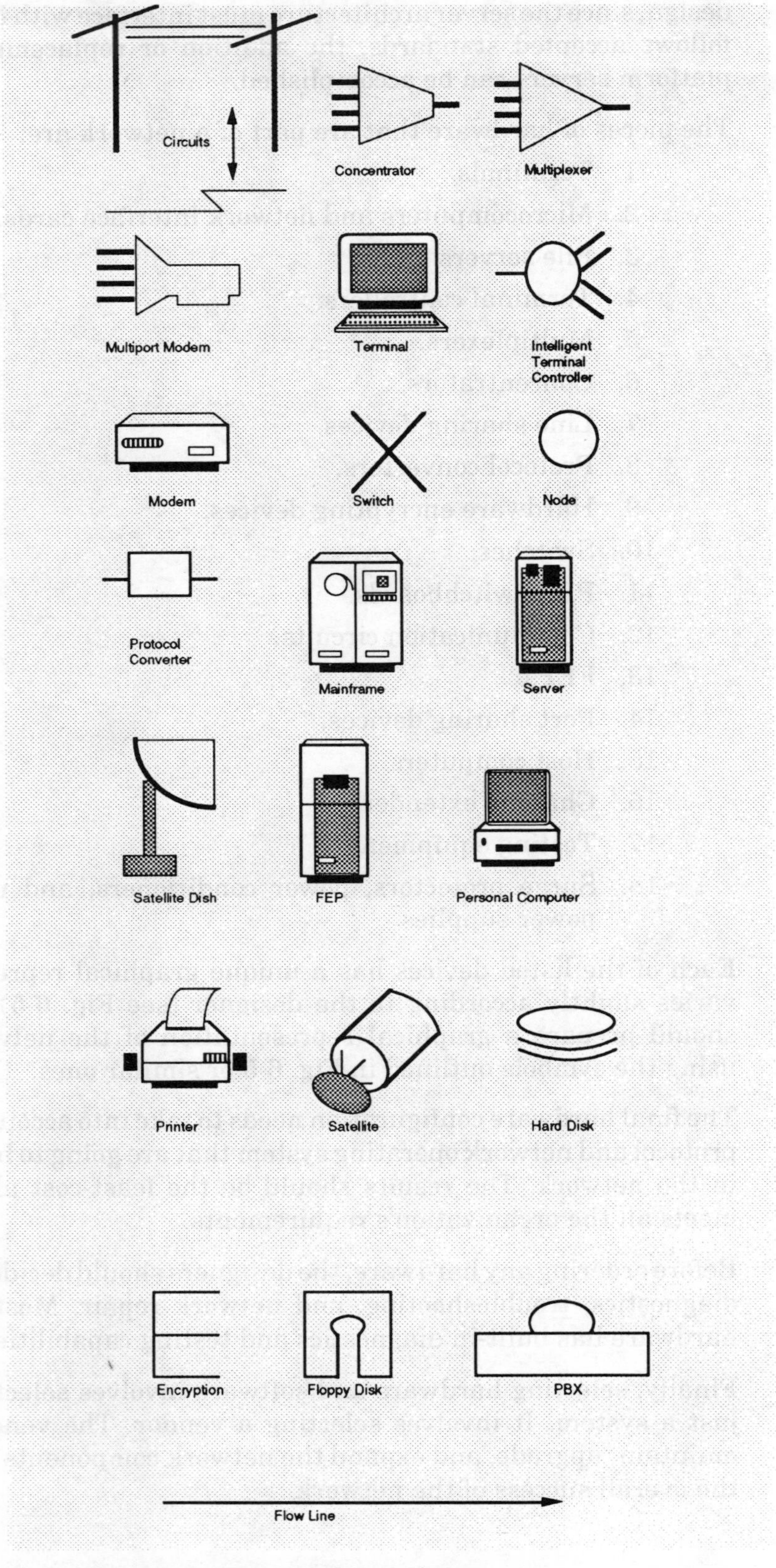

Fig. 6-5. Symbols of network hardware

Implementation

During the implementation phase the individual components of the network are purchased and installed. This phase can be divided into:

1. **Software acquisition.** If a new network is being implemented, the necessary network operating system, application software, managing software, and communication protocols must be procured. A useful tool in software and hardware procurement is a request for proposal (RFP). The RFP is based on the network requirements produced in the investigation step of the feasibility study. In response to a RFP come bids from potential vendors. The bids are evaluated, using specified criteria, and one is selected.
2. **Hardware acquisition.** Hardware procurement can be done from the same software vendor or a third party vendor may be used. Some software can run on a multitude of computer hardware configurations (sometimes called platforms). Deciding on the software first helps narrow the selection of a hardware vendor.
3. **Installation.** During or after the hardware and software acquisition, the individual components need to be assembled into what will become the network. The final product of this phase is an operational network system.
4. **Testing.** Testing should be conducted in an integrated fashion. That is, hardware and software should be tested simultaneously as they are implemented, trying to process to maximum work loads whenever possible. This will provide statistics that indicate the best and worst possibilities of network efficiency. It will also provide feedback for fine-tuning the network before it becomes fully operational. Integrated testing ensures that all parts of the system will function together properly.

   Testing should be performed using test plans developed during the design phase of the life cycle. There must be a complete and extensive test plan that produces test results reflecting the operation of the network under real life situations. These results are necessary if management is to trust and accept the network.
5. **Documentation.** Even though documentation is placed at this stage in the life cycle, it should be an integral part of each phase in network design. Reports that document every aspect of the network, from its conception until final implementation, must be present for audit trail purposes and must always accompany the network. These documents can take the form of reference manuals, maintenance manuals, operational and user manuals, and all the reference materials used in the feasibility study.

6. **Switch-over.** The switch-over step consists of moving all transactions from the old system to the new system. The final product of this step is the active working network. The switch-over plan must include milestones that need to be reached during the transition period and contingency plans in case the new system does not meet operational guidelines.

The Request for Proposals

Once the network has been designed, but before implementation can proceed, the specific vendors must be selected. A formal approach is to send a request for proposal (RFP) to prospective vendors. The RFP is a document that asks each vendor to prepare a price quotation for the configuration described in the RFP. Some RFPs give vendors great latitude in how the proposed system should be implemented. Others are very specific and expect detailed technical data in response from the vendor.

The format of a RFP can vary according to how specific the document needs to be. However, as a general rule, a RFP contains the following topics.

- **Title pages.** This identifies the originating organization and title of the project.
- **Table of contents.** Any lengthy document should have a table of contents to provide a quick reference to specific topics.
- **Introduction.** This is a brief introduction that includes an overview of the organization for which the final product is intended, the problem to be solved, schedule for the response to the RFP, evaluation and selection criteria, installation schedules, and operation schedules.
- **RFP response guidelines.** The RFP guidelines for responding to it establish the schedule for the selection process, the format of the proposal, how proposals are evaluated, the time and place of proposal submission, when presentations are made, and the time for the announcement of the winner or winners.
- **Deadlines.** The deadline and place for submitting responses to the RFP must be stated clearly throughout the proposal. The deadlines should also include equipment delivery dates and the date to commence operations.
- **Response format.** The format of the response to the RFP depends on the user. Normally, responses come in two separate documents. One document contains the specific technical details of the proposed system. The other volume has the financial and contractual details of the contract.
- **Evaluation criteria.** The RFP needs to include guidelines for the vendors on how the responses will be evaluated. It should include the items that are the most important on a prioritized

list. This allows the vendors to provide further information on these items in their responses. Typically, vendor responses include the following items:

1. System design.
2. System features.
3. Upgrade capabilities.
4. Installation methods.
5. Installation schedule.
6. Testing methods.
7. Maintenance agreements.
8. Cost of items.
9. Payment schedule.
10. System support.
11. Warranty coverage.
12. Training options.

This is the largest portion of the RFP. It describes the problems that need to be solved. Solutions to these problems should not be included in this section. Rather, the vendors should be allowed to propose their own solutions.

Maintenance and Upgrade

The last phase in the life cycle of the network is the maintenance and upgrade of the components of the network. During the maintenance and upgrade period the system is kept operational and fine-tuned to keep adequate performance levels and fix system problems.

The products of this phase are change and upgrade requests, updates to existing documentation to reflect changes in the network, and reports and statistics from the monitoring and control functions of the network.

At some point in the life of the system, the new network in its own turn will be replaced or phased out. This final stage in the life cycle leads to the beginning of a new life cycle as the organization goes through the same process to find a replacement or upgrade to the existing system.

Network Security

An important responsibility of network managers is maintaining control over the security of the network and the data stored and transmitted by it. The major goals of security are to prevent computer crime and data loss.

Detection of security problems in a network is compounded by the nature of information processing, storage, and the transmission system in the network. For example:

1. Data is stored on media not easily readable by people.
2. Data can be erased or modified without leaving evidence.
3. Computerized records do not have signatures to verify authenticity or distinguish copies from originals.
4. Data can be accessed and manipulated from remote stations.
5. Transactions are performed at high speeds and often without human monitoring.

The threat of the loss of the data stored in the network is sufficient reason for implementing methods and techniques to detect and prevent loss. It is important to incorporate the security methods during the design phase of the life cycle rather than add them later. Although no system is completely sealed from outside interference, the following methodologies will help in preventing a breach in network security.

Physical Security

The main emphasis of physical security is to prevent unauthorized access to the communications room, network control center, or communications equipment. This could result in damage to the network equipment or tapping into the circuits by unauthorized personnel.

The room or building that houses network communication equipment should be locked, and access should be restricted by network managers. Terminals should be equipped with locks that deactivate the screen and keyboard switch. In some situations, instead of keys and locks, a programmable plastic card can be used. The locking mechanism that accepts the card may be programmed to accept passwords, in addition to the magnetic code in the card.

Encrypting

With many networks using satellite and microwave relays for transmitting data, anyone with an antenna can pick up the transmission and have access to the data being transmitted. One method to safeguard the information transmitted through the airwaves and even data transmitted through wires is called encrypting or ciphering.

Encrypting involves the substitution or transposition of the bits that represent a known data message. The level of encrypting can be of any complexity and it is usually judged by a work factor. The higher the work factor, the more complex the cipher or encrypting.

As shown in Fig. 6-6, an encrypting system (also called a cryptosystem) between a sender and a receiver consists of the following elements:

1. A message to be transmitted and protected.
2. A large set of invertible cryptographic transformations (ciphers) applied to the message to produce ciphertext and later to recover the original message by applying the inverse of the cipher to the ciphertext.
3. The key of the cryptosystem that selects one specific transformation from the set of possible transformations.

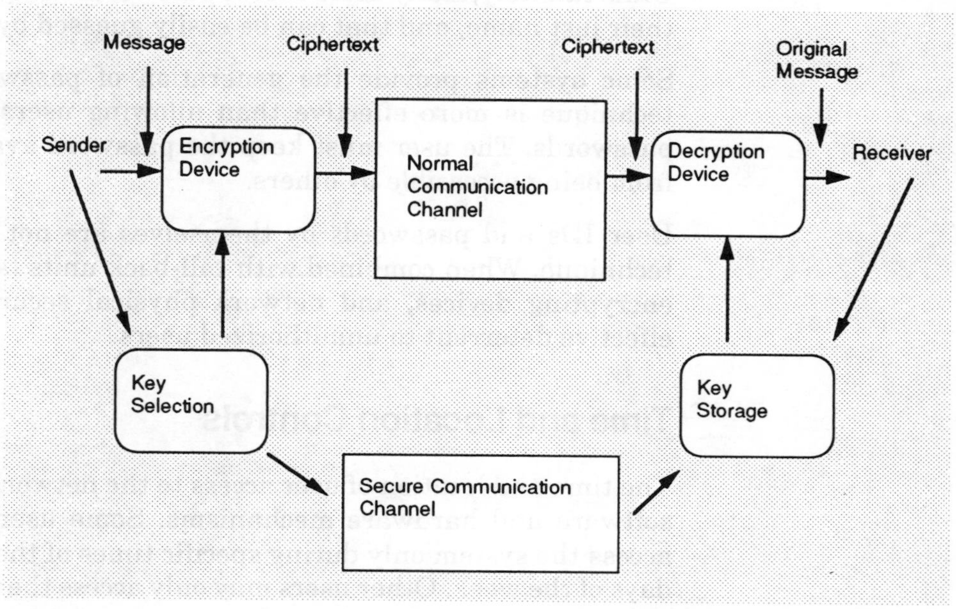

Fig. 6-6. Encrypting system

A cryptosystem is effective only if the key is kept secret and the set of ciphers is large enough that the correct key could not be guessed or determined by trial-and-error techniques.

The National Bureau of Standards has set a data encrypting standard (DES). The DES effectiveness derives from its complexity, the number of possible keys (over 10^{16}), and the security of the keys used. The DES transformation is an iterative nonlinear block product cipher that uses 64-bit data blocks. It is implemented on special purpose microcircuits that have been developed for DES and are available commercially. The DES encrypting algorithm is used in reverse for decrypting the ciphertext. The key is also a 64-bit word, 8 of which are parity bits; therefore, the effective key length is 56 bits (see hardware encrypting in chapter 3).

The suitability of a type of encrypting algorithm for applications in a data network depends on the relevant characteristics of the applications running in the system, the characteristics of the chosen algorithm, and the technical aspects of the network. Even though the purpose of encrypting is to secure data, the effect of the cryptosystem on the network is equally important. A cryptosystem that provides excellent security may deteriorate the performance of the network to unacceptable levels.

User !dentification and Passwords

User identification (ID) and passwords are the most common, and at times the easiest to break, security systems employed in networks. The user ID is provided by the network manager when the user profile is added to the network. The password is normally at the user's discretion. Unfortunately, many users choose passwords that are too simple, such as their last name, and that can be easily guessed by trial and error.

Some systems provide the generation of passwords for users. This technique is more effective than allowing users to define their own passwords. The user must keep the password available, but protect it from being accessible by others.

User IDs and passwords by themselves are not an effective security technique. When combined with call-back units (see chapters 2 and 3), encrypting devices, and network physical security, they provide an effective deterrent to unauthorized users.

Time and Location Controls

The time and location of user access to the network can be controlled by software and hardware mechanisms. Some users may be allowed to access the system only during specific times of the day and on specified days of the week. Other users may only access the system from specified terminals. Although such measures are an inconvenience to users, they help in managing data flow and in monitoring the network usage.

Time controls are performed on individuals by having a user profile in the network that determines the day and time intervals during which the user can access the system. Location controls are enforced by having a terminal profile. The terminal profile identifies the terminal and sets up specific paths that the terminal can follow to access selected data. No matter who the user is on the terminal, the terminal profile can be given a higher priority to override the user profile.

Switched Port and Dialing Access

The most vulnerable security point on a network is switched ports that allow dial-in access. They are a security risk because they allow any person with a telephone and terminal to access the system. To enhance the security of switched ports with dial-in access, they should be operational only during the time when transactions are allowed, instead of 24 hours per day. A call-back unit (see chapter 3) can be used to deter unauthorized calls and to ensure that calls are made only from authorized locations.

The telephone numbers of the switch should be safeguarded and only be available to personnel who must have access to them. User identification and password enforcement takes on a higher priority with dial-in access. In systems that contain critical data, a person-to-person authentication as well as application-to-user authentication should be used.

Audit Logs

Transaction logs are an important aspect of network security. Every login attempt should be logged, including date and time of attempt, user ID and password used, location, and number of unsuccessful attempts. In some situations, after a number of unsuccessful login attempts are made, the data described above may be displayed on an operator console for immediate action.

Many of the above methods can be incorporated into a system including extensive audit trails that collect the necessary information required to determine who is accessing the system. However, audit trails are worthless unless network managers study them and monitor the network.

Viruses

A computer virus is an executable computer program that propagates itself, using other programs as carriers, and sometimes modifies itself during or after replication. It is intended to perform some unwanted function on the computer system attached to the network.

Some viruses perform simple annoying functions such as popping up in the middle of an application to demonstrate that they are there. Other viruses are more destructive by erasing or modifying portions of programs or critical data. They are typically introduced into network computers by floppy disk based software that was purchased or copied. Many of the known viruses enter networks through programs or data downloaded from electronic bulletin boards. Some are deposited on networks by the creator of the virus. Other viruses migrate from network to network through gateways and other interconnecting hardware.

Viruses can be monitored and eliminated at the user level with the use of antivirus software. This type of application program searches files and looks for known computer viruses, alerting users of their presence. At this point, the user has the option to eliminate the virus or take some other security action. This process can take place on a stand-alone machine that the user has access to before introducing the application in the network. Additionally, the user can also run a virus scanning program from a directory in the network. The program will them scan the user's floppy disk and report any suspicious files.

At the system manager level, virus protection can be be accomplished by using a network statistical program with a virus detection component that is designed to run as the network operating system is active. This type of application watches for signs of a virus and alerts the LAN manager at the first symptom. The program warns the LAN manager when application or data files show any change from the original. An example of this type of application is TGR Software's SCUA Plus.

It is important to note that antivirus software does not identify all viruses circulating. This type of software can only work on known viruses and offers little protection against new or unknown viruses. On a regular basis, the makers of antivirus software provide upgrades that contain protection against new computer viruses that were created since that last release of the virus protection program.

Disaster Recovery Planning

The increased use of computer systems and data communication networks has expanded the need for a realistic disaster plan. The network manager needs to be involved in such planning and should have knowledge in the areas that follow:

1. The need for disaster planning.
2. Computer backup approaches.
3. Network backup approaches.
4. The characteristics of a disaster backup strategy.
5. Planning processes of the organization.
6. The impact of a data network disaster on the organization.

Planning for a disaster is much like planning for a new system. It requires goals, objectives, design, implementation, testing, documentation, and maintenance. Producing a good disaster plan requires significant organizational skills. However, LAN developers and LAN managers should also concentrate on disaster prevention measures. Good prevention measures may allow the disaster recovery plan to never go into effect. Some of these measures and others not outlined below will make the recovery process easier and protect users' information.

1. Adequate surge protectors. All computers in the network should be protected with surge protectors that can react to a large voltage spike in at least one or two nanoseconds. This type of device normally costs about $100, so it can be expensive to outfit a network with many workstations. However, when compared with the cost of a workstation, they are worth the price.

2. Servers must be protected with a UPS. A UPS protects against voltage surges and drops. In many networks, the server contains invaluable data that a company can't function without.

Protecting the data is one of the most important functions of the LAN manager. Additionally, the UPS also allows the proper shutdown of the network in case of a loss of power.

3. Communication line protectors and filters. Computers connected to modems and telephone lines also need a protection from incoming noise and surges that may travel through the phone lines.
4. Protect cables. All cabling must be protected and placed in locations where a user cannot accidentally tamper with the line.
5. Adequate backups. Continuous and comprehensive backups will ensure that all data and programs are safeguarded. If possible, during a period of network inactivity, the backup and recovery plans outlined below should be rehearsed.

Characteristics of the Disaster Recovery Plan

A disaster plan must meet certain criteria, including:

1. Reliability.
2. Operability.
3. Response time to activate the plan.
4. Cost effectiveness.

Reliability. Whatever the strategy taken to safeguard the network and the data stored on it, the organization must be confident that, in case of a disaster, the plan will work. Confidence can be achieved by using proven techniques to replace network media in case of a failure.

The best plans are those that are kept simple. The plan needs to be tested in order to ensure that the information in the system is secured. Any disaster plan is suspect without proper testing.

Operability. The methods used for recovering from a disaster should be consistent with the normal methods of backup and restore that are used in the routine management of the network. This ensures that, in case of failure, trained personnel will be able to restore the system quickly and without errors. Additionally, the plan should be well documented and distributed to appropriate personnel.

Response time to activate the plan. The recovery plan must be capable of being activated within the time constraints imposed by the network. In some cases, backup networks are activated on a temporary basis until the stricken facility is restored to an acceptable operational level. The network design must be flexible to allow for time-sensitive considerations.

Cost effectiveness. The recovery plan must be cost effective since it will be idle for most of the network life. However, in a disaster situation, the backup system must also be flexible enough for long-term use if necessary.

Disaster Recovery Methodologies

Extensive planning and research are required to produce an effective disaster recovery plan. Some of the concerns that a manager may want to address in preparing a recovery plan follow:

1. Create a list of the critical applications. This will require involvement from top management. The items on the list should be prioritized, and their impact on the firm should be analyzed.
2. Determine the required recovery time for the organization.
3. Determine the critical nodes in the network.
4. Analyze the critical work load for each node, and create a transaction profile for it.
5. Analyze the use of shared communication facilities and alternate methods of information transfer.
6. Obtain best vendor and carrier lead-time estimates for a backup network.
7. Identify facilities that exceed the recovery time. That is, these facilities are critical and the recovery time exceeeds the allowable down time. These must be restored first.
8. Determine costs.
9. Have the vendor develop a plan to connect users with planned backup networks.
10. List all cable and front end requirements.
11. Make a list of equipment that can be shared, such as modems.
12. List all facilities that can be provided at the recovery site in case of a prolonged down time.
13. List all support personnel available for recovery.
14. List all dial-up facilities at the recovery site.

The Planning Process

The disaster recovery plan may be divided into strategic and implementation sections. The strategic section lists the goals, design objectives, and strategies for network recovery. The implementation section describes the steps to take during the recovery process. Some of the major items to be included in the plan are provided below.

1. List all assumptions and objectives, and the methodology for implementing the objectives.

2. List all tasks to be performed before, during, and after a disaster.
3. Put together a technical description of any backup networks.
4. List all personnel involved in the recovery phase and their responsibilities.
5. Describe how the recovery site will be employed.
6. Make a list of critical nodes and their profiles.
7. Make a list of vendors and carriers who will supply facilities and backup.
8. Make a list of alternate sources of equipment and supplies.
9. Create all necessary network diagrams.
10. Make a list of all required software, manuals, testing, and operational procedures of backup networks.
11. Diagram all backup circuits.
12. Describe procedures for updating the recovery plan.

A commitment to an effective disaster recovery plan must have the support of top management. They must be aware of the consequences of the failure of such a plan. A team consisting of a coordinator and representatives from management is required to continually upgrade the plan as facilities are added and modified, if the firm is to be protected.

Network Management

For a network to be effective and efficient over a long period of time, a good network management plan must be created. The network management plan must have two goals:

1. The plan should prevent problems where possible.
2. The plan should prepare for problems that will most likely occur.

A comprehensive plan needs to include the following duties:

1. Monitor and control hard disk space.
2. Monitor network workload and performance.
3. Add to and maintain user login information and workstation information.
4. Monitor and reset network devices.
5. Perform regular maintenance on software and data files stored in the servers.
6. Make regular backups of data and programs stored in the servers.

Managing Hard Disk Space

The server's hard disk is one of the network's primary commodities. Files for network based programs are stored on the hard disk. Print jobs that are sent from workstations to network printers are stored on the hard disk in a queue before they are printed. And in some networks, personal files and data are stored on the network hard disk.

If the hard disk space fills up, then print jobs can't be printed, users can't save their data files, and data files may be corrupted since data manipulation can't be accomplished.

Disk space must be available at all times for legitimate users of the network. The hard disk space must be checked every day. Growth of users' files should be controlled to ensure that a single user won't be monopolizing the hard disk. Unwanted files must be deleted, and when heavy disk fragmentation occurs, all files could be backed up and the disk reformatted. This will allow defragmentation of files in the hard disk and provide for more efficient access to data in the server's hard disk. Some networks allow the use of software to repack files in the hard disk and eliminate file fragmentation. When possible, such tools should be used. However, all files should be backed up first before using a defragmentation software application in case something goes wrong.

Monitoring Server Performance

The performance of the LAN's server will determine how quickly the server can deliver data to the user. The servers must be monitored to ensure that they are performing at their peak.

Several factors determine the response of a server. One of these factors is the number of users that are attached to the system. The more users a server has to deal with, the slower its response time. If a specific application has a large amount of users, then the server that contains the application could be dedicated to serve only such a program. Other servers could be used to distribute the load of other programs that users may require.

Additionally, the server's main memory (RAM) should be monitored to make sure that it is used efficiently. Many servers use RAM as disk buffers. These buffers cannot function if there isn't sufficient memory to run the network operating system and the buffers. If a server has to reduce the number of buffers required for I/O, then the overall performance of the network will suffer.

Most networks provide tools that show statistical data about the use of the network and outline potential problems. An experienced network administrator uses these statistics to ensure that the network operates at its peak level at all times.

Maintaining User and Workstation Information

Network users have network identification numbers that can be used to monitor security and the growth of the network. A network manager must keep a log of information about the network users such as login ID, node address, network address, and some personal information such as phone, name, and address. Also, network cabling, workstation type, configuration, and purpose of use should be kept in records.

This information can be stored in a database, and used to detect problems with data delivery, make changes to users' profiles, workstation profiles, and accounts, and support other tasks.

Monitoring and Resetting Network Devices

A network consists not only of servers and workstations but also of printers, input devices such as scanners, and other machines. Some devices may need to be reset daily (such as some type of gateways), while other devices require periodic maintenance.

Some types of electronic mail routers may need to be monitored on an hourly basis to make sure that the communication device is working properly. In either case, all devices should be monitored periodically, and a schedule of reset and maintenance should be created to ensure that all network devices work when a user requests them.

Maintaining Software

Software applications, especially database application, need regular maintenance to rebuild files and reclaim space left empty by deleted records. Space not used must be made available to the system and in many cases index files will have to be rebuilt.

Additionally, as new software upgrades become available, they need to be placed in the network. After an upgrade is placed in the network, file cleanup may have to take place, and also any incompatibilities between the new software and the network will need to be resolved.

Also, as e-mail messages become old they will have to be deleted and the space they occupy made available to the system. The same type of procedure will have to be performed as users are added or deleted from the network.

Making Regular Backups

Backups of user information and data must be made on a periodic basis. If a server's hard disk fails, a major problem could occur if inadequate backups exist.

Backups of server information is normally placed on tapes or cartridges. Tapes and cartridges offer an inexpensive solution to backup needs and can hold large amounts of information. Their capacity ranges from 20 megabytes to as much as 2,200 megabytes.

Writing information from the server's hard disk to a tape or cartridge is a slow process. Network managers should have automated backup procedures and a tape system that offers 1 to 3 megabytes of transfer speed per minute.

Summary

The life cycle of a network is an important planning consideration. One significant aspect is the technological changes that will have to be dealt with during the useful life of the network. Each network is a representation of the technology at the time of its design and implementation.

During the course of its life cycle, a network passes through the following phases:

1. The feasibility study involves the subphases of problem definition and investigation. The problem definition attempts to find the problems that exist in the organization that caused management to initiate the study. The investigation subphase involves gathering input data to develop a precise definition of the present data communication conditions and to uncover problems.
2. The analysis phase uses the data gathered in step 1 to identify the requirements that the network must meet if it is to be a successful implementation.
3. During the design phase, all the components that will comprise the network are developed.
4. The implementation phase consists of the installation of the hardware and software that make up the network system. Also, during this phase all training and documentation materials are developed.
5. During the maintenance and upgrade phase the network is kept operational and fine-tuned by network operations personnel. Additionally, updates of software and hardware are performed to keep the network operating efficiently and effectively.

One of the most important requirements in network design is response time. Response time is the total time that expires between sending an inquiry from a workstation or terminal and receiving the response back at the workstation.

One of the major uses of the data gathering process is in developing a network topology. The load and site data are used as input for network modeling programs. These programs are application software that model a network using mathematical models.

The network operating system and the protocols that the host can handle limit the number and types of application software programs that can be used on a network. These limitations can be overcome with the acquisition of protocol converters and FEPs.

The type of software purchased for the network will determine the operation of the network, whether it uses asynchronous or synchronous communication, full-duplex or half-duplex communication, and the speed of transmission. Additionally, the limitations imposed by the software will determine the types of other networks that can be interfaced with. The network designer should select a protocol that is compatible with the ISO seven-layer model and one that can grow as the network grows. The protocol is a crucial element of the overall design, since the server architecture must interface with it.

Once the network has been designed, the specific vendors must be selected. A formal approach is to send a request for proposal (RFP) to prospective vendors. The RFP is a document that asks each vendor to prepare specifications and a price quotation for the configuration described in the RFP.

An important responsibility of network managers is maintaining control over the security of the network and the data on it. The major goals of security measures are to prevent computer crime and data loss. Some of the data losses can be the result of computer viruses. A computer virus is an executable computer program that propagates itself, using other programs as carriers, and sometimes modifies itself during or after replication. It is intended to perform some unwanted function on the computer system attached to the network. Viruses can be monitored and eliminated with the use of antivirus software.

Another method to safeguard the information transmitted is called encrypting or ciphering. User IDs and passwords by themselves are not an effective security technique. When combined with call-back units, encrypting devices, and network physical security, they provide an effective deterrent to unauthorized users.

The time and location of user access to the network can be controlled by software and hardware mechanisms. Although such measures are an inconvenience to users, they help in providing access to data by monitoring communication sessions and access during critical times. The most vulnerable security point on a network is switched ports that allow dial-in access. To enhance the security of switched ports with dial-in access, they should be operational only during the time when transactions are allowed. A call-back unit can be used to ensure that calls are made only from authorized locations.

The increasing use of computer systems and data communication networks requires that managers need a realistic disaster plan. The network manager needs to be involved in the planning and should have knowledge in:

1. The need for disaster planning.
2. Computer backup approaches.
3. Network backup approaches.
4. The characteristics of a disaster backup strategy.
5. Planning processes of the organization.
6. The impact of a data network disaster on the organization.

Planning a disaster recovery system requires goals, objectives, design, implementation, testing, documentation, and maintenance. A disaster plan must meet certain criteria, including:

1. Reliability.
2. Operability.
3. Response time to activate the plan.
4. Cost-effectiveness.

For networks to be effective and efficient over a long period of time, a good network management plan is needed. The network management plan must have two goals:

1. The plan should prevent problems where possible.
2. The plan should prepare for problems that will most likely occur.

A comprehensive plan needs to address the following tasks:

1. Monitor and control hard disk space.
2. Monitor network workload and performance.
3. Add to and maintain user login information and workstation information.
4. Monitor and reset network devices.
5. Perform regular maintenance on software and data files stored in the servers.
6. Make regular backups of data and programs stored in the servers.

Questions

1. Briefly describe the life cycle phases for network design.
2. Name four items that should be included in the report produced at the end of the feasibility study.
3. Why is network response time important?

4. What is network modeling?
5. What is the purpose of message analysis?
6. Name ten hardware items that are part of a network.
7. What are the steps of the implementation phase?
8. What are the major sections of an RFP?
9. Briefly describe encryption.
10. Why are passwords and user IDs not enough security for a network?
11. What is a virus? How can it be detected?
12. Why should there be a disaster recovery plan for a data communications network?
13. Name four characteristics of a disaster recovery plan.
14. Name four major items that should be included in the recovery plan.

Projects

Objective

There are two different projects in this section. Project 1 provides some general guidelines for troubleshooting a small local area network. Before expensive testing methods are used to find problems with LANs, the guidelines provided below may find and correct a problem in a more efficient manner. The second project is the study of the design and installation of a local area network for the computer laboratory.

Project 1. Troubleshooting a LAN

Troubleshooting a LAN is accomplished by using an established methodology of problem determination and recovery through event login and report techniques. Some troubleshooting techniques will be explained in later chapters in this book. However, sometimes the best planned approach does not work. The following suggestions may accomplish what the scientific methods can't do. Try to follow them in the order that they are listed.

1. If the problem appears to be on the network, try turning the power to network devices off and on in a systematic manner. Turn off the power to routers, gateways, and network modems. After turning the power off, wait approximately 30 seconds and turn the power back on. Sometimes a device gets "hung-up" because of an electrical malfunction or an instruction that it cannot execute.
2. If the problem appears to be in your workstation, turn the machine off and reboot the computer.

3. Check for viruses in the file server and your workstation.
4. Reload the network software, and any other software that controls devices such as gateways.
5. Swap out devices, cables, connectors, and network interface cards on your machine and then across the network.
6. Reconfigure the user profile in the network server.
7. Add more memory to the file server.

If the above suggestions do not work and the LAN manuals do not offer any other possibilities, then call the LAN vendor.

Project 2. Study of a Local Area Network

Go to the school's data processing center or any other site where a local area network may be in operation. Carefully document the following topics by questioning network managers and by observing the LAN in operation.

1. Describe the hardware that constitutes the LAN. Use the following check list as a guide.
    a. Is the network a peer-to-peer network or a dedicated file server network?
    b. What models of server(s) are available?
    c. What is the internal configuration of the server(s) (i.e., amount of RAM, disk space, processor speed, coprocessor speed, number of floppy drives and types, etc.)?
    d. What models of workstations are available?
    e. What is the internal configuration of the workstations (i.e., amount of RAM, disk space, processor speed, coprocessor speed, number of floppy drives and types, etc.)?
    f. What make, model, and type of network interface card is being used?
    g. What is the network configuration? Why was this type choosen?
    h. What models and types of printers are available to network users?
    i. Are there any gateways to other networks? If yes, what type and models are available?
    j. What are the physical limitations of the network (i.e, number of users, maximum distance of transmission)?
    k. What type of transmission medium is being used? Why was this type chosen?

2. What network operating system is in place? Why was this type chosen?
3. How do the users interact with the software stored in the network?
4. What type of work is normally accomplished by the workstations?
5. How do users perform network operations such as printing, copying files, and so forth?
6. What are the maintenance policies?
7. Are there any support fees? If yes, what type and amount?
8. What is the cost of adding stations?
9. What is the cost of adding a server?
10. What are the system management procedures in place and their cost?
11. How are software licensing agreements handled?
12. What type of upgrades or modifications are planned for the next three years?

After all the material is compiled, create a report indicating your findings about the status of the local area network. The report should consist of at least five pages, but it will probably be much longer.

After completing the report on the actual LAN, provide suggestions for improving the system without increasing the current costs. For each suggestion, provide evidence in the form of interviews, data compiled from magazines, or vendor specification sheets. Is there a way to provide a better service and lower the costs? What problems do you anticipate with this network during the next three years? How can a solution be in place before serious interruption of LAN services take place?

7

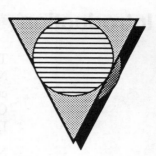

Introduction to Novell NetWare

Objectives

1. Understand the basic hardware components required to install NetWare.
2. Obtain an overview of the software components of NetWare.
3. Understand Novell's shell.
4. Understand the concept of drive mappings.
5. Understand the concept of trustee and trustee's rights.

Key Terms

Client Computer	Drive Mapping
Login Script	NetWare
Network Interface Card	Search Drive
Server Computer	Trustee
Trustee Rights	User Environment

Introduction

This chapter introduces a network operating system known as Novell NetWare. It will introduce concepts that will be more thoroughly discussed in later chapters. Originally designed for computers running the CP/M operating system, Novell quickly adapted NetWare for use on the IBM PC. This move ensured NetWare's success.

NetWare's primary components on a PC are the network interface card (NIC), and two programs collectively known as the NetWare shell. The NIC physically connects the client (user's) computer to a file server where data can be shared by all the users on the network. The shell allows the user to treat the file server as if it were a disk drive attached to his client computer. Ordinary DOS commands can be used on the file server and several additional functions are available. The user can create drive mappings and search drives, which allows more effective use of the data and programs on the file server. That data can be protected by assigning the proper trustee rights to the other users on the network.

Overview of NetWare

Little remains constant in the world of networking. Network operating systems, hardware components, and topologies have changed rapidly over the last several years to keep pace with advancing technology and consumer demand. Novell, Inc. has performed better than most at maintaining a saleable product and a share of the market. Novell's original network product, however, did not do well. The system was a file server and network operating system software, with serial cables to connect to client computers running the CP/M operating system. The product line was expanded somewhat, but the company went bankrupt. Novell's reorganization, however, took place at an opportune point in history. The introduction of the IBM PC gave Novell an entirely new market. Novell's operating system was eventually rewritten to allow the IBM PC to be used as both the file server and the client. Novell has introduced many software and hardware products since then, and now controls the largest single share of the networking market with Novell NetWare. "NetWare" refers to all of Novell's network operating system products.

Novell NetWare was originally designed around hardware using a star topology to communicate with a single file server. The file server simply allowed client computers to store and share files. This structure has influenced all of Novell's products to date. NetWare has become largely hardware independent, allowing many topologies and file servers to be used simultaneously, but communication on the network is still handled almost entirely through a primary file server. Two client computers may be connected directly to each other by a network cable, but for a file to be transferred from one to the other, that file must first be sent to the file server, then to the target client computer. Of course, the network provides many other functions, but they are generally centered around the idea of a client computer connected to a file server.

By far, the most common client on a Novell network is an IBM PC or PC-compatible computer running DOS. DOS is the software that handles all of the low-level functions of the computer such as reading and writing to the disk drives, loading and executing application programs, and handling input from the keyboard. When running an application program such as a word processor, DOS allocates memory, reads the program from the disk drive and then allows the program to begin. The application program can then use the resources of the computer through what are known as DOS function calls. For instance, there are many different types of printers and dozens of companies manufacturing them. To the application program, this is irrelevant. It will simply make a DOS function call to write data to the printer and DOS will handle the output to the device.

Since even DOS can't "know" the details of every peripheral device one might attach to a computer, including a network, programs known as drivers are often used to help DOS provide a common environment for application programs to work in. Attaching a Novell network to a computer is a good example of this and essentially involves three components: the network interface card or NIC, a program called IPX, and another program called NET#, where # indicates the version of DOS already running on the computer.

The NIC is the hardware that is physically connected to the network, much like a telephone is the piece of hardware that is physically connected to the telephone network. It generates the proper electrical signal to communicate on the particular type of network being used. It may even use pulses of light or radio waves to send signals across the network.

IPX is an abbreviation for Internetwork Packet Exchange. The IPX program controls the operation of the NIC so that a common protocol is used throughout the network. Since there are hundreds of types and brands of NICs, IPX is built using drivers specific to each. IPX is actually hardware dependent, but, since drivers are available for all types of NICs, NetWare itself can still claim to be hardware independent.

NET# controls communication between DOS and IPX. Since there are several versions of DOS, NetWare comes with several versions of the NET# program: NET2, NET3, NET4, XMSNET2, XMSNET3, XMSNET4, EMSNET2, EMSNET3, and EMSNET4. The XMS prefix refers to Extended Memory System and the EMS prefix refers to Expanded Memory System. These are not different DOS versions, but significant extensions to DOS. The different versions of the NET# program allow it to take advantage of functions specific to each operating system version and memory extension. The NET# program is therefore operating system dependent.

Together the IPX and NET# make up the NetWare shell which is a complete interface between DOS and NetWare. The word "shell" refers to an interface provided to users to allow them to interact with the computer in a "natural" manner. This "shields" users from the complex low level operations of the computer and the network. Therefore, the network shell protects the user from having to know how to interact directly with the network.

The User Environment

Network Drives

The NetWare shell allows DOS and the user to treat the file server as a disk drive attached to the client computer. DOS assigns a drive letter to each of the disk drives physically attached to the computer. A and B designate floppy disk drives while C, D, and so on represent hard disk drives. On a typical system, with two floppy disk drives and a hard disk drive, DOS would assign A, B, and C to the those disk drives. When the NetWare shell programs are loaded, another drive letter is made available to the user. Typically, F is used to designate the first network drive. Ordinary DOS commands like DIR (which displays a list of the files on the disk) and CHDIR (which moves access to a different area of the disk) can be used on the network drive F. In addition, application programs can make ordinary DOS function calls to carry out their functions on the network drive as if it were a hard disk attached to the computer. The network drive is the hard disk on the file server, the same hard disk accessed by every other user on the network.

Fig. 7-1 shows three computers, a file server and two client computers. The first client has local disk drives A, B, and C. It also has access to drive F, which is actually on the file server. The second client has only one local disk drive, but can also access drive F.

DOS Directories

In DOS you can create directories to organize the data on a disk. A directory contains files grouped together on the disk. Every disk has what is called the root directory even though it is not referred to it as "root" in a DOS command. Since a "\" (a backslash) is used to separate directory names, a backslash with no name is considered the root directory.

Fig. 7-2 shows how a hard disk might be organized. The files in the root directory could be listed by typing the DIR command. The DIR command lists the files in the current directory. In this case DIR C: would list the files COMMAND.COM, IPX.COM, NET3.EXE and a directory called WORD. The files in the directory WORD could be displayed by typing DIR C:\WORD and pressing the ENTER key. WORD.COM and LETTER.DOC would be listed. Another way to view the list of files in the WORD directory would be to use the CHDIR command. CHDIR stands for change directory and can be abbreviated further by using only CD. If you were to type CD C:\WORD, the current directory would be changed to the WORD directory and DIR C: would list the files WORD. COM and LETTER.DOC. In this way the drive letter C moves around the disk drive pointing to different areas. Just as the root directory contains a directory called WORD, the WORD directory could contain another directory and so on.

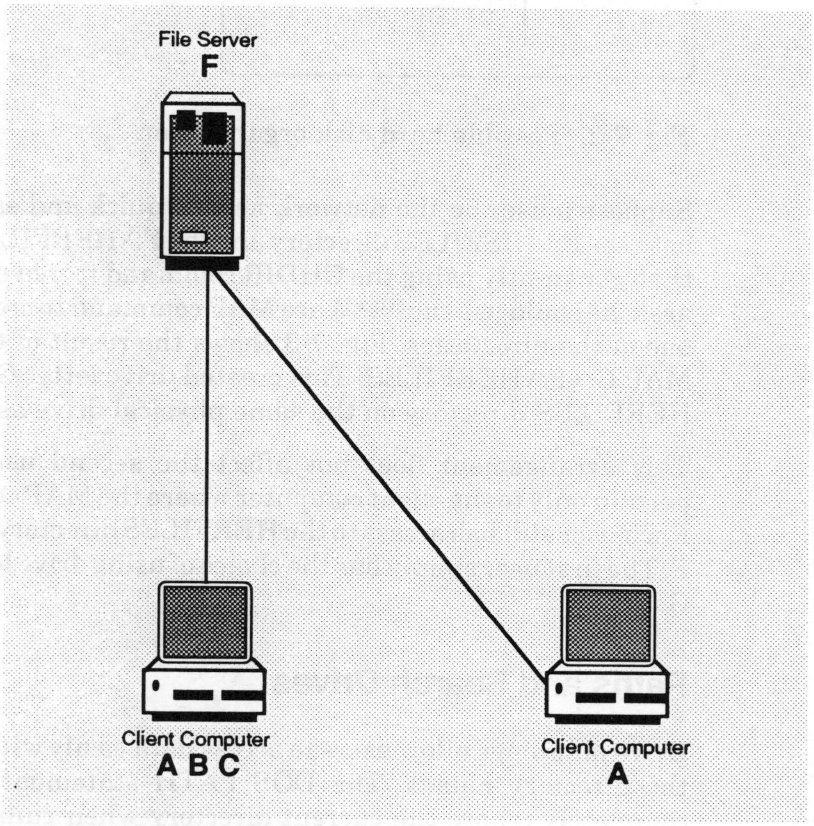

Fig. 7-1. Client computers network to a server

The same commands can be used on the network drive F. In Fig. 7-1 the first computer could create a directory called F:\HISFILES by using the MKDIR command. MKDIR stands for make directory and can be abbreviated further by using only MD. By typing the command MD F:\HISFILES, the first user can create a place to store files on the file server. The user at the second computer could type MD F:\HERFILES. Now, if either computer user typed DIR F:, both directory names would be listed.

Drive Mappings

With directories containing directories and every user on the network creating directories, the directory structure can become quite complex.

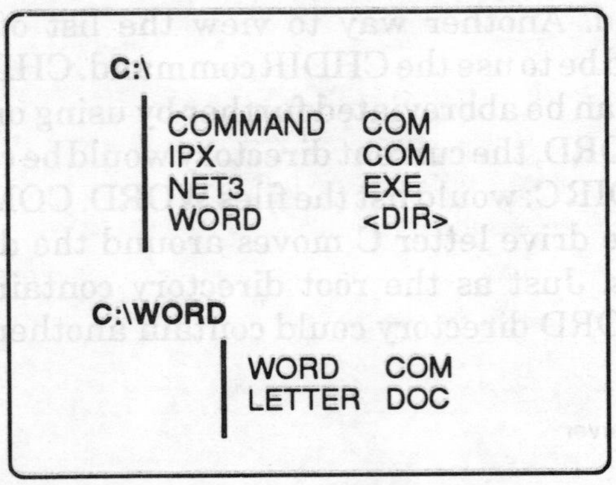

Fig. 7-2. Possible hard disk organization

Suppose a user on the network needed quick and easy access to files in both the F:\HISFILES directory and the F:\HERFILES directory. Rather than constantly using the CHDIR command to move drive F to the other area, he could use the NetWare MAP command to create a drive letter for one of the directories. Fig. 7-3 shows the result of the first user typing MAP G:=F:\HERFILES. This created drive letter G which points to the HERFILES directory on the same physical drive as F:\HISFILES.

This arrangement does not affect the second user. Drive mappings pertain only to the client computer where the MAP command was issued. Each user still has access to the HERFILES directory through drive letter F. The first user simply has the choice of using drive letter F or drive letter G.

Paths and Search Drives

Drive mappings allow users to access data easily without worrying about the directory names. The DOS PATH statement allows the user to completely ignore the current directory when running programs. NetWare combines these functions in the search drive. Ordinarily, to execute a program, it must reside in the current directory or the full path must be used when referring to the program. The "path" is the complete directory name where the program resides. Referring to Fig. 7-3, the first user may have a program in the HISFILES directory called WORD.COM. If the current directory is F:\HERFILES, he would have to type F:\HISFILES\WORD to execute the WORD program. DOS provides a means to shorten this in the PATH command. The PATH command tells the computer where to look for a program if it can't be found in the current directory. If the first user types PATH F:\HISFILES he can use all the programs in the HISFILES directory without typing the entire path. He could simply type WORD and the computer would look in the current directory first, then look in the HISFILES directory and find, and then execute, the program. Multiple directories can be included in the PATH command to instruct the computer to search several areas for the program. The command PATH F:\HERFILES;F:\HISFILES would tell the computer to search the current directory first (as it always does), then the F:\HERFILES directory, and lastly the F:\HISFILES directory. A NetWare search drive is a drive mapping that is automatically inserted in the PATH.

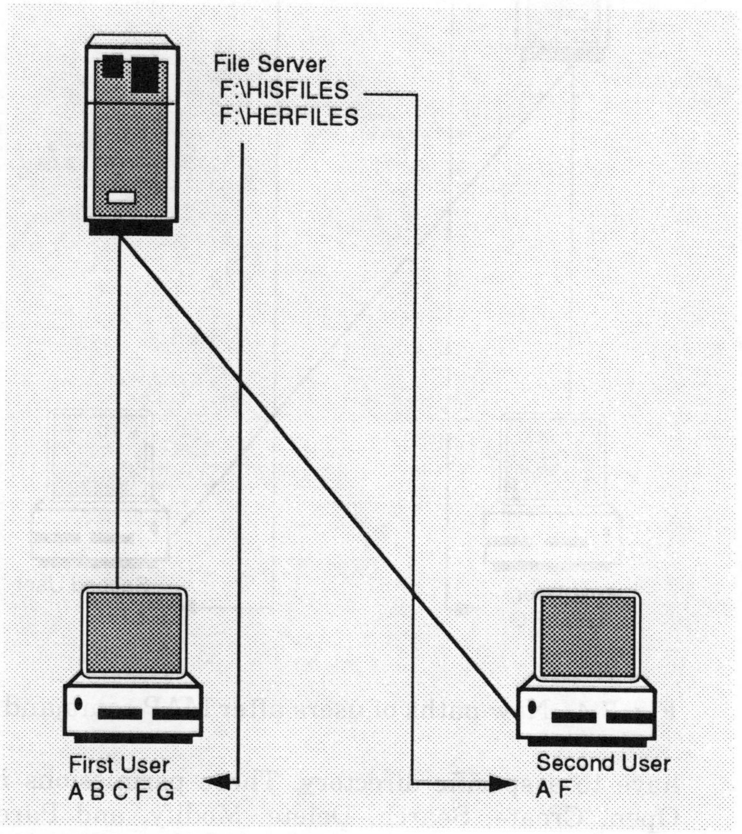

Fig. 7-3. Paths for different network users

In Fig. 7-4, the second user has typed the command MAP S1:=F:\HISFILES. This NetWare command automatically chooses a drive letter starting from the end of the alphabet and maps it to the directory indicated. But the drive letter is more than the pointer used in the other drive letters, it is also a PATH to the directory. The second user can use drive letter Z as she would any other drive letter, but if she is using drive A, for instance, she needs only to type WORD to run the program contained in the F:\HISFILES directory.

Trustee Rights

NetWare allows users to share data or to restrict access to data. Trustee rights allow access to specific directories on the file server. Without trustee rights to a certain directory, a user cannot access the data in that directory. Trustee rights are composed of several permissions a user may

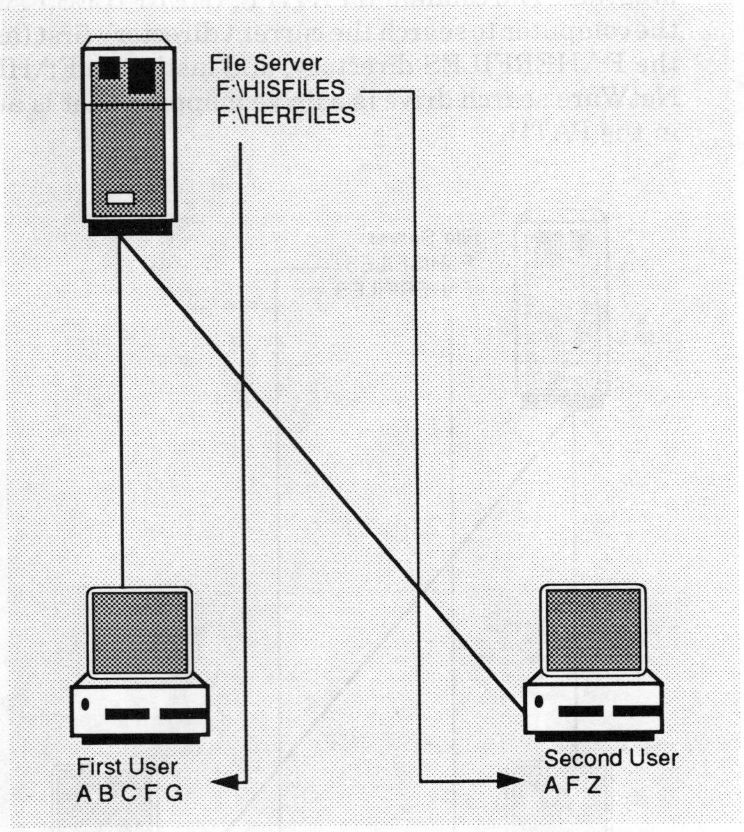

Fig. 7-4. New paths of users after MAP command

have to a specific directory. These permissions include Read, Write, Open, Create, Search, Delete, Modify, and Parental. Each of these permissions may be granted or denied to a user. The meanings of these permissions or rights are listed:

Read. The user can read from open files in the directory.

Write. The user can write to open files in the directory.

Open. The user can open files in the directory.

Create. The user can create files in the directory.

Search. The user can search for files in the directory. This means he or she can also see the files in a directory list.

Delete. The user can delete the files in the directory.

Modify. The user can modify the Attribute of the file. The Attribute of a file indicates what access anyone has to the file.

Parental. The user can grant the rights he or she has to a directory to other users.

Fig. 7-5 shows the trustee rights each of the users has to the file server using the first letter of the above listed rights. The first user has all rights except Parental to the F:\HISFILES directory. He can use all of the files there any way he wants, but he cannot grant those rights to any other users. He only has Read, Open, and Search rights in the F:\HERFILES directory. This means he can only read from the data there, not change it or add to it. The second user has all rights to the F:\HERFILES directory. She could even grant additional rights in that directory to the first user. Her access to the F:\HISFILES directory is restricted to Write, Open, Create, and Search. This allows her to create new files in the directory but not to read or change the files already there.

Fig. 7-5. Trustee rights for users

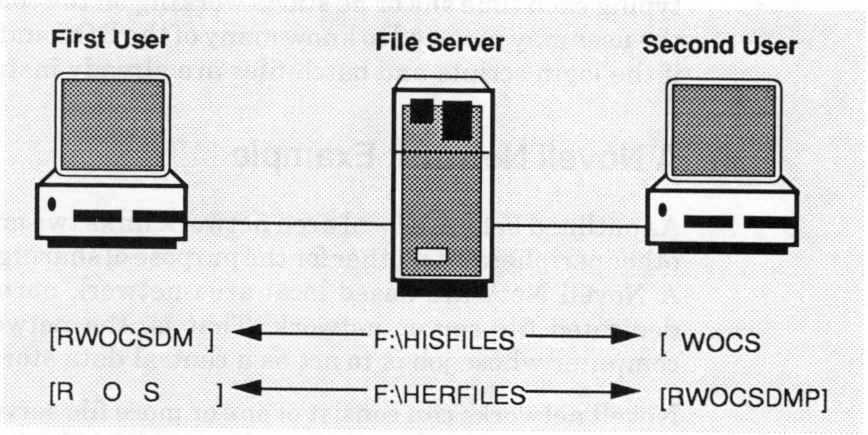

Batch Files and Login Scripts

Many of the commands described above could become quite tedious if you had to type them every time you used the computer. This is why DOS provides a means for storing these commands in a file known as a batch file. A batch file is a list of commands that can be executed by entering the file name.

For instance, if a user needed to execute the commands listed in Fig. 7-6, those commands could be stored in a file called START.BAT. The ".BAT" portion of the name is called the extension and, in this case, indicates that the file is a batch file. With this file in the current directory the user only needs to type Start. The computer will read the file and execute the commands listed in it.

```
MAP G= F\HERFILES
CHDIR F:\HISFILES
PATH G:
WORD
```

Fig. 7-6. Commands for the batch file START.BAT

NetWare provides a similar function in the form of login scripts. Login scripts are lists of commands that are executed when a user logs into NetWare. Logging in identifies the user to the network so trustee rights can be established. A user might type LOGIN USER1, then a password. NetWare would verify the password is correct, establish the trustee rights for the user, then execute the login script for that user. Each user may have a different login script and the login script may execute batch files.

Together, batch files and login scripts free the user from a great deal of typing each time she or he starts working on the computer. Additionally, the user may not need to know many of the DOS and NetWare commands if the login scripts and batch files are already installed.

A Novell Network Example

As outlined before, a local area network links two or more computers and other peripherals together for the purpose of sharing data and equipment. A Novell NetWare based local area network normally is considered a dedicated file server network. That is, the network has at least one computer whose job is to act as a central data storage system.

Novell networks can consist of one or more file servers, each with dozens of workstations, multiple shared printers, and other devices that can be attached to the file server or workstations.

A small office network or a teaching laboratory can be established easily by creating one for the first time or by using existing networks. The basic components are as follows:

1. A file server (IBM AT or higher model or IBM-compatible computer) with at least 2 megabytes of RAM and a hard disk (preferably with a minimum of 80 megabytes of storage).
2. Network interface cards (NICs) for the server and the workstations.
3. Transmission media (twisted pair, coaxial, or other type according to the type of NICs used).
4. Novell NetWare 2.2 or higher.
5. A printer should also be added to the network (preferably more than one).

If a Novell NetWare based network is not already available, the process to install one consists of the steps outlined in chapter 6. (The list below provides a general review of the process.)

1. Find a location for the server.
2. Find a location for the workstations.
3. Configure each NIC to contain a unique network address.
4. Install the NIC in each of the workstations and servers that will make up the nodes of the network.

5. Connect each node with the medium chosen.
6. Write down all the hardware that makes up the network.
7. Install the NetWare network operating system and use the data from item 6 to answer NetWare's requests.

Fig. 7-7 displays a possible configuration for such a laboratory or work environment. If the network is used to provide instructions on the use of commands and network management, a program called LANSKOOL from Lan Fan Technologies, Inc. may be a good addition to the system. This program allows the instructor to project his or her workstation screen on the screen of other users for the purpose of answering questions or for instructional needs.

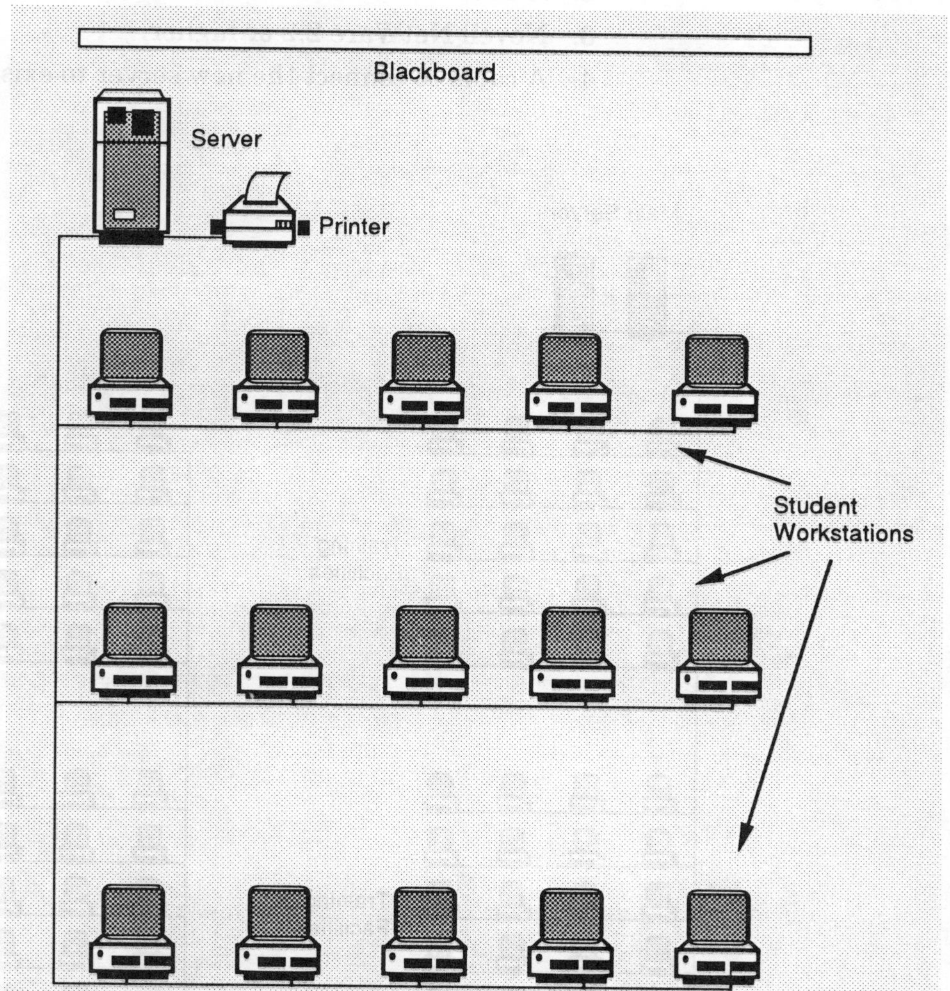

Fig. 7-7. Possible network configuration for training users

The other scenario consists of a Novell network that already exists. It is expensive to purchase additional workstations, materials, and space if all that is required is a laboratory or room for providing training to users. If a current network is in place with user's workstations available, all that is needed is an additional server that can function as a training server for the users. This server can be connected to the existing wiring and, after NetWare is installed in it, training can be conducted using existing workstations. Fig. 7-8 shows this scenario. The equipment required for this situation is as follows:

1. A file server (IBM AT or higher model or IBM-compatible computer) with at least 2 megabytes of RAM and a hard disk (preferably with a minimum of 80 megabytes of storage).
2. A network interface card (NIC) for the server.
3. Novell NetWare 2.2 or higher.
4. A cable to connect the new server to existing wire.

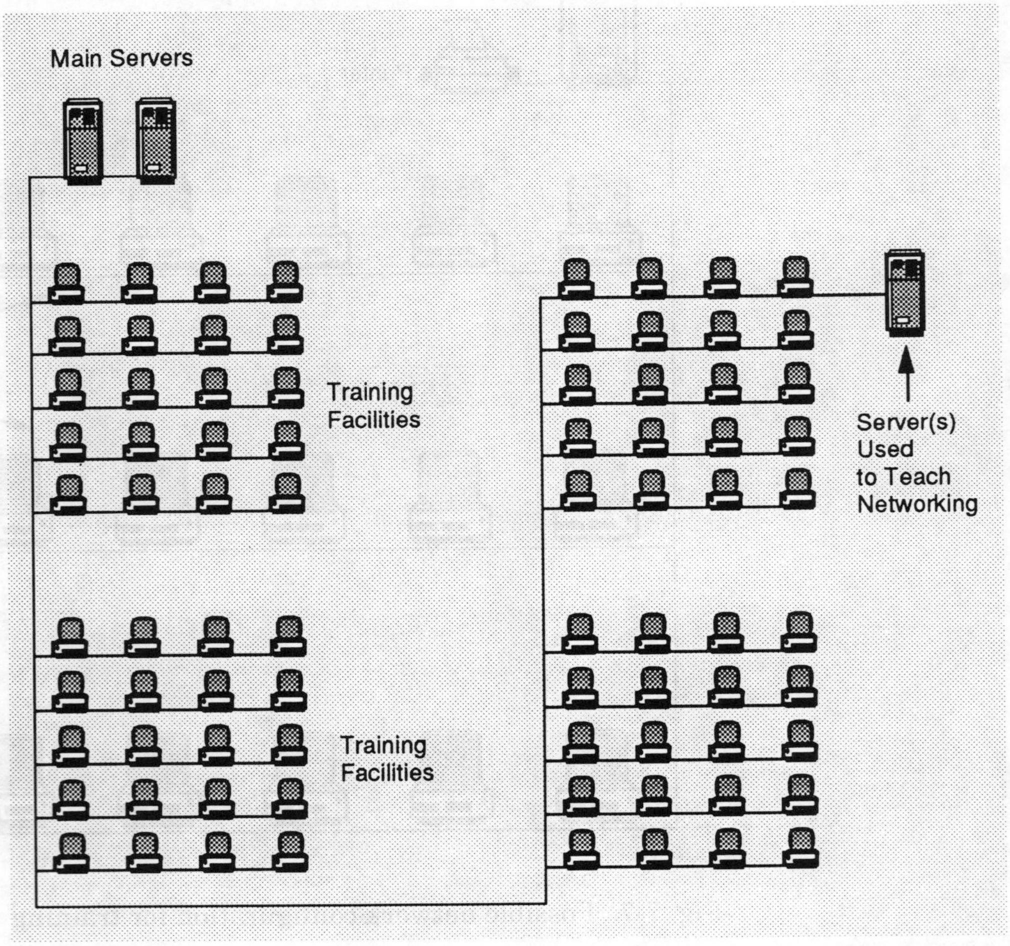

Fig. 7-8. Additional configuration for setting up a network to train users

The process to install the server is as follows:

1. Find a location for the server. If it is going to be used for training, then probably the classroom is a good place. After a training session is over the keyboard should be locked for additional protection.
2. Install the NIC in the server and, if required, provide a unique address.
3. Connect the server to existing network transmission media.
4. Install NetWare in the server and provide a unique server name.

The process to install NetWare is provided in the next chapter in this book. After the server goes on line, users that need training will simply attach their workstation to the server. Any commands issued, and any modifications to the environment stay in the training server without affecting the rest of the users and file servers. The server can be configured so that users can attached themselves to other servers.

Summary

NetWare provides access to a file server by many client computers through the hardware and software on each computer. The hardware consists of a network interface card or NIC. Under DOS, the NIC is controlled by a program called IPX. Another program, NET#, provides the interface to DOS. With the NIC, IPX and NET# in place, the file server appears to the client computer as a disk drive attached to the client computer. DOS commands can be used to create and access directories on the file server.

IPX and NET# make up the NetWare shell that serves as the interface between the computer operating system and the network operating system. The NetWare shell allows DOS and the user to treat file servers as a disk drive attached to the client computer. This protects the user from having to learn new commands and makes using the network a natural extension of the user's workstation.

With the use of batch files, login scripts, drive mappings, paths, and search drives, users of the network can customize their environments without affecting other network users. In this manner, users can modify their own network operating environments to increase their efficiency. In addition, security of the network and user files are enhanced by the use of passwords and trustee rights. Trustee rights determine the type of access privileges that each user posseses.

Questions

1. What does DOS stand for?
2. What are the three components needed for attaching a computer to a Novell network?
3. Under DOS, files may be stored in different areas on the same disk. What are these areas called?
4. What does CHDIR stand for?
5. What NetWare command changes the assignment of drive letters?
6. What does the PATH command tell the computer?
7. A user on a Novell network must have a set of permissions to use a directory on the file server. What are these permissions called?
8. If a user has Read, Open, and Search rights in a directory, can she store data there? Why or why not?
9. DOS allows a list of commands to be entered in a file. What is this type of file called?
10. A user only executes his login script once in a session. When?

Project

Objective

Before NetWare can be installed on a system, a listing of hardware, users, and other resources must be recorded. Also, all steps taken during the installation process must to be recorded in case something goes wrong and an audit needs to occur.

Additionally, knowing the applications, directories, users, and workstations on the network will help in maintaining the network, and in performing future upgrades or expansions that may be required.

Creating a Novell NetWare Log Book

A typical log book contains the information outlined below. One should be created for each server.

Name of the server.

Type of hardware.

Date of installation.

Name of installer.

Operating system:

Name and version of the operating system in use.

Installation date of the operating system.

Name of the operating system installer.

Server:

Purchase date of the server.

Server's network address.

Location of the server.

Volume:

Volume(s) name(s) in the server.

Volume disk number.

Volume(s) size(s).

Users' workstations:

Users' names.

Users' locations.

Users' network addresses.

Users' workstation types.

Users' workstation RAM.

Users' workstation disk options.

Users' workstation graphics boards and monitors.

Users' workstation hardware options (other).

Applications:

Name of the applications in use.

Application's vendor.

Application's purchase date.

Application's version number.

Application's memory requirements.

Application's disk space requirements.

Additional log information.

Using the above as a guideline and a word processor, create a NetWare log book and fill in the information requested for the network that you will be installing during the hands-on portion of this class. Make sure that all information is correct because once the network is set up, it is difficult and time consuming to correct major errors or omissions in the setup process.

8

NetWare Installation

Objectives

1. Understand the NetWare menu system.
2. Understand the shell generation process.
3. Be able to create a valid NetWare shell using SHGEN.
4. Understand the network generation process.
5. Be able to configure NetWare.
6. Be able to install NetWare.

Key Terms

Hard Disk
Hard Disk Controller
File Server
Network Card
NetWare Shell
RAM
SHGEN
Tape Backup
Workstation

Introduction

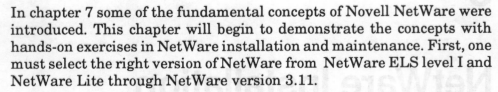

In chapter 7 some of the fundamental concepts of Novell NetWare were introduced. This chapter will begin to demonstrate the concepts with hands-on exercises in NetWare installation and maintenance. First, one must select the right version of NetWare from NetWare ELS level I and NetWare Lite through NetWare version 3.11.

The version number 3.11 represents more than just improvements on the original. NetWare versions through 2.2 are designed to operate on an IBM compatible with an 80286 or faster central processing unit (CPU). The 80286 CPU is the microprocessor chip that controls the operation of the computer. Beginning with version 3, NetWare has required a more powerful CPU. NetWare version 3 was originally called NetWare 386 because it required a machine based on the Intel 80386 CPU. When Novell made NetWare available for computers other than IBM compatibles, they changed the name to NetWare version 3. Even though each version must be written for each type of computer it is to be run on, Novell wanted to show that the network operating system was not limited to an 80386 processor. Many versions are now available from Novell which cover a variety of hardware platforms and user needs.

One significantly different version is the System Fault Tolerant version or SFT version. It includes features to ensure data integrity that previous versions did not have. The three most important features are Disk Mirroring, Disk Duplexing, and Transaction Tracking.

Disk Mirroring uses two hard disks attached to the same hard disk controller. All the data is written to both hard disks in exactly the same way. If one of the hard disks should fail, the other contains all the data.

Another method for ensuring the hard disk data remains intact is called Disk Duplexing. It uses two controller cards and two hard disks. Again the data is duplicated on the second hard disk, but it is sent to it separately so failures in the controller card will not damage the data on both hard drives.

Transaction Tracking helps ensure data accuracy by keeping an ongoing record of past changes to the data on the disk. If a user is in the process of making several changes to a database when, for instance, there is a power failure, the changes can be "rewound" so they can be verified.

For IBM-compatible computers, the least expensive and least functional system is NetWare Lite. It is intended for very small networks with limited ability. The most expensive and most functional version is NetWare Version 3.11. It provides a wide range of functions including connectivity to other types of networks. It is also available in versions that provide the same functions with a smaller number of workstations attached. At the writing of this book, Novell had condensed its offerings by selling NetWare versions 2.15, 2.2, and 3.11, and NetWare Lite only.

Because of its availability in existing classrooms and its intermediate level of functionality, and the fact that almost 70 percent of all Novell networks in the work market use V2.15, Novell Advanced NetWare 2.15 will be the model that the remainder of this text will focus on. However, since there are only a few minor differences between V2.15 and 2.2, all commands and exercises in this book will work with either version of NetWare. Whenever a difference exists, an effort is made to inform the reader of it. Also, with the exception of the installation procedure, which is simpler in V3.11, all commands and exercises in this book will also work with NetWare 3.11.

Installing NetWare

Novell has worked very hard to provide the installer with a menu-driven interface that allows easy selection of important options or a relatively simple "default" installation in which the NetWare installation program determines how NetWare should be installed. Both methods require the installer to have some information and experience.

The installer must have a complete list of the hardware on the file server, including information on the type of hard disk and the type of network card to be used. NetWare's control of the file server depends on its being able to communicate with each peripheral device accurately.

Communication with most devices depends on three pieces of information, the ROM address, the RAM address, and the interrupt number. The computer's memory is arranged so it can be accessed through use of an address. The memory consists of two types, RAM, random access memory, and ROM, read only memory. Random access means the computer can choose any address and read or write to that area of memory without sequentially reading all the memory before it. Read only memory can also be accessed randomly but the computer can only read from it. Many peripheral devices have RAM or ROM on them that is added to the computer's existing memory. The addresses where the memory is added must be known by NetWare, and therefore the installer.

The CPU spends most of its time reading from memory and executing the instructions it finds there. Some devices, however, must interrupt this process so the CPU can perform some special, critical task. A network interface card, for example, must interrupt the CPU so incoming data can be dealt with. Each device needing access is assigned an Interrupt Request Line number. The number and the RAM and ROM addresses are often selectable on the device so the person installing the equipment can make sure that each device does not use another's address or interrupt number. The Interrupt Request Line number used in each peripheral must also be recorded for use during installation.

Often the equipment on the file server will require special drivers supplied by the manufacturer. A driver is a program written to control a specific peripheral such as a tape drive. Novell may not have supplied the driver for a particular unit. If it is intended to be used with NetWare, the manufacturer of the tape drive must supply the driver on diskettes. These drivers must be available at the time of installation. Similar information for each type of workstation on the network will also be needed. The following are items that the network administrator needs to be concerned with before installing NetWare. Use the list below to collect and record this information.

For the file server the information required is as follows.

1. **File server**. The make and model type of the computer that will be used as a file server.
2. **Hard disk type.** Manufacturers and model numbers of all hard disks attached to the file server.
3. **Hard disk controller type.** Manufacturers and model numbers of the controller cards used with the hard disks, including RAM and ROM addresses and Interrupt Request Lines used.
4. **Network card type.** Manufacturers and model numbers of the network interface cards used, including RAM and ROM addresses and Interrupt Request Lines used.
5. **Tape backup type.** Manufacturers and model numbers of the tape drive units installed, including RAM and ROM addresses and Interrupt Request Lines used.
6. **Types of printers attached to file server.** Manufacturers and model numbers of the printers that will be attached to the file server and the ports, LPT or COM, that will be used with each.

For the workstation the information required is as follows:

1. **Workstation manufacturer and model**. The make and model type of the computer that will be used as a workstation.
2. **Random access memory (RAM).** Amount of conventional memory. Conventional memory is the memory below 640K. The installer also needs to know the amount of extended or expanded memory. Extended memory and expanded memory are different conventions for using memory above 640K. If the workstation has 1 megabyte of RAM the memory between 640K and 1 megabyte is extended memory and not normally addressable by DOS. Some programs, including NetWare, can use this memory. If the workstation has more than 1 megabyte of RAM it might be extended or expanded. The expanded memory conventions allow programs to switch blocks of data back and forth between the expanded memory region and the conventional memory region below 640K.

3. **DOS version.** The DOS versions used on all workstations to be attached to the network.
4. **IBM or compatible.** Some of the installable options in NetWare are specific to IBM computers.

The installer should be familiar with DOS. Much of the setup after installation of the file server requires a complete understanding of DOS directories, commands, and batch files.

Installation Preparation

Before installing any program, including a network operating system, backup copies of the distribution diskettes should be made. NetWare is not copy protected, so DOS commands can be used to make copies.

To make the copies, have the number of original disks plus two or three extras. They must be the same type of disks as the NetWare distribution disks. NetWare is shipped on either 3 1/2 or 5 1/4 inch disks, each size being either high density or low density. The extra disks may be needed if some of the new disks do not format correctly.

Attach the label stickers to the blank disks if needed, and set the write protect tabs on the original disks. When a disk is write protected the computer cannot write to or change any information on the disk. On 3 1/2 inch disks the write protect tab is the small sliding tab on the corner of the disk. It should be set in the open position so the hole goes through the disk. On a 5 1/4 inch disk, the write protect tab is a small sticker that covers the hole in the side of the disk; the disk is protected when the tab is on. The procedures to make the backup copies is the same as for ordinary DOS files. Step by step instructions are provided in the hands-on section of this chapter.

NetWare Menus

All NetWare menu utilities are designed around a few relatively simple rules of operation. Understanding how these menus work is essential since many of them change as you use them. In some utilities, completing an option makes another option available. Also, the menus may include different items depending on how the utility was started.

Fig. 8-1 shows an example of the opening menu of the NetWare Shell Generation utility or SHGEN. Along the top is a box that indicates the name and version of the utility and may also display the date and time. No information in this box can be changed by the user.

Near the bottom of the screen is an instructional box that indicates the next action the user can take. It is usually highlighted in an outstanding color and may appear and disappear as needed. Notice that some boxes are drawn with a single line while others are drawn using double lines. Any single-line box in a NetWare menu utility contains information that the user cannot change. The box on the left side of the screen shows this utility main menu. It consists of a bright double line with various options inside. To select an item, use the arrow keys to move the highlighted bar to the option desired, then press the ENTER key.

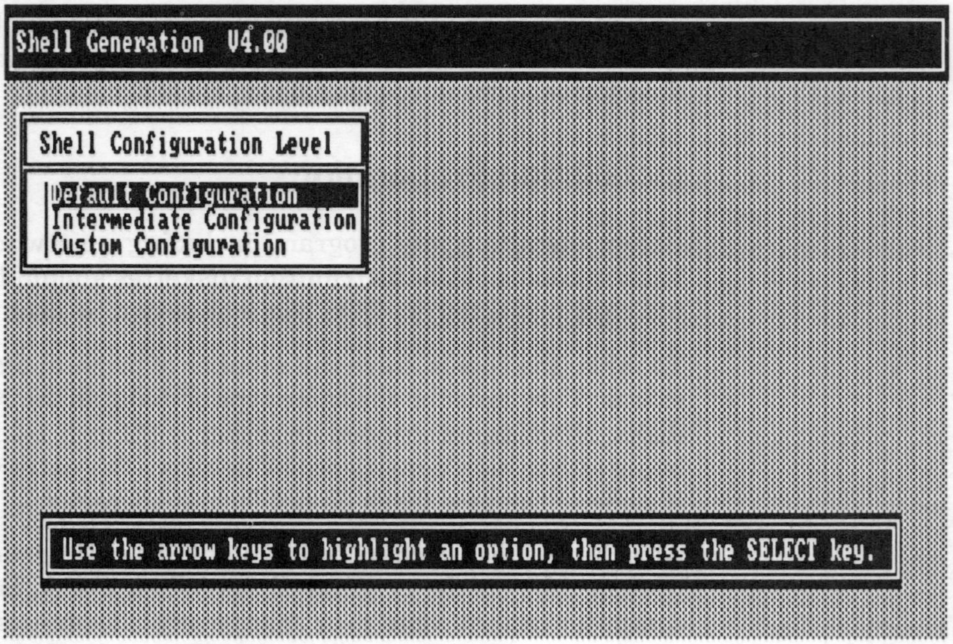

Fig. 8-1. Screen displaying the Shell Generation utility

If there are more items than can fit in the box, a small arrow pointing down will appear in the lower left of the box. Notice the instructional box at the bottom of the screen refers to the SELECT key. Another method for selecting options from a list is to begin typing the name of the option. The highlighted bar will move to the appropriate option as you type.

The NetWare menus often use Novell's names for the keys rather than the commonly accepted name for the key. For example, the SELECT key is the ENTER key on the keyboard. The following list shows the Novell names for certain keys and their functions.

1. **Select.** The ENTER or RETURN key. The SELECT key is used to choose an item from a list.
2. **Help.** The F1 key. This key will provide information on the options currently available to the user. Pressing F1 twice shows the uses of all the function keys.
3. **Modify.** The F3 key. Some highlighted options can be changed by pressing the F3 key. If an option can be changed this way, a new box will appear for the user to put the new information in.
4. **Mark.** The F5 key. Some menu commands can be executed on multiple items. The F5 key marks the items in a list so the next command will affect them all.

5. **Accept.** The ESCAPE key. This is the most unusual feature of the NetWare menus, because it seems backwards from computer conventions. After making selections in a menu, the user presses the ESCAPE key to return to the previous menu. Rather than discarding the changes the user made, this choice accepts and saves them.
6. **Cancel.** The F7 key. This key returns to the previous menu without saving the options selected.
7. **Insert.** The INSERT key. This key is used to insert a new item in a list. If it is allowed at that point in the menu, the user will be prompted for an item to place in the list.
8. **Delete.** The DELETE key. This key will delete an item from a list.
9. **Exit.** ALT/F10. This key combination exits the menu utility without saving any pending information and without prompting the user with "Are you sure?". (Often, however, changes are saved as they are made.)

Creating a NetWare Shell

The installation process begins with the generation of an appropriate NetWare shell. As discussed earlier the shell is the software interface to the rest of the network. NetWare builds the shell programs by combining the shell program code with the drivers for the particular network card being used. NetWare is shipped with drivers for many different brands of network cards, using standards such as Ethernet and Token-Ring. Drivers are also included for many nonstandard or proprietary cards such as StarLAN.

The shell programs are usually loaded onto a bootable disk to make access to the network as easy as possible. A bootable disk is a disk that the DOS system files have been previously loaded onto. The disk may also be known as a boot disk. To create a NetWare boot disk you will need the copies of the NetWare disks, a DOS disk, a blank disk, and any special driver disk that your network interface card may require. You will need a blank disk for each type of computer you intend to make a boot disk for.

The Shell Generation Program

The Shell Generation program, SHGEN, can be started with commands that tell it to operate differently than when started by typing SHGEN only. These commands are entered as command line arguments. When you type the name of the program, you include commands on the same line before you press enter. For instance, to begin the Shell Generation program to generate a new shell, you would type SHGEN -N. The "-" simply begins the list of arguments; the "N" indicates you wish to generate a new shell.

All of the commands except "N" are used to skip certain menus in the SHGEN program. The following list summarizes the options available. Only one "-" is needed to begin the list on the command line.

1. "N". Start a new shell generation session. The SHGEN program will not use any data already on the disk.
2. "D","I", or "C". Only one of these options may be used. They select between different levels of operation that can be used: "D" for Default, "I" for Intermediate, "C" for Custom.
3. "S". Standard floppy disk method.

A copy of the latest version of IPX.OBJ should be placed on the SHGEN-1 disk before beginning. The next step is to place a copy of the NetWare disk labeled SHGEN-1 in drive A:. If the computer has a diskette drive B:, then a copy of the AUXGEN disk is placed there. The next step is to invoke the Shell Generation utility by typing SHGEN -N at the DOS prompt. The main menu of the Shell Generation utility should appear as it does in Fig. 8-1. Many of the NetWare utilities have different levels of operation that can be used. The level of use will depend on your knowledge and experience, and on the level of detail that is needed to accomplish the task. The Shell Generation utility, as stated before, offers three levels of operation: Default, Intermediate and Custom.

The Default level can be used in most cases but may not give you the options you need. It allows you to select a driver from a list for the network interface card you are using. The list contains only those cards that Novell has supplied drivers for on the NetWare disks. The Intermediate level allows you to select drivers supplied by the network card manufacturer. The Custom level is intended for use by people who will be generating many different but similar shells. It allows the creation and editing of Resource Sets. Resource Sets are collections of options the installer can save and use later.

The next menu displayed is the SHGEN Run Options menu as shown in Fig. 8-2. This menu gives you the options of running the SHGEN program from floppy disks (Standard method), a hard disk, or a network drive. A network drive is the drive on the file server that is accessible on an existing network. The hard disk and network drive methods are most useful when you need to prepare many different network shells. In many cases, the appropriate NetWare disks may have been loaded already onto a hard disk or network drive.

The Standard method is the most often used. In this case, the computer provides the installer with prompts that indicate when to insert other disks as needed. If the NetWare disks have already been loaded onto the hard disk, then one of the other methods of installation must be used. But this is done only if preparations have been made by the instructor. Fig. 8-3 shows the available options for this level of configuration.

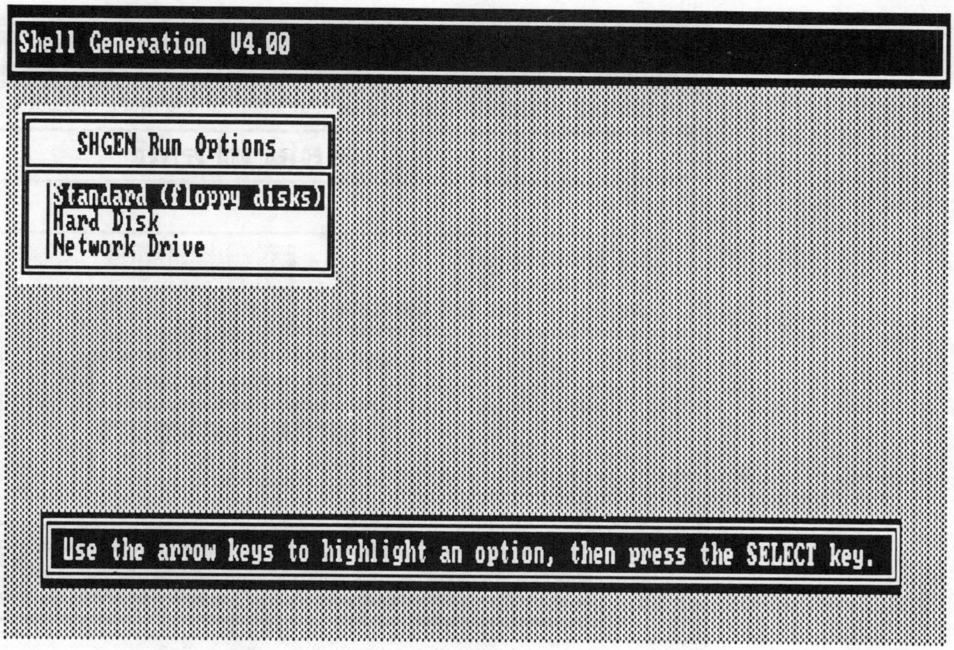

Fig. 8-2. The SHGEN Run Options screen

After the proper option is selected, the screen in Fig. 8-4 will appear. The Shell Generation program is allowing the installer to select among any LAN drivers prepared earlier with this program or LAN drivers on a separate disk. At this point, the installer needs to choose Load and Select Item. Then a prompt to enter the LAN drivers disk will appear.

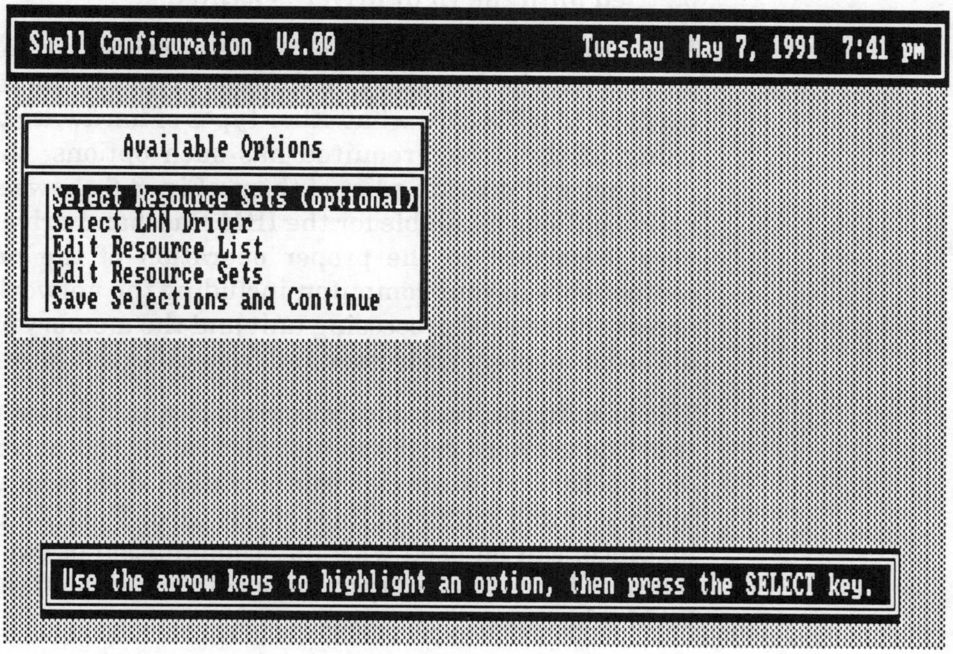

Fig. 8-3. Available options for the Standard method

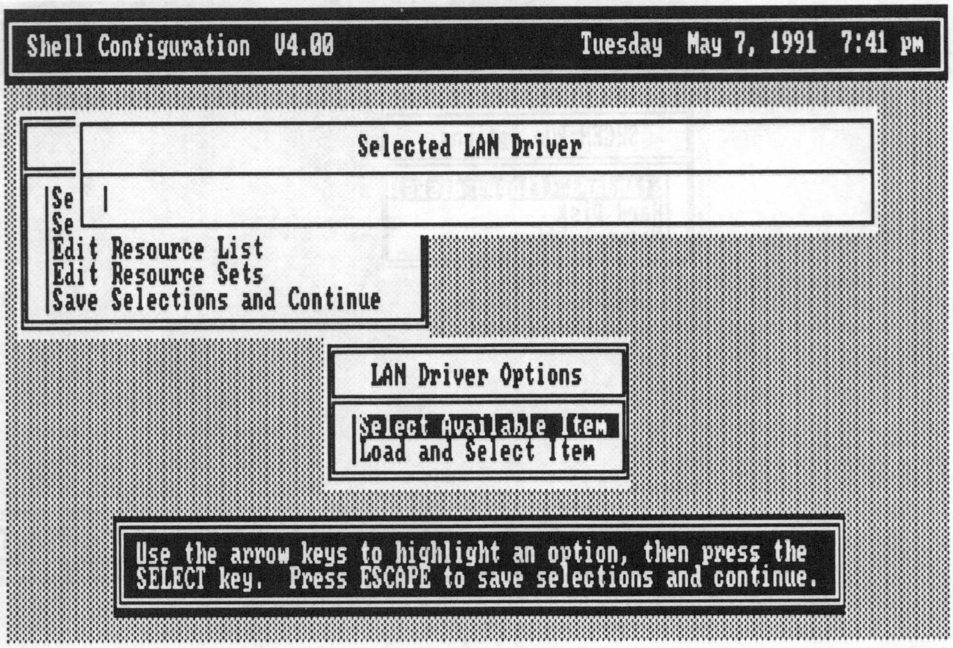

Fig. 8-4. Dialog box to select a LAN driver

If NetWare drivers were supplied with the network interface card, the disk is inserted now. If not, the NetWare disk labeled LAN_DRV_001 is inserted into the drive. Either way, a list of driver names will appear. The arrow keys are used to scroll through the list until the right type of network interface card is found. Different LAN_DRV disks may need to be tried until the right driver is located.

Many drivers may be configured with several different options. These options may be necessary for different types of the same manufacturer's cards or to tell a card what other types of hardware the computer will be using. If the driver required has such options, the Shell Generation program will provide a list of them. Fig. 8-5 shows some of the configuration options available for the IBM Baseband driver. These options are very important to the proper operation of the network card. Many components in your computer, including the network interface card, can access the central processing unit and the memory of the computer from different memory addresses and from different Interrupt Request Lines.

The specific address and Interrupt Request Lines were defined at the time the network card was installed in the computer. Switches were set on the card or a special configuration disk was used to set specific addresses and interrupt lines on the card. The IBM Baseband driver, for instance, can be used with any combination of two different Interrupt Request Lines (the IRQ numbers listed on the left) and several different RAM addresses.

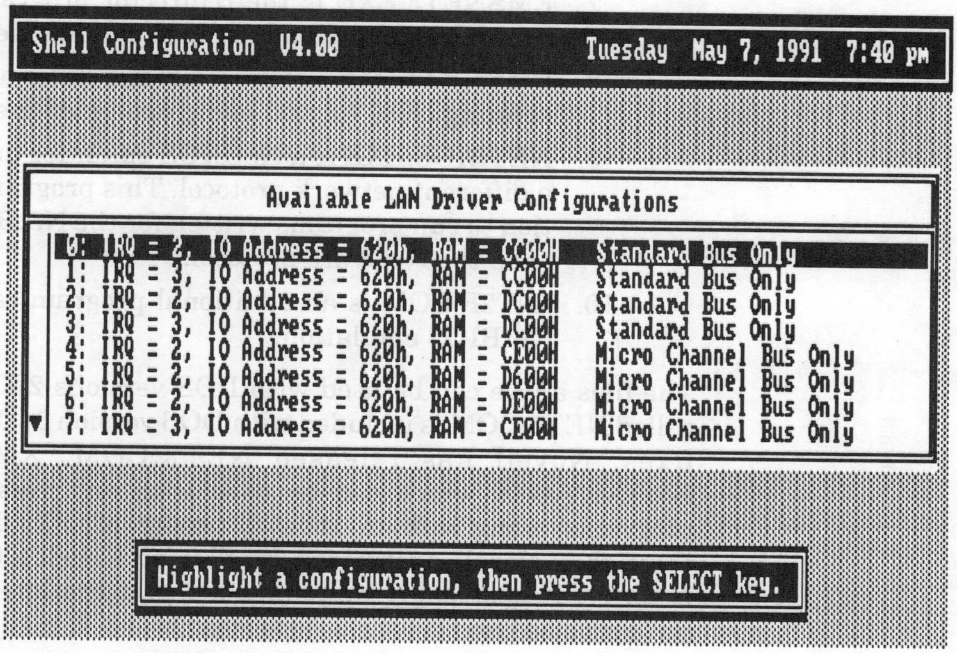

Fig. 8-5. Configuration options for the IBM Baseband driver

The option that is on the required network card must be selected. Refer to the checklist created earlier to determine the correct option. Also listed are options for either Standard Bus or Micro Channel Bus cards. After the appropriate option is selected the Shell Generation program will construct the network shell.

The shell, as stated earlier, consists of two parts, a program called IPX.COM and a program called NETX.COM. SHGEN is the only program needed to create IPX.COM, but other programs that may be needed later are also on the SHGEN-1 disk.

The program files available as shell components are as follows:

1. IPX.COM is the network card driver. This is the program that actually operates the network card and is the only one SHGEN creates.
2. NET4.COM is the redirector program for workstations running DOS 4.x. It is called the redirector because it redirects requests from the user to the network.
3. NET3.COM is the redirector program for workstations running DOS 3.x.
4. NET2.COM is the redirector program for workstations running DOS 2.x.
5. XMSNET3.EXE is the redirector program for workstations running DOS 3.x and using extended memory.
6. XMSNET4.EXE is the redirector program for workstations running DOS 4.x and using extended memory.

7. EMSNET3.EXE is the redirector program for workstations running DOS 3.x and using expanded memory.
8. EMSNET4.EXE is the redirector program for workstations running DOS 4.x and using expanded memory.
9. NETBIOS.EXE is a NetBIOS emulator program. NetBIOS is a different network protocol. This program allows a workstation to run programs written for the NetBIOS protocol rather than the NetWare protocol.
10. INT2F.COM is an additional program required when using NetBIOS emulation.

The files above can be used with DOS versions 2.X through 4.X. A file called NET5.COM is included with DOS version 5. Due to numerous bug fixes, Novell has released NETX.COM, XMSNET.EXE, and EMSNET.EXE which can be used with any version of DOS. These programs, along with an updated version of IPX.OBJ, can be obtained through a Novell authorized reseller or Novell's Compuserve forum, Netwire. It is strongly recommended that the latest versions of these programs be used.

The program will ask the installer if he or she wants to download the shell files to a floppy disk. If SHGEN is being executed from a hard disk or network drive, the answer is "yes." On-screen instructions will appear that will guide the installer on how to download the shell files to the boot disk created earlier.

If SHGEN is being executed from floppy disks, the SHGEN program needs to be exited. In this case the appropriate DOS commands must be used to copy the shell files from the SHGEN-1 disk to the boot disk created earlier. A copy of the IPX.COM file and the NETX file appropriate to the system being installed will be required. The hands-on sections of this book contains several scenarios that indicate the steps to be performed to complete this process.

Configuring NetWare

Before loading NetWare onto a file server it must be configured for the type of hardware on the file server. The hard disk, tape drive, type of network card and any other component needed by NetWare must be specified. This information is used by the Network Generation utility, NETGEN, to create the network operating system and utilities.

While running NETGEN many of the menus will include the option to Exit Netgen. In most cases the selections made up to that point are saved and the process can be stopped and resumed later. The necessary NetWare files will be created only when all the information has been entered. After creating the files, NETGEN will load them onto the file server. Some of the utilities needed to run NetWare do not need to be configured to the hardware involved. NETGEN will load these programs onto the file server as well, prompting you for the disks as needed.

NETGEN can be run in different ways just as SHGEN could, either from floppy disks, from a hard disk, from a network drive, or from a RAM disk. A RAM disk is a disk drive emulation program that allows files to be stored in memory as if they were on a disk drive. In order to accommodate all possible hardware configurations, this exercise will use the simplest method, which is running from floppy disks. During the configuration process, NETGEN will prompt you many times to insert a particular disk. The NETGEN program will store the selections made on the NetWare installation disks. After configuring the NetWare files, NETGEN must be run on the computer functioning as the file server. Until then, the program only needs a computer with at least 640K of RAM and one or two diskette drives of the same type as the NetWare installation diskettes. The computer must be booted from DOS, with a CONFIG.SYS file containing the following lines:

FILE=20

BUFFERS=15

With your computer booted and your copies of the NetWare installation disks available, you are ready to beginning the configuration process. Step by step instructions of this process are provided in the hands-on section of this chapter. After the NETGEN program is executed successfully, NetWare will be configured for the system it will be running on. The next step is to use NETGEN to prepare the server's disk.

The NETGEN program has the same command line options as the SHGEN program does, but the Intermediate level is not available in NETGEN. The options are as follows.

1. "N". Start a new network generation session. The NETGEN program will not use any data already on the disk.
2. "D" or "C". Only one of these options may be used. They select between different levels of operation that can be used: "D" for Default and "C" for Custom.
3. "S". Standard floppy disk method.

To run NETGEN, the command NETGEN -N is entered at the DOS prompt. This starts a new session and NETGEN's first menu should appear as shown in Fig. 8-6. If, during the course of this process, you need to exit NETGEN, restart it later without the "-N".

This menu offers the choice of using either the Default Configuration level or the Custom Configuration level. The primary advantage to using the Custom level is the ability to create Resource Sets. These are sets of features and equipment a file server might have. By creating Resource Sets that contain commonly used items, an installer can be prepared to

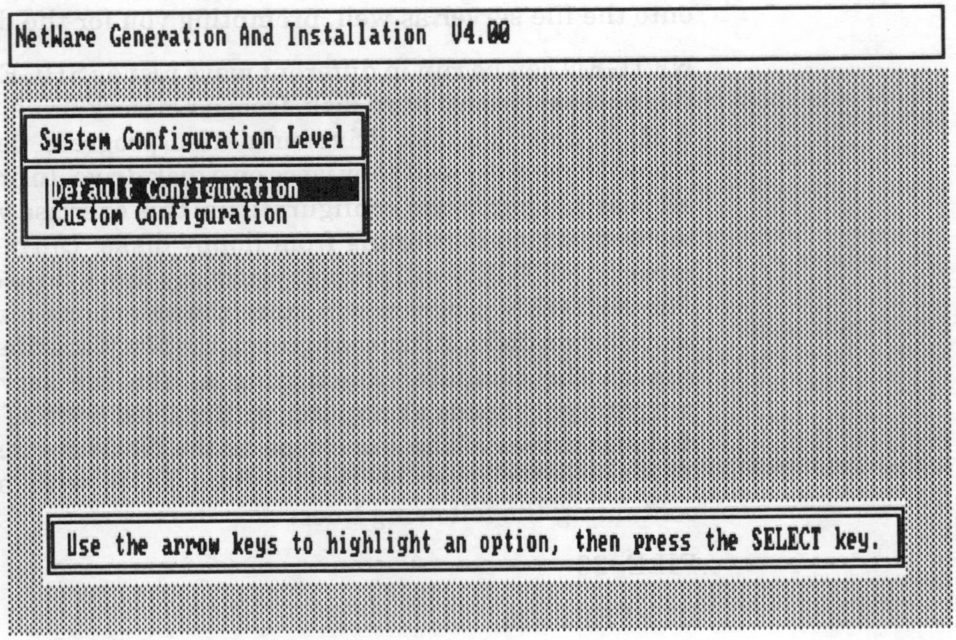

Fig. 8-6. NETGEN first menu

quickly choose the configurations for a variety of file servers. To install just one file server, the Default level is selected by highlighting Default Configuration.

The Run Options menu appears next. In this case the Standard method is typically selected, taking the installer to the next menu. The next menu, Network Generation Options, seems rather redundant, but will later have more selections to choose from. To proceed with a standard installation, the Select Network Configuration is highlighted.

When the menu titled Available Options appears, the Set Operating System options is normally selected. A screen similar to Fig. 8-7 will appear. The menu box on the left shows the key components for generating NetWare, and all of them will be selected in time. The menu box on the right shows the options available at this time, but the key words are Dedicated and Nondedicated.

A NetWare file server can be run in one of two basic modes. The Dedicated mode uses all the resources of the computer, so that computer cannot be used for any other purpose. It acts only as a file server, and the data on its hard disk can only be accessed through a workstation. It isn't running DOS, but only the network operating system, NetWare. The Nondedicated mode allows the file server to be used simultaneously as a workstation. A user could login and access the data on the server as if it were connected by a cable. The computer is still running NetWare but it has also loaded DOS. This mode gives you one more workstation, but puts the entire network at risk because the user could unintentionally cause the computer to lock up or "crash".

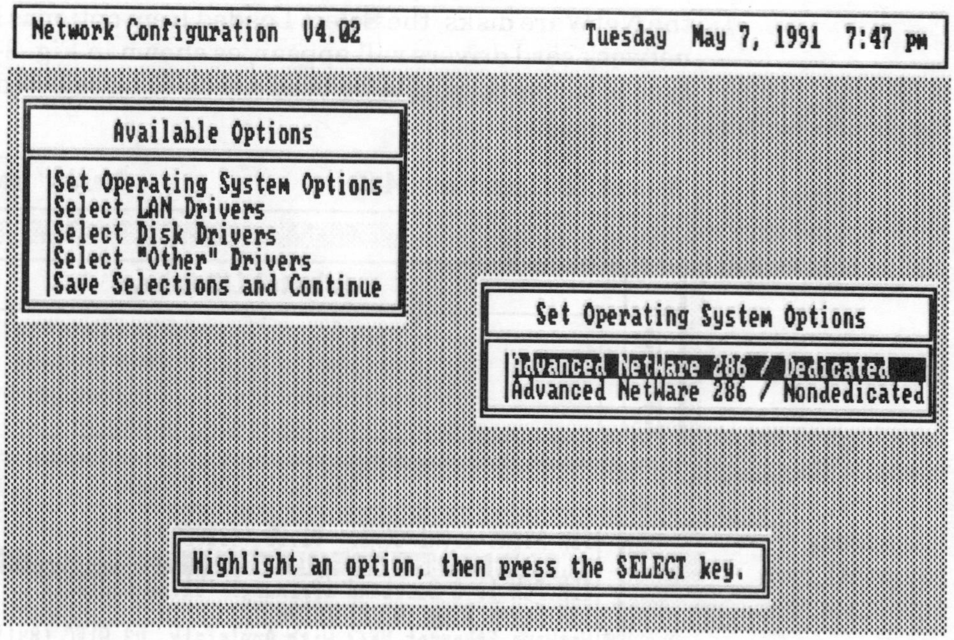

Fig. 8-7. Screen showing dialog box to set operating system options

A file server running Nondedicated mode also requires more memory. These restrictions make the Nondedicated mode useless in most situations. Because of this, the option NetWare/Dedicated mode is usually selected. The next item on the Available Options menu is Select LAN Drivers. After this item is highlighted, the screen shown in Fig. 8-8 will be displayed.

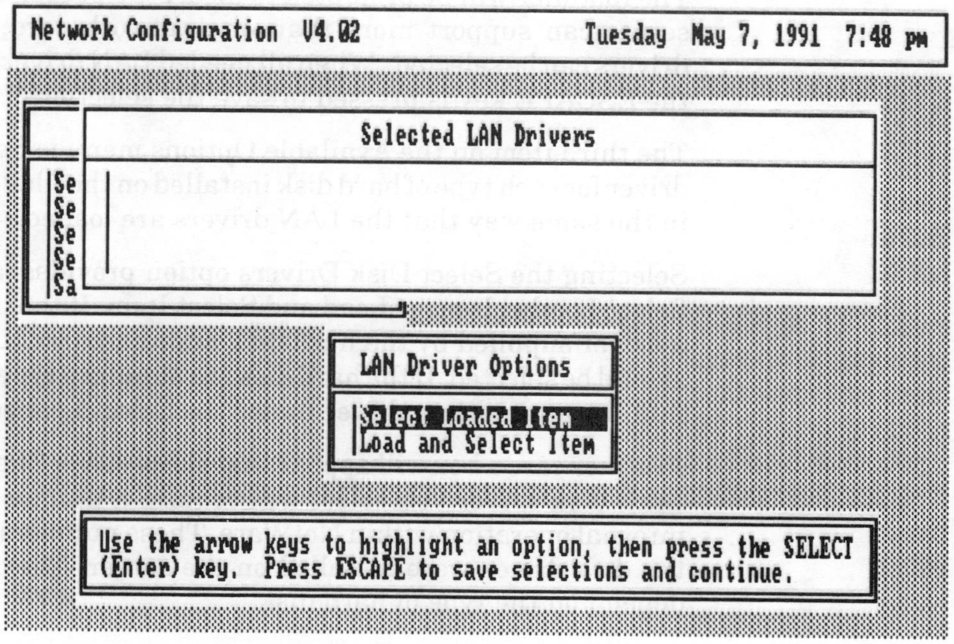

Fig. 8-8. Screen displaying LAN driver options

If the driver for the type of network card being installed was included on the NetWare disks, the Select Loaded Item option is highlighted. A list of network card drivers will appear, as shown in Fig. 8-9. At this point, the type of network card to be used needs to be selected from the menu.

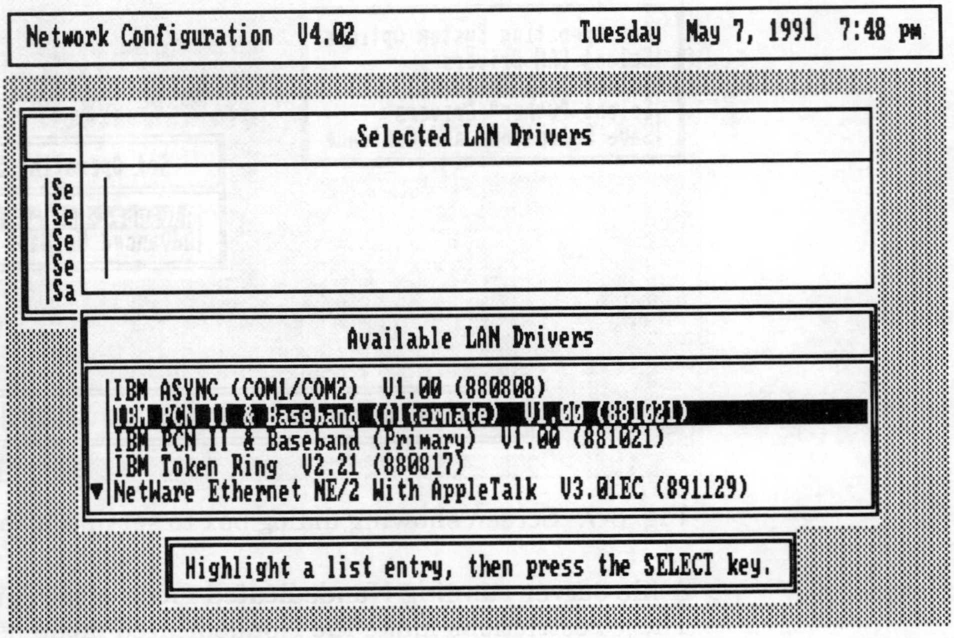

Fig. 8-9. Dialog box displaying network card drivers

If the driver for the right network card was supplied by the card manufacturer, the Load and Select Item option needs to be highlighted. The installer will be prompted to insert the proper disk. A NetWare file server can support more than one network card, so additional LAN drivers can be selected. When all needed LAN drivers have been selected, the ESCAPE key is pressed to save the selections.

The third item on the Available Options menu is Select Disk Drivers. A driver for each type of hard disk installed on the file server must be loaded in the same way that the LAN drivers are loaded.

Selecting the Select Disk Drivers option provides, again, the options of Select Loaded Item or Load and Select Item. If the installer needs to use a driver supplied by the hard disk manufacturer, Load and Select Item should be selected. If the hard disk is a standard type, the installer should find the appropriate driver under the Select Loaded Item option.

In either case a box will appear that simply says Channel: as in Fig. 8-10. Each disk driver you select will require a unique channel number for internal operation within NetWare. These numbers were assigned when the disk drives were installed on the server. They start with zero and depend on the type of hard disk.

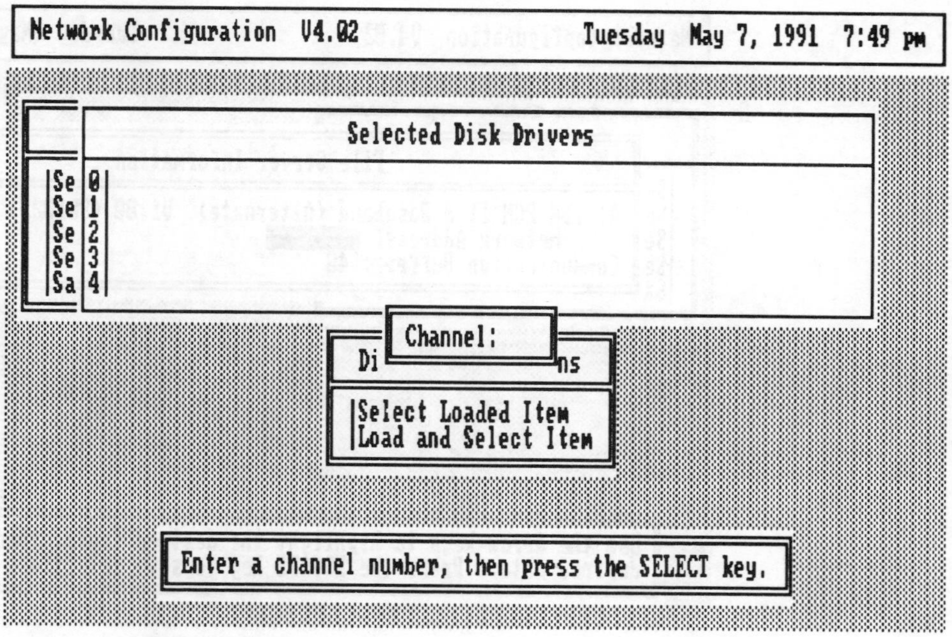

Fig. 8-10. Dialog box to select channel number for disk drivers

The next step in the installation is to enter the appropriate number. The number 0 is entered if there is only one hard disk in the server and the installer is not sure about the number. With more than one hard disk in the server, the installer will need to know the channel numbers and enter them at the appropriate time. When the installer is finished with the selections for disk drivers, the ESCAPE key needs to be pressed to save the selections and continue.

The fourth option on the Available Options menu is Select "Other" Drivers. Only select this item if there is some other device, such as a tape backup unit, attached to the file server.

After selecting the last option, Save Selections and Continue, the box shown in Fig. 8-11 will appear. These two fields, Network Address and Communication Buffers, must be filled in before installation can continue.

The network address is an eight-digit hexadecimal number that identifies the network associated with the network card shown. As a hexadecimal number the network address can be any combination of the digits 0 through 9 and the letters A through F and must include at least one nonzero digit. For instance, 012F4067, 01ABCDEF, and A10BEEF0 are all valid network addresses. You need only specify a number that is unique in that file server and any other network it may be bridged to in the future, so avoid obvious numbers such as 00000001.

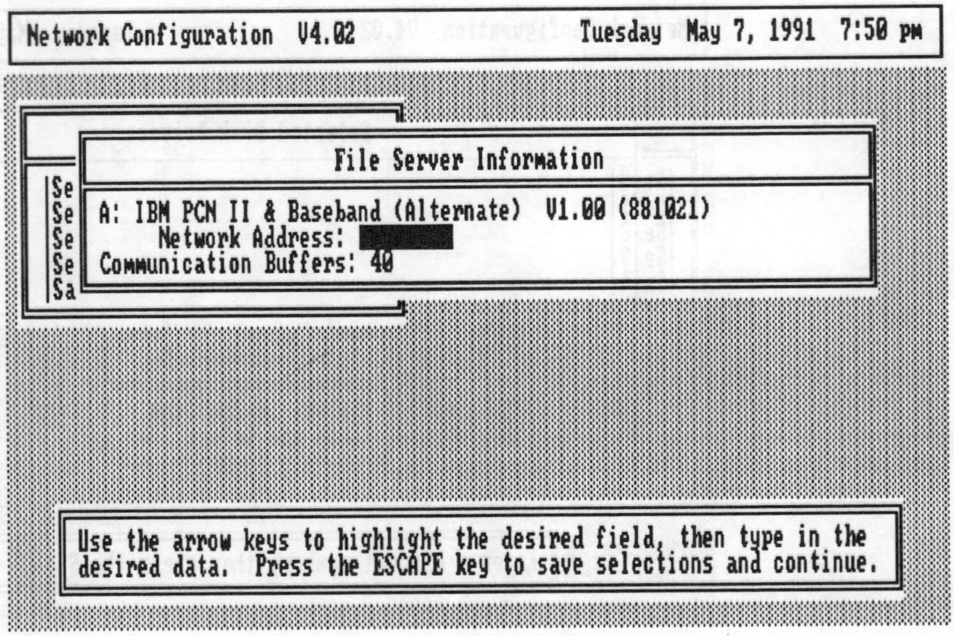

Fig. 8-11. Dialog box displaying file server information

If, however, one of the network cards is a part of an existing network, you must specify the same number as that network. Fig. 8-12 shows why it might be necessary to use the network number from another network. The network number actually specifies a network cabling system rather than a server. File server A is attached to network 00000001 and network 00000002. If the new file server B is to be attached to network 00000002, the network card in file server B must be given the number 00000002.

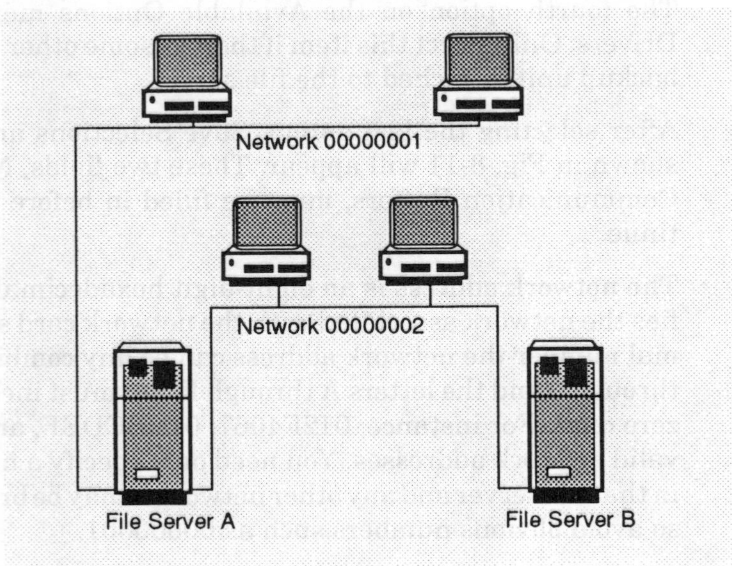

Fig. 8-12. Two networks showing their unique identification numbers

Now the installer must enter a network number appropriate for the network being installed in order to proceed. The other field in this box, Communication Buffers, cannot be given an arbitrary value. The number is used by NetWare to determine how much memory it needs to allocate for network communication packets. The number can be from 10 to 150 but the Novell recommendation is to add 40 to the expected number of workstations.

After entering a value for the communication buffers, a screen similar to the one in Fig. 8-13 will show what selections have been made. Pressing ESCAPE accepts these selections, and a box asking if the installer wishes to continue installation will appear. Answering yes provides another Default/Custom menu. In most situations, the Default Configuration is selected.

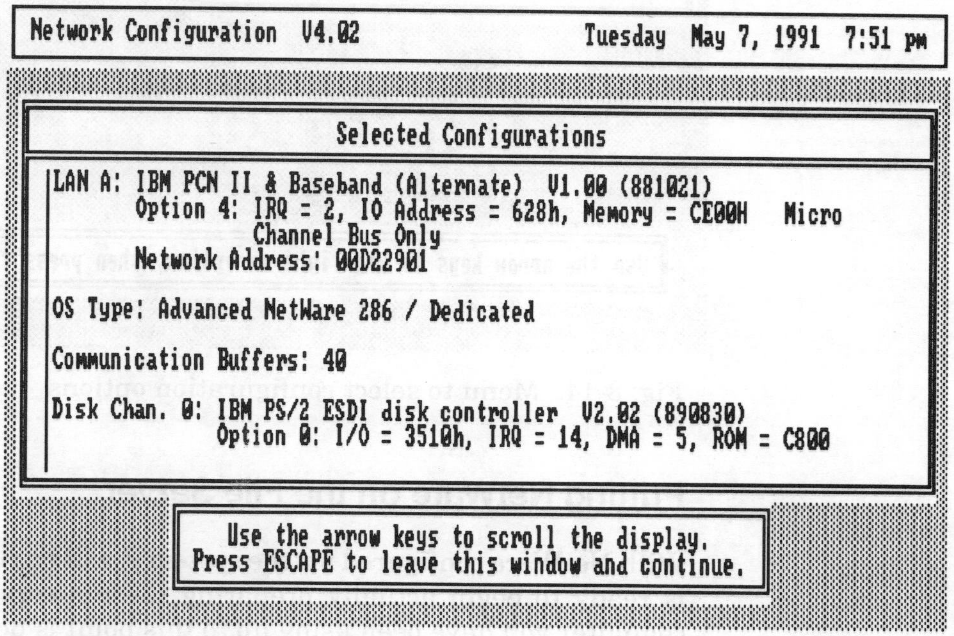

Fig. 8-13. Screen displaying selections made during installation

The Network Generation utility may need to verify some of the previous selections such as Run Options. The installer needs to respond to these as was previously done. Some drivers have more than one possible configuration. NETGEN will detect whether the drivers you have selected require a particular configuration to be selected. Fig. 8-14 shows the menu used when configuration options need to be selected.

If Select Network Configuration appears on the menu, it should be selected. This option will only appear if the drivers chosen can be configured for different addresses, IRQ lines, or bus types. The LAN configurations will probably be the same as the configurations used during the shell generation process, but may be different if there is more than one network card in the file server. Refer to the checklist created earlier.

After selecting all the configurable options for all the drivers in the system, an option for NetWare Installation will appear in the Network Generation Options menu.

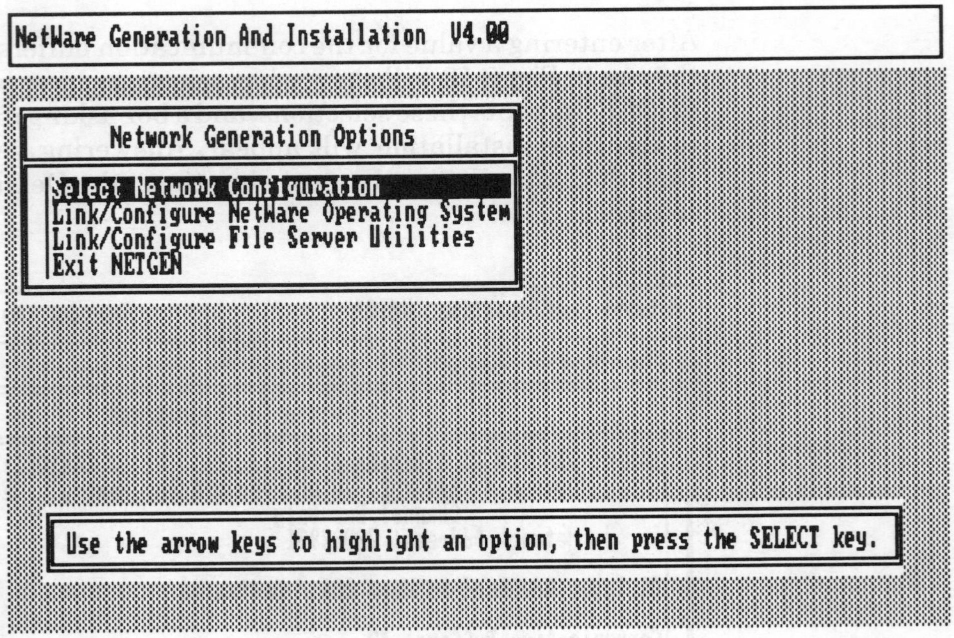

Fig. 8-14. Menu to select configuration options

Putting NetWare on the File Server

With NetWare configured for the system it will be running on, NETGEN is ready to begin actually preparing the file server hard disk. If the computer you have been using up to this point is not the file server, you must exit NETGEN. The NETGEN program can be started on the file server without losing the configuration data by not using the "-N" command line option. To run the NetWare utility COMPSURF, you would also exit NETGEN.

The Comprehensive Surface analysis program performs a low-level format of the hard disk to detect any physical flaws on the disk surface. COMPSURF can be run from within the NETGEN program by selecting the Analyze Disk Surface option from the Network Generation Options menu when using custom installation. However, COMPSURF can take several hours to complete, and it is usually impractical to run with the rest of the installation process left pending. It is also impractical in a classroom when many people may need to use the same computer during a day. If it is necessary for you to run COMPSURF, NETGEN has configured a version of the program for your type of hard disk, which is now on the Utilities diskette. The COMPSURF program erases all data on the hard disk and leaves it completely blank. The installation of NetWare on a computer also erases all data that may have been on the computer's hard disk by creating a new partition table and directory structure.

Selecting NetWare Installation from the NETGEN menu begins this process. Again, the installer is given the options of default or custom installation.

The custom installation allows you to modify such things as the partition table and NetWare's Hot Fix area. Modifying the partition table would allow you to have the NetWare area and a DOS area, or any other operating system, on the same hard disk. Such an arrangement is not recommended in most situations since the file server would have to be running in nondedicated mode, or the network would have to be brought down in order to access the other operating system. The Hot Fix area on a NetWare server is a portion of the hard disk that NetWare uses to replace other areas of the disk that become unusable during operation. When NetWare writes data to the hard disk, it reads it again to verify that the write was performed successfully. If the data cannot be read as it was written, NetWare marks that area of the disk as bad and writes the data to the Hot Fix area. Since this operation is completely automatic there is rarely any reason to modify the Hot Fix area.

Since the default installation is the most common, the option Select Default Installation should be chosen. NETGEN will ask the installer to verify the hard disks to be used by NetWare. Then it will ask for a file server name as shown in Fig. 8-15. The file server name must be unique in the network, between 2 and 45 characters long, and consist of only alphabetic characters, numeric characters or the "." (period). The period cannot be the first character. SERVER1, FIRST.SERVER, and NETWARE1992 are examples of valid server names. At this step, the name of the file server should be typed.

Under the default installation, the installer will be asked if he or she wants to use the printer and communication ports on the file server for network printers. Answering Yes to both will leave all the options open for later. Finally, select Continue Installation and Netgen will start loading the necessary files onto the hard disk. This process will vary widely depending on the size of disks and level of installation you are using. NETGEN will ask for all of the NetWare disks as it loads the NetWare system files and utilities onto the hard disk.

Eventually the installation will be complete and the installer will be asked if he or she wishes to exit NETGEN. The answer should be Yes. If all has gone well, when the file server is rebooted by pressing the "Ctrl", "Alt" and "Del" key simultaneously, it will load NetWare and operate as a file server. Fig. 8-16 shows the initialization screen of a NetWare file server. If NetWare detected any problems while loading, they would be displayed here. The Mounting Volume SYS message indicates NetWare is loading the directory information from the hard disk volume called SYS. Volumes are physical sections of the server hard disk, and, in this version of NetWare, can be only 225 megabytes or less. A hard disk larger than 225 megabytes would be broken up into additional volumes. NetWare automatically named the hard disk volume SYS. The messages Checking Bindrey and Checking Queues show NetWare is checking the system files for errors. Initializing LAN A appears while NetWare is testing the primary network it is attached to. If NetWare does not load successfully, three general areas of problems could be at fault.

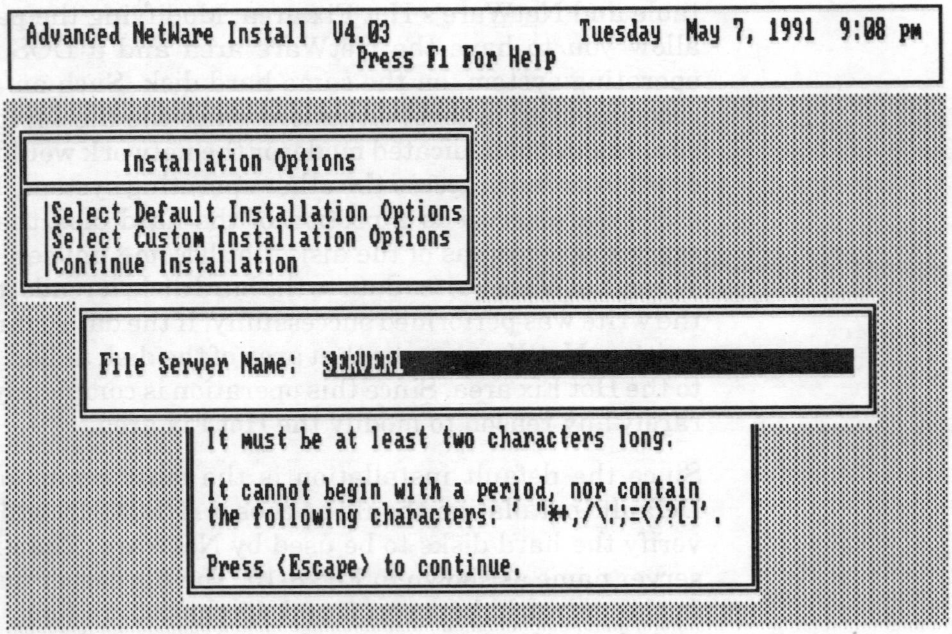

Fig. 8-15. Dialog box to enter the file server's name

First, the file server hardware could be defective. This is very unlikely since you were able to boot it. If no NetWare messages are displayed on the screen, the file server may not be able to read the hard disk or it is stopping at some point in its Power On Self Test.

Second, there could be a defect in the way the network cabling system is configured. If there is a break in a cable or the cable is not plugged in properly, NetWare will not be able to initialize the network. A message will be displayed on the screen if that happens.

Third, NetWare may not be configured properly for the type of hard disk or network card. The file server may have to be booted with DOS again and the NETGEN program run again to correct the problem.

Logging onto the File Server

Assuming the file server is up and running and the cabling system is complete, a workstation should now be able to login to the server. To

```
Mounting Volume SYS

Checking Bindrey
Checking Queues
Initializing LAN A




Novell Advanced NetWare 286 v2.15 12/11/88
(C) Copyright 1983, 1988 Novell Inc.
All Rights Reserved.


APRIL 23, 1991        7:03:21 am
:
```

Fig. 8-16. Initialization screen of NetWare file server

login, a workstation needs to be booted with the NetWare boot disk created earlier. At the A> prompt, the IPX program is executed by typing IPX. If the IPX program loads successfully, the NETX program appropriate to the DOS version needs to be loaded. If DOS version 3.x is being used, for instance, NET3 is typed. When the NETX program loads successfully, typing F:, pressing the ENTER key, typing DIR, and pressing the ENTER key provides a list of the directories in the server.

The screen now shows the LOGIN directory on the file server. The LOGIN directory is where users are placed when they are connected but not logged into the file server. If the installer is the first user to login to this file server, the only user name available is SUPERVISOR. It is the supervisor that creates all other user names allowed to login to the server.

Logging in as the supervisor is achieved by typing LOGIN SUPERVISOR and pressing the ENTER key. A prompt by the LOGIN program to enter a password will appear. Pressing ENTER indicates that the installer does not have a password.

Typing DIR F:\ and pressing the ENTER key shows that even though this is a new file server, it is not an empty one. NetWare has created four directories called SYSTEM, LOGIN, MAIL, and PUBLIC. The SYSTEM directory contains the NetWare program files that actually run the network. The LOGIN directory contains the LOGIN program and other programs or data files a user might need before logging into the network. The MAIL directory contains a directory for each user. Each of those directories contains files that are used by NetWare to maintain the user's account. The user does not normally directly access the data. Instead, a program such as a network mail program stores data for each user in these directories (transparent to the user). The fourth directory created by NetWare is the PUBLIC directory. It contains all the NetWare utilities that users, including the supervisor, use to manage their accounts and files. In the following chapters those utilities will be further explored.

Before leaving any network terminal, a user, especially the supervisor, should logout. Making this a habit is an important component of network security. The LOGOUT program is used to close the user's account on the file server, but it does not completely disconnect the workstation.

To logout, the command LOGOUT is typed at the F> prompt and the ENTER key is pressed. At this stage, workstations can access the LOGIN directory and its contents, but not actually be logged in. The workstation can be turned off without fear of leaving files open on the server.

Typically a network file server is left turned on all the time. This is because the most stressfull part of the operation of any computer equipment is turning it on or off. If it is necessary to turn the server off, the DOWN command must be entered at the file server keyboard. It ensures that all files the workstations might have left open are closed and that any files the server was using are closed. The DOWN command also informs workstations and other servers on the network that the server is no longer available. The file server can be safely turned off after it has responded to the DOWN command.

Hands-on NetWare Installation

Installation Preparation

Making Backup Copies with a Dual Disk Drive Computer -- Two disk Drives of the Same Type

If the computer being used to make the backup copies has two disk drives of the same type specified as A and B (e.g., two 3 1/2 inch drives or two 5 1/4 inch drives), follow the instructions below. If the computer has only one disk drive, skip to the Single Disk Drive instructions.

1. Boot the computer with a DOS disk. The DOS disk should be write protected to help protect against computer viruses.
2. Type **DISKCOPY A: B:** and press the [Enter←] key.

The DISKCOPY program will instruct you to insert the source disk in drive A: and the target disk in drive B:. The original NetWare disk is the source disk and one of the blank disks is the target.

3. Press the [Enter←] key when the disks are inserted and the copy process will begin.

When the copy has been successfully made, the DISKCOPY program will ask you if you would like to copy another.

4. Answer Yes by pressing [Y] and pressing the [Enter←] key. You will be prompted to insert source and target disks again.
5. Remove the two disks you started with and write the name of the original on the copy. Insert the second source disk and another blank disk. Continue this process with all of the NetWare distribution disks.

Making Backup Copies with a Single Disk Drive Computer

A single disk drive computer will probably have a hard disk installed and will only need to be turned on to be booted with DOS.

1. Type **DISKCOPY A: A:** and press the [Enter←] key.
2. The computer will ask you to insert the source disk in drive A. Press the [Enter←] key when ready.

The computer will read the disk and then ask for the target disk to be put in Drive A. It then writes to the target disk and may ask for the source disk again. This process continues until the copy is complete. Copying disks with a single disk drive takes a little longer because you may have to change the diskette several times to make one copy. Copy all the NetWare disks, writing the name of each original on its copy.

Creating the Boot Disk

Before continuing with the installation process a bootable disk needs to be created. The most straightforward way of doing this is to format the disk with the /S option.

1. Boot the computer with the DOS diskette
2. Type **FORMAT A: /S** and press the [Enter←] key. The format program will prompt you to insert a new diskette.
3. Insert the blank disk in drive A: and press the [Enter←] key when ready.

The new disk will be formatted and the DOS system files will be placed on the diskette so it is bootable. When the format process is complete, label the disk NetWare Boot Disk. Later we will place in this disk the NetWare files required to boot the machine and attach it to the network.

Creating the Shell with the Shell Generation Program

1. Insert your copy of the NetWare disk labeled SHGEN-1 in drive A:. If you have a diskette drive B: insert the AUXGEN disk there.
2. Type **SHGEN -N** and press the [Enter←] key.

The main menu of the Shell Generation utility should appear as it does in Fig. 8-1.

3. Highlight the Intermediate Configuration Level by highlighting that option with the ARROW keys and pressing Enter.

The next menu displayed is the SHGEN Run Options menu as shown in Fig. 8-2.

4. If the disk is already loaded, highlight the Standard method and press the Enter key.

Using the Standard method, the computer will prompt you when to insert other disks as needed. Select one of the other methods only if preparations have been made by the instructor. Fig. 8-3 shows the available options for this level of configuration.

5. Highlight the Select LAN Driver option and press the Enter key.
6. Highlight Load and Select Item and press the Enter key.

You will be prompted to enter the LAN drivers disk.

7. If NetWare drivers were supplied with your network interface card, insert the disk now and press the esc key. If not, insert the NetWare disk labeled LAN_DRV_001 and press the esc key. Either way, a list of driver names will appear.
8. Use the ARROW keys to scroll through the list until you find your type of network interface card. You may need to try another LAN_DRV disk to find the right driver.
9. Highlight the option that is on your network card and press the Enter key. Refer to the checklist created earlier to determine the correct option. Also listed are options for either Standard Bus or Micro Channel Bus cards.

After selecting the appropriate option, the Shell Generation program will construct the network shell.

10. If you are running SHGEN from a hard disk or network drive, the program will ask you if you want to continue to download the shell files to a floppy disk. Answer Yes, and follow the on-screen instructions to download the shell files to the boot disk created earlier.
11. If you are running SHGEN from floppy disks, exit the SHGEN program. Use the appropriate DOS commands to copy the shell files from the SHGEN-1 disk to the boot disk you created earlier. You will need the IPX.COM file and the NETX file appropriate to your system. The DOS commands will vary depending on your hardware but here are a few examples.

Two Diskette Drives of the Same Type

With two disk drives of the same type, the following instructions can be used to copy the network shell files to your boot disk.

With the SHGEN-1 disk in drive A: and the your boot disk in drive B:

1. Type **COPY A:IPX.COM B:** and press the [Enter←] key.
2. Type **COPY A:NET*.* B:** and press the [Enter←] key.

One Diskette Drive and a Hard Disk

If one diskette drive and a hard disk are available, use these instructions to copy the files.

1. Insert the SHGEN-1 disk in drive A:.
2. Type **COPY A:IPX.COM C:** and press the [Enter←] key.
3. Type **COPY A:NET*.* C:** and press the [Enter←] key.
4. Remove the SHGEN-1 disk and replace it with your boot disk.
5. Type **COPY C:IPX.COM A:** and press the [Enter←] key.
6. Type **COPY C:NET*.* A:** and press the [Enter←] key.

Two Diskette Drives of Different Types

With two diskette drives of different types, it is nessesary to copy the files to another blank disk first.

1. Insert a formatted, blank diskette in drive B:.
2. Insert the SHGEN-1 disk in drive A:
3. Type **COPY A:IPX.COM B:** and press the [Enter←] key.
4. Type **COPY A:NET*.* B:** and press the [Enter←] key.
5. Remove the SHGEN-1 disk from drive A: and replace it with your boot disk.
6. Type **COPY B:IPX.COM A:** and press the [Enter←] key.
7. Type **COPY B:NET*.* A:** and press the [Enter←] key.
8. Type **COPY A:NET*.* B:** Press the [Enter←] key.

Configuring NetWare

To configure NetWare for the system that it is going to be running on, the network generating program NETGEN must be executed.

1. Type **A:** and press the [Enter←] key.
2. Insert the disk labeled NETGEN into drive A:.
3. Type **NETGEN -N** and press the [Enter←] key.

This starts a new session and NETGEN's first menu should appear as shown in Fig. 8-6. If, during the course of this process, you need to exit NETGEN, restart it later without the "-N".

4. Select the Default level by highlighting Default Configuration and pressing the Enter key.

The Run Options menu should appear next.

5. Highlight Standard method and press the Enter key.
6. Highlight Select Network Configuration and press the Enter key.

The computer will ask you to insert the AUXGEN, NETGEN, and GENDATA disks several times respectively into one of the floppy drives. Follow the instructions on the screen and insert the proper disk when the computer asks for it. When the computer obtains all of the data necessary, the Available Options menu will appear.

7. When the menu titled Available Options appears, highlight Set Operating System Options and press the Enter key. Your screen should appear very similar to Fig. 8-7.
8. Highlight the NetWare/Dedicated mode and press the Enter key.
9. The next item on the Available Options menu is Select LAN Drivers. Highlight this item and press the Enter key. The screen should appear, as seen in Fig. 8-8.
10. If the driver for your type of network card was included on the NetWare disks, highlight the Select Loaded Item option and press the Enter key. A list of network card drivers will appear as in Fig. 8-9. Highlight your type of network card and press the Enter key. If your network card did not come with a NetWare driver disk, then refer to step 11 below.
11. If the driver for your network card was supplied by the card manufacturer, highlight the Load and Select Item option and press the Enter key. You will be prompted to insert the proper disk.
12. Highlight your card from the list provided and press the Enter key.

A NetWare file server can support more than one network card so you can select additional LAN drivers.

13. When all needed LAN drivers have been selected and loaded, press the esc key to save your selections.

The third item on the Available Options menu is Select Disk Drivers. A driver for each type of hard disk installed in the file server must be loaded in the same way that the LAN drivers are loaded.

14. Highlight the Select Disk Drivers option and press the Enter key.

15. Again you are given the options of Select Loaded Item or Load and Select Item. If you need to use a driver supplied by your hard disk manufacturer, highlight Load and Select Item and press the [Enter←] key. If the hard disk is a standard type, you should find the appropriate driver under the Select Loaded Item option and press the [Enter←] key.

In either case a box that simply says Channel: will appear as in Fig. 8-10. Each disk driver you select will require a unique channel number for internal operation within NetWare. These numbers were assigned when the disk drives were installed on the server. They start with zero and depend on the type of hard disk.

16. Enter the appropriate number. Enter **0** if there is only one hard disk in the server and you are not sure about the number. With more than one hard disk in the server you will need to know the channel numbers and enter them at the appropriate time.
17. Also, you will need to highlight the type of disk controller from the list on the screen. When you are finished with the selections for disk drivers and disk controllers, press the [esc] key to save your selections and continue.

The fourth option on the Available Options menu is Select "Other" Drivers. Only select this item if there is some other device, such as a tape backup unit, attached to the file server.

18. Highlight the last option, Save Selections and Continue, and press the [Enter←] key.

The box shown in Fig. 8-11 will appear. These two fields, Network Address and Communication Buffers, must be filled in before you can continue. Refer back to the beginning of this chapter for the parameters that need to go in these fields.

19. Enter a network address appropriate for your network and press the [Enter←] key.
20. Enter the number of communication buffers needed for your network or accept the default provided by the computer and press the [Enter←] key. After entering a value for the communication buffers option, press the [esc] key, and a screen similar to the one in Fig. 8-13 will show what selections have been made.
21. Press the [esc] key to accept these selections and a box asking you if you wish to continue installation will appear.
22. Highlight Yes and press the [Enter←] key.

The computer will ask you to insert several of the NetWare disks multiple times. The disks that you will need at this point are AUXGEN, ADOBJ, GENDATA, LAN_DRV_001, DSK_DRV_001, OSEXE_1 NETGEN, UTILEXE, and UTILOBJ. Follow the instructions on the screen that indicate which disk needs to be placed in the disk drive.

The Network Generation utility may need to verify some of your previous selections such as Run Options. Respond to these as you did previously. Some drivers have more than one possible configuration. NETGEN will detect whether the drivers you have selected require a particular configuration to be selected. Fig. 8-14 shows the menu that will appear if configuration options need to be selected.

23. If Select Network Configuration appears on the menu, highlight it and press the [Enter←] key. This option will only appear if the drivers you have chosen can be configured for different addresses, IRQ lines, or bus types. The LAN configurations will probably be the same as the configurations used during the shell generation process, but may be different if there is more than one network card in the file server. Refer to the checklist created earlier.

After selecting all the configurable options for all the drivers in your system, an option for NetWare Installation will appear in the Network Generation Options menu.

Stopping Place

Time limitations may require you to stop the installation process and continue later. If you need to stop,

1. Press the [esc] key until the Exit NETGEN? message appears on the screen.
2. Press the [Y] and [Enter←] keys.

Installing NetWare

If it was necessary for you exit NETGEN, restart it now by inserting the NETGEN disk in drive A and following the instructions below.

1. Type **NETGEN** and press the [Enter←] key. Highlight NetWare Installation and press the [Enter←] key. Again, you are given the options of default or custom installation.
2. Highlight Default Installation and press the [Enter←] key.

NETGEN will ask you to verify the hard disks to be used by NetWare.

3. If the list is correct press the [esc] key.

Next, the computer will ask for a file server name as in Fig. 8-15. The file server name must be unique in the network, between 2 and 45 characters long and consist of only alphabetic characters, numeric characters or the "." (period). The period cannot be the first character.

4. Type in your file server name and press the [Enter←] key.

A screen to verify all entries will be displayed.

5. Press the [esc] key if all entries are correct.

Next, printer port options will appear, asking which ports will be used for network printers. Normally, LPT1 is used as a network printer.

6. Highlight LPT1 and press the [Enter←] key.
7. Highlight Continue Installation and press the [Enter←] key.

You will be asked if you want to install the NetWare software in the file server.

8. Highlight the Yes option and press the [Enter←] key.

If everything goes well, the message "The cold boot loader has been successfully installed" will appear on the screen. Next the computer will ask you to insert the GENDATA disk into the disk drive.

9. Insert the GENDATA disk in one of the floppy drives and press any key.

The computer will ask you to insert the OSEXE_1 disk into the disk drive.

10. Insert the OSEXE_1 into one of the floppy drives and press any key.

A message "NET$OS.EXE successfully installed" should appear on the screen. At this point, you will be asked to insert the SYSTEM, GENDATA, BRUTILS, SUPER_TUTOR (supervisor tutorial), USERTUTOR_1 (user tutorial), PUBLIC_1, PUBLIC_2, PUBLIC_3, PUBLIC_4, PUBLIC_5, and PROGRAMS_1 into the disk drive multiple times. Follow the instructions on the screen and insert the proper disk when the computer asks for it. If everything goes well, the message "Systems files successfully installed" will appear on the screen. Also, the computer will ask you to insert the NETGEN disk into one of the floppy drives.

11. Insert the NETGEN disk in the drive and press any key. The installation of NetWare is completed.

After the installation is completed, you will be asked if you wish to exit NETGEN.

12. Answer Yes and press the [Enter←] key. If all has gone well, when you reboot the file server by pressing the [Ctrl] [alt] [delete] keys simultaneously, it will load NetWare and operate as a file server.

Logging onto the File Server

1. Boot a workstation with the NetWare boot disk created earlier.
2. At the A> prompt, type **IPX** and press the [Enter←] key.
3. If the IPX program loads successfully, run the NETX program appropriate to the DOS version you are using. If you are using DOS version 3.x, for instance, type NET3 and press the [Enter←] key.

If you are using the latest versions of the NETX program in a multiple server environment, each time you load the NETX program add PS=SERVER1 to the command line, for the remainder of this book. For instance, if the NETX program is to be used, type NETX PS=SERVER1 and press the Enter key.

4. When the NETX program loads successfully, type F: and press the Enter key, then type **DIR** and press the Enter key.
5. Type **LOGIN SUPERVISOR** and press the Enter key. You will be prompted to enter a password by the LOGIN program. Press the Enter key to indicate that you do not have a password.
6. Type **DIR F:** and press the Enter key.

You will see that even though this is a new file server, it is not an empty one. NetWare creates four directories: SYSTEM, LOGIN, MAIL and PUBLIC.

Before leaving any network terminal, a user, especially the supervisor, should logout. Making this a habit is an important component of network security. The LOGOUT program is used to close the user's account on the file server, but it does not completely disconnect the workstation.

7. Type **LOGOUT** at the F> prompt and press the Enter key.
8. Type **DIR** and press the Enter key. Again, the workstation can access the LOGIN directory and its contents, but it is not actually logged in. The workstation can be turned off without fear of leaving files open on the server.

The file server must be shut down using the DOWN command. It insures that all files the workstations might have left open are closed and that any files the server was using are closed. The DOWN command also informs workstations and other servers on the network that the server is no longer available.

9. Go back to the file server and type **DOWN** and press the Enter key. The file server can be safely turned off.

Summary

NetWare must be installed for both the workstation and the file server. The Shell Generation program, SHGEN, is used to create a proper IPX.COM program for the type and configuration of the network card in the workstation. That program is then placed on a bootable disk with the appropriate NETX program. The version of NETX used depends on the version of DOS used and whether the workstation has expanded or extended memory.

The file server is prepared with the Network Generation program, NETGEN. It is used to configure NetWare to the type of network card used, type of hard disk used, and any other device attached to the file server. The configuration process can be done on any computer. Once NetWare is configured properly, NETGEN must be run on the computer intended to be the file server. It will erase all data on the hard disk and place the NetWare system files and utilities there.

With the file server completely installed and running, a user can login by running the IPX program and the appropriate NETX program on any connected workstation.

Questions

1. In a NetWare utility menu, can the user change data in a box made with a double line?
2. In most NetWare menus, what key is pressed to accept the selections and return to the previous menu?
3. Does a NetWare boot disk need DOS on it in addition to the NetWare shell programs?
4. What command line option is used to start a new session in both SHGEN and NETGEN programs?
5. Is 00000001 a valid network address?
6. Should the COMPSURF program be run before or after NetWare has been installed on the file server?
7. Is FILESERVER-1 a valid server name?
8. What are the four directories created on the file server during the installation process?

Projects

Objective

The following projects are designed to familiarize you with the process of booting a workstation, logging into the network, and using the help facility available in NetWare.

Project 1. Logging into NetWare

1. Boot a workstation with the appropriate disk.
2. Run the appropriate IPX and NETX programs.
3. Type **DIR F:** and notice the number of bytes free listed at the bottom of the screen.

4. Login as the SUPERVISOR. Press [shift][print screen] to record the results.
5. Type **DIR F:** and notice the number of bytes free listed at the bottom of the screen. Why is this figure larger than the one shown earlier?

Project 2. Using the NetWare's Help Facility

NetWare contains an extensive help facility that contains extensive information about NetWare commands, concepts, utilities, and messages.

1. Login as the user GUEST.
2. Type **HELP** and press the [enter] key.

To navigate in any of the help screens use the TAB key.

3. Press the [tab] key until it is under the triangle marker at the left of Using the Network option and press the [enter] key.
4. Press the [tab] key until the cursor moves to Logging In and Out and press the [enter] key.

Read about the login procedure and make any notes that you deem necessary.

5. Press the [tab] key until the cursor reaches Login Scripts and press the [enter] key.

Read about the login scripts and make any notes that you deem necessary.

6. When you finish reading the information, press the [esc] key several times until the NetWare OS screen is displayed. Another method to exit the help facility is to press the [Ctrl][esc] keys.

The help facility can also be accessed by typing HELP followed by the command, utility, message, or concept that you want to investigate.

7. Type **HELP login** and press the [enter] key.

You will see the earlier login help screen.

8. Practice viewing and reading several other NetWare commands.

9

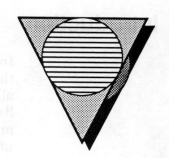

The SYSCON Utility and Login Scripts

Objectives

1. Understand the importance of the System Configuration utility, SYSCON.
2. Understand the functions of each of the main menu selections in SYSCON.
3. Understand the purpose of a login script.
4. Understand login script commands.
5. Understand how to use login script variables.
6. Be able to login and logout of a file server.
7. Be able to create a user using SYSCON.

Key Terms

Account Balance
Groups
Passwords
SYSCON
File Server
Login Script
Rights
Trustees

Introduction

In the last chapter Novell NetWare was installed on the file server and the workstation was booted with the network shell. That arrangement allowed the user supervisor to login to the file server and view the files listed there. Now it must be set up to allow other users to login and easily manage their files and directories. The NetWare System Configuration utility SYSCON is used to accomplish this. With it the supervisor can create user accounts and groups of user accounts. Each account or group can have different access rights, legal login times, and other attributes. Many of the controls used to set up the user's environment are executed when the user logs in through the use of a login script. It can set the user's drive mappings, check various conditions at the time the user logs in, and write messages to the screen.

Syscon

Introduction

SYSCON allows the network supervisor to create, change, and delete users and groups of users in addition to enabling many other functions. It is by far the most important utility Novell provides with NetWare, since it used to set up the most fundamental aspects of the network. As with many NetWare utilities, some menu options only appear for the supervisor. But the users can choose other menu options themselves to view and change their accounts.

Fig. 9-1 shows SYSCONs' main menu, which is labeled Available Topics. These topics comprise the essentials of managing the network as a whole. Starting from the top of the menu, SYSCON's primary functions are:

1. Accounting
2. Change Current Server
3. File Server Information
4. Group Information
5. Supervisor Options
6. User Information

The SYSCON Options

Accounting

NetWare is capable of tracking how much each user uses the network. The supervisor can set up each account to be charged a certain rate for various functions of the network. This process is referred to as accounting

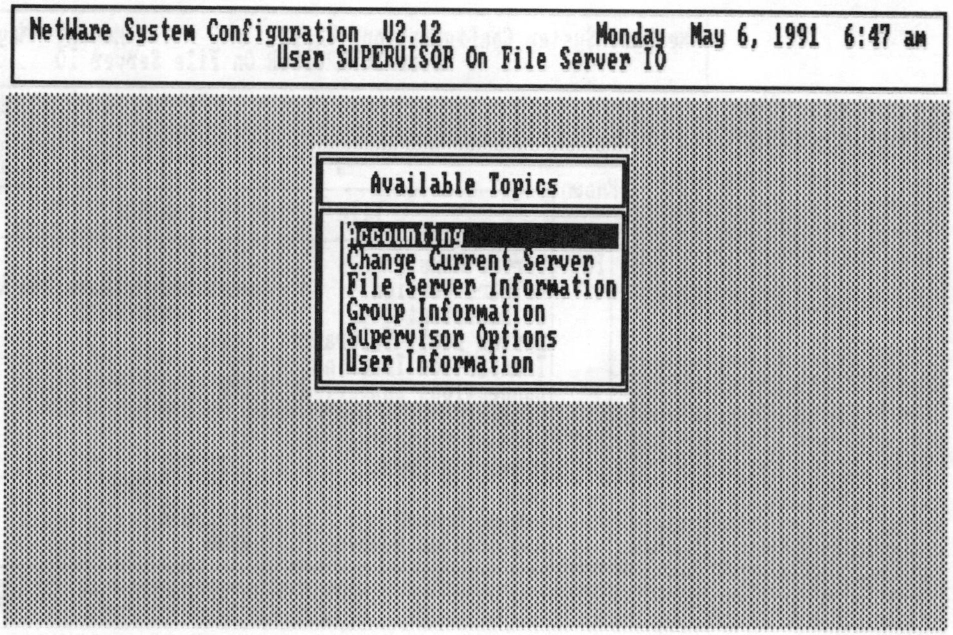

Fig. 9-1. SYSCON's main menu

because it is often used by companies who want to charge each department for its use of the network.

Change Current Server

With the SYSCON program, the supervisor can operate up to eight file servers. He or she can perform all of the functions provided by SYSCON on each of the file servers attached to the network but not simultaneously. The supervisor must select the file server to be used, then create users or make other changes to each individual file server. Some other networks, most notably Banyon VINES, allow the supervisor to create users and groups that can login to any server attached to the network.

File Server Information

This option displays a list of information about the file server currently selected. Fig. 9-2 shows a typical File Server Information box. Note that it is a single line box, which means that the information in it cannot be changed.

Group Information

This selection displays a list of groups of users on this server. Each group name in the list can be selected to display a list of options available. The options are very similar to those available for individual users. Using carefully arranged groups, the supervisor can avoid many details when creating individual accounts and can make changes to the attributes of many users by making changes to the groups they belong to. Fig. 9-3 shows the list of groups on the left and the options available after a group

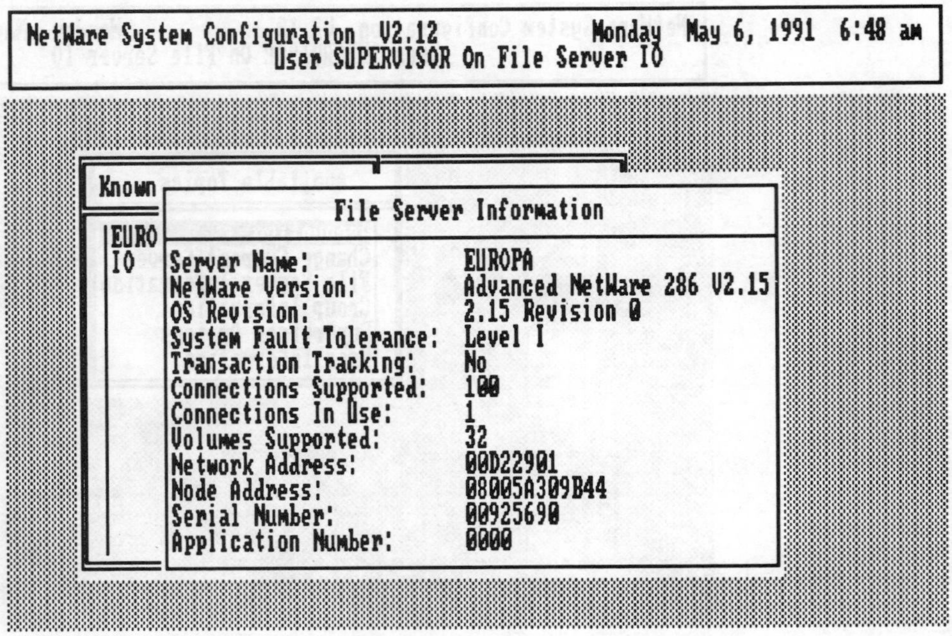

Fig. 9-2. File Server Information box

has been selected on the right. Notice that create and delete a group are not listed as options. As in most of the NetWare utilities, creating a new item is accomplished by pressing the INSERT key and deleting an item is accomplished by highlighting it and pressing the DELETE key.

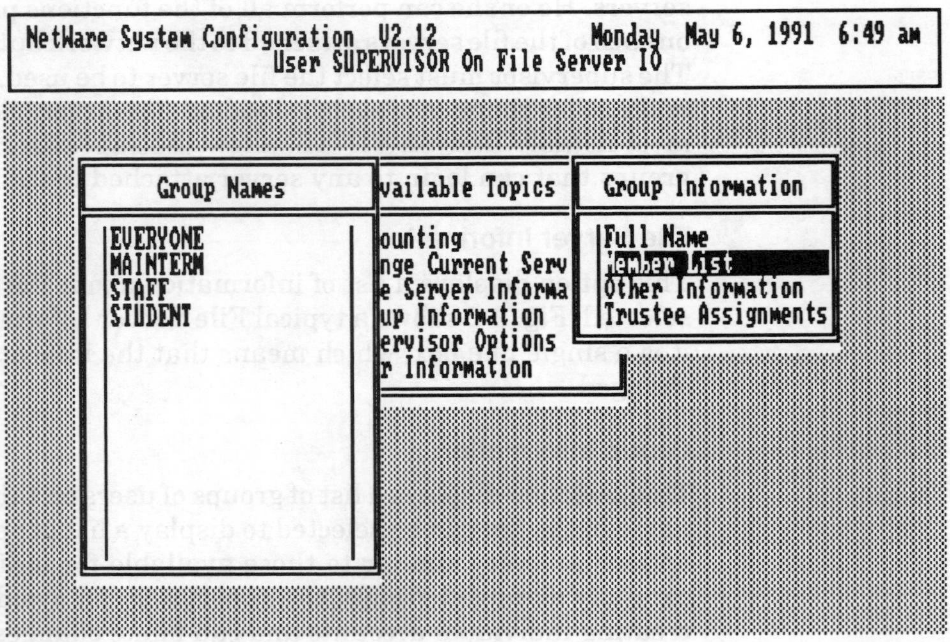

Fig. 9-3. Screen displaying group information for a file server

Supervisor Options

Not all the information needed for setting up a user account needs to be entered for each user or even each group. The supervisor has several options that can be used to establish defaults that will be in effect for each new user created. For instance, if the supervisor wanted login time restrictions for all of the new users, he or she could set those defaults from the Supervisor Options menu shown in Fig. 9-4. The defaults set in this menu do not affect existing users.

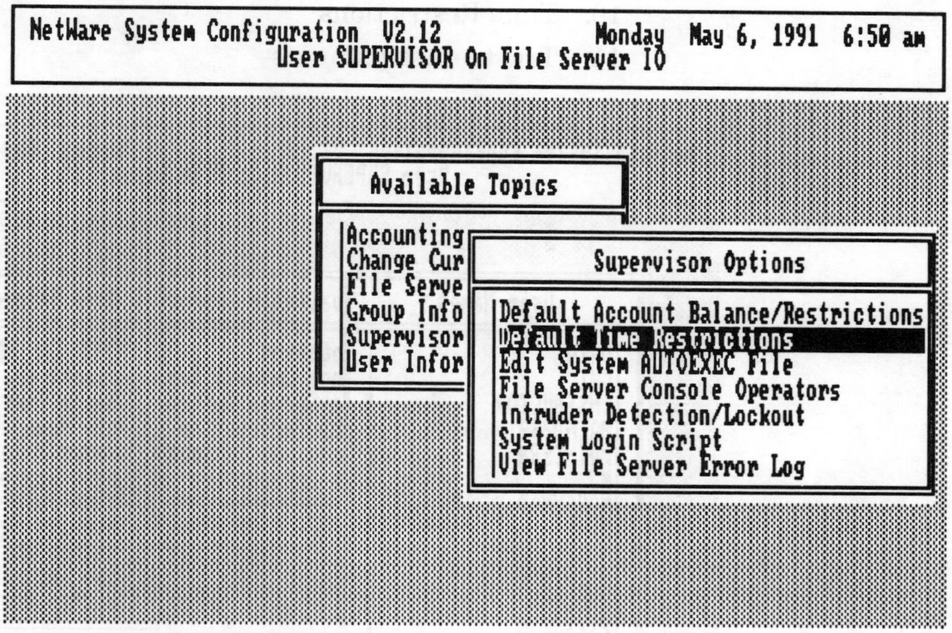

Fig. 9-4. Screen displaying the Supervisor Options menu

User Information

As in Group Information the User Information option displays a list of existing user names. The supervisor can press INSERT to create a new user, press DELETE to delete a listed user, or highlight a user name and press the ENTER key to select it. Pressing ENTER on a highlighted user name brings up the User Information menu, as shown in Fig. 9-5. This menu provides the most important options for running the network. From here the supervisor controls the most fundamental options a user has.

The User Information Options

The User Information menu allows the supervisor to set up individual accounts and assign different attributes to each. The options available in this menu are:

1. Account Balance
2. Account Restrictions

3. Change Password
4. Full Name
5. Groups Belonged To
6. Login Scripts
7. Other Information
8. Security Equivalences
9. Station Restrictions
10. Time Restrictions
11. Trustee Assignments

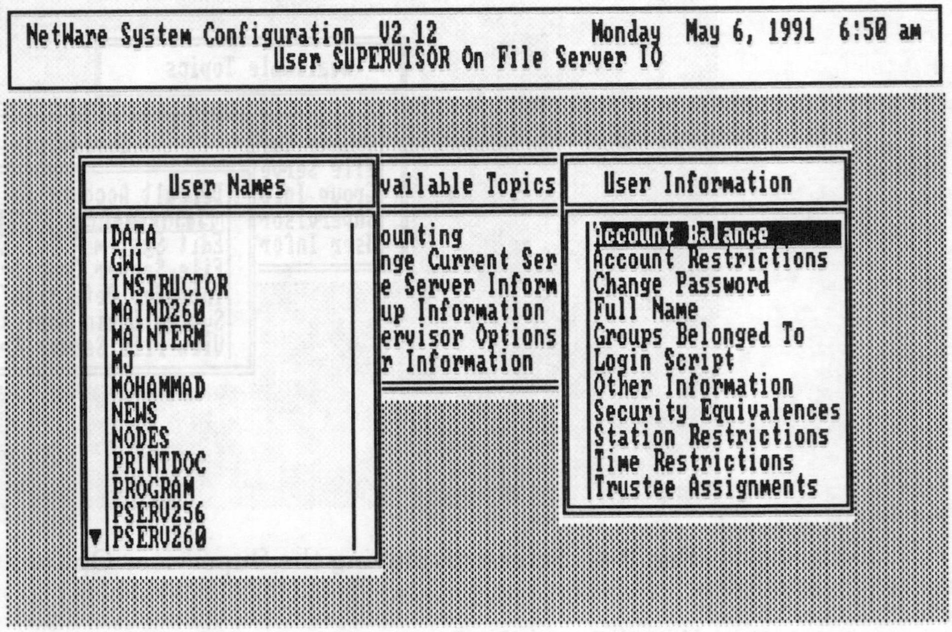

Fig. 9-5. The User Information Menu

Account Balance

As noted in the Accounting section of SYSCON's main menu, the supervisor may choose to charge the user for many of the network functions. The charges for all the different network services are drawn on the user's account balance. The Account Balance option allows the supervisor to set a limit on the account, view the current account balance, or set the account to unlimited. If the user has a limited account balance he or she can use any chargeable services only if the account balance is below the limit set by the supervisor. By marking the account unlimited, the supervisor can keep a record of the services without interfering with regular use of those services.

Account Restrictions

There are seventeen separate options that can be set from the Account Restrictions menu as seen in Fig. 9-6. All of these options except Account Disabled can be set under the Supervisor Options as Default Account Balance/Restrictions (see Fig. 9-4). These options include the ability to restrict an account to a certain period of time, limit the number of people that can be logged in under a single user name, and limit the use of a password. The user can be forced to use a password or allowed to log in without one. With a password he or she may or may not be allowed to change it, or may be forced to change it at specified intervals.

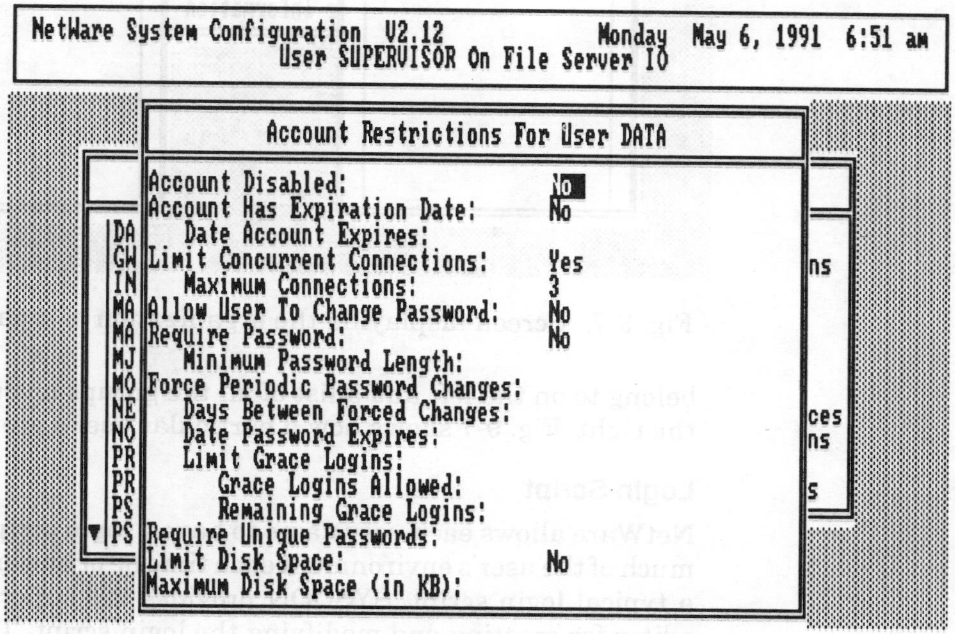

Fig. 9-6. The Account Restrictions menu

Change Password

An important part of network security is the ability to frequently change the user's password. The user can change it or the supervisor can change it using this option. Note that neither the user nor the supervisor can view an existing password, but can only change it.

Full Name

For accounting purposes a Full Name can be assigned to each user name. While a user name may be something like JSMITH the full name might be JOHN MAXIMILIAN SMITH.

Groups Belonged To

Each user may belong to several groups or to no groups at all. When selected, this option displays a list of all the groups the user does not

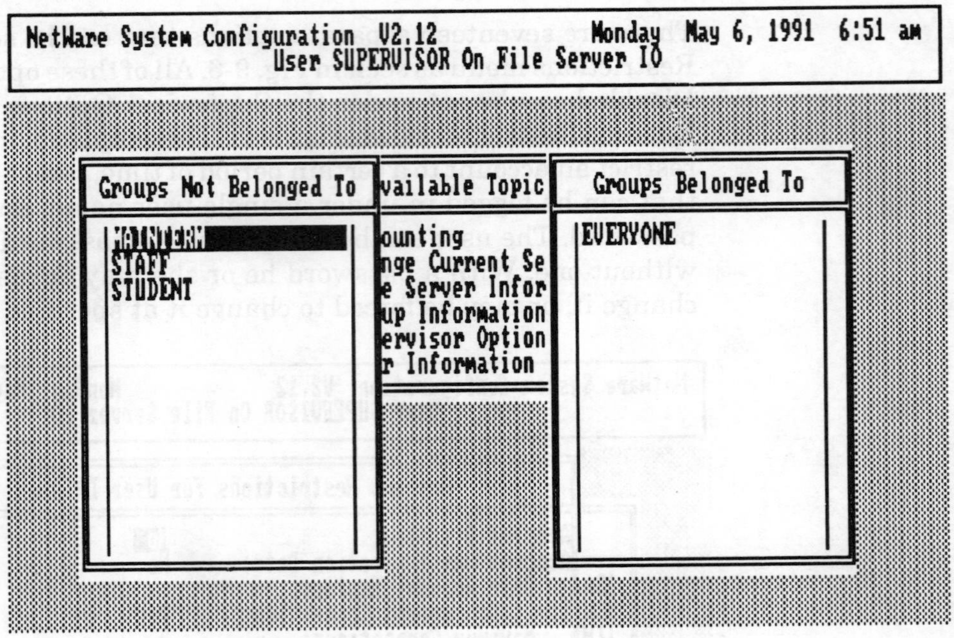

Fig. 9-7. Screen displaying the organization of a particular user group

belong to on the left and a list of all the groups a user does belong to on the right. Fig. 9-7 shows how a particular user's groups might stack up.

Login Script

NetWare allows each user name to have a login script which establishes much of the user's environment each time he or she logs in. Fig. 9-8 shows a typical login script. SYSCON provides the supervisor with a simple editor for creating and modifying the login script. This login script performs several mapping operations such as mapping the \SOFTWARE\DATA directory to appear as the root directory of drive F. Then it sets two DOS environment variables to certain values from the NetWare login variables %STATION and %P_STATION. A message is displayed to the user, and lastly the EXIT command sends a command to DOS to display a directory listing. All of these commands are executed each time the user DATA logs in. NetWare does not require each user to have a login script since the supervisor can set a System Login Script in the Supervisor Options menu. (See Fig. 9-4) However, it is very important that each user be given a login script for security reasons.

A weakness in NetWare is in its handling of login scripts and user mail. Specifically, they are both stored in the same directory. Since every other user on the network must have write access to the mail directory in order to leave mail, those other users could conceivably create a login script and copy it to any user who did not already have a login script.

```
NetWare System Configuration  V2.12              Monday  May 6, 1991  6:51 am
                              User SUPERVISOR On File Server IO

                         Login Script For User DATA

MAP DISPLAY Off
MAP ERRORS ON
BREAK ON
map root f:=sys:\software\data
map v:=Io/vol1:
map p:=sys:\public
dos set st="%STATION"
dos set node="%P_STATION"
write "****** Please be sure the data placed in this section *******"
write "****** can be legally distributed to students.        *******"
write " "
write ">>>>>>> NOTE: I am in the process of upgrading the network "
write "        shell software.  The new shell allows you to access "
write "        F:\SOFTWARE\DATA as if it were F:\ . "
WRITE "----------------- SERVER IO ----------------------"
exit "dir /w"
```

Fig. 9-8. A typical login script

Other Information

This option displays information such as the date the user last logged in, disk space usage information, and the user ID number.

Security Equivalences

After assigning all the directory rights and groups for one user, the supervisor may wish to duplicate those rights for another user. To do this, the supervisor can select Security Equivalences after creating the new user. From there the supervisor simply selects the name of an existing user or group from a list.

Station Restrictions

Each network interface card on the network has a unique number consisting of the network number and the node number. Together they are known as the network address. The supervisor can restrict a user to logging in only at specific network addresses, which means effectively only at specific computers.

Time Restrictions

In addition to restricting a user to specific computers, the supervisor can also restrict a user to certain times of the day on certain days of the week. Fig. 9-9 shows the chart used by the supervisor to assign these times. Each asterisk represents a half hour interval. Here, user DATA is given access to the network nearly all day six days a week, but only four and a half hours in the afternoon on Sunday.

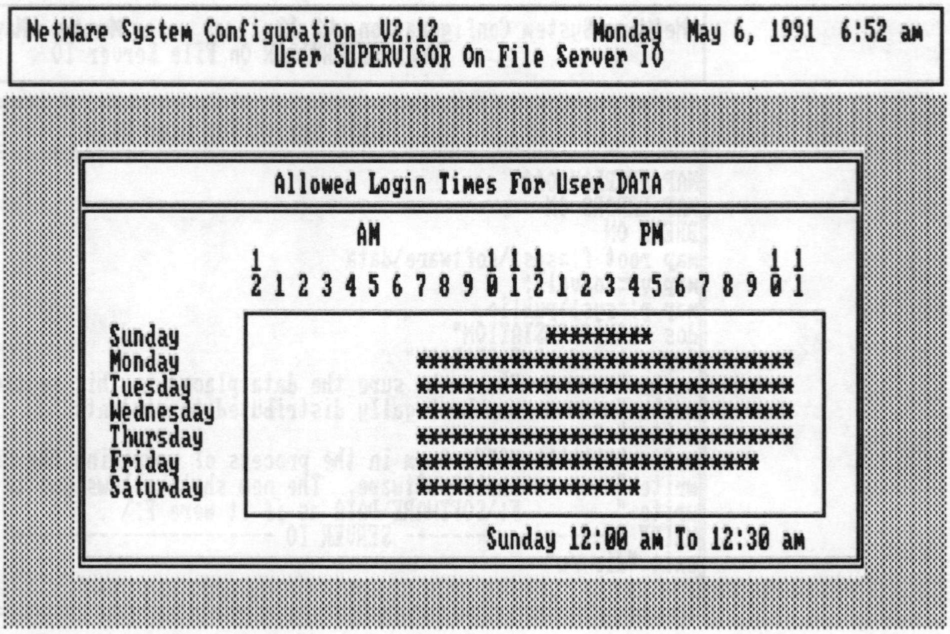

Fig. 9-9. Chart used to assign time restrictions

Trustee Assignments

When a user is given any access to a directory on the file server he or she is known as a trustee of that directory. The supervisor must assign the user as a trustee to each directory he or she will need any access to. The supervisor must also assign which rights the user will have in each directory. This is the most direct way of making a user a trustee of a directory, but there are two other ways. First, the user could have been a member of a group that is a trustee. Second, the user could be made a Security Equivalent of a user with access to a certain directory. Either way, a user must be given explicit access to a directory to have any rights there.

Fig. 9-10 shows user DATA's trustee assignments. It does not show trustee assignments that DATA may have from being a member of a group or from being a Security Equivalent to another user. From the screen in Fig. 9-10 the supervisor has four options. First, by selecting a directory listed and pressing ENTER the supervisor can modify the rights user DATA has to one of those directories. Second, the supervisor can press DELETE on a directory to completely remove the user as a trustee. Third, the INSERT key can be used to add a new directory to the list. And fourth, the ESCAPE key accepts any changes made, and SYSCON returns to the User Information menu.

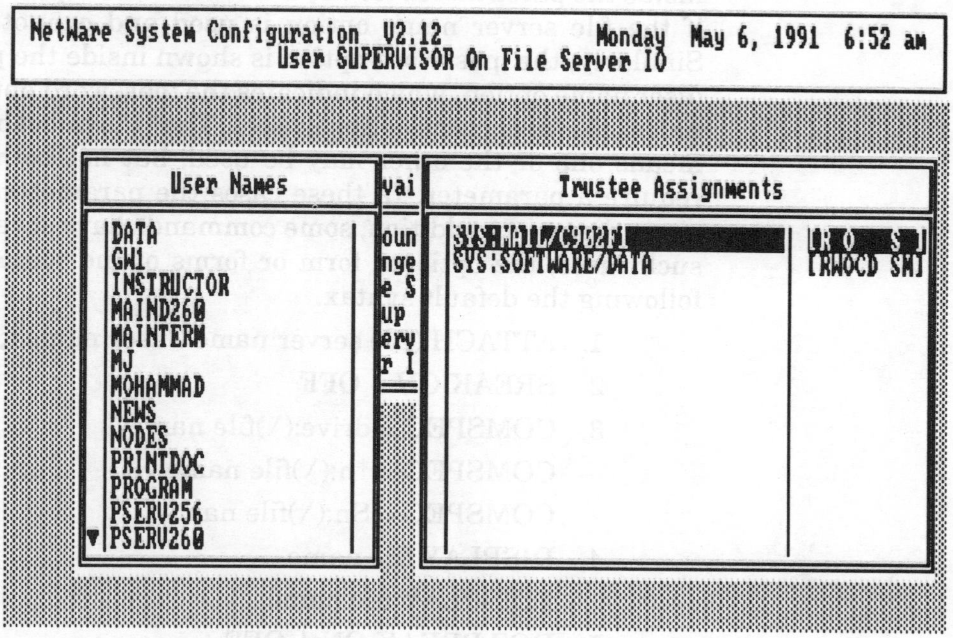

Fig. 9-10. Trustee assignments for user DATA

Login Scripts

As mentioned earlier, every time a user logs in, NetWare is capable of running a login script. Its function is to issue all the commands needed to set up the user's environment. The environment, in this case, refers primarily to the drive mappings created for the user, but there are many other commands available in login scripts for customizing the login.

The login script is essentially a program that the supervisor writes using a strict set of rules and commands available. A user might type LOGIN JSMITH at the F> prompt after loading the appropriate network drivers. The LOGIN program checks the user name given and executes the login script found in the user's MAIL directory. If no login script is there, the system login script set up by the supervisor using SYSCON (see Fig. 9-4) is executed. Many of the commands that can be used in a login script can also be used from the command line. In other words, if the appropriate PATHs have been established, a user can issue several of the commands by typing the name of the command at the F> prompt. The ATTACH command is a good example. The ATTACH command can be used in a login script and a program called ATTACH.EXE resides in the F:\PUBLIC directory. ATTACH.EXE performs exactly the same function as the ATTACH command in a login script.

The following is a list of login script commands and their uses. Items listed in parentheses are options that may be used. Notice the /user name option in the ATTACH command listed first. Since this option is shown inside the parentheses for the file server name option it can be used only if the file server name option is used and cannot be used by itself. Similarly, the ;password option is shown inside the parentheses for the /user name option, which indicates the ;password option cannot be used unless the /user name option in used. The "|" symbol between two options means one or the other may be used, but not both. Some commands require a parameter. In these cases the parameters are not shown in parentheses. In addition, some commands have several other forms. In such cases, the optional form or forms of the command are displayed following the default syntax.

1. ATTACH (file server name (/user name (;password)))
2. BREAK ON | OFF
3. COMSPEC = drive:(\)file name
   COMSPEC = *n:(\)file name
   COMSPEC = Sn:(\)file name
4. DISPLAY file name
   FDISPLAY file name
5. DOS BREAK ON | OFF
6. (DOS) SET name="value"
7. DOS VERIFY ON | OFF
8. DRIVE drive letter:
   DRIVE *drive number:
9. EXIT ("file name")
10. #program name with command line options
11. FIRE PHASERS number TIMES
12. IF condition (AND condition) THEN command
    IF condition (AND condition) THEN BEGIN
    commands
    END
13. INCLUDE file name
14. MACHINE = "name"
    MACHINE NAME = "name"
15. MAP
16. PAUSE
    WAIT
17. PCCOMPATIBLE
    COMPATIBLE
18. REMARK remark statement
    REM, *, or ; are all remark statements
19. WRITE "comment to be displayed"

ATTACH

Ordinarily a user logs in to a single file server using the LOGIN command. The ATTACH command in a login script attaches the user to another file server that may be on the same network. This command can also be executed from the command line. Suppose user JSMITH has an account with the same password on two file servers on the network called FS_ONE and FS_TWO. JSMITH's workstation is normally connected to FS_ONE but he usually needs access to FS_TWO also. An ATTACH command could be placed in the login script of his account on FS_ONE that reads;

ATTACH FS_TWO

The LOGIN program will execute the ATTACH command and login JSMITH to FS_TWO using the same user name and password that was used on FS_ONE.

Another possibility is that JSMITH might log into any one of many workstations that may be connected to either file server, and he needs access to both servers. If he logs in at a workstation that is already connected to FS_ONE he would need to use the ATTACH command to log into FS_TWO. Likewise if the workstation is already connected to FS_TWO he would ATTACH to FS_ONE. In this case an ATTACH command would exist in the login scripts for both of the accounts. Each would ATTACH to the other file server. On FS_ONE the login script would read;

ATTACH FS_TWO

And on FS_TWO the login script command would be;

ATTACH FS_ONE

The other options of the ATTACH command are used only if the user name or password is different on the other file server. If user JSMITH's supervisor changed her mind about how much access he should have to FS_TWO, she could remove his account there and insist that he use another account for such purposes called STAFF with a password of PICNIC. JSMITH's login script on FS_ONE would now read;

ATTACH FS_TWO/STAFF;PICNIC

The login script for the STAFF account would not need an ATTACH command.

BREAK

The BREAK command controls how the keyboard responds during execution of the login script. If the command BREAK ON is used, the login script can be halted by holding down the CONTROL key and pressing BREAK. The BREAK key may also be labeled SCROLL LOCK. If the command is in the form BREAK OFF the execution of the login script cannot be stopped with CONTROL-BREAK.

COMSPEC

The COMSPEC command can be very important to the proper operation of the workstation. DOS always keeps a pointer (called the COMSPEC environment variable) to the file containing the command processor program. The command processor provided with every version of DOS is a program called COMMAND.COM. DOS must be told where this file is located because it must often be reloaded into memory after the execution of a program. Ordinarily when a computer is booted the COMSPEC variable is set to point to the COMMAND.COM that was used to boot the computer. If the computer was booted from floppy disk drive A:, the COMSPEC variable would probably read

COMSPEC=A:\COMMAND.COM.

But if the boot disk was then removed, COMMAND.COM would no longer reside where the COMSPEC variable points to. If this computer were on a network, the COMSPEC variable could be set to point to a copy of COMMAND.COM on a network drive, where it cannot be removed.

The COMSPEC login script command allows the variable to be set automatically when the user logs in. In its simplest form, the command COMSPEC = drive:(\)file name sets the COMSPEC variable to a value such as

COMSPEC = F:COMMAND.COM

where F: has already been mapped to a directory containing a copy of COMMAND.COM. The drive option can indicate any drive letter that exists at the time the COMSPEC command is executed.

The two other forms of the command allow the COMSPEC variable to be set to a value that is indicated at the time the login script is executed. The "*n:" in the second form listed above indicates a drive number that might be used in the login script. The command might read;

COMSPEC = *2:COMMAND.COM

The result is to set the COMSPEC variable to point to a copy of COMMAND.COM in a directory on the second network drive, already mapped to whatever the drive letter may be. The "Sn:" in the third form of the command indicates a search drive number. Under NetWare, a special type of drive mapping called a search drive can be made to allow the computer to automatically search a directory for a program that is not in the current directory. When mapping such a search drive the user maps a search drive number such as S1: or S2:. NetWare designates the associated drive letter by starting at the end of the alphabet, so S1: becomes drive letter Z: and S2: becomes Y: unless those letters are already in use. By using a command such as

COMSPEC = S1:COMMAND.COM

the supervisor can ensure that the COMSPEC variable points to the first search drive already assigned, without knowing what drive letter it is using.

In any of the three forms of this command, the drive letter used should point to the directory containing the COMMAND.COM program, because the command only accepts twelve characters after the drive specification. With this restriction a command such as

COMSPEC = S1:\DOS\COMMAND.COM

would not be legal. The path \DOS\COMMAND.COM is too long.

DISPLAY

Using the DISPLAY command, a message can be displayed on the screen each time a user logs in. The message is contained in a file represented by the file name option in the command. The file name can include a complete directory path such as;

DISPLAY F:\PUBLIC\MESSAGE.TXT

DISPLAY is used when the file contains only the ASCII characters that are to be displayed. FDISPLAY is used when the file contains control characters placed there by a word processing program that are not intended to be displayed. FDISPLAY will filter out these characters before printing the message on the screen.

(DOS) BREAK

DOS also has a BREAK command. This login script command sets the DOS environment variable to BREAK ON or BREAK OFF.

(DOS) SET

The SET command is used to set any DOS environment variable to any value. These values can be checked later by other login script commands, batch file commands, or other programs. This command is identical in function to the DOS command SET. The only differences are the optional word DOS and the use of quotation marks around the value in the login script command. Some examples are:

DOS SET USER="JANE"

SET ROOM="D229"

SET PROMPT="PG"

Several login script variables can be used to place special values in an environment variable. These variables will be discussed later.

DOS VERIFY

The DOS VERIFY flag can be set so that each time a file is copied DOS will read the newly created copy and compare it with the original to ensure it is correct. The login script command DOS VERIFY can be used to turn this feature on or off.

DRIVE

The drive command is used to set the default drive. Normally the default drive is the first network drive, usually drive F. With the DRIVE drive letter: command it can be set to any valid local or network drive letter. The DRIVE *drive number: form of the command is used to set the default drive to a number indicating the order in which the drive was mapped. For instance, the command

DRIVE *1:

would set the default drive to the first network drive letter, which might be F.

The command

DRIVE C:

could be used to set the default drive to be the local hard disk drive C:

EXIT

The EXIT command is used to terminate a login script and to start another program. It is often necessary to start another program, usually a menu program, at the conclusion of the login script. When the LOGIN.EXE program finishes processing the login script, it can pass control on to any executable program named in the parameter "file name". For example, if user JSMITH needed a menu program called MENU.EXE executed each time he logged in, the last line in his login script might be

EXIT "F:MENU"

The item in quotes can actually be any DOS command as long as it is fourteen characters or less in length. Therefore in addition to any executable program, any batch file or DOS internal command can be used. For example, suppose a user simply needed a directory listing each time he logged in. The last line in the login script would be

EXIT "DIR /W"

The login script for user DATA in Fig. 9-8 uses the EXIT command in this way. Since the option in quotes is sent directly to DOS, drive numbers cannot be used. Also, programs that terminate and stay resident should not be used.

#Program name with command line options

The "#" symbol is known as the External Program Execution command. This command tells the LOGIN program to temporarily suspend its operations, load and run the program named. When the program is finished, control is returned to the LOGIN program and the login script resumes execution at the next line. The program called by the External Program Execution command must have either an .EXE or .COM extension, but it can be called from any directory with any command line options it needs. The login script command

#F:\APPS\LOTUS\LOTUS COLOR.SET

loads and executes a program called LOTUS from the F:\APPS\LOTUS directory and passes the command line parameter COLOR.SET to it. As with the EXIT command, terminate and stay resident programs are excluded.

The example above, however, would be a very unusual case since after the user exited the LOTUS program, control would return to the LOGIN program and the rest of the login script would be executed.

FIRE PHASERS

The FIRE PHASERS command is used to catch the user's attention by generating a science fiction like sound. The "number" parameter tells the login script how many times to make the sound. The command

FIRE PHASERS 3 TIMES

would cause the alarm to sound three times.

IF Statement

This command structure allows the login script to test conditions and execute different commands based on the result. The command executed as a result of the comparison can be any valid login script command. In the diagram of the IF THEN structure above, the "condition" represents a true or false comparison of two items. The comparison will always be in the form

ITEM OPERATOR ITEM

where the operator tests the relationship between the two items. In the first form of the command a single command is executed as the result of any number of comparisons, if they are all true. In the second form of the command, the key word BEGIN is used to start a list of commands to be executed. The key word END is used to indicate the end of the list of commands. Between the BEGIN and END may be any number of commands that will be executed only if all the conditions are true. The command will accept many different operators in the testing of the two items, as shown below:

To represent equal	To represent not equal
IS	IS NOT
=	!=
==	<>
EQUALS	#
	DOES NOT EQUAL
	NOT EQUAL TO

Four more relationships can be tested using the following operators. Either the symbols on the right or the words on the left may be used in the IF THEN command.

IS GREATER THAN	>
IS LESS THAN	<
IS GREATER THAN OR EQUAL TO	>=
IS LESS THAN OR EQUAL TO	<=

Several pairs of items can be compared using the AND operator. Also, the AND operator may be replaced with a comma. Comparisons such as these are possible:

IF DAY_OF_WEEK IS "Monday" AND HOUR >= "09" THEN SET NOW="*"

This command tests whether a variable DAY_OF_WEEK is equal to Monday and checks whether a variable HOUR is greater than or equal to 9. If both conditions are true a DOS environment variable NOW is given a value of "*".

IF DAY > THAN "15", DAY_OF_WEEK IS NOT "Sunday"
THEN BEGIN
FIRE PHASERS 2 TIMES
DOS SET REMIND="Pay the bills today!"
END

This command checks to see if the day of the month is greater than 15 and makes sure the day of the week is not Sunday. If those conditions are met, the alarm will sound two times and a DOS environment variable is set to the string "Pay the bills today!".

The variables DAY, DAY_OF_WEEK and HOUR are login script variables that are set before execution of the login script. Many more such variables are available for use in the IF THEN command as well as other commands. The following is a complete list of the login script variables available:

Variable	Possible Values
AM_PM	(am or pm)
DAY	(01 - 31)
DAY_OF_WEEK	(Sunday - Saturday)
ERROR_LEVEL	(0 - 255)
FULL_NAME	(The user's full name recorded in SYSCON)
GREETING_TIME	(Morning, Afternoon, Evening)
HOUR	(1 - 12)
HOUR24	(00 - 24)
LOGIN_NAME	(The user's login name)

Variable	Possible Values
MACHINE	(The name of the workstation type of computer)
MEMBER OF	(The MEMBER OF variable is a special case in that it is not used with a comparison operator. It is used to check if the user is a member of a given group.)
MINUTE	(00 - 59)
MONTH	(01 - 12)
MONTH_NAME	(January - December)
NDAY_OF_WEEK	(1 - 7 where Sunday is 1 and Saturday is 7)
NEW_MAIL	(YES or NO indicating whether new mail is waiting for the user)
OS	(The operating system running on the users' workstation)
OS_VERSION	(The version number of a DOS workstation)
P_STATION	(The physical node number of the workstation)
SECOND	(00 - 59)
SHELL_TYPE	(A code number indicating the type of network shell running on the user's workstation)
SHORT_YEAR	(The last two digits of the year)
SMACHINE	(A shortened name for the workstation type)
STATION	(The connection number assigned to the workstation)
YEAR	(The year)

INCLUDE

This login script command tells the login script to pull in a second file as a part of the currently executing login script. When the commands are finished executing in the second login script, control is returned to the calling login script. Each script file can call other script files to a maximum of ten login scripts.

Nesting login scripts in this way can be very helpful if there are many different users who all need a section of their login script to be the same.

MACHINE

The MACHINE command sets the MACHINE variable to a name intended to represent the type of workstation computer being used. The two forms of the command are equivalent.

MAP

The MAP command is used to display or set the drive mappings of the workstation. It assigns drive letters to directories on the file server or drives on the local workstation or displays those assignments. There are fourteen separate forms of this command, each requiring a complete description. This command is another in which the login script variables can be used. Directory names used in the MAP command can contain login script variables preceded by a "%".

Suppose a directory has been created for each user with the user's name being the name of the directory. For user JSMITH the directory would be F:\JSMITH. A directory for each user is usually referred to as a user's home directory. Each user might need a drive letter assigned to his or her home directory in the login script. To do this a MAP command could be placed in each user's login script that includes the login script variable LOGIN_NAME.

MAP H:=F:\%LOGIN_NAME

When LOGIN.EXE executes this command it will replace the %LOGIN_NAME with the individual user's name and, in the case of user JSMITH, the result would be

MAP H:=F:\JSMITH

giving the user a new drive letter H: that points to the F:\JSMITH directory.

In its simplest form, the MAP command alone displays all drive letter assignments, including the drive letters assigned to local disk drives. The command

MAP drive:

displays the directory or local drive that the drive letter listed points to.

MAP drive:=directory

sets the drive letter listed to point to the directory listed. The directory may contain the volume name.

MAP drive:=directory ; drive:=directory ; ...

shows that multiple drive letter assignments may be made following a single MAP command. Each assignment is separated by a semicolon.

MAP directory

changes the current drive letter to point to the directory listed. The directory may contain a volume name.

MAP drive:=

assigns the drive letter listed to point to the current directory.

MAP drive:=drive:

assigns the drive letter on the left to point to the directory pointed to by the drive letter on the right.

MAP INSERT search drive:=directory

creates a new search drive pointing to the directory listed.

MAP DEL drive:

deletes the drive letter assignment.

MAP REM drive:

removes the drive letter assignment. Exactly the same as the MAP DEL command.

MAP DISPLAY OFF

instructs LOGIN.EXE not to display the drive mappings made when the user logs in. Ordinarily the drive mapping are displayed.

MAP DISPLAY ON

explicitly tells the LOGIN.EXE program to display the drive mappings when the user logs in.

MAP ERRORS OFF

instructs LOGIN.EXE not to display any error messages that may be generated as a result of an incorrect MAP command in the login script. Ordinarily all errors would be displayed.

MAP ERRORS ON

explicitly tell the LOGIN.EXE program to display all error messages concerning MAP commands in the login script.

PAUSE

The login script command PAUSE works exactly the same as the DOS batch file command of the same name. It halts execution of the login script and displays the message "Strike a key when ready...". After the user presses a key the login script is resumed at the next command. The word WAIT may be used for the same function.

PCCOMPATIBLE

This command is only necessary when the workstation has been set to identify itself incorrectly as not being an IBM PC-compatible computer. It allows other commands in the login script to treat the workstation as compatible, even though the login script variables MACHINE and SMACHINE may indicate a different type of computer. The two forms of the command, PCCOMPATIBLE and COMPATIBLE are, of course, completely compatible.

REMARK

Often the supervisor will wish to place remarks or comments in the text of the login script that are not intended to be executed. These might include explanations of a particularly complex IF THEN structure, the need for various drive mappings, or a message for future supervisors. Either of the four forms of the REMARK command will prevent LOGIN.EXE from attempting to execute the remark statement following it.

WRITE

The WRITE command is roughly equivalent to the PRINT command in the BASIC programming language or the ECHO command in a batch file. It displays the text following it on the user's screen at the time it is executed. The easiest way to use the WRITE command is to simply put a message in quotes.

WRITE "Welcome to file server FS_ONE."

The WRITE command above would tell the user which file server he or she just logged in to. But WRITE commands can be much more flexible. The text to be displayed can use the same login script variables that the IF THEN command can use. As in the MAP command the variable is preceded by a "%" to tell the LOGIN.EXE program to convert it to the value it represents. In the command

WRITE "Welcome %LOGIN_NAME, to file server FS_ONE."

the %LOGIN_NAME would be converted to the user name. In the case of user JSMITH, the message displayed would read;

Welcome JSMITH, to file server FS_ONE.

The login script variables can also be used outside the quotes without the preceding "%". The command

WRITE "Welcome ";LOGIN_NAME;", to file server FS_ONE."

is exactly equivalent to the write command above. Notice that a semicolon is used to separate the components of the text when a variable is used outside the quotes and without the "%".

In addition to the login script variables, there are four special symbols that may be used within the quotes to control the format of the text printed on the screen.

Symbol	Description
\r	(Carriage return. Causes the cursor to return to column one on the same line of the screen.)
\n	(New line. Causes the cursor to go to the first column of the next line. The cursor will automatically go to a new line at the end of a WRITE command.)
\"	(Embedded quotation mark. Must be used to display a quotation.)
\7	(ASCII character seven. Causes a beep sound to be generated.)

The WRITE command below shows the effects of some of these symbols.

```
WRITE "HAPPY\n  \"BIRTHDAY\"\n      ";LOGIN_NAME
```

For user JSMITH, the output on the screen would look like this:

```
HAPPY
  "BIRTHDAY"
      JSMITH
```

The login script commands listed above give the supervisor a very powerful language to meet the user's needs. With them a user's environment can be constructed to allow him or her to use the network freely or to take the user directly into an application. The possibilities are endless.

In the next section of this chapter, SYSCON will be used to create users, assign them trustee rights, and create login scripts.

Hands-on NetWare

In the previous chapter, Novell NetWare was completely installed on a file server. But the installation of the NetWare software was only a small part of creating a usable network. The structure of the directories, the creation of user accounts, the setting up of network printers, and many other tasks will require much more work and thought. A network's supervisor is the one who must consider how the network will be used and determine how best to serve each user, while maintaining overall system continuity and security.

When NetWare is installed a user account is automatically created called SUPERVISOR. It has complete trustee rights over the entire server and permission to use all menus in each of the NetWare utilities. Originally the account has no password, so the first thing that should be done on any newly installed Novell network is to give the user SUPERVISOR a password. To do this, the file server must be running, and a workstation must be booted with the proper network drivers. In this section you will prepare the server and workstation for operation, login to the network, start the SYSCON utility, and give the account SUPERVISOR a password of FIRST. All commands shown here are written in upper case characters for clarity. However, they can be entered as either upper or lower case.

Preparing the Network for Operation

1. Prepare the server for operation by simply turning it on. A message saying that the LAN is initializing and the volumes are being mounted should appear.
2. At a network workstation, boot the workstation with the appropriate DOS boot disk. To do this, insert the boot disk created in chapter 8 into drive A. If the computer is off, simply turn it on. If the computer is on, hold down the [Ctrl] and [alt] keys and press the [delete] key. The computer should read the disk and display a message showing the DOS version being used. An A> prompt should be at the left of the screen.
3. The network drivers must now be loaded into memory. Type **IPX** and press the [Enter←] key. A message should appear confirming that the IPX program has successfully loaded.
4. Type the name of the appropriate NET# program needed. The "#" symbol here represents the number of the DOS version being used. Your screen should say what version the computer was just booted with. If the version is 2.1 type **NET2** and press the [Enter←] key. If the version is 3.3 type **NET3** and press the [Enter←] key.

If the workstation booted successfully and the network drivers were loaded successfully, the screen should appear similar to the one in Fig. 9-11. The DOS version, the version and type of IPX, and the version of the NET# program may all be different. The "A>" prompt shows the default drive is still the local drive A:. To perform any network operations it is necessary to access the network drive. The network drivers automatically assign the first drive letter to the network drive based on the next letter available after the letters reserved by the workstation for local drives. DOS reserves drive letters A - E unless the DOS LASTDRIVE command is used, or there are more than five disk drives on the workstation. The next drive letter available on almost all DOS workstations is then F.

Logging In

Once the network drivers have been loaded, the workstation is attached to the file server, but no one is logged in. Logging in tells the file server who the user is and how much access that user has.

1. Type F: and press the [Enter←] key. At this point no user is logged in, so the workstation has only limited access to the server.

2. Type **DIR** and press the [Enter ←] key. The files available to all workstations, whether a user is logged in or not, should scroll by. They are stored in a directory already created by NetWare called F:\LOGIN.

3. Type **LOGIN SUPERVISOR** and press the [Enter ←] key. The LOGIN program prompts the user for whatever information it is not given before attempting to actually log the user on to the network, so an "Enter Password" message is displayed next. Press the [Enter ←] key without any other characters to indicate that there is no password for that user. (When you type the password, the characters typed are not displayed on the screen.)

```
Enter new date (mm-dd-yy):
Current time is 11:14:43.93
Enter new time:


The IBM Personal Computer DOS
Version 3.30 (C)Copyright International Business Machines Corp 1981, 1987
             (C)Copyright Microsoft Corp 1981, 1986

A>ipx
Novell IPX/SPX v3.01 Rev. B (900605)
(C) Copyright 1985, 1990 Novell Inc.  All Rights Reserved.

LAN Option: IBM PCN II & Baseband  V1.10 (880526)
Hardware Configuration: IRQ = 2, IO Address = 620h, RAM = CE00H   Micro Channel
Bus Only

A>net3
NetWare V3.01 rev. B - Workstation Shell for PC DOS V3.x
(C) Copyright 1983, 1988 Novell, Inc.  All Rights Reserved.

Attached to server IO
Wednesday, July 24, 1991    11:15:01 am
A>
```

Fig. 9-11. Screen displaying a successful load of network drivers

Starting the SYSCON Utility

The SYSCON utility is a program on the file server stored in a directory called F:\PUBLIC. It is used for much of the setup and maintenance a supervisor must do.

1. Type **CD\PUBLIC** and press the [Enter ←] key.

2. Type **DIR** and press the [Enter ←] key. This step is included to familiarize you with the environment of the file server. A directory listing of all the files the NetWare installation program has placed in the PUBLIC directory should scroll by. The list is quite long and represents all the NetWare utilities

a general user might need. The SYSCON utility is here because a user can view or modify many of his or her own attributes.

3. Type **SYSCON** and press the [Enter←] key. SYSCON's main menu should appear, similar to the screen in Fig. 9-12.

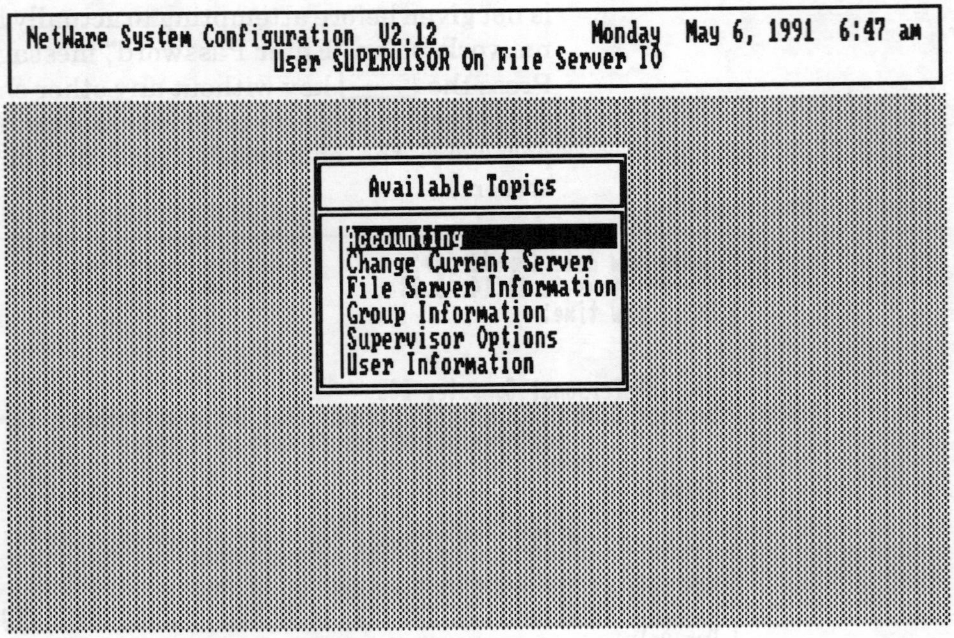

Fig. 9-12. The SYSCON main menu

Changing a User Password

Each user account on a NetWare file server can be given a password. The password is intended to be kept secret so that only a certain person or set of people can access the account. The user's name is intended to be public so everyone on the network can interact with the user through electronic mail or other network services. The supervisor's account is a special case in two respects. It is absolutely important that unauthorized people do not use the supervisor account, and it is absolutely critical that the supervisor does. If a user forgets his password the supervisor can change it to a new one. But if the supervisor forgets his or her own password, and has not created a supervisor-equivalent user, NetWare must be reinstalled. A good idea is to write down the supervisor password and place it in a sealed envelope. Then place the envelope in a secure place such as a locked cabinet or vault.

Remember that, in a NetWare utility, an item can be highlighted by moving the cursor or by typing the name of the item to be selected. A list of users on a large network can be quite long, so the easiest way to find the supervisor account is to type SUPERVISOR. The cursor will move to the first occurrence of the letters typed. For instance, when "S" is typed the alphabetically first user name that begins with "S" will be highlighted. If the only other name that began with "S" was SUE, it would stay highlighted until the "P" in the word supervisor was typed.

1. Move the cursor down to User Information and press the Enter key. The list of user accounts should appear.
2. Press the Enter key when the user name SUPERVISOR has been highlighted and the User Information box will be displayed on the right side of the screen.

Notice that there are now three menu boxes of the screen. Only one menu is active at any one time, and SYSCON tells the user which one by highlighting the border of the active box.

3. Move the cursor down to the option Change Password and then press the Enter key. Another box will appear at the bottom of the screen as shown in Fig. 9-13.

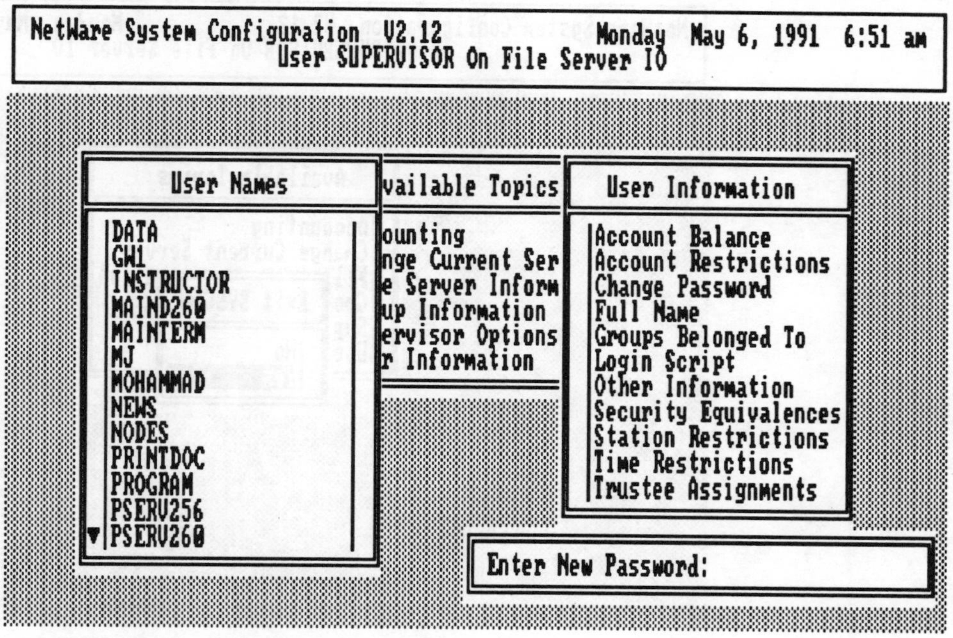

Fig. 9-13. Screen displaying dialog box to change the password

The Change Password option will not display the old password, it only prompts for a new one. If fact, there is no method for finding out what a current password is. Even as a password is typed, it is not displayed on the screen. When Enter is pressed after typing a password, the password box flickers away for an instant and returns. The password must be typed a second time for verification. If the two entries do not match, the user must start over.

4. In either upper or lower case letters, type **FIRST** for a password and press the Enter key.

5. Type **FIRST** again to verify and press the Enter key. When this operation has been completed the cursor will return to the User Information menu.

Testing the Password

Presumably, the password has been set to the word FIRST, but, as with any complex system, nothing can be believed until it has been tested. In some situations the supervisor will create all user passwords and not allow any changes. In others, the supervisor only creates an initial password. After the user has logged in, he or she may be allowed to change it. In either case, a good supervisor will test everything possible. To test a password, the user must log out of the network, then log back in.

1. Press the Esc key three times. This should take SYSCON to its final menu box, as shown in Fig. 9-14.

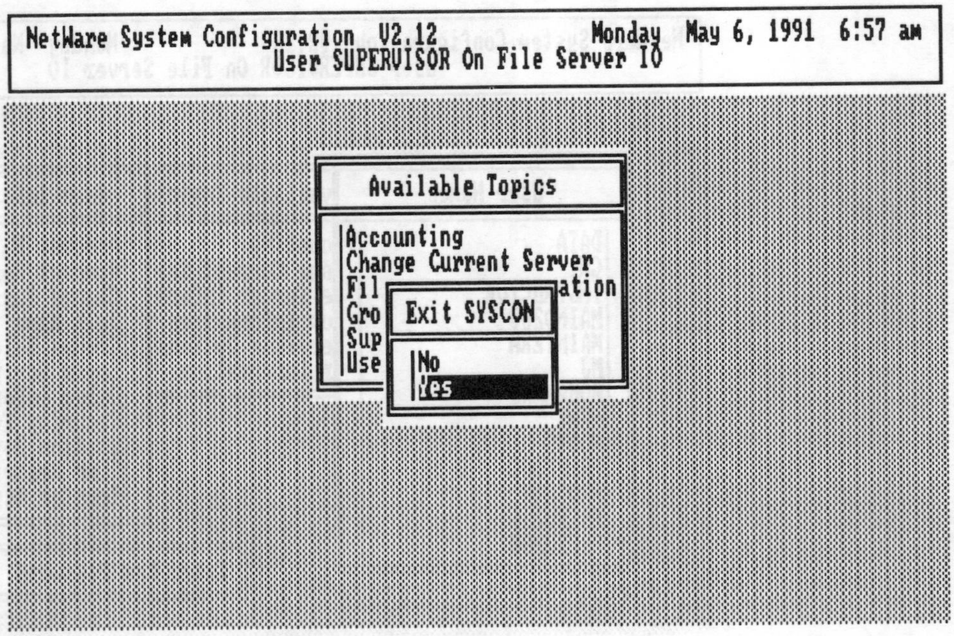

Fig. 9-14. Exit option from the SYSCON utility

2. Select Yes to exit SYSCON by pressing Y and the Enter key.
3. At the F> prompt type LOGOUT and press the Enter key. A message should appear saying what time user SUPERVISOR logged out, from which station, and from which server.
4. At this point the workstation is still attached to the file server. Type **DIR** and the listing of the F:\LOGIN directory should scroll by as it did earlier in the Logging In section.
5. Type **LOGIN SUPERVISOR** and press the Enter key.
6. Type **FIRST** at the password prompt and press the Enter key.

The word FIRST will not appear on the screen as it is typed. If you were able to login successfully, the password was correctly entered in SYSCON twice and in the LOGIN program once. As a general rule, after changing a password, if you cannot login using the password, try variations of misspellings of the word.

7. To complete the exercise, type **LOGOUT** again and press the Enter← key.

After installing NetWare and giving the account SUPERVISOR a suitable password, the system supervisor should use the actual SUPERVISOR account as little as possible. For maximum security, new user accounts should be created that allow the supervisor to perform the tasks required of him or her at lower security levels. The supervisor account is simply too important and powerful to use frequently. In the next section a new user will be created. This user will be able to perform all supervisor tasks needed for the rest of the exercises in this book.

Creating a User Account

Only the supervisor or a supervisor equivalent can create accounts. The last section ended by giving the supervisor account the password FIRST. That account and password must be used again to create supervisor equivalent accounts that each student in the network classroom can use. The file server and the workstation must be running, and the network drivers should be loaded on the workstation for the following steps.

Enter SYSCON

1. Type **F:** and press the Enter← key.
2. Type **LOGIN SUPERVISOR** and press the Enter← key.
3. Type **FIRST** at the password prompt and press the Enter← key. The word FIRST will not appear on the screen as it is typed.
4. Type **CD\PUBLIC** and press the Enter← key.
5. Type **SYSCON** and press the Enter← key.
6. Highlight Accounting and press the Enter← key.
7. If an Install Accounting? message appears, type Y and press the Enter← key.
8. Press the Esc key.

The User Information Menu

Creating a new user in SYSCON involves using the User Information Menu. This menu is not reached directly, it appears only after a user name has been selected. If the user name does not yet exist, it must be inserted into the list of user names. When the User Information option is selected from the SYSCON main menu, the list of names appears first. After a name has been selected or inserted, the User Information menu allows the supervisor to establish the users' attributes such as trustee rights, group status, and login scripts.

1. Move the cursor to the User Information line and press the [Enter] key. The list of users should appear on the left of the screen.
2. Press the [Ins] key. A box asking for a new user name should appear in the center of the screen.
3. To establish a unique user name for each student on the network, type in your first initial and last name, then press the [Enter] key. A message could appear informing you that name already exists. If it does, try a different form of your name.
4. Press the [Enter] key.

When a user name has been successfully entered, the user's name should be in the list of users on the left and the User Information menu should be on the right. In the following sections, most of the options in the User Information menu will be used.

Checking the Account Balance

Depending on how other options may have been set, this user may be charged for connect time. By setting charge rates and account balances the supervisor can limit the time a user is connected to the network or how many of the network services a user can access without checking with the supervisor. When creating a new user, it is important to ensure that the account balance allows the user to login.

1. Highlight Supervisor Options in the SYSCON menu and press the [Enter] key.
2. Highlight Accounting and press the [Enter] key.
3. Answer Yes when asked to install the accounting features.
4. Highlight the Account Balance line in the User Information menu and press the [Enter] key. A small box similar to the one in Fig. 9-15 should appear.
5. Move the cursor to the line that reads Allow Unlimited Credit.
6. Press the [Y] and [Enter] keys.
7. Press the [Esc] key to accept the changes and return to the User Information menu.

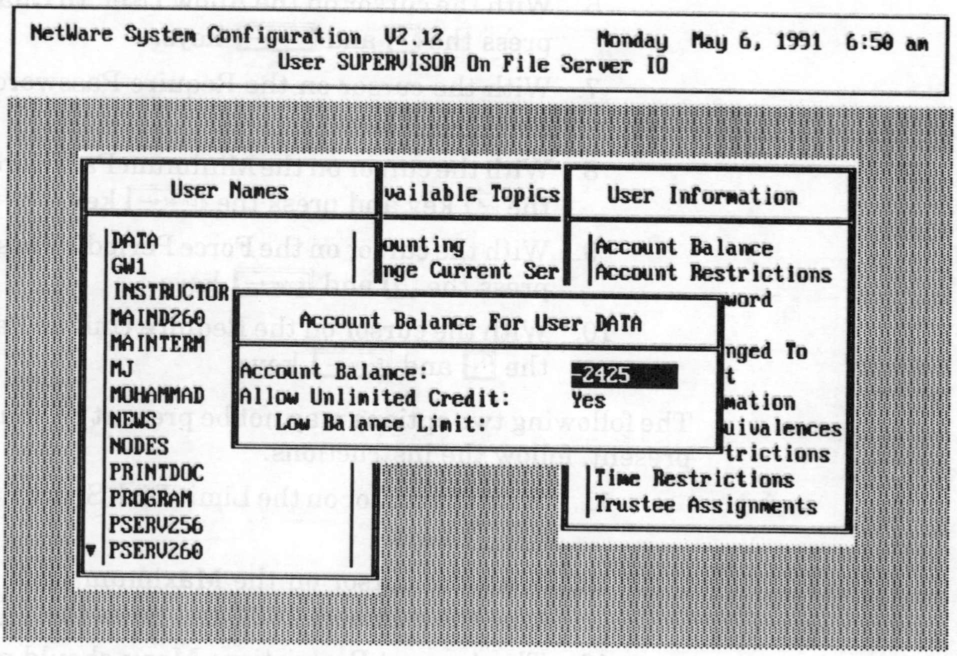

Fig. 9-15. Account balance dialog box

The Account Restrictions Menu

This screen allows you to change many of the very fundamental attributes of the account. The cursor can be moved up or down the list of account restrictions. When an item is highlighted, a new value can be simply typed in. The ESCAPE key is used to accept the changes after all modifications have been made. Follow the instructions below to ensure that all of the values are correct. Move the highlighted area to the appropriate field by pressing the up or down cursor keys.

1. Move the cursor to the Account Restrictions line of the User Information menu and press the [Enter] key. A large box should appear with the title Account Restrictions For User DATA.
2. The field at the end of the Account Disabled line should now be highlighted. Press the [N] and then [Enter] keys.
3. Press [N] and then [Enter] on the Account Has Expiration Date line. Without an expiration date, the cursor will skip to the Limit Concurrent Connections field when the down cursor key is pressed.
4. Press the [Y] and [Enter] keys. The cursor should move to the Maximum Connections field.
5. Press the [1] and [Enter] keys. With a one in this field only one workstation can be logged in under this user name.

6. With the cursor on the Allow User To Change Password field, press the [Y] and [Enter←] keys.
7. With the cursor on the Require Password field, press the [Y] and [Enter←] keys.
8. With the cursor on the Minimum Password Length field, press the [4] key and press the [Enter←] key.
9. With the cursor on the Force Periodic Password Changes field, press the [N] and [Enter←] keys.
10. With the cursor on the Require Unique Passwords field, press the [N] and [Enter←] keys.

The following two options may not be present on your system. If they are present, follow the instructions.

11. With the cursor on the Limit Disk Space field, press the [Y] and [Enter←] keys.
12. With the cursor on the Maximum Disk Space (in KB) field, type the numbers 1024 and press the [Enter←] key.
13. The Account Restrictions Menu should now look like the one shown in Fig. 9-16. Press the [esc] key to accept these changes and return to the User Information menu.

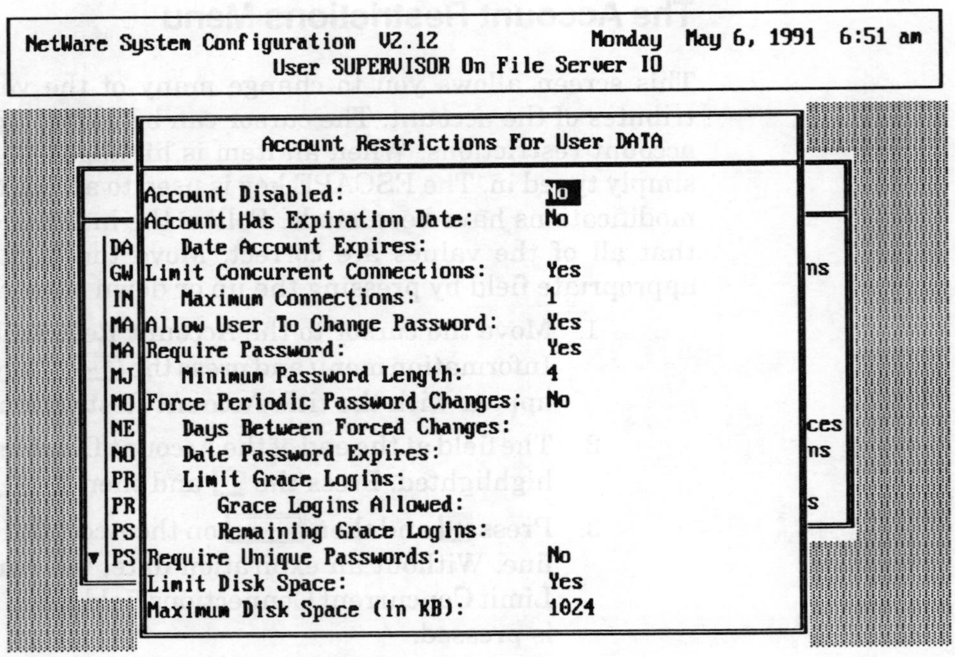

Fig. 9-16. Account restriction dialog box

Creating a Password

This account will need to be password protected just as the supervisor account is. Ordinarily a password should be unusual and not associated with the user in any way. For the purpose of this exercise the same password will be used on all accounts.

1. Highlight the Change Password option on the User Information menu and press the [Enter←] key.
2. Type the word **FIRST** in the box provided and press the [Enter←] key. The word will not show on the screen as it is typed.
3. For verification the password must be entered again. Type the word **FIRST** and press the [Enter←] key.

Creating a Login Script

To facilitate this user's access to the network, a login script can be created which maps search drives to frequently used directories. The directories that would be helpful are F:\PUBLIC, F:\SYSTEM and F:\LOGIN. Other information may be put in a login script that displays a message when the user logs in.

The following steps create a login script that maps the proper search drives and displays an interesting message.

1. Select the Login Script option from the User Information menu by highlighting Login Script and pressing the [Enter←] key.

Since this user does not have a login script, SYSCON offers to make a copy of another login script. A Copy Login Script From box appears to allow you to type in the name of another user with a login script.

2. Press the [Enter←] key to indicate that no other login script is to be used. A blank screen similar to the one in Fig. 9-17 should appear.

At this point, any login script can be typed in. Within the large box the cursor can be moved freely about with the arrow keys. The login script can be any length because the screen inside the box will scroll as it is filled up. Also, the INSERT and DELETE keys function much as they would in any full screen editor.

3. Type **MAP S1:=SYS:\PUBLIC** and press the [Enter←] key.
4. Type **MAP S2:=SYS:\SYSTEM** and press the [Enter←] key.
5. Type **MAP S3:=SYS:\LOGIN** and press the [Enter←] key.
6. Type **IF DAY_OF_WEEK IS "Monday" WRITE "Monday Again!"** and press the [Enter←] key.
7. Type **WRITE "Another %DAY_OF_WEEK %GREETING_TIME."** and press the [Enter←] key.

8. Press the [Esc] key. A box will appear asking you if you want to save the changes.
9. Press the [Y] and [Enter ←] keys. The User Information menu should reappear.

The SYS: in the above login script commands specifies a volume on the file server. Volumes are major divisions of the file server's hard disk.

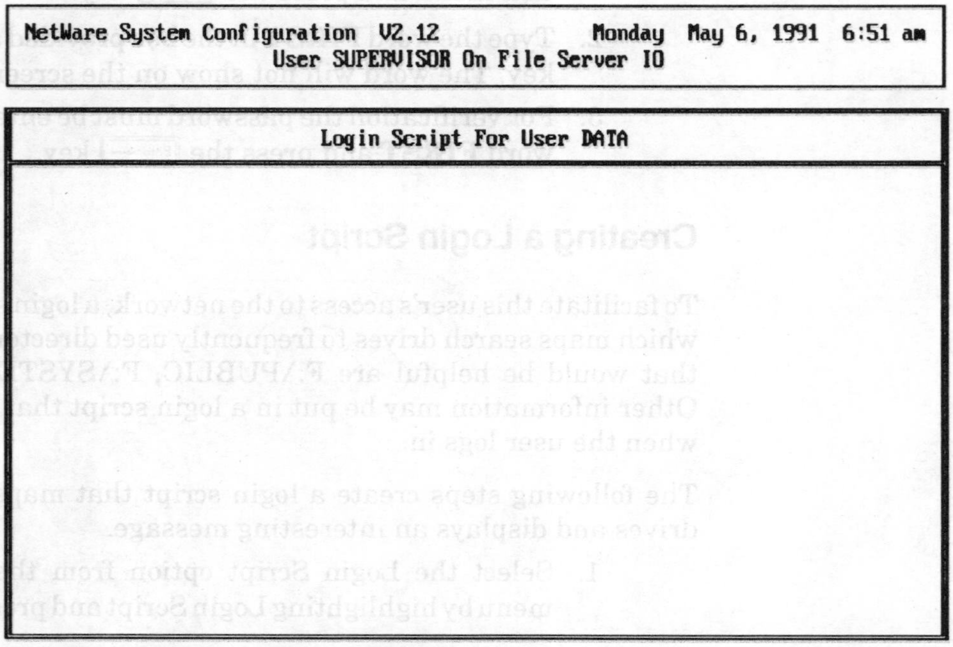

Fig. 9-17. Data entry screen for creating login scripts

Setting the Security Equivalences

On any NetWare network, there should be at least one account that has a security equivalence to user SUPERVISOR. That other account should be used most of the time that supervisor maintenance is required. In this exercise the student account will be given supervisor security equivalence.

1. Highlight the Security Equivalences option in the User Information menu and press the [Enter ←] key. A list of current security equivalences for this user will appear on the right side of the screen as it does in Fig. 9-18.
2. Press the [Ins] key.
3. Type the word **SUPERVISOR**. As the word SUPERVISOR is typed the highlighted bar will move along a list of users and groups of users until user SUPERVISOR is marked.

4. Press the Enter key on the user SUPERVISOR. SUPERVISOR will be added to the list of security equivalences.
5. Press the esc key to accept the changes and return to the User Information menu.

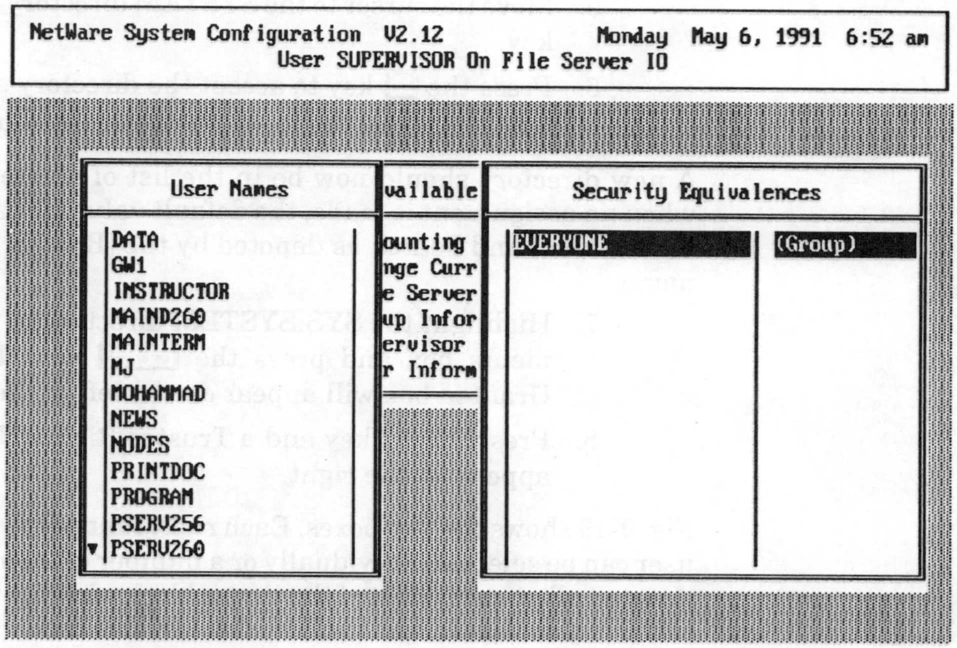

Fig. 9-18. Screen displaying security equivalences for a user

Setting Trustee Assignments

Directory access rights are called Trustee Assignments in NetWare. Each user with privileges in a certain directory is said to be a trustee of that directory. In this example the user being created is equivalent to user SUPERVISOR and so is automatically given trustee rights in all directories. However, most users will not be given such rights. The following steps demonstrate the process of modifying the trustee privileges of a user.

1. Highlight the Trustee Assignments option of the User Information menu and press the Enter key. The current Trustee Assignments for this user will be displayed on the right of the screen.
2. To add a trustee assignment to this list, press the ins key twice.

A long box labeled Directory In Which Trustee Should Be Added will appear near the top of the screen. The complete directory name could be typed in at this point, but SYSCON allows you to select from the available directories also.

3. Move the cursor to the name of the file server being used for this exercise and press the [Enter←] key.
4. With volume SYS highlighted, press the [Enter←] key. A list of directories should appear.
5. Move the cursor to the SYSTEM directory and press the [Enter←] key.
6. Press the [esc] key to accept the directory as it is shown in the long box along the top of the screen and press the [Enter←] key.

A new directory should now be in the list of trustee assignments. But when an assignment is made, the default values for access right are only Read, Open, and Search as denoted by the [R O S] after the directory name.

7. Highlight the SYS:SYSTEM directory in the Trustee Assignments box and press the [Enter←] key. The Trustee Rights Granted box will appear on the left of the screen.
8. Press the [ins] key and a Trustee Rights Not Granted box will appear on the right.

Fig. 9-19 shows the two boxes. Each right that needs to be granted to this user can be selected individually or a number of them can be marked and granted all at once. Most of the time a block of rights will need to be given to a user, so that is what will be done in this case.

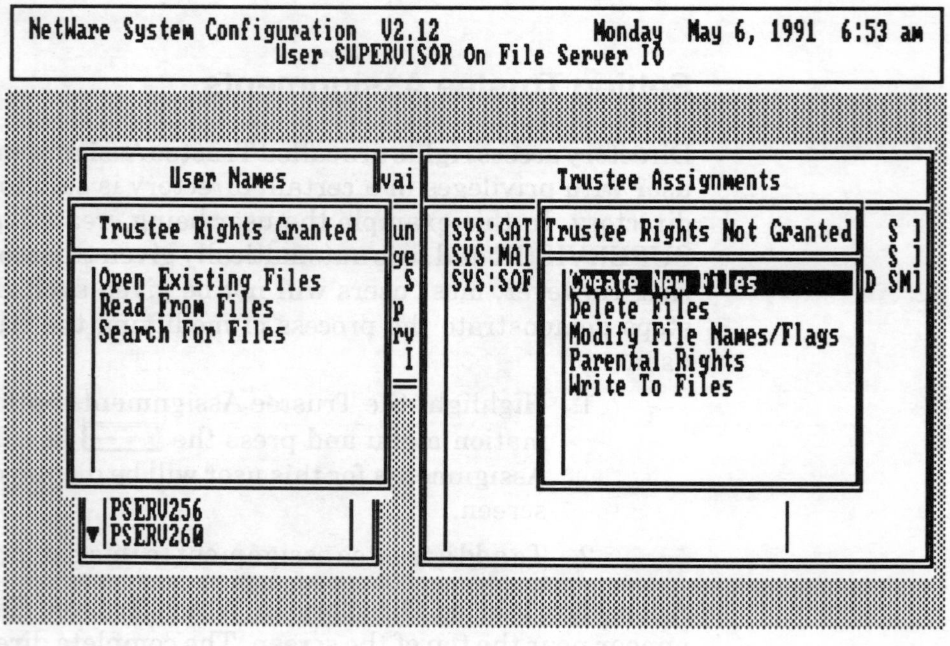

Fig. 9-19. Dialog box to assign rights to trustees

9. Press the [F5] function key.
10. Press the [↓] key to move the highlighted bar to the next trustee right not granted, which will be swapped to the other box.
11. Press [F5] again.
12. Continue marking the trustree rights not granted until they are all marked.
13. Press the [Enter←] key. The rights not granted should move to the rights granted box.
14. Press the [Esc] key twice and the User Information menu should reappear.

Testing the New Account

This user should now be set up to be able to perform any task the supervisor might need to do. But again, the job is not finished until it has been tested. To do this the current user, SUPERVISOR, must logout and the new user login.

1. Press the [Esc] key three times until the Exit SYSCON? box appears.
2. Press the [Y] and [Enter←] keys.
3. Type **LOGOUT** and press the [Enter←] key.
4. Type **LOGIN** and the name you gave to the user just created on the same line and press the [Enter←] key.
5. Type the password given to the user just created, **FIRST**, and press the [Enter←] key.

For now it will be assumed that if the user can log in, the account has been set up correctly.

6. Type **LOGOUT** and press the [Enter←] key.

Summary

The most important aspect of managing a network involves the creation of user accounts. These accounts control how and when the user will be able to use the network. With the System Configuration utility, SYSCON, the supervisor can create accounts that allow users to do the work they need to do and provide them with login scripts that set up helpful environments. The login script commands and variables available allow the supervisor to create very complex programs that can take different actions based on who the user is, the time of day, and other factors.

When creating a user, the supervisor can specify user equivalences. The new user can be given security equivalence to any user or group already on the server, including the supervisor.

Questions

1. How can a supervisor record how much time a user spends on the network?
2. How can a supervisor save time when creating individual user accounts and also be able to easily make changes to collections of users?
3. In a network with many file servers running NetWare version 2.15, can the supervisor update the user accounts on all the file servers simultaneously?
4. Under which of SYSCON's main menu options can the supervisor set default values for all users created?
5. How can the supervisor affect the user's environment each time the user logs in?
6. What can the supervisor do if a user forgets his password?
7. What should the supervisor do to ensure the security of the SUPERVISOR account?
8. Explain the function of the following lines in a login script:

   IF DAY IS EQUAL TO "29" AND MONTH = "02" THEN BEGIN

   WRITE "Today is special!"

   END.

Projects

Objective

The following projects will provide additional practice on how to create a user and login scripts. Login scripts provide a mechanism by which the system manager can customize the network and thereby make using the system easier for users.

Project 1. Using the SYSCON Utility

1. Use the SYSCON utility to create a new user. Use your initials as the name of the user.
2. Give the new user Read, Open, and Search rights to the SYS:\LOGIN, SYS:\SYSTEM, and SYS:\PUBLIC directories.

3. Create a login script for the user that maps the drive letters F:, G:, and H: to the directories listed above.
4. Add statements to the login script that print the message "Today is April Fools Day" if the user logs in on that day.
5. Exit the SYSCON utility. Set your workstations date to April 1 by typing DATE 05/01/92 and pressing the [enter] key.
6. Login as the new user. Use the [shift][print screen] keys to record the results of the login script.
7. Use the DATE command to set the date back to the current date.
8. While still logged in as the new user, start the SYSCON utility and attempt to create another user.
9. Exit the SYSCON utility and login under the supervisor equivalent account.
10. Start the SYSCON utility and delete the new user.
11. Exit the SYSCON utility

Project 2. More Login Scripts

1. Using the SYSCON utility create two new users, US1 and US2.
2. Give them the same rights as GUEST and assign US1 to a new group named DATABASE.

The rest of exercise should be created from the SYSCON utility under the Supervisor Options/System Login Script options.

3. Turn the map display off.
4. Type the basic login script commands.
5. Type all mappings to the basic applications in the system.
6. Make sure that everyone's first network drive is mapped to his or her home directory.
7. Type a greeting to be displayed when a user logs in.
8. Type the commands neccessary to display the type and version of the operating system.
9. Type the commands neccessary to display the current date and time of day.
10. Type the commands neccessary that will execute a subroutine if the user is a member of the DATABASE group.
11. Type the commands neccessary to remind all users of a meeting that begins at 12:00 noon every day of the week.
12. Turn the map display on and display the mappings at the end of the script.
13. Login as both new users (one at a time) and test the script.

10

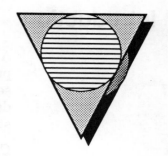

Security, Organization, and Management

Objectives

1. Understand the need for organization in the network.
2. Know the advantages of organizing users into groups.
3. Learn the available trustee rights.
4. Understand the available file attributes.
5. Understand the main menu functions of the FCONSOLE program.
6. Be familiar with the four levels of security.
7. Know how to assign restrictions to a user's account.
8. Know how to create groups.
9. Know how to use FCONSOLE to observe network activity.

Key Terms

Data Organization
FCONSOLE
Groups
Levels of Security
Trustee Rights
Directory Rights
File Attributes
Group Hierarchy
Passwords

Introduction

A network may have many functions. It may have electronic mail, shared printers, or shared modems. But all of these functions are usually secondary to providing users with shared disk space for programs and data. In addition to the shared space, most users will need to be able to store data in a private area.

Creating a structure in which users can access the shared data they need and protect their private data is the supervisor's most challenging task. Usually programs and data must be placed in different areas with different access rights. Different users will have many different needs, normally disposing them into groups of users. Under NetWare, the supervisor can grant trustee rights to these groups and still be able to customize the accounts of each user. The principle of allowing some users access to data while restricting other users is known as network security. NetWare establishes security at four levels, through passwords, trustee rights, directory rights, and file attributes. This multilevel approach allows the supervisor to customize the security requirements to fit any need.

Careful management of the users and their data must involve backing up the data. Backing up the data on the file server is important to preserve both the application software and the NetWare files. In addition to managing file software, the supervisor must maintain control over the network as a whole. Part of this can be done using the File Server Console program FCONSOLE.EXE.

Four Levels of Security

There are four main levels of security. These are

1. Passwords.
2. Trustee rights.
3. Directory rights.
4. File attributes.

Passwords

Each NetWare account can be given a password. The password is a string of characters that the user types in when he or she logs in. The LOGIN.EXE program compares the login name and password to those stored by NetWare. If they match, the user is allowed access to the account. The login name is intended to be known by everyone while the password is kept secret by the user.

The supervisor can give the user a password or allow the user to choose one the first time he or she logs in. After it has been entered, neither the user nor the supervisor can view it. If it is forgotten, the only way to access the account is for the supervisor to change it. In the System Configuration program, SYSCON.EXE, the supervisor can set defaults concerning passwords for all new accounts. Fig. 10-1 shows the Supervisor Options menu in SYSCON. By selecting Default Account Balance/Restrictions, the supervisor can access the menu shown in Fig. 10-2. This menu is almost identical to the Account Restrictions menu that can be accessed for each user. It shows the restrictions that can be placed on the user's password.

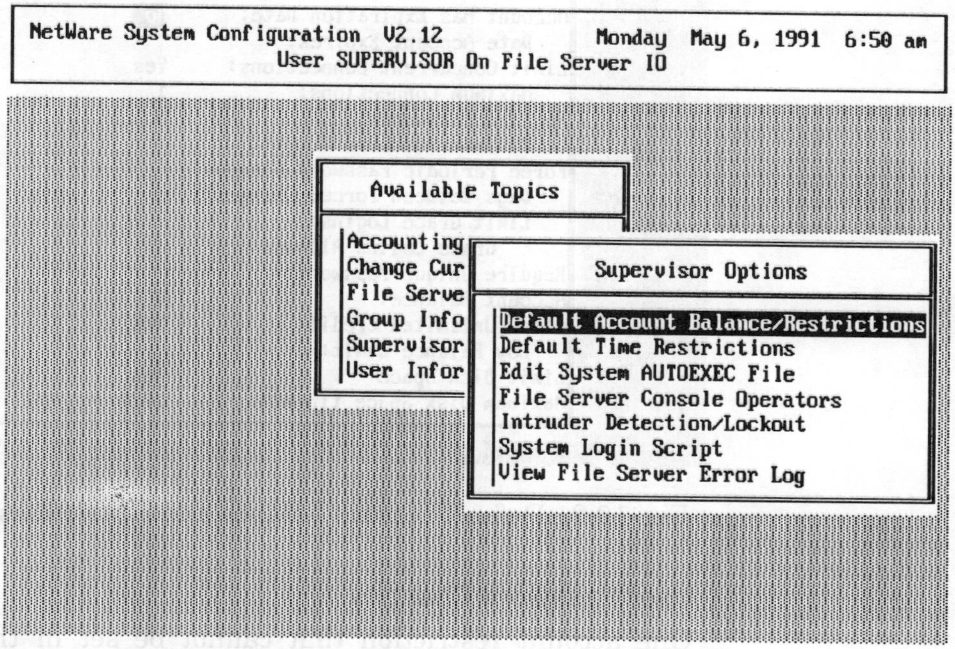

Fig. 10-1. Supervisor options menu in SYSCON

Minimum Password Length

The account can be required to have a password or not required to. If it does have a password, a minimum length can be set. The default minimum password length is 5 characters; the maximum is 128 characters.

Force Periodic Password Changes

A password is effective only if it is secret. If the same password is used for a very long time, the opportunity for an unauthorized person to discover it may be increased. This is why the account can be set to periodically force the user to change the password. If this feature is set, after the specified number of days has passed LOGIN.EXE will automatically prompt the user for a new password when he or she logs in. The account can be set to allow a certain number of grace logins that prompt the user for a new password but do not require one. If the Require Unique Passwords option is set to YES the user must enter a different password each time. NetWare remembers the last eight passwords so one could begin repeating passwords after the eighth password is used. While using the same password for too long may allow someone to discover it, forcing the user to change it too frequently may also force the user to write it down too often or to use obvious words.

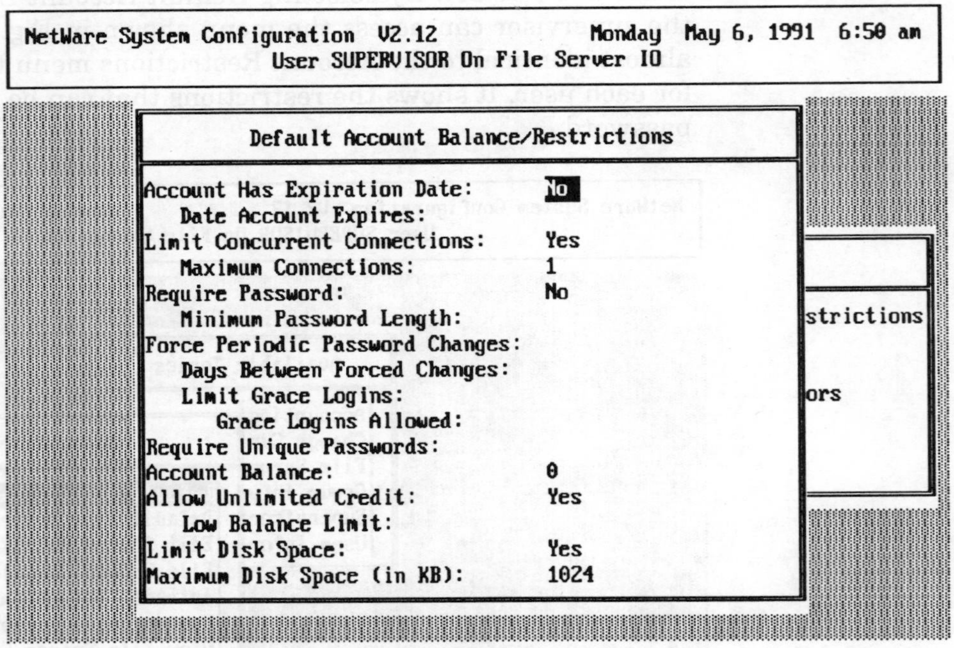

Fig. 10-2. Default account balance and restrictions dialog box

User Password Changes

One account restriction that cannot be set in the Default Account Restrictions/Balances menu is Allow User to Change Password. This can only be set in the User Information menu for each individual user. If the option Allow User to Change Password is set to No, the supervisor must enter a password for each user.

Trustee Rights

Each user must be given trustee rights through his or her individual account or through a group to have any access to the server at all. When a user is given some access to a directory, he or she is said to be a trustee of that directory. Fig. 10-3 shows the trustee rights for user DATA in a directory called SYS:GATE\GW. The column on the right of the Trustee Assignments shows all of the rights given to the user in each directory. The Trustee Rights Granted box on the left is really a menu allowing the supervisor to insert new rights or delete existing ones.

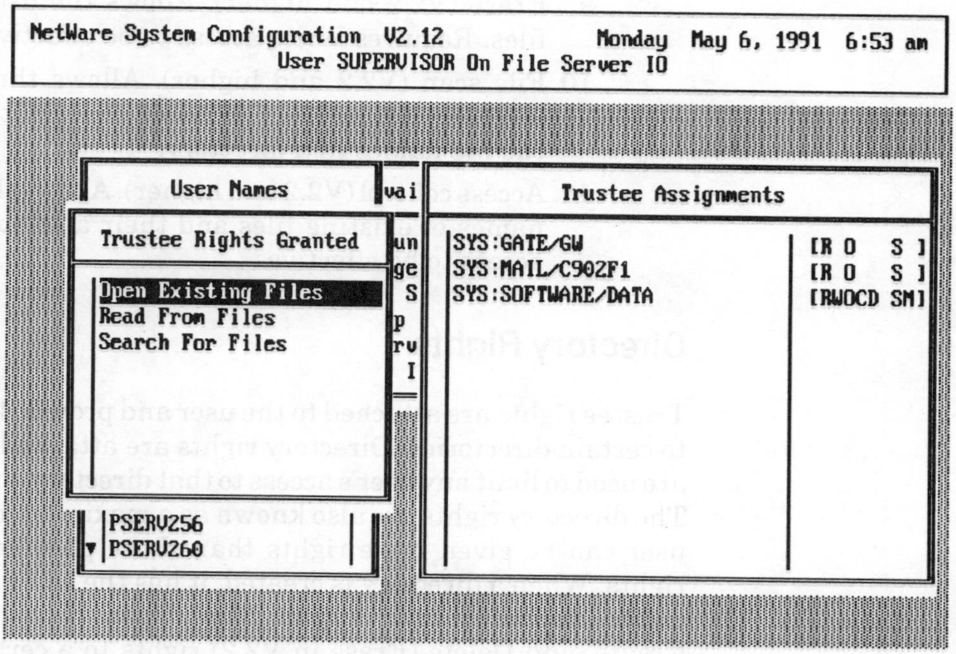

Fig. 10-3. Trustee rights for user DATA

The rights that can be given are:

1. Read (all versions). Allows the user to read from files in the directory. Usually requires Open and Search rights to be effective.
2. Write (all versions). Allows the user to write to files in the directory. Usually requires Open and Search rights to be effective.
3. Open (V2.15 and lower). Allows user to open files that already exist in the directory. It requires either Read or Write rights in order to be effective.
4. Create (all versions). Allows the user to create new files in the directory. Requires Write access in order to be effective.
5. Delete (V2.15 and lower). Allows the user to delete existing files. Requires Write access to be effective.
6. Parental (V2.15 and lower). Allows the user to grant other users rights to directory space. The user can only grant rights that he or she has to a certain directory. This right also allows the user to change the maximum rights mask.
7. Search (V2.15 and lower). Allows the user access to the directory listing itself. Without this right the user cannot even see the file names in a directory.
8. Modify (all versions). Allows the user to change the names of existing files and their attributes. Requires Write access to be effective.

9. Erase (V2.2 and higher). Allows the user to delete existing files. Requires Write access to be effective.
10. File scan (V2.2 and higher). Allows the user access to the directory listing itself. Without this right, the user cannot see the file names in a directory.
11. Access control (V2.2 and higher). Allows the user to change the names of existing files and their attributes. Requires Write access to be effective.

Directory Rights

Trustee rights are attached to the user and provide that user with access to certain directories. Directory rights are attached to the directory and are used to limit any user's access to that directory, except the supervisor. The directory rights are also known as a maximum rights mask, since no user can be given more rights than those permitted by the directory rights. When a directory is created, it has the same rights as the trustee rights. Suppose a user is given Read, Open, Search (File scan in V2.2), Create, and Delete (Erase in V2.2) rights to a certain directory. If the supervisor removes Delete from the directory, the user will no longer be able to delete files in that directory even though Delete is still listed as one of her trustee rights.

File Attributes

Information stored on the file server is stored in files. These files can have several different attributes that may further inhibit the user's access or track the use of the file. Attributes limit what a user can do with a file in much the same way that directory rights limit what can be done with the files in a directory. For instance, a file can have a Read Only attribute, which means the user cannot write to it or delete it. The file is said to be "flagged" Read Only. If the user has the Modify File Name/Flags right, he or she can remove the Read Only flag from the file using either the DOS Attrib command or the NetWare Flag command. This allows the supervisor or the user to safeguard certain files against accidental changes or deletions, while still being able to make those changes if necessary. If the user does not have the Modify File Name/Flags right, he or she cannot remove the Read Only attribute. This would give the supervisor the ability to protect individual files in a directory. The file attributes available in NetWare version 2.15 and above are as follows:

1. Read Only (V2.15 and lower). The file and its file name cannot be changed or deleted.
2. Read/Write. The file and its file name can be changed or deleted. The Read/Write attribute is simply the absence of the Read Only attribute.

3. Shareable. The file can be read by several users simultaneously.
4. Hidden. The file name is hidden from directory searches so it is not listed in the DOS DIR command. Unlike the DOS file attribute Hidden, a program file flagged Hidden cannot be executed.
5. System. The file is one of the operating system files. It cannot be deleted or changed by the user.
6. Transactional. This attribute is only available for SFT (System Fault Tolerant) Advanced NetWare. It is a safety feature that is usually applied to a database file. NetWare ensures that changes to the file are either completed or not made at all in case of an interruption during the process.
7. Indexed. The file server will keep an index in memory, indicating the file's position on the hard disk. This can improve access time to very large files.
8. Read Audit. The user will be charged for reading this file.
9. Write Audit. The user will be charged for writing to this file.
10. Modified Since Last Back Up (V2.15 and lower). Set by the system, this flag indicates whether the file will need to be backed up again.
11. Execute Only. The file, which must have an .EXE or .COM extension, can be executed only. The program cannot be copied. This attribute cannot be removed once set.
12. Archive Needed (V2.2 and higher). Identifies files modified after last backup. It is assigned automatically.

There are three utility programs that can be used to set file attributes, the DOS program ATTRIB.EXE and the NetWare utilities FLAG.EXE and FILER.EXE. Fig. 10-4 shows how the FILER.EXE program displays attribute information for a file. This particular file has only the Read/Write and System attributes.

A right must be listed as a directory right and a trustee right for a given user to be effective. The result of the two sets of rights is called the effective rights of a user in a directory.

Organization

Types of Users

When NetWare was installed, it automatically created a user account called SUPERVISOR. The person who assumes the role of supervisor is responsible for the smooth operation of the entire network. It is the supervisor's job to ensure easy and productive access to the network. A user must be given an account with access to the necessary directories and files. Most users will need drive mappings to particular directories. A typist in an office, for example, may need only read access to the directory containing a word processing program and write access to a document directory. A casual user or a user whose uses of the network are not very well defined may also need a menu system and may not be given permission to alter his or her account. A more sophisticated user may want to be able to control as much of his or her account as possible. In addition, this user may want to be able to configure the software he or she is using. A typist probably would not need to be able to change the configuration of the word processing program, but the office manager might.

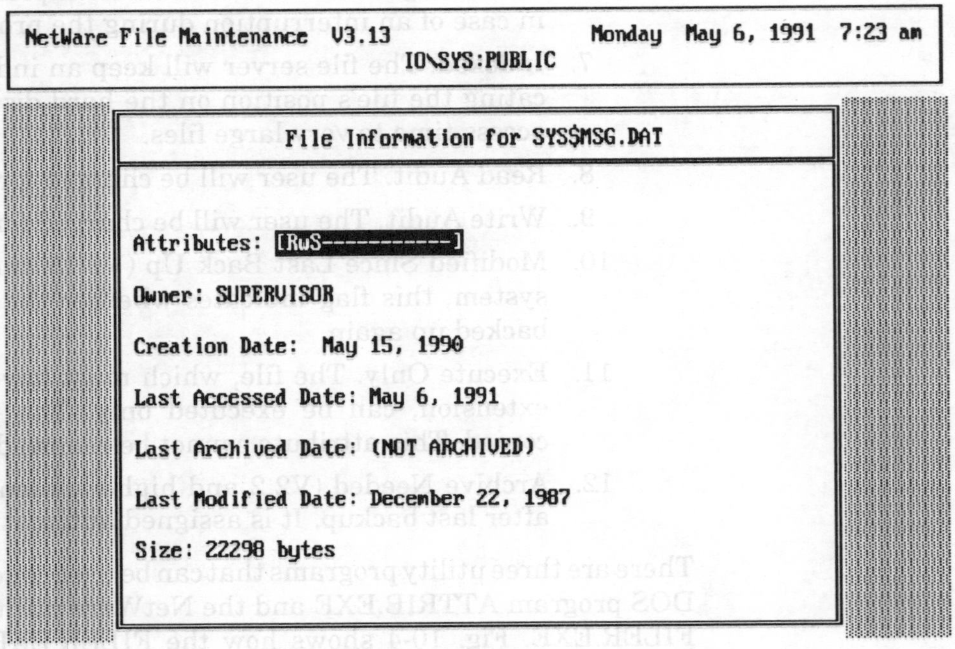

Fig. 10-4. File information stored in SYS$MSG.DAT

If it is a large office there may be many people needing the same access rights and menus. One solution is to have all the typists log in under the same user name. An account called TYPIST could be set up which allows several users to be logged in at the same time. This one account could have everything a typist might want, and all the typists would share the same directory space, software, and data. This situation could work well as long as the typists could agree on how their directory space was to be handled. Having everyone login using the same login name can be inconvenient, however. Individual typists may need a more customized environment to work with. Electronic mail and other messages could not be sent to individuals.

Groups

With various users needing different attributes to their accounts, individual accounts would have to be created. But since many users may need the same access rights, it is possible to create groups of users that can be given the same rights. A group could be created called TYPIST rather than an individual account. The group would be given the rights, and then each member of the group TYPIST in the office would be made a user in that group. Each typist in the office could have his or her own login name, login scripts, passwords and other attributes. Each member of the group TYPIST, for example, may have programs he or she wants in addition to the word processing software provided by the company. If the supervisor sets up the accounts properly, the users could have private areas on the file server to store their programs. Some of the members of the group TYPIST may wish to share some of their private directory space with only certain other individuals, not everyone in the group TYPIST. Users can make these modifications themselves assuming the supervisor has set up their accounts correctly and they know how.

Group Hierarchy

NetWare does not explicitly provide for groups of groups, but the same thing can be accomplished logically. Suppose there were several office managers overseeing the network users. They would need access to everything the members of the group TYPIST have plus additional space for confidential employee information. A group called MANAGER could be created that has only the additional rights needed. A manager would then belong to both groups, MANAGER and TYPIST. A member of the board might need even more information available. That position might need access to pending contracts, for instance. A group called BOARD would give those members access to very critical data only, but since a member of the board might not need to see the work in progress by the members of the group TYPIST, he or she might be a member of the group BOARD and MANAGER and not TYPIST. In this way a hierarchy of users can be established so changes can be made to each group according to the functions they require.

Data Organization

The way data is organized on the file server hard disk can greatly influence the efficiency of the network. Since the supervisor is responsible for providing the users with a convenient working environment, he or she must arrange the items stored on the server in a way that will make it easy for the user to access them. This implies that it must be easy for the supervisor to assign the proper rights in order to maintain security. The items on the server would need to be arranged by function, as much as possible, with data, application software, operating system software, NetWare public utilities, and NetWare system software in separate areas.

Types of Data

All of the above items may be referred to as data. However, in this context, data is the information created and stored by the user. Application software is the set of programs used to create the data. The operating system consists of DOS and its program utilities such as FORMAT.COM and CHKDSK.COM. NetWare has several public utilities that are intended to be used by any user who knows how, since they cannot harm the accounts of anyone else. Other utilities, software, and data used only by NetWare itself or the supervisor is known as system software.

Suppose a company had the same types of users as above with members of the group TYPIST, managers, and board members. Since each user has his or her own account, the supervisor might be tempted to arrange the directories something like the way shown in Fig. 10-5.

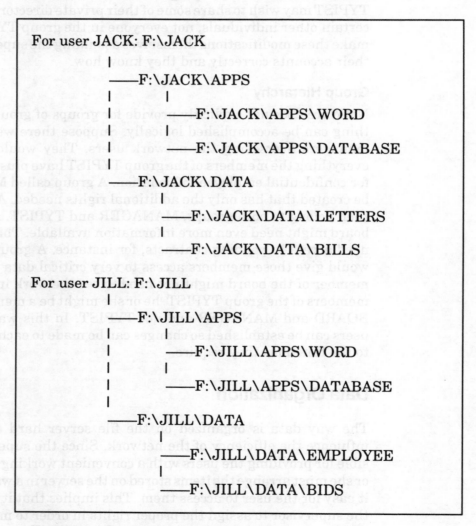

```
For user JACK: F:\JACK
          |
          ——F:\JACK\APPS
          |       |
          |       ——F:\JACK\APPS\WORD
          |       |
          |       ——F:\JACK\APPS\DATABASE
          |
          ——F:\JACK\DATA
                  |
                  ——F:\JACK\DATA\LETTERS
                  |
                  ——F:\JACK\DATA\BILLS

For user JILL: F:\JILL
          |
          ——F:\JILL\APPS
          |       |
          |       ——F:\JILL\APPS\WORD
          |       |
          |       ——F:\JILL\APPS\DATABASE
          |
          ——F:\JILL\DATA
                  |
                  ——F:\JILL\DATA\EMPLOYEE
                  |
                  ——F:\JILL\DATA\BIDS
```

Fig. 10-5. Directory arrangement

In Fig. 10-5 user JACK is a member of the group TYPIST who needs access to a word processing program and a database program. JACK stores only low security letters and bills in his data directory. JILL on the other hand, is a manager and needs to use the same type of software but must store very sensitive data such as employee evaluations and contract bids. JACK could be made a trustee with full rights in the F:\JACK\DATA directory and only read rights in the F:\JACK\APPS directory. JILL would then need similar rights in the directories under F:\JILL. But she would also need full access to JACK's data directory. Since there are usually more members of the group TYPIST than managers supervising them, JILL would need full rights to all the members of the group TYPIST.

The network supervisor would have to list each of the members of the group TYPIST data directories under JILL's trustee assignments. Also, the software that each of these users needs is being duplicated, wasting space and installation time. A more efficient approach would be to put all the software under one directory and all the data under another.

```
For all users:

   ——F:\SYSTEM
   |
   ——F:\PUBLIC
   |
   ——F:\APPS
   |     |
   |     ——F:\APPS\WORD
   |     |
   |     ——F:\APPS\DATABASE
   |
   ——F:\DATA\MANAGER
   |     |
   |     ——F:\DATA\MANAGER\EMPLOYEE
   |     |
   |     ——F:\DATA\MANAGER\BIDS
   |
   ——F:\DATA\TYPIST
         |
         ——F:\DATA\TYPIST\LETTERS
         |
         ——F:\DATA\TYPIST\BILLS
```

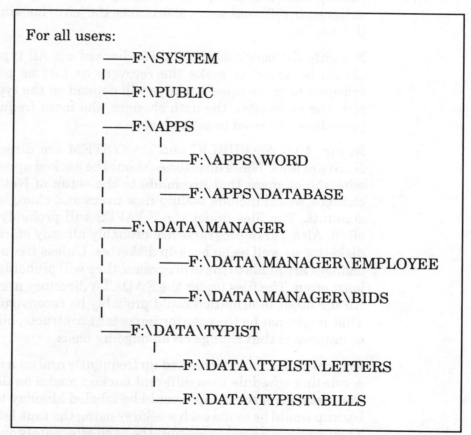

Fig. 10-6. A more efficient directory arrangement

Fig. 10-6 shows a better directory structure. Under this structure the group called MANAGER would have read and write access to the entire F:\DATA directory and read access to the F:\APPS directory. The group TYPIST would have read and right access to only the F:\DATA\TYPIST directory, and it would also have read access to the F:\APPS directory.

With these groups created, there could be as many members of the group TYPIST and as many managers as necessary. JACK may not have any explicit trustee rights but instead belongs to the group TYPIST. JILL also might have no trustee assignments listed in her account but her membership in the MANAGER group would give her all the rights she needs.

Backing up Data

Often the supervisor must manage all the types of data for the users. Critical data should periodically be stored on a diskette or tape to ensure its safety. Backing up the data, as it is called, serves two main functions. First, it allows the user to retrieve information that may have been changed or deleted in the normal course of operations. Second, it saves information that could be lost if a disaster were to strike the file server. A hardware failure could destroy all the information on the file server. If the data were backed up in a timely manner, it could be restored using the backup diskettes or tapes. Arranging the data so that it can be easily assigned to different users also makes the job of backing up the information easier.

Not only the user's data should be backed up. All types of information should be saved to make the recovery as fast as possible. The time schedule to make these backups will depend on the type of data. Generally, the more often the data changes, the more frequently the backup procedure will need to take place.

In Fig. 10-6, F:\PUBLIC and F:\SYSTEM are directories containing NetWare files. These directories should be backed up at a rate consistent with the changes that are made to the setup of NetWare itself. Such changes would include adding new users and changes to existing user accounts. The files under the F:\APPS will probably not change very often. Also, these programs are probably already stored on the original diskettes as well as on backup diskettes. Unless frequent configuration changes are made to these programs, they will probably be backed up the least often. The files under the F:\DATA directory are the most critical. All the other information could probably be reconstructed if necessary. That might not be the case for important contracts, billing information, or databases that change on an ongoing basis.

Critical data should be backed up frequently and on a rotating schedule. A rotating schedule uses different backup media on different intervals. For instance, a set of tapes could be labeled Monday through Friday. A backup would be made each weekday using the tape labeled for that day. Then, two additional tapes could be used alternately on Saturday. Two or more tapes could be used alternately at the end of each month.

A schedule like this is necessary to be reasonably sure of having a good set of backup tapes at any given moment since the backup hardware and media can also fail, producing unreadable copies. Also, and this is the more frequent problem, a user may ask for a file to be restored that was erased days or weeks ago. With a rotating schedule such as this, the supervisor has a good chance of finding the file the user wanted.

The exact schedule used in a particular installation would of course depend on many factors, including the nature of the business and the amount of data. There may even be data on the server that was placed there for the purpose of being backed up. Many users may wish to copy data from their local hard disk or floppies to the file server for safe keeping. On the server, it becomes the network supervisor's responsibility to back it up. In actual practice there would also be a backup made at regular intervals that would be archived. That is, the tape would not be used to make another backup, but rather it would be placed in long term storage.

Network Management

Introduction to FCONSOLE

Network control might be considered a fifth level of security. A Novell Network is a very complex system. Almost all of the functions of the system are controlled through the file server. With a program called FCONSOLE, which stands for File Server Console, much of the network activity can be controlled or at least observed. Most of the functions of the FCONSOLE program are available at the file server itself, but in a less attractive format. Also many more functions are available at the file server.

By observing the processes on the server, as well as the activities of the users, a supervisor can sometimes avoid problems or catch them as they start. With FCONSOLE, critical values that may not have been set correctly in installation can be detected. Users can be monitored and disconnected if they cause trouble. Users can also be warned of problems that require their immediate attention.

The SYSCON utility can be used to establish other network control features. User accounts can be set to be restricted to certain workstations or certain times of the day. These restrictions and FCONSOLE's monitoring abilities give the supervisor a great deal of power in determining how, when, and where the network will be used.

FCONSOLE Management Options

Fig. 10-7 shows FCONSOLE's main menu. FCONSOLE is to network management what SYSCON is to network security. Following, the different management options that can be performed with FCONSOLE are explained. In NetWare version 3.XX not all of the FCONSOLE options are available. Four of the options below (File/Lock Activity, LAN

Driver Information, Purge All Salvageable Files, and Statistics) will not work. Equivalent functions are available using V3.XX MONITOR utility, which is run from the server console.

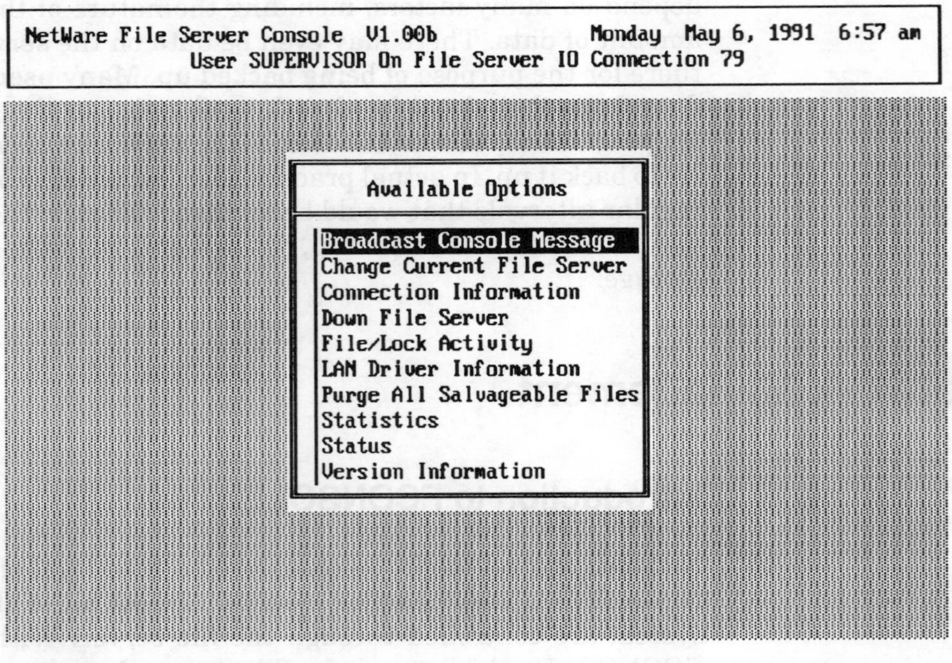

Fig. 10-7. FCONSOLE's main menu

Broadcast Console Message

The supervisor can send a short message to every workstation attached to the server. The message sent appears on the bottom line of the workstation screen. Any program that may have been running at the time is temporarily halted until the user presses the keys CTRL-ENTER. Only very critical messages should be broadcast in this way since it is very interruptive to everyone on the network.

Change Current File Server

The biggest advantage to using the FCONSOLE program over entering similar commands at the file server itself is that it can be used from any workstation connected to a file server. The Change Current File Server option displays a list of servers the workstation is attached to as shown in Fig. 10-8. Here the file servers are named after two of Jupiter's moons, EUROPA and IO. When a new file server is selected, all the other options pertain to the new server only.

Connection Information

One of FCONSOLE's most important functions is to provide information on the users actually logged in at the moment. When Connection Information is selected a list of users currently logged in appears on the left, as it does in Fig. 10-9. In this case, user SUPERVISOR is the only person

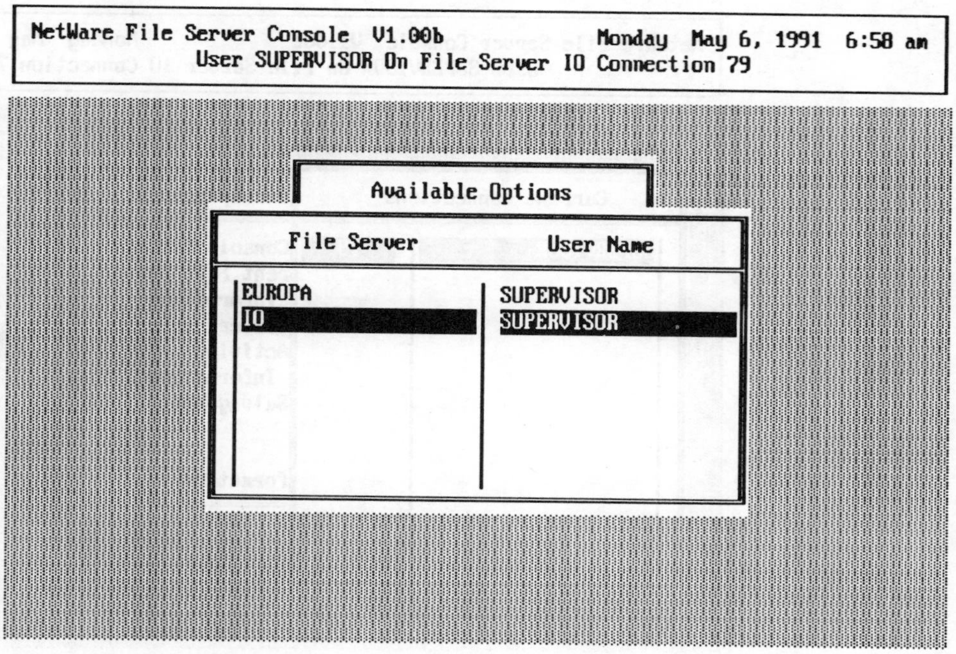

Fig. 10-8. List of servers that the workstation is attached to

logged in. The second column in the Current Connections box shows the connection number. Each station attached to a file server is assigned a connection number. The first workstation to attach is given the value 1, the second 2, and so on. The file server uses these numbers to identify the station. If the server is not turned off, the numbers lose their sequence. From Fig. 10-9 it can be seen that 78 other workstations were attached to the server before the user SUPERVISOR's workstation was attached. Then they were disconnected.

The connection number is temporally assigned to a workstation, not a user. Many users may log on and off the same workstation during the day. Assuming the workstation was never disconnected from the file server, all the users would use the same connection number.

When one of the users is selected, the Connection Information menu appears on the right as in Fig. 10-10. These options allow the supervisor to send a message to the user, disconnect the user, or examine various aspects of the user's usage of the file server.

Down File Server

As noted in Chapter 8, the file server must be properly shut down in order to close any open files. This option shuts down the server after prompting for verification.

File/Lock Activity

A NetWare network allows programs to communicate with each other to some degree. The messages are simple but important. The File/Lock

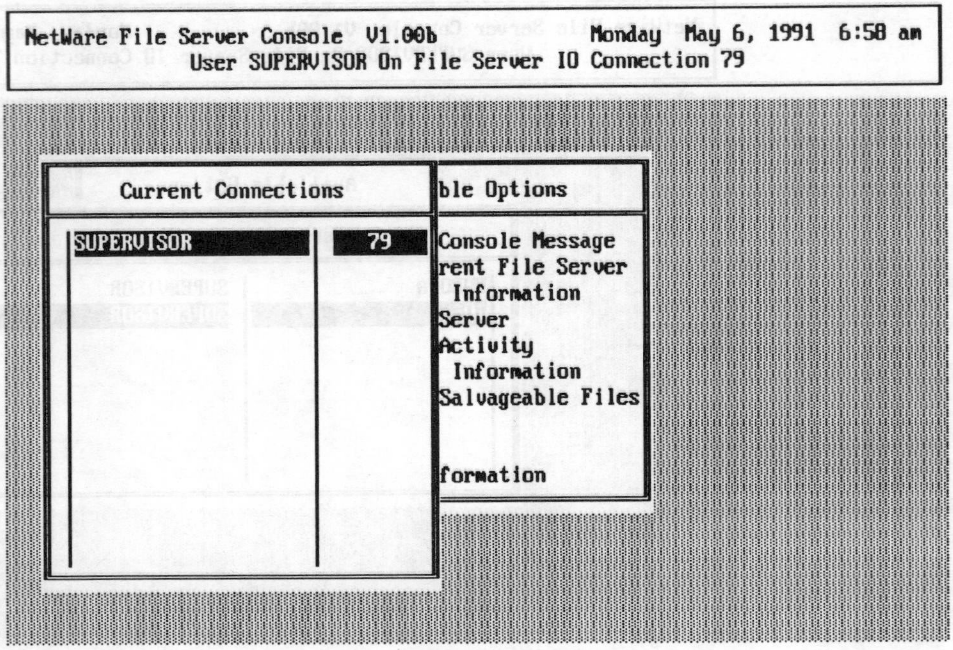

Fig. 10-9. List of current connections to the server

Activity has three types of messages that might be posted. These messages are flags that one program may post so another program running on another workstation will take some other action. The File/Physical Records Information option shows information on individual files that a program may be accessing. The Logical Lock Information option provides information on a group of resources a program has allocated. Semaphore Information shows the status of general purpose flags a program may post. Another program running on another workstation would have to "know" the meanings of these flags in order to take the proper action.

LAN Driver Information

This option displays information about the network interface card drivers used on the file server.

Purge All Salvageable Files

When a file on a NetWare file server is deleted using the DOS DEL or ERASE commands, it is not actually erased. Its directory entry is simply removed from the list. The directory entries for deleted files are saved for each user until that user issues another DEL command. These files can be either returned to the directory with a program called SALVAGE or removed permanently with the PURGE program. The Purge All Salvageable Files option permanently erases all the deleted files for all users.

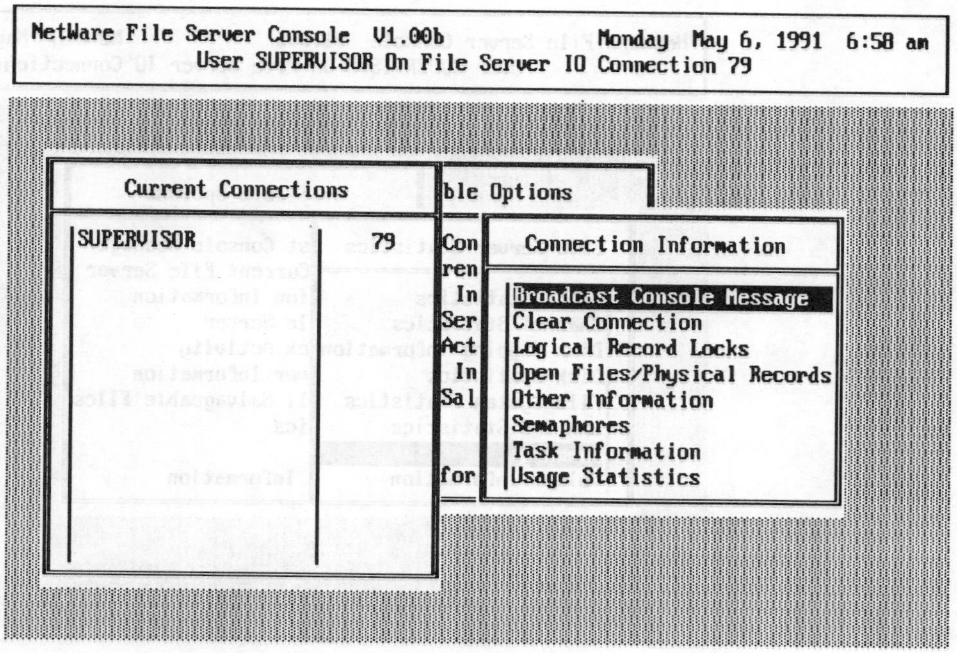

Fig. 10-10. Screen displaying the Connection Information menu

Statistics

This option opens the File Server Statistics menu as in Fig. 10-11. The options listed can sometimes be helpful in identifying problems with the file server. Each gives detailed information about the operation of a component as it is happening. The Summary option places the most critical information from each of the other options on one screen as shown in Fig. 10-12.

The third line inside the File Server Statistics Summary box, for instance, shows that 97 percent of the disk requests were serviced from the cache. This means that most of the time, when a workstation asked for data on the server, that data had already been read from the disk and stored in memory. Reading the data from memory is much faster that reading it from the disk again. Other figures on this screen might be very important for a supervisor to know.

The chart in the lower half of the box shows many of the network resources. These resources have maximum values that the supervisor must watch carefully. If the value in the Peak Used column gets too close to the maximum, action may need to be taken. Usually, NetWare must be reinstalled using the Intermediate or Custom Installation options to change a maximum. The second item listed in the chart, Open Files, shows a peak used of 276. In early releases of NetWare the default maximum was 250. With version 2.15 and above, the maximum was raised to 508. Without the change, some users would have been able to login but not use any software.

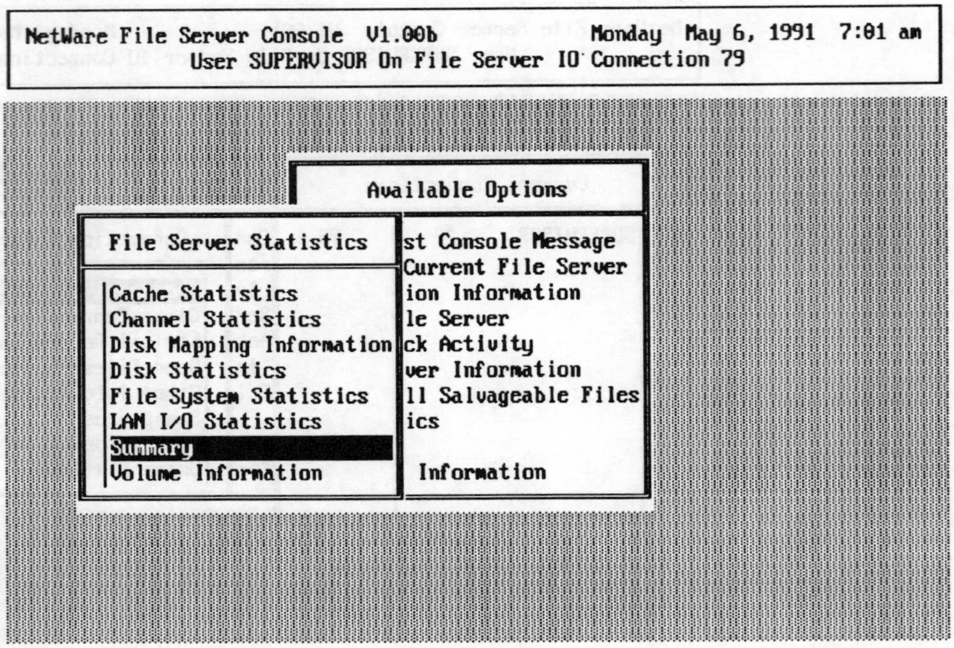

Fig. 10-11. File Server Statistics menu

```
NetWare File Server Console  V1.00b              Monday  May 6, 1991   7:01 am
              User SUPERVISOR On File Server IO Connection 79

                        File Server Statistics Summary

File Server Up Time:  13 Days  0 Hours  5 Minutes 35 Seconds
Number Of File Service Processes:       4  Current Server Utilization:        0%
Disk Requests Serviced From Cache:    97%  Packets Routed:                    0
Total Packets Received:        16,240,574  File Service Packets:              5
Total Number Of Cache Buffers:        487  Dirty Cache Buffers:               0
Total Server Memory:            4,062,208  Unused Server Memory:          2,048

                         Maximum        Peak Used   Currently In Use
Routing Buffers:             150               14          0
Open Files:                  508              276         11
Indexed Files:               100                0          0
Transactions:                N/A              N/A        N/A
Bindery Objects:             500              134        132
Connections:                 100               91          1
Dynamic Memory 1:         17,786           12,370        896
Dynamic Memory 2:         53,212           12,558      4,180
Dynamic Memory 3:         47,104            1,132        274
```

Fig. 10-12. File server statistics provided by the Summary option

Status

The Status option on FCONSOLE's main menu has only four components, as seen in Fig. 10-13; Date, Time, Allow New Users To Login, and Transaction Tracking. These can be changed by highlighting the item and typing in a new value. The date and time will, of course, need occasional adjustment. Allow New Users To Login might be set to No near the end of a day or a few minutes before the server must be brought down for some other reason. Transaction Tracking simply displays that this feature is not available in this case.

Version Information

This option displays the exact version the file server is running. FCONSOLE permits the supervisor to examine, manage, and control much of what a file server does. In the next section, FCONSOLE and other utilities will be used to demonstrate some of the processes needed to run a secured and well organized network.

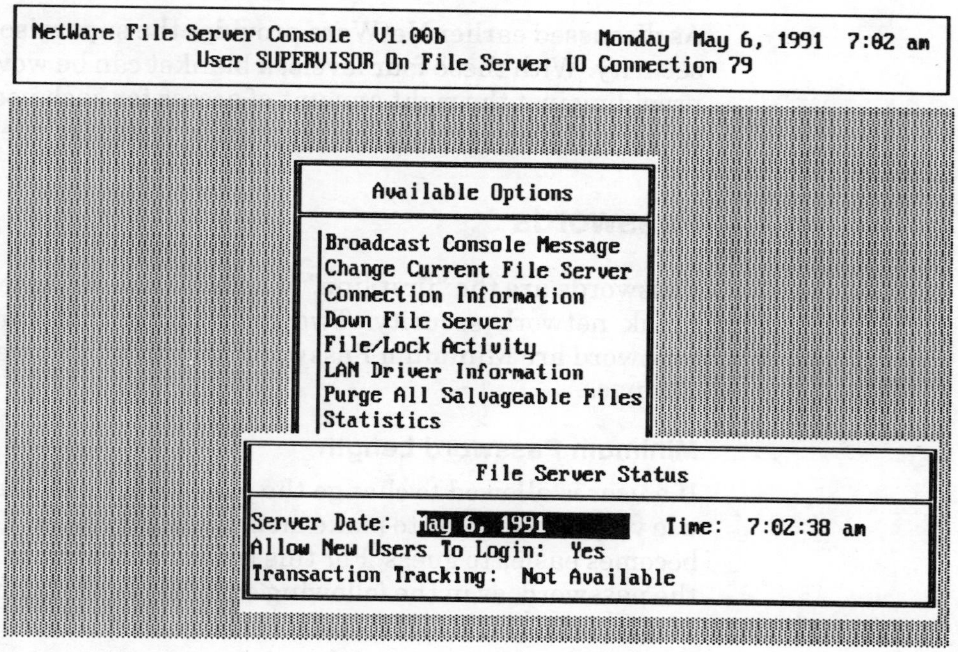

Fig. 10-13. Screen displaying the components of the Status option

Hands-on NetWare

In order to complete the hands-on section of this chapter, the file server and a workstation should be ready to use.

1. The file server must be on.
2. A workstation must be booted and the appropriate network drivers must be loaded.
3. Network Drive F: should be the default drive at the workstation.
4. The user account created in the previous chapter must still be available.

5. In the example below, TYPE THE NAME OF YOUR ACCOUNT WHERE USER JSMITH IS USED. For instance, if the instructions read "Type LOGIN JSMITH", you should type LOGIN followed by the name of the account you created earlier.

Each numbered set of instructions can be completed at different times, as long as they are finished in order. For instance, the exercise on Minimum Password Length must be completed before the exercise on Force Periodic Password Changes.

Four Levels of Security

As discussed earlier NetWare provides the supervisor with four levels of security. With these four levels, a blanket can be woven around the data providing just the right amount of access for each user. The instructions below will demonstrate the properties of each of the four levels.

Passwords

Passwords are the "first line" of defense against intentional attempts to break network security. Two restrictions that can be placed on the password are Minimum Password Length and Force Periodic Password Changes.

Minimum Password Length

If a user is allowed to change the password, he or she may be tempted to use very short words to make memorizing it easier. Unfortunately it also becomes easier to guess. For this reason a minimum length can be set on the password, as in the following exercise. A program called SETPASS is available in the F:\PUBLIC directory that allows the user to quickly change his or her password.

1. Type **F:** and press the Enter key
2. Type **LOGIN** and your user name, then press the Enter key. The password prompt should appear.
3. Type **FIRST** and press the Enter key.
4. Type **SETPASS** and press the Enter key.
5. A prompt should appear asking for your old password. This ensures that no one could change your password while you were momentarily away from your workstation.
6. Type **FIRST** and press the Enter key. The word FIRST will not appear on the screen.
7. Type **1ST** again and press the Enter key.
8. For verification, type **1ST** again and press the Enter key.

9. A message asking you if the password should be synchronized on all attached servers should appear. If the account exists on other file servers that are now attached, the SETPASS program can change those passwords as well.
10. Press the [Y] and [Enter←] keys as in Fig. 10-14. The SETPASS program will attempt to change the passwords but then find that the new password is too short.
11. Type **LOGOUT** and press the [Enter←] key to end this session.

```
F>SETPASS

Enter your old password:
Enter your new password:
Retype your new password:
Would you like to synchronize your passwords on all attached servers? (Y/N) Y

Synchronizing all passwords...

The new password was too short, password not changed.

F>
```

Fig. 10-14. Screen display of output generated by SETPASS

Force Periodic Password Changes.

Forcing a user to periodically change his or her password is considered an important component of password security. However, changing the password too often makes it difficult to remember. The steps below illustrate the process of setting Force Periodic Password Changes and what happens when the password expires.

1. Type **F:** and press the [Enter←] key
2. Type **LOGIN** and your user name, then press the [Enter←] key. The password prompt should appear.
3. Type **FIRST** and press the [Enter←] key.
4. Type **SYSCON** and press the [Enter←] key.
5. Use the [↓] key to highlight User Information and press the [Enter←] key.
6. Type the name of your user account. When your account name is highlighted, press the [Enter←] key.
7. Press the [↓] key to highlight Account Restrictions and press the [Enter←] key.
8. Move the cursor with the [↓] key until the value for Force Periodic Password Changes is highlighted.
9. Press the [Y] and [Enter←] keys. The Account Restrictions menu should appear similar to the one shown in Fig. 10-15. Here a 40-day interval has been set until the next required change.
10. Highlight the date on the Date Password Expires line using the [↓] key.

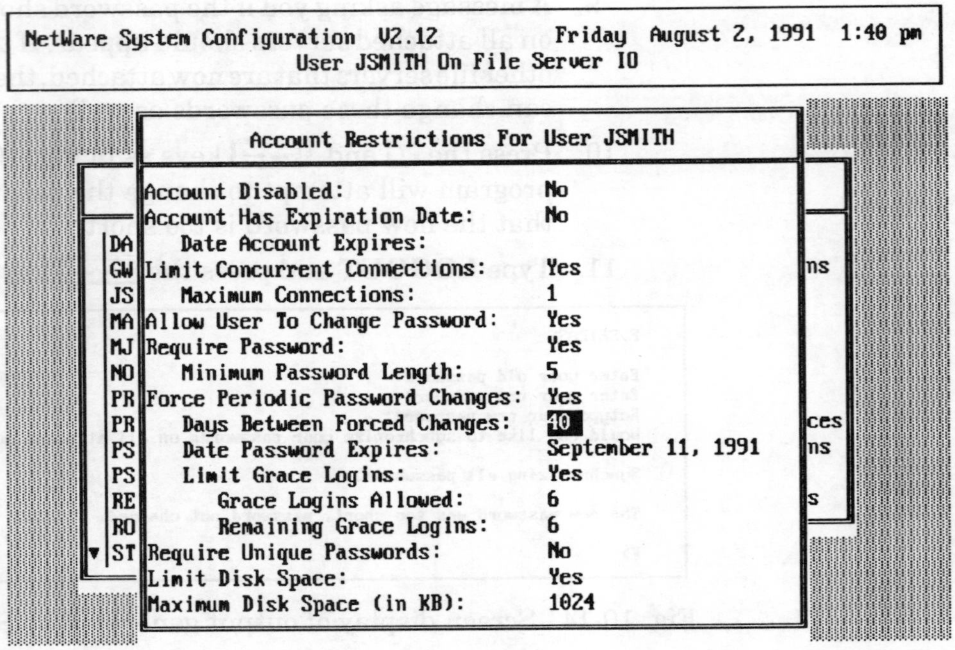

Fig. 10-15. Account Restrictions menu

11. Look at the date shown in the upper right corner of the screen. It should be the current date. Type in the day before the day shown as the current date on your screen. In Fig. 10-16 the current date is August 2, 1991. For the purpose of this exercise, user JSMITH typed in AUGUST 1, 1991 to indicate that the password has expired.
12. Press the [Esc] key four times until the EXIT box appears.
13. Press the [Y] key and then press the [Enter] key.
14. Type **LOGOUT** and press the [Enter] key. The file server should respond with a message indicating the login time and the logout time.
15. Type **LOGIN** and your user name, then press the [Enter] key. The password prompt should appear.
16. Type **FIRST** and press the [Enter] key. Since the password expired yesterday, a message will appear asking you if you would like to change it.
17. Press the [Y] and the [Enter] keys as in Fig. 10-17.
18. Type **SECOND** as your new password. The word SECOND will appear as it is typed. Press the [Enter] key.
19. Type **SECOND** and press the [Enter] key to verify the change.
20. Type **LOGOUT** and press the [Enter] key to end this session.

```
NetWare System Configuration  V2.12          Friday  August 2, 1991  1:40 pm
                    User JSMITH On File Server IO

              Account Restrictions For User JSMITH
     Account Disabled:                         No
     Account Has Expiration Date:              No
  DA    Date Account Expires:
  GW Limit Concurrent Connections:             Yes                ns
  JS    Maximum Connections:                   1
  MA Allow User To Change Password:            Yes
  MJ Require Password:                         Yes
  NO    Minimum Password Length:               5
  PR Force Periodic Password Changes:          Yes
  PR    Days Between Forced Changes:           40                 ces
  PS    Date Password Expires:                 AUGUST 1,1991      ns
  PS    Limit Grace Logins:                    Yes
  RE       Grace Logins Allowed:               6                  s
  RO       Remaining Grace Logins:             6
  ST Require Unique Passwords:                 No
     Limit Disk Space:                         Yes
     Maximum Disk Space (in KB):               1024
```

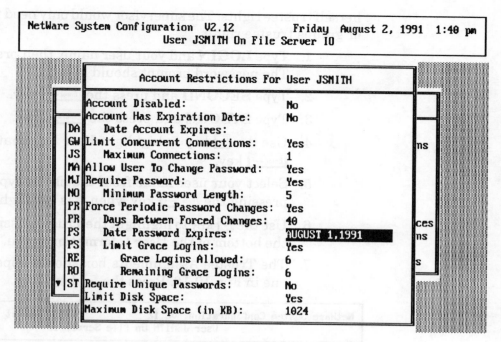

Fig. 10-16. Key sequence for typing the current date

```
F>LOGOUT
JSMITH logged out from server IO connection 77
Login  Time:  Friday  August 2, 1991  1:38 pm
Logout Time:  Friday  August 2, 1991  1:41 pm


F>LOGIN JSMITH
Enter your password:

Password for user JSMITH on server IO has expired.
Would you like to change your password? (Y/N) Y
Enter your new password:
Retype your new password:
IO/JSMITH: Your password has been changed.

F>
```

Fig. 10-17. Key sequence required by user to change the password

Trustee Rights

The second level of security, trustee rights, requires the most work on the part of the supervisor. SYSCON is used to identify each directory the user or group has trustee rights in. In the following steps you will use your account to give yourself trustee rights in a new directory. This exercise would never be done quite this way in the real world since the supervisor (or a user with supervisor equivalence) does not need to give himself or herself trustee rights. The supervisor would only need to give other users or groups trustee rights.

1. Type **LOGIN** and your user name, then press the [Enter←] key. The password prompt should appear.
2. Type **SECOND** and press the [Enter←] key.
3. Type **SYSCON** and press the [Enter←] key.
4. Use the [↓] key to highlight User Information and press the [Enter←] key.
5. Select your user name from the list by typing the name and pressing the [Enter←] key when it is highlighted.
6. Use the [↓] key to highlight the Trustee Assignments option at the bottom of the User Information menu.
7. The Trustee Assignments box should appear, similar to the one in Fig. 10-18. Press the [Ins] key.

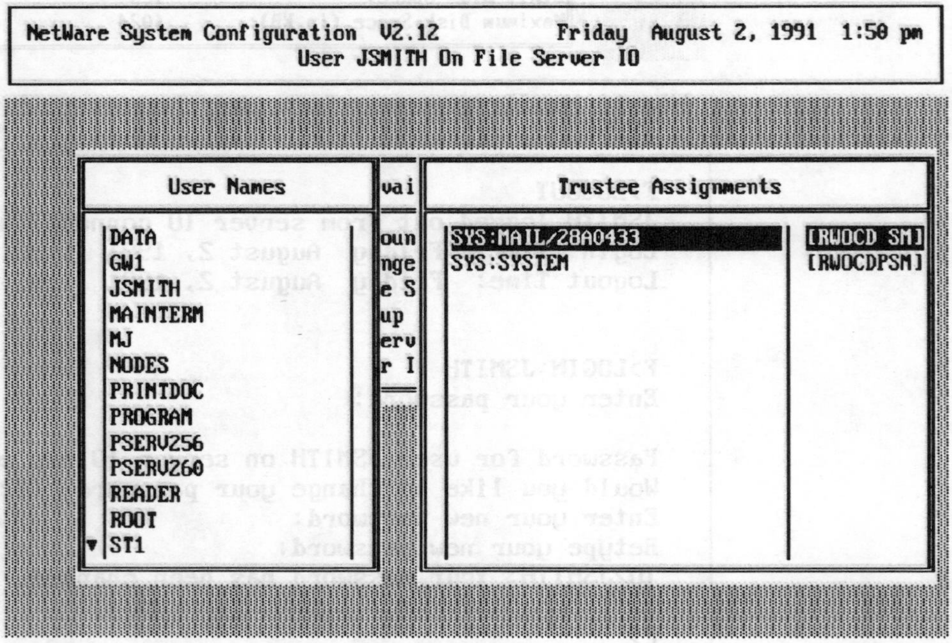

Fig. 10-18. Trustee Assignment dialog box

8. A long box labeled Directory In Which Trustee Should Be Added should appear along the top of the screen. The complete directory name can be typed in at this point but SYSCON offers a method for selecting the directory from a list.
9. Press the [Ins] key again and the file servers available will be listed.

10. If there is more than one file server listed, use the arrow keys to highlight the one you are using. Fig. 10-19 shows user JSMITH's file server as File Server IO at the top of the screen and indeed IO is the only file server listed in the File Servers/ Local Drives box.

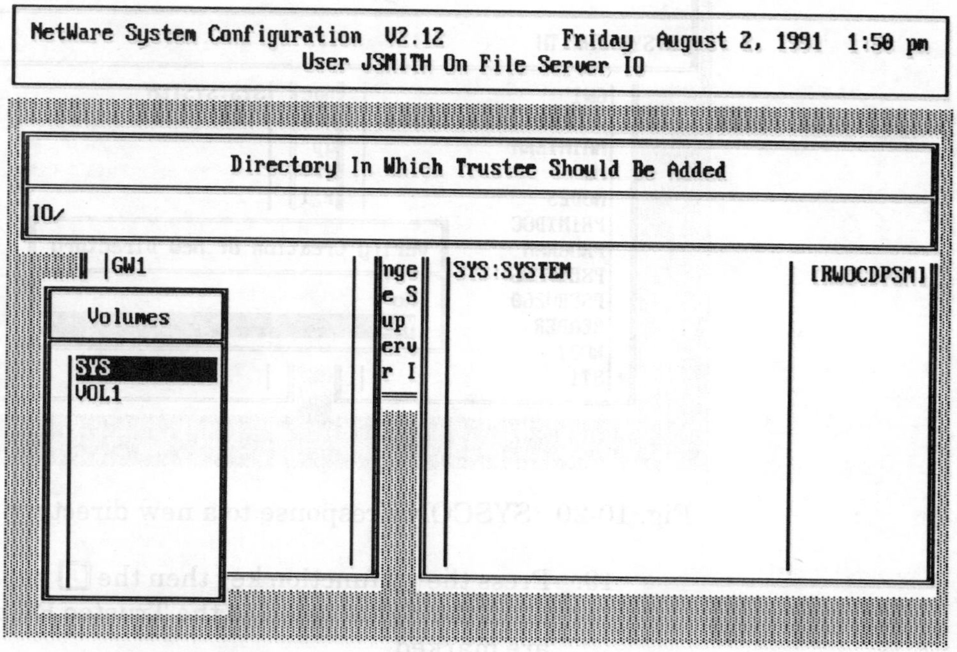

Fig. 10-19. User JSMITH's file server

11. Press the [Enter ←] key with the proper file server name highlighted.
12. Press the [Enter ←] key. This chooses the first volume on the file server.
13. Do not do this, but by pressing the [Enter ←] key to select a directory, any directory on the server can be chosen.
14. Press the [Esc] key. The cursor should return to the long Directory In Which Trustee Should Be Added box.
15. Type the name of your user account and press the [Enter ←] key.
16. Fig. 10-20 shows how SYSCON responds to a new directory. Press the [Y] and [Enter ←] keys. The new directory is now listed in the Trustee Assignments box with rights Read, Open and Search.
17. Highlight the new directory with the ARROW keys and press the [Enter ←] key.
18. With the Trustee Rights Granted Box on the left of the screen press the [Ins] key.

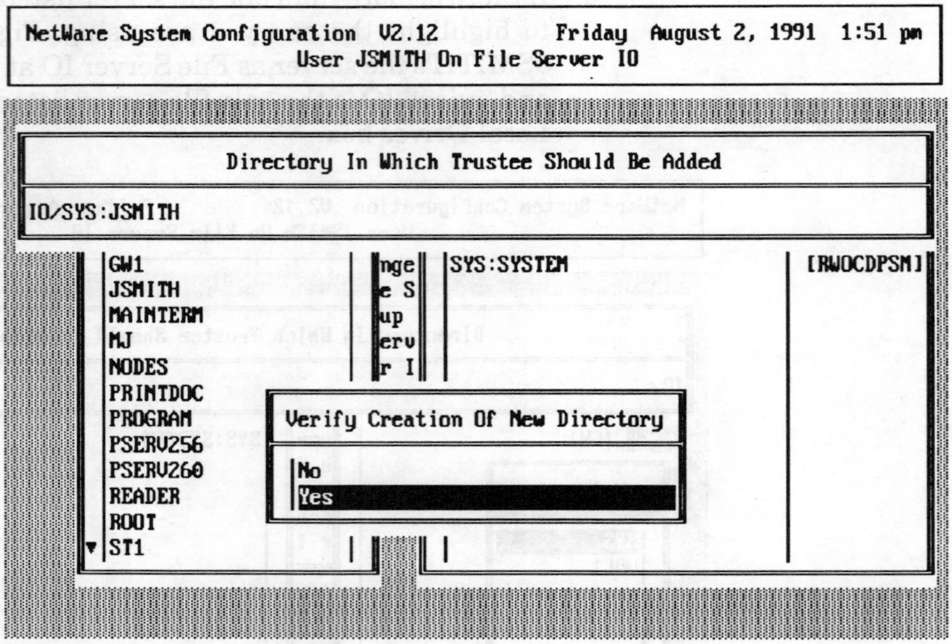

Fig. 10-20. SYSCON's response to a new directory

19. Press the F5 function key then the ↓ key. Continue this until all of the rights listed in the Trustee Rights Not Granted box are marked.
20. Press the Enter← key. All of the rights should move to the trustee rights granted box. Press the Enter← key again to accept these changes.
21. All of the rights should now be listed for the directory with your name as they are for user JSMITH in Fig. 10-21.
22. The user now has complete access to the directory. A directory such as this is referred to as the user's home directory. It is clearly identified as belonging to this particular user and the user has full rights in it. Press the esc key five times until the Exit box appears, then press the Y and Enter← keys.
23. Type **LOGOUT** and press the Enter← key to end this session.

Directory Rights

The supervisor can set each user's access rights to particular values in particular directories. The user automatically has the same rights in any subdirectory. For instance, user JSMITH in the example above was given complete rights to the JSMITH directory. If any directories are created below the JSMITH directory, user JSMITH will have complete rights to those as well.

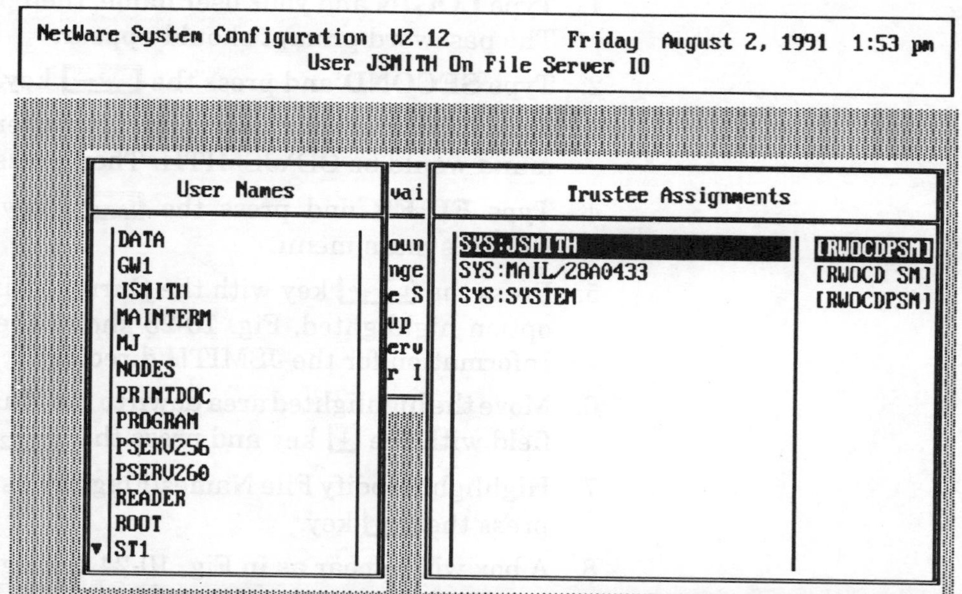

Fig. 10-21. All rights for user JSMITH

Often, in a large directory structure, there may be one or two directories that need to be restricted so that all users are denied certain rights. Directory rights can be removed to create a maximum rights mask that restricts all users except the supervisor. The directions below illustrate how the NetWare utility program FILER is used to make the directory rights changes.

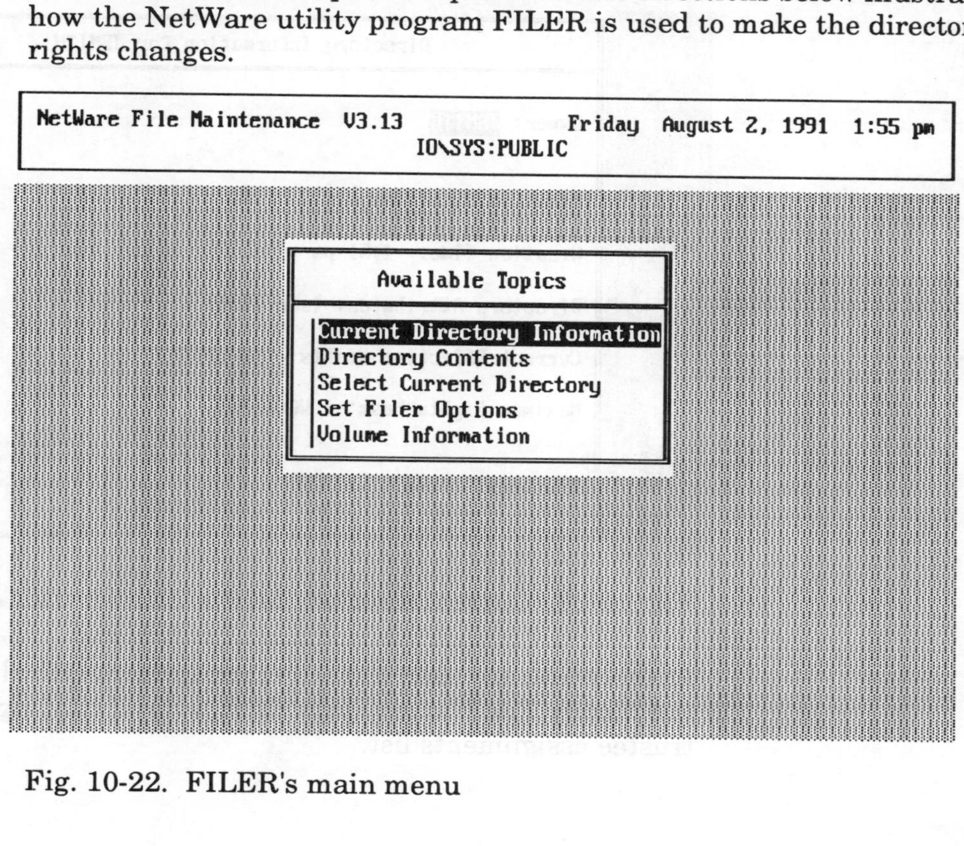

Fig. 10-22. FILER's main menu

1. Type **LOGIN** and your user name, then press the [Enter←] key. The password prompt should appear.
2. Type **SECOND** and press the [Enter←] key.
3. Type **CD** and your user name. For user JSMITH the command would be CD\JSMITH. Then press the [Enter←] key.
4. Type **FILER** and press the [Enter←] key. Fig. 10-22 shows FILER's main menu.
5. Press the [Enter←] key with the Current Directory Information option highlighted. Fig. 10-23 shows the Current Directory Information for the JSMITH directory.
6. Move the highlighted area down to the Maximum Rights Mask field with the [↓] key and press the [Enter←] key.
7. Highlight Modify File Names/Flags by using the [↓] key, then press the [delete] key.
8. A box will appear as in Fig. 10-24 asking for conformation to revoke the right. Press the [Y] and [Enter←] keys.
9. Press the [esc] key three times until the Exit Filer box appears.

11. Press the [Y] and [Enter←] keys.

10. Type **LOGOUT** and press the [Enter←] key to end this session.

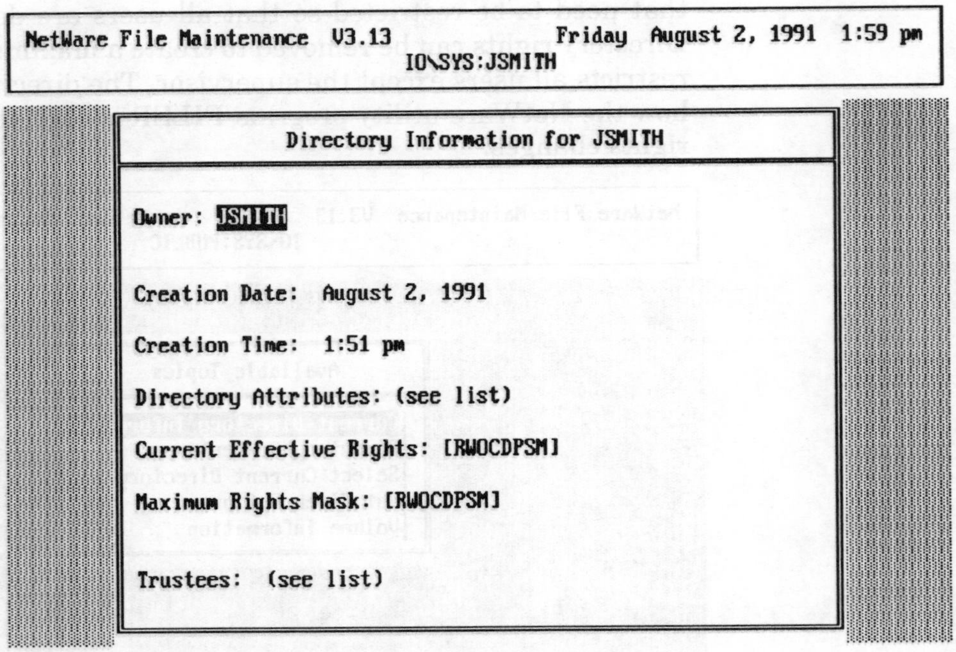

Fig. 10-23. Current directory information for user JSMITH

At this point, any user other than supervisor-equivalent users are denied the Modify File Names/Flags right, even if that right is listed in their trustee assignments list.

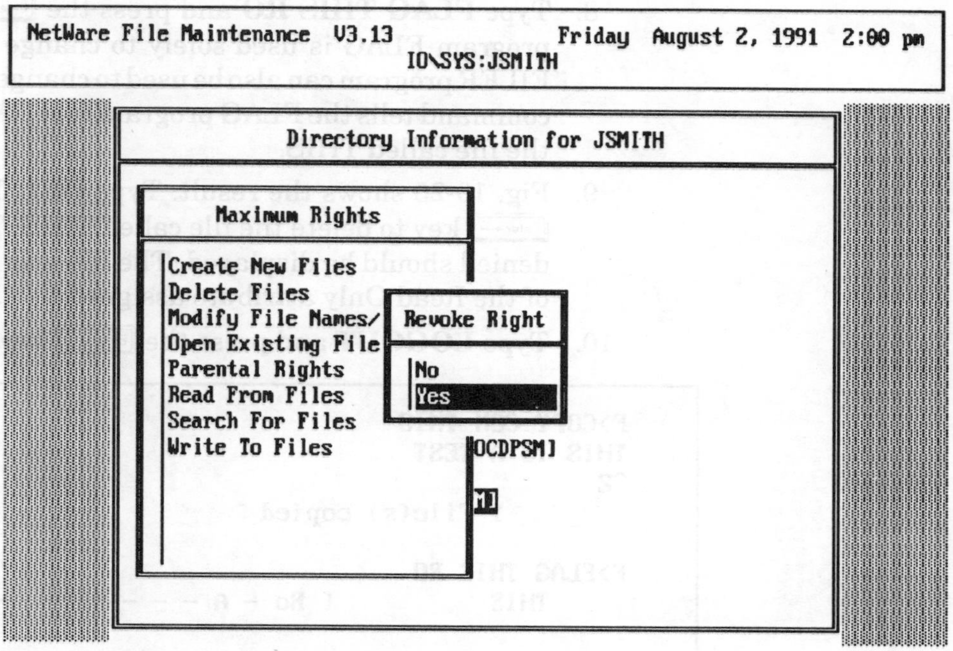

Fig. 10-24. Dialog box to revoke rights

File Attributes

File attributes could be said to be the last line of defense in security since often they are used to prevent accidental erasure or changes to files. With a file flagged as Read Only, no user, including the supervisor, can change or delete the file. If the user has the Modify File Names/Flags right in the directory, the Read Only attribute can be set to Read Write, which then allows changes. The following short exercise demonstrates this point.

1. Type **LOGIN** and your user name, then press the Enter key. The password prompt should appear.
2. Type **SECOND** and press the Enter key.
3. Type **CD** and your user name. For user JSMITH the command would be CD\JSMITH. Then press the Enter key.
4. Type **COPY CON THIS** and press the Enter key. This DOS command instructs the computer to copy a file from the console to a file called THIS. In other words the next thing you type will go into the file THIS.
5. Type **THIS IS A TEST** and press the Enter key.
6. Hold down the control key and press the Z key. This character combination marks the end of the file.
7. Press the Enter key. The message 1 File(s) copied should appear.

8. Type **FLAG THIS RO** and press the [Enter←] key. The utility program FLAG is used solely to change file attributes. The FILER program can also be used to change file attributes. This command tells the FLAG program to set the Read Only flag on the file called THIS.
9. Fig. 10-25 shows the result. Type **DEL THIS** and press the [Enter←] key to delete the file called THIS. The message Access denied should be displayed. The file was not deleted because of the Read Only attribute assigned to it.
10. Type **LOGOUT** and press the [Enter←] key to end this session.

```
F>COPY CON THIS
THIS IS A TEST
^Z
        1 File(s) copied

F>FLAG THIS RO
   THIS          [ Ro - A - - - - - - - - - -- -- ]

F>
```

Fig. 10-25. Screen displaying rights provided by the FLAG utility

Effective Rights

The combination of trustee rights and directory rights is called a user's effective rights. The effective rights are those rights that are granted in both the user trustee assignments and the directory rights. To prove this, a non-supervisor-equivalent user account is needed. The following steps create such a user.

1. Type **LOGIN** and your user name, then press the [Enter←] key. The password prompt should appear.
2. Type **SECOND** and press the [Enter←] key.
3. Type **SYSCON** and press the [Enter←] key.
4. Press the [↓] key to highlight the User Information option and press the [Enter←] key.
5. Press the [Ins] key and a box requesting a new user name will appear as it does in Fig. 10-26.
6. Type your user name followed by a **1** on the same line. User JSMITH typed JSMITH1 for a new user name. Press the [Enter←] key after typing the name. Press the [Enter←] again to select the name from the list.
7. Select Account Restrictions from the User Information menu by moving the highlighted bar to that option and pressing the [Enter←] key.

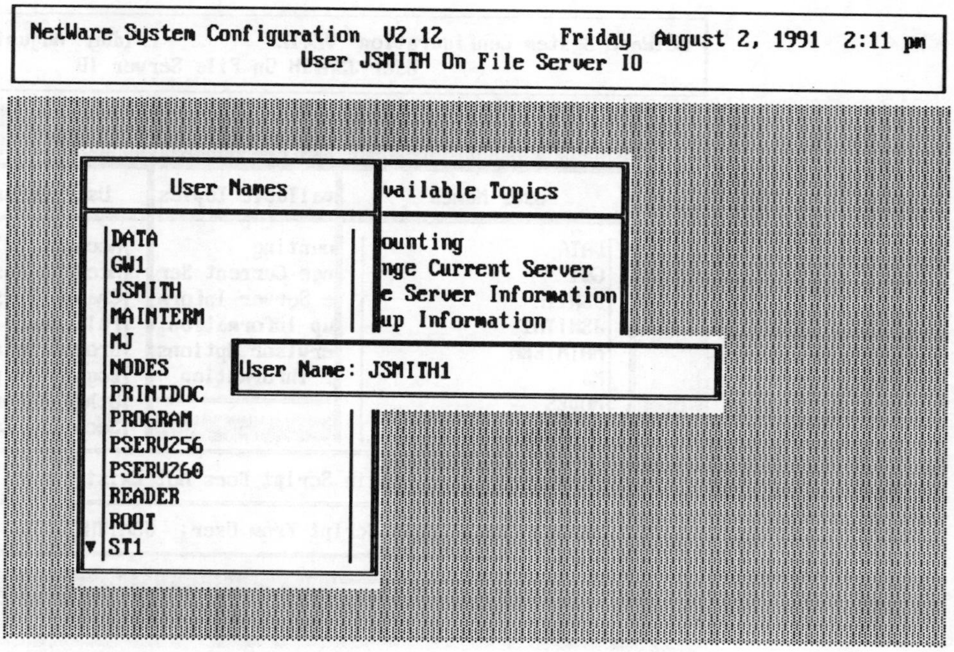

Fig. 10-26. Dialog box to request a new user name

8. Move the cursor down to the Require Password option with the [↓] key.
9. Press the [N] and [Enter ←] keys.
10. Press the [esc] key to return to the User Information menu.
11. Press the [↓] key to highlight Login Script and press the [Enter ←] key. A message box will appear as it does in Fig. 10-27.
12. This box allows the supervisor to copy a login script from any other user to the user just created. To copy your login script, simply use the [backspace] key to remove the 1 at the end of the name displayed and press the [Enter ←] key.
13. The Login Script editor should now appear. With the cursor in the upper left corner of the box, press the [Enter ←] key once.
14. Move the cursor back up to the top line and type **MAP F:=SYS:** but do not press the [Enter ←] key. This line maps the drive letter F to the root directory of the volume SYS.
15. For further practice in the editor, use the ARROW keys to move to the second line of the login script. Then move the cursor between the word MAP and the S1.
16. Type **INS** leaving at least one space on each side. INS stands for insert which means that this drive letter is to be inserted in the list with any others that might exist. This way it will not replace any that already exist.
17. Type the letters **INS** after the MAP statement on the remaining two lines as well.

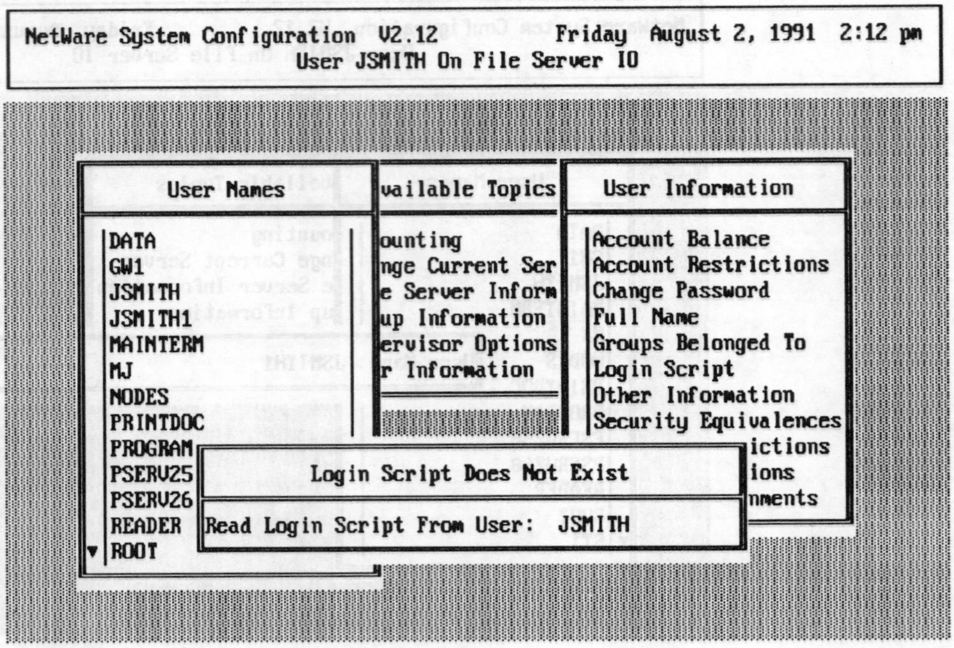

Fig. 10-27. Login script creation error message

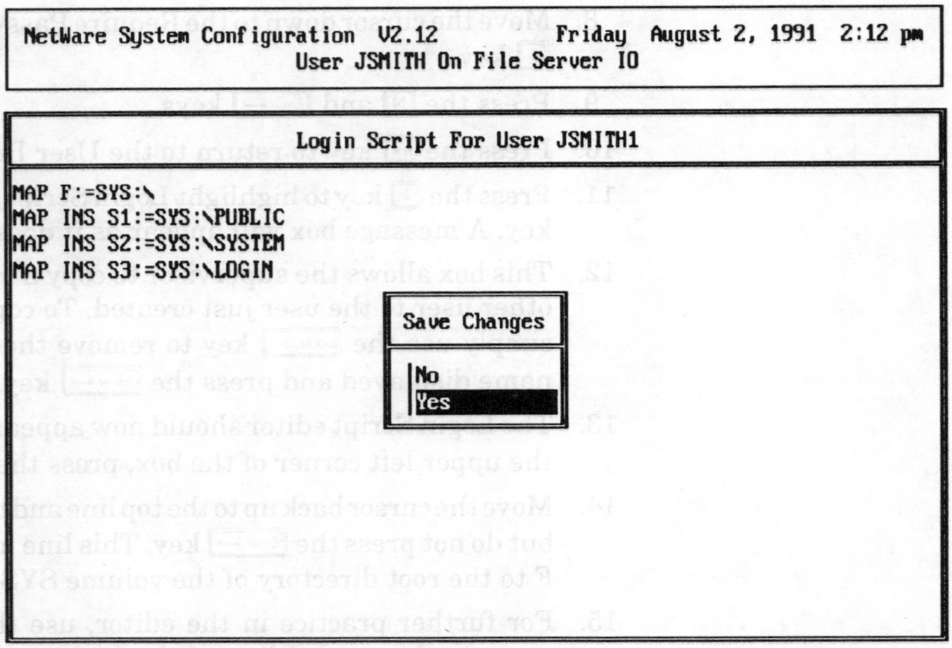

Fig. 10-28. Save changes dialog box

18. Press the [Esc] key. The Save Changes box should appear as it does in Fig. 10-28.
19. Press the [Y] and [Enter] keys.

20. Next the new user must be given trustee rights. Select Trustee Rights from the User Information menu by pressing the ↓ key to highlight the proper line and pressing the Enter key.
21. Press the Ins key.
22. Type **SYS:** followed by your user name. This is the home directory created earlier. User JSMITH would type **SYS:\JSMITH**. Press the Enter key when the line has been typed in.
23. With the new directory in the Trustee Assignments box highlighted, press the Enter key.
24. With the Trustee Rights Granted Box on the left of the screen, press the Ins key.
25. Press the F5 key, then the ↓ key. Continue this until all of the rights listed in the Trustee Rights Not Granted box are marked.
26. Press the Enter key. All of the rights should move to the trustee rights granted box.
27. Press the Esc key.
28. Press the Ins key.
29. Type **SYS:PUBLIC** and press the Enter key.
30. Press the Ins key.
31. Type **SYS:SYSTEM** and press the Enter key.
32. Press the Esc key four times. When the Exit box appears, press Y and press the Enter key.
33. Type **LOGOUT** and press the Enter key to end this session.

In the example, user JSMITH1 was given all the trustee rights in the \JSMITH directory but the effective rights should be different. The following steps test the effective rights of the new user.

1. Type **LOGIN** followed by your user name and a **1**. User JSMITH would type **LOGIN JSMITH1**. Then press the Enter key.
2. Type **CD** followed by your user name. User JSMITH would type CD \JSMITH. Then press the Enter key.
3. A file called THIS with the Read Only attribute should still exist in this directory. As a supervisor equivalent, your first account could override the maximum rights mask and change the attribute. The new user cannot. Type **FLAG THIS RW** and press the Enter key.

The command FLAG THIS RW tells the FLAG program to change the attribute of the file called THIS to Read/Write. Since this directory does not have the Modify Files Names/Flags right, the FLAG program responds with:

You don't have rights to change :

THIS [Ro - A - - — - - — —]

The message shows the file you tried to change and its current attributes, Read Only and Archive.

4. Type **LOGOUT** and press the [Enter←] key to end this session.

Groups

The new account created in the previous section was not given sup rvisor equivalence. Therefore, the only rights available were those granted in the Trustee Assignments list. Since it can become tedious to maintain many users accounts when new directories are added, NetWare provides the ability to assign users to a group, and then simply grant the group trustee rights. The following example illustrates the use of groups when assigning trustee rights.

1. Type **LOGIN** and your user name, then press the [Enter←] key. The password prompt should appear. Use the original account, not the username1 account.
2. Type **SECOND** and press the [Enter←] key.
3. Type **SYSCON** and press the [Enter←] key.
4. Use the [↓] key to move to the Group Information Option and press the [Enter←] key.
5. Press the [Ins] key and a box asking for a new group name will appear.
6. Type the name of the account you are now using. User names and group names can be the same. Press the [Enter←] key after typing in the name.
7. With the new group name highlighted, press the [Enter←] key. The Group Information menu should appear.
8. Use the [↓] key to highlight Member List and press the [Enter←] key.
9. Press the [Ins] key and a Not Group Members list will appear.
10. Type the name of your user account followed by a **1**. In the example the user name is JSMITH1. Press the [Enter←] key when the name is highlighted.
11. The name should move to the Group Members box as it did in Fig. 10-29. Press the [Esc] key to return to the Group Information menu.

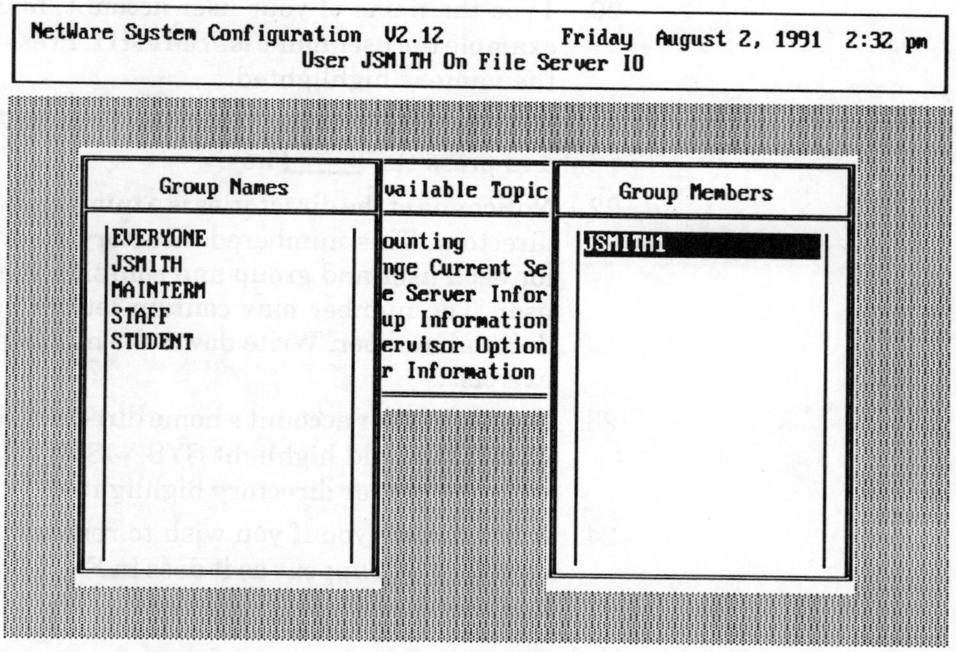

Fig. 10-29. Screen displaying JSMITH1 moved to the Group Members dialog box

12. Use the [↓] key to highlight Trustee Assignments and press the [Enter] key, then press the [Ins] key.
13. Type **SYS:** followed by your user name. This is the home directory created earlier. User JSMITH would type **SYS:\JSMITH**. Press the [Enter] key when the line has been typed.
14. With the new directory in the Trustee Assignments box highlighted, press the [Enter] key.
15. With the Trustee Rights Granted box on the left of the screen, press the [Ins] key.
16. Press the [F5] function key then the [↓] key. Continue this until all of the rights listed in the Trustee Rights Not Granted box are marked.
17. Press the [Enter] key. All of the rights should move to the Trustee Rights Granted box. Press the [Ins] again to accept these changes.
18. Press the [Esc] key three times to return to SYSCON's main menu called Available Topics.
19. Use the [↓] key to highlight User Information and press the [Enter] key.

20. Type the name of your user account, followed by a 1. In the example the user name is JSMITH1. Press the [Enter] key when the name is highlighted.
21. Use the [↓] key to highlight the Trustee Assignments option and press the [Enter] key.
22. Notice one of the directories is a number listed under the MAIL directory. This numbered directory is automatically created for each user and group and contains the login script for the user. The number may contain letters because it is a hexadecimal number. Write down the number for use later in the exercise.
23. Highlight your account's home directory. In the example, user JSMITH would highlight SYS:\JSMITH. Press the [delete] key with the proper directory highlighted.
24. A box asking you if you wish to remove the trustee from the directory will appear as it does in Fig. 10-30. Press the [Y] key and then press the [Enter] key.

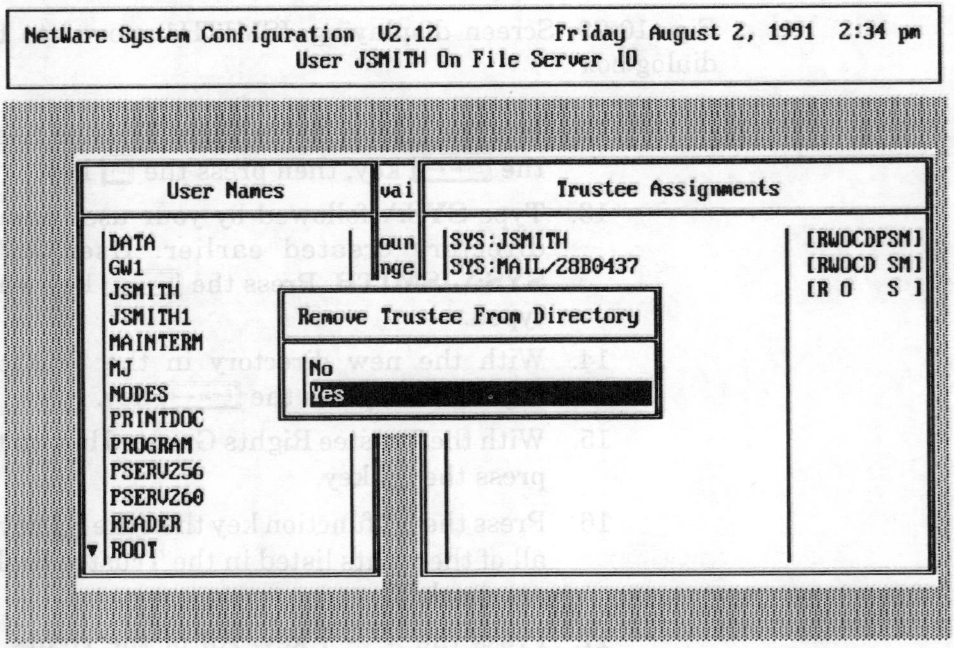

Fig. 10-30. Dialog box used to remove trustee from a directory

25. Press the [esc] key to return to the User Information menu.
26. Use the ARROW keys to highlight Login Script and press the [Enter] key.
27. Move the cursor to the end of the last line in the login script and press the [Enter] key to create a new line.

28. Type in the new line as it appears in Fig. 10-31, except use the name of the group you created earlier in place of JSMITH. Your group name should also be in quotes.

```
NetWare System Configuration V2.12          Friday  August 2, 1991  2:41 pm
                         User JSMITH On File Server IO

                         Login Script For User JSMITH1

MAP F:=SYS:\
MAP INS S1:=SYS:\PUBLIC
MAP INS S2:=SYS:\SYSTEM
MAP INS S3:=SYS:\LOGIN
IF MEMBER OF "JSMITH" WRITE "WE HAVE BEEN WAITING FOR YOU %LOGIN_NAME"
```

Fig. 10-31. Login script for user JSMITH1

29. Press the [Esc] key and then press [Y] and press the [Enter] key to save these changes.
30. Press the [Esc] key three times until the Exit box appears, then press the [Y] and [Enter] keys.
31. Before testing the new login script, it may be of some interest to see where it is located. Type **CD\MAIL** followed by the number you wrote down earlier in this exercise. For user JSMITH the command would be CD \MAIL\28B0437. Press the [Enter] key at the end of the command.
32. Type **DIR** and press the [Enter] key. The login script and a backup of the old login script should appear as files in the directory.
33. Type the command **TYPE LOGIN** and press the [Enter] key. This DOS command displays the contents of the file called LOGIN and should appear similar to the one shown in Fig. 10-32.
34. Type **CD** and press the [Enter] key.
35. Type **LOGIN** followed by your account name and a **1**. In the example the command would be LOGIN JSMITH1. Press the [Enter] key at the end of the line.

When the new user logs in, the login script will identify the account as a member of the group and print the message:

WE HAVE BEEN WAITING FOR YOU JSMITH1

On your screen JSMITH1 will of course be replaced with the name of your account. JSMITH1 is now a member of the group called JSMITH. It is in the group trustee assignments list where the user is assigned trustee rights to the \JSMITH directory. Many more members could be added to the group without assigning individual trustee rights to that directory.

36. Type **LOGOUT** and press the Enter← key to end this session.

```
F>CD \MAIL\28B0437

F>DIR

 Volume in drive F is SYS
 Directory of  F:\MAIL\28B0437

LOGIN            154   8-02-91   2:38p
LOGIN    BAK     152   8-02-91   2:37p
        2 File(s)    921600 bytes free

F>TYPE LOGIN
MAP F:=SYS:\
         MAP INS S1:=SYS:\PUBLIC
                          MAP INS S2:=SYS:\SYSTEM
                                         MAP INS S3:=SYS:\LOGIN

IF MEMBER OF "JSMITH" WRITE "WE HAVE BEEN WAITING FOR YOU %LOGIN_NAME"
F>
```

Fig. 10-32. Contents of file LOGIN

Network Control

The FCONSOLE utility is helpful in observing the functioning of the network as well as establishing control over the use of the network. It provides information on the file server and on the use of the file server. The following instructions illustrate some of the uses of the FCONSOLE utility.

1. Type **LOGIN** and your user name, then press the Enter← key. The password prompt should appear. Use the original account, not the username1 account.
2. Type **SECOND** and press the Enter← key.
3. Type **FCONSOLE** and press the Enter← key. The FCONSOLE main menu should appear, similar to the one in Fig. 10-33.
4. Move the highlighted bar down with the ↓ key to highlight the Connection Information option and press the Enter← key.
5. Type the name of your user account. The highlighted bar will move to your name. Press the Enter← key.

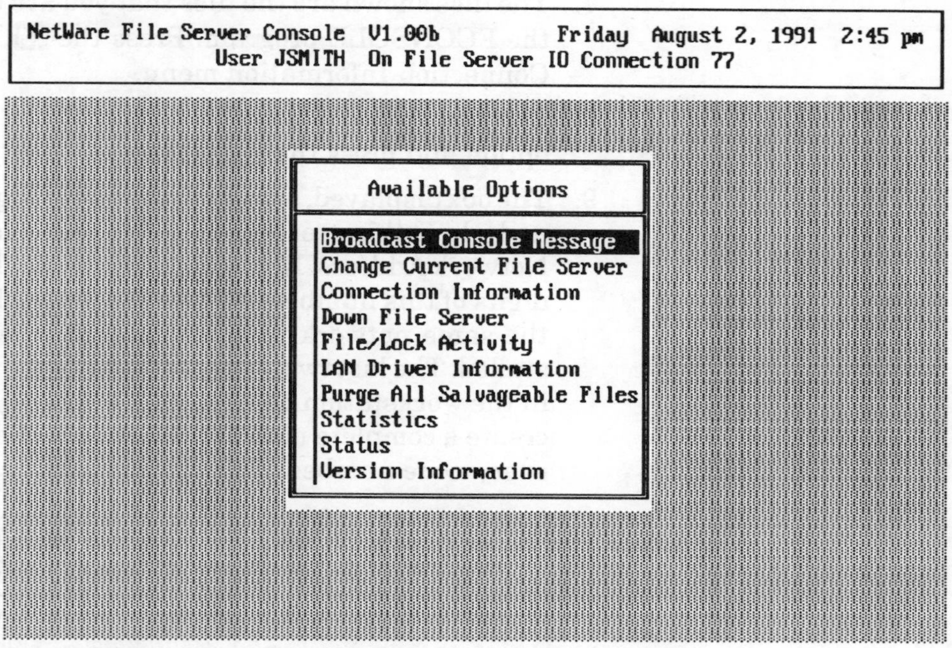

Fig. 10-33. FCONSOLE main menu

6. Fig. 10-34 shows what user JSMITH's screen looks like. Highlight the Open Files/Physical Records option and press the Enter key.

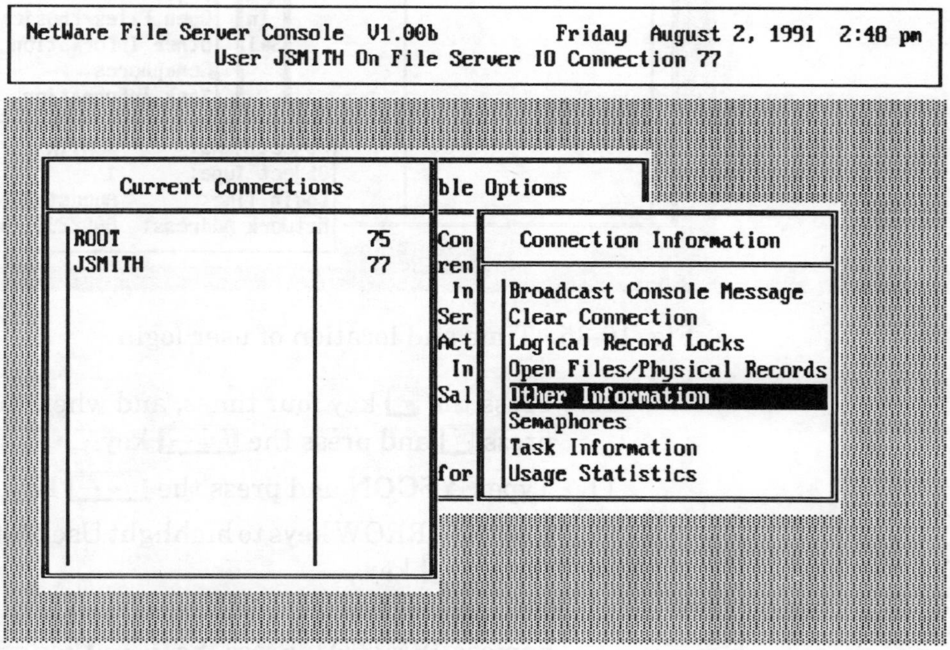

Fig. 10-34. FCONSOLE display of user account JSMITH

7. The files shown are the files that you are using while running the FCONSOLE program. Press the [Esc] key to return to the Connection Information menu.
8. Use the ARROW keys to highlight the Other Information option and press the [Enter] key.
9. The box displayed, similar to the one in Fig. 10-35, shows when and where this user logged in. Write down the number labeled Network Address. Remember to include the ":". The first eight digits of this number indicate the network being used. This is the same network number entered when NetWare was installed. The last twelve digits identify the actual network card in the workstation being used. Ordinarily a supervisor would create a complete map of the network showing the location of every node number.

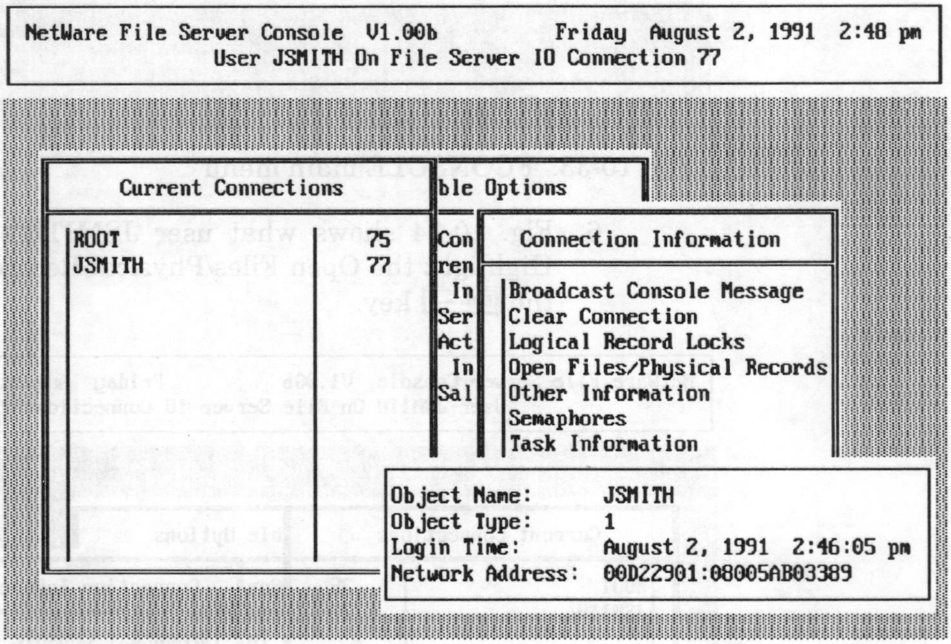

Fig. 10-35. Time and location of user login

10. Press the [Esc] key four times, and when the Exit box appears, press [Y] and press the [Enter] key.
11. Type **SYSCON** and press the [Enter] key.
12. Use the ARROW keys to highlight User Information and press the [Enter] key.
13. Type the name of your account and a 1. In the example the name is JSMITH1. Press the [Enter] key with the correct name highlighted.
14. Use the [↓] key to highlight the Station Restrictions option and press the [Enter] key.

15. Press Ins. A box labeled Network Address will appear.
16. Type in the first eight digits of the number you wrote down earlier and press the Enter key. A box will appear as it does in Fig. 10-36. This box allows the supervisor to restrict the user to any workstation on the network indicated by the network number.

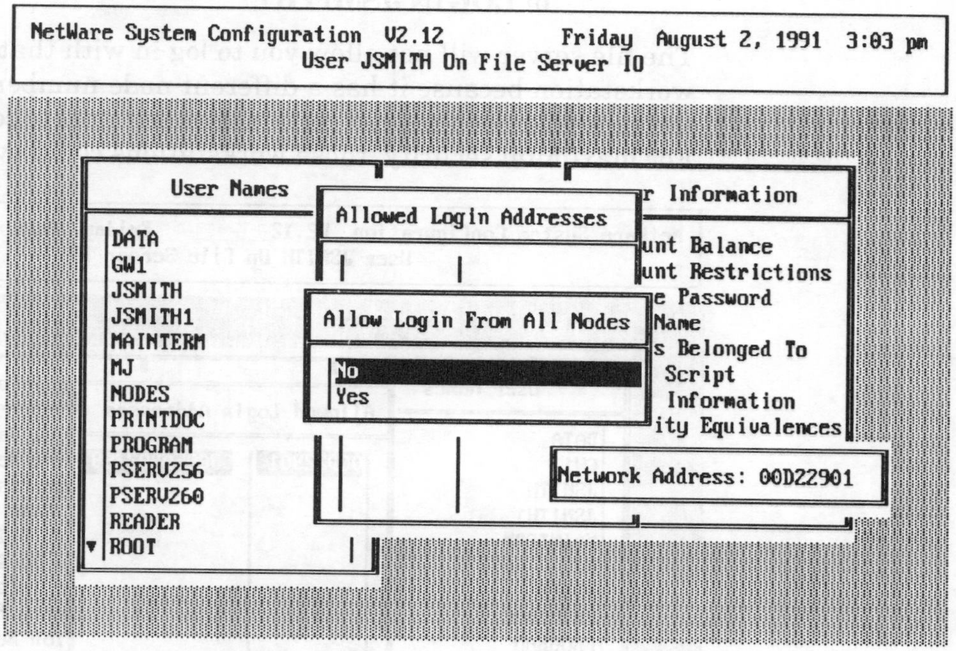

Fig. 10-36. Dialog box used to restrict a user to a workstation

17. Type N and press the Enter key to indicate that further restrictions apply.
18. A Node Address box will appear below the Network Address box. Type in the last twelve digits of the Network Address you wrote down earlier. Do not include the ":", it only separates the two components of the number. Press the Enter key at the end of the number. Notice that Novell is not consistent with what it calls the Network Address. In FCONSOLE the Network Address was the entire twenty digit number and in SYSCON the Network Address is only the network number portion. Both numbers are represented in hexadecimal format, which is why they contain numbers and letters.
19. The Allowed Login Address box should now show the number you just typed in and no others. Fig. 10-37 shows the only address where user JSMITH1 is allowed to login to be network number 00D22901, node number 08005AB03389.
20. Press the Esc key four times. When the Exit box appears, press Y and press the Enter key.

21. The Network Address this user is restricted to is the address of the workstation you are now using. Type **LOGOUT** and press the [Enter ←] key.
22. Trade workstations with a student next to you or simply move to a vacant workstation. At the new workstation type **LOGIN** followed by your user name and a 1. User JSMITH would type in **LOGIN JSMITH1**.

The file server will not allow you to log in with that account at the new workstation because it has a different node number. With this feature, the supervisor can restrict certain user accounts to certain workstations. For maximum security, those workstations could even be diskless.

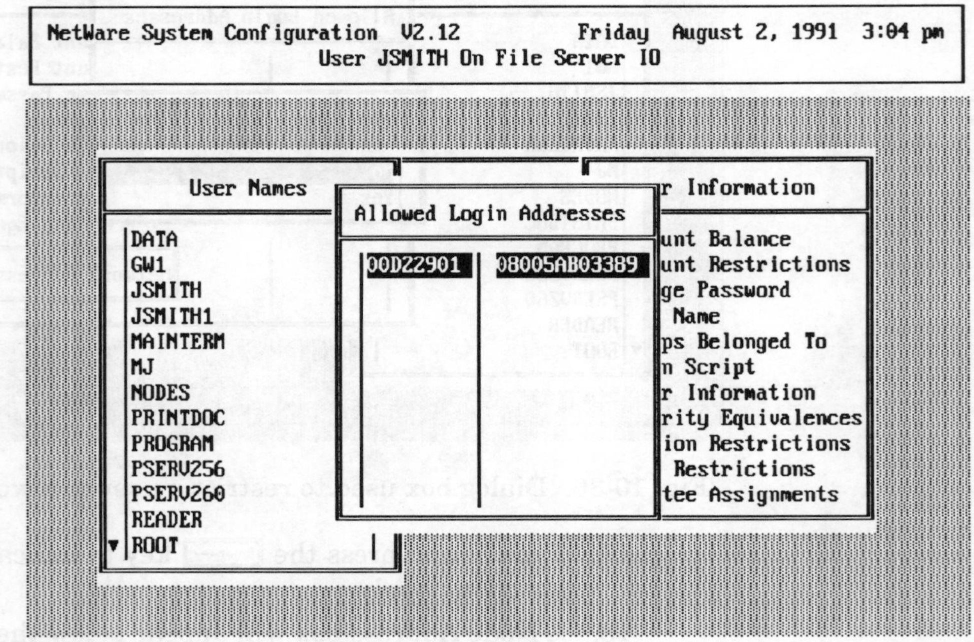

Fig. 10-37. Dialog box displaying the address where user JSMITH is allowed

Summary

Network security is broken down into four levels; passwords, trustee rights, directory rights, and file attributes. The supervisor can put certain restrictions on the password that are intended to force the user to maintain a secure password. The only rights a user has in a given directory are those granted by the supervisor. These rights will be listed in the user's trustee assignments, or the user must belong to a group with the proper rights. The rights granted can be masked by directory rights. All users except the supervisor are restricted by the maximum rights mask placed on a directory. File attributes are primarily used to prevent accidental damage to files because the attributes apply to the supervisor as well as the other users. With the proper rights in a directory, the file attributes can be changed. The combination of all the rights and restrictions a user has in a given directory is known as the effective rights. Users usually fall into categories that require different rights and restrictions. NetWare provides the ability to put these users into groups that can be given the same rights as the users. The groups can then be structured to allow the supervisor to easily make changes to many user accounts by changing only the group account.

Information on the server must be organized as well. Programs and operating system software should be placed in one region and data created by the users in another. This structure has several advantages. The software and data can be more easily shared. The trustee assignments can be more easily standardized and the supervisor can more easily isolate the data that must be backed up on a regular basis.

Controlling how, when, and where users use the network could be called the fifth level of security. With the FCONSOLE utility the supervisor can observe the files accessed by users and see what workstations they are using. SYSCON can then be used to restrict the user to certain workstations, times and directories.

Questions

1. List the four levels of security.
2. Describe what might be considered a fifth level of security.
3. Can any user change his or her password?
4. What trustee rights are automatically granted to any user?
5. A user has all trustee rights in a directory but still cannot access the files in it. What is preventing him from using the files?
6. A user checks her own Trustee Assignments list and finds that the only directory listed is her MAIL directory, yet she is able to use many different programs on the server. How can this be?
7. Where is a user's login script stored on the server?
8. How can the supervisor identify the workstation a user is logged into?
9. Ordinarily, which should be backed up more often, a database file or the NetWare system files?

Projects

Objective

The following projects provide additional practice in establishing security and trustee rights. Additionally, it provides more hands-on practice with the FCONSOLE utility and login scripts.

Project 1. FCONSOLE and Trustee Rights

1. Use the SYSCON utility to create a new user. Use your initials as the name of the user.
2. Select Trustee Assignments and write down the full MAIL directory.
3. Give the new user Read, Open and Search rights to the SYS:\LOGIN, SYS:\SYSTEM, and SYS:\PUBLIC directories. Do not give the user a login script.
4. Examine the trustee assignments of the account you are currently using. Write down the full MAIL directory.
5. Exit the SYSCON utility.
6. Use the DOS COPY command to copy the file called LOGIN from the MAIL directory of the supervisor-equivalent account to the MAIL directory of the new account.
7. Log in as the new user. Record the results with the [shift] [print screen] keys.
8. From another workstation, login under the supervisor-equivalent account.
9. Start the FCONSOLE utility.
10. Use the Connection Information menu to clear the new user account on the other workstation.
11. Use [shift] [print screen] keys to record the message that appears at the first workstation.
12. Exit FCONSOLE and start the SYSCON utility.
13. Delete the new user acount.

Project 2. Practicing the MAP command

1. Given the directory structure below, write the MAP commands needed to map the drive letter H: to the numbered directories.

```
F:\———|
      |-ACCOUNTS
      |  |
      |  |-RECEIVE (1)
      |  |-PAY (2)
      |
      |-PERSONEL
      |  |
      |  |-ARCHIVE
      |  |   |
      |  |   |-FULLTIME (3)
      |  |   |-PARTTIME
      |  |
      |  |-CURRENT
      |      |-FULLTIME
      |      |-PARTTIME (4)
```

2. Write the MAP command needed to ensure the correct version of DOS is used with a COMPAQ computer runing MS DOS version 3.1. Assume the necessary directories are in place.
3. Create a new user. Give the new user a login script that prints "Happy Birthday" on your birthday.
4. Create a directory structure similar to the following:

```
F:\———|
      |-(Your User Name)
          |
          |-SECURE
          |  |
             |-DATA
```

Using the SYSCON utility create a new user with all trustee rights to the directory (Your User Name) except Parental and Modify. Use a different utility to make the contents of the SECURE directory inaccessible to the user. Use the [shift] [print screen] keys at each step and remove the directories and the user when you are finished.

11

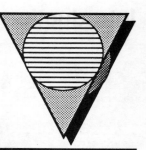

Workstation Customization

Objectives

1. Know the command line options available with some versions of IPX.COM and NET#.COM.
2. Understand the use of extended and expanded memory by the network driver programs.
3. Understand the use of login script variables to create a search path to DOS directories.
4. Understand the concept of remote reset.
5. Recognize the problems that can occur when using an AUTOEXEC.BAT file during remote reset.
6. Know how to create a boot image file.
7. Know how to use a BOOTCONF.SYS file.

Key Terms

AUTOEXEC.BAT	DOS
DOS Directories	DOSGEN
IPX.COM	MAP
NetBIOS	NET#.COM
Remote Reset	Workstation Shell

Introduction

In previous chapters, attaching workstations to the network was shown to be simple. Booting the workstation and loading the IPX and NET# programs sufficed to connect the workstation to a file server. This general purpose strategy works well only when the task being done on the network is relatively simple. If the user needs access to DOS programs such as COMMAND.COM, however, the proper DOS version of the program must be stored somewhere on the server and automatically identified by the workstation. Or the workstation may have extended or expanded memory that could be used to free more conventional memory for application programs. Finally, many workstations could take advantage of a feature known as remote reset. This feature allows workstations to boot from the file server rather than from a diskette in drive A or a hard disk. All these features can be utilized if the workstation is customized, so a few techniques for accomplishing this are well worth learning.

Customizing NetWare

Network Drivers

Access to a Novell network requires two programs to be loaded into memory in the workstation. The programs are IPX.COM and NET#.COM where the # stands for the DOS version used on the workstation. The IPX.COM program controls the network card being used in the workstation, and it was customized during the installation of NetWare. The NET#.COM program is the interface between DOS and the network. It monitors the operations of the user and redirects commands to the network card that involve the network. For this reason the NET#.COM program is generally known as the network redirector.

IPX.COM

Both IPX.COM and NET#.COM have command line parameters that can be used to check or set certain options. IPX.COM's parameters are as follows:

1. I. The "I" parameter causes the program to display information about the version of IPX.COM without loading the program.
2. D. The "D" parameter displays all the options available with this version of IPX.COM. These are the same options that must be selected after the network card driver is chosen during installation. Fig. 11-1 shows the options available for a particular network card during installation. Fig. 11-2 shows

the options available using the "D" parameter. An "*" indicates the option chosen during installation. This option does not work with some older versions of IPX.

3. O#. The "O" parameter is used with a number to select and load a particular option. For instance, IPX O2 loads option 2 of this version of IPX.COM. This option does not work with some older versions of IPX.

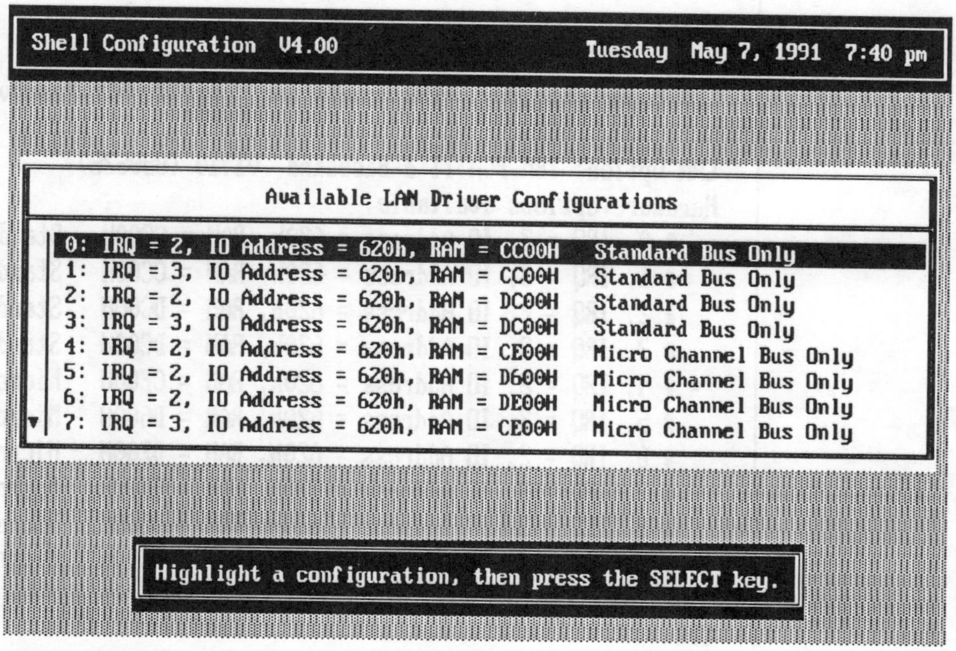

Fig. 11-1. Options available for a network card during installation

NET#.COM

Since the network redirector must operate in a number of different environments, NET#.COM is actually provided in a number of different forms; NET#.COM, XMSNET#.EXE and EMSNET#.EXE. The last two of these are used on computers with more than 640K of RAM. XMSNET#.EXE is used on computers with extended memory and EMSNET#.EXE is used on computers with expanded memory. The two types of memory represent two different addressing schemes used to overcome DOS's inherent 640K limit.

The network redirector programs also have command line parameters. NET#.COM, XMSNET#.EXE and EMSNET#.EXE can all use the following parameters.

1. I. The I parameter causes the program to display information about the version of the redirector without loading the program.

2. U. The U parameter unloads the program from memory. This option does not work with some older versions.
3. PS=. In a multi-file-server environment, the network drivers will attach to the first available file server. The PS= parameter is used to indicate a Preferred Server as in PS=SERVER1. This option does not work with some older versions.

```
C>IPX D
Novell IPX/SPX v3.01 Rev. B (900605)
(C) Copyright 1985, 1990 Novell Inc.  All Rights Reserved.

LAN Option: IBM PCN II & Baseband  V1.10 (880526)
Hardware options available:
   # 0. IRQ = 2, IO Address = 620h, RAM = CC00H   Standard Bus Only
   # 1. IRQ = 3, IO Address = 620h, RAM = CC00H   Standard Bus Only
   # 2. IRQ = 2, IO Address = 620h, RAM = DC00H   Standard Bus Only
   # 3. IRQ = 3, IO Address = 620h, RAM = DC00H   Standard Bus Only
 * # 4. IRQ = 2, IO Address = 620h, RAM = CE00H   Micro Channel Bus Only
   # 5. IRQ = 2, IO Address = 620h, RAM = D600H   Micro Channel Bus Only
   # 6. IRQ = 2, IO Address = 620h, RAM = DE00H   Micro Channel Bus Only
   # 7. IRQ = 3, IO Address = 620h, RAM = CE00H   Micro Channel Bus Only
   # 8. IRQ = 3, IO Address = 620h, RAM = D600H   Micro Channel Bus Only
   # 9. IRQ = 3, IO Address = 620h, RAM = DE00H   Micro Channel Bus Only

C>
```

Fig. 11-2. Options available to a network card using the D parameter

Both extended memory and expanded memory require drivers to allow DOS access to these areas. Microsoft's extended memory driver is called HIMEM.SYS and it is included with several software products, including Windows and DOS. The expanded memory driver is very hardware specific and is included only with an expanded memory card. Both drivers are included as statements in the workstation's CONFIG.SYS file. The CONFIG.SYS file is a text file DOS uses for commands that must be executed at the time DOS loads.

The network redirector programs, NET#.COM, XMSNET#.EXE and EMSNET#.EXE were included with NetWare for DOS versions 2, 3, and 4, with XMSNET#.EXE and EMSNET#.EXE available for versions 3 and 4 only. NET5.COM is packaged with MS DOS version 5, along with drivers for several other networks. Due to several software bugs, Novell has released NETX.COM, XMSNETX.EXE and EMSNETX.EXE. These three programs are not DOS version specific. They are available from Novell's Compuserve forum Netwire, or through a Novell authorized dealer.

DOS Directories

In a large network there may be many different types of workstations running many different versions of DOS. The utility programs for each of those DOS versions are sensitive to the version loaded into the computer. Each program, such as FORMAT.COM or CHKDSK.COM, checks which version the computer is running before it executes. For instance, if the FORMAT.COM program from MS DOS 3.1 was started on a computer running PC DOS 3.3 the program would print "Incorrect DOS version." on the screen and then halt.

The result is that if the DOS files for the workstations are to be loaded on the file server, a directory must be created for each of the types of DOS versions that might be used by the workstations. The most critical of the DOS files stored in this way is the DOS command interpreter COMMAND.COM. It is loaded by DOS when the computer is booted and must be frequently reloaded during normal operation. DOS uses the COMSPEC environment variable to record the location of this program. Ordinarily, the COMSPEC variable is set when the computer is booted. If, for instance, the computer was booted from a DOS disk in drive A:, the COMSPEC variable would probably be set to A:\COMMAND.COM. Unfortunately, the DOS disk must often be removed from drive A: to make room for other program or data disks. When DOS needs to reload COMMAND.COM, it will display the message "Insert diskette with COMMAND.COM and strike any key when ready" on the screen and wait for the user to respond.

Network workstations must often be booted from a diskette, so setting the COMSPEC variable to point to a copy of COMMAND.COM on the file server can save a great deal of time for the user. The problem is of course setting it to point to the correct version of COMMAND.COM. NetWare provides facilities for doing just that. The login script variables OS, OS_VERSION, and MACHINE can be used to locate the DOS files at the time the user logs in to the network.

These variables are automatically set when the network drivers are loaded. Once set, they can be used by the login script to MAP network drive letters to appropriate directories. For instance, if an IBM PC running DOS version 3.3 were to logon to the network, the OS variable would be set to MSDOS, the OS_VERSION variable would be set to V3.30, and the MACHINE variable would be set to IBM_PC. All the user accounts on the file server could have a line in their login scripts like this:

```
MAP S1:=SYS:\PUBLIC\%MACHINE\%OS\%OS_VERSION
```

The search drive, S1, would be mapped to a different directory on the file server for each different value of MACHINE, OS, and OS_VERSION. The supervisor need only ensure that there is a directory containing the correct DOS version for each workstation that logs in. After this line has been executed, the S1 can be used to set the COMSPEC variable.

```
COMSPEC=S1:COMMAND.COM
```

In actual practice these two lines would probably be placed in the System Login Script, where they would be executed for every user.

Customizing the Workstation Shell

The network drivers are collectively known as the shell. The shell surrounds the DOS interface to allow commands that should be handled by the network to be rerouted to the network. There are many different ways in which the shell can be customized to work effectively on a given workstation.

The SHELL.CFG File

In addition to configuring the IPX.COM program and choosing the correct NET#.COM program, several options can be set using a file called SHELL.CFG. The SHELL.CFG file is a simple text file stored on the workstation computer. Each of the network drivers checks this file for configuration commands. Many of the commands available are quite esoteric and are used primarily to patch compatibility problems with other software running on the workstation. The following is a partial list of SHELL.CFG commands.

1. LONG MACHINE TYPE. Sets the MACHINE login script variable. The default value for this variable is IBM_PC.
2. SHORT MACHINE TYPE. Sets the SMACHINE login script variable. The default value for this variable is IBM. The length cannot exceed four characters. A value of CMPQ, standing for Compaq, will cause the Novell utilities to use a black and white color pallet.
3. LOCAL PRINTERS. Sets the number of printers reserved by the workstation. The most valuable use of this command is to set it to a value of 0 on workstations that do not have any printers. This prevents the computer from locking up when the Print-Screen key is pressed.
4. PREFERRED SERVER. The PREFERRED SERVER command is used to name a specific file server. If the specified file server is not available, the shell will attach to the next available server.
5. SHOW DOTS. An ordinary NetWare directory does not contain the "." and ".." entry as a DOS directory. With the SHOW DOTS command set to ON the "." and ".." entries will be shown. This is especially important when using mouse driven programs that require the user to select ".." to move through the directory structure.

NetBIOS

Novell recognizes the fact that many different networks exist. Among them are networks designed to emulate IBM's original NetBIOS standard. Many network applications were and are written to use the

NetBIOS standards for network communications. Novell has provided a program called, not surprisingly, NETBIOS.EXE that emulates the NetBIOS standard. With this program and another called INT2F.EXE installed, application programs can use NetBIOS network function calls or Novell's IPX/SPX network function calls.

Remote Reset

In some environments, strict network security is required. In these situations diskless workstations can be used to prevent most users from copying data from the server to a diskette on the workstation. The problem, of course, is to boot a computer with no disk drives. The solution is called remote reset, remote boot, or sometimes remote program load. With this feature, a computer can be booted from a file on a network drive rather than from a local disk drive.

Essentially, the workstation is tricked into thinking that the file on the server is a boot disk in drive A. Remote boot is also very helpful for workstations with only floppy disk drives since it eliminates the need for a customized boot diskette to be located near each workstation. Another advantage is that upgrades to a computer's DOS or the network drivers can be made from the network without the need for the supervisor to visit each workstation.

Setting up remote boot involves four steps. These are outlined below.

1. The network card must be prepared for remote boot. Only certain network cards can support remote boot. These cards have a ROM (read only memory) chip that requests boot information from the server. Many network cards have sockets for remote boot ROM chips, but the chips are not usually sold with them. Most network cards that are capable of remote boot require a switch to be set on the card or a setup program to be run that sets the card to remote boot mode.
2. A boot disk must be prepared for the workstation that is to be set for remote boot. DOS, the network drivers, and any other programs that are to be loaded when the computer boots must be copied to the disk. The proper AUTOEXEC.BAT, CONFIG.SYS, and SHELL.CFG files must be prepared and copied to the disk.
3. A program on the file server called DOSGEN must be used to copy all the data on the boot disk to a file on the server called a boot disk image file. The default name for this file is NET$DOS.SYS but it can be changed to something more meaningful such as ROOM1.SYS.
4. If more than one boot image file is needed, another file must be created that indicates which workstations are to use which boot image files. The file, which is named BOOTCONF.SYS, is simply a list of network addresses and the boot image file each needs.

Remote Reset Setup

The Network Card

Preparing the network card for remote boot will be different on each card. Some cards will require only a switch to be set on the card. Many cards have setup programs that are used to set the card to remote boot mode. Other cards will need a remote boot ROM to be inserted in a socket on the card.

The Boot Disk

Some special considerations must be made when preparing a boot disk for remote boot. The problem stems from the unusual behavior of the computer while it is using remote boot.

Without remote boot, the computer will search for a bootable disk. Assuming there is a disk in drive A:, the computer first loads the DOS system files and reads the CONFIG.SYS file for device drivers or other instructions. Next the AUTOEXEC.BAT file is executed. A network boot disk will have an AUTOEXEC.BAT file that loads the appropriate network drivers, IPX.COM and NET3.COM, for example. Once these programs are loaded the next line in the AUTOEXEC.BAT file would be executed. Suppose the following lines are in the AUTOEXEC.BAT file.

```
IPX
NET3
LOGIN JSMITH1
```

Since the computer is booting off the A drive, drive A is the default drive. When the IPX instruction in AUTOEXEC.BAT is executed, the computer will first search only the root directory of drive A to locate and load this program. The same is true for the NET3 and LOGIN JSMITH1 instructions. Note that after the NET3 program is loaded, drive letter F: is available to the user. When the LOGIN JSMITH1 instruction is executed, the default drive is still A, even though the workstation has been attached to the server.

The same sequence of events occur when remote boot is used; however, the computer is "fooled" into reading the boot image file as if it were a disk in drive A. The difference comes after the NET3 program is loaded. As soon as a formal connection is made to the file server, the remote boot process is abandoned and the default drive is left at drive F. Novell considers this a "bug" in the shell software, but new releases of the shell programs have not corrected the problem in all cases.

Even though the remote boot process is essentially over, the AUTOEXEC.BAT file is still executing. Unfortunately DOS has not stored the entire file in memory. Only a byte offset of the next instruction in the batch file is stored. With the remote boot process ended, the AUTOEXEC.BAT file is no longer available since it cannot be read from the boot image file. Additionally, DOS does not recognize that the default drive has been changed. The result is that the computer will attempt to read the next instruction in the AUTOEXEC.BAT from the F:\LOGIN directory.

If there were no more instructions in the file, that is, if NET3 were the last line, the workstation would simply display the F> prompt and be ready for the user to login. Often, however, there are additional instructions that must be executed after the workstation is connected to a file server. In the example above the command LOGIN JSMITH1 is intended to provide an automatic login at the workstation. To accommodate this one workstation, a copy of the AUTOEXEC.BAT file could be placed in the F:\LOGIN directory. This would not be a satisfactory solution, since every workstation that uses remote boot and needs instructions executed after being connected to the server would encounter the same AUTOEXEC.BAT file.

```
Workstation #1
AUTOEXEC.BAT in boot image file
   IPX
   NET3
   LOGIN JSMITH1
Workstation #2
AUTOEXEC.BAT in boot image file
   IPX
   NET3
   LOGIN SUSAN
On file server
F:\LOGIN\AUTOEXEC.BAT
   IPX
   NET3
   CAPTURE
```

Fig. 11-3. Different AUTOEXEC.BAT files

Fig. 11-3 shows three different AUTOEXEC.BAT files. The first two represent files in the boot image prepared for workstations #1 and #2. The third is the file in the F:\LOGIN directory. After the NET3 instruction in each of the workstation files is executed, those workstations are connected to the file server. They will be "fooled" into executing the next line in F:\LOGIN\AUTOEXEC.BAT on the server. The last line in workstation #1s' AUTOEXEC.BAT, LOGIN JSMITH1, and the last line in workstation #2s' AUTOEXEC.BAT, LOGIN SUSAN would be lost. Each would execute the CAPTURE command in F:\LOGIN\AUTOEXEC.BAT.

There are two solutions to this problem, the first, and most widely used, is to provide a different batch file for each boot disk. The second solution is to ensure that the F:\LOGIN\AUTOEXEC.BAT file will execute different instructions based on information received from the workstation boot image file.

Providing a different batch file for each boot disk is a little more involved than it would first seem. The computer booting up will need to return to the batch file after any programs in it are executed. For instance, if the batch file had a LOGIN statement in it, the computer would need to find the batch file after the LOGIN statement was executed. But the LOGIN script might have changed the current directory. For this reason the batch file being used by the computer during the remote boot process should exist in three places, in the boot disk image file, in the \LOGIN directory, and in the directory that the login script leaves as the default directory when it finishes.

To create the proper boot image file, a complete boot disk should be prepared. DOS, the network shell programs, and an appropriate AUTOEXEC.BAT file should be placed on a disk. To accommodate all of the boot disk image files that might exist on the server, the AUTOEXEC.BAT file is divided into two batch files. AUTOEXEC.BAT simply starts another batch file with a unique name. On the boot disk, the AUTOEXEC.BAT file would have a single line such as JSMITH.BAT. The other file, JSMITH.BAT, would contain all the appropriate instructions for starting the workstation on the network. This file would also be the one that must be duplicated in all three locations mentioned above, the boot disk, the \LOGIN directory, and the default directory left after the login script executes.

The second solution to the problem of multiple boot image files involves the creation of an AUTOEXEC.BAT file on the file server that can accommodate different instructions depending on which boot image file calls it. Creating these batch files requires a better understanding of DOS batch files and the remote boot process.

In Fig. 11-4 all three AUTOEXEC.BAT files have been changed. Three new DOS batch file commands have been used, the SET command, the REM command, and the "%" symbol. The SET command places the text to the right of the "=" in the variable on the left of the "=". This variable is known as an environment variable and is stored in the workstations' memory. The REM command is called a remark and is used simply to put a comment in the file. It and any text that follows it on the same line are not executed by the computer. The "%" symbol is called a replacement symbol. In a batch file, the environment variable contained inside two "%" symbols is replaced with the contents of the variable. In workstation #1's file, for instance, the last line, %NEXT%, would be replaced with the contents of the variable NEXT, LOGIN JSMITH1.

```
Workstation #1
AUTOEXEC.BAT in boot image file
  SET NEXT=LOGIN JSMITH1
  REM *
  IPX
  NET3
  %NEXT%
Workstation #2
AUTOEXEC.BAT in boot image file
  SET NEXT=LOGIN SUSAN
  REM ***
  IPX
  NET3
  %NEXT%
On the file server
F:\LOGIN\AUTOEXEC.BAT
  REM ****************
  REM ***
  IPX
  NET3
  %NEXT%
```

Fig. 11-4. Updated batch files

In this case, however, the last line of workstation #1's AUTOEXEC.BAT file will never be executed. But the same replacement will take place when the last line of F:\LOGIN\AUTOEXEC.BAT is executed. The environment variable NEXT will still have the value in it from the first line in workstation #1's AUTOEXEC.BAT.

Followed from the beginning, this is what will happen to workstation #1.

1. When the workstation is turned on or re-booted, the network interface card requests boot information from the server.
2. The file server sends a copy of the boot image file to the workstation. That file is treated as if it were a disk in drive A of the workstation.
3. The workstation loads DOS and begins to execute AUTOEXEC.BAT.
4. The first line, SET NEXT=LOGIN JSMITH1, creates a variable called NEXT and stores the value LOGIN JSMITH1 in it.

5. The second line, REM *, is a remark and is not executed.
6. The third and fourth lines load the network drivers IPX and NET3.
7. The instant NET3 has loaded successfully, the workstation is attached to the file server and the boot image file is abandoned.
8. The workstation reads its next command from the file server in the file F:\LOGIN\AUTOEXEC.BAT. This is when the REM statements become important. The next command is not necessarily the fifth line in the batch file. It is the command located at the same byte offset as the next command in workstation #1's AUTOEXEC.BAT. There are 34 characters in workstation #1's AUTOEXEC.BAT file up to the end of the fourth line NET3. Adding a carriage return and line feed character to each line brings the total number of bytes to 42 through the end of the fourth line. The REM statements are used to ensure that the fifth line starts at byte offset 43 in each of the three files. The REM statement in the second line of workstation #2's file has two more asterisks in it than the similar line in workstation #1's file because the line SET NEXT=LOGIN SUSAN is two characters less than the line SET NEXT=LOGIN JSMITH1. The first two lines of F:\LOGIN\AUTOEXEC.BAT are there to occupy the space that the first two lines in each of the workstation's files use.
9. Since the byte offsets of the files are aligned properly, the next statement executed by workstation #1 is the fifth line in F:\LOGIN\AUTOEXEC.BAT. The %NEXT% is replaced with the value of the NEXT variable and LOGIN JSMITH1 is executed.
10. The login script for user JSMITH1 takes over and any instructions located there are executed.

The files in this example represent just one way in which environment variables can be used to make individual workstations work differently.

Using DOSGEN

Once created, the information on the boot disk must be converted to a special type of file known as a boot image. The file consists of all the information, including the DOS system files, the network driver programs, and the AUTOEXEC.BAT on the boot disk, converted to a form that the file server can store and send to the workstation when necessary. The NetWare utility program for doing this is called DOSGEN.EXE. The following syntax is used with DOSGEN:

DOSGEN drive [file name]

The drive specified must be a floppy disk drive on the local computer. The file name is optional but must end with a .SYS extension. If no file name is given, DOSGEN will convert the information on the disk to a file called NET$DOS.SYS. The boot disk itself is not changed. NET$DOS.SYS is also the default name that a workstation will use when remote booting. The DOSGEN program is located in the F:\SYSTEM directory on the file server and all boot image files must be stored in the F:\LOGIN directory.

DOSGEN works with any bootable DOS diskette except DOS version 5 and higher. Novell has provided a program called RPLFIX.COM that is used to repair a DOS 5 boot image file already created with DOSGEN. RPLFIX.COM (Remote Program Load Fix) is available on Novell's Compuserve forum Netwire, or through a Novell authorized dealer.

BOOTCONF.SYS

Customizing each boot disk means that each workstation will need a separate boot image file. A file called BOOTCONF.SYS is used to store the names of all the boot image files and the network addresses where each will be used. BOOTCONF.SYS must be located in the F:\LOGIN directory and is a simple text file in the form:

List 0Xnetwork number,node number=boot image file name

A typical line in BOOTCONF.SYS might look something like the following:

List 0X00D22901,08005A6A34F1=ROOM1.SYS

BOOTCONF.SYS can contain as many lines as needed. When a workstation is using remote boot, BOOTCONF.SYS is searched for a line with that workstation's address. If the address is found, the boot image file specified is used. If the address is not found, the file NET$DOS.SYS is used.

Hands-on NetWare

In order to complete the tutorials in the remaining half of this chapter, the file server and a workstation should be ready to use.

1. The file server must be on.
2. The user account created in the previous chapter must still be available.
3. The network boot disk created earlier must be available.
4. The NetWare SHGEN disks must be available.
5. A complete set of DOS diskettes must be available. DOS version 5 must be used in some sections. The MEM command must be available for these sections.
6. The latest releases of the network shell programs should be obtained. New versions of IPX.OBJ, NETX.COM, XMSNETX.EXE, and EMSNETX.EXE are available through Novell's Compuserve forum Netwire or through a Novell authorized reseller.

7. In the examples below TYPE THE NAME OF YOUR ACCOUNT WHERE USER JSMITH IS USED. For instance, if the instructions read "Type LOGIN JSMITH", you should type LOGIN followed by the name of the account you created earlier.

Memory Usage

One of the most important concerns when attaching a DOS computer to any network is the amount of RAM that will be used by the network drivers. In some cases the network drivers use so much memory that application programs cannot run. This of course makes the network worse than useless. The amount of memory used by different networks varies widely from as much as 100K to as little as 10K. Also, the amount of memory used by a single network can vary depending on the options used and the way the drivers are loaded into memory. NetWare is no exception. Many different configurations are possible, and each leaves different amounts of conventional memory free. Conventional memory is all memory up to 640K. All DOS programs must use some of this area during some time in their operation. Other areas of memory, high memory, extended memory, and expanded memory, can only be used in addition to the 640K region, which is what makes it so critical. On a computer with 640K or less of memory, the choices are somewhat limited. The following tutorial demonstrates memory usage in these computers.

Computers with 640K or Less of RAM

In the following tutorial, a workstation with 640K of memory is used. Any workstation with at least 256K could be used. Additional memory will not present a problem.

1. Boot the computer with a DOS diskette by placing the disk in drive A: and pressing the [Ctrl], [alt], and [delete] keys simultaneously.
2. Enter the date and time as requested.
3. Type **CHKDSK** and press the [Enter←] key. The CHKDSK program will show the disk space information and memory usage similar to that in Fig. 11-5. The last two set of numbers at the bottom show the total amount available to DOS and the amount currently unused. In this case the CHKDSK program shows 580224 bytes of free memory with only DOS loaded.
4. Remove the DOS diskette from drive A and replace it with the network boot disk.
5. Type **IPX** and press the [Enter←] key.
6. Type **NET#** and press the [Enter←] key, where the "#" symbol is the DOS version you are currently running. For instance, if you are using DOS 3.1, type NET3.

7. With both network drivers loaded, return the DOS disk to drive A, type **CHKDSK**, and press the Enter← key. The CHKDSK program should report significantly less memory in the "bytes free" section. The missing memory is being used by the network drivers. Write down the figure shown for "bytes free" for comparison later.
8. Again replace the DOS diskette with the network boot disk. Type **NETBIOS** and press the Enter← key, then type **INT2F** and press the Enter← key. These two programs provide the NetBIOS emulation for application programs that require it.
9. Return the DOS disk to drive A, type **CHKDSK** and press the Enter← key. The "bytes free" figure should be even lower. The memory occupied by these two programs could be significant, and they should not be used unless NetBIOS emulation is required.

The example above represents a worst-case situation in which the drivers must be placed entirely in conventional memory. Many programs not originally intended to operate in a networked environment would not have enough memory to run. A computer with at least 1 megabyte of memory can be configured to preserve much more conventional memory.

```
Microsoft(R) MS-DOS(R) Version 5.00
             (C)Copyright Microsoft Corp 1981-1991.

A>chkdsk
Volume Serial Number is 2247-13FC

    362496 bytes total disk space
     71680 bytes in 2 hidden files
    211968 bytes in 8 user files
     78848 bytes available on disk

      1024 bytes in each allocation unit
       354 total allocation units on disk
        77 available allocation units on disk

    655360 total bytes memory
    580224 bytes free

A>
A>
A>
A>
A>
```

Fig. 11-5. Output produced by the CHKDSK program

Computers with 1 Megabyte or More of Memory.

DOS programs are typically limited to the 640K conventional memory region, but a number of methods have been created to use more. On a computer with 1 megabyte of memory, some of the 360K (actually 384K) above conventional memory (called high memory) can be used by DOS, if an appropriate extended memory manager program is implemented. Microsoft's HIMEM.SYS device driver is the most readily available of these programs. The instructions below demonstrate how high memory can be used to save conventional memory.

Using HIMEM.SYS and XMSNET#

1. Boot the workstation with the network boot disk by inserting the disk in drive A and simultaneously pressing the Ctrl, alt, and delete keys.
2. Copy the HIMEM.SYS device driver to the network boot disk.
3. Ensure that the network boot disk is in drive A.
4. Type the following lines, pressing the Enter key at the end of each line.

   COPY CON CONFIG.SYS
   DEVICE=HIMEM.SYS
5. While holding down the Ctrl key, press the Z key, then press the Enter key.
6. Boot the workstation by simultaneously pressing the Ctrl, alt, and delete keys.
7. Type **IPX** and press the Enter key.
8. Type **XMSNET#** and press the Enter key where the "#" represents the DOS version number you are using.
9. Replace the network boot disk with a DOS disk containing the CHKDSK program.
10. Type **CHKDSK** and press the Enter key.

The number of bytes free should be significantly larger in this case than in the previous example with only IPX and NET# loaded. The extra space available in conventional memory is made possible by the network shell program XMSNET# loading itself primarily into the high memory region between 640K and 1 megabyte. Write down the figure shown for "bytes free" for comparison later.

DOS Version 5

DOS version 5 offers other ways to use the high memory area. Most of the DOS code itself, as well as any other memory resident programs such as network drivers can be loaded into the high memory area. The following exercises demonstrate the benefits in conventional memory savings using DOS 5 on a computer with at least 1 megabyte of memory. A bootable DOS 5 disk will be needed.

1. Copy the IPX.COM and NETX.COM programs to the bootable DOS 5 disk.

2. Copy the following files from the original DOS 5 disks to the bootable disk; HIMEM.SYS, EMM386.EXE, CHKDSK.EXE, MEM.EXE and MORE.COM.
3. Ensure that the DOS 5 disk is in drive A and type the following lines, pressing the [Enter←] key after each line.

   COPY CON CONFIG.SYS
   DEVICE=HIMEM.SYS
   DEVICE=EMM386.EXE NOEMS
   DOS=HIGH,UMB
4. While holding down the [Ctrl] key, press the [Z] key, then press the [Enter←] key.

The CONFIG.SYS file is being used in this case to load programs that will manage the high memory area and to load DOS into that area. The HIMEM.SYS device driver manages the use of all the memory above 640K. The EMM386.EXE program is being used to allow DOS programs access to the high memory area between 640K and 1 megabyte. The DOS command instructs DOS to load itself into the high memory area and to allow other programs to be loaded there as well.

5. Boot the workstation with the DOS 5 disk by simultaneously pressing the [Ctrl], [alt], and [delete] keys.
6. Enter the date and time as requested.
7. Type **LOADHIGH IPX** and press the [Enter←] key. LOADHIGH, which can be abbreviated LH, is a DOS 5 command that attempts to load the program into the high memory area.
8. Type **LOADHIGH NETX** and press the [Enter←] key.
9. Type **CHKDSK** and press the [Enter←] key. Compare the "bytes free" figure with the number obtained when using conventional memory only. This amount should be much larger.
10. Type **MEM/C | MORE** and press the [Enter←] key. The | MORE portion of this command is necessary only because the output from the MEM /C command will be longer than 25 lines displayed on the monitor.

This command displays memory usage in a more complete form than the CHKDSK command. The first screen shows programs running in conventional memory. MSDOS, HIMEM, EMM386, and COMMAND should be listed there.

11. Strike any key to advance to the next screen of output from the MEM/C command. A list of programs loaded into high memory should appear. SYSTEM, IPX, and NETX should be shown in high memory. The MSDOS shown in conventional memory and the SYSTEM shown in high memory are both portions of DOS code.

Note that the XMSNET# and the EMSNET# programs are not used in this example because DOS is being used to load the programs in high memory. With this configuration, these programs would not find any memory available for their use.

The exercises above demonstrate the memory savings using the proper network shell programs, particularly when using DOS 5.

The SHELL.CFG File

When the network shell is loaded, a file called SHELL.CFG is searched for in the current directory. This file contains instructions to the shell programs regarding how they are to be loaded. One of the most important functions of the SHELL.CFG file is to set login script variables to values that reflect the type of computer being used. The variable MACHINE can be used to specify a certain type of computer. This variable can be critical when preparing a login script if the login script needs to set a search drive to a directory containing DOS program files.

In preparation for exercises involving the SHELL.CFG file, directories must be created on the server for each type and version of DOS being used. The following instructions show how this is done. These instructions need to be performed only once on a file server for each DOS version.

1. Boot the workstation with the appropriate network boot disk.
2. Type **IPX** and press the [Enter←] key.
3. Type the name of the network redirector you will be using and press the [Enter←] key. NETX will work for all situations but the appropriate NET# program can also be used.
4. Type **F:** and press the [Enter←] key.
5. Type **LOGIN** followed by the name of the supervisor-equivalent account you created earlier and press the [Enter←] key.
6. Type **CD\PUBLIC** and press the [Enter←] key.
7. If your workstation is an IBM computer type MD IBM_PC and press the [Enter←] key. If your workstation is an IBM compatible running a machine-specific version of DOS, use the name of the computer shorted to eight characters or less instead of IBM_PC. For instance, if the workstation is a Compaq computer type MD COMPAQ and press the [Enter←] key.
8. Type **CD** followed by the name of the computer you used in the previous step and press the [Enter←] key.
9. Type **MD MSDOS** and press the [Enter←] key. Use MSDOS in the command even if you are using PC DOS.
10. Type **CD MSDOS** and press the [Enter←] key.

11. Type **MD V** followed by the version number of the DOS you are using and press the Enter key. For instance if you are using PC DOS version 3.31, type MD V3.31 and press the Enter key. If you are using MS DOS version 5, type MD V5.00 and press the Enter key.
12. Type **CD V** followed by the version number you used in the previous command.
13. Insert the first DOS disk of the version you are using in drive A:.
14. Type **COPY A:*.* F:** and press the Enter key.
15. Repeat the previous step for each DOS disk needed for that version of DOS. For instance, PC DOS 3.3 on 3 1/2 inch disks requires two disks to be copied to drive F:.

With the appropriate DOS version placed on the file server, the SHELL.CFG file should be created to ensure the correct version is used. Also, additional login script commands should be used to map the DOS directory to a search drive. The following instructions should be used to update the SHELL.CFG file with the appropriate commands:

1. Place the network boot disk in drive A:.
2. Type **COPY CON SHELL.CFG** and press the Enter key.
3. Type **LONG MACHINE TYPE=** followed by the name of the computer used in the creation of the DOS directory and press the Enter key. For instance, for an IBM PC type LONG MACHINE TYPE=IBM_PC and press the Enter key.
4. Type **SHOW DOTS ON** and press the Enter key.
5. Hold down the Ctrl key and press the Z key, then press the Enter key.

The SHELL.CFG file should now be on the network boot disk. The next time IPX and NETX are loaded, the commands in this file will take effect. In the following steps, SYSCON is used to change the login script to include a map command that uses information provided by the SHELL.CFG file.

1. Boot the workstation with the network boot disk by simultaneously pressing the Ctrl, alt, and delete keys.
2. Enter the date and time as requested.
3. Type **IPX** and press the Enter key.
4. Type the name of the network redirector you will be using and press the Enter key. NETX will work for all situations, but the appropriate NET# program can also be used.
5. Type **F:** and press the Enter key.

6. Type **DIR** and press the [Enter←] key. Notice the entries for "." and ".." at the top of the directory listing. These are the dots referred to in the SHOW DOTS ON command in the SHELL.CFG file.
7. Type **LOGIN** followed by the name of supervisor-equivalent account you created earlier and press the [Enter←] key.
8. Type **SECOND**, the password used for this account, and press the [Enter←] key.
9. Type **SYSCON** and press the [Enter←] key. SYSCON's main menu should appear as shown in Fig. 11-6.

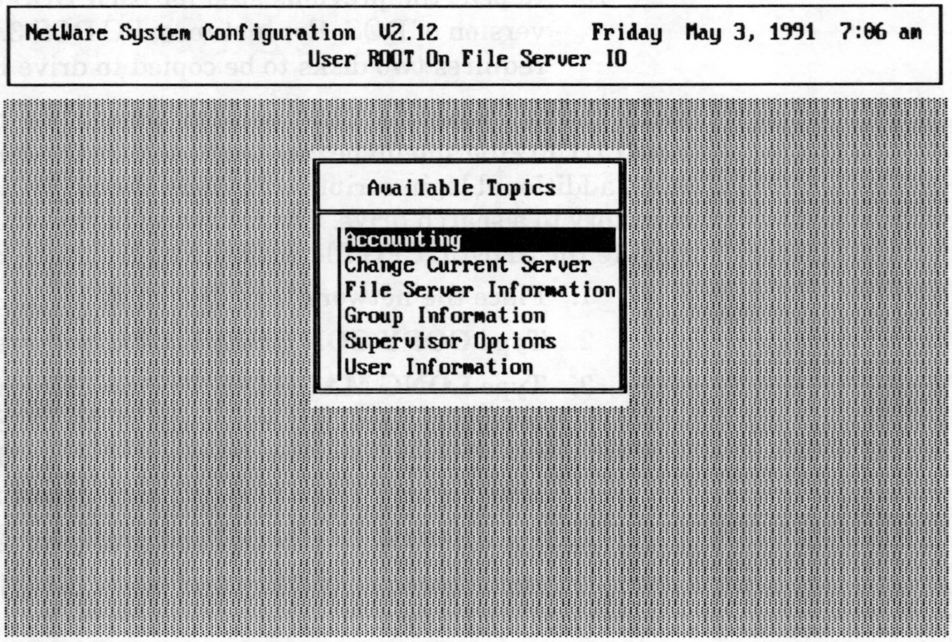

Fig. 11-6. SYSCON's main menu

10. Move the cursor to the User Information option and press the [Enter←] key.
11. Type the name of the account you are now using. The cursor should move to highlight the name. Press the [Enter←] key when the proper name is highlighted.
12. Type **L** to highlight Login Script and press the [Enter←] key.
13. Within the Login Script editor, move the cursor to the right-most position in the last line and press the [Enter←] key.
14. Type the following line exactly as it appears below, then press the [Enter←] key.

MAP S4:=SYS:PUBLIC\%MACHINE\%OS\%OS_VERSION

15. Type the following line exactly as it appears below, then press the Enter key.

    COMSPEC=S4:COMMAND.COM

16. Press the Esc key.
17. Press the Y key, then press the Enter key.
18. Press the Esc key three times until the Exit SYSCON menu appears.
19. Press the Y key then press the Enter key.
20. Type **LOGOUT** and press the Enter key.
21. Type **LOGIN** followed by the name of your account, and press the Enter key.
22. Type **SECOND**, the password used for this account, and press the Enter key.
23. The new login script should give you access to the DOS directory appropriate to the version of DOS you are now using. To test the availability of the DOS programs, type **CHKDSK A:** and press the Enter key. If the drive mapping has been made correctly, the CHKDSK program will report the status of the disk in drive A.

The user now has a search path to the NetWare utility programs as well as DOS programs such as CHKDSK and FORMAT. If appropriate directories are created for all of the DOS versions that might be used on the workstations, the user can login at any workstation and still have a search path to the DOS files needed by that workstation. In other words, the search path to the DOS directory is dependent on the DOS version used at a particular workstation.

Remote Reset

With the remote reset feature, also called remote boot or remote IPL, a workstation can boot from a file on the server rather than from a diskette. This is extraordinarily beneficial in environments where there are many computers without a hard disk to boot from. The supervisor can avoid the tedium of maintaining a boot disk for each workstation which can become lost, damaged, or infected with a computer virus. Remote reset also makes possible a diskless workstation for use in environments where strict data security is required.

Remote reset is only possible when using network interface cards that are specifically designed for it. In addition, most network cards that can employ remote reset require a switch to be physically set on the card. Some network cards require the switch to be set using a program on a setup disk provided with the computer or the card. The following exercises assume the proper hardware settings have been made for remote boot. Remote reset will only work on a computer that has no other physical disk to boot from. Therefore, if the workstation being used to test remote boot has a hard disk, it must be configured as nonbootable.

Installing remote reset will require some cooperation between students using the server. Since there is only one BOOTCONF.SYS file and one AUTOEXEC.BAT file on the server, these files may need to be created only once or updated by an individual for all others. The BOOTCONF.SYS file will contain the network addresses of all the workstations using remote boot. Follow the instructions below to determine the address of the workstation you are currently using.

1. Type **LOGIN** and your user name, then press the Enter← key. The password prompt should appear.
2. Type **SECOND** and press the Enter← key.
3. Type **FCONSOLE** and press the Enter← key. The FCONSOLE main menu should appear, similar to the one in Fig. 11-7.

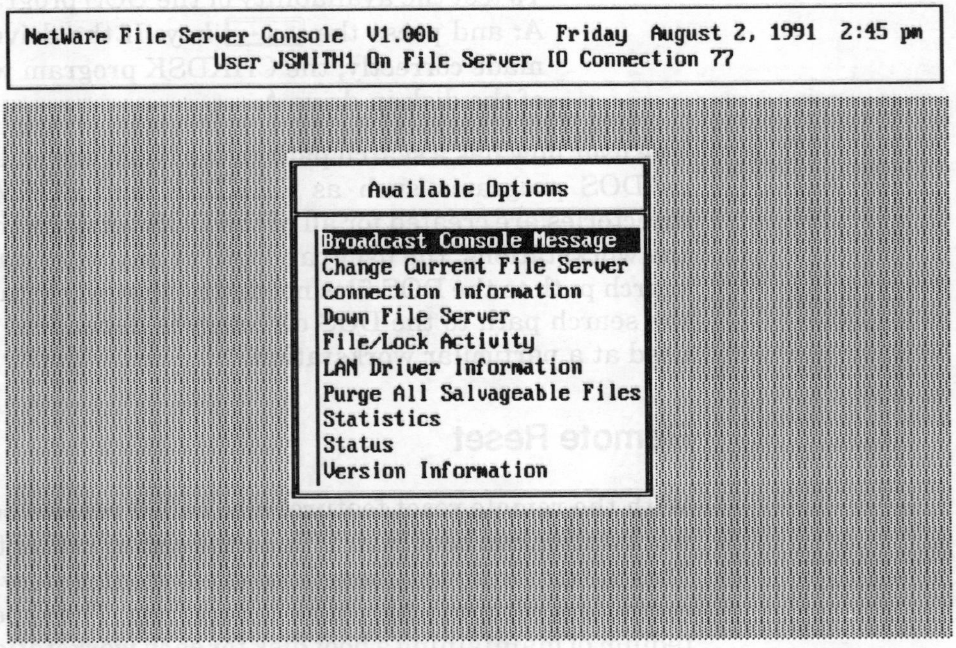

Fig. 11-7. FCONSOLE's main menu

4. Move the highlighted bar to the Connection Information option and press the Enter← key.
5. Type the name of your user account. The highlighted bar will move to your name. Press the Enter← key.
6. Use the ARROW keys to highlight the Other Information option and press the Enter← key.

7. The box displayed shows when and where this user logged in. Write down the number labeled Network Address. Remember to include the ":". The first eight digits of this number indicate the network being used. This is the same network number entered when NetWare was installed. The last twelve digits identify the actual network card in the workstation being used. Later in this chapter, when this number is used, you must be using the same workstation.
8. Press the [esc] key four times until the Exit FCONSOLE menu appears.
9. Press [Y], then the [Enter] key.
10. Type **LOGOUT** and press the [Enter] key to end this session.

For this exercise the last eight digits of the node number will be used as the name for the boot image file. Ordinarily a name would be used that indicates the location or type of computer being used. For instance, the file might be called ROOM222.SYS or COMPAQ#1.SYS. The .SYS extension is required by NetWare. By using the a portion of the node number as the name, the chance of accidental duplications of node numbers in the BOOTCONF.SYS file can be greatly reduced.

The next task is to create an appropriate AUTOEXEC.BAT file to be placed on the boot disk. Often a complementary AUTOEXEC.BAT needs to be placed in the F:\LOGIN directory on the file server. The file server AUTOEXEC.BAT must be usable by all the workstations using remote boot. Remember the necessity of a general purpose AUTOEXEC.BAT on the file server is considered to be a bug by Novell and may be fixed in the version of the network shell you are using. To simplify this exercise, a short AUTOEXEC.BAT file will be used that does not have any commands after the network shell is loaded. No file server AUTOEXEC.BAT will then be needed. Follow the steps below to create an AUTOEXEC.BAT file for the boot disk and to create a boot image file on the file server.

1. If necessary, boot the workstation by placing a network boot disk in drive A and pressing the [Ctrl], [alt], and [delete] keys simultaneously.
2. Enter the date and time as required.
3. Type the following line exactly as shown, pressing the [Enter] key after each line.

   COPY CON AUTOEXEC.BAT
   IPX
4. Type the name of the network shell program you are using and press the [Enter] key. NETX will work in all situations.
5. Hold down the [Ctrl] key and press the [Z] key, then press the [Enter] key.

6. Type **AUTOEXEC.BAT** and press the Enter key. This will test the AUTOEXEC.BAT file and load the network driver programs.
7. Type **F:** and press the Enter key.
8. Type **LOGIN** followed by the name of your account and press the Enter key.
9. To ensure that you are in the proper directory, type **CD\LOGIN** and press the Enter key.
10. Verify that the disk in drive A is the network boot disk with the proper network driver programs, the SHELL.CFG file, and the AUTOEXEC.BAT file.
11. Type **DOSGEN A:** followed by the last eight digits of the node number of the workstation you are now using followed by .SYS, then press the Enter key. For example, if the network address written down earlier was 00D22901:08005A5A0123, the command would be DOSGEN A: 5A5A0123.SYS.

An additional step is required for DOS 5 users. A program called RPLFIX.COM must be obtained from Novell's Compuserve forum, Netwire, or from a Novell authorized reseller.

With the RPLFIX program on a disk in drive A:, type A:RPLFIX followed by the name of your boot image file, then press the Enter key. For instance, if your boot image file name is 5A5A0123.SYS, the command would be A:RPLFIX 5A5A0123.SYS.

12. A BOOTCONF.SYS file must be created to tell NetWare which boot image file is to be sent to which workstation. This file could be completely entered by an individual using the proper format to indicate the names of the boot image files. A complete BOOTCONF.SYS file might look something like the following.

    List 0X00D22901,08005A6A3491=5A6A3491.SYS
    List 0X00D22901,08007A6A44F1=7A6A44F1.SYS
    List 0X00D22901,08005A6A348B=5A6A348B.SYS
    List 0X00D22901,08005A6B14FC=5A6B14FC.SYS
    List 0X00D22901,08005A6A3A11=5A6A3A11.SYS
    List 0X00D22901,08005A6A24F7=5A6A24F7.SYS
    List 0X00D22901,08005B6AF4E1=5B6AF4E1.SYS
    List 0X00D22901,08005A6A34F2=5A6A34F2.SYS

The first two characters of each line, 0X, are required to indicate that the other characters represent a hexadecimal number. The next eight characters are the network number of the network being used. The characters between the "," and the "=" are the individual workstation node numbers and finally, the characters following the "=" are the names of the boot image files.

An alternate method of creating the BOOTCONF.SYS file would be to have each student append the line required for his or her workstation by using a command in the following format.

ECHO 0X00D22901,08005A6A3491=5A6A3491.SYS >> BOOTCONF.SYS

This command must be entered while still logged in under your supervisor-equivalent account and with F:\LOGIN as the current directory. The network address, node address, and boot image file name in the command above would be replaced with the numbers for your workstation.

Testing Remote Reset

With the BOOTCONF.SYS file created, the only step left is to test the remote reset.

1. Type **LOGOUT** and press the Enter← key.
2. Remove any disk that may be in disk drive A.
3. Boot the computer by pressing the Ctrl, alt, and delete keys simultaneously.
4. The workstation should boot as if it were using the boot disk created earlier without prompting for the date and time.
5. To completely test the remote boot feature, type **F:** and press the Enter← key.
6. Type **LOGIN** followed by your account name and press the Enter← key.
7. If the login was successful, type **LOGOUT** and press the Enter← key.

Summary

The workstations on a network may have different types and amounts of memory. To take full advantage of the memory available, these differences must be taken into account when loading the network driver programs. NET# or NETX can be used on any computer, but by using EMSNET# or XMSNET# the memory available for application programs can be significantly increased. DOS version 5 can also be used to increase available memory by loading the network driver programs into high memory.

Workstations may also use different versions of DOS. Each of the different versions must be loaded onto the file server with appropriate login script commands to make the DOS files available to the user.

Some network cards can take advantage of a NetWare feature called remote reset, which allows the workstation to boot from the file server rather than a floppy or hard disk. In this process, a fully customized boot disk is copied to a file on the server using a program called DOSGEN. If more than one boot image file is needed, a file called BOOTCONF.SYS is used to correlate the workstation with the boot image file.

Questions

1. Can the XMSNETX program be used to conserve memory on a computer with 640K of RAM?
2. Under what situations can the network shell program NETX.COM be used?
3. What are the two ways a particular file server can be specified in a multi-file-server environment?
4. What circumstances would require a user to load the NET-BIOS and INT2F programs?
5. Why is it important that the login script variables MACHINE, OS, and OS_VERSION have the proper values for a given workstation?
6. The remote reset process can abandon the AUTOEXEC.BAT file in the boot image file and use another. Where is this other copy of AUTOEXEC.BAT located?
7. What is the name of the program used to create a boot image file?
8. What information does the BOOTCONF.SYS file contain?

Projects

Objective

The following projects provide additional practice creating automated processes in order for users to access the network and to remotely boot a file. They enhance earlier hands-on exercises on these topics.

Project 1. Automating User Logins

1. Create a new user with the SYSCON utility. Use the appropriate login script variables to display the workstation type, operating system, and operating system version each time the user logs in. Do not give the user a password. Use the [shift] [print screen] keys to record the results.
2. Change the login script so that the SET command is executed during the login script. The SET command is an internal DOS command, not a program name. To execute an internal DOS command, use the following syntax:

   COMMAND /C command name

The COMMAND is the DOS command interpreter COMMAND.COM. The /C tells COMMAND.COM to execute the internal DOS command that follows. Use [shift][print screen] to record the results.

3. Using the DOSGEN program, create a boot image file that logs in the user created above. Use [shift][print screen] to record the results.

Project 2. Creating a Remote Boot File

1. Create a remote boot file for your workstation. Use only one command in the AUTOEXEC.BAT file. That command should be the name of another batch file with a unique name that exists both on the boot disk and in the F:\LOGIN directory.
2. Modify the remote boot file above to login to a user account.
3. Create a login script that assigns the drive letter M: to one of three different subdirectories, MORNING, AFTERNOON, and EVENING, depending on the time of day.
4. Modify the login script of the account used above to start another program such as a word processor or the FILER utility.

12

Network Printing

Objectives

1. Understand the concepts of network printing.
2. Learn how network printers can be attached to the network.
3. Understand the use of printing structures to direct data and control printers.
4. Learn how to install a print server and print queue.
5. Learn how to send data to a network printer.

Key Terms

Bridges
CAPTURE
PCONSOLE
Queue
Server Printing
Boot Disk
Print Server
PRINTCON
Remote Printing

Introduction

Often an important function of a network is printer sharing. Printing across a network involves loading special software on the workstation that remains resident along with the other network drivers. The software intercepts output that a normal application such as a word processor sends to the workstation's printer port. That data is then sent across the network to a printer attached to another computer. With a network, many users can send output to the same printer. Or users may wish to select among different types of printers available on the network. NetWare has supported network printing since its earliest versions, but lacked many important features. Several third-party products offered capabilities that made network printing a much more valuable resource. With later versions of NetWare, however, some of these features have been introduced as separate utilities.

The printers can be attached to the network in four ways. They can be connected to the file server, to a NetWare bridge, to a dedicated print server, or to a remote print server.

To accommodate the many users and printers that might be on a network, Novell has created a number of structures that are used to control what gets printed and where it gets printed. These structures are print forms, print devices, print queues, and print job configurations.

Printing in a Novell Network

File Server Printing

NetWare networks are very centralized in that almost all activity is handled through the file server. Therefore, the file server is a natural place to begin network printing. In the installation of NetWare on the file server, the network installation program NETGEN asks if printers will be attached. Answering Yes allows NETGEN to configure NetWare to use the printer ports on the file server. NETGEN also creates a print queue for each printer port. A print queue allows several users to submit data to the network printer at once. The data is stored until a printer is free. On a server with one printer port, NETGEN creates a print queue called PRINTQ_0 for a printer defined as PRINTER0. On a server with two printer ports, there would be an additional queue called PRINTQ_1 for PRINTER1 and so on. To use the same menu utilities that are used to control printers at other locations, a print server Value-Added Process, or VAP, must be installed on the file server. The VAP is essentially another program that runs on the server in addition to NetWare. Even without the VAP, there are several commands that can be entered at the file server keyboard that control network printing on printers attached to the file server.

NetWare Bridge Printing

A Novell program called BRIDGE can be loaded onto a computer to allow networks of different types to be connected. Up to four different types of network cards can be placed in the bridge. The BRIDGE program then redirects information from one network to the other when necessary. This bridge server can also run the print server VAP.

Print Server Printing

It is often inconvenient for a variety of reasons to use a file server for printing. Perhaps most importantly, the users who may need access to the printer may not be users who should have access to the file server. In other words, it may be dangerous to have the file server where an unskilled individual might try to reboot it in an attempt to restart the printer or run some other software. Physical proximity to the server can also create a noise problem if the network supervisor, the file server, and a loud printer are all located in the same room. Another reason to avoid attaching the printers to the file server is simply that printers usually require a great deal of maintenance while file servers do not. A file server may run for months without being turned off or even touched. Frequent installation and removal of printers or printer ports could disrupt the file server. A dedicated print server can be used to avoid these concerns by placing the printers, paper, cables, and noise in a separate location.

The print server can be any computer on the network with at least 360K of memory and up to sixteen printer ports. With remote reset it does not even need any disk drives. The computer runs a program called PSERVER that sends the output to the printers attached to it. Since a print server requires only minimal hardware, it is a good investment to make if there are to be several network printers.

Remote Printing

A print server can direct data to sixteen different printers but those printers do not need to be physically attached to it. With the proper software loaded on a workstation, the workstation's printer becomes a network printer. Authorized users anywhere on the network can send data to be printed on the workstation's local printer without disturbing the normal operation of the workstation. The remote printer software is a memory resident program that uses approximately 9K of memory and allows other applications to run. It operates similar to the way the DOS PRINT command works, operating "in the background" while the workstation's user runs another application in foreground, such as a word processor. Using remote printing, a printer that is usually accessed by a single workstation can be set up to be accessible by anyone on the network. The greatest disadvantage to this system is its vulnerability. If the user reboots or causes an operating system crash, the remote printing software will no longer be available and will have to be reloaded to continue printing.

Wherever the printer is located, the same tools can be used to access and control it. These tools or printing structures can be used to control all aspects of printing, such as which printer is to used, what print style is to be used, and who will have access to the printer.

Print Forms

Print forms are the simplest of the printing structures. They represent the type of paper the printer will use. Fig. 12-1 shows a Forms Definition Form in the Printer Definition Utility program PRINTDEF. As seen here, the only important information to the printer is the length and width of the paper. The name of the form might represent much more to the printer operator. For instance, one form might be called CHECK and another BILL. While they may be the same size, they are definitely different.

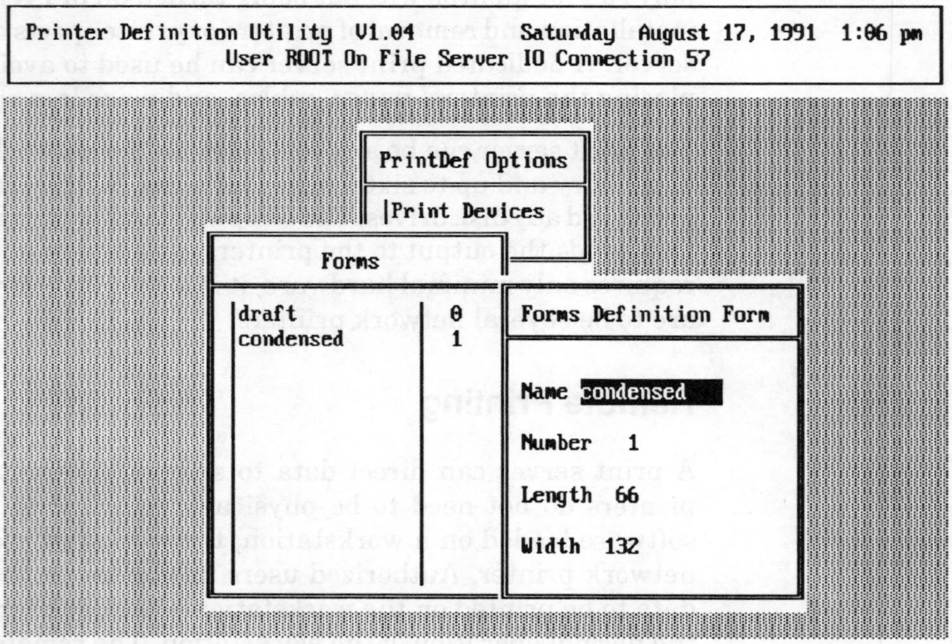

Fig. 12-1. The Forms Definition Form dialog box

Print Devices

Since each type and brand of printer may have a different set of control codes, NetWare uses the print device structure to define each printer. Fig. 12-2 shows the Print Device Options of the PRINTDEF program. The three options Edit Print Devices, Import Print Device, and Export Print Device refer to the use of printer definition files. When Import Print Device is chosen, the PRINTDEF program prompts the user for a directory. With the proper directory chosen, the program displays a list of printer definition files. Novell has provided files for most popular printers. The arrow in the lower left corner of the Available .PDFs box indicates that more files are available than are shown. The files contain the codes that each printer uses for each of its functions. For instance, the CIT120D.PDF file contains the codes a Citizen 120D printer uses for bold, italics, and underline printing. Selecting one of these files causes it to be stored in a separate file, where the information can be used by the other printing structures.

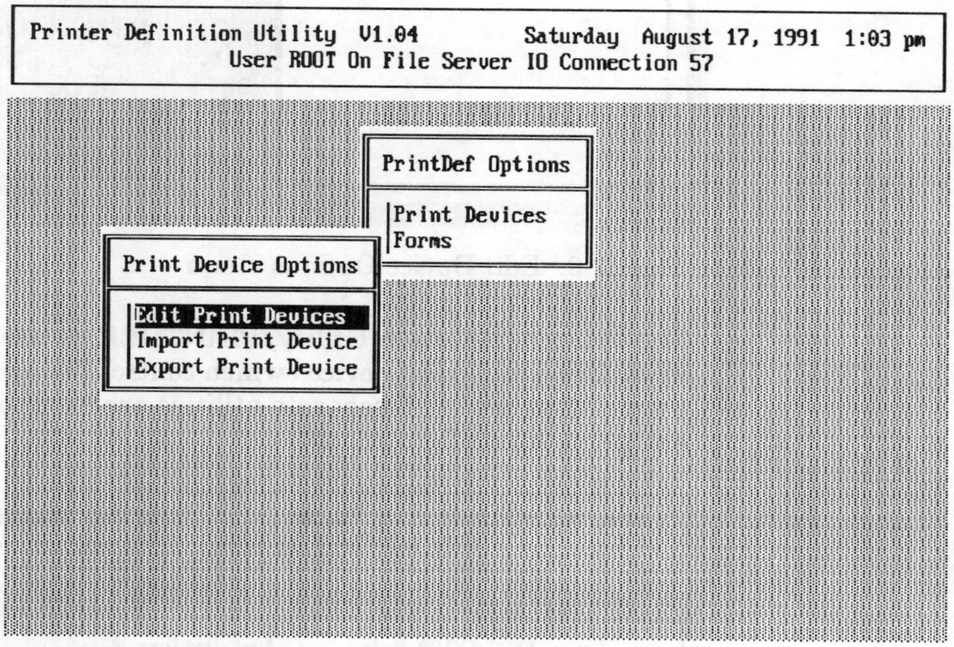

Fig. 12-2. Print Device Options menu

The print devices can also be edited to provide more functions or to create completely new printer device files. After the Edit Print Devices option is selected, a box containing the Defined Print Devices shows the printers that have already been loaded. Fig. 12-3 shows the Edit Device Options menu that appears when one of the devices is selected. Both of the options listed represent control codes that might be sent to the printer. Device Modes refers to a set of codes that might be sent as a setup before printing, while Device Functions represents the specific codes sent for a single printer command. After selecting Letter Quality, the functions that make up the Letter Quality mode are displayed. In this case it is only one, also called letter quality. Fig. 12-4 shows the control codes for the function letter quality. This box is intended only to display the functions. To edit them, the Edit Print Functions option must be selected from the Edit Device Options menu.

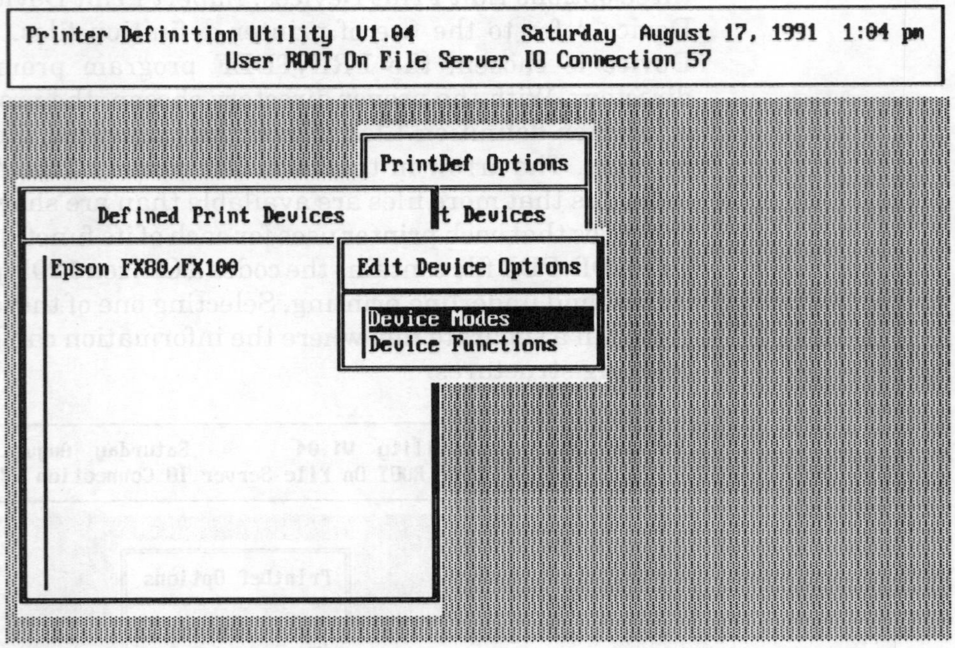

Fig. 12-3. Edit Device Options menu

The Printer Definition Utility, PRINTDEF, is used to create and edit print forms and print devices which control the printer. To control how the printers are used, separate utilities are used to create print queues and print job configurations.

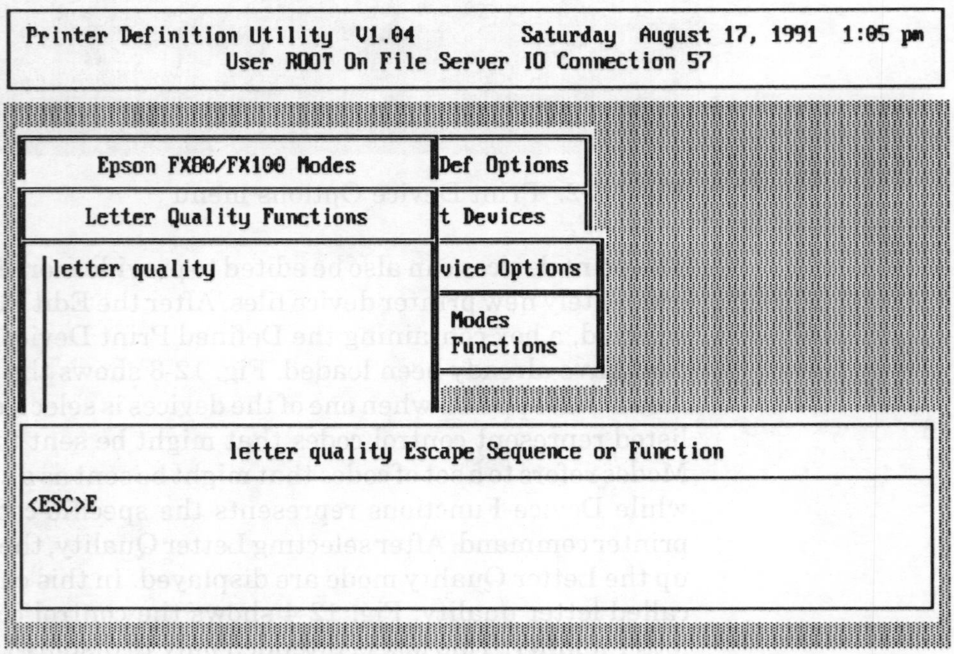

Fig. 12-4. Dialog box for the control codes for the letter quality function

Print Queues

Obviously, if everyone on the network sent data to a network printer at once, problems would arise. A system must be created to allow the data from each user to be stored and printed when the printer becomes available. Print queues provide this function and more. The NetWare Print Console utility, PCONSOLE, is used to create and maintain print queues and print servers. Fig. 12-5 shows PCONSOLE's main menu. The first option simply allows the user to select another file server. The second option displays a list of existing print queues. When one is selected, the Print Queue Information menu appears. These options control the who, what, where, and when of the queue. The following is a description of each of the selections.

1. Current Print Job Entries. This option displays a list of the print jobs waiting to print on the selected print queue. In this case a print job is data that a user has sent to be printed. A print job is any set of output sent to the printer. This term is easily confused with a print job configuration, which is a certain set of network printing options.

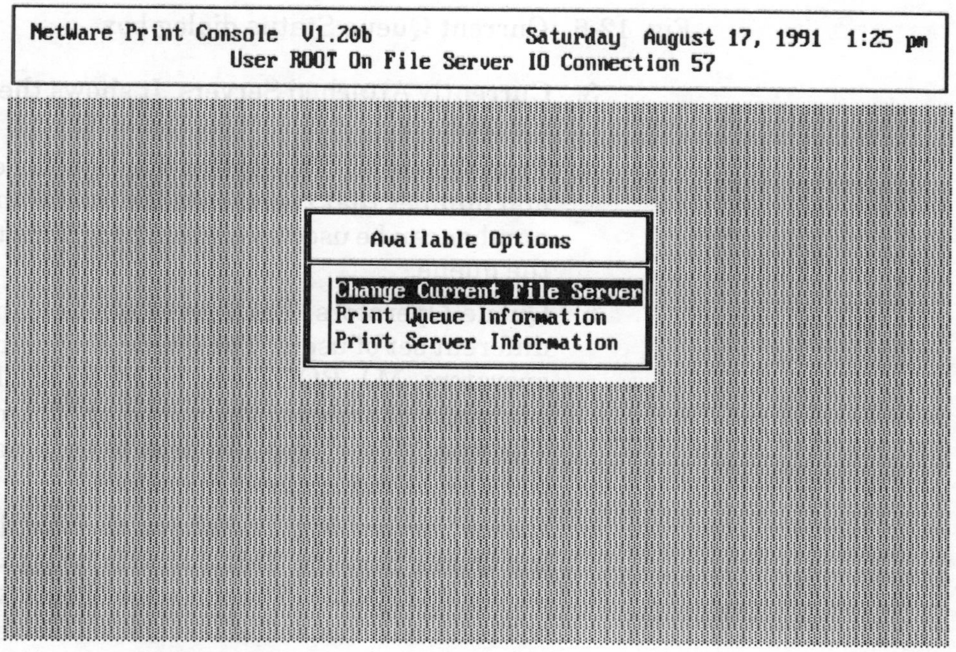

Fig. 12-5. PCONSOLE's main menu

2. Current Queue Status. Shown in Fig. 12-6, the Current Queue Status box displays how many jobs are waiting to print and how many print servers are attached to the queue. The Operator Flags section allows the operator to turn certain features of the queue on and off. Most importantly, it allows the operator to turn off access to the queue altogether.

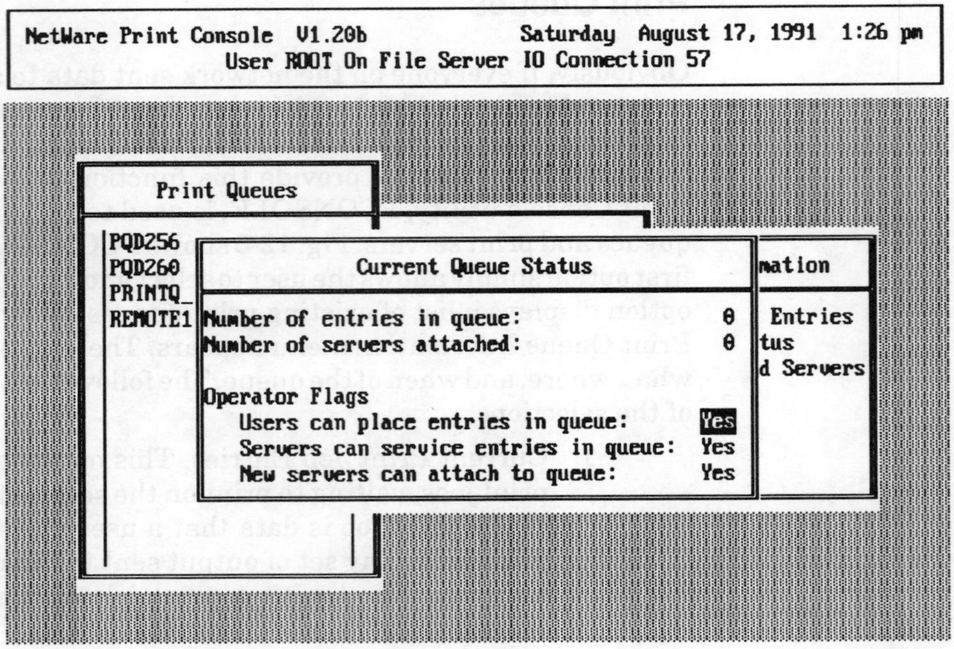

Fig. 12-6. Current Queue Status dialog box

3. Currently Attached Servers. It shows the servers attached to a queue.
4. Print Queue ID. This option displays the eight digit hexadecimal number that represents the queue on the file server. The number can be used by custom programs to access and control the queue.
5. Queue Operators. Each print queue can be controlled by a different set of users. The queue shown in Fig. 12-7 has three operators, MJ, ROOT and SUPERVISOR. Only these users can make changes to the queue or control jobs in the queue. The word "User" appears next to each name because groups can also be made queue operators.
6. Queue Servers. Fig. 12-8 shows the box displayed after selecting Queue Servers. This queue is being serviced by the print server PSERV256. The message "Print Server" appears next to the name because file servers can also service print queues.
7. Que Users. Each queue can be restricted to certain users or groups of users. This box shows the users and groups who have access to a queue.

The last item on PCONSOLE's main menu is Print Server Information. This item is, of course, quite important in network printing. However, to complete the topic of printing structures, another program, the Configure Print Jobs utility PRINTCON, must be considered.

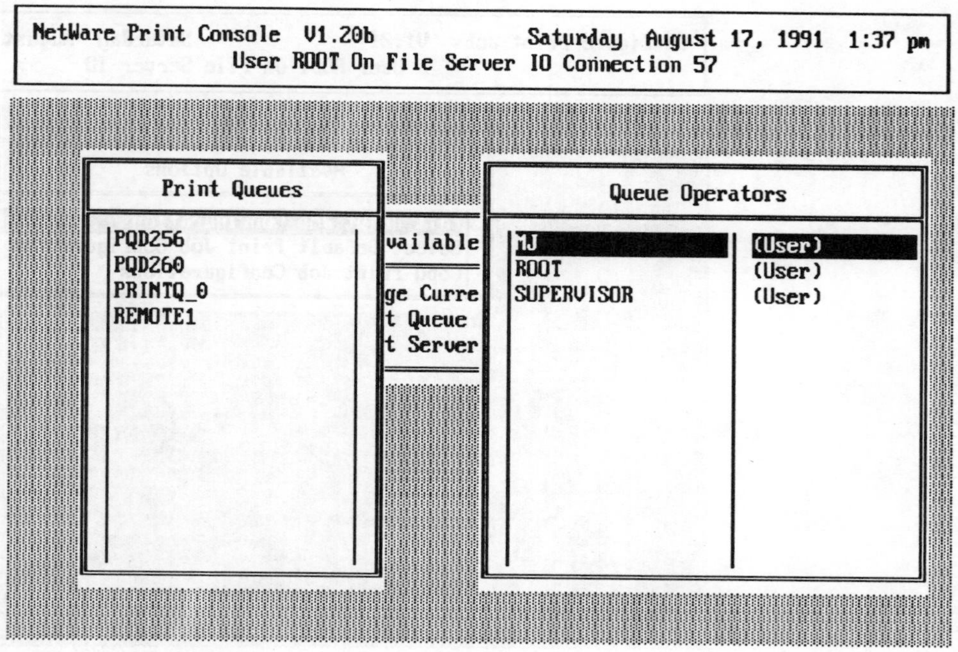

Fig. 12-7. A queue with three operators

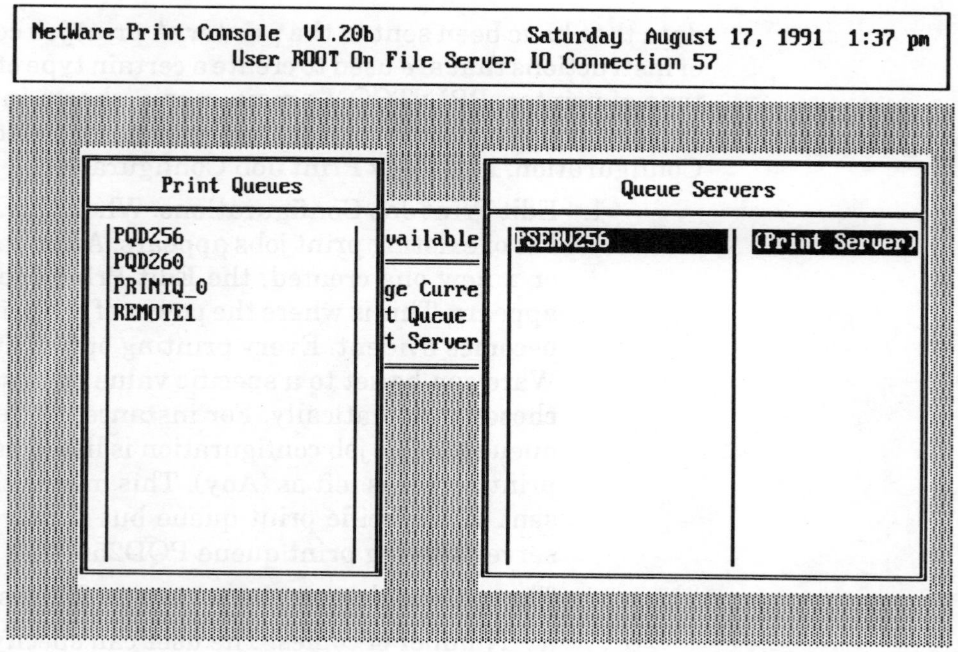

Fig. 12-8. Dialog box displaying a queue and its print server

Print Job Configurations

PRINTCON allows users to create print job configurations. Notice that this terminology refers to a printing structure, not to individual sets of

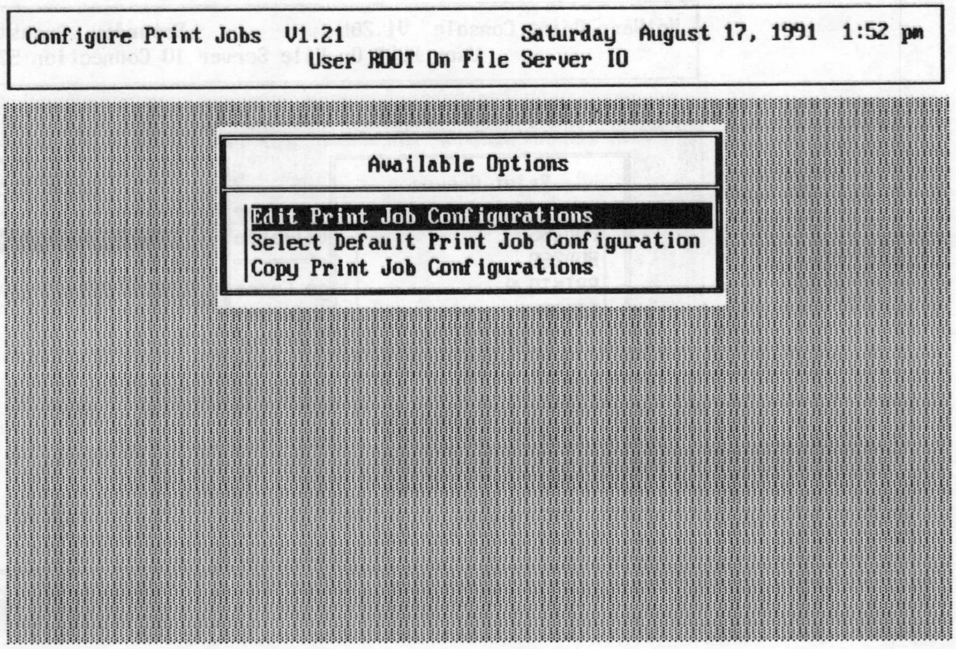

Fig. 12-9. PRINTCON's main menu

data that have been sent to the printer. A print job configuration is a set of instructions that are used to create a certain type of output on a certain type of printer. PRINTCON's main menu, shown in Fig. 12-9, has only three selections; Edit Print Job Configurations, Select Default Print Job Configuration, and Copy Print Job Configurations.

1. Edit Print Job Configurations. When this option is selected, a list of existing print jobs appears. After one has been selected or a new one created, the Edit Print Job Configuration box appears. This is where the power of the print job configuration becomes evident. Every printing option available under NetWare can be set to a specific value or in some cases left to be chosen automatically. For instance, in the left column, print queue for this job configuration is listed as PQD256 while the print server is left as (Any). This means that the data will be sent to a specific print queue but it may print on any print server serving print queue PQD256.

   The options that can be set are as follows:

   a. Number of copies. The user can specify how many times a certain set of data will be printed.
   b. File contents. This option helps NetWare determine how to handle the data.

c. Tab size. Often in a text document, a tab character is used to represent a certain number of spaces. The number of spaces is then left to the printer to determine. This option tells NetWare to convert those tab characters into the specified number of spaces.

d. Suppress form feed. Another character often present in text files is the form feed character. It tells the printer to advance to the next page. Since NetWare can handle this function, too many form feeds may be sent to the printer. Suppressing the form feed character allows NetWare to fully control the page advance.

e. Notify when done. When this option is set to "Yes" a message is sent to the user after the data sent has been printed.

f. Local printer. Simply used to specify how many printers the workstation has connected directly.

g. Auto endcap. Output sent to a network printer is stored in the print queue first. The data is not printed until an ENDCAP message is sent. With the Auto endcap feature set to "Yes", output from a certain application is sent to the printer when that application finishes executing. In other words, a word processor such as Word Star can send data to the queue, but that data will not be sent to the printer until the user exits Word Star. With Auto endcap set to "No", the data would not be printed until the user issues an ENDCAP command.

h. File server. Displays the file server being used.

i. Print queue. Shows which queue the data will be sent to.

j. Print server. Shows which print server the data will be sent to.

k. Device. Shows which device definition will be used.

l. Mode. Shows which mode the device will be in. The mode is dependent on the device used.

m. Form name. Shows which form will be used.

n. Print banner. A banner printed in extra large characters can be printed at the top of the output for identification. Normally when a banner is included, the name of the user and the file name are used in the banner. Here, the name of the user and the file name can be given different values.

o. Enable timeout/timeout count. Used to set the number of seconds to wait after an application has finished sending output to the printer before sending that data on to the print server.

2. Select Default Print Job Configuration. PRINTCON's second main menu option allows the user to specify a certain print job configuration to be always used unless another is specified.
3. Copy Print Job Configuration. Print job configurations allow individuals to customize how their output will be printed by the network. Unfortunately, the configuration must be set up for each user and cannot be extended to a group as with most NetWare functions. However, the Copy Print Job Configurations option allows print job configurations to be copied to other users one user at a time.

NetWare offers print forms, print devices, print queues, and print job configurations to allow the process of printing on the network to be completely customized. These features are useless, of course, without printers attached to the network and a means for sending data to them.

Attaching the Printer

The printers can be attached to the network in essentially four different ways: on a print server, on a file server, to a NetWork bridge, and on a workstation as a remote printer. By far the most versatile method for attaching printers to the network is to install a print server. The print server is simply a computer running a program called PSERVER.EXE. This program directs the data that has been queued on the file server to the printers that are physically attached to it. It may also direct data to printers attached to workstations. The PCONSOLE program is used again to configure print servers. Fig. 12-10 shows the print servers already available on the file server. Selecting one of them displays the Print Server Information menu, as shown in Fig. 12-11. Each of its options is explained below.

1. Change Password. A password can be set on the print server to prevent unauthorized changes.
2. Full Name. The Full Name option can be used to provide a more descriptive name for the print server.
3. Print Server Configuration. This option displays another menu as shown in Fig. 12-12. Its four options are as follows:
   a. File Servers Serviced. Displays the file servers this print server will accept print jobs from. The current file server does not need to be listed.
   b. Notify List for Printer. Printers require frequent maintenance. A print server can detect when a printer goes off-line and notify a user. The Notify List for Printer option is used to set which users will be notified about problems with each printer.

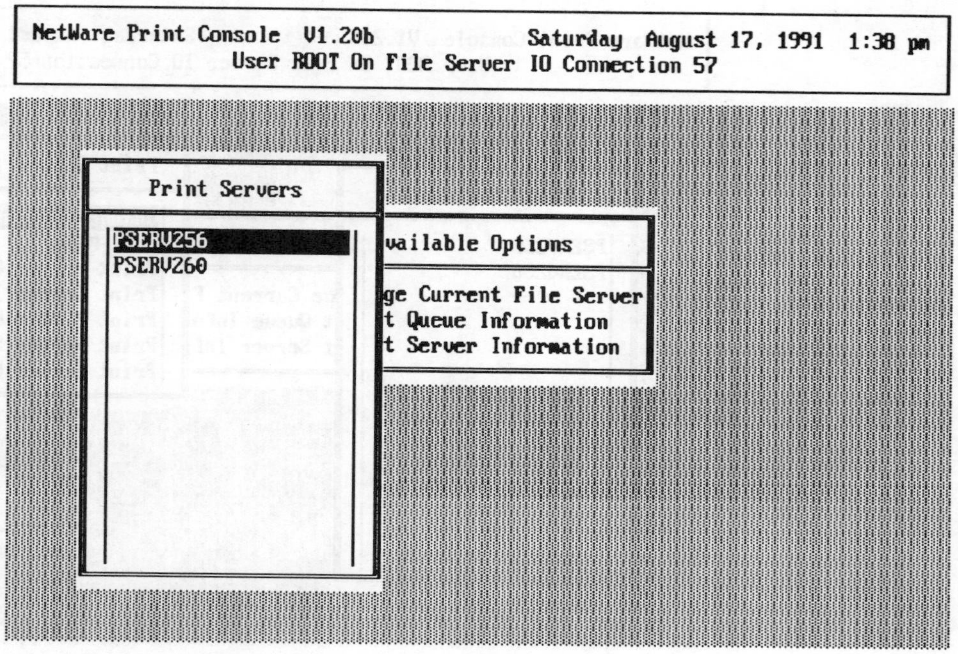

Fig. 12-10. Print servers available to users

c. Printer Configuration. When selected, this option displays a list of the sixteen printers that can be connected to a single print server. By selecting any of these, a Printer Configuration box appears. These options tell the print server how the printer is physically attached.

d. Queues Serviced by printer. When this option is selected, a list of defined printers appears. Selecting a printer shows which print queues send data to that printer.

4. Print Server ID. This option simply displays the NetWare Object Identification number.
5. Print Server Operators. This option displays a list of users or groups authorized to change the status of the print server selected. Users can be added to or deleted from this option.
6. Print Server Status/Control. Displays status and allows some control over the print server.
7. Print Server Users. Displays a list of users and groups allowed to send data to the selected print server. Users can be added to or deleted from this option.

The PRINTDEF, PCONSOLE, and PRINTCON utilities are used to manipulate how data is to be sent to the available network printers. Sending the data to be printed can be accomplished in four ways: using the PCONSOLE utility, using a command line utility called NPRINT, using a command line utility called CAPTURE, or by using an application program designed to use network printers.

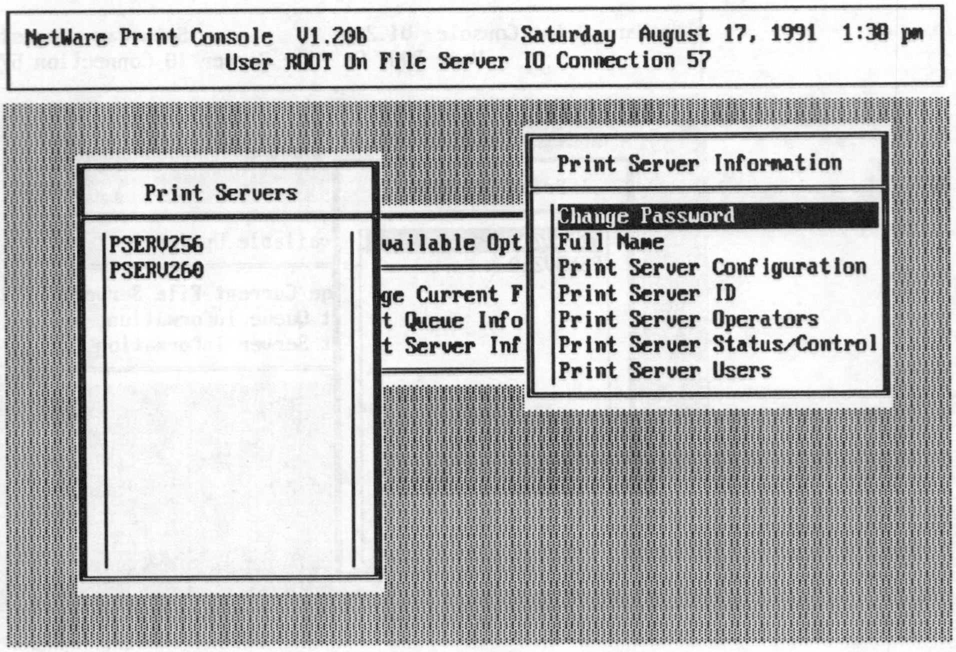

Fig. 12-11. The Print Server Information menu

Printing with PCONSOLE

The PCONSOLE program provides much of the control needed for network printing, including manipulating the jobs waiting to be printed. With it, print jobs can be added or deleted directly from the print queue.

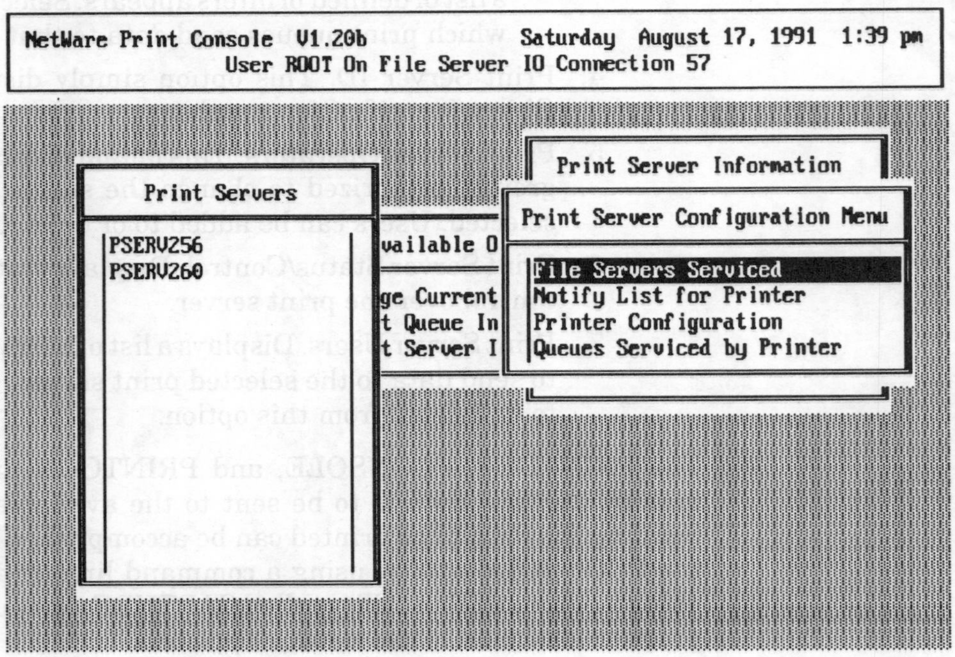

Fig. 12-12. Print Server Configuration menu

Selecting Current Print Job Entries in the Print Queue Information menu of PCONSOLE displays the print jobs printing or waiting to be printed. Pressing the INSERT key allows the user to select a file to be printed. This method of sending data to be printed assumes that a file has been created that contains any special characters that may be needed for underlining, boldface fonts, or other special effects. Such a file is known as a print file. Many application programs allow their output to be sent to a print file.

Printing with NPRINT

The NPRINT utility also requires a print file to already exist. A command of NPRINT THISFILE would send the file called THISFILE to the default print queue. The NPRINT program has several command line options that allow the print forms, print queues, and print job configurations to be specified.

Printing with CAPTURE

Almost any application can be used with network printers using the CAPTURE program. It is a memory resident program that intercepts data that the workstation sends to its printer ports, and redirects that data to a print queue. The CAPTURE program can be used in three different ways: in conjunction with the ENDCAP program, with the AUTO ENDCAP feature, or with the TIMEOUT feature.

The ENDCAP program is used to turn off redirection of the printer data. It essentially unloads the CAPTURE program from memory and places the data in the print queue. Notice that the data is only stored, not put in the queue, until the ENDCAP program is run. This way a user may send data to the network printer in many separate pieces. When the ENDCAP command is given, all the data is placed in the queue.

With the AUTO ENDCAP feature of the CAPTURE program enabled, the CAPTURE program automatically unloads itself after an application has been run. The data is then sent on to the print queue. For instance, if a user wants to send data to a network printer using a word processor, he or she would first run the CAPTURE program, then start the word processing program. Any printing that is done from the word processing program is stored until the user exits the word processing program. It is only then that the data is placed in the print queue.

Using the TIMEOUT feature allows the user's data to be sent to the print queue while the user is still in the application program. A timeout period is given in seconds that tells the CAPTURE program when to send the data that it has captured on to the print queue. The CAPTURE program waits the time specified after the last output has been captured before placing the data in the print queue.

Suppose a spreadsheet program is being used with the TIMEOUT feature set to 15 seconds. When the user requests a chart to be printed, the output is stored, and a timer starts counting after the last byte is captured. If the user prints another chart less than 15 seconds later, the data will continue to be stored. The data will be sent to the print queue only when a time longer than 15 seconds passes between print requests.

Making the timeout period too short may break up data that should be printed together. For instance, it may take longer than 15 seconds for the second chart in a single report to be calculated. Someone else's data could be placed in the queue between the first and second charts.

Making the period too long may cause data that the user intended to be printed separately to be printed together instead. If the user wanted the charts to be printed separately, he or she would have to watch the clock until the 15 seconds had passed before printing the second chart. This is not usually a problem since most applications would advance to the next page before printing the second time. A period longer than a few seconds may also be a source of frustration for the user. Even when only one person is sending data to be printed, he or she must wait for the data to be captured, wait the timeout period, then wait for the print server to start processing the data in the queue. These delays can add up to a long enough time that the user may wonder if there is a problem with the printer.

The last and easiest way to send data to a network printer is to use an application program that is designed to send its output to a print queue on a NetWare network.

Hands-on NetWare

In order to complete the following exercises, the file server and at least two workstations should be ready to use.

1. The file server should be on.
2. The boot disk created earlier should be available.
3. Backup copies of the NetWare Print Server diskettes should be available.
4. The accounts created earlier should be available.

Installing the Print Server Software

The Print Server software is provided as a separate utility with its own disks and manuals. Novell has included batch files that copy the software to the appropriate directories on the file server. The program is then accessed by a networked computer that will operate as the print server. The following instructions need to be executed only once to prepare the file server with the Print Server software.

1. Boot the workstation with the appropriate network boot disk by placing the disk in drive A and simultaneously pressing the Ctrl, alt, and delete keys. Enter the date and time if prompted.
2. The network driver programs should have been loaded by the AUTOEXEC.BAT file on the diskette. If they were not, type **IPX** and press the Enter← key. Then type **NETX** and press the Enter← key. NETX can be replaced with the appropriate network shell program for your memory configuration and DOS version.
3. Type **F:** and press the Enter← key.
4. Type **LOGIN** followed by your supervisor-equivalent login name and press the Enter← key.
5. Type in the password for this account and press the Enter← key.
6. Type **CD\PUBLIC** and press the Enter← key.
7. Insert your backup copy of the NetWare Print Server diskette in disk drive A.
8. Type **A:** and press the Enter← key.
9. Type **PS-COPY ALL** and press the Enter← key. Unlike most commands, the ALL must be in either all upper case or all lower case letters. The PS-COPY batch file will copy the print server software as well as new versions of the printing menu utilities to the PUBLIC directory of the file server.
10. For exercises using remote printing, type **PS-COPY RPRINTER F:** and press the Enter← key. This command must also be entered in either all upper case or all lower case letters.
11. To end this session type **LOGOUT** and press the Enter← key.

The operations above only copy the necessary software to the file server. Configuring the software for use as a print server involves considerably more effort. Each student will be able to use the following steps to create and run the print server software. However, to thoroughly test the configuration, the workstation must have a printer attached and another workstation must be available to send data to be printed. If there are limited workstations with printers, each student can configure his or her print server from another workstation, then move to one with a printer to actually run it. If every student workstation has a printer attached then finding one workstation to act as a server and another to send data should not be difficult.

Preparing the Boot Disk

A new line must be added to the SHELL.CFG file on the boot disk in order for the print server to operate properly. The print server software will not be loaded for several steps to come, but the change will not affect normal

normal operation of the workstation. The following instructions prepare the network boot disk for use by a print server.

1. Boot the workstation with the appropriate network boot disk by placing the disk in drive A and simultaneously pressing the Ctrl, alt, and delete keys.
2. Enter the date and time if prompted.
3. Ensure that the network boot disk is in drive A and that it is not write protected.
4. Type **ECHO SPX=50 >> A:SHELL.CFG** and press the Enter key. The >> symbol in the command appends SPX=50 to the end of the existing SHELL.CFG file.

Configuring the Print Server and Print Queue

The long list of steps below create a new print server and a new print queue. These operations can be carried out at any workstation.

1. Boot the workstation with the appropriate network boot disk by placing the disk in drive A and simultaneously pressing the Ctrl, alt, and delete keys. Enter the date and time if prompted.
2. The network driver programs should have been loaded by the AUTOEXEC.BAT file on the diskette. If they were not, type IPX and press the Enter key. Then type NETX and press the Enter key. NETX can be replaced with the appropriate network shell program for your memory configuration and DOS version.
3. Type **F:** and press the Enter key.
4. Type **LOGIN** followed by your supervisor-equivalent login name and press the Enter key.
5. Type the password for this account, and press the Enter key.
6. Type **CD\PUBLIC** and press the Enter key
7. Type **PCONSOLE** and press the Enter key.
8. Select Print Server Information by using the cursor keys to highlight that option and pressing the Enter key.
9. Press the ins key. A box requesting a new print server name should appear, as shown in Fig. 12-13. Here the print server name LASER has been added.
10. Type **PS** followed by your login name. For instance, if your login name is JSMITH, type PSJSMITH and press the Enter key. The PS is simply used to indicate Print Server; it is not a required prefix.
11. With the new name highlighted, press the Enter key.

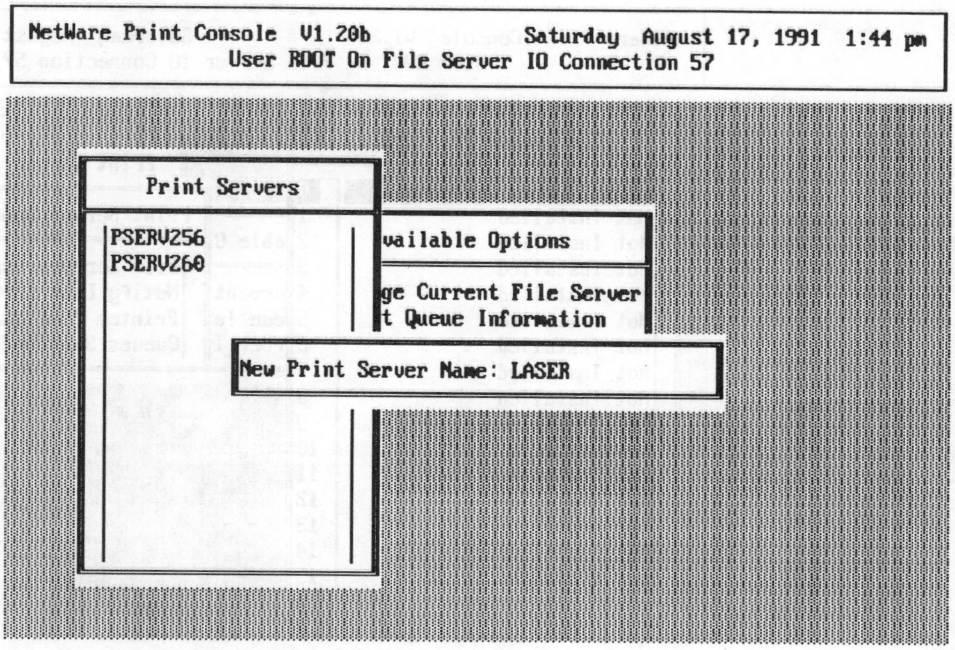

Fig. 12-13. Dialog box to request a new print server

12. Select Print Server Configuration in the Print Server Information box by using the cursor keys to highlight that option and pressing the [Enter] key.
13. Select Printer Configuration in the Print Server Configuration menu by highlighting that option with the cursor keys and pressing the [Enter] key. Your screen should appear similar to Fig. 12-14.
14. With the first Not Installed message highlighted, press the [Enter] key.
15. Move the cursor to the field labeled Type: and highlight the words Defined Elsewhere. Press the [Enter] key.
16. A list of possible printer ports should be displayed as they are in Fig. 12-15. Use the cursor keys to highlight the printer port your printer is attached to. The first one on the list, Parallel, LPT1, is the most common.
17. With the correct printer port highlighted, press the [Enter] key.
18. If the printer port you selected was Serial, additional options will have to be set. Only if you have selected a Serial port, use the cursor keys to move to the fields labeled Baud rate:, Data bits:, Stop bits:, Parity:, and Use X-On/X-Off: and place the correct values in each. The values shown are the most common, but your printer may need different settings.
19. Press the [esc] key to leave the Printer 0 configuration menu.
20. Press the [Y] and [Enter] keys to save the changes.

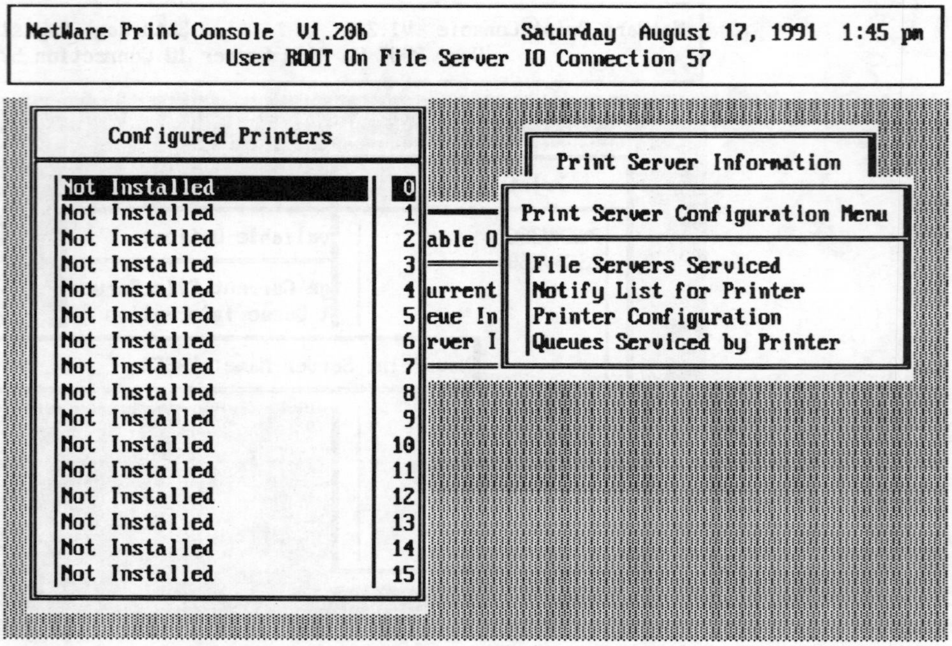

Fig. 12-14. Output produced by the Print Server Configuration menu

21. Press the [esc] key twice to return to the Print Server Information box.
22. Use the cursor keys to highlight Print Server Operators and press the [Enter] key.
23. Press the [ins] key.

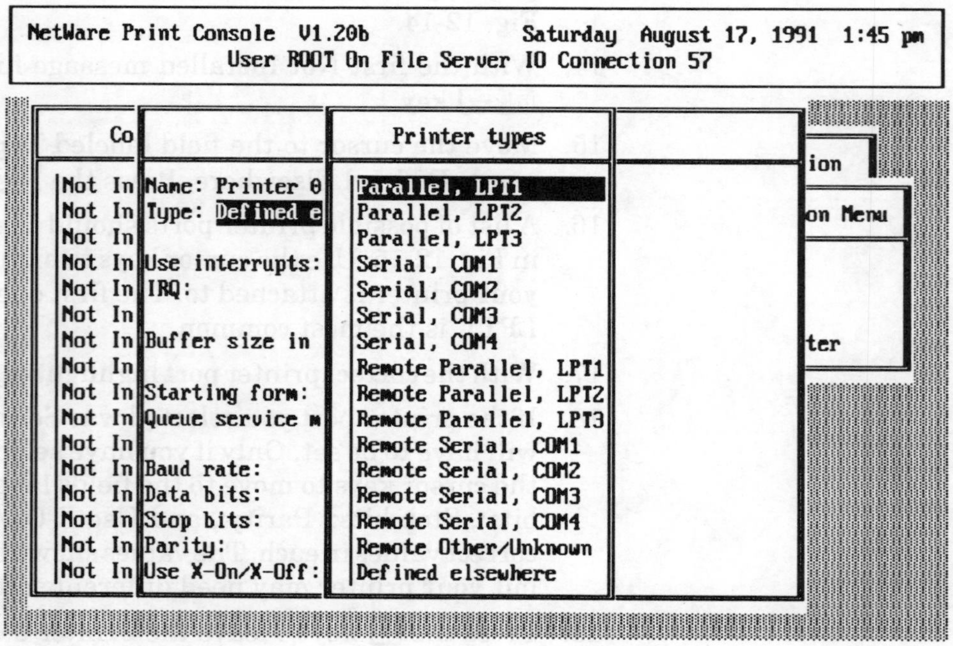

Fig. 12-15. List of printer ports

24. Type the name of your user account. The highlighted bar should move to your name, but it will stop when it reaches the group of the same name. Highlight the correct account name with (User) displayed in the right column and press the [Enter←] key.
25. Press the [esc] key to return to the Print Server Information box.
26. Highlight Print Server Users and press the [Enter←] key.
27. Verify that the group EVERYONE has been made a user of this print server and press the [esc] key.
28. Press the [esc] key twice to return to PCONSOLE's main menu.

When creating a new print server and print queue combination, something of a chicken and egg problem arises. You cannot finish configuring the print server without the print queue, and you cannot finish configuring the print queue without the print server. The reason for this complexity is that one queue can send data to several print servers and one print server can receive data from several queues. The following instructions create a new print queue and assign it to the new print server.

29. Highlight the Print Queue Information Option and press the [Enter←] key.
30. Press the [ins] key.
31. Type **Q**, followed by your account name, and press the [Enter←] key. For instance, if your account name is JSMITH, type QJSMITH and press the [Enter←] key. The "Q" is simply used to indicate a queue. It is not a required prefix.
32. With the new print queue name highlighted, press the [Enter←] key. The Print Queue Information box should appear as shown in Fig. 12-16.
33. Highlight Queue Servers and press the [Enter←] key.
34. Press the [ins] key to view the list of available servers, as shown in Fig. 12-17.
35. Type the name of your print server and press the [Enter←] key. Your print server's name is PS, followed by your account name.
36. Press the [esc] key.
37. Highlight Queue Operators and press the [Enter←] key.
38. Press the [ins] key.
39. Type the name of your user account. The highlighted bar should move to your name, but it will stop when it reaches the group of the same name. Highlight the correct account name with (User) displayed in the right column and press the [Enter←] key.

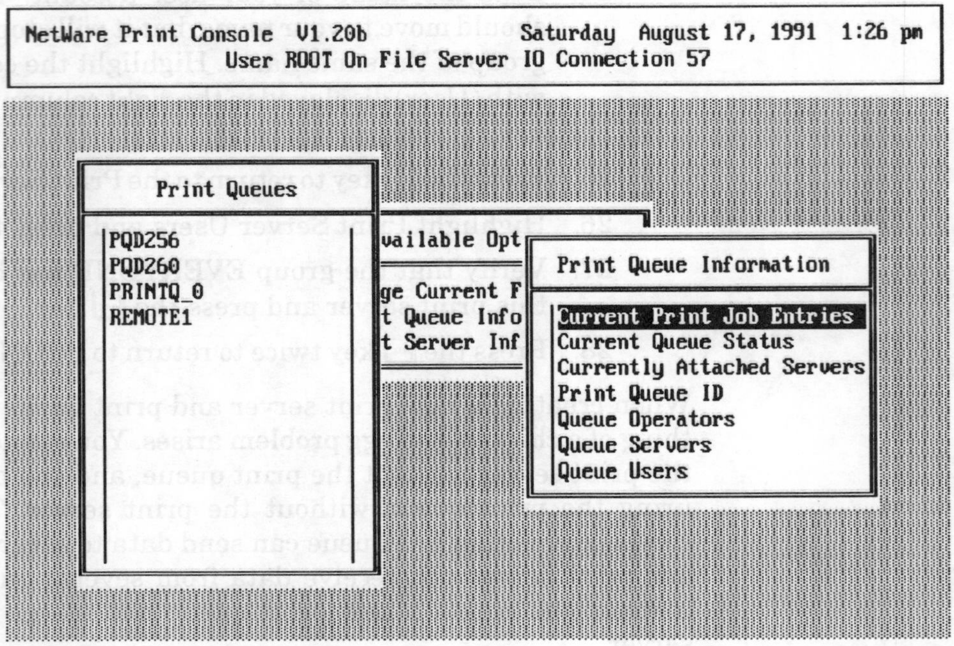

Fig. 12-16. The Print Queue Information dialog box

40. Press the [Esc] key to return to the Print Queue Information box.
41. Highlight Print Queue Users and press the [Enter] key.
42. Verify that the group EVERYONE has been made a user of this print queue and press the [Esc] key.

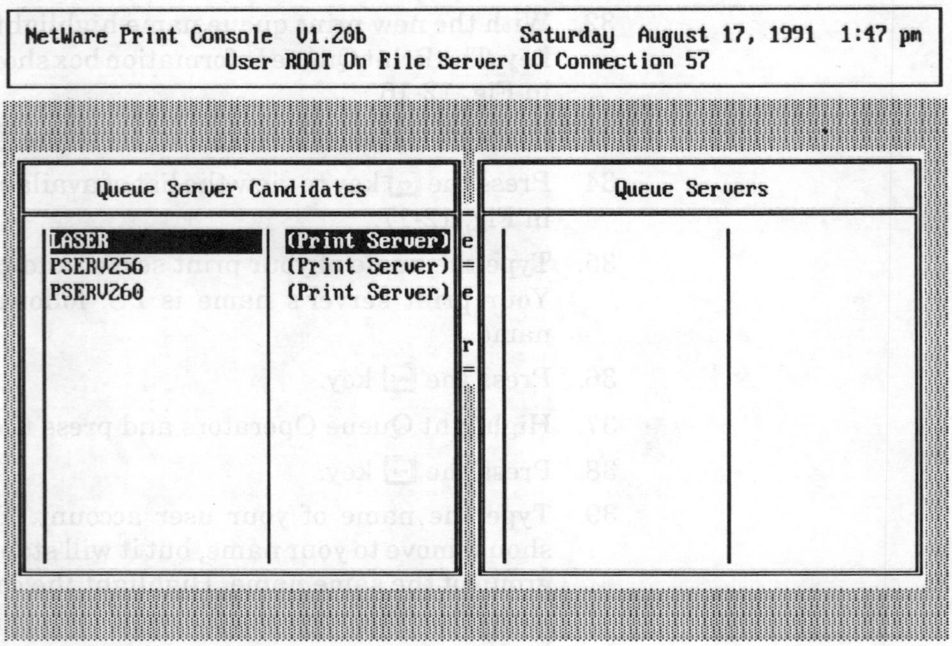

Fig. 12-17. List of available servers

43. Press the [Esc] key twice to return to PCONSOLE's main menu.
44. Highlight Print Server Information again and press the [Enter] key.
45. Type the name of your print server and press the [Enter] key. Your print server's name is PS, followed by your account name.
46. In the Print Server Information box, move the cursor down to the Print Server Configuration option and press the [Enter] key.
47. In the Print Server Configuration menu, move the cursor down to the Queues Serviced by Printer option and press the [Enter] key.
48. Press the [Enter] key with the printer you defined earlier highlighted.
49. Press the [Ins] key to view the list of available queues.
50. Type the name of your print queue and press the [Enter] key. Its name is **Q** followed by the name of your account.
51. Since several queues can be assigned to a single server, a priority number can be given to each queue. This feature permits a special queue to be created for "rush" print jobs. Press the [Enter] key to accept the priority shown.
52. Press the [Esc] key six times until the Exit PCONSOLE prompt appears.
53. Press the [Y] and [Enter] keys. The print server is now ready for operation.
54. Type **LOGOUT** and press the [Enter] key to end this session.

Running PSERVER

With the Print Server software loaded onto the file server and configured using the PCONSOLE program, the print server can be started by running the PSERVER program on any workstation with a sortable printer. The following operations start the print server.

1. Boot the workstation with the appropriate network boot disk by placing the disk in drive A and simultaneously pressing the [Ctrl], [Alt], and [Delete] keys. Enter the date and time if prompted.
2. The network driver programs should have been loaded by the AUTOEXEC.BAT file on the diskette. If they were not, type **IPX** and press the [Enter] key. Then type **NETX** and the [Enter] key. NETX can be replaced with the appropriate network shell program for your memory configuration and DOS version.
3. Type **F:** and press the [Enter] key.

4. Type **LOGIN** followed by the name of your NON-supervisor-equivalent account and press the Enter key. This account name was created using your first initial, last name, and a 1. For instance, if your supervisor-equivalent account was called JSMITH, the non-supervisor account was called JSMITH1.
5. Type the password for this account and press the Enter key.
6. Type **CD\PUBLIC** and press the Enter key.
7. Type **PSERVER** followed by the name of your print server and press the Enter key. Your print server's name is PS followed by your account name. PSERVER's screen should appear similar to the one in Fig. 12-18.
8. The status of the printer is displayed in the upper left corner of the screen. Press any key to display the status of the other eight possible printers. Press any key again to return to the first eight printers.
9. The boot disk may be removed from disk drive A.

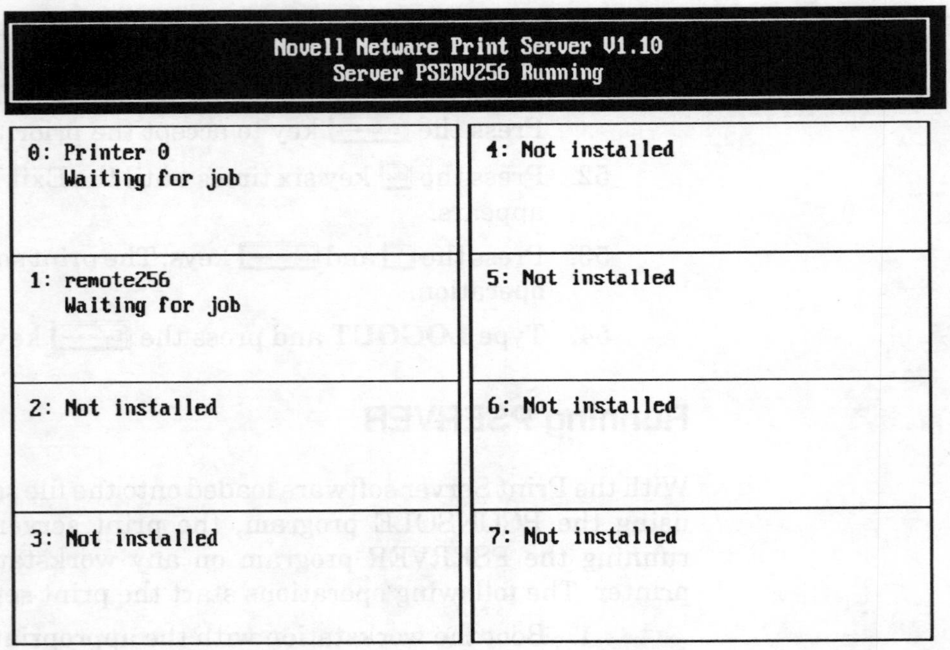

Fig. 12-18. The PSERVER main screen

Sending Output to the Print Server

The Print Server is up and running. All that remains is to test it. Leave the print server software running and move to another workstation. Follow the directions below to send data to the print server.

1. Boot the workstation with the appropriate network boot disk by placing the disk in drive A and simultaneously pressing the Ctrl, alt, and delete keys.
2. Type **F:** and press the Enter key.
3. Type **LOGIN** followed by your supervisor-equivalent login name and press the Enter key.
4. Type the password for this account, and press the Enter key.
5. Type **F:** and press the Enter key.
6. Type **NPRINT A:SHELL.CFG /Q=** followed by the print queue created earlier, then press the Enter key. For example, if your supervisor-equivalent account is JSMITH, the command would be NPRINT A:SHELL.CFG /Q=QJSMITH.
7. In a few moments the contents of the SHELL.CFG file should print on the printer attached to the print server. Note that this method of network printing does not interfere with the use of the printer on the workstation.
8. Type **CAPTURE /Q=** followed by the print queue name and /NA, then press the Enter key. For instance, the command might look like CAPTURE /Q=QJSMITH /NA. The CAPTURE program loads into memory and remains resident. The /NA stands for No Autoendcap.
9. Type **COPY A:SHELL.CFG LPT1:** and press the Enter key. Ordinarily, this DOS command would send the contents of the SHELL.CFG file to the local printer. With the CAPTURE program loaded, the output is stored until the ENDCAP command is issued.
10. Type **ENDCAP** and press the Enter key. The contents of the SHELL.CFG file will print at the print server in a few moments.
11. To end this session, type **LOGOUT** and press the Enter key. The print server can be turned off or re-booted.

Configuring the Print Server for Remote Printing

Additional printers can be connected to the print server, even printers that are not physically attached to it. With a program called RPRINTER running on a workstation, the workstation's local printer becomes a network printer. Use the directions below to configure the print server for a remote printer, restart the print server, and start the RPRINTER program on a workstation.

1. Boot the workstation with the appropriate network boot disk by placing the disk in drive A and simultaneously pressing the Ctrl, alt, and delete keys.
2. Type **F:** and press the Enter key.

3. Type **LOGIN** followed by your supervisor-equivalent login name and press the Enter← key.
4. Type the password for this account, and press the Enter← key.
5. Type **PCONSOLE** and press the Enter← key.
6. Move the cursor to Print Server Information and press the Enter← key.
7. Type the name of your print server. Press the Enter← key when the proper name is highlighted.
8. Move the cursor to the Print Server Configuration option and press the Enter← key.
9. Move the cursor to the Printer Configuration option of the Print Server Configuration menu and press the Enter← key. A list of printers attached to this print server should appear as it does in Fig. 12-19.

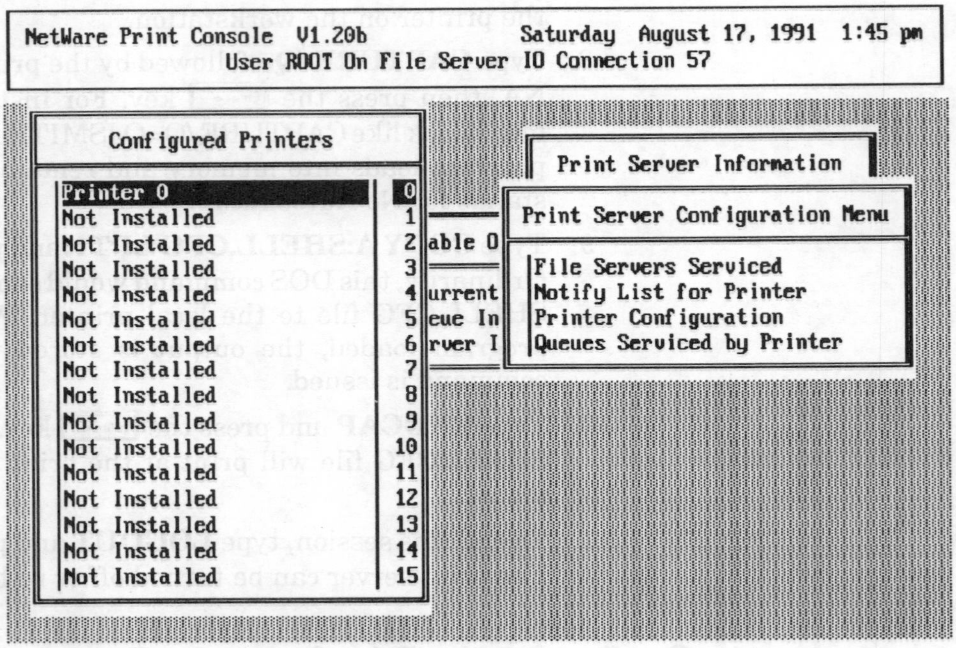

Fig. 12-19. List of printers attached to the server

10. Move the cursor to the first available Not Installed message and press the Enter← key.
11. Move the cursor to the Type: Defined elsewhere message and press the Enter← key.
12. Move the cursor to the Remote Parallel, LPT1 option in the Printer types box, as shown in Fig. 12-20, then press the Enter← key.
13. Press the esc key twice until the Save Changes menu appears.
14. Press the Y and Enter← keys.

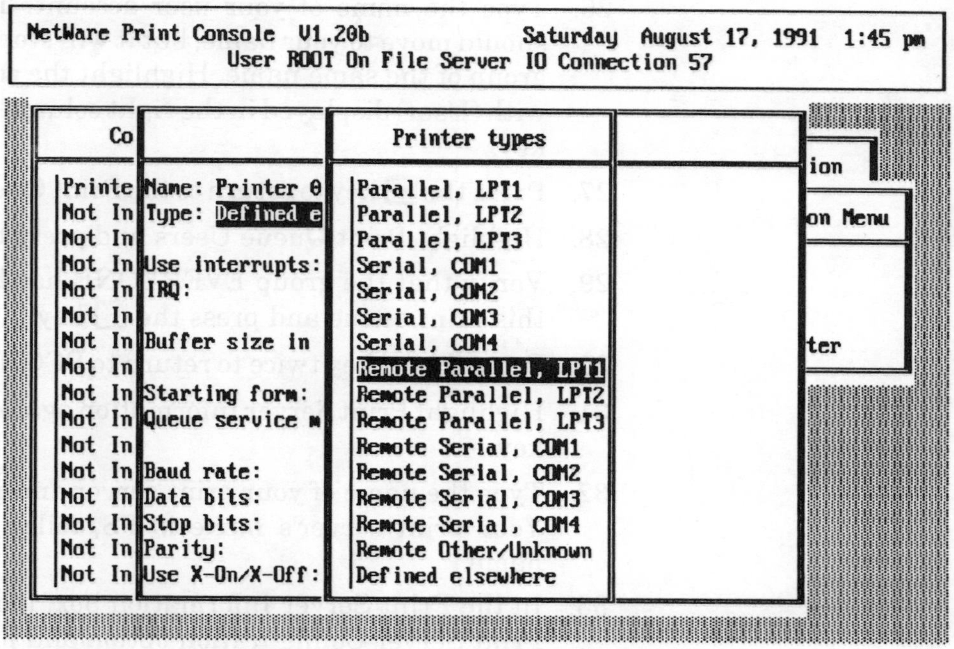

Fig. 12-20. Selecting a port for the printer

15. Press the Esc key four times to return to PCONSOLE's main menu of available topics
16. Highlight the Print Queue Information option and press the Enter key.
17. Press the Ins key to enter a new print queue name.
18. Type **R** followed by your account name and press the Enter key. For instance, user JSMITH would type RJSMITH and press the Enter key.
19. With the new print queue name highlighted, press the Enter key.
20. Move the cursor to highlight Queue Servers and press the Enter key.
21. Press the Ins key to view the list of available servers.
22. Type the name of your print server and press the Enter key. Your print server's name is PS, followed by your account name.
23. Press the Esc key.
24. Move the cursor down to highlight Queue Operators and press the Enter key.
25. Press the Ins key.

26. Type the name of your user account. The highlighted bar should move to your name, but it will stop when it reaches the group of the same name. Highlight the correct account name with (User) displayed in the right column and press the [Enter] key.
27. Press the [esc] key to return to the Print Queue Information box.
28. Highlight Print Queue Users and press the [Enter] key.
29. Verify that the group EVERYONE has been made a user of this print queue and press the [esc] key.
30. Press the [esc] key twice to return to PCONSOLE's main menu.
31. Highlight Print Server Information again and press the [Enter] key.
32. Type the name of your print server and press the [Enter] key. Your print server's name is PS, followed by your account name.
33. In the Print Server Information box, move the cursor to the Print Server Configuration option and press the [Enter] key.
34. In the Print Server Configuration menu, move the cursor down to the Queues Serviced by Printer option and press the [Enter] key.
35. Move the cursor down to the remote printer defined as Printer 1 earlier and press the [Enter] key.
36. Press the [ins] key to view the list of available queues.
37. Type the name of your remote printer queue and press the [Enter] key. The remote printer queue name is R followed by your account name.
38. Press the [Enter] key to verify the Priority.
39. Press the [esc] key six times until the "Exit PCONSOLE" menu appears.
40. Press the [Y] and [Enter] keys.

Running PSERVER with a Remote Printer

The print server now has the capability of supporting a remote printer anywhere on the network. Any workstation that loads the RPRINTER program and selects the proper print server and printer will operate as the remote print server. The following steps restart the print server, which will control the remote printer.

1. Boot the workstation with the appropriate network boot disk by placing the disk in drive A and simultaneously pressing the [Ctrl], [alt], and [delete] keys. Enter the date and time if prompted.

2. The network driver programs should have been loaded by the AUTOEXEC.BAT file on the diskette. If they were not, type **IPX** and press the Enter key. Then type **NETX** and the press the Enter key. NETX can be replaced with the appropriate network shell program for your memory configuration and DOS version.
3. Type **F:** and press the Enter key.
4. Type **LOGIN** followed by the name of your NON-supervisor-equivalent account and press the Enter key. This account name was created using your first initial, last name, and a 1. For instance, if your supervisor-equivalent account was called JSMITH, the non-supervisor account was called JSMITH1.
5. Type **SECOND**, the password for this account, and press the Enter key.
6. Type **CD\PUBLIC** and press the Enter key.
7. Type **PSERVER** followed by the name of your print server and press the Enter key. Your print server's name is PS, followed by your account name.
8. Remove the boot disk from drive A.

Running RPRINTER

With the new improved version of the Print Server program running, move to a new workstation that has a local printer. Follow the instruction below to install the RPRINTER program.

1. Boot the workstation with the appropriate network boot disk by placing the disk in drive A and simutaneously pressing the Ctrl, alt, and delete keys.
2. Type **F:** and press the Enter key.
3. Type **LOGIN** followed by your supervisor-equivalent login name and press the Enter key.
4. Type the password for this account, and press the Enter key.
5. Type **RPRINTER** and press the Enter key. The remote printer program should display a list of print servers.
6. Type the name of your print server and press the Enter key. The remote printers available for that print server should be displayed.
7. Select the name of your remote printer by pressing the Enter key. The message "** Remote printer now installed **" indicates that the RPRINTER program has been successfully installed.

Sending Output to the Remote Printer

The printer attached to the workstation can still be used by the workstation, but data being sent to the workstation by the print server will also be printed. Two methods can be used to test this situation. One is to have another student at another workstation send data to the remote printer. The other method is to use a network printing utility to send data to the same workstation as a remote printer. The following steps will work equally well at another workstation or at the same workstation. These instructions assume the workstation is still logged in.

1. Type **NPRINT A:SHELL.CFG /Q=** followed by the remote print queue created earlier, then press the Enter key. For example, if your supervisor equivalent account is JSMITH, the command would be NPRINT A:SHELL.CFG /Q=RJSMITH.
2. In a few moments the contents of the SHELL.CFG file should print on the printer attached to the remote print server. Note that this method of network printing does not interfere with the use of the printer on the workstation.
3. Type **CAPTURE /Q=** followed by the remote print queue name and /NA, and then press the Enter key. For instance, the command might look like CAPTURE /Q=RJSMITH /NA. The CAPTURE program loads into memory and remains resident. The "/NA" stands for No Autoendcap.
4. Type **COPY A:SHELL.CFG LPT1:** and press the Enter key. Ordinarily, this DOS command would send the contents of the SHELL.CFG file to the local printer. With the CAPTURE program loaded, the output is stored until the ENDCAP command is issued.
5. Type **ENDCAP** and press the Enter key. The contents of the SHELL.CFG file will print at the remote print server in a few moments.
6. To end this session, type **LOGOUT** and press the Enter key. The print server can be turned off or rebooted.

Summary

One of the most often used features of a network is sharing printers. A Novell network allows printers located on the file server, on a bridge server, on a dedicated print server, or on a remote print server to be accessed by any user or group with authorization. Print forms, print devices, print queues, and print job configurations are all tools that can be used to control how and where data is to be printed. Data can be sent to a network printer in four ways; with the PCONSOLE utility, with the NPRINT command, with the CAPTURE command, or with an application program designed to send data to a network printer.

Questions

1. What is considered to be the most versatile way to attach a printer to the network?
2. Can a print form be used to specify which printer will be used?
3. Can a print device be used to define a special font such as bold?
4. Can a print job configuration be used by a group?
5. How many printers can be attached to a print server?
6. If a print server has only one printer port, but two printers attached, where is the second printer?
7. Can a single print queue feed data to more than one printer?
8. In what ways is a remote printer vulnerable?

Projects

Objective

The following projects provide additional practice with the basic networking printing facilities of NetWare. Additionally, the second project provides more hands-on tranining in creating print queues and sending print jobs accross the network.

Project 1. Basic Network Printing

1. Use the PRINTDEF utility to ensure that the driver for the printer attached to the print server created earlier is available on the system. The driver will need to be imported only once for the file server being used.
2. Use the PRINTDEF utility to create a print form called 132_COL that uses a form width of 132 columns. The form will need to be created only once for the file server being used.
3. Use the PRINTCON utility to create a print job configuration called CONDENSED that specifies the print device, the print mode, and the print form. Use the print device name of the printer attached to your print server, the condensed mode of that printer, and the 132-column form.
4. Use the NPRINT utility to print the AUTOEXEC.BAT file on your boot disk with the print job CONDENSED. The syntax of the NPRINT command is

   NPRINT filename /J=print_job_name

Project 2. Advanced Network Printing

1. Create a print queue with a unique name on an existing print server. Be sure to include your user name as a print queue operator.
2. Set the printer to OFF LINE. Send a file to the print queue, then use the PCONSOLE utility to remove the file from the queue. Put the printer back on line.
3. Try the same operation as above, but send your data to a classmates' print queue. You should not be able to remove the print job.

13

Installing Network Application Software

Objectives

1. Understand the benefits of LAN based software.
2. Learn techniques to install LANs.
3. Learn techniques to make LANs more accessible to users.
4. Understand how to install shared software on a LAN.

Key Terms

Attributes	Application Software
Batch File	Data Sharing
Executable Only	Group
Menu	Network Software
Read	Read Only
Rights	Server
Submenu	Variables

Introduction

Assuming Novell NetWare has been installed correctly, that appropriate users and login scripts have been created, and all network printing functions needed have been installed, there is only one item missing -- application software. The primary purpose of the network is to deliver the software that users need to their workstations. All of the other setup involved means nothing to the users if they cannot easily access the word processors, databases, spreadsheets, and other programs they need to do their jobs. Novell supplies a program with NetWare called MENU.EXE that can produce attractive, easy to use menus that blend smoothly with the other Novell utilities. Unfortunatly, it does not work in all situations. In some cases, it is necessary to use DOS batch files to serve as menus. It is also possible to purchase programs designed specifically to operate as NetWare menus.

The software that is to be accessed by these menus falls into three catagories: network incompatible, network compatible, and network aware. Network incompatible software is software that cannot be run from the file server. It might, however, still need to be called from the workstation's local hard disk in a menu system. Network compatible programs have no difficulty running on the file server, but they do not take advantage of the network for services such as network printing or mail. Programs that do take advantage of these services are known as network aware.

Personal computers derive their usefulness from the software that they are capable of running. This software includes word processors, spreadsheets, databases, graphics, and others. Local area networks enhance the usefulness of the personal computer. Therefore, it is important to understand the capability of the personal computer in running applications in a local area network environment.

Most popular software applications in the market have network versions of their individual products. Knowing how to install software products in a network is a must for any network administrator. This chapter provides some guidelines and examples on how to install this type of software and how to create menus that simplify the network to the users.

Using Application Software in a Network

Benefits

There are many reasons for using network versions of software on a local area network. Some of the most compelling are:

1. Sharing of software.
2. Sharing of data.

3. Sharing system resources.
4. Security and backups.
5. Easier maintenance and upgrades.

Sharing Software

Imagine an office that has 20 employees, all using personal computers with word processing, spreadsheet, and database software. If each user is to have individual copies of software, there must a legally purchased copy of each package for each user.

Another solution is to purchase network versions of all software products and install a single copy of each on a local area network connecting all users. Purchasing a network version of a software product is, in many situations, less expensive than buying individual copies for each user.

Additionally, there isn't the need to keep track of 20 copies of the same software product. Only one copy needs to be administered.

Sharing Data

With Network copies of software programs, the data generated by one user can be used by other users in a "transparent" mode. That is, all users can work with the same data file as if it were their own. With individual copies of software, data generated on one workstation must be physically moved from one machine to another. In the case of sales, inventory departments, and others, this type of data transfer creates problems with outdated versions of files and with duplication of efforts and data.

Sharing System Resources

Network versions of software also save on hard disk space. Instead of using space on multiple users' hard disks, the software can be placed on the network server's hard disk. This allows the software and data to be shared by everyone in a local area network.

Security and Backup

Individual copies of software on multiple workstations are difficult to safeguard from unauthorized individuals. It is relatively easy to go to a person's desk and damage or change data files.

Using the security resources of a network, software can be safeguarded by installing passwords, trustee rights, and file attributes. This enhances the safety of data files and programs in a manner that is almost impossible with individual software.

With multiple users working with stand-alone programs, backing up software becomes a difficult task. Users are not always prompt when it comes to backing up important software and data. Using the network resources, software and data can be backed up from a single location with a minimal amount of effort. This also enhances security since the latest copy of a file is assured when using the latter method.

Easy Maintenance and Upgrades

In many situations users of a particular package do not have the latest updates or modifications. Sometimes this is due to a lack of time to install software upgrades, and other times there is a lack of funding to purchase the latest release of a product.

If network software is used, only one upgrade copy of the software needs to be installed and/or modified to get the latest features. Also, in large corporations with many users, the cost of upgrading a network version of a software product can be substantially less than purchasing individual copies of the same program.

Choosing Servers

If the network consists of only one server, then the choice of where to install shared software is easy. However, if multiple servers are available, a decision must be made as to which server will hold the shared software.

There are several possibilities for multiple server networks. Assume that a network consists of two servers. One possibility is to purchase two copies of the software and install one on each server. Another possibility is to purchase a third server and place all shared software on it. Or all shared software can be installed in one of the servers and let users of the other server attach themselves to the one that has the software (see Fig. 13.1).

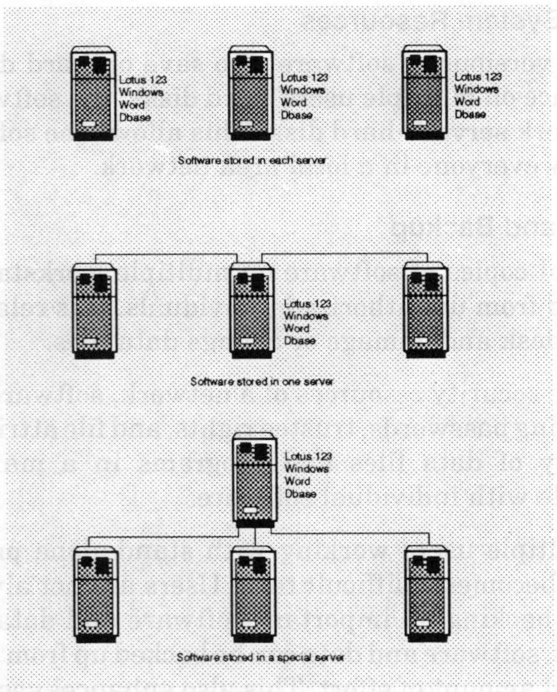

Fig. 13-1. Possible combinations of shared servers

Each of these approaches has its pros and cons. If a copy is purchased for each server, then the expense of the extra copy may be higher than having a network version of the software and a license for all possible users. Additionally, there is the need to keep security and maintenance of the same software product on multiple servers.

Placing all shared software on a single server may prove to be too much for a computer acting as the server. Too many users can slow the response time of the server to unacceptable levels.

Acquiring an individual server to place all shared software on is the most elegant solution. However, in many situations this is not economically feasible.

A final possibility is to spread all shared software among the available servers. This allows the purchase of a single network version of a software product along with a license for the number of users involved. This method also allows the load created by the shared software to be spread evenly among all available servers (see Fig. 13.2).

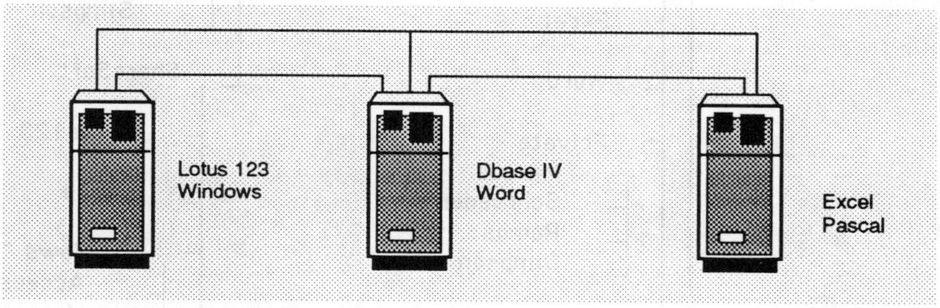

Fig. 13-2. Dividing software evenly among three servers

Choosing a Directory for Shared Software

In addition to choosing the server where the shared software is to reside, the directory structure of this server must be decided. There are several possibilities. One is to place all shared programs under the main or root directory. The other possible solution is to create a directory under the root directory and name this subdirectory SHARESOF, PROGRAMS, or something that indicates its purpose (see Fig. 13.3 for two such subdirectories).

The first solution may not be the best approach. One problem is that the root directory may become cluttered as new programs are added to the server. This makes the task of maintenance and backup more difficult since each shared program name must be identified during backups.

The second method is the better one. During backup procedures the entire shared software subdirectory can be backed up with a single command. Additionally, establishing security rights over one subdirectory is easier than over multiple subdirectories.

A more complex task is when some software is supposed to be "public domain" and other software is to be secured. The words "public domain" mean that all programs or data in the subdirectory are available to all users for downloading to their workstation and there are no restrictions imposed on how they use it. Even though such software is shared, it should not share a parent directory with programs and data that require large measures of security.

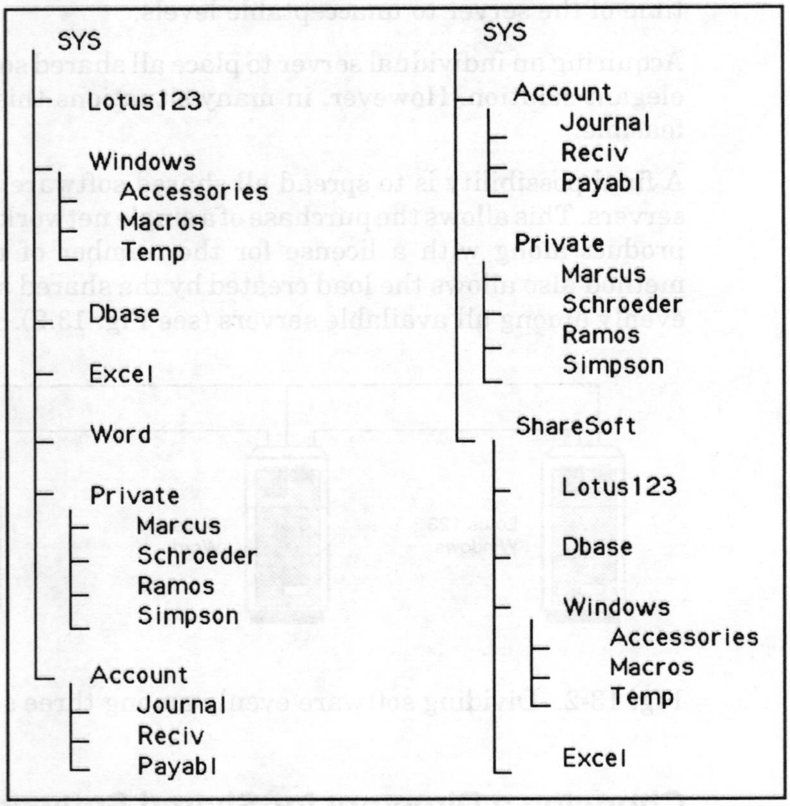

Fig. 13-3. Directory structure for shared programs

Accessing Shared Programs

Several NetWare tools allow a system manager to determine the access rights and privileges of the network users. As a rule, users should be able to work with networked software as if it were an individual program on their workstation. They should be able to change certain software parameters, such as type of printer, in the same manner as they would if they had a personal copy of the program. Also, users should be able to create data files and store them without the need to learn complex network commands. All of this should take place with the shared programs safeguarded from accidental deletions or deliberate alterations by users without the proper authorization.

A list of all users needs to be made, specifying their software needs, hard disk space, requirements, and rights. Also, for each data file and software program, attributes such as Shareable or Read Only need to be identified. This also needs to be performed for all subdirectories and the programs stored inside of them. When a program is Shareable, its parent directory should also be Shareable. The parent directory attributes typically determine what can be done with the programs and files stored inside of it.

Granting NetWare Rights

Most shared software comes with documentation that indicates in detail the types of rights to provide to program users. If a list is not available, the network administrator must decide what rights to provide.

The goal is to provide users access to the program without allowing them to change or delete the files that make up the program. If the software package to be installed provides no documentation, then a possible model is to place the software in the SYS:PUBLIC directory. This directory contains program files that all users must be able to run but not change.

All users on a NetWare system have, by default, Read, Open, and Search rights to the SYS:PUBLIC directory. If the shared software to be installed provides little or no information as to the rights to provide to programs and files, the rights of Read, Open, and Search can be provided as a first try. The programs should then be tested to make sure that they perform correctly. If errors are encountered, a trial and error procedure of assigning rights may have to be undertaken until the proper rights are provided.

Group Rights

If a large number of users have the same rights, such as a class in a college, a group can be created instead of creating individual users. Then group rights can be provided that affect all the users that belong to the group. For example, if an accounting class needs access to an accounting package, and no one else needs to use the programs, a group ACCOUNTING can be created. The group can have a homogeneous password, ID, and rights. When a user uses the accounting password and ID, he or she will be granted all rights for the group and access to the programs accordingly. This eliminates the need to create several dozen accounts, thus reducing the overhead of the network and making maintenance less difficult for network administrators.

Many network administrators create a group for each program that requires some type of access control. Each group is then given rights to its respective program. Finally, users are placed in the appropriate program group.

Program File Attributes

Files in a NetWare based network can be given any of the file attributes outlined in earlier chapters. Generally, most files are made Shareable and Read Only. Files that are shareable are available to multiple users at any time that they are desired. If a file is not Shareable and a user is accessing the file, other users must wait for the first user to complete using the file before they can gain access to it. In other words, it can be used by only one user at a time. If the file is made Shareable, multiple users can use it at the same time.

Making a program Read Only protects it from accidental deletion and modification, even by users that have delete privileges, such as the supervisor.

Another type of file attribute is Execute Only. This attribute can be given to executable files in order to prevent them from being copied. While this attribute is on, users can execute the program but cannot copy it to their own disks or subdirectories.

Using Application Programs in a Network Environment

Most software written for IBM compatibles can be divided into three catagories, network incompatible, network compatible, and network aware.

Network incompatible software cannot be used at all while it is stored on a file server. Usually the problem involves the program's use of low-level operations to control the disk drive or access its own files. These low-level operations access the hardware of the computer directly, rather than using the DOS function calls that NetWare has redirected to the file server. Other problems can arise when the program is simply incompatible with the resident network driver programs, although this situation is rare. In that case the program cannot be run on a computer that is attached to the network. When the software can be run with the network drivers loaded, but not on the network, it is necessary to install it on the workstation's hard disk. A complete menu system would also offer selections to the user to run this software, as well as network software.

Network compatible software includes all programs that can be run on the network, even though they might not be network specific versions. Many programs have no install options that indicate what drive letter the program is running on. These programs can simply be copied to a network directory. Others, such as older versions of WordStar, can be installed on any drive letter A - Z using the appropriate install procedures. This is often the easiest type of program for the network supervisor to install. Still others may be programmed to always look on a certain disk drive for their files, for instance on drive C. In this case, the NetWare MAP command can be used to map drive letter C to the appropriate network directory. The programs in this category must be handled very carefully in regard to federal copyright laws. Under almost all license agreements accompanying the software, one copy of the software must be owned for each user accessing the program.

Network aware programs have been written to detect and sometimes take advantage of a network. Many programs released in the last few years are designed specifically to detect that they are running on a network and to allow only one user to access them. This prevents users from illegally using more copies of the software than they own. Usually, special multiuser versions of such programs are available that allow five, ten or some other number of users to access the software simultaneously. The multiuser versions are always more expensive than single-user versions, of course. But they are less expensive than an equal number of single-user copies. Other programs are written to take advantage of the network environment. These programs offer electronic mail, quick messages, easy use of network printers, or network use of a common database.

Installing Shared Software

Installing Microsoft Windows

Microsoft Windows is a graphical environment for IBM personal computers and compatibles running under the MS-DOS operating system. Windows creates a new working environment on top of MS-DOS, thus shielding the user from having to memorize operating system commands.

It is important to understand that Windows is not a replacement for MS-DOS. It is just a graphical shell that becomes the interface between the computer and the user. Additionally, individuals that plan to use Microsoft Windows should have some knowledge of the basic input/output operations performed by the computer.

To install Windows on a Novell network, a shared copy of the program must be placed in the network. Then copies of some Windows files need to be placed on user disks. This is done by using the command SETUP/N during the installation process. The directory where some of the Windows files are placed is a personal directory for the user that must be present in order to run Windows.

By maintaining their own copies of these files, users can customize the Windows environment without affecting the shared files located in the network and used by all individuals working with Windows.

To place Windows in the network, the network administrator attaches it to a server on the network. Then the directory where Windows will reside is accessed, and a series of commands are given to copy the proper files to the server. These commands are outlined in the hands-on portion of this chapter.

Accessing Windows

Users can access Windows applications easier by placing entries in the SETUP.INF file that indicate the application and the access mechanism for a specific program. The SETUP.INF file is included with Windows and becomes a permanent file in the shared Windows directory.

By placing entries in the SETUP.INF file, applications can be added to the Program Manager's groups and their settings can also be modified or customized. In this manner, if an application needs to be added to the user's Program Manager window, a title and the path for the application must be placed in the SETUP.INF file.

In addition to the title and path, an icon file name or icon number may also be included in the SETUP.INF file entry for a program application. If an icon is not specified, the displayed icon will be one from the application file.

Guidelines for Using Windows on a Novell Network

Using Windows on a Novell network is simplified by following these steps:

1. Start the network first, then start Windows. That is, make sure that the workstation is attached to the network server, and that the user is logged in.
2. Personal files should not be kept in a shared file directory.
3. Always use the same network drive letter used when Windows was installed. If Windows was installed in drive H, use drive H when trying to access Windows.
4. When attaching to a printer, always use the same port for that specific printer.

By following these guidelines, using Windows in a Novell network becomes a much simpler task.

Customizing NetWare

All programs in a NetWare file server should be made easy to access by all users. The process followed in accessing network based software consists of the following steps.

1. The user workstation must attach to the file server that contains the shared programs.
2. A drive letter must be mapped to the directory where the required program resides.
3. The command required to start a program must be given.
4. After the program is used, it must be exited.
5. The drive letter mapped in step 2 needs to be deleted.

6. The user logs out of the file server that contains the shared software.

These steps are difficult to perform by most users, in addition to being cumbersome to use on a continuous basis. The solution is to create a batch file and place it in the SYS:PUBLIC where all users can have access to it.

An example of a typical batch file to start a copy of Lotus 123 from a server named SERVER2 may consist of the following lines.

```
ATTACH SERVER2/GUEST
MAP H:=SERVER2/SYS:SHARESOF\LOTUS123
H:
LOTUS
LOGOUT SERVER2
```

In this example, the first line attaches a user who has the login name GUEST to the server whose network name is SERVER2. A drive H is mapped to the directory that stores Lotus 123. The program is executed with the command LOTUS, and when the user exits the program, the user is logged out of the server SERVER2.

Batch files are used when shared programs are stored on special servers to which the user must attach in order to run the programs. Although network managers create much more complicated batch files, the above example illustrates the use of such a file to access programs stored in a network file server.

Although batch files protect the user from needing to know the intricacies of NetWare commands to attach to file servers and map directories, the use of menus further enhances the usability of the network. Using menus provides easy access to shared software for new or inexperienced users.

Novell has a menu building system that can be used for most situations and needs. Many commercially available programs can also be used for this purpose. With menus, users can start batch files by selecting a letter or a number from a list of choices. The menu then transfers execution to the batch file. When the batch file terminates executing, control is returned to the menu and it is automatically displayed back on the screen. Creating menus requires extra effort from the network administrator, but in the long run menus tend to increase network usage by making users feel comfortable with the hardware.

The Novell Menu System

Novell provides a program with NetWare called MENU.EXE that can be used to create custom menus. MENU.EXE is placed in the \PUBLIC directory. The program uses ASCII script files to display colorful menus, similar to those used in the NetWare utilities. The script files can be written with any ASCII text editor. Once written, the MENU program is used to interpret them. For example, suppose an ASCII text file called START.MNU contains the following:

```
%Available Options
1. Syscon
    SYSCON
2. Fconsole
    FCONSOLE
```

The command MENU START would load and execute the MENU program. The MENU program would load and interpret the instructions in the START.MNU file. MENU.EXE assumes the file name listed on the command line has a .MNU extension. The "%" on the first line indicates the title of the menu. Text that begins in the first column without a "%" indicates a menu selection. Any other text that does not start in the first column is considered the instructions that are to be executed for the preceding menu selection. The instructions can be any legal DOS command or program name with three exceptions. First the LOGOUT command must be preceded by a "!" to operate properly. Second, DOS batch files should not be called by the menu. Third, memory resident programs should not be loaded from the menu. The file shown above results in the menu shown in Fig. 13-4. The menu thus created follows many of the same rules as other Novell menus. For instance, the "2." on the line with the Fconsole menu option does not have any special meaning to the MENU.EXE program but by typing a "2" in the menu, the Fconsole line is highlighted. This is because, as in any Novell menu, typing the menu selection highlights the option. The arrow keys can also be used to move the highlighted area to the desired option. In either case, ENTER is pressed to select the option highlighted. Even the F1 key operates the same as in other Novell menus. Fig. 13-5 shows the first panel of the help screen shown when F1 is pressed in the START.MNU menu. Pressing F1 again displays the second help panel as in Fig. 13-6. Unfortunately not all of the keys listed work when using custom menus. To exit a custom menu such as START.MNU, the ESCAPE key is pressed. A familiar "Exit" menu will be displayed as it is in Fig. 13-7.

The menus created with MENU.EXE can be customized further by using parameters on the menu title line. Three parameters can be used to indicate the vertical placement of the menu, the horizontal placement, and the color palette used. For instance, if the first line in START.MNU were changed to "%Available Options,10,60,5", the center of the menu would be placed 10 lines from the top of the screen and 60 columns from the left edge of the screen. The "5" on the end of the line indicates that color palette 5 is to be used. Palette 5 denotes black and white text only. Note that the vertical and horizontal distances are measured from the center of the menu. The result is shown in Fig. 13-8. Additional color palettes can be created using the NetWare COLORPAL program.

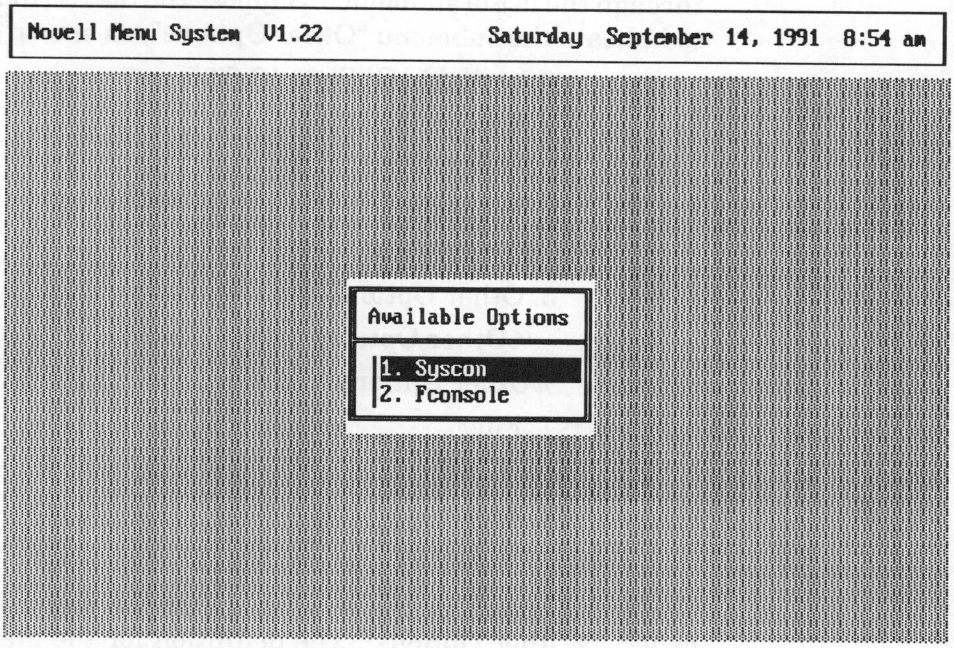

Fig. 13-4. Menu created by batch file

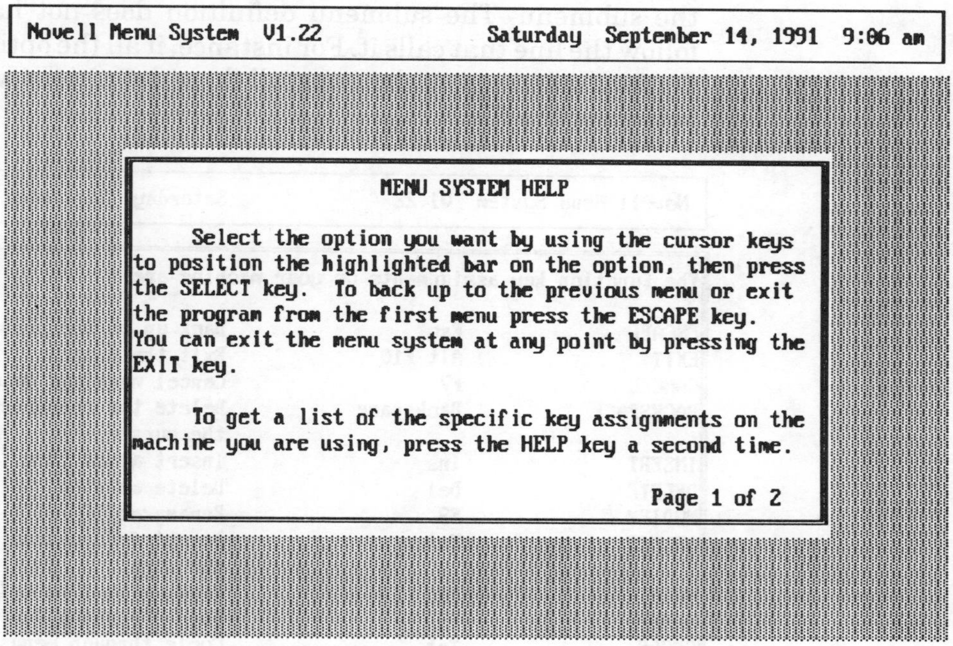

Fig. 13-5. First panel of help screen

Submenus

The START.MNU example above is, of course, a very simple menu. The MENU.EXE program is capable of producing much more complex menus through the use of submenus. Suppose the file START.MNU is expanded to indicate the submenu "Other Options", as shown below.

```
%Available Options,10,60,5
1. Syscon
   SYSCON
2. Fconsole
   FCONSOLE
3. Other Options
   %Other Options
%Other Options
1. Filer
   FILER
2. Session
   SESSION
```

The third option in the Available Options menu executes something called "%Other Options". The definition for the menu "Other Options" immediately follows. A line starting with a % in the first column defines a menu. A line that starts with a % but does not begin in column one calls the submenu. The submenu definition does not have to immediately follow the line that calls it. For instance, if all the options in the Available Options menu were submenus, all three definitions would be listed at the bottom of the file.

Novell Menu System V1.22 Saturday September 14, 1991 9:09 am

The function key assignments on your machine are:

ESCAPE	Esc	Back up to the previous level.
EXIT	Alt F10	Exit the program.
CANCEL	F7	Cancel markings or edit changes.
BACKSPACE	Backspace	Delete the character to the left of the cursor.
INSERT	Ins	Insert a new item.
DELETE	Del	Delete an item.
MODIFY	F3	Rename/modify/edit the item.
SELECT	Enter	Accept information entered or select the item.
HELP	F1	Provide on-line help.
MARK	F5	Toggle marking for current item.
CYCLE	Tab	Cycle through menus or screens.
MODE	F9	Change Modes.
UP	Up arrow	Move up one line.
DOWN	Down arrow	Move down one line.
LEFT	Left arrow	Move left one position.
RIGHT	Right arrow	Move right one position

Fig. 13-6. Second panel of help screen

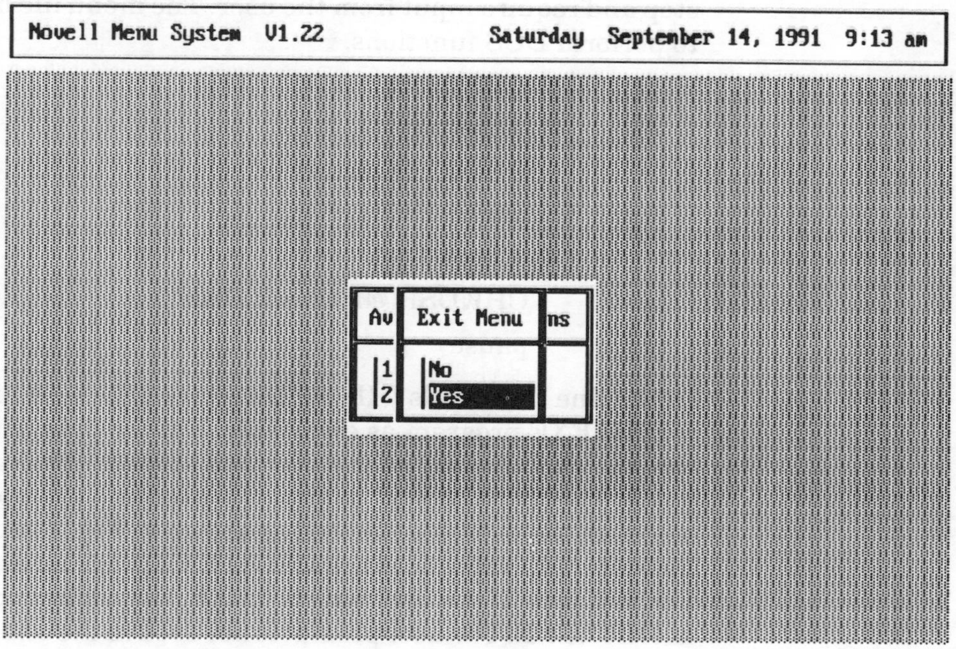

Fig. 13-7. Exit menu created by the batch file

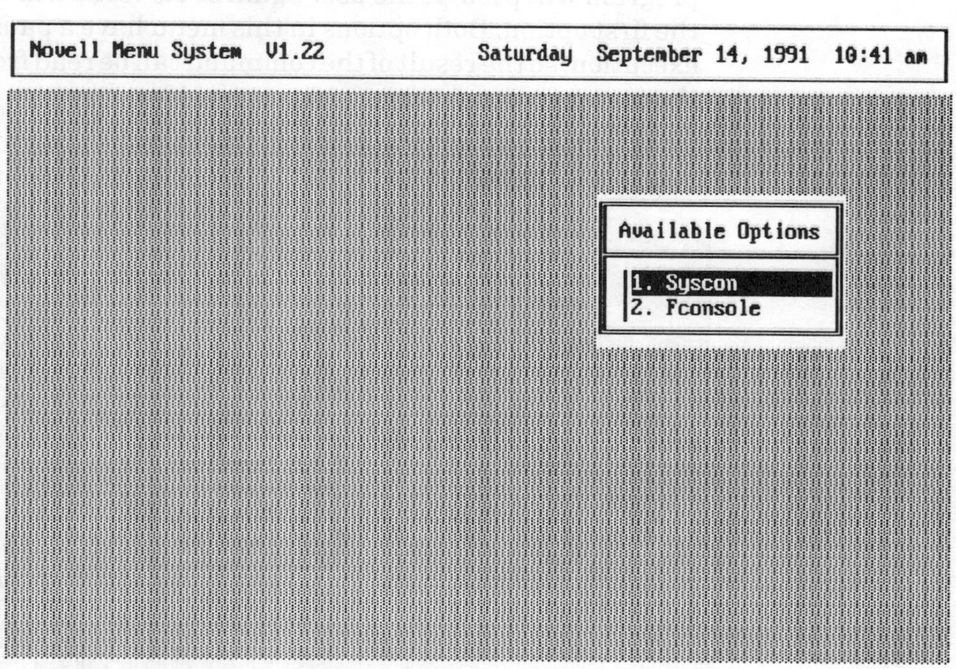

Fig. 13-8. Screen generated by the command %Available Options,10,60,5

Menu Variables

The Novell menu system also allows the user to enter text that the menu can then take some action on. Variables can be used to force the menu to stop and require input from the user. The menu file below uses variables to perform DOS functions.

```
%DOS functions
1. Directory
   DIR @1"Directory of"
   pause
2. Check Disk
   CHKDSK @1"Check Disk"
   pause
```

In the line that reads DIR @1"Directory of", the @1 is recognized by the MENU.EXE program as a variable. Rather than attempting to execute the line exactly as it is, the program stops and asks the user to input a value. The "Directory of" in quotes is used as a prompt for the user. When selected, the user is prompted as shown in Fig. 13-9. Only after the user has entered a value does the MENU.EXE program execute the command. For instance, if the user enters *.EXE, the command would be executed as DIR *.EXE. The user prompt is not used in the command. In the second option, Check Disk, the @1 variable is used again but the MENU.EXE program will prompt the user again so its value will not be retained from the first option. Both options in this menu have a pause statement to halt execution, so the result of the command can be read from the screen before the menu screen returns.

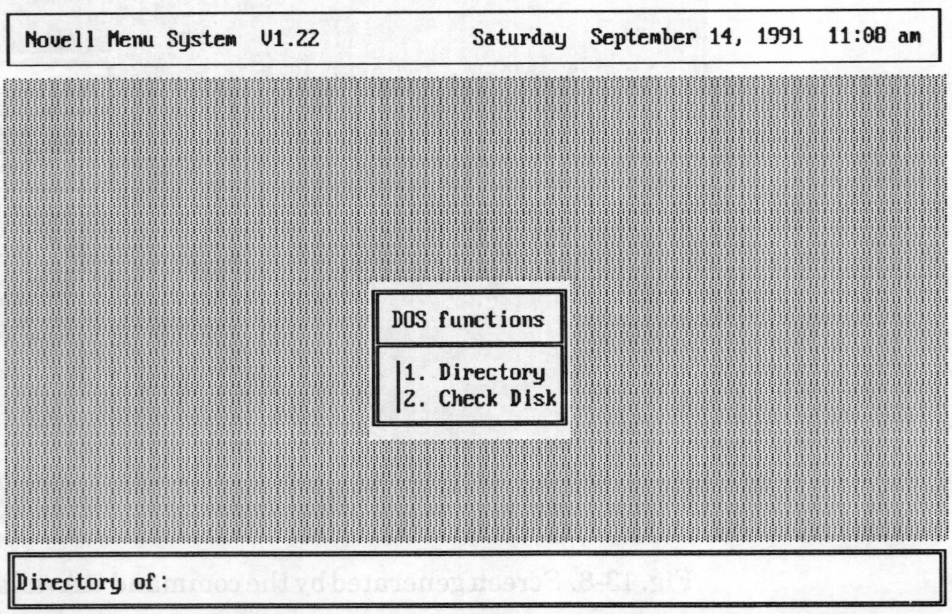

Fig. 13-9. Screen generated by batch file in menu variables section

Problems with MENU.EXE

As impressive as MENU.EXE is at creating menus, it has two very significant flaws. First, memory resident applications cannot be loaded from it. Attempting to load a resident program can cause the computer to "crash." Second, it does not operate well with DOS batch files. If a batch file calls MENU.EXE, the first menu option selected causes control to be returned to the batch file. When the batch file finishes, control goes back to MENU.EXE, and the menu screen reappears. Also, if a menu file calls a batch file, only the batch file will be executed in that menu option. Commands that appear after the batch file name in a certain menu option will not be executed. Other commercial programs are available for creating menus on a Novell network.

Batch File Menus

Novell's menu system is colorful and allows the supervisor to create menus that match the NetWare Utilities, but its inability to load memory resident programs makes it impossible to use in many situations. In a diverse environment where there may be dozens of programs available to use on the file server, loading and unloading memory resident programs becomes quite important. The NetWare CAPTURE program is a good example. In a truly friendly environment, the user would need the option of redirecting the printer output to a network printer or a local printer. This is accomplished by either loading the CAPTURE program or unloading it with the ENDCAP program. Such memory resident programs also use memory that then cannot be used by the primary application. General purpose resident programs such as Sidekick can consume a large amount of memory, too much for some other programs to run in what is left. In addition, memory resident programs often collide with each other or with the primary application, causing a system crash. For example, many programs require a mouse and a memory resident mouse driver program, but others such as Microsoft Windows are capable of running without a memory resident mouse driver program and will crash if one is present. If the user is not permitted to install memory resident programs as they are needed and remove them when possible, he or she will be forced to logout and re-boot the workstation frequently, causing frustration and delays.

Fortunately, complex menus can be created using only DOS batch commands. Consider the batch file, MYMENU.BAT below.

```
@ECHO OFF
IF "%1" == "" GOTO SCREEN
IF "%1" == "a" GOTO A
IF "%1" == "A" GOTO A
IF "%1" == "b" GOTO B
IF "%1" == "B" GOTO B
IF "%1" == "c" GOTO C
```

```
IF "%1" == "C" GOTO C
ECHO %1 is not a valid menu option.
goto screen
:A
CAPTURE
CD Z:\SHARESOF\WORDSTAR
WORDSTAR %2
CD\
ENDCAP
GOTO SCREEN
:B
CD Z:\SHARESOF\LOTUS
LOTUS %2
GOTO SCREEN
:C
CD Z:\SHARESOF\WP
WP %2
GOTO SCREEN
:SCREEN
CLS
ECHO Type MENU followed by:
ECHO ____________________________
ECHO   A    for WordStar
ECHO   B    for Lotus
ECHO   C    for WordPerfect
ECHO ____________________________
```

This batch file starts three different programs when the user types MYMENU A, MYMENU B, or MYMENU C. The menu screen itself is displayed when the user types MENU. Any DOS commands can be used to start the program or prepare for it. For example, the WORDSTAR option includes the CAPTURE and ENDCAP commands. The %1 in the first few lines of the batch file represents the item typed immediately after the word MENU. The %2 in the lines that call the application programs represents the second item typed after the word MYMENU. For instance, if the user types MYMENU A LETTER.DOC, the WORDSTAR program would execute with the word LETTER.DOC as its parameter. Notice that no PATH statement is used and no MAP statement is used. Instead, the drive letter Z, which is assumed to have been created earlier, is moved to point to the appropriate directory. When a search drive is created, it starts at the end of the alphabet to choose an available drive letter -- in this case drive letter Z. By simply changing the directory that drive letter Z points to, the search path is changed as well.

Hands-on Installing Shared Software and Creating Menus

Part I

Installing Microsoft Windows

To install shared software on a Novell network, you should login as the supervisor.

1. Type **Login Supervisor** and press the Enter key.
2. Type the password required to login as the supervisor.

We are going to install Windows as a shared program to be used by all network users. Therefore, a good place to put the Windows files is a subdirectory that branches off from the main directory or one that branches off from the public directory. For this exercise you will take the latter approach.

We may decide later to install additional shared software; therefore, we will create a subdirectory called SHARESOF. The subdirectory SHARESOF will contain subdirectories for each shared application that may need to be installed.

3. Type **cd\public** and press the Enter key.
4. Type **MD SHARESOF** and press the Enter key.

This creates the shared directory where all the applications subdirectories will reside.

5. Type **CD SHARESOF** and press the Enter key.
6. Type **MD WINDOWS** and press the Enter key.

This creates the Windows subdirectory.

7. Type **CD WINDOWS** and press the Enter key.
8. Type **COPY CON EXPALL.BAT** and press the Enter key.
9. Type **a:** and press the Enter key.
10. Type **for %%i in (*.*) do f:\public\sharesof\windows\expand %%i f:\public\sharesof\windows\%%i** and press the Enter key.
11. Type **f:** and press the Enter key.
12. Press the Ctrl and Z keys simultaneously.
13. Insert the Microsoft Windows Disk 2 in drive A.
14. Type **COPY A:EXPAND.EXE F:\PUBLIC\SHARESOF\WINDOWS** and press the Enter key.

15. Insert the Microsoft Windows Disk 1 in drive A.
16. Type **EXPALL A:*.* F:\PUBLIC\SHARESOF\WINDOWS** and press the [Enter ←] key.
17. Place the Microsoft Windows Disk 2 in drive A and repeat step 16.
18. Repeat step 17 for the remaining disks of Microsoft Windows.

After the last disk is copied to the file server, the files installed need to be made Shareable and Read Only.

19. Type **flag f:\public\sharesof\windows*.* shareable,read-only** and press the [Enter ←] key.

Installing Windows in Users' Disks

Microsoft Windows is now installed in the file server under the subdirectory Windows. The actual path to the Windows files is

f:\public\sharesof\windows.

Users will need only a few of the files residing in the above directory in order to use the application. These files will reside in the user's directory or on the hard disk. To prepare Windows in a user directory or hard disk follow the steps below.

1. Login to the network with the user name and password.
2. Type **cd\public\sharesof\windows** and press the [Enter ←] key.
3. Type **setup/n** and press the [Enter ←] key.
4. Press the [Enter ←] key.

The computer will respond with a default path and directory suggesting where files should reside.

5. Type the path and name of the directory where Windows will be installed. In this example we assume that the user has a hard disk on his or her workstation. Therefore, type **c:\windows** and press the [Enter ←] key.
6. Continue to follow the installation instructions displayed on the screen by the setup program. You will need to verify the equipment that the setup program thinks you have and plan to use with Windows. If there are no hardware problems, Windows will install some required files on the user's disk and the installation will stop normally.

To facilitate using the Windows program, an entry should be made in the login script for this user. This entry will map a search drive to the Windows subdirectory. This helps in accessing the shared files required to run the application.

7. Logout of the user account and login as a supervisor.
8. Type **SYSCON** and press the Enter key.
9. Highlight User Information from the SYSCON menu and press the Enter key.
10. Highlight the name of the user to receive the changes in the login script and press the Enter key.
11. Highlight Login Script and press the Enter key.
12. Type **MAP S4:SYS:\PUBLIC\SHARESOF\WINDOWS** and highlight Yes when asked if you want to save the changes.
13. Press the esc key four times.
14. Highlight Yes when asked if you want to exit SYSCON.

Windows is now installed. To access it, the user types

W: and press the Enter key.

WIN and press the Enter key.

After exiting Windows, the user needs to type

F: and press the Enter key.

CD\PUBLIC and press the Enter key.

To make it a little easier, a batch file as the one below can be placed in the PUBLIC directory and be given the attributes Shareable and Read Only. The batch file is

```
W:
WIN
F:
CD\PUBLIC
```

Part II

The Novell Menu System

The following instructions offer practice in using the Novell menu program.

1. Boot the workstation, if not already on, with the appropriate network boot disk by placing the disk in drive A and simultaneously pressing the Ctrl, alt, and delete keys. Enter the date and time if prompted.
2. The network driver programs should have been loaded by the AUTOEXEC.BAT file on the diskette. If they were not, type **IPX** and press the Enter key. Then type **NETX** and the Enter key. NETX can be replaced with the appropriate network shell program for your memory configuration and DOS version.

3. Type **F:** and press the [Enter] key.
4. Type **LOGIN** followed by your supervisor-equivalent login name and press the [Enter] key.
5. Type the password for this account, and press the [Enter] key.
6. Type **CD** followed by your account name and press the [Enter] key. For instance if the account name is JSMITH, the command would be CD\JSMITH followed by the [Enter] key.
7. A menu file can be created with any ASCII text editor or by using the DOS COPY CON command. If you do not have an appropriate text editor, type COPY CON MYMENU.MNU and press the [Enter] key.
8. Type the following lines, either imeadiately following the COPY CON MYMENU.MNU command or in your text editor. Type each line exactly as it appears, pressing the [Enter] key at the end of each line.

```
%Available Options,10,20
1. Syscon
   SYSCON
2. Fconsole
   FCONSOLE
3. Other Options
   %Other Options
%Other Options,17,60
1. Directory
   DIR @1"Directory of"
   PAUSE
2. Check Disk
   CHKDSK @1"Chkdsk"
   PAUSE
```

9. If you are using the COPY CON MYMENU.MNU command, hold down the [Ctrl] key and press the [Z] key. If you are using a text editor, save the file under the name MYMENU.MNU.
10. Type **MENU MYMENU** and press the [Enter] key. The Available Options menu should appear as it does in Fig. 13-10.
11. With the the Syscon option highlighted, press the [Enter] key. Syscon's main menu should appear.
12. Press the [esc] key, then the [Y] and [Enter] keys. You should return to your menu.
13. Press the [3] key then the [Enter] key. The Other Options menu should appear in the lower right of the screen as it does in Fig. 13-11.
14. Highlight the Check Disk option and press the [Enter] key. The Chkdsk : prompt should appear at the bottom of the screen as in Fig. 13-12.

15. Ensure that a diskette is in drive A and type **A:**, then press the [Enter] key. The CHKDSK program should run and display data about your diskette.
16. Press any key to return to the Other Options menu.
17. Press the [esc] key to return to the Available Options menu.
18. Press the [esc] key.
19. Press the [Y] key, then the [Enter] key to exit your menu.
20. To end this session, type **LOGOUT** and press the [Enter] key.

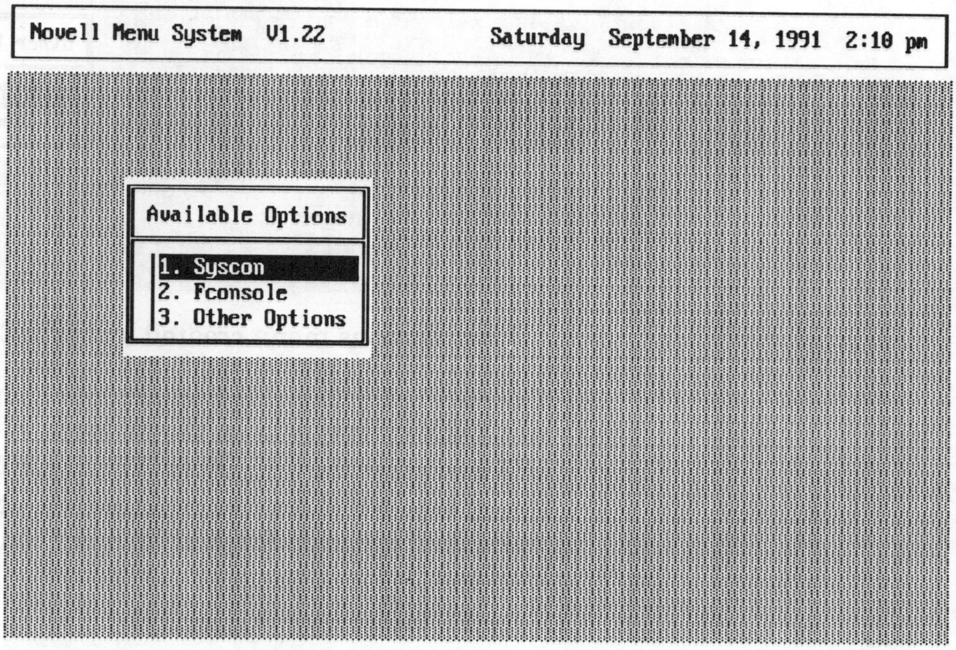

Fig. 13-10. Available options menu created by the MYMENU.MNU

Batch Files

The following steps demonstrate how some of the same features can be built into a batch file rather than the Novell menu program. It is often necessary to use batch files, even if they are not as attractive as the menus created with MENU.EXE.

1. Boot the workstation, if not already on, with the appropriate network boot disk, by placing the disk in drive A and simultaneously pressing the [Ctrl], [alt], and [delete] keys. Enter the date and time if prompted.

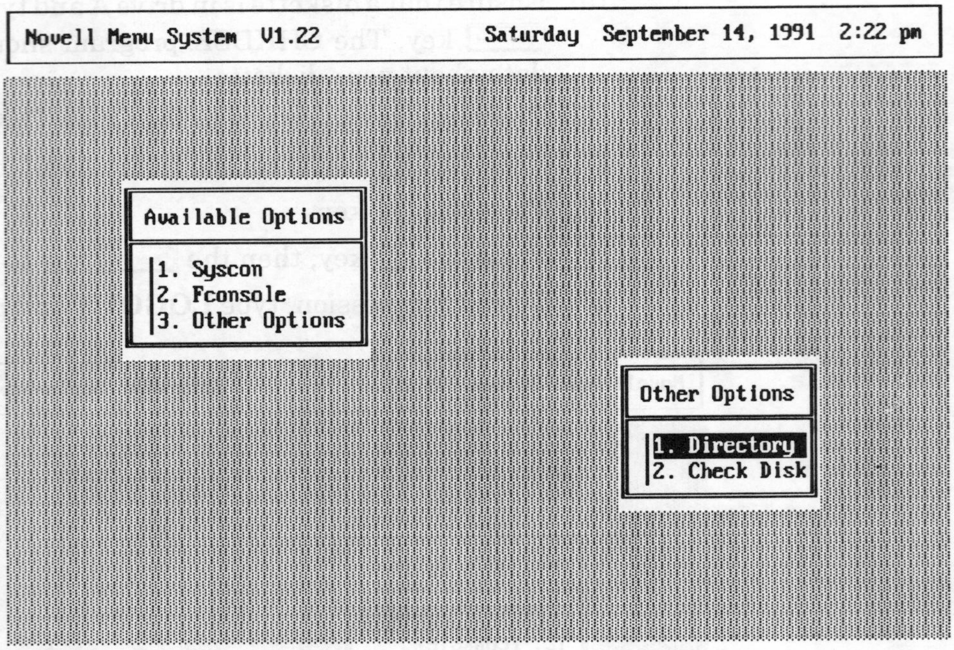

Fig. 13-11. Other Options menu created by MYMENU.MNU

2. The network driver programs should have been loaded by the AUTOEXEC.BAT file on the diskette. If they were not, type **IPX** and press the Enter key. Then type **NETX** and press the Enter key. NETX can be replaced with the appropriate network shell program for your memory configuration and DOS version.
3. Type **F:** and press the Enter key.
4. Type **LOGIN** followed by your supervisor-equivalent login name and press the Enter key.
5. Type the password for this account, and press the Enter key.
6. Type **CD** followed by your account name and press the Enter key. For instance if the account name is JSMITH, the command would be CD\JSMITH followed by the Enter key.
7. The batch file can be created with any ASCII text editor or by using the DOS COPY CON command. If you do not have an appropriate text editor, type **COPY CON M.BAT** and press the Enter key.
8. Type the following lines, either immediately following the COPY CON M.BAT command or in your text editor. Type each line exactly as it appears, pressing the Enter key at the end of each line.

@ECHO OFF
IF "%1" == "" GOTO SCREEN
IF "%1" == "a" GOTO A

```
IF "%1" == "A" GOTO A
IF "%1" == "b" GOTO B
IF "%1" == "B" GOTO B
IF "%1" == "c" GOTO C
IF "%1" == "C" GOTO C
ECHO %1 is not a valid menu option.
goto screen
:A
SYSCON
GOTO SCREEN
:B
FCONSOLE
GOTO SCREEN
:C
CHKDSK %2 %3
GOTO SCREEN
:SCREEN
CLS
ECHO Type M followed by:
ECHO ________________
ECHO   A         Syscon
ECHO   B         Fconsole
ECHO   C drive:  Chkdsk
ECHO ________________
```

9. If you are using the COPY CON M.BAT command, hold down the Ctrl key and press the Z key. If you are using a text editor, save the file under the name M.BAT.

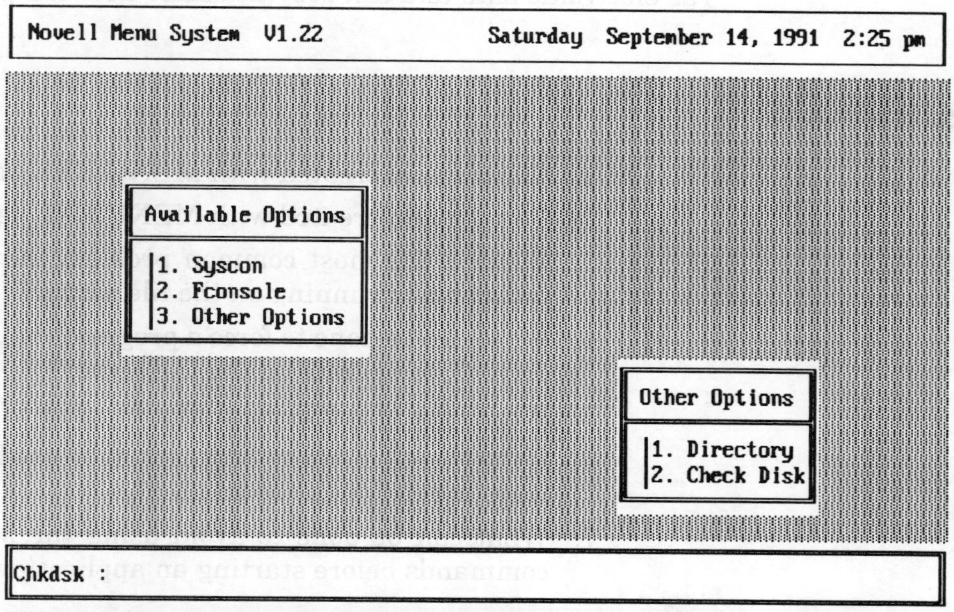

Fig. 13-12. Screen displaying the Chkdsk: prompt

10. Type **M** and press the Enter key. A menu should appear at the top of the screen.
11. Type **M A** and press the Enter key. Syscon's main menu should appear.
12. Press the esc key and then press the Enter key. The batch file menu should be displayed.
13. To end this session, type **LOGOUT** and press the Enter key.

Summary

The efficiently installed network is useless without easy access to the application programs it is intended to deliver. Often this implies that a menu system is needed to allow users to select the programs they need. Novell supplies a program that can be used to create such menus, but it does not work in all situations. Often, batch files must be used instead.

Most programs can be put into one of three categories: network incompatible, network compatible, and network aware. The network incompatible software might be installed on the workstation's local hard disk where it could be included in the menu system. Network compatible programs are often the easiest to install but are the most dangerous from a legal perspective, because a copy of the software must be purchased for each user accessing the program on the server. Network aware software often eliminates the legal issue by using the network to restrict the number of users accessing it. Network aware programs can also offer features such as electronic mail and can provide easier network printing.

Questions

1. Can a menu created with MENU.EXE have submenus?
2. Can a menu created with MENU.EXE call a batch file?
3. What is the most common problem that makes a program incapable of running on the file server?
4. What can be done to force a program that looks for its files on drive C, to operate on the file server?
5. What type of software cannot be used with MENU.EXE?
6. If the Novell menu system cannot be used, what are two other ways menus might be created?
7. What can be done to avoid using the MAP and the PATH commands before starting an application in a menu?

Projects

Objective

The following projects provide additional practice installing application software in a Novell based network. In addition, the projects provide practice creating menus.

Project 1. Installing Microsoft Excel on the File Server

Excel is a spreadsheet developed by Microsoft Corporation to run under the Microsoft Windows environment. Before Excel can be installed, a shared version of Windows needs to be present in a network file server. Excel can be installed in a directory in the file server. Then it can be executed on any computer that has access to this file directory.

To install Excel on a Novell network server, the Microsoft Excel Setup program needs to be executed. When the Setup program asks for the name of a directory where Excel is to be installed, the name of a previously created and shareable directory has to be provided to the program.

All files in the above directory can have the attributes of Shareable, Execute, and Read Only. This will allow multiple network users to access the program simultaneously.

In addition to using Novell's network security mechanisms to protect Excel generated documents, users can provide additional safeguards using one or more of the following methods:

1. Allow only authorized users to open a document. This is done by saving the document with a password using the Save As command. Only people that are given the password can access the document.
2. Prevent unauthorized editing of a document. Using the Format Cell Protection command, cells can be locked. Then using the Options Protect Document command, the document should be given a password for further security.
3. Hide cells by setting the column width or row height to zero for the columns containing the cells to be protected.

Project 2. Installing Microsoft Word for Windows on the File Server

Microsoft Word for Windows is a word processor that runs under the Microsoft Windows environment. The Word program files can be stored in a shareable directory in the file server. Any workstation that has access to the directory can run the Word program.

For Word to work properly, an entry needs to be made in the file WIN.INI that indicates the Word options. Word also has its own version of WIN.INI. It is called WINWORD.INI. This file contains the settings for some Word menus and utilities.

Microsoft Word for Windows looks for WINWORD.INI in the directory specified in WIN.INI, the Word directory, or the directory from which Word was executed. If it doesn't find one, it will create it. Finally, the entry "NOVELLNET=YES" needs to be added to the Word for Windows section of the WIN.INI file.

Project 3. Creating Directories and Menus

1. A company has three divisions, Sales, Manufacturing, and Business Services. The Sales division has two departments, Accounting and Transportation. The Manufacturing division has three departments, Accounting, Transportation, and Quality Control. The Business Services division has three departments, Accounting, Personnel, and Secretarial. Each division stores its own data but they share all the software possible. Draw a directory structure that might be suitable for this company's file server.
2. In this company, the Business Services division collects all the data it needs from the other divisions directly from their directories. The other divisions, however, should not be able to read each other's data or modify Business Services' data. Write the trustee rights that should be given to a typical user from each of the divisions.
3. Use the MENU program to create a menu that provides access to at least three other programs.
4. Create a menu that prompts the user for a local drive to be mapped to a network directory. The options should be as follows:

   a. Map drive A: to the LOGIN directory.

   b. Map drive B: to the LOGIN directory.

   c. Map drive C: to the LOGIN directory.

   d. Delete local drive mapping.

14

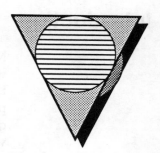

Additional Connectivity Topics

Objectives

1. Understand the concept of electronic mail and know its importance in the business environment.
2. Understand bulletin boards and their use in the business environment.
3. Recognize the importance of media conversion and file transfer.
4. Know the different types of media conversion problems.
5. Understand different techniques for solving media conversion problems.

Key Terms

- Bulletin Board
- E-mail
- Electronic Transfer
- File Transfer
- Information Service
- Media Conversion
- X.400 Standard
- X.25 Standard

Introduction

Many topics related to network use are becoming commonplace in the work environment. These items include electronic mail, electronic bulletin boards, and facsimile technology. Even though these subjects were not part of the mainstream of corporate America until recently, they are quickly making an impact on the way we perform electronic transactions with the personal computer.

These topics are difficult to place in a traditional book on data communications, even in the new networking topics. Therefore, they are treated independently in this chapter. However, it should be noted that such applications are quickly becoming part of the daily routines that we perform in our professional and personal lives.

Electronic Mail

Computer networks provide the necessary tools for a new type of industry -- electronic mail services. The main function of electronic mail services is to serve as a centralized clearing house for electronic messages. These messages can be grouped according to the purpose for which they are intended. Some of these are:

1. E-mail.
2. Electronic data interchange.
3. Electronic fund transfer.

E-mail

Electronic mail (e-mail) provides the ability to transmit written messages over short or long distances instantaneously through the use of a microcomputer or terminal attached to a communication network. The people communicating through electronic mail do not have to be on-line at the same time. Each can leave messages to the other and retrieve the replies at later times. Fig. 14-1 shows the screen for a commercial e-mail service (used by the Prodigy service).

Electronic mail has the capability to forward messages to different locations, send word processor or spreadsheet documents to any user of the network, and transmit the same message to more than one user by using a mail list. A mail list contains the names and electronic mailbox addresses of people that the message is sent to. The electronic mail system reads the names and addresses from the list and sends the message to all users on the mail list. Electronic mail services improve corporate and individual communications significantly.

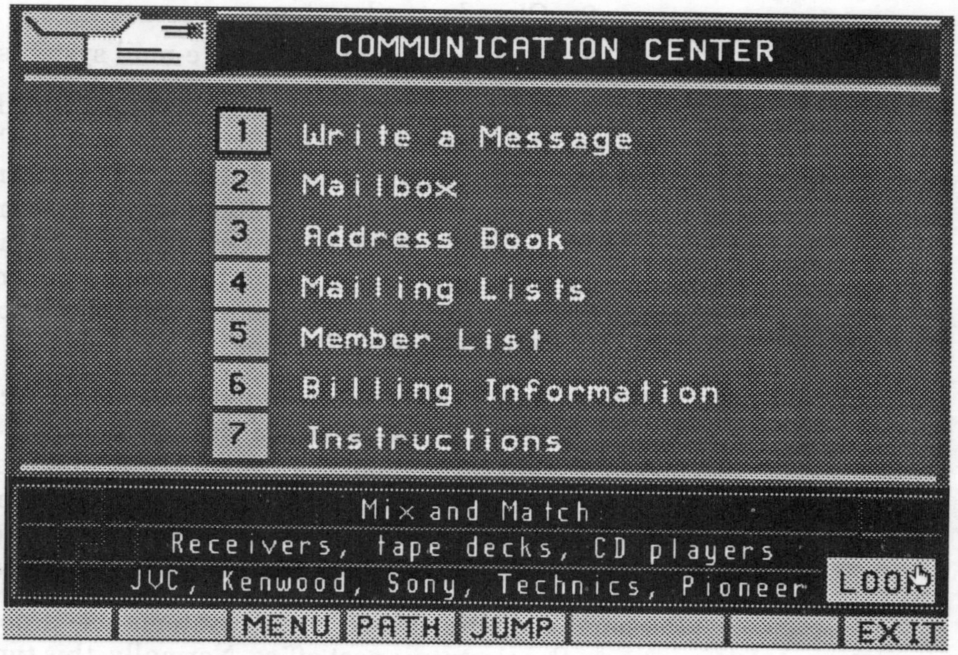

Fig. 14-1. E-mail screen for a commercial information service

Electronic Data Interchange

Electronic data interchange is computer-to-computer communications among different enterprises for the purposes of performing daily business operations. Corporations send inventory information to suppliers, invoices to customers, and checks to banks, to name but a few uses. Before the advent of computer networks, all transactions were performed by using paper and postal delivery. With electronic data interchange, all of these business transactions can be performed electronically and almost instantaneously.

Electronic Fund Transfer

The ability to transfer funds electronically from one financial institution to another has become a necessity in today's banking world. Commercial banks transfer millions of dollars daily through their electronic fund transfer (EFT) system. The large number of transactions that are made every day by banks require the use of computers and communication networks to increase speed and cost efficiency.

Types of E-mail Systems

E-mail systems can be categorized into

1. Public and private commercial e-mail carriers.

2. Closed e-mail systems.
3. Personal computer based e-mail systems.

Private commercial e-mail carriers are specialized carriers that lease telephone lines from public carriers such as AT&T or set up their own networks. They support selected users that perform business with the network company directly and often provide customized enhancements applicable to needs of their users. One example of a private carrier is IBM. Public carriers, on the other hand, take calls from any user that needs or wants to access the network. Some examples of public carriers are GTE Telenet and Tymeshare's Tymnet.

A closed e-mail system allows individuals within a company to exchange messages. It is called a closed system because the documents and messages sent throughout the system are available only to the employees of the company. In many cases, a minicomputer or mainframe acts as the e-mail server and router. Any terminal or microcomputer attached to the server can access the e-mail system and send or receive messages.

Personal computer based e-mail systems use a personal or microcomputer as the electronic post office. Normally, this type of e-mail system is part of a PC-based local area network. A workstation on the network can send any type of electronic message to another workstation by "attaching" the message to the address of the receiving microcomputer. The address in most instances is nothing more than the network name of the user that is to receive the message.

The X.400 Standard

As the makers of e-mail system proliferate, several international associations have created standards that allow different e-mail systems to communicate with each other. One of the fastest emerging and most important standards is called X.400. It was established by the Comite Consultatif Internationale de Telegraphique et Telephonique (CCITT). Many vendors, including IBM, Telenet, and DEC have announced support for this standard, which is used extensively in the international community.

X.400 specifies data transmission in the form of messages and the information that accompanies the message. Using the X.400 communication standards, network nodes can send and receive information from one another without the need of a central host computer. X.400 also allows for the transmission of multimedia messages such as voice, graphics, and FAX messages.

Some of the services provided by the X.400 standard are:

1. Message identification.
2. Time of submission.
3. Indication of the type of content.

4. Access management.
5. Delivery notification.
6. Nondelivery notification.
7. Multiple destination delivery.
8. Importance indication.
9. Primary and copy receivers indication.
10. Reply requested indication.
11. Encryption indication.

The X.25 Standard

The CCITT has also published a wide area network standard called the X.25. The X.25 standard governs much of the public bulletin board industry and is used extensively in the United States by most public data networks, such as Tymenet and Telenet.

A network using X.25 is a packet switching network. The data is placed into packets before transmission across the WAN. In addition, the X.25 protocol is "transparent." As long as the receiving computer understands the data sent by the sender computer, the communication takes place.

This transparency allows X.25 packets to be encapsulated in other protocols such as IBM's SNA. This allows diverse systems to use the same wide area network system.

In addition, a LAN may access public and private WANs through the use of an X.25 gateway. Most X.25 gateways for a PC-based LAN consist of a PC, a wide area communications board, communications software, and a synchronous modem.

Functions of an E-mail Package

All e-mail systems provide a basic set of features that are composed of creating, sending, receiving, reading, and printing documents. In addition to these functions, most e-mail systems have enhanced capabilities that vary according to the maker of the product. Also, many new systems have a help feature that provides a list and explanation of all features available.

Although the following list does not contain all features available in sophisticated systems, it describes some of the commonly available services that most new e-mail programs offer.

1. Create a message. Messages need to be created before they can be sent. Although large documents will probably be created using an independent word processor, e-mail packages have text editing capabilities that allow for the creation of small

documents or messages that can then be sent electronically to other users.

2. Send a message. Messages and documents can be sent through e-mail systems with different levels of priority. Most systems support first class, registered, and normal mail. A document sent with the registered mark in it may require an acknowledgment of the recipient, in the form of a message back to the sender. In this manner, the sender will know the time and date the receiver read the message.

   In addition, mail can be sent regular, express, or immediately. Immediate mail is delivered within seconds of being sent. Express mail is collected electronically at various points and forwarded to its destination at regular intervals through the day or when the activity on the network has declined. Regular mail is collected electronically and sent to its destination when the charges are the lowest or the activity of the network is low.

3. Receive a message. Documents sent electronically are placed in the receiver's "electronic mailbox." In some systems, this mailbox is called a "basket." There could be incoming baskets and outgoing baskets. Mail can be read from the incoming basket and sent from the outgoing basket. Notification of new mail in the incoming basket is done automatically on most systems by displaying a message on the screen when the user logs in.

4. Read the message. Messages can be read by the recipient in the order that they reach the incoming basket or in some prioritized order. Also, messages can be deleted or stored for further reading.

5. Print the message. Messages can be printed provided that a network printer is available or that a printer is attached to the terminal of microcomputer that is being used for communications.

New e-mail systems contain some additional features. Some of these are:

1. Time of submission.
2. Indication of the type of content.
3. Delivery notification.
4. Nondelivery notification.
5. Multiple destination delivery.
6. Importance indication.
7. Primary and copy receivers indication.
8. Reply requested indication.

Choosing an E-mail System

Although three different types of e-mail systems are available, some basic questions should be answered before an organization purchases or leases e-mail services. Even though the type of questions that a service provider must answer are complex and extensive, the following list provides a general framework by which a decision could be made.

1. What other mail system will you need to communicate to?
2. Can mail be prioritized?
3. What tools are available for finding a message?
4. What security measures are available to keep the communications private?
5. What word processors does the system support?
6. What other software programs does it support (e.g., Lotus 123, graphics programs, etc.)?
7. What are the workstation requirements?
8. Does it support office functions such as electronic calendars, automatic forwarding, alerts and alarms, etc.
9. What is the speed of transmission?
10. What is the monthly fee?
11. Are there any surcharges?
12. What "user friendly" features does it have?
13. Can users check their mail from remote locations?
14. What backup options are available?

Bulletin Boards

The electronic bulletin board system (BBS or EBBS) consists of a computer system that is used to store, retrieve, and catalog messages sent in by the general public with the use of a terminal or microcomputer and a modem. The telephone company provides the link between the person using the BBS and the computer that is the host of the BBS. The main reason for their existence is for people to leave messages to others. Also, some BBS are now being used for group conferencing. They offer a variety of messages and services to their users. Some of these services are electronic "chat" with other users, making airline reservations, playing games, and sending and receiving messages.

Types of Bulletin Boards

Computerized bulletin boards offer a wide variety of services and physical setups. However, they can be categorized into three major areas:

1. Large commercial bulletin boards. Sometimes called information utility services, this type of bulletin board offers both general and specialized information that is organized and cross-referenced, much like subjects are in libraries. Items are organized into databases. These BBS offer several categories of services such as access to news, legal libraries, stock prices, electronic mail services, conferencing, and games.
2. Local area public bulletin boards. This type of bulletin board is a dial-up system that serves a limited geographical area. They are operated by individuals out of their homes and by local computer clubs. They act as message clearing houses for individuals with common interests. Typically there are no fees for the use of this type of bulletin board, and if a fee is charged, it is nominal.
3. Specialized bulletin boards. This type of bulletin board is set up by corporations to serve a particular need of the company employees. For example, a company may set up a BBS so its sales agents can obtain instant communication with other personnel.

Components of an Electronic Bulletin Board

All electronic bulletin boards have several elements in common. These elements include:

1. Modem. A modem (or several modems) is necessary to allow users to connect to the EBBS. The caller will also be required to have a modem connected to his or her computer to perform the connection.
2. Telephone lines. Commercial EBBS may have hundreds of modems, while local or PC-based EBBS may have only one or two phone lines. The phone lines become the transmission medium for the connection between modems. Although some EBBS are attached to networks and don't use the public phone carriers as the physical connecting media, most EBBS use the phone lines as their transmission medium.
3. High-capacity computer. The EBBS would not be possible without the use of a computer. The size of storage that the computer possesses is important for the electronic bulletin board service. The larger the disk space, the longer the messages that can be stored, and the more messages that can be stored.

4. EBBS software. All the hardware needs to be controlled by software. The EBBS software not only controls communications, but facilitates the management of the entire operation. Good bulletin board software contains a series of utilities that facilitate the maintenance, operation, backup, and security of the system.
5. System operator. The system operator (sysop) is responsible for installing software, setting up the EBBS menu, answering questions, solving problems, and monitoring the activity of the bulletin board.

Services Provided

The services provided by an electronic bulletin board differ according to the type of company that provides the service. Commercial bulletin board services provide most of the services listed:

1. Message centers.
2. News services.
3. Shopping services.
4. Specialized clubs.
5. Entertainment services (games, etc.).
6. Electronic mail.
7. Banking services.
8. Travel services.
9. Various professional services.
10. Conferencing.
11. Electronic libraries.

Popular Electronic Bulletin Board Systems

Quite a few commercial and public BBS are in operation across the USA. Some offer a large variety of services and are also called information services. Some of the best known are

1. Dow Jones News/Retrieval Services
2. CompuServe
3. GEnie
4. DIALOG
5. Prodigy

Dow Jones News/Retrieval Services

The Dow Jones News/Retrieval Services is a collection of business, economic, financial, investment, and general-interest news oriented toward the uses and needs of businesses. It is operated by the Wall Street Journal.

It contains the full text of several major business publications such as the Wall Street Journal and Barron's. This service provides some of the most comprehensive business and financial news of all information services in the industry.

In addition, it provides its members with brokerage services, e-mail facilities, national and international news, travel information services, weather, and other general interest services.

To sign up for this information service system, call or write to

Dow Jones News/Retrieval
Dept LB, Box 300
Princeton, NJ 08543
609-520-4650

CompuServe

CompuServe Information Service is a public on-line service that provides private communications, database services, network services, and general interest services for businesses, financial institutions, government agencies, and individuals of all types.

The range of topics available is rather large and includes e-mail, news, sports, weather, travel, electronic shopping, entertainment, home services, family services, education, technology services, and business services. In addition, CompuServe is used as a gateway to other services.

To sign up for this information service system, call or write to

CompuServe
5000 Arlington Centre Blvd.
Columbus, OH 43220
800-848-8199

GEnie

GEnie is an acronym for General Electric Network for Information Exchange. It provides services for e-mail, news, entertainment, home services, reference services, business services, and other general interest services.

To sign up for this information service system, call or write to

GEnie
GE Information Services, Dept. 2B
401 North Washington St.
Rockville, MD 20850
800-638-936

DIALOG

DIALOG provides access to over 150 million records of information. They include financial information, statistical information, and bibliographic reference information. The information provided by DIALOG comes directly from private, public, and government publishers.

To sign up for this information service system, call or write to

DIALOG Information Services
3460 Hillview Ave.
Palo Alto, CA 94304
800-334-2564

Prodigy

Prodigy is a general information service provider with topics that include news, sports, finance services, business services, e-mail, recreational services, travel, home banking, electronic shopping, access to the Dow Jones News/Retrieval, bibliographic information, and other services.

Prodigy is one of the fastest growing information services, and it has been geared toward the home user that wants to explore and use professional services at low costs. Fig. 14-2 shows the entry screen for this service during a particular day.

To sign up for this information service system, call or write to

Prodigy Membership Services
445 Hamilton Ave.
White Plains, NY 10601
800-284-5933

Media Conversion and File Transfer

Media conversion refers to the transfer of data and information from one physical entity to another. A document typed on a word processor may need to be shared with other users that have incompatible systems. In such situations, time and effort can be saved if there is some methodology by which the document can be transferred from one system to a different system without having to retype the document and with minimal effort.

Fig. 14-2. Entry screen for the commercial information service PRODIGY

Incompatibility creates problems in the following situations:

1. New computers are added to an office, and the new machines are incompatible with the old machines at the operating system level or at the physical (hardware) level.
2. Various departments or users within a department use different and incompatible equipment.
3. Users produce documents on home computers or portables that have disks that can't be used at the office.
4. Documents need to be transferred among companies that have different equipment.
5. Users have the same equipment, but use different software programs to produce their documents. A document from one package is often incompatible with other packages.

Conversion Problems

Physical Media Conversion

Since the introduction of the first personal computer, different types of storage media have been available with the introduction of new advanced products. Initially, personal computers used magnetic tape (cassette) to store documents. Then the first floppy disks were available in the Apple II, IBM PC, and other home computers. These initial disks were capable of storing data up to 160,000 bytes per disk. However, data written on a disk by one type of computer (e.g., IBM PC) could not be read by drives on a different computer (e.g., Apple II). There wasn't an effective means by which documents could be easily exchanged among users of the different computers.

In today's business world, the most common types of media conversion that are required among PC users are as follows:

1. Conversion from an 8 inch disk to a 5 1/4 inch disk (IBM format).
2. Conversion from a 5 1/4 inch disk to a 3 1/2 inch disk (IBM format).
3. Conversion from a 5 1/4 inch disk low-density to a 5 1/4 inch disk high-density (IBM format).
4. Conversion from a 3 1/2 inch disk double-density to a 3 1/2 inch high-density (IBM format)
5. Conversion between IBM formats and Apple Macintosh format.

The incompatibility between the IBM format and the Apple formats lies in the process used to store data on the disk by the respective computer manufacturers. IBM and Apple use different techniques for placing document data on the floppy disks. Therefore, a document saved with an IBM version of a word processor can't be read directly by the same Apple version of the word processor.

Document Conversion

Although users may use the same computer to produce documents, they may use different types of software products. Each document-generating program has it owns unique manner of formatting and saving the document with formatting codes.

As an example, consider a document created with WordPerfect. If this document needs to be incorporated into another document that is being prepared with Word, the formatting codes for bold face, underline, and so forth created with WordPerfect will not transfer to Word. Word will try to interpret the formatting codes as part of the data and produce a document that is incorrect. If the document is transferred without any formatting codes, then the problem of formatting is placed on a single user.

Protocol Conversion

Protocol conversion deals with documents that are transferred among computers that use different protocols such as ASCII and EBCDIC. Also, it applies to documents sent over communication lines. A document created on an ASCII based computer will have to be translated by some protocol converter before it can be understood properly by an EBCDIC based computer.

Solving Conversion Problems

The easiest way to solve conversion problems is to have a single vendor for all equipment used in the office. In many situations, though, this is impossible. Even with a single vendor, there are file and media conversion problems. However, a single vendor environment goes a long way in minimizing conversion problems. Some solutions to the conversion problems outlined above are presented next.

1. Conversion from an 8 inch disk to a 5 1/4 inch disk (IBM format).

   Conversion from a 5 1/4 inch disk to a 3 1/2 inch disk (IBM format).

   Conversion from a 5 1/4 inch disk low-density to a 5 1/4 inch disk high-density (IBM format).

   Conversion from a 3 1/2 inch disk double-density to a 3 1/2 inch high-density (IBM format).

   The easiest way to solve these problems is to have a machine with one type of drive (such as an 8 inch drive) and a drive of a different type (such as a 5 1/4 high-density drive). In this case, the data from one disk is copied to the other using the operating system commands for copying and data transfer. When two drives of the desired type are not available, telephone lines or direct connection through the RS-232 can be used, along with a communications program. Some projects in previous chapters describe how this process can be accomplished.

2. Conversion between IBM format and Apple Macintosh format. This type of conversion can be performed by using the Macintosh superdrive that is standard on all new Macintosh computers, and using the Apple file exchange program. By selecting the Apple File Exchange folder under the System Additions folder, a screen is displayed that shows on one side the files and folders on the Mac, and on the other files and directories on the IBM PC. Highlighting the names of the files to transfer and the direction of transfer, that is IBM->Mac or Mac->IBM, causes the transferring to take place.

   The above process works well when the number of files to be transferred is small. However, if a large number of files needs to be transferred between an IBM PC or compatible and a Macintosh, a commercial software product such as Maclink Plus/PC may prove to be a more efficient solution. This product allows an IBM PC or compatible and a Macintosh computer to transfer files using the telephone lines or a direct connection. The process for both options is the same, the only difference is that with the first a phone number must be dialed. The project at the end of this chapter uses this product to transfer documents between incompatible media.

3. Document conversion. Converting a document from one format to another can be accomplished with the use of format converting software. Several commercial software packages such as Keyword 7000 can convert a document from one format such as Wordstar to another format such as DisplayWrite.

   Additionally, some word processors, spreadsheets, and other document-generating software programs are capable of reading many different formats. This provides enhanced flexibility to the users since a document can be generated with one type of word processor and loaded into another without the loss of formatting.

4. Protocol conversion. Documents that are produced in one protocol can be transferred to another computer using a different protocol with the aid of a protocol converter. A protocol converter is a device that connects between a computer and the communication line to other systems. The protocol converter performs all the character conversions necessary for the receiving computer to obtain the proper codes for the characters that make up the document.

5. Hard copy to electronic format conversion. There are situations where a document that is already on paper needs to be converted into electronic format. One device that can be used for this purpose is a scanner. A scanner can transfer written text or a picture on paper into an electronic document. The document can be saved in a variety of formats and incorporated into other documents.

   Also, a figure or text scanned into an electronic document can be sent as a FAX document using a computer equipped with a FAX board. A FAX board allows a PC to act as a FAX machine. That is, it can send and receive documents, unattended, through the telephone lines. The main difference between a stand-alone FAX machine and a computer equipped with a FAX board lies in how the document is placed in the FAX machine for sending. A stand-alone FAX machine can receive documents that are on any type of paper. To send a FAX using a FAX board and a computer, the document must be first converted into electronic format.

Facsimile Technology and the Personal Computer

A facsimile (FAX) terminal is able to transmit an exact picture of a hard copy document over telephone lines anywhere in the world. It is a quick and inexpensive way to send documents any place where there is a telephone line and another FAX machine. In the earlier days of FAX machines, the speed of transmission was slow, documents were fed into the machine manually, and the quality of the output was poor. In newer facsimile machines, all of these problems have been corrected or improved.

FAX machines are divided into four major groups, according to their technology and speed.

1. Group 1 is the oldest of the FAX machines. It required manual document feed and manual communication links. It required between four and six minutes to send a document and the output quality was very poor.
2. Group 2 FAX machines were developed in the 1970s. They showed speed transmission improvements over group 1 machines. This type of facsimile could transmit a document in one to three minutes.
3. Group 3 FAX machines are high-speed terminals. They are capable of transmitting a document in less than a minute. Also, these types of machines have automatic document feeders, automatic dialing, automatic connection, laser quality output, and other advanced features.
4. Group 4 FAX machines are the latest generation of facsimile devices. They use digital telephone networks to increase the speed of transmission and the options available.

Most newer FAX machines are group 3 or 4. The group 3 machines can transmit a page in approximately one minute or less. Group 4 machines can transmit an 8 1/2 by 11 inch page in approximately 20 seconds. Additionally, group 4 FAX machines have a higher image transmission quality.

Signals from a digital facsimile device can be read into a computer and stored inside of it because they are made up of bits. This has led to the development of FAX boards that can be added to microcomputers. With these boards, any document created on a personal computer can be transmitted to any FAX machine through phone lines. Messages sent by FAX machines can also be received by the FAX boards inside microcomputers and a picture of the document can be stored on a disk or sent to an attached printer.

If a FAX board is used, documents that need to be sent must be scanned using a desktop scanner. The scanner will produced a graphical image and store it in the hard disk of the computer that contains the FAX board. Using software, the phone number of a receiving FAX machine or computer with a FAX board is dialed. After the receiving machine answers the phone call, the document is sent and printed on the FAX machine or stored in the local disk of the receiving computer.

If a document is produced with a software package that can create documents that are readable by the computer with the FAX board, then the scanner is not required. For example, a document can be created with a word processor or spreadsheet, using a computer with a FAX board. After the document is created and saved, it can be transmitted directly from the hard disk of the computer to a receiving FAX machine or computer equipped with a FAX board.

The Facsimile Transmission Process

To use a facsimile device the following equipment is required:

1. Two compatible units, one unit at the sending location and the other at the receiving location.
2. Two phone ports, one at the sending location and the other at the receiving location.
3. If the machines are not equipped with dialing and phone receiving capability, then two telephones will be required, one at the sending location and the other at the receiving location.
4. Paper for the sending and receiving documents. In some cases plain paper can be used; in others, special types of paper need to be used. It depends on the machines.

Transmitting a FAX Document

To transmit a document using facsimile equipment, the following steps can be taken:

1. Make sure that both units are powered and with paper.
2. Place the document to be sent in the transmitting or sending machine.
3. Using the phone capabilities of the FAX machine or a telephone attached to it, dial the phone number of the receiving FAX machine.
4. After a dial tone is received, press the Send button on the machine.
5. After the message has been received, hang up the telephone.

If a computer with a FAX board is used, the process is as follows:

1. Create the document and store it on the hard disk of the computer containing the FAX board.
2. Run the FAX communication software that comes with the FAX board.
3. Using the dialing utilities of the software, dial the phone of the receiving station. It doesn't matter whether the receiving station is a FAX machine or a computer equipped with a FAX board.
4. Use the command in the software to send the document.

The document will be read from the disk and sent through the phone lines to the receiving station.

Summary

New contemporary topics in networks include the use of electronic mail, bulletin boards, media conversion, and facsimile technology.

The main function of electronic mail services is to be a centralized clearing house for electronic messages. These messages can be grouped according to the type of purpose for which they are intended. These types are:

1. E-mail.
2. Electronic data interchange.
3. Electronic fund transfer.

Electronic mail (e-mail) provides the ability to transmit written messages over short or long distances instantaneously through the use of a microcomputer or terminal attached to a communication network. Electronic data interchange is computer-to-computer communications among different enterprises for the purposes of performing daily business operations. Electronic fund transfer is the ability of computer networks to perform financial transactions without the need to perform hard currency exchanges.

The electronic bulletin board system (BBS or EBBS) consists of a computer or microcomputer that is used to store, retrieve, and catalog messages sent in by the general public through their modems. The telephone company provides the link between the person using the BBS and the host computer of the BBS. The main reason BBSs exist is for people to leave messages for others. Also, some BBSs are now being used for group conferencing. They offer a variety of messages and services to their users.

Media conversion refers to the transfer of data and information from one physical entity to another. A document typed on a word processor may need to be shared with other users that have incompatible systems. In such situations, time and effort can be saved if there is some methodology by which the document can be transferred from one system to a different system easily, without having to retype the document.

A facsimile (FAX) terminal is able to transmit an exact picture of a hard copy document over telephone lines anywhere in the world. It is a quick and inexpensive way to send documents any place where there is a telephone line and another FAX machine. The speed, quality, and convenience has greatly improved since the early days of FAX machines.

Questions

1. What is e-mail?
2. What types of electronic mail are available to corporations?
3. What features can be found on most e-mail systems?
4. What is a bulletin board system?
5. What is an information service?
6. What functions are provided by commercial bulletin board systems?
7. Name four commercial information services.
8. What is the X.400 standard? Why is it important?
9. What is media conversion?
10. Describe two methods that can be used to transfer data between two incompatible machines.
11. What is the purpose of a FAX machine?
12. Briefly describe the different generations of FAX technology.

Project

File Transfer between an IBM PC and a Macintosh Using Maclink Plus/PC

The Maclink Plus/PC package contains all the materials required to perform file transfers between an IBM PC or compatible and a Macintosh computer. The connection to transfer the document can be either directly through a cable that connects both machines using their respective serial ports or through telephone lines and a pair of modems.

For this exercise, we will assume that the connection is made through the serial cables of both computers. Before the transfer can be made, the software must be installed in the Macintosh and the PC. The installation is accomplished through the following instructions.

1. Copy the Mac disk to the Apple File Exchange folder that is contained in the System Additions folder.
2. Copy the IBM PC disk to a subdirectory in the PC.

After the software is copied, the machines need to be linked together.

3. Using the serial cable provided, attach one end to the modem or printer port located on the back of the Macintosh.
4. Attach the other end to the serial port of the IBM PC.

Now you are ready to execute the programs that will allow you to transfer the files.

5. Access the folder that contains the Maclink Plus/PC files.

You will get a screen that contains a window showing the contents of the Apple File Exchange folder. Your screen will look like Fig. 14-3.

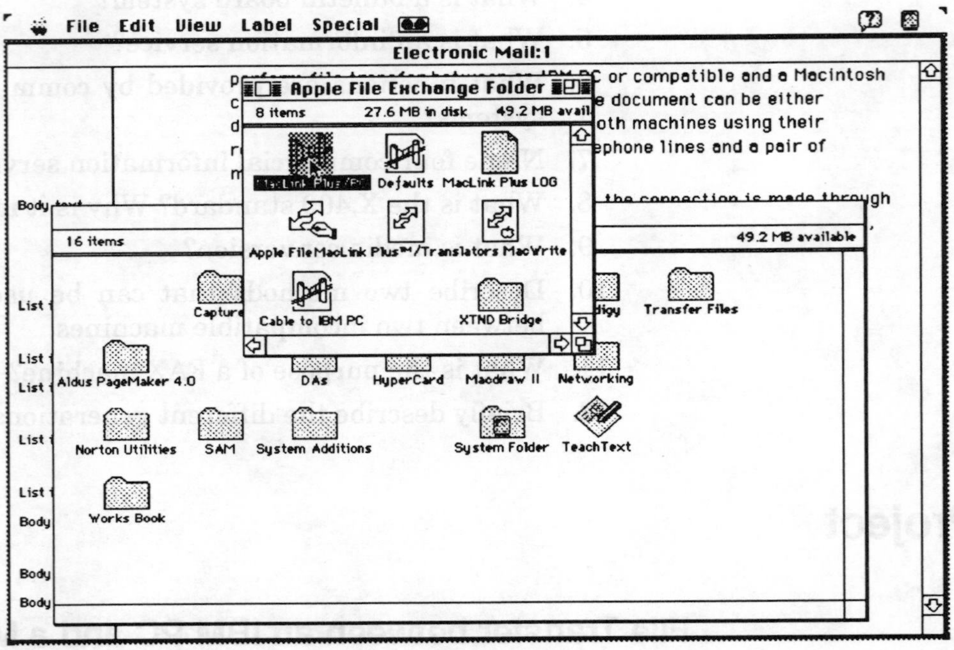

Fig. 14-3. The Apple File Exchange folder

6. Double click on the program icon Maclink Plus/PC.
7. The initial Maclink Plus/PC screen will appear.
8. Run the Maclink program in the PC by typing ML and pressing the ENTER key in the subdirectory containing the program.

The PC and the Mac need to have the same communication settings for them to work together. The Mac screen should look like Fig. 14-4. The modes of communication are Maclink Mode, Desktop Mode, Terminal Mode, and Maclink Answer Mode. For this exercise the Maclink Mode is the one you want. In this mode, files can be transferred and translated between your Mac and a remote computer running Maclink Plus software.

The Desktop Mode allows the translation of files using the Macintosh super drive. The Terminal Mode operates similarly to the Maclink Mode, except that it allows the connection of two computers using the telephone lines. The Answer Mode allows Maclink Plus running on the Mac to answer the call of another computer using Maclink Plus.

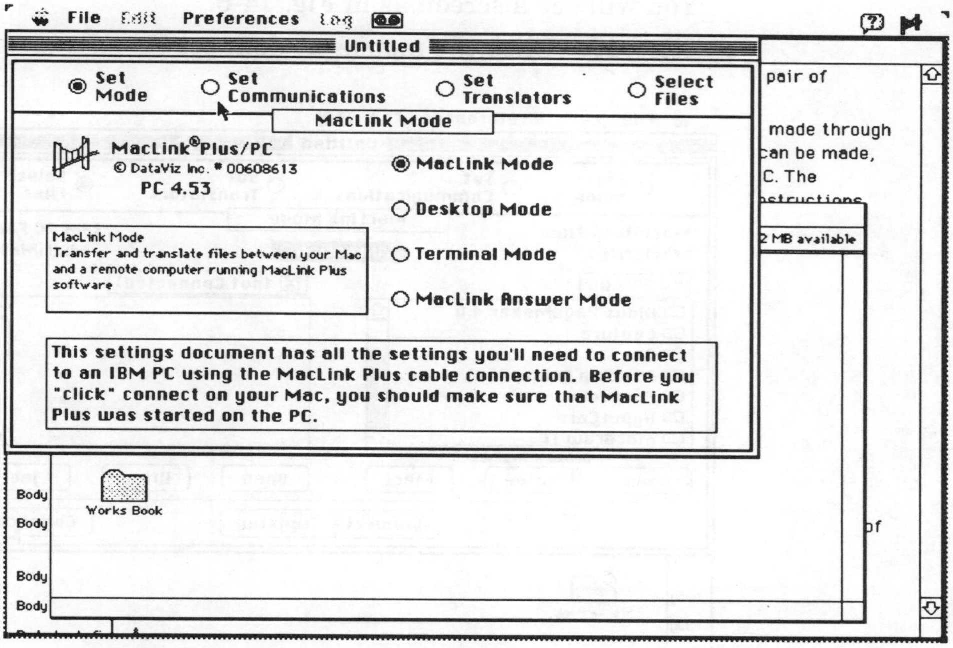

Fig. 14-4. The Maclink screen

9. Select Set Communications by clicking the mouse on this choice.
10. Make sure that the PC and the Mac have the same settings as in Fig. 14-5
11. Next click the mouse on Select Files.

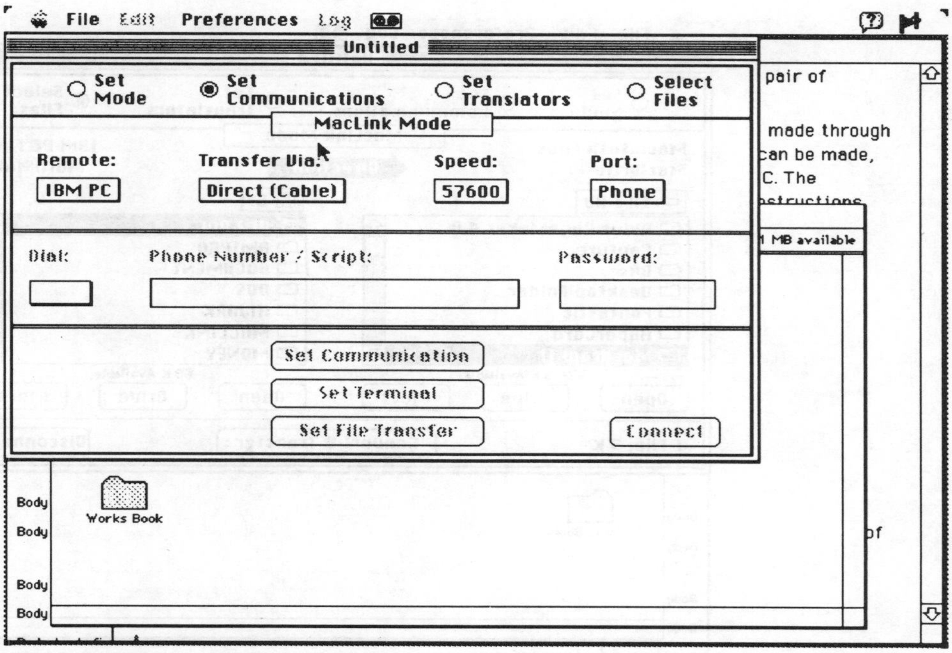

Fig. 14-5. Communication settings

You will see a screen as in Fig. 14-6.

12. Click the mouse on Connect

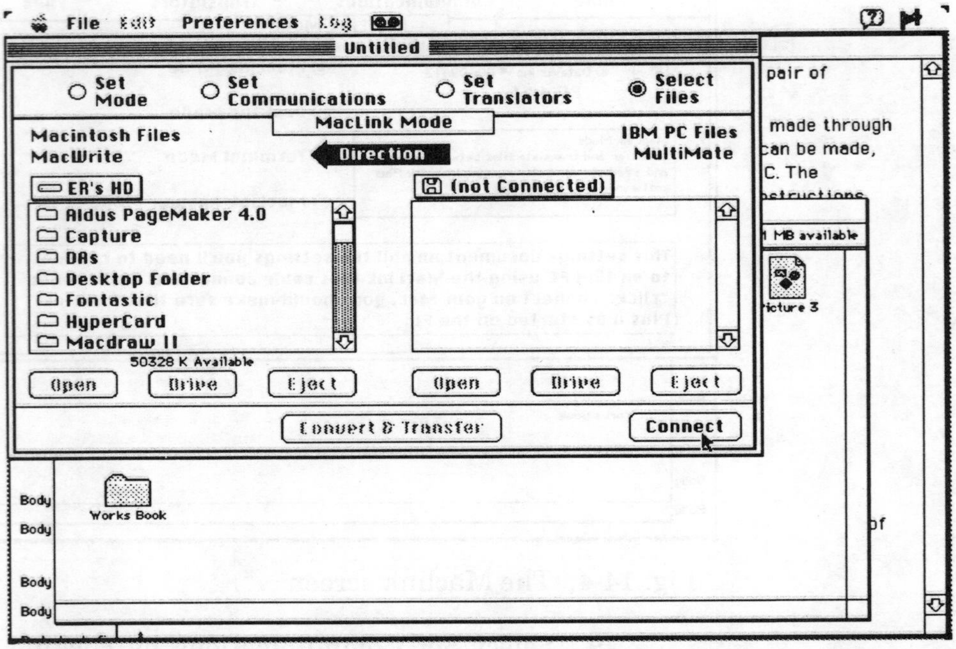

Fig. 14-6. Select files menu to initiate the file transfers

The next screen should look similar to Fig. 14-7. In the figure, the left side shows the hard disk and folders in the Macintosh. The right side displays the files on the PC's hard disk.

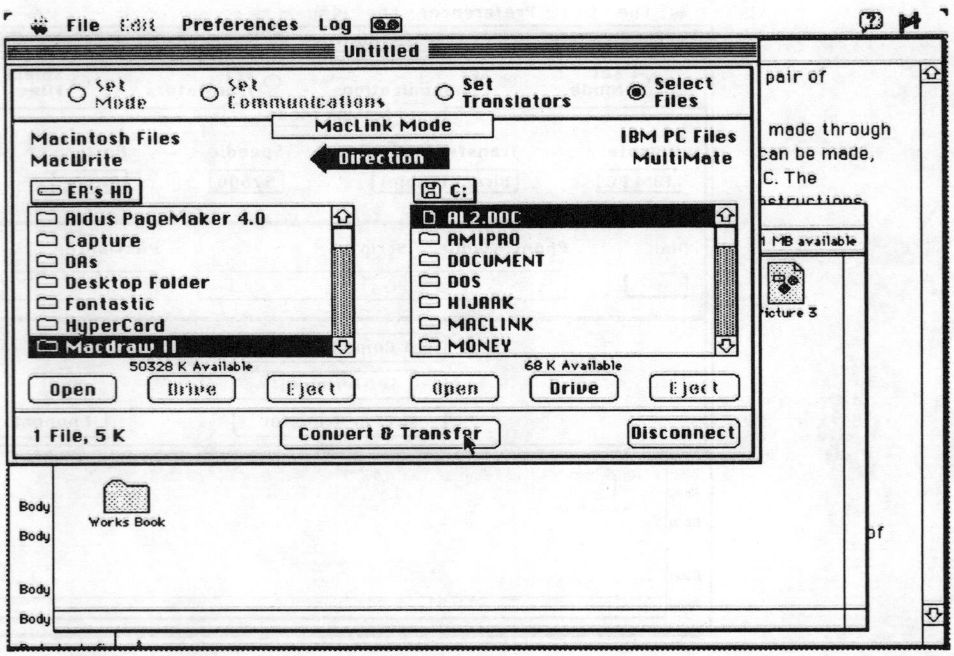

Fig. 14-7. Screen displaying files on the Macintosh and the PC

13. Select the file on the PC that you want to transfer to the Mac by clicking the mouse on it.
14. Select the folder in the Mac where the file will be placed by clicking the mouse on the folder's name.
15. Click the mouse on Convert & Transfer.

The file will be transferred from the PC to the Mac. To transfer from the Mac to the PC the process can be reversed by instructing the software in the Mac to answer the call of the PC. This is done by clicking the mouse on Maclink Answer Mode in the Mac and selecting connect from the PC console.

Appendix A

NetWare Commands, Rights, and Attributes Summary

The following tables display the most commonly used NetWare commands, rights, and attributes. There are four sets of tables:

Table 1 (a through d) displays the summary of the commands.

Table 2 displays the summary of NetWare rights.

Table 3 displays the summary of file attributes.

Table 4 displays the summary of directory attributes.

The first table indicates the command, followed by a code that indicates whether the command can be issued from a workstation or if it has to be given from the server. If the code is W, it indicates that the command can be given from a workstation. If it has a S, then it must be issued from the server. The third column provides a description of the command.

The second, third, and fourth tables contain only two columns each. The first column indicates the right or attribute, and the second column is a description of the right or attribute.

Command	W/S	Description
ATOTAL	W	Provides a summary of server resource usage
ATTACH	W	Connects to another server
BINDFIX	W	Repairs damaged bindery files
BINREST	W	Restores bindery files copied before running BINDFIX
BROADCAST	S	Sends a message to workstations
CAPTURE	W	Redirects output to a network printer
CASTOFF	W	Blocks the receipt of messages sent by workstations
CASTON	W	Enables the receipt of messages sent by workstations
CHKVOL	W	Display volume information
CLEAR MESSAGE	S	Clear the message area
CLEAR STATION	S	Disconnects a workstation from the server
COLORPAL	W	Sets up colors of Netware menus
CONFIG	S	Display the server's configuration
CONSOLE	W	Changes from workstation to console on nondedicated PC
DISABLE LOGIN	S	Prevents users from logging into the server
DISK	S	DIsplay information about server's disk
DISKSET	W	Sets up a disk coprocessor board
DISMOUNT	S	Deactivates a volume
DISPLAY NETWORKS	S	Displays all available networks
DISPLAY SERVERS	S	Displays all available servers
DOS	S	Changes from console to workstation on nondedicated PC
DOWN	S	Terminates server activity

Table 1a

Command	S/W	Description
ENABLE LOGIN	S	Enables users to log in
ENDCAP	W	Cancels the CAPTURE command
FCONSOLE	W	Manages servers and monitors their performance
FILER	W	File and directory manager
FLAG	W	Enables file attributes
FLAGDIR	W	Enables directory attributes
GRANT	W	Gives rights to directories and files
HELP	W	Displays help information
HIDEFILE	W	Hides a file from user viewing
LARCHIVE	W	Archives server files to a local disk
LISTDIR	W	List subdirectories below current directory
LOGIN	W	Logs into a server
LOGOUT	W	Logs out from a server
LRESTORE	W	Restores server files from a local disk
MAKEUSER	W	Adds users to the server
MAP	W	Assigns drive letters to volumes and directories
MENU	W	Runs script files
MONITOR	W	Displays server statistics
MOUNT	S	Mounts a volume
NAME	S	Displays the server name
NARCHIVE	W	Archives server files to another volume on server
NCOPY	W	Copies files

Table 1b

Command	S/ W	Description
NDIR	W	Provides information about files and directories
NPRINT	W	Print files on network printers
NRESTORE	W	Restores files from another volume in server
NVER	W	Provides version number of Netware
OFF	S	Clears the server display
PAUDIT	W	Displays server accounting data
PCONSOLE	W	Manages network printers
PRINTCON	W	Creates print job configurations
PRINTDEF	W	Configures printer definition, functions, and modes
PRINTER	S	Manages printers on server
PURGE	W	Removes erased files from server
QUEUE	S	Manages queues
REMIRROR	S	Remirrors a pair of duplexed server disks
REMOVE	W	Removes users as trustees
RENDIR	W	Renames a directory
RESET ROUTER	S	Forces server to relearn list of other servers and routers
REVOKE	W	Removes directory or file from users
RIGHTS	W	Displays a file or directory rights
SALVAGE	W	Recovers deleted files
SECURITY	W	Show security problem areas
SEND	W	Sends a message to another user
SESSION	W	Manages drive mappings

Table 1c

Command	S/ W	Description
SET TIME	S	Updates the date and time in server
SET PASS	W	Changes passwords
SHOWFILE	W	Makes hidden files visible to users
SLIST	W	List network servers
SMODE	W	Sets the search mode of EXE file
SPOOL	S	Maps queues to printers
SYSCON	W	Manages login names, scripts, and user accounts
SYSTIME	W	Shows server time and matches workstation time
TIME	S	Shows server data and time
TLIST	W	Shows the directory of a trustee
TRACK OFF	S	Turns off server tracking
TRACK ON	S	Turns on server tracking
UNMIRROR	S	Unmirrors a matched pair of disks in server
UPS	S	Monitor operation of uninterruptible power supply
USERDEF	W	Adds users to the network
USERLIST	W	Shows users logged into a server
VAP	S	Shows a list of VAPs loaded
VERSION	S	Show the Netware version
VOLINFO	W	Shows disk space statistics
VOLUMES	S	Shows statistics about server's volumes
VREPAIR	W	Repairs a damaged server volume
WHOAMI	W	Display information about connected user

Table 1d

NetWare Rights	Description
READ	Allows users to read the contents of a file
WRITE	Allows users to modify the contents of a file
OPEN	Allows users to open a file
CREATE	Allows users to create files in a directory
DELETE	Allows users to delete an existing file
PARENTAL	Allows users to create or remove subdirectories under a specified directory and provide other users with rights to it
SEARCH	Allows users to list a directory contents
MODIFY	Allows users to rename or change attributes of a file or subdirectory

Table 2

Directory Attributes	Description
HIDDEN	Makes the directory invisible
SYSTEM	Makes the directory invisible and reserves it for system use
PRIVATE	Prevents users from seeing subdirectories

Table 3

File Attributes	Description
ARCHIVE	This attribute is turned on when a file has been changed by a program
EXECUTE ONLY	Files can be executed but not copied
HIDDEN	Makes files invisible to users
INDEXED	Makes access to large files more efficient
READ ONLY	File cannot be modified or deleted
SHAREABLE	File can be accessed by multiple users at a time
SYSTEM	Makes file invisible and reserves file for system use
TRANSACTION	Makes the file able to work with Novell's transaction tracking system.

Table 4

Appendix B

NetWare for Macintosh

NetWare for Macintosh software allows Macintosh computers running AppleShare to be connected to a NetWare file server. This type of connection can be made only if the file server is running Netware 2.15 or above.

By connecting to a NetWare file server, Macintosh users can store their files on the NetWare file server, access DOS files, and print to Apple printers using NetWare's printing tools. In addition, network users that are running under DOS can access Macintosh files and print on Apple printers.

To DOS users, the Macintosh files look like DOS files. To Macintosh users, DOS files appear in Macintosh form. However, in order to use the same files between the two machines, the same type of software must be installed for the Mac and the DOS machine. For example, Microsoft Word has a version for DOS and a version for the Macintosh.

How NetWare for Macintosh Works

Macintosh computers use a protocol and file management format called the Apple File Protocol (AFP). The NetWare equivalent of AFP is called the NetWare Core Protocol (NCP). In order for the Macintosh to use a NetWare file server, a bridge must exist between the two protocols so both systems can communicate with each other.

This bridge is provided by a file services Value-Added Process (VAP) and a LAN driver VAP in the file server. Once the file services VAP is installed in the network server, the server becomes a file server gateway or bridge between the two systems. The VAP is an application that runs on top of NetWare. It allows third-party programs and processes to be linked to NetWare and then executed from the file server while the network is operational.

Print services are provided by installing print services VAP and queue services VAP in the bridge or file server. Once this step is done, the file server also becomes a print service gateway.

Typically, the file services and print services are installed in separate bridges due to memory limitations. With the advent of 80386 based computers and their use of protected mode and large memory capacity, both services can be installed in the same bridge.

After the file and print services VAP are installed, they act as a translator between AFP and NCP. This is known as the Service Protocol Gateway (SPG). When the AFP request from a Macintosh workstation is sent to the file server, the SPG translates it to an NCP request that the file server can work with. In the same manner, any request made by DOS based machines are translated by the SPG into a request that the AFP can understand. (See Fig. B-1).

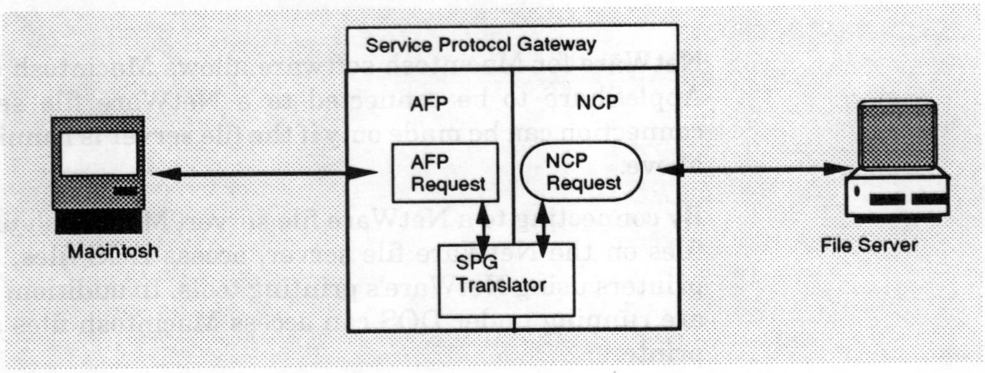

Fig. B-1. Macintosh and file server connected through a SPG

Hardware Requirements

The Netware for Macintosh VAPs can be installed on a server or external bridge running NetWare 2.15C or above. The complete hardware components required to run NetWare for Macintosh are as follows.

1. A NetWare file server or one or two Netware bridges. The following computers will work:

   Novell 286B file server.
   Novell 386AE file server.
   IBM PC AT or compatible.
   Compaq 386 or compatible.
   IBM PS/2 models 50 and above with a minimum of 2 megabytes of RAM

2. One or more Macintosh workstations. The Macintosh computers supported are as follows:

   Macintosh IIXX series computers.
   Macintosh SE and SE/30.
   Macintosh Plus.
   Macintosh Classic.
   Macintosh 512K Enhanced.

3. Cabling. Ethernet, LocalTalk, PhoneNet, or other third parties can be used.
4. File server or bridge network interface cards.

Software Requirements

The following software is required to run NetWare for Macintosh:

1. NetWare 2.15C or above.
2. File services VAP drivers and board drivers.
3. Print services VAP and the queue gateway VAP.
4. AppleTalk-compatible board driver.
5. The MACSETUP program and the NetWare for Macintosh diskettes.
6. The Macintosh System Tools diskette set V6.0 or above.
7. The Netware Control Center application located in the Macintosh Utilities diskette.
8. The Netware desk accessory located in the Macintosh System Tools set.

Planning a Network

Most networks that use the Macintosh use either LocalTalk cabling or Ethernet cabling. The hardware configuration varies according to which cabling schema will be implemented.

LocalTalk Cabling

In LocalTalk cabling is used, the network can be attached directly to the file server or to the bridges. Fig. B-2 shows this type of configuration. Additionally, AppleTalk network interface cards (NICs) have to be installed in the file server or bridges. The cable will go directly from the AppleTalk connector in the back of the Macintosh to the file server as in the figure.

Ethernet Cabling

If Ethernet cabling is used, then the configuration in Fig. B-3 can be used. Ethernet network interface cards need to be installed in the file server or bridges. In addition, EtherTalk cards will also have to be installed in the Macintosh workstations if they are to be attached to the Ethernet cable.

With this schema, Apple printers will have to be attached to the file server using LocalTalk cabling. A LocalTalk network can be connected to an Ethernet network with the use of a third party gateway.

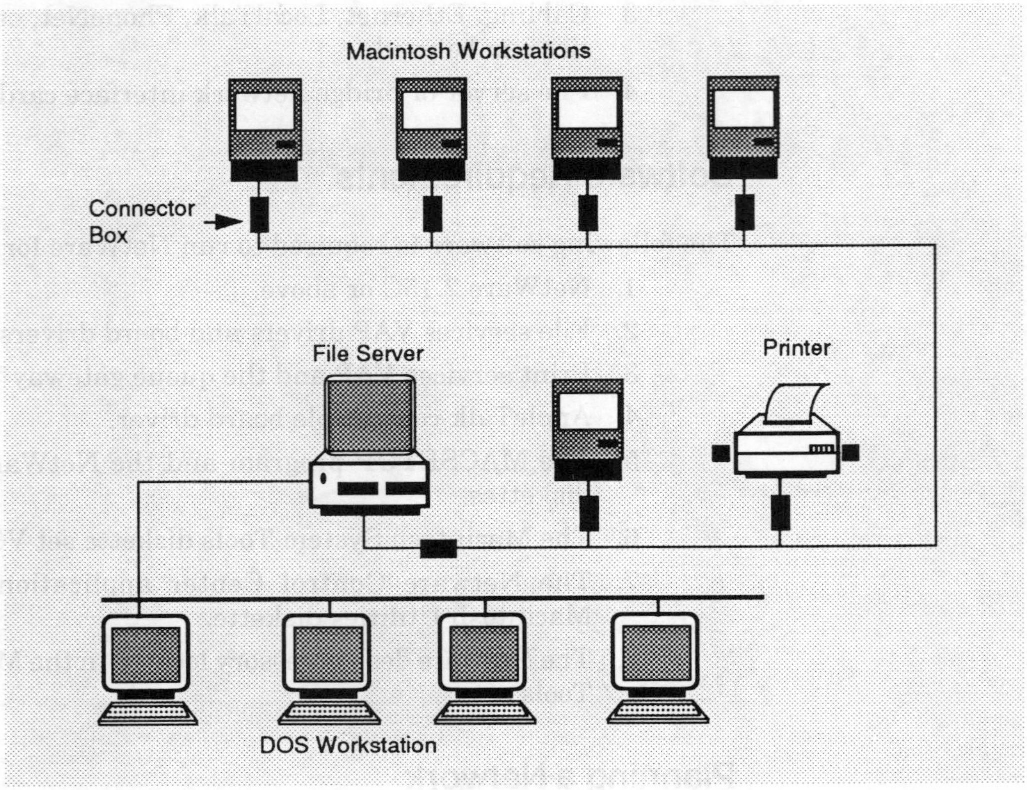

Fig. B-2. Macintosh connected to a file server via AppleTalk

Installing NetWare for Macintosh

Follow the instructions below to install NetWare for Macintosh.

1. Install the NICs and attach cables.
2. The first step is to run NETGEN or BRGEN. If a file server is to contain NetWare for Macintosh VAPs, NETGEN needs to be executed. If the NetWare for Macintosh is to be installed in bridges, BRGEN needs to be executed.
3. After the screen for either NETGEN or BRGEN is displayed, select the driver that correspond to the board that you will be using in the file server or bridges. With LocalTalk cabling, the NetWare for Macintosh driver should be the last driver selected. LAN A should not be selected as the driver in this case.
4. Follow the installation instructions provided on the screen until a LAN driver configuration needs to be selected. If a Novell NL1000 board is selected, I/O address 240h should be selected.
5. Continue with the instructions provided on the screen that indicate how to proceed with the installation with NETGEN or BRGEN.

6. After NETGEN or BRGEN finish, run MACSETUP.

MACSETUP will have to be executed each time a new NetWare file server is to be added, a host is to be added, or a print queue is to be added. MACSETUP will configure file services and print services. Follow the instructions on the screen provided by MACSETUP to complete the installation.

7. After MACSETUP completes installing file and printer services, boot the file servers or bridges.

Note: for further installation details, consult the NetWare for Macintosh supplements that come with the NetWare package.

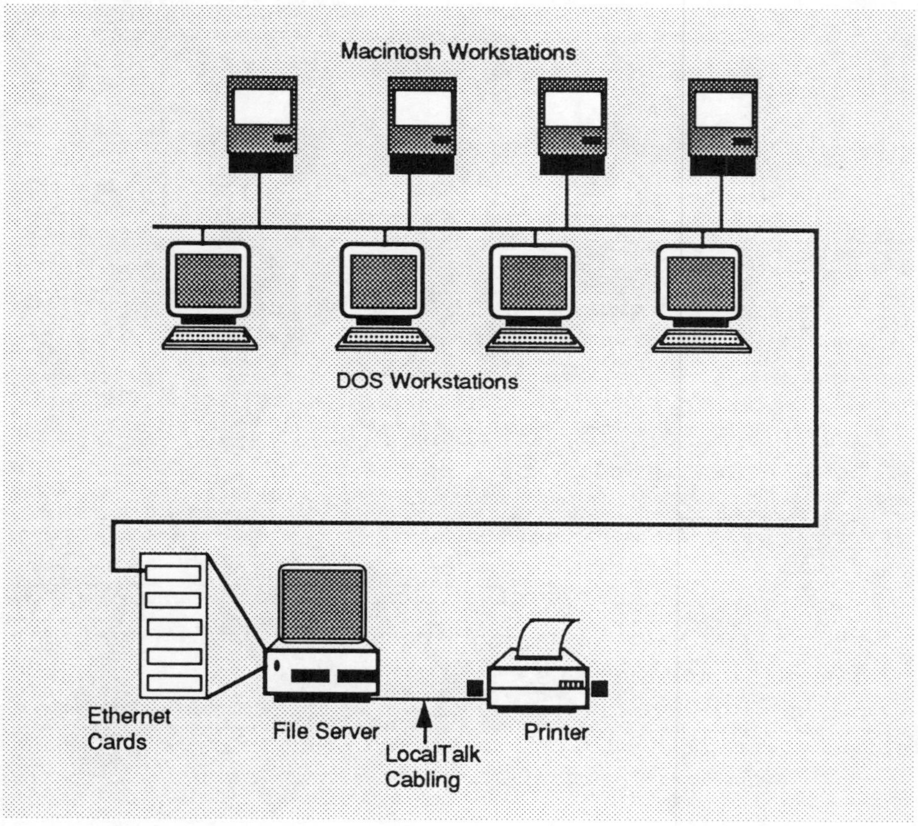

Fig. B-3. Workstations connected via Ethernet

Appendix C

Vendors of Gateways and Related Products

C-Slave/286 and XBUS4/AT
Alloy Computer Products Inc.
165 Forest St.
Marlboro, MA 01752
508-481-8500

MultiComAsyncGateway
Multi-Tech Systems Inc.
2205 Woodale Dr.
Mounds View, MN 55112
800-328-9717

Telebits ACS
Telebit Corp
115 Chesapeake Terr.
Sunnyvale, CA 94089
800-835-3248

386/Multiware
Alloy Computer Products Inc.
165 Forest St.
Marlboro, MA 01752
508-481-8500

ComBridge
Cubix Corp.
2800 Lockheed Way
Carson City, NV 89706
800-829-0550

FlexCom
Evergreen Systems Inc.,
120 Landing Ct.
Suite A
Novato, CA 94945
415-897-8888

ChatterBox 4000
J&L Information Systems Inc.
9238 Deering Ave.
Chatsworth, CA 91311
818-709-1778

Access Server
Novell Inc. Comm. Products
890 Ross Dr.
Sunnyvale, CA 94089
800-453-1267

Vendors of EBBS and Related Products

Accunet
The Major BBS
Galacticom Inc.
4101 SW 47th Ave., #101
Fort Lauderdale, FL 33314
305-583-5990

Oracomm-Plus
Surf Computer Services, Inc.
71-540 Gardess Rd.
Rancho Mirage, CA 92270
619-346-1608

PCBoard
Clark Development Co.
3950 S. 700 East, #303
Murray, UT 84107
800-356-1686

RemoteAccess
Continental Software
195 Adelaide Terr.
Perth, Australia, 6000
USA contact 918-254-6618

Searchlight
Searchlight Software
Box 640
Stony Brook, NY 11790
516-751-2966

TBBS
eSoft Inc.
15200 E. Girard Ave., #2550
Aurora, CA 80014
303-699-6565

Vendors of Routers, Bridges, and Related Products

Eicon Router for NetWare
Eicon Technology Corp.
2196 32nd Ave.
Montreal, Quebec H8T 3H7 Canada
514-631-2592

G/X25 Gateway & Bridge 64
Gateway Communicatons Inc.
2941 Alton Ave.
Irvine, CA 92714
800-367-6555

Microcom LAN Bridge 6000
Microcom Systems Inc.
500 River Ridge Dr.
Norwood, MA 02062
800-822-8224

LAN2LAN/Mega Router
Newport Systems Solutions Inc.
4019 Westerley Pl, #103
Newport Beach, CA 92660
800-368-6533

NetWare Link/X.25
Novell Inc.
122 East 1700 South
Provo, UT 84606
800-638-9273

NetWare Link/T1
Novell Inc.
122 East 1700 South
Provo, UT 84606
800-638-9273

POWERbridge
Performace Technology
7800 IH 10, W. 800
Lincoln Center
San Antonio, TX 78230
800-825-5267

Vendors of E-Mail Products

cc:Mail Gateway
Lotus Development Corp.
2141 Landings Dr.
Mountain View, CA 94043
800-448-2500

Beyond Mail
Beyond Inc.
38 Sidney St.
Cambridge, MA 02139
617-621-0095

@Mail
Beyond Inc.
38 Sidney St.
Cambridge, MA 02139
617-621-0095

MailMAN
Reach Soft. Corp.
330 Portrero Ave.
Sunnyvale, CA 94086
408-733-8685

Microsoft Mail for PC Networks
Microsoft Corp.
1 Microsoft Way
Redmont, WA 98052
206-882-8080

Microsoft Mail
Microsoft Corp.
1 Microsoft Way
Redmont, WA 98052
206-882-8080

Office Works Comm. Option
Data Access Corp.
14000 SW 119 Ave.
Miami, FL 33186
800-451-3539

WordPerfect Office
WordPerfect Corp.
1555 N. Technology Way
Orem, UT 84057
800-451-5151

3+Open Mail
3Com Corp.
3165 Kifer Rd.
Santa Clara, CA 95052
800-638-3266

Vendors of Fax Gateways and Related Products

NetFax Board
All the Fax, Inc.
917 Northern Blvd.
Great Neck, NY 11021
800-289-3329

FaxPress 2000
Castelle
3255-3 Scott Blvd.
Santa Clara, CA 95051
800-359-7654

GammaFax CPD
GammaLink
133 Caspian Court
Sunnyvale, CA 94089
408-744-1430

Facsimile Server
Interpreter, Inc.
11455 West 48th Ave.
Wheat Ridge, CO 80033
800-232-4687

Vendors of Network Management Products

PreCursor
The Alridge Co.
2500 City West Blvd., Suite 575
Houston, TX 77042
800-548-5019

StopCopy Plus
BBI Computer Systems
14105 Heritage Lane
Silver Spring, MD 20906
301-871-1094

Stop View
BBI Computer Systems
14105 Heritage Lane
Silver Spring, MD 20906
301-871-1094

SiteLock
Brightwork Development, Inc.
766 Shrewsbury Ave.
Jerral Center West
Trenton Falls, NJ
800-552-9876

Certus LAN
Certus International
13110 Shaker Sq.
Cleveland, OH 44120
800-722-8737

Saber Meter
Saber Software Corp.
Box 9088
Dallas, TX 75209
800-338-8754

EtherPeek
AG Group
2540 Camino Diablo
Walnut Creek, CA 94596
415-937-2479

LocalPeek
AG Group
2540 Camino Diablo
Walnut Creek, CA 94596
415-937-2479

NetPatrol Pack
AG Group
2540 Camino Diablo
Walnut Creek, CA 94596
415-937-2479

Net Watchman
AG Group
2540 Camino Diablo
Walnut Creek, CA 94596
415-937-2479

ARCserve for NetWare 286
Cheyenne Software, Inc.
55 Bryant Ave.
Roslyn, NY 11576
800-243-9462

ARCserve for NetWare 386
Cheyenne Software, Inc.
55 Bryant Ave.
Roslyn, NY 11576
800-243-9462

Network Supervisor
CSG Technologies, Inc.
530 William Penn Place
Suite 329
Pittsburgh, PA 15219
800-366-4622

Retrospect Remote
Dantz Development Corp.
1400 Shattuck Ave., Suite 1
Berkeley, CA 94709
415-849-0293

LANVista 100
Digilog, Inc.
1370 Welsh Rd.
Montgomeryville, PA 18936
800-344-4564

PhoneNET Manager's Pack
Farallon Computing, Inc.
2000 Powell St.
Emeryville, CA 94608
415-596-9000

NetWare Early Warning System
Frye Computer Systems, Inc.
19 Temple Place, 4th Floor
Boston, MA 02111
800-234-3793

NetWare Management
Frye Computer Systems, Inc.
19 Temple Place, 4th. Floor
Boston, MA 02111
800-234-3793

LANWatch
FTP Software, Inc.
26 Princess St.
Wakefield, MA 01880
617-246-0900

LANprobe
Hewlett-Packard Co.
5070 Centennial Blvd.
Colorado Springs, CO 80919
719-531-4000

Network Advisor
Hewlett-Packard Co.
5070 Centennial Blvd.
Colorado Springs, CO 80919
719-531-4000

OpenView
Hewlett-Packard Co.
5070 Centennial Blvd.
Colorado Springs, CO 80919
719-531-4000

ProbeView
Hewlett-Packard Co.
5070 Centennial Blvd.
Colorado Springs, CO 80919
719-531-4000

LANanlyzer
Novell, Inc.
122 East 1700 South
Provo, UT 84606
800-453-1267

Lantern
Novell, Inc.
122 East 1700 South
Provo, UT 84606
800-453-1267

Lantern Service Monitor
Novell, Inc.
122 East 1700 South
Provo, UT 84606
800-453-1267

Access/One
Ungermann-Bass, Inc.
3900 Freedom Cir.
Santa Clara, CA 95052
800-873-6381

NetDirector
Ungermann-Bass, Inc.
3900 Freedom Cir.
Santa Clara, CA 95052
800-873-6381

LattisNet Advanced Network Management
Synoptics Communication, Inc.
Box 58185
Santa Clara, CA 95052
408-988-2400

LattisNet Basic Network Management
Synoptics Communication, Inc.
Box 58185
Santa Clara, CA 95052
408-988-2400

LattisNet System 3000
Synoptics Communication, Inc.
Box 58185
Santa Clara, CA 95052
408-988-2400

Network Control Engine
Synoptics Communication, Inc.
Box 58185
Santa Clara, CA 95052
408-988-2400

Vendors of Network Operating Systems and Related Products

LANtastic
Artisoft, Inc.
575 E. River Rd., Artisoft Plaza
Tucson, AZ 85704
602-293-6363

LANsoft
ACCTON Technology Corp.
46750 Fremont Blvd., Suite 104
Fremont, CA 94538
415-226-9800

VINES
Banyan Systems, Inc.
120 Flanders Rd.
Westboro, MA 01581
508-898-1000

PC/NOS
Corvus Systems, Inc.
160 Great Oaks Blvd.
San Jose, CA 95119
800-426-7887

LANsmart
D-Link Systems, Inc.
5 Musick
Irvine, CA 92718
714-455-1688

OS/2 Ext. Ed.
IBM Corp.
Old Orchard Rd.
Armonk, NY 10504
800-426-2468

EasyNet NOS/2 Plus
LanMark Corp.
Box 246, Postal Station A
Mississauga, ON
CD L5A 3G8
416-848-6865

LAN Manager
Microsoft Corp.
One Microsoft Way
Redmont, WA 98052
800-426-9400

NetWare
Novell, Inc.
122 East 1700 South
Provo, UT 84606
800-453-1267

Commercial Information Services

BIX
One Phoenix Mill Lane
Peterborough, NH 03458
800-227-2983

Compuserve
Box 20212
Columbus, OH 43220
800-848-8199

Dialog Information Service, Inc.
3460 Hillview Ave.
Palo Alto, CA 94304
800-334-2564

General Videotext Corp.
Three Blackstone St.
Cambridge, MA 02139
800-544-4005

GEnie
401 N. Washington St.
Rockville, MD 20850
800-638-9636

NewsNet
945 Haverford Rd.
Bryn Mawr, PA 19010
800-345-1301

Prodigy Services Co.
445 Hamilton Ave.
White Plains, NY 10601
800-776-3449

Quantum Computer Services
8619 Westwood Center Dr., Suite 200
Vienna, VA 22182
800-227-6364

SprintMail
12490 Sunrise Valley Dr.
Reston, VA 22096
800-736-1130

Public Communication Networks
Accunet
AT&T Computer Systems
295 N. Maple Ave.
Basking Ridge, NJ 07920
800-222-0400

CompuServe Network Services
CompuServe Inc.
5000 Arlington Centre Blvd.
Columbus, OH 43220
800-848-8199

IBM Information Network
IBM Corp
3405 W. Dr. Martin Luther King, Jr. Blvd.
Tampa, FL 33607
800-727-2222

Infonet
Infonet Services Corp.
2100 East Grand Ave.
El Segundo, CA 90245
800-342-5272

Mark*Net
GE Corp.
Information Services Div.
401 N. Washington St.
Rockville, MD 20850
800-433-3683

SprintNet Data Network
US Sprint
12490 Sunrise Valley Dr.
Reston, VA 22096
800-736-1130

Tymnet Global Network
BT North America Inc.
2560 N. 1st St., Box 49019
San Jose, CA 94161
800-872-7654

Vendors of Data Switches, PBXs, and Related Products

AISwitch Series XXX
Applied Innovation, Inc.
651-C Lakeview Plaza Blvd.
Columbus, OH 43085
800-247-9482

MDX
Equinox Systems, Inc.
14260 Southwest 119th Ave.
Miami, FL 33186
800-328-2729

Instanet6000
MICOM Communications Corp.
Box 8100
4100 Los Angeles Ave.
Simi Valley, CA 93062-8100
800-642-6687

Data PBX Series
Rose Electronics
Box 742571
Houston, TX 77274
800-333-9343

Gateway Data Switch
SKP Electronics
1232-E S. Village Way
Santa Ana, CA 92705
714-972-1727

INCS-64
Western Telematic, Inc.
5 Sterling
Irvine, CA 92178
800-854-7226

Slimline Data Switches
Belkin Components
14550 S. Main St.
Gardena, CA 90248
800-223-5546

MetroLAN
Datacom Technologies, Inc.
11001 31st Place, West
Everett, WA 98204
800-468-5557

Intelligent Printer Buffer
Primax Electronics Inc.
2531 West 237th St., Suite 102
Torrance, CA 90505
213-326-8018

Data Switches
Rose Electronics
Box 742571
Houston, TX 77274
800-333-9343

ShareNet 5110
McComb Research
Box 3984
Minneapolis, MN 55405
612-527-8082

Aura 1000
Intran Systems, Inc.
7493 N. Oracle Rd., Suite 207
Tucson, AZ 85704
602-797-2797

Logical Connection
Fifth Generation Systems, Inc.
10049 N. Reiger Rd.
Baton Rouge, LA 70809
800-873-4384

Vendors of Network Remote Access Software and Related Products

Distribute Console Access Facility
IBM Corp.
(Contact IBM sales rep.)
800-426-2468

PolyMod2
Memsoft Corp.
1 Park Pl.
621 NW 53rd St., #240
Boca Raton, FL 33487
407-997-6655

Remote-OS
The Software Lifeline Inc.
Fountain Square, 2600 Military Trail, #290
Boca Raton, FL 33531
407-994-4466

Vendors of TCP/IP Hardware and Related Products

Isolink PC/TCP
BICC Data Networks
1800 W. Park Dr., Suite 150
Westborough, MA 01581
800-447-6526

PC/TCP Plus
FTP Software, Inc.
26 Princess St.
Wakefield, MA 01880
617-246-0900

TCP/IP for OS/2 EE
IBM
Old Orchard Rd.
Armonk, NY 10504
800-426-2468

10Net TCP
Digital Comm. Assoc.
10NET Comm. Div.
7887 Washington Village Dr.
Dayton, OH 45459
800-358-1010

WIN/TCP for DOS
Wollongong Group, Inc.
Box 51860
1129 San Antonio Rd.
Palo Alto, CA 94303
800-872-8649

PC/TCP Thernet Comm.
UniPress Software, Inc.
2025 Lincoln Hwy.
Edison, NJ 08817
800-222-0550

Vendors of Zero Slot LANs, Media Transfer Hardware and Software, and Related Products

LANtastic Z
Artisoft, Inc.
575 E. River Rd.
Artisoft Plaza
Tucson, AZ 85704
602-293-6363

PC-Hookup
Brown Bag Software
2155 S. Bascom, Suite 114
Campbell, CA 95008
800-523-0764

Brooklyn Bridge
Fifth Generation Systems
10049 N. Reiger Rd.
Baton Rouge, LA 70809

LapLink
Traveling Software, Inc.
18702 N. Creek Pkwy.
Bothell, WA 98011
800-662-2652

FastLynx
Rupp Corp.
7285 Franklin Ave.
Los Angeles, CA 90046
800-852-7877

MasterLink
U.S. Marketing, Inc.
1402 South St.
Nashville, TN 37212
615-242-8800

Glossary

ASCII. The acronym for American Standard Code for Information Interchange. This is a standard code for the transmission of data within the US. It is composed of 128 characters in a 7-bit format.

Account Boot Disk. A disk used to load DOS into the computer when it is turned on.

Asynchronous. A communication that places data in discrete blocks that are surrounded by framing bits. These bits show the beginning and ending of a block of data.

Baud. The rate of data transmission.

Bandwidth. This is the capacity of a cable to carry data on different channels or frequencies.

Baseband. A network cable that has only one channel for carrying data signals.

Bit. An abbreviation for binary digit. A bit is the smallest unit of data.

Bridge. A device that connects different LANs so a node on one LAN can communicate with a node on another LAN.

Broadband. A network cable with several channels of communication.

Bus Topology. A physical layout of a LAN where all nodes are connected to a single cable.

Byte. Normally a combination of 8 bits.

BOOTCONF.SYS. A file on the file server used to indicate which boot image file each workstation will use.

CAPTURE. A NetWare utility program used to redirect output from a printer port on the workstation to a network printer.

Coaxial Cable. A cable consisting of a single metal wire surrounded by insulation, which is itself surrounded by a braided or foil outer conductor.

COMPSURF. A NetWare utility program that prepares a hard disk for use in a NetWare file server. Its name stands for COMPrehensive SURFace analysis.

Computer. An electronic system that can store and process information under program control.

Control Code. Special nonprinting codes that cause electronic equipment to perform specific actions.

CONSOLE. The file server.

CPU. Central processing unit. The "brains" of the computer; that section where the logic and control functions are performed.

Device Driver. A software program that enables a network operating system and the DOS operating system to work with NICs, disk controllers, and other hardware.

Directory Rights. Access attached to directories on a NetWare file server.

Driver. A memory resident program usually used to control a hardware device.

FCONSOLE. A NetWare utility program used to monitor file server and workstation activity.

Full Duplex. In full duplex communication, the terminal transmits and receives data simultaneously.

Fiber-Optic Cable. A data transmitting cable that consists of plastic or glass fibers.

File Attributes. Access rights attached to each file.

File Server. A computer running a network operating system that enables other computers to access its files.

Gateway. A device that acts as a translator between networks that use different protocols.

Group. A collection of users.

Group Rights. Rights given to a collection of users.

Half Duplex. In half duplex communication, the terminal transmits and receives data in separate, consecutive operations.

Handshaking. A set of commands recognized by the sending and receiving stations that control the flow of data transmission.

Interface. A communication channel that is used to connect a computer to an external device.

Internetwork Packet Exchange (IPX). One of the data transmission protocols used by NetWare.

LAN. Local area network. A network that encompasses a small geographical area.

LOGIN. A NetWare utility program that allows users to identify themselves to the network.

Login Script. A series of statements executed each time a user logs into a NetWare network.

MAP. Association of a logical NetWare drive letter with a directory.

Modem. An electronic device that converts digital data (modulates) from a computer into analog signals that the phone equipment can understand. Additionally, the modem converts analog (demodulates) data into digital data.

NetBIOS. A network communication protocol that NetWare can emulate.

NETGEN. A NetWare utility program used to configure and load NetWare onto a file server.

NetWare. A network operating system produced by Novell Incorporated.

Network Address. A hexadecimal number used to identify a network cabling system.

NIC. The network interface card is a circuit board that is installed in the file server and workstations that make up the network. It allows the hardware in the network to send and receive data.

Node. A workstation, file server, bridge, or other device that has an address on a network.

Novell. A company based in Provo, Utah, that produces the NetWare network operating system.

NPRINT. A NetWare utility program used to send a file directly to a network printer. Its name stands for Network PRINT.

Packet. A discrete unit of data bits transmitted over a network.

Password. A secret word used to identify a user.

PCONSOLE. A NetWare utility program used to configure and operate print servers. Its name stands for Print server CONSOLE .

Print Devices. Definition files for different type of printers to be used on a print server.

Print Forms. Definitions of different types of paper size to be used on a print server.

Print Job Configurations. Complete descriptions of how a file is to be printed on the network.

Print Queues. Definitions of the order in which and where a file is to be printed on the network.

Print Server. A computer running the PSERVER program that allows it to accept files to be printed from other workstations.

PRINTCON. A NetWare utility program used to create print job configurations.

PRINTDEF. A NetWare utility program used to create and edit print device files.

Protocol. The conventions that must be observed in order for two electronic devices to communicate with each other.

PSERVER. The NetWare Print SERVER program.

RAM. Random access memory.

Remote Print Server. A computer running the RPRINTER program, enabling it to print output from other network workstations and operate as a normal workstation.

Remote Reset. The process of loading DOS and the network drivers from the file server.

Ring Topology. A network configuration that connects all nodes in a logical ring-like structure.

ROM. Read only memory

RPRINTER. The program that allows other workstations to print to a workstation's printer.

Shell. Under NetWare, the network drivers.

SHELL.CFG. A file used on a workstation to configure the network drivers as they are loaded into memory.

Star Topology. A network configuration where each node is connected by a single cable link to a central location, called the hub.

Synchronous. A method of communication using a time interval to distinguish between transmitted blocks of data.

SYSCON. A NetWare utility program used to establish users and their rights on the file server. Its name stands for SYStem CONfiguration.

Trustee Rights. Rights given to users to access directories on the file server.

Topology. The manner in which nodes are connected on a LAN.

Token. The data packet used to carry information on LANs using the ring topology.

User. Under NetWare, the definition of a set of access rights for an individual.

Uninterruptible Power Supply. A device that keeps computers running after a power failure, providing power from batteries for a short period of time.

VAP. A value-added process to the NetWare operating system provided by a third party vendor.

Wide Area Network. A network that encompasses a large geographical area.

Workstation. A computer attached to the network.

X.25. A communication protocol used on public data networks.

Index

World Development Report 1984

Published for The World Bank
Oxford University Press

Oxford University Press
NEW YORK OXFORD LONDON GLASGOW
TORONTO MELBOURNE WELLINGTON HONG KONG
TOKYO KUALA LUMPUR SINGAPORE JAKARTA
DELHI BOMBAY CALCUTTA MADRAS KARACHI
NAIROBI DAR ES SALAAM CAPE TOWN

First printing July 1984

ISBN 0-19-520459-X cloth
ISBN 0-19-520460-3 paperback
ISSN 0163-5085

The Library of Congress has cataloged this serial publication as follows:
World development report. 1978–
[New York] Oxford University Press.
v. 27 cm. annual.
Published for The World Bank

1. Underdeveloped areas—Periodicals. 2. Economic development Periodicals I. International Bank for Reconstruction and Development.

HC59.7.W659 *330.9'172'4* *78–67086*